# ACCA

# Audit and Assurance (AA)

## Practice & Revision Kit

For exams in September 2022, December 2022, March 2023 and June 2023

First edition 2007
Fifthteenth edition February 2022

ISBN 9781 5097 4758 0
(previous ISBN 9781 5097 3808 3)
e-ISBN 9781 5097 4464 0

**Cataloguing-in-Publication Data**
A catalogue record for this book
is available from the British Library

**Published by**

BPP Learning Media Ltd
BPP House, Aldine Place
London W12 8AA

www.bpp.com/learningmedia

Printed in the United Kingdom

Your learning materials, published by BPP Learning
Media Ltd, are printed on paper obtained from
traceable sustainable sources.

We are grateful to the Association of Chartered
Certified Accountants for permission to reproduce past
examination questions. The suggested solutions in the
Practice & Revision Kit have been prepared by BPP
Learning Media Ltd, except where otherwise stated.

BPP Learning Media is grateful to the IASB for permission
to reproduce extracts from the International Financial
Reporting Standards including all International
Accounting Standards, SIC and IFRIC Interpretations
(the Standards). The Standards together with their
accompanying documents are issued by:

The International Accounting Standards Board (IASB) 30
Cannon Street, London, EC4M 6XH, United Kingdom.
Email: info@ifrs.org  Web: www.ifrs.org

**Disclaimer:** The IASB, the International Financial
Reporting Standards (IFRS) Foundation, the authors and
the publishers do not accept responsibility for any loss
caused by acting or refraining from acting in reliance on
the material in this publication, whether such loss is
caused by negligence or otherwise to the maximum
extent permitted by law.

# Contents

## Finding questions

### Revising Audit and Assurance

## Questions and answers

## Exam practice

### Mock exam 1 (September 2016)

### Mock exam 2 (Specimen exam)

### Mock exam 3 (December 2016 exam)

### Mock exam 4 (Sep/Dec 2021 Hybrid exam)

## Review for

# Question index

The headings in this checklist/index indicate the main topics of questions, but questions are expected to cover several different topics.

Questions set under the old syllabus *Audit and Assurance* (F8) and *Audit and Internal Review* (AIR) exams are included because their style and content are similar to those which appear in the Audit and Assurance exam. The questions have been amended to reflect the current exam format.

BPP LEARNING MEDIA

BPP
LEARNING MEDIA

| | Marks | Time allocation Mins | Page number Question | Page number Answer |
|---|---|---|---|---|
| **Sample questions from the examining team** | | | | |
| 221-222  March 2019 | 4 | 7 | 120 | 323 |
| 223-244  June 2019 | 4 | 7 | 121 | 324 |
| 225-226  September 2019 | 4 | 7 | 123 | 325 |
| 227-228  December 2019 | 4 | 7 | 124 | 325 |
| 229-230  March 2020 | 4 | 7 | 125 | 326 |
| 231-232  July 2020 | 4 | 7 | 126 | 326 |

Mock exam 1 (September 2016)

Mock exam 2 (Specimen Exam)

Mock exam 3 (December 2016)

Mock exam 4 (Section B: Sep/Dec 2021 Hybrid Exam)

# Topic index

Listed below are the key Audit and Assurance syllabus topics and the numbers of the questions in this Kit covering those topics. If you need to concentrate your practice and revision on certain topics or if you want to attempt all available questions that refer to a particular subject, you will find this index useful.

BPP LEARNING MEDIA

| Syllabus topic | Question numbers |
|---|---|
| Non-current assets | 48, 49, 71(c), 100-101, 112(c), 119-121, 153(b), 154(b), 155(a), 157(a)-(b), 185, 195, 198, 208, 209 |
| Outsourcing | 76(c) |
| Payables and accruals | 150(b)-(c), 152(b), 156(a)-(c) |
| Professional scepticism and judgment | 71(a) |
| Provisions and contingencies | 50, 107(d), 126-127, 151(c), 152(b) |
| Purchases systems | 87-89, 99, 108(b), 111(b)-(c), 116(c)-(d), 135-136, 150(a) |
| Quality management | 7, 162, 216 |
| Receivables and revenue | 38-39, 43, 49, 51, 54, 81(e), 102-104, 109(b), 139-141, 143, 151(a)-(b), 152(b), 153(c), 154(c), 155(b), 158(a), 159, 170, 176 |
| Sales systems | 109(a) & (d), 145-148 |
| Sampling | 131 |
| Share capital | 47 |
| Subsequent events | 153(d), 164-168, 193 |
| Understanding the entity | 42, 46 |
| Value for money audit | 91, 112(a)-(b) |
| Wages systems | 92-93, 107(b), 108(c), 110(a), (c)-(d), 117(a)-(b), (d), 201 |
| Written representations | 41, 42, 169, 171 |

# The exam

## Computer-based exams

It has only been possible from exams in June 2019 for candidates to sit Applied Skills exams as a computer-based exam (CBE). Applied Skills exams are all computer-based exams.

# Introduction to Audit and Assurance (AA)

## Overall aim of the syllabus

This exam requires students to develop knowledge and understanding of the process of carrying out the assurance engagement and its application in the context of the professional regulatory framework.

## Brought forward knowledge

The *Audit and Assurance* syllabus assumes prior knowledge and understanding of the accounting topics in *Financial Accounting* (with the exception of group financial statements). A summary of such knowledge is included in the Essential reading in the AA Workbook.

## The syllabus

The broad syllabus headings are:

A  Audit framework and regulation
B  Planning and risk assessment
C  Internal control
D  Audit evidence
E  Review and reporting
F  Employability and technology skills

## Main capabilities

On successful completion of this exam, candidates should be able to:

- Explain the concept of audit and assurance and the functions of audit, corporate governance, including ethics and professional conduct.

- Demonstrate how the auditor obtains and accepts audit engagements, obtains an understanding of the entity and its environment, assesses the risk of material misstatement (whether arising from fraud or other irregularities) and plans an audit of financial statements.

- Describe and evaluate internal controls, techniques and audit tests, including IT systems to identify and communicate control risks and their potential consequences, making appropriate recommendations. Describe the scope, role and function of internal audit.

- Identify and describe the work and evidence obtained by the auditor and others required to meet the objectives of audit engagements and the application of the International Standards on Auditing (ISAs).

- Explain how consideration of subsequent events and the going concern principle can inform the conclusions from audit work and are reflected in different types of auditor's report, written representations and the final review and report.

- Demonstrate employability and technology skills.

# Displaying the right qualities and avoiding weaknesses

In order to pass Audit and Assurance it is important that you get some of the basics right. These include the following:

## Read the question

Again this sounds obvious but is absolutely critical. When you are reading the question think about the following:

- Which technical area is being tested?

  This should let you identify the relevant areas of technical knowledge to draw on.

- What am I being asked to do?

  (We will take a more detailed look at the wording of requirements later.)

- Are there any key dates?

  This is important in questions on inventory. If the inventory count takes place at a time other than the year-end you need to be aware of this.

- What is the status of your client?

  For example is it large or small, is it a new or existing client? This might affect issues such as risk.

- What is the nature of the business?

  This is particularly relevant in planning questions as it will have an impact on risk areas.

- How many marks are allocated to each part of the question so approximately how many points do I need to make?

When you think about the number of points you need to achieve you need to consider this in relation to the requirement. If you are asked for explanation it is likely that you will score more marks per point than if you are simply asked for a list of points.

You also need to think about the order in which you read information in the question. Particularly in Section B it is important that you read the requirement first so that as you read through the rest of the information you are aware of the key matters/issues which you are looking out for. For example if you are asked for risks in a scenario you can try to identify as many risk factors as possible as you read the detailed information.

## Understand the requirements

It is important that you can understand and differentiate between the requirements and terms that the examining team typically uses. Here are some examples:

| Requirement | Meaning |
| --- | --- |
| Explain | Make a point clear, justify a point of view |
| Describe | Give an account of something, including the key features |
| Define | Give the meaning of |
| Recommend | Advise the appropriate actions to pursue in terms the recipient will understand |
| Discuss | Critically examine an issue |
| List | Normally punchier points than 'explain' or 'discuss' |
| Illustrate | Explain by using examples |
| Audit procedures/audit tests | Actions |
| Enquiries | Questions |
| Evidence | Source (eg document) and what it proves |

## Think and plan

No matter how well prepared you are, you are going to have to do some thinking in the exam. Obviously you will be under time pressure but, if used effectively, thinking and planning time should not be seen as a waste of time.

Generating ideas can often be a problem at this stage. Remember that your knowledge of key ISAs can serve as a good starting point.

In audit evidence questions you may think about the financial statement assertions (completeness, accuracy, existence etc). You could also think about the different types of procedures (inspection, observation, inquiry, confirmation, recalculation/reperformance and analytical procedures).

In risk questions it might be helpful to think about the different elements of risk (inherent risk, control risk, detection risk).

Repeating this knowledge will not be sufficient in most cases to pass the question but these ideas can form a very sound basis for developing a good answer.

Keep going back to the requirement and make sure that you really are answering the question. One of the most common errors in auditing exams is identifying the correct point but using it in the wrong way. Make sure that your answer is focused on the requirements. It may be tempting to write everything you know about a particular point but this will not help you to pass the exam. This 'scattergun' approach will attract few, if any, marks.

## Producing your answer

Although much of the hard work has been done by the time you get to this stage you need to think carefully about how you put down each point. The way you make the point can make a difference to the number of marks scored. You need to make sure your answers do not suffer from a lack of clarity and precision. This is particularly the case regarding questions on audit evidence. For example, lists of tests stating 'check this' and 'check that' without explaining what is being checked and why is likely to score few marks. If you find it difficult to gauge the right level of detail try to imagine that you are explaining the procedure to a junior member of staff. Would they be able to perform the procedure based on your description?

Think about your style. A well-structured answer with clearly identifiable points is generally preferable to long paragraphs of text. However, do not fall into the trap of producing note-form answers. This is rarely sufficiently detailed to score marks.

# Format of the exam

The exam format is the same irrespective of the mode of delivery and will comprise two exam sections:

| Section | Style of question type | Description | Proportion of exam (%) |
|---------|------------------------|-------------|------------------------|
| A | Objective test (OT) case | 3 questions × 10 marks<br>Each question will contain 5 subparts each worth 2 marks | 30 |
| B | Constructed response (written questions) | 1 question × 30 marks<br>2 questions × 20 marks | 70 |
| Total | | | 100 |

Section A questions will be selected from the entire syllabus. The responses to each question or subpart in the case of OT cases are marked automatically as either correct or incorrect by computer.

Section B questions will mainly focus on the following syllabus areas but a minority of marks can be drawn from any other area of the syllabus

- Planning and risk assessment (syllabus area B)
- Internal control (syllabus area C)
- Audit evidence (syllabus area D)

The responses to these questions are human marked.

For exam sittings from September 2019 onwards, questions have used a dating convention whereby the 'current' date is 1 July 20X5.

## Additional information

The study guide provides more detailed guidance on the syllabus and can be found by visiting the exam resource finder on the ACCA website: www.accaglobal.com/uk/en/student/exam-support-resources.html

# Helping you with your revision

## BPP Learning Media – Approved Content Provider

As an ACCA **Approved Content Provider**, BPP Learning Media gives you the **opportunity** to use revision materials reviewed by the ACCA examining team. By incorporating the ACCA examining team's comments and suggestions regarding the depth and breadth of syllabus coverage, the BPP Learning Media Practice & Revision Kit provides excellent **ACCA approved** support for your revision.

These materials are reviewed by the ACCA examining team. The objective of the review is to ensure that the material properly covers the syllabus and study guide outcomes used by the examining team in setting the exams in the appropriate breadth and depth. The review does not ensure that every eventuality, combination or application of examinable topics is addressed by the ACCA Approved Content. Nor does the review comprise a detailed technical check of the content as the Approved Content Provider has its own quality assurance processes in place in this respect.

BPP Learning Media does everything possible to ensure that material is accurate and up to date when sending to print. In the event that any errors are found after the print date, they are uploaded to the following website: www.bpp.com/learningmedia/Errata.

## Question practice

Question practice under timed conditions is absolutely vital. We strongly advise you to create a revision study plan which focuses on question practice. This is so that you can get used to the pressures of answering exam questions in limited time, develop proficiency in the Specific AA skills and the Exam success skills. Ideally, you should aim to cover all questions in this Kit, and very importantly, all four mock exams.

To help you plan your revision, we have provided a full topic index which maps the questions to topics in the syllabus (see page ix).

## Making the most of question practice

At BPP Learning Media we realise that you need more than just questions and model answers to get the most from your question practice.

- Our **Top tips** included for certain questions provide essential advice on tackling questions, presenting answers and the key points that answers need to include. .

- We include **marking guides** to show you what the examining team rewards.

- We include **comments from the examining team** to show you where students struggled or performed well in the actual exam.

## Attempting mock exams

There are four mock exams that provide practice at coping with the pressures of the exam day. We strongly recommend that you attempt them under exam conditions. **Mock exam 1** is the September 2016 exam; **Mock exam 2** is the Specimen exam; **Mock exam 3** is the December 2016 exam and **Mock exam 4** includes the Section B questions from the September / December 2021 Hybrid exam.

## Topics to revise

The Audit and Assurance exam assumes knowledge of Financial Accounting. It is important, therefore, that candidates can apply the knowledge they have gained in Financial Accounting to the Audit and Assurance exam.

All questions are compulsory so you must revise the **whole** syllabus. Since the exam includes three 10 mark OT case questions (each comprising five OT questions of 2 marks each) in Section A, you should expect questions to cover a large part of the syllabus. Selective revision **will limit** the number of questions you can answer and hence reduce your chances of passing. It is better to go into the exam knowing a reasonable amount about most of the syllabus rather than concentrating on a few topics to the exclusion of the rest.

In Section B, all questions will require a written response but there may be questions requiring the calculation and interpretation of some basic ratios in the context of audit planning or review.

In short, remember that **all** the questions in this exam are compulsory. Therefore, we **strongly advise** that you do not selectively revise certain topics – any topic from the syllabus could be examined. Selective revision will limit the number of questions you can answer and hence reduce your chances of passing this exam.

## Question practice

Practising as many exam-style questions as possible will be the key to passing this exam. You must do questions under **timed conditions** and ensure you write full answers to the discussion parts as well as doing the calculations.

Avoid looking at the answer until you have finished a question. Your biggest problem with Audit and Assurance questions may be knowing how to start, and this needs practice.

Also ensure that you attempt all four mock exams under exam conditions. Gaining the easy marks in this exam tend to fall into two categories.

## Objective test questions (OTs) in Section A

Some OTs are easier than others, particularly MCQs. Answer those that you feel fairly confident about as quickly as you can. Come back later to those you find more difficult. This could be a way of making use of the time in the examination most efficiently and effectively.

Make sure that you understand the wording of OTs before selecting your answer.

## Discussions in Section B questions

A Section B question may separate discussion requirements from calculations, so that you do not need to do the calculations first in order to answer the discussion part. This means that you should be able to gain marks from making sensible, practical comments without having to complete the calculations.

Discussions that are focused on the specific organisation in the question will gain more marks than regurgitation of knowledge. Read the question carefully and more than once, to ensure you are actually answering the specific requirements.

Pick out key words such as 'describe', 'evaluate' and 'discuss'. These all mean something specific.

- 'Describe' means to communicate the key features
- 'Evaluate' means to assess the value
- 'Discuss' means to examine in detail by argument

Clearly label the points you make in discussions so that the marker can identify them all rather than getting lost in the detail.

Provide answers in the form requested. Use a report format if asked for and give recommendations if required.

## Tackling Objective Test Case Questions

You will see a variety of question styles in addition to MCQs, including number entry, multiple response and drag and drop.

First, read the whole case scenario. Make a note of any specific instructions or assumptions, such as key dates.

Then skim through the requirements of the five questions. The questions are independent of each other and can be answered in any order.

Some of the questions will be easier than others. For example, you may be asked to identify risks to independence from a given scenario.

Other questions will be more difficult and/or complex. There are two types of question that may take you longer to answer.

The first more time-consuming question is one where you are asked to consider two related issues. The best approach to adopt here is a step-by-step approach, dealing with each issue in turn. For example you could be asked to consider whether a potential adjustment is material and the impact of this on the audit report based on circumstances set out in the scenario. The first step would be to assess the materiality of the adjustment using your technical knowledge, but also applying any information given to you in the scenario. Having made a decision it should be possible to discount at least one of the distracters. Then think about the impact on the auditor's report. Does the audit opinion need to be modified or not? If it is, is the issue pervasive or not? If possible, try to come to your own conclusion before looking at the options available, then check whether your answer is one of the options listed. (Obviously if you are struggling looking at the remaining available options may help to jog your memory.) Having selected your answer always check the remaining distracters to ensure that you haven't made a common mistake.

The second more time-consuming question is one where you are asked to consider a number of statements and identify which one (or more) of them is correct. Make sure that you read each statement at least twice before making your selection. Be careful to follow the requirements of the question exactly, for example if you are asked to identify **two** correct statements. Make sure that you have spotted any negative questions, eg 'Which **TWO** of the following are **NOT**....'

# Analysis of past exams

The table below provides details of when each element of the syllabus has been examined in the most recent sittings.

From December 2016, the ACCA have released a 'sample' exam every two sittings which shows only questions set in Section B of the exam.

| Workbook chapter | | Mar/ Jun 2021 | Sep/ Dec 2020 | Mar/ Jun 2020 | Sep/ Dec 2019 | Mar/ Jun 2019 | Sep/ Dec 2018 | Mar/ Jun 2018 | Sep/ Dec 2017 | Mar/ Jun 2017 |
|---|---|---|---|---|---|---|---|---|---|---|
| | Audit framework and regulation | | | | | | | | | |
| 1 | The concept of audit and other assurance engagements | | | | | | | | | |
| 2 | External audits | | | | | | | | | |
| 3 | Corporate governance | | | | | B Q16d | | | | |
| 5 | Professional ethics and ACCA's Code of Ethics and Conduct | B Q17a | B Q16d | B Q16a, b | | | | | B Q16a | B Q16c |
| | Planning and risk assessment | | Q B16a | | | | | | | |
| 6 | Obtaining and accepting audit engagements | | | | | | | | | |
| 6 | Objective and general principles | B Q17c | | | | | | | | |
| 6 | Assessing audit risks | B Q17b | B Q16b | B Q16c | B Q16b | B Q17 | B Q16c | B Q17b | B Q17c | B Q16a, b |
| 6 | Understanding the entity and its environment | | | | | | B Q16a, b | | | |
| 6 | Fraud, laws and regulations | | | B Q18c | B Q16a | | | B Q17a | | |
| 7 | Audit planning and documentation | | | | | | | | B Q17a, b | |
| | Internal control | | | | | | | | | |
| 9 | Internal control systems | B Q16c | | | | B Q16a | | B Q16a | B Q16b | B Q18a |

| Workbook chapter | | Mar/ Jun 2021 | Sep/ Dec 2020 | Mar/ Jun 2020 | Sep/ Dec 2019 | Mar/ Jun 2019 | Sep/ Dec 2018 | Mar/ Jun 2018 | Sep/ Dec 2017 | Mar/ Jun 2017 |
|---|---|---|---|---|---|---|---|---|---|---|
| 9 | The use and evaluation of internal control systems by auditors | B Q16a | B Q17a | | | | | | | |
| 10 | Tests of controls | B Q16b | B Q17 | B Q17 | B Q17 | B Q16b | B Q17b | B Q16a, b | B Q16c | B Q18b |
| 10 | Communication on internal control | | | | | | B Q17a | | | |
| 4 | Internal audit and governance and the differences between external and internal audit | | | | | | | | | |
| 4 | The scope of the internal audit function, outsourcing and internal audit assignments | | | | | | | B Q16c | | |
| 8 | Financial statement assertions and audit evidence | | | | | | | | | |
| 11 | Audit procedures | | | | | | | | | |
| 11 | Audit sampling and other means of testing | | | | | | | | | |
| 12-17 | The audit of specific items | B Q16d, B Q18a, b, c | B Q16c, B Q18a, b, c | B Q16d, B Q18a, b | B Q16d, c, B Q18 a, b | B Q16c, B Q18a, b, c | B Q16d, e, B Q18a, b | B Q16d, B Q18a, b, c | B Q16d, B Q18a, b, c | B Q17a, c d |
| 11 | Computer-assisted audit techniques | | | | | | | | | B Q17b |
| 12 | The work of others | | | | | | | | | |

| Workbook chapter | | Mar/Jun 2021 | Sep/Dec 2020 | Mar/Jun 2020 | Sep/Dec 2019 | Mar/Jun 2019 | Sep/Dec 2018 | Mar/Jun 2018 | Sep/Dec 2017 | Mar/Jun 2017 |
|---|---|---|---|---|---|---|---|---|---|---|
| 18 | Not-for-profit organisations | | | | | | | | | |
| 19 | Subsequent events | | | | | B Q18d | | | | |
| 19 | Going concern | | | | B Q18c, d | | B Q18c | | | |
| 19 | Written representations | | | | | | | | | |
| 19 | Audit finalisation and the final review | | | | | | | | | |
| 20 | Auditor's reports | B Q18d | B Q18d | B Q18d | | | B Q18d | B Q18d | B Q18d | B Q17e |

# Essential skills areas to be successful in Audit and Assurance

We think there are three areas you should develop in order to achieve exam success in Audit and Assurance (AA):

(1)    Knowledge application

(2)    Specific AA skills

(3)    Exam success skills

These are shown in the diagram below:

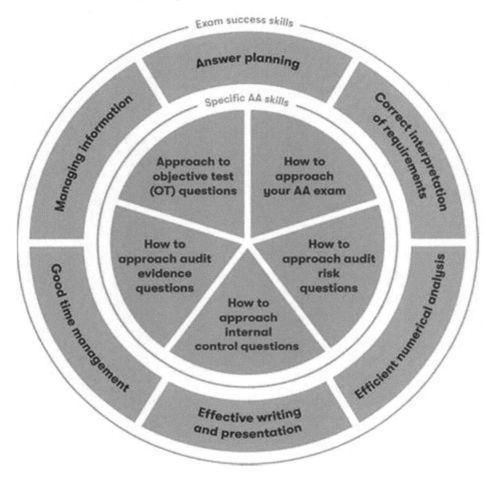

BPP
LEARNING
MEDIA

# Specific AA skills

These are the skills specific to AA that we think you need to develop in order to pass the exam.

In this Workbook, there are five skills checkpoints which define each skill and show how it is applied in answering a question. A brief summary of each skill is given below:

### Skill 1: How to approach your AA exam

Passing AA is about a combination of exam technique with detailed knowledge. Therefore, it is important that you plan your approach to the exam, and practise this approach, before you sit your exam.

A step-by-step technique for ensuring that you have a **planned approach to your AA exam** is outlined below:

**Step 1**    Attempt Section A first. Read the requirements to each of the OT questions before reading the OT case scenario.

Do not rush through this section of the exam.

**Step 2**    Then attempt Section B. Skim through all three questions and attempt them in your order of preference. Read all requirements in detail and use the scenario fully.

Skills Checkpoint 1 in the BPP Workbook covers this technique in detail.

### Skill 2: How to approach audit risk questions

In the exam, it is highly likely that you will need to attempt a scenario based question on audit risk.

**Step 1**    Allow some of your allotted time to read the requirement and the scenario. Don't rush into starting to write your answer.

Start by analysing the requirements so that you know what you are looking for when you read the scenario.

**Step 2**    Re-read the scenario and set out an answer plan using the risks you identify as you read through. Work through each paragraph of the scenario identifying specific audit risks. Each risk is worth one mark and the auditor's response is also worth one mark, so you would need five properly explained risks and responses to gain ten marks.

**Step 3**    Where there are more than the required number of audit risks, choose those that you can best explain.

Describe the audit risk in detail explaining the potential impact on the financial statements. Also remember to explain the practical steps the auditor would take and the work they would do.

Start each point in a new section.

Skills Checkpoint 2 in the BPP Workbook covers this technique in detail through application to an exam-standard question.

### Skill 3: How to approach internal control questions

Similarly, to Skill 2, it is likely that you will need to attempt a scenario based question on internal controls in your exam.

A step-by-step technique for attempting such questions is outlined below.

**Step 1**     Allow some of your allotted time to read the requirement and the scenario. Don't rush into starting to write your answer.

Start by analysing the requirements so that you know what you are looking for when you read the scenario.

**Step 2**     Re-read the scenario and set out an answer plan using the points you identify as you read through.

Work through each paragraph of the scenario identifying specific points to make, for example deficiencies. Each deficiency is worth one mark and the recommendation is also worth one mark, hence why you would need six properly explained deficiencies and recommendations to gain 12 marks.

**Step 3**     Often there are more than the required number of deficiencies in a scenario, therefore choose the ones for which you can provide a recommended control.

Explain the deficiency in terms of its impact on the entity. Also remember to explain the recommendation, what internal control should be implemented and by whom.

Start each point in a new section.

Skills Checkpoint 3 in the BPP Workbook covers this technique in detail through application to an exam-standard question.

## Skill 4: How to approach audit evidence questions

These questions can appear in both sections of the exam. It is very important that you discern exactly what the requirement is asking for and that you use any scenario provided in the exam.

A step-by-step technique for approaching audit evidence questions is outlined below.

**Step 1**     Identify exactly what you are being asked for in the requirement: audit procedures, tests of controls or substantive procedures.

Also identify whether the requirement is testing audit procedures that relate to a particular assertion.

**Step 2**     Now that you have understood what the requirement demands you are much better placed to answer it. Consider the following:

Is there a scenario you should use?

Can you remember the accounting treatment for the item? Would that give you a starting point?

What audit procedures have you learnt/used at work?

Can you use the mnemonic AEIOU to help you to generate audit procedures?

**Step 3**     Write out your audit procedure using the 'verb-document-reason' approach.

What do you want to be done (eg recalculate, agree, vouch)?

To which document (eg invoice, physical asset, board minutes)?

Why (eg to ensure that receivables are recoverable (valuation))? You might choose to link this to an assertion.

Start each audit procedure on a new line.

Skills Checkpoint 4 in the BPP Workbook covers this technique in detail through application to a sample of exam-standard questions.

## Skill 5: Approach to objective test (OT) questions

Section A comprises 30% of the exam and consists of three OT case questions. Candidates can be tempted to rush through this section in order to make up time for Section B however this is a risky approach because there are a lot of marks you could lose.

A step-by-step technique for approaching OT questions is outlined below:

**Step 1**     **Answer the questions you know first.**

If you're having difficulty answering a question, move on and come back to tackle it once you've answered all the questions you know. It is often quicker to answer discursive style OT questions first, leaving more time for calculations. The AA exam doesn't have many calculations but you may be asked to calculate financial statement ratios.

**Step 2**     **Answer all questions.**

There is no penalty for an incorrect answer in ACCA exams, there is nothing to be gained by leaving an OT question unanswered. If you are stuck on a question, as a last resort, it is worth selecting the option you consider most likely to be correct, and moving on. Make a note of the question, so if you have time after you have answered the rest of the questions, you can revisit it.

**Step 3**     **Read the requirement first!**

The requirement will be stated in bold text in the exam. Identify what you are being asked to do, any technical knowledge required and what type of OT question you are dealing with. Look for key words in the requirement such as "which TWO of the following," or "which of the following is NOT".

Skills Checkpoint 5 in the BPP Workbook covers this technique in detail through application to an exam-standard question.

## Exam success skills

Passing the AA exam requires more than applying syllabus knowledge and demonstrating the specific AA skills. It also requires the development of excellent exam technique through question practice.

We consider the following six skills to be vital for exam success. The skills checkpoints show how each of these skills can be applied in the exam.

## Exam success skill 1

### Managing information

Questions in the exam will present you with a lot of information. The skill is how you handle this information to make the best use of your time. The key is determining how you will approach the exam and then actively reading the questions.

### Advice on developing Managing information

### Approach

The exam is three hours long. There is no designated 'reading' time at the start of the exam.

However, one approach that can work well is to start the exam by spending 10–15 minutes carefully reading through all of the questions to familiarise yourself with the exam.

Once you feel familiar with the exam consider the order in which you will attempt the questions; always attempt them in your order of preference. For example, you may want to leave to last the question you consider to be the most difficult.

If you do take this approach, remember to adjust the time available for each question appropriately – see Exam success skill 6: Good time management.

If you find that this approach doesn't work for you, don't worry because you can develop your own technique.

### Active reading

You must take an active approach to reading each question. In Section B questions in particular, focus on the requirement first, making a note of key verbs such as 'explain' and 'discuss', to ensure you answer the question properly. Then read the rest of the question, making notes on important and relevant information you think you will need.

# Exam success skill 2

## Correct interpretation of the requirements

The active verb used often dictates the approach that written answers should take (eg 'explain', 'discuss'). It is important you identify and use the verb to define your approach. The correct interpretation of the **requirements** skill means correctly producing only what is being asked for by a requirement. Anything not required will not earn marks.

## Advice on developing the Correct interpretation of the requirements

This skill can be developed by analysing question requirements and applying this process:

**Step 1**   **Read the requirement**

Firstly, read the requirement a couple of times slowly and carefully and note the active verbs. Use the active verbs to define what you plan to do. Make sure you identify any sub-requirements.

**Step 2**   Read the rest of the question

By reading the requirement first, you will have an idea of what you are looking out for as you read through the case overview and exhibits. This is a great time saver and means you don't end up having to read the whole question in full twice. You should do this in an active way – see Exam success skill 1: Managing Information.

**Step 3**   Read the requirement again

Read the requirement again to remind yourself of the exact wording before starting your written answer. This will capture any misinterpretation of the requirements or any missed requirements entirely. This should become a habit in your approach and, with repeated practice, you will find the focus, relevance and depth of your answer plan will improve.

# Exam success skill 3

## Answer planning: Priorities, structure and logic

This skill requires the planning of the key aspects of an answer which accurately and completely responds to the requirement.

## Advice on developing Answer planning: Priorities, structure and logic

Everyone will have a preferred style for an answer plan. For example, it may be a mind map, bullet pointed lists or simply making some notes. Choose the approach that you feel most comfortable with, or, if you are not sure, try out different approaches for different questions until you have found your preferred style.

# Exam success skill 4

## Efficient numerical analysis

This skill aims to maximise the marks awarded by making clear to the marker the process of arriving at your answer. This is achieved by laying out an answer such that, even if you make a few errors, you can still score subsequent marks for follow-on calculations. It is vital that you do not lose marks purely because the marker cannot follow what you have done.

## Advice on developing Efficient numerical analysis

There are not many marks available for numbers in the AA exam, however you may need to calculate ratios such as the receivables collection period. This skill can be developed by applying the following process:

**Step 1**   **Use a standard proforma working/formula where relevant**

If answers can be laid out in a standard proforma or using a standard formula then always plan to do so. This will help the marker to understand your working and allocate the marks easily. It will also help you to work through the figures in a methodical and time-efficient way.

**Step 2**     **Show your workings**

Keep your workings as clear and simple as possible and ensure they are cross-referenced to the main part of your answer. Where it helps, provide brief narrative explanations to help the marker understand the steps in the calculation. This means that if a mistake is made you do not lose any subsequent marks for follow-on calculations.

**Step 3**     **Keep moving!**

It is important to remember that, in an exam situation, it can sometimes be difficult to get every number 100% correct. The key is therefore ensuring you do not spend too long on any single calculation. If you are struggling with a solution then make a sensible assumption, state it and move on.

# Exam success skill 5

## Effective writing and presentation

Written answers should be presented so that the marker can clearly see the points you are making, presented in the format specified in the question. The skill is to provide efficient written answers with sufficient breadth of points that answer the question, in the right depth, in the time available.

### Advice on developing Effective writing and presentation

**Step 1**     **Use headings.**

Using the headings and sub-headings from your answer plan will give your answer structure, order and logic. This will ensure your answer links back to the requirement and is clearly signposted, making it easier for the marker to understand the different points you are making. Making your headings bold will also help the marker.

**Step 2**     **Write your answer in short, but full, sentences.**

Use short, punchy sentences with the aim that every sentence should say something different and generate marks. Write in full sentences, ensuring your style is professional.

**Step 3**     **Do your calculations first and explanation second.**

Questions sometimes ask for a discussion or explanation with suitable calculations. The best approach is to prepare the calculation first then add the explanation.

Performing the calculation first should enable you to explain what you have done.

# Exam success skill 6

## Good time management

This skill means planning your time across all the requirements so that all tasks have been attempted at the end of the three hours available and actively checking on time during your exam. This is so that you can flex your approach and prioritise requirements which, in your judgement, will generate the maximum marks in the available time remaining.

### Advice on developing Good time management

The exam is three hours long, which translates to 1.8 minutes per mark. Therefore a 20-mark requirement should be allocated a maximum of 36 minutes to complete your answer before you move on to the next task. At the beginning of a question, work out the amount of time you should be spending on each requirement and write the finishing time next to each requirement on your exam. If you take the approach of spending 10–15 minutes reading and planning at the start of the exam, adjust the time allocated to each question accordingly.

### Keep an eye on the clock

Aim to attempt all requirements, but be prepared to move on if your answer is not going as planned. The challenge for many is sticking to planned timings. Be aware this is difficult to achieve in the early stages of your studies and be ready to let this skill develop over time. If you find yourself running short on time and know that a full answer is not possible in the time you have, consider recreating your plan in overview form and then add key terms and details as time allows. Remember, some marks may be available, for example, simply stating a conclusion which you don't have time to justify in full.

## Question practice

Question practice is a core part of learning new topic areas. When you practice questions, you should focus on improving the Exam success skills – personal to your needs – by obtaining feedback or through a process of self-assessment.

Sitting this exam as a computer-based exam and practicing as many exam-style questions as possible in the ACCA CBE practice platform will be the key to passing this exam. You should attempt questions under timed conditions and ensure you produce full answers to the discussion parts as well as doing the calculations. Also ensure that you attempt all mock exams under exam conditions.

ACCA have launched a free on-demand resource designed to mirror the live exam experience helping you to become more familiar with the exam format. You can access the platform via the Study Support Resources section of the ACCA website navigating to the CBE question practice section and logging in with your my ACCA credentials.

# Questions

# BJM Co                                                    18 mins

The following scenario relates to questions 1–5.

You are an audit senior of YHT & Co and have worked on the external audit of BJM Co (BJM), an unlisted company, since your firm was appointed external auditor two years ago.

BJM owns a chain of nine restaurants and is a successful company. BJM has always been subject to national hygiene regulations, especially in relation to the food preparation process. Non-compliance can result in a large fine or closure of the restaurant concerned.

The board of BJM has recently notified you that the national hygiene regulations have been updated and are now much more stringent and onerous than before.

With this in mind, the board has asked your firm to conduct a review of BJM's compliance with hygiene regulations, in order to allow the board to assess whether the appropriate processes have been implemented at each of the nine restaurants. The review is not expected to include the provision of accounting advice or the preparation of figures in the financial statements.

The work is likely to be very lucrative. Your firm has sufficient experience to undertake the above review engagement.

1    Despite running a successful company, BJM's board has often needed to be reminded of some fundamental principles and you often have to explain key concepts.

     Which of the following statements best defines the external audit?

     O    The external audit is an exercise carried out by auditors in order to give an opinion on whether the financial statements of a company are fairly presented.

     O    The external audit is an exercise carried out in order to give an opinion on the effectiveness of a company's internal control system.

     O    The purpose of the external audit is to identify areas of deficiency within a company and to make recommendations to mitigate those deficiencies.

     O    The external audit provides negative assurance on the truth and fairness of a company's financial statements.

2    The board has also struggled to differentiate between its responsibilities and those of the external auditor in circumstances such as the prevention and detection of fraud and error, and compliance with regulations.

     Which of the following statements best describes YHT & Co's responsibility regarding BJM's compliance with hygiene regulations, in line with ISA 250 (Revised) *Consideration of Laws and Regulations in an Audit of Financial Statements*?

     O    YHT & Co should actively prevent and detect non-compliance with the regulations.

     O    YHT & Co should perform specific audit procedures to identify possible non-compliance.

     O    YHT & Co should obtain sufficient appropriate audit evidence about BJM's compliance with the regulations as they have a direct effect on the financial statements.

     O    YHT & Co does not have any responsibility as the hygiene regulations do not have a direct effect on the financial statements.

3   The partner responsible for the review of hygiene compliance has informed you that the engagement is an assurance engagement.

Which of the following would **NOT** have been relevant to the partner in forming this opinion?

- O   The existence of a three-party relationship
- O   The existence of suitable criteria
- O   The determination of materiality
- O   The subject matter

---

4   The partner responsible for the review engagement has asked you to tell him what level of assurance you believe YHT & Co should provide, and also what type of opinion the firm should give.

What is the level of assurance and type of opinion that can be provided on this review engagement?

| | Level of assurance | Report wording |
|---|---|---|
| O | Reasonable | Positive |
| O | Reasonable | Negative |
| O | Limited | Positive |
| O | Limited | Negative |

---

5   The audit engagement partner has told you that the independence threats arising from YHT & Co performing the review engagement should be monitored carefully.

Which of the following is likely to cause the audit engagement partner most concern?

- O   According to the ACCA *Code of Ethics and Conduct*, YHT & Co is prohibited from providing other assurance services to an audit client.
- O   The review engagement is likely to give rise to a self-review threat, as the outcomes of the review could form the basis of the financial statements which the audit team will audit.
- O   The lucrative nature of the review engagement may make the external audit team less inclined to require management to make adjustments or to issue a modified audit opinion, for fear of losing the review engagement.
- O   If the new review engagement causes YHT & Co's fee income from BJM to exceed 15% of the firm's total fees, the ACCA *Code of Ethics and Conduct* states that the new engagement must be turned down.

---

(Total = 10 marks)

# Conoy

The following scenario relates to questions 6–10.

Conoy designs and manufactures luxury motor vehicles. It is not a listed company, but its board has recently decided that it would like to improve its corporate governance in order to apply best practice. Conoy's shares are held equally by six shareholders, four of whom are also executive directors. The remaining two shareholders are not involved with Conoy, other than as shareholders.

Conoy has an internal audit department which is managed by Adrian Muse, the chief internal auditor. Adrian frequently comments that Conoy's board does not understand his reports, and does not provide sufficient support for his department and for the company's system of internal control. RWG & Co, Conoy's external auditors, have also expressed concern in this area.

Adrian has submitted a proposal to the board to establish an audit committee, and this is currently under consideration. The proposed membership of the audit committee is:

- Adrian Muse (chief internal auditor)
- Penny Dinty (existing executive director with some financial expertise)
- Sharon Header (proposed new non-executive director)
- Fredrick Rowe (proposed new non-executive director)

The board is also considering a significant expansion of the company. However, the company's bank is concerned by the standard of financial reporting as Conoy's finance director recently left the company. The board is delaying providing the bank with financial information until a new finance director has been appointed.

As part of its commitment to the effectiveness of the external audit process, the chair of Conoy's audit committee, Leslie Schiff, is keen to ensure that the external audit makes use of the latest auditing techniques. She has heard about data analytics routines, but is unsure exactly what they entail.

In addition, Leslie has expressed an interest in understanding the processes used by RWG & Co to ensure that the Conoy audit is conducted to the required standards of quality. She mainly deals with, Karolina Hernandez, the engagement partner but is unsure how responsibilities are divided up within the team performing the audit.

6    RWG & Co is required to adhere to quality management standards in relation to the audits it performs.

Use the drop down lists to complete the following sentence to correctly describe the auditor's responsibilities in accordance with ISA 220 *Quality management for an audit of financial statements*.

The engagement partner is responsible for the [          ] of the audit.

In relation to the audit of Conoy, an engagement quality review [          ] in order to comply with auditing standards.

Options for drop down list:

First list:

| direction |
| --- |
| review |
| direction and review |
| direction, supervision, performance and review |

Second list:

| may be performed, but is not mandatory |
| --- |
| is required |
| is required only if the auditor is not independent |

---

7    ISA 220 *Quality Management for an Audit of Financial Statements* states that the engagement partner is ultimately responsible for the audit.

The following statements concern the quality management of the audit of Conoy. Indicate whether each statement represents a strength or a deficiency of the quality management of the audit?

| | Strength | Deficiency |
|---|---|---|
| The audit team as a whole takes collective responsibility for the audit. | ☐ | ☐ |
| At the audit planning meeting, Karolina Hernandez emphasised that each member of the audit team is required exercise professional scepticism through the Conoy audit. | ☐ | ☐ |
| Karolina Hernandez is scheduled to review the formal written communications to be sent to Conoy's management after the date of the auditor's report. | ☐ | ☐ |

8    In relation to the proposed membership of the audit committee, state whether each proposed member should be included or not.

| Proposed member | Include in audit committee | Do not include in audit committee |
|---|---|---|
| Adrian Muse | ☐ | ☐ |
| Penny Dinty | ☐ | ☐ |
| Sharon Header | ☐ | ☐ |
| Fredrick Rowe | ☐ | ☐ |

9    Which of the following statements best describes why having an audit committee could help Conoy raise additional finance by addressing the concerns of the bank?

○    The independent non-executive members of the audit committee can provide guarantees to the bank concerning Conoy's financial viability.

○    The audit committee will have at least one member who has relevant financial experience. This person will be able to stand in as Conoy's finance director before a new finance director is appointed.

○    The audit committee will have at least one member who has relevant financial experience, so that they can monitor the integrity of the financial statements.

○    The audit committee will review all the available evidence to substantiate information in financial reporting, thus improving the credibility of the financial statements.

10    The following statements concern the auditor's use of data analytics routines is true. Indicate whether each statement is false?

|  | True | False |
|---|---|---|
| A key drawback of data analytics software is that it is difficult to tailor to each particular audit client | ☐ | ☐ |
| Data analytics routines enable auditors to examine complex data using simple visualisation techniques | ☐ | ☐ |
| Although powerful, data analytics routines must be applied to strictly limited quantities of data so as to extrapolate correctly from a sample | ☐ | ☐ |

(Total = 10 marks)

# Stark                                                                18 mins

The following scenario relates to questions 11–15.

You are an audit manager of Ali & Co and have just been assigned the audit of Stark Co (Stark). Stark, a listed company, provides investment advice to individuals, and is regulated by the relevant financial conduct authority.

Mr Day, a partner in Ali & Co, has been the audit engagement partner for Stark for the previous nine years and has excellent knowledge of the client. Mr Day has informed you that he would like his daughter Zoe to be part of the audit team this year; Zoe is currently studying for her first set of exams for her ACCA qualification.

In an initial meeting with the finance director of Stark, you learn that the audit team will not be entertained on Stark's yacht this year; instead, he has arranged a balloon flight costing less than one-tenth of the expense of using the yacht and hopes this will be acceptable.

Ali & Co has always carried out tax advisory work for Stark. The tax advisory services do not have an impact on the figures reported in the financial statements. The finance director has stated that he feels strongly that the firm that offers taxation services this year should charge a fee which is based on a percentage of tax saved. He also trusts that your firm will accept a fixed fee for representing Stark in a dispute regarding the amount of sales tax payable to the taxation authorities.

11    From a review of the information above, your audit assistant has highlighted some of the potential risks to independence in respect of the audit of Stark.

(1)    Mr Day would like his daughter Zoe to be part of the audit team
(2)    Audit team to be offered a balloon flight
(3)    Tax fee to be based on a percentage of tax saved
(4)    Firm to represent Stark in a dispute with the tax authorities

Which of the following options best identifies the valid threats to independence and allocates the threat to the most appropriate category?

|  | Advocacy | Intimidation | Self-interest |
|---|---|---|---|
| O | (3) and (4) | (3) only | (1) and (2) |
| O | (4) only | (3) only | (2) and (3) |
| O | (3) only | (3) and (4) | (2) only |
| O | (3) and (4) | (1) and (4) | (1) and (2) |

12  In relation to the audit team being offered a balloon ride:

Which of the following actions should be taken to ensure the firm complies with ACCA's *Code of Ethics and Conduct*?

○   The gift may be accepted as Stark has taken appropriate measures to reduce the value of the gift compared to previous years.

○   The value of the gift should be assessed to determine whether it is of material value to the financial statements.

○   The gift should only be accepted if its value is trivial and inconsequential to the recipients.

○   Only the audit engagement partner and audit manager should accept the gift.

13  In relation to the audit engagement partner holding the role for nine years:

Which of the following safeguards should be implemented in order to comply with ACCA's *Code of Ethics and Conduct*?

○   An independent review partner should be appointed to the audit.

○   The audit engagement partner should be removed from the audit team but may serve as the engagement quality reviewer.

○   Ali & Co should not audit Stark for a five-year period.

○   The audit engagement partner should be removed from the audit team.

14  Mr Day's daughter, Zoe, is currently learning about International Standards on Auditing (ISAs) in her studies. She has asked you for clarification of the following.

Which is the correct order of the following stages involved in the development of an ISA?

(1)  Distribution of exposure draft for public comment

(2)  Consideration of comments received from the public

(3)  Approval by IAASB members

(4)  Establishment of task force to develop draft standard

(5)  Discussion of proposed standard at a public meeting

○   1, 5, 4, 3, 2

○   2, 4, 1, 3, 5

○   4, 5, 1, 2, 3

○   5, 4, 2, 1, 3

15  Zoe is also concerned that Ali & Co might breach confidentiality were the audit firm to represent Stark in its dispute with the tax authorities.

Which of the following statements best reflects the auditor's duty of confidentiality?

○   Auditors must never, under any circumstances, disclose any matters of which they become aware during the course of the audit to third parties, without the permission of the client.

○   Auditors may disclose any matters in relation to criminal activities to the police or taxation authorities, if requested to do so by the police or a tax inspector.

○   Auditors may disclose matters to third parties without their client's consent if it is in the public interest, and they must do so if there is a statutory duty to do so.

○   Auditors may only disclose matters to third parties without their client's consent if the public interest or national security is involved.

(Total = 10 marks)

# Tangerine Tech Co (Mar/Jun 16) (amended)    18 mins

The following scenario relates to questions 16–20.

You are an audit manager of Satsuma & Co and have been assigned to the audit of Tangerine Tech Co (Tangerine), a company which is planning to list on a stock exchange within six months. The listing rules of the stock exchange require compliance with corporate governance principles, and the directors are unsure whether they are following best practice in relation to this. They have asked the audit engagement partner for their view on this matter.

Tangerine's board is comprised of six executive directors, a non-executive chairman and three other non-executive directors (NEDs). The chairman and one of the NEDs are former directors of Tangerine and on reaching retirement age were asked to take on non-executive roles. The company has established an audit committee, and all NEDs are members including the chairman who chairs the committee. All four members of the audit committee were previously involved in sales or production related roles.

All of the directors have been members of the board for at least four years. As the chairman does not have an executive role, he has sole responsibility for liaising with the shareholders and answering their questions. The company has not established an internal audit function to monitor internal controls.

16    Which of the following features are corporate governance deficiencies which Tangerine Co would need to address prior to their listing?

(1)    The chairman has sole responsibility for liaising with shareholders.

(2)    The company has not established an internal audit function.

(3)    The chairman and one of the NEDs are former executive directors of Tangerine Co.

O    1 and 2 only

O    1 and 3 only

O    2 and 3 only

O    1, 2 and 3

---

17    The audit engagement partner's review has identified the following additional corporate governance deficiencies:

(1)    All the directors have been members of the board for at least four years.

(2)    The board is comprised of six executive and four non-executive directors.

Which of the following would the audit engagement partner recommend to address these deficiencies to ensure compliance with corporate governance principles?

| | Deficiency 1 | Deficiency 2 |
|---|---|---|
| O | The directors should be subject to annual re-election | At least 50% of the board, excluding the Chair, must be comprised of non-executive directors whom the board considers to be independent |
| O | The directors must be reappointed annually by the chairman | At least 75% of the board must be comprised of executive directors |
| O | The directors should be subject to annual re-election | At least 75% of the board must be comprised of executive directors |
| O | The directors must be reappointed annually by the chairman | At least 50% of the board, excluding the Chair, must be comprised of non-executive directors whom the board considers to be independent |

Questions    9

18    The audit engagement partner has assessed the make-up of the audit committee.

      Which of the following would be valid conclusions from this assessment?

      (1)    It is acceptable for the chairman to chair the audit committee.

      (2)    A new member of the audit committee with relevant financial experience must be recruited.

      O    1 only

      O    2 only

      O    1 and 2

      O    Neither 1 nor 2

19    The directors are aware that in accordance with corporate governance provisions they have responsibilities for internal control but are unclear as to the extent of these responsibilities.

      Which of the following correctly describes their responsibilities?

| | To review internal controls annually | To report on internal controls to shareholders |
|---|---|---|
| O | No | No |
| O | Yes | No |
| O | No | Yes |
| O | Yes | Yes |

20    The board of Tangerine is considering establishing an internal audit function.

      Which of the following factors would be relevant in making this decision?

      (1)    It would help the audit committee to discharge its responsibilities for monitoring internal control.

      (2)    The board would no longer need to take responsibility for the prevention and detection of fraud and error.

      (3)    The costs of establishing an internal audit function should be considered against the benefits gained.

      O    1 and 2 only

      O    1 and 3 only

      O    2 and 3 only

      O    1, 2 and 3

                                                                    (Total = 10 marks)

# LV Fones (Jun 10) (amended)                    18 mins

The following scenario relates to questions 21–25.

You are the audit manager of Jones & Co and you are planning the audit of LV Fones Co, a listed company, which has been an audit client for four years and specialises in manufacturing luxury mobile phones.

During the planning stage of the audit you have obtained the following information. The employees of LV Fones Co are entitled to purchase smartphones at a discount of 10%. The audit team has in previous years been offered the same level of staff discount.

During the year the financial controller of LV Fones was ill and hence unable to work. The company had no spare staff able to fulfil the role and hence a qualified audit senior of Jones & Co was seconded to the client for three months to cover the work of the financial controller. The audit engagement partner has recommended that the audit senior work on the audit as he has good knowledge of the client. The fee income derived from LV Fones was boosted by this engagement and, along with the audit and tax fee, now accounts for 16% of the firm's total fees (15.7% last year).

From a review of the correspondence files you note 60% of last year's audit fee is still outstanding.

Based on the information above you have summarised some of the potential risks to independence in the audit of LV Fones as follows.

(1)     The audit team has been offered a discount on luxury phones.
(2)     The audit senior was seconded to LV to cover for the financial controller.
(3)     Total fees from LV is over 15% of the total fees of the firm for the second consecutive year.
(4)     Fees are overdue in respect of last year's audit.

21     Which of the following options best identifies the valid potential threats to independence in the audit of LV Fones and allocates the threat to the most appropriate category?

| | Self-interest | Self-review |
|---|---|---|
| O | 1 and 2 only | 3 and 4 only |
| O | 3 and 4 only | 1 and 2 only |
| O | 1, 3 and 4 | 2 only |
| O | 3 only | 1, 2 and 4 |

22     You have also discovered that the audit engagement partner and the finance director have known each other socially for many years, and in fact went on holiday together last summer with their families to the finance director's villa.

Which **TWO** threats to independence are raised by this relationship and what safeguards should be applied?

| | Threats | Safeguards |
|---|---|---|
| O | Familiarity and self-interest | Jones & Co to resign as auditors |
| O | Self-review and intimidation | Rotation of audit engagement partner |
| O | Self-review and intimidation | Jones & Co to resign as auditors |
| O | Familiarity and self-interest | Rotation of audit engagement partner |

23    In relation to the audit team being offered a 10% discount on mobile phones:

Indicate whether the following statements are true or false, in accordance with ACCA's *Code of Ethics and Conduct*.

|  | True | False |
|---|---|---|
| The audit team can accept the discount as it is on the same terms as that offered to staff | ☐ | ☐ |
| Junior members of the audit team are allowed to accept the discount, but the audit manager and audit engagement partner should not | ☐ | ☐ |
| Unless the value of the discount is trivial and inconsequential to the audit team members, the offer should be declined | ☐ | ☐ |
| The audit team is only allowed to accept a discount of up to 5% | ☐ | ☐ |

---

24    Which of the following steps must Jones & Co take, as the fees from LV have exceeded 15% for the last two years?

(1)    Resign from the audit
(2)    Disclose the matter to those charged with governance
(3)    Arrange for a pre- or post-issuance review

○    1 only
○    2 only
○    3 only
○    2 and 3

---

25    The finance director of LV has made some enquiries about the other services that Jones & Co may be able to assist with.

In the table below indicate whether Jones & Co would or would not be able to provide the other services.

|  | Service can be provided | Service cannot be provided |
|---|---|---|
| Design and implementation of IT systems over financial reporting | ☐ | ☐ |
| Assistance with preparation of tax return | ☐ | ☐ |
| Accounting services | ☐ | ☐ |
| Recruiting service for the position of credit controller | ☐ | ☐ |

---

(Total = 10 marks)

# Orange (Jun 12) (amended)

The following scenario relates to questions 26–30.

You are the audit manager of Currant & Co and you are planning the audit of Orange Financials Co (Orange), which specialises in the provision of loans and financial advice to individuals and companies. Currant & Co has audited Orange for many years.

The directors are planning to list Orange on a stock exchange within the next few months and have asked if the audit engagement partner can attend the meetings with potential investors. In addition, as the finance director of Orange is likely to be quite busy with the listing, he has asked if Currant & Co can produce the financial statements for the current year.

During the year, the assistant finance director of Orange left and joined Currant & Co as a partner. It has been suggested that due to his familiarity with Orange, he should be appointed to provide an independent partner review for the audit.

Once Orange obtains its stock exchange listing it will require several assignments to be undertaken; for example, obtaining advice about corporate governance best practice. Currant & Co is very keen to be appointed to these engagements, however, Orange has implied that in order to gain this work Currant & Co needs to complete the external audit quickly and with minimal questions/issues.

The finance director has informed you that once the stock exchange listing has been completed, he would like the engagement team to attend a weekend away at a luxury hotel with his team, as a thank you for all their hard work. In addition, he has offered a senior member of the engagement team a short-term loan at a significantly reduced interest rate.

Orange is aware that subsequent to the stock exchange listing it will need to establish an audit committee, and has asked for some advice in relation to this.

26 As part of your planning work you have identified a number of potential risks to independence.

Indicate whether each of the following potential risks could give rise to an advocacy threat.

|  | | Yes | No |
| --- | --- | --- | --- |
| (1) | The audit engagement partner has been asked to attend meetings with potential investors. | ☐ | ☐ |
| (2) | Currant & Co has been offered the opportunity to provide other services to Orange Financials. | ☐ | ☐ |
| (3) | Currant & Co has been asked to produce the financial statements of Orange Financials. | ☐ | ☐ |
| (4) | There is a suggestion that a partner who previously worked for Orange Financials should be the review partner. | ☐ | ☐ |

27 Currant & Co has been offered work by Orange Financials. This is dependent on the audit being completed with minimal issues.

Which **TWO** of the following threats does this situation create?

☐ Intimidation

☐ Self-interest

☐ Familiarity

☐ Advocacy

28 The finance director has made two offers to members of the audit team:

(1)    Weekend away

(2)    Loan at reduced rates

Which of the following correctly summarises which of the offers, if any, can be accepted?

|  | (1) | (2) |
|---|---|---|
| O | Accepted | Accepted |
| O | Accepted | Not accepted |
| O | Not accepted | Accepted |
| O | Not accepted | Not accepted |

29 In accordance with ACCA's *Code of Ethics and Conduct* you have concluded that if you win the additional work you will need to disclose the proportion of fees obtained from Orange Financials to those charged with governance and conduct a post-issuance review.

Which of the following explains the basis for your conclusion?

O    Total fees from Orange Financials will make up more than 10% of Currant & Co's total fees for the first time since your appointment.

O    Total non-audit fees from all Currant & Co's clients make up more than 5% of the total fees of the firm.

O    Total fees from Orange Financials make up more than 15% of Currant & Co's total fees for the second consecutive year.

O    The disclosure and review are required in all circumstances where services other than audit are offered, irrespective of the level of fees.

30 The board has noted down a number of statements relating to the audit committee and has asked you to confirm whether their understanding is correct.

Indicate whether the following statements are true or false.

|  | True | False |
|---|---|---|
| The audit committee should be made up of independent non-executive directors | ☐ | ☐ |
| The audit committee normally appoints the external auditors at the AGM | ☐ | ☐ |
| The audit committee monitors and reviews the internal audit function | ☐ | ☐ |
| The audit committee sets out the scope of the external auditor's work | ☐ | ☐ |

(Total = 10 marks)

# SGCC

The following scenario relates to questions 31–35.

You are an audit manager in HTQ & Co. One of your clients, SGCC, has recently become a listed company and has asked for your advice regarding the changes they should make to achieve appropriate compliance with corporate governance codes.

## The board

Mr Sheppard is the Chief Executive Officer and Chairman of the board of SGCC. He appoints and maintains a board of five executive and two non-executive directors. While the board sets performance targets for the senior managers in the company, no formal targets are set for each director and no review of board policies is carried out. Board salaries are therefore set and paid by Mr Sheppard based on his assessment of all the board members, including himself, and not their actual performance.

## Internal controls

Internal controls in SGCC are monitored by the senior accountant, although the company assumes that, as external auditors, your firm will carry out a detailed review of internal controls. SGCC does not have an internal audit department or an audit committee.

Annual financial statements are produced, providing detailed information on past performance.

31    From a review of the information above, your audit assistant has highlighted some deficiencies in SGCC's corporate governance arrangements, especially in relation to the composition of the board.

Which of the following actions would be appropriate to improve SGCC's corporate governance compliance?

    ○    SGCC should appoint an external consultant to review board policies.

    ○    SGCC should appoint a new chief executive officer or board chairman.

    ○    SGCC should create a remuneration committee to oversee the appointment of new directors.

    ○    SGCC should implement a formal and rigorous evaluation of its directors' performance once every two years.

32    Which of the following statements is correct with regards to the composition of the board at SGCC?

    ○    SGCC should appoint three new non-executive directors to the board.

    ○    SGCC should reappoint two of its executive directors as non-executive directors.

    ○    SGCC should appoint three new executive directors to the board.

    ○    SGCC should reappoint three of its executive directors as non-executive directors.

33  Your audit assistant does not feel that SGCC's approach to internal controls is sufficiently robust to comply with corporate governance principles and has drawn up a list of recommendations.

Which **TWO** of the following recommendations are valid?

☐ SGCC should establish an audit committee with at least four directors as is required for all listed companies.

☐ SGCC must establish an internal audit department as is required for all listed companies.

☐ Once SGCC has an audit committee and an internal audit department, the head of the internal audit department should report to the audit committee.

☐ SGCC should not rely on the external audit to inform them of deficiencies in internal controls.

34  You are aware that SGCC is considering establishing an internal audit department.

With which of the following activities should the internal audit function **NOT** be involved?

○ Monitoring of management's performance

○ Reviewing adequacy of management information for decision-making purposes

○ Taking responsibility for the implementation of a new sales ledger system

○ Assessing compliance with regulation relevant to SGCC

35  If SGCC's board decides to establish an internal audit department then it will also need to decide whether it will employ members of staff directly, or will outsource the department to an external firm. You have found a list in your study notes of the advantages of outsourcing as compared to the advantages of employing staff directly. The list includes the following points:

(1) Greater availability of specialist industry skills as required

(2) Flexibility regarding staff numbers in response to changing circumstances

(3) Elimination of direct training costs

(4) Development of skills increasing the human resource strength of the entity

For each consideration, indicate whether it relates to the employment of internal auditors by SGCC, or to the outsourcing of the department.

| Consideration | | Employed | Outsourced |
|---|---|---|---|
| (1) | Greater availability of specialist industry skills as required | ☐ | ☐ |
| (2) | Flexibility regarding staff numbers in response to changing circumstances | ☐ | ☐ |
| (3) | Elimination of direct training costs | ☐ | ☐ |
| (4) | Development of skills increasing the human resource strength of the entity | ☐ | ☐ |

(Total = 10 marks)

BPP
LEARNING
MEDIA

PLANNING AND RISK ASSESSMENT

Questions 36–81 cover Audit planning and risk assessment, the subject of Part B of the BPP Workbook for Audit and Assurance.

# Bridgford                                                              18 mins

The following scenario relates to questions 36–40.

You are an audit senior of Ovette & Co and your firm has recently been appointed as the auditor to Bridgford Products (Bridgford), a large company which sells televisions, DVD players and Blu-ray Disc players to electrical retailers.

You are planning the audit for the year ended 31 January 20X9 and your audit manager has asked you to produce both the audit strategy document and the detailed audit plan, including an assessment of materiality.

In order to assist you in your planning work you have visited Bridgford, where you obtained the following information.

Sales have increased during the year ended 31 January 20X9 following a move to attract new customers by offering extended credit. The new credit arrangements allow customers three months' credit, rather than the one-month credit period allowed previously. As a result of this change, you have calculated that the receivables collection period has increased from 49 days to 127 days.

Bridgford installed a new computerised inventory control system, which began operating on 1 June 20X8. Since the inventory control system records both inventory movements and current inventory quantities, Bridgford is proposing to use the inventory quantities on the computer to value the inventory at the year-end rather than carrying out an inventory count.

The production director informed you that in the last month or so there have been reliability problems with the company's products which have resulted in some customers refusing to pay for the products.

As part of the planning process you also undertake a risk assessment. Based on the information you have obtained to date you have identified several audit risks which you feel your team will need to address. The first risk relates to the extended credit terms offered by Bridgford to its customers, and the recent product reliability problems resulting in customers' refusal to pay.

A second audit risk relates to the computerised inventory control system which was implemented on 1 June 20X8. You are concerned about whether data was accurately transferred into the new system, and whether it is sufficiently reliable to determine the quantity of inventory for the year-end financial statements.

36  The audit manager has requested that you cover a number of specified areas in the audit planning documentation.

For each area, indicate whether the information would be included in the audit strategy document or in the detailed audit plan.

| Area | Audit strategy document | Detailed audit plan |
|---|---|---|
| (1) The availability of the client's data and staff (including internal audit) | ☐ | ☐ |
| (2) The allocation of responsibility for specific audit procedures to audit team members | ☐ | ☐ |
| (3) The audit procedures to be undertaken for each area of the financial statements | ☐ | ☐ |
| (4) The potential for using automated tools and techniques to gather evidence | ☐ | ☐ |

37    You have set the level of materiality for the financial statements as a whole, and now need to determine performance materiality.

Which of the following statements about performance materiality is **NOT** true?

   O     Performance materiality is used to reduce the risk that the aggregate of uncorrected and undetected misstatements exceeds materiality for the financial statements as a whole to an acceptable level.

   O     Performance materiality refers to the amounts set by the auditor at higher than the materiality level for particular classes of transactions, account balances or disclosures where the materiality level might otherwise mean that such items are not tested.

   O     Once the level of materiality for the financial statements as a whole has been set, a lower level of performance materiality is determined by the auditor using their professional judgement.

   O     The performance materiality level is affected by the auditor's understanding of the entity and the nature and extent of misstatements identified in prior audits.

---

38    ISA 520 *Analytical Procedures* states that where analytical procedures identify fluctuations or relationships that are inconsistent with other relevant information or that differ significantly from the expected results, the auditor shall investigate the reason for this.

Which of the following auditor responses to the increase in the receivables collection period of Bridgford is the **LEAST** relevant?

   O     Make enquiries of management to understand the likely reason why the receivables collection period exceeds the extended credit period

   O     Perform detailed substantive testing on the aged receivables listing, to determine whether any amounts should be written off

   O     Perform a trend analysis on current year and prior year monthly revenue, to identify whether revenue is overstated as a result of fraud or error

   O     Perform further working capital ratio analysis, to determine the effect of the extended credit on Bridgford's cash position

---

39    Which of the following statements summarises your key concern regarding the risk relating to the extended credit terms and refusal of certain customers to pay?

   O     That the directors may have prepared Bridgford's financial statements on the going concern basis when this is not applicable

   O     That the financial statements include amounts due from credit customers which are not valid debts

   O     That there are balances due from credit customers which have not been included in the financial statements

   O     That the financial statements include balances due from credit customers which are not recoverable

---

40    Which **TWO** of the following procedures are relevant responses to the risk that inventory quantities are misstated by the new computerised inventory system?

☐ Review a sample of purchase requisitions to determine whether the quantity of inventory held per the inventory system was verified before the requisition was approved

☐ Determine how often inventory counts are performed and the level of corrections required to the inventory system

☐ Review sales prices of inventory sold after the year end to identify inventory where cost exceeds net realisable value

☐ Test the operation of the inventory system using CAATs

(Total = 10 marks)

# EuKaRe (Dec 08) (amended)                    18 mins

The following scenario relates to questions 41–45.

You are an audit senior of TEY & Co and are responsible for planning the audit of EuKaRe for the year ended 30 September 20X8.

EuKaRe is a charity which was established over five years ago. The charity's aim is to provide support to children from disadvantaged backgrounds who wish to take part in sports such as tennis, badminton and football.

EuKaRe has a detailed constitution which explains how the charity's income can be spent. The constitution also notes that expenditure relating to the administration of the charity cannot exceed 10% of the charity's income in any year. EuKaRe currently employs 3 permanent members of staff. At present, 100 volunteers work for EuKaRe: some commit up to 3 days a week and others help out on an ad hoc basis. The organisation, including its finance department, is primarily run by volunteers.

The charity's income is derived wholly from voluntary donations. Sources of donations include the public in the form of cash collected in buckets by volunteers in shopping areas, and from generous individuals.

41    Based on your understanding of the nature of EuKaRe, you have identified that income is received primarily in the form of cash and this will affect audit risk.

By clicking on the relevant box indicate whether the following statements regarding the effect on audit risk are true or false.

| | True | False |
|---|---|---|
| Detection risk will increase due to the increased risk of cash donations being misappropriated and revenue being overstated | True | False |
| Inherent risk will increase as the nature of EuKaRe's transactions means that income may be misstated either in error or deliberately. | True | False |
| Control risk will increase as internal controls may be weak due to the large number of volunteers used by EuKaRe | True | False |
| Business risk will increase due to the level of volunteers used by EuKaRe | True | False |

42 Your audit partner has highlighted to you that it is imperative that TEY & Co acts in line with ISA 315 *Identifying and Assessing the Risks of Material Misstatement*. This means it must identify and assess the risks of material misstatement at both the overall financial statement level and the assertion level, for classes of transactions, events and their related disclosures, and account balances and their related disclosures.

Indicate which of the following statements gives a true explanation of why ISA 315 requires a risk assessment to be carried out at the planning stage?

| | True | False |
|---|---|---|
| The risk assessment will help the audit team gain an understanding of the entity for audit purposes | ☐ | ☐ |
| The risk assessment will enable the audit senior to produce an accurate budget for the audit assignment | ☐ | ☐ |
| The risk assessment will form the basis of the audit strategy and the detailed audit plan | ☐ | ☐ |
| Once the risks have been assessed, TEY & Co can select audit team members with sufficient skill and experience to maximise the chance of those risks being addressed | ☐ | ☐ |

43 You have identified several audit risks which you feel your team will need to address. One such audit risk relates to the risk that income may be understated in the financial statements. You are concerned that not all income may be recorded.

Which of the following statements is **NOT** a valid response to this audit risk?

○ Obtain a breakdown of the income recorded from the cash that was collected in buckets, and vouch a sample of entries back to the volunteer in order to determine which volunteer collected the relevant donations

○ Perform analytical procedures on the level of donations in shopping areas per volunteer

○ Review the internal controls relating to cash collected in buckets to determine whether buckets are sealed, sequentially numbered and signed in and out by EuKaRe's volunteers

○ Observe the counting and recording of proceeds from collections, to determine whether appropriate segregation of duties is in place

44 Another identified audit risk is the susceptibility of EuKaRe's business to fraud due to the high levels of cash involved.

Use the drop down lists to complete the following sentence to correctly describe the auditor's responsibilities in accordance with ISA 240 *The Auditor's Responsibilities Relating to Fraud in an Audit of Financial Statements*.

The auditor is not responsible for the [＿＿＿＿＿＿＿＿＿＿] of fraud or error.

However, they are responsible for obtaining [＿＿＿＿＿＿＿＿＿＿] that the financial statements are free from material misstatement whether caused by fraud or error.

Options for drop down list:

First list:

Detection
Prevention
Prevention or detection

Second list:

Absolute assurance
Evidence
Reasonable assurance

45    The audit manager has noted in the detailed audit plan that EuKaRe's control environment may be weak.

Which **TWO** of the following statements are valid reasons as to why EuKaRe may have a weak control environment?

☐   EuKaRe has a detailed constitution which explains how the charity's income can be spent.

☐   EuKaRe's finance department relies on volunteers who may not have accounts experience.

☐   A high proportion of the income of EuKaRe is cash.

☐   Understaffing in the finance department at certain times is due to the ad hoc nature of volunteer working hours.

(Total = 10 marks)

# South                                                    18 mins

The following scenario relates to questions 46–50.

You are an audit senior of KLT & Co, and your firm has recently been appointed as the auditor to South, a private company that runs seven supermarkets in the UK. You are currently planning your firm's audit of South and are shortly due to make a preliminary visit to South's head office.

Four months before the year end, the company installed a new till system in all supermarkets. The new till system is linked to the accounting system at head office and automatically posts transactions to the accounting system. Previously journals were made manually based on totals on till rolls. The cost of the new till system which South has capitalised as a non-current asset.

The audit engagement partner has also said that she has is concerned that the new till system may not be reliable, and that consequently not all sales have been recorded, resulting in an understatement of revenue. She is also concerned that staff may not yet be familiar with the system, leading to an increased risk of errors relating to data entry.

Finally, after a number of people living close to one of South's stores became seriously ill, the source of the illness was traced back to meat the customers had purchased from South. Legal proceedings were commenced against South by a number of customers during the financial year, demanding $1m in compensation.

46    Indicate which **TWO** of the following statements describe the objectives of planning the audit of South.

☐   To ensure appropriate attention is devoted to important areas of the audit

☐   To assist in the co-ordination of work done by any auditor's experts

☐   To ensure that the audit engagement is only accepted if this is permissible by the ACCA *Code of ethics and conduct*

☐   To ensure the audit is completed within budget restraints

47    You are about to begin work on the share capital section of the South audit file.

Match each of the following audit procedures to the financial statement assertion to which it is most closely related.

| Procedure | Assertion |
|---|---|
| Recalculate the closing balance on the share capital account | Presentation |
| Review financial statement notes | Completeness |
| Review Memorandum and Articles of Association and compare their requirements with issued share capital | Accuracy, valuation and allocation |
| Read minutes of board meetings for evidence of share issues | Existence |

48    In relation to the capitalised costs of the new till system, you are concerned that South may have included within the capitalised costs some items which are revenue in nature, leading to the overstatement of non-current assets.

Which of the following statements is a valid response to this audit risk?

O    Obtain a copy of the training manual relating to the new till system and discuss with directors the extent of training staff have received on the new system

O    Agree the capitalised costs from the trial balance back to invoices to confirm their value

O    Inspect invoices capitalised within the cost of the new till system to determine whether they are directly attributable to the cost of the new till system

O    Recalculate the depreciation charged on the new till system

49    The audit engagement partner has stated that the new till system may not be reliable.

Which **TWO** of the following statements represent valid responses to this audit risk?

☐    Perform analytical procedures by comparing daily/weekly sales by store with both the prior year and with expectations, in order to determine whether any unusual patterns have occurred following the installation of the new system

☐    Vouch the sales revenue per the system to the till receipts to confirm the accuracy of the sales

☐    Obtain a copy of the training manual relating to the new till system and discuss with directors the extent of training staff have received on the new system

☐    Agree sales revenue from till receipts to the cashbook to determine the accuracy of till receipts

50  You plan to review the legal correspondence relating to the claims made by those customers to whom South sold contaminated meat.

Which **TWO** of the following are valid objectives of this audit procedure?

☐ To determine whether South's reputation will have been damaged within the local area

☐ To confirm whether there are deficiencies in South's internal controls relating to food hygiene

☐ To assess whether a provision for customer compensation is required in South's financial statements

☐ To determine whether disclosure of the nature and financial effect of the legal claim is required in South's financial statements

(Total = 10 marks)

# Mason                                    **18 mins**

The following scenario relates to questions 51–55.

You are an audit senior of IBN & Co and you are planning the audit of Mason Air Services Co (Mason) for the year ended 31 December 20X3.

Mason is a company that provides specialist helicopter support to public services, such as the police force and the ambulance service. Mason has four of these contracts, which contain very similar terms and are equal in value. Mason owns and maintains the helicopter fleet which is held at cost. Each aircraft carries specialist equipment and is operated by a highly skilled specialist pilot. Under the terms of these contracts Mason charges the customer an annual fee to cover the maintenance, storage and testing of the aircraft and equipment. The annual fee is payable in advance each year with the first annual payment being paid on the date the contract commences.

Mason has not purchased any new helicopters during the year to 31 December 20X3; however, there has been a lot of refitting, replacement and adding of specialist equipment to some of the existing aircraft. This has been necessary to keep up with the latest developments in search and rescue, and to maintain the aircraft to the high standard required under the contracts in place.

The original purchase of each aircraft was funded with a secured loan carrying substantial interest charges. The loan is in the process of being renegotiated and the bank has indicated that finance costs will increase further. Furthermore, the directors have told you that Mason's contract with the police force expires in March 20X4, at a time when, in the wake of government cuts, the police are trying to substantially reduce the amount they pay. It is thought that the contract will be put out to tender, and it is possible that another aircraft provider may also bid for the contract.

Mason also holds around $2 million of aircraft spares which are included within inventory. Mason sells the aircraft spares to amateur flying associations. Aircraft spares which are not sold after three years are scrapped.

Approximately one-quarter of this value is made up of specialist equipment taken out of aircraft when it was replaced by newer or more advanced equipment. Such specialist equipment is transferred from non-current assets to inventory without adjustment, and continues to be recognised at amortised cost.

51    In relation to the specialist helicopter support contracts, which of the following statements summarises a key audit risk?

    ○    Mason's assets could be undervalued if the market value of the helicopter fleet exceeds its cost.

    ○    Mason could breach the terms of its contracts with its customers and be liable to pay penalties, so provisions may be understated

    ○    Revenue may be overstated if it is recognised according to the contract date rather than over the relevant accounting period.

    ○    An expert valuer is required to value the helicopters in the financial statements.

---

52    Given the large amount of refitting of existing aircraft, you are concerned that property, plant and equipment may be overstated in the financial statements.

    Indicate which **TWO** of the following statements represent valid responses to this audit risk?

    ☐    Perform a proof in total calculation of the depreciation charge for the year and investigate any significant differences

    ☐    Review minutes of training meetings to determine whether the pilots have been trained how to use the specialist equipment

    ☐    Obtain a breakdown of the capitalised costs and agree a sample of items to invoices to determine the nature of the expenditure

    ☐    Inspect management's review of whether the value of the aircraft has been impaired

---

53    In relation to Mason's secured loan, which is the **MOST** important audit risk that should be documented in the detailed audit plan?

    ○    Disclosure relating to the secured loan may be omitted from the financial statements.

    ○    Mason's going concern status may be at risk if the contract is not renewed.

    ○    Interest charges may be understated.

    ○    The bank will rely on the audited financial statements when deciding whether to renew the loan.

---

54    Which **TWO** of the following are valid responses to the fact that Mason's contract with the police force is due for renewal?

    ☐    Review Mason's contracts with its other three customers to determine whether they contain a break clause, in order to determine the likelihood of losing any further contracts to other aircraft providers

    ☐    Contact the police force directly and request confirmation as to whether the contract is to be renewed

    ☐    Review the short-term and long-term funding facilities which are available to Mason

    ☐    Consider whether the financial statements contain appropriate disclosures in relation to the matter

---

55    In relation to the aircraft spares held by Mason, indicate which of the following correctly
      describe areas of audit concern?

|  | Audit concern | Not audit concern |
|---|:---:|:---:|
| Non-current assets | ☐ | ☐ |
| Inventory | ☐ | ☐ |
| Completeness | ☐ | ☐ |
| Accuracy, valuation and allocation | ☐ | ☐ |

(Total = 10 marks)

# Severn                                                                    18 mins

The following scenario relates to questions 56–60.

You are an audit manager of Rivers & Co. Your firm has been invited to tender for the audit of
Severn Co, a listed company. Your firm does not have any other listed clients, and Severn Co will
represent the biggest client of your firm (by client annual revenue) if your tender is successful.

A member of the audit committee of Severn Co informed your audit engagement partner that
the current auditors were not being invited to stand for re-election as the audit committee felt
that the relationship between the firm and the company had begun to lose objectivity due to
overfamiliarity. You have reviewed past financial statements of Severn Co and have noted that the
company applies IFRS, and that the audit committee reports on its responsibilities with regard to
internal control annually. The director confirmed that the board would be happy to confirm their
responsibilities in writing with Rivers & Co as they are aware of the relevant audit requirements.

56    The audit engagement partner has asked you to prepare some information ready for the
      tender.

      Identify, by clicking on the relevant box in the table below, if the following items should be
      included in, or excluded from, the tender for the audit of Severn Co.

| The proposed fee for the initial audit of Severn Co | INCLUDE | EXCLUDE |
|---|:---:|:---:|
| A description of Rivers & Co, including the curriculum vitae of key staff likely to be assigned to the client | INCLUDE | EXCLUDE |
| Overall level of materiality to be used in the audit | INCLUDE | EXCLUDE |
| A summary of potential other services Rivers & Co could provide to Severn Co | INCLUDE | EXCLUDE |

57    You have identified a number of issues which should be considered prior to tendering for a
      new client.

      Given what you already know of Severn Co, which **TWO** of these are most important to
      consider further prior to tendering for the audit?

      ☐  The firm is independent of the potential client

      ☐  The firm has the appropriate resources to conduct the audit of the potential client

      ☐  The preconditions of audit will be met

      ☐  The outgoing auditors will give Rivers & Co access to working papers

Your firm has tendered for the engagement and has been successful. You have been asked to follow through the acceptance procedures for the firm.

58    You are reappraising whether it is appropriate for the firm to accept the engagement.

Which of the following issues arising would cause Rivers & Co to decline the engagement?

○    The engagement letter not being received by Rivers & Co

○    Rivers & Co losing a major client meaning Severn's audit fee would represent 20% of annual firm income

○    A reply from the outgoing auditors stating that they declined to seek reappointment to the audit of Severn Co due to a disagreement over accounting policies

○    A request from Severn Co that the audit be carried out in March, when Rivers & Co already works at maximum capacity

59    You are drafting an engagement letter in respect of Severn Co, and are aware that ISA 210 *Terms of Audit Engagements* requires certain issues to be included.

Indicate which of the following issues must be included in the engagement letter?

|  | Include in engagement letter | Do not include in engagement letter |
|---|---|---|
| Scope of the audit | ☐ | ☐ |
| Responsibilities of management of Severn Co | ☐ | ☐ |
| Timetable for the provision of accounting information by Severn Co | ☐ | ☐ |
| Fees and billing arrangements | ☐ | ☐ |

60    Before accepting the audit of Severn Co, Rivers & Co should [                    ]. Once the audit has been accepted, then Rivers & Co should begin to [                    ].

Options for drop down list:

First list:

Obtain references concerning directors

Submit the letter of engagement

Appoint a quality reviewer

Second list:

Obtain references concerning directors

Submit the letter of engagement

Determine audit materiality levels

(Total = 10 marks)

# Goofy Co (Jun 11) (amended)

The following scenario relates to questions 61–65.

You are an audit manager in NAB & Co, a large audit firm which specialises in the audit of retailers. The firm currently audits Goofy Co (Goofy), a food retailer, but Goofy's main competitor, Mickey Co (Mickey), has approached the audit firm to act as auditors. Both Goofy and Mickey are listed companies. Goofy is concerned that if NAB & Co audits both companies then confidential information could pass across to Mickey.

The audit engagement partner for Goofy has been in place for approximately six years and her daughter, Emma, has just accepted a job offer from Goofy as a warehouse manager. Emma's employment contract states that if a bonus is to be paid it will be awarded as shares in Goofy rather than in cash. Goofy is offering NAB & Co a 5% bonus on top of the audit fee if this year's audit can be completed three weeks earlier than last year. This is to reduce the demands on the finance director's time as he is busy working on other projects.

61    The ACCA *Code of Ethics and Conduct* requires that an external auditor implement appropriate safeguards to ensure that a conflict of interest is properly managed.

Which **TWO** of the following actions should NAB & Co take regarding the potential confidentiality issue?

☐    Inform the audit committees of both Goofy and Mickey of the potential conflict of interest and obtain their consent to act for both parties

☐    Use separate audit teams for each audit with a common independent review partner to determine whether confidentiality has been maintained

☐    Draw up confidentiality agreements to be signed by the board of directors of Goofy and Mickey

☐    Prevent unauthorised physical access to the information relating to both company audits

---

62    From a review of the information above, your audit assistant has highlighted some potential risks to independence in respect of the audit of Goofy.

Indicate the appropriate category to which each of the threats to independence should be allocated.

| Threat to independence | | Familiarity | Self-interest |
|---|---|---|---|
| (1) | Audit engagement partner has been in the position for six years | ☐ | ☐ |
| (2) | Audit engagement partner's daughter works for Goofy | ☐ | ☐ |
| (3) | Audit engagement partner's daughter's bonus would be in the form of shares | ☐ | ☐ |
| (4) | 5% bonus offered if audit is completed three weeks earlier than last year | ☐ | ☐ |

---

63    NAB & Co has decided that it would like to accept nomination as Mickey's auditors and Mickey's existing auditors have agreed to resign rather than be removed from office. The audit manager in charge of the tender has set out a list of procedures that the firm must undertake before Mickey can be approved as an audit client.

(1)    Ensure that the existing auditor's resignation has been properly conducted

(2)    Communicate with Mickey's existing auditors

(3)    Submit an engagement letter to Mickey's management

(4)    Perform client screening procedures, including an assessment of Mickey's risk profile

Drag each of the four options below to the right hand side to show the correct order in which the above procedures should be undertaken.

| Procedure | | Order | |
|---|---|---|---|
| (1) | Ensure that the existing auditor's resignation has been properly conducted | (1) | |
| (2) | Communicate with Mickey's existing auditors | (2) | |
| (3) | Submit an engagement letter to Mickey's management | (3) | |
| (4) | Perform client screening procedures, including an assessment of Mickey's risk profile | (4) | |

64    Before NAB & Co can accept appointment as Mickey's auditors it must determine whether the preconditions for an audit are met and obtain management's agreement that it acknowledges and understands its responsibilities.

Which of the following is **NOT** included in the agreement obtained by the auditor?

O    Management's responsibility for preparing the financial statements

O    Management's responsibility for internal control to enable the preparation of financial statements which are free from material misstatement

O    Management's responsibility to provide the auditor with all information relevant to the preparation of the financial statements

O    Management's responsibility to prevent and detect fraud

65  Indicate which of the following statements are true regarding the regulation of the audit profession?

| | | |
|---|---|---|
| The auditor has the right of access to the books, records and vouchers of the company | TRUE | FALSE |
| The auditor has the right to be heard at general meetings on matters relating to the audit | TRUE | FALSE |
| The auditor is appointed by, and answerable to, those charged with governance of the company | TRUE | FALSE |
| An auditor can be removed by a simple oral resolution in line with the common law | TRUE | FALSE |

(Total = 10 marks)

# Carlise                                                18 mins

The following scenario relates to questions 66–70.

You are an audit senior of UYE & Co and your firm is the external auditor of Carlise, a large private company that runs major sports venues in the UK. Carlise has a year end of 31 December and you are currently planning the interim audit of Carlise for the six months ended 30 June 20X4.

This year you will have another audit senior, James, who has recently joined UYE & Co, working with you. James did not work on any interim audits with his previous audit firm, and your audit manager has asked you to train him to use the different approach used in interim audits.

James has drawn up the following list of audit procedures:

(1)     Update documentation relating to Carlise's accounting systems which has been prepared in prior year audits.

(2)     Obtain third-party confirmations relating to receivables, payables and cash at bank.

(3)     Review the directors' assessment of whether Carlise is a going concern. Consider whether the assumptions made by the directors are reasonable and whether it is appropriate to prepare the accounts on the going concern basis.

(4)     Perform preliminary analytical procedures in order to identify any major changes in the business or unexpected trends.

In July 20X4 Carlise established an internal audit department. The board is still planning the exact responsibilities the internal audit department will have, but it is likely that, among other things, they will be involved in monitoring the internal controls relating to Carlise's online ticket sales system.

It is the policy of UYE & Co that audit files for both interim and final audits are assembled within 60 days of the date when the auditor's report was signed. The files are then locked and cannot be amended after this date, but it is sometimes deemed necessary for further minor procedures to be added to the files after the auditor's report is issued. The files are then retained for 3 years, at which time they are disposed of securely.

66    Indicate whether the procedures identified by James above will be conducted during the interim or the final audit.

| Audit procedures | | Interim audit | Final audit |
|---|---|---|---|
| (1) | Update documentation relating to Carlise's accounting systems which has been prepared in prior year audits. | ☐ | ☐ |
| (2) | Obtain third-party confirmations relating to receivables, payables and cash at bank. | ☐ | ☐ |
| (3) | Review the directors' assessment of whether Carlise is a going concern. Consider whether the assumptions made by the directors are reasonable and whether it is appropriate to prepare the accounts on the going concern basis. | ☐ | ☐ |
| (4) | Perform preliminary analytical procedures in order to identify any major changes in the business or unexpected trends. | ☐ | ☐ |

67    During the interim audit, you performed internal controls testing and the results of these indicate that, to date, the control environment is strong and internal controls are operating effectively.

James has asked you to explain the factors that will determine the extent of further work on internal controls that will need to be performed at the final audit.

Which of the following should be taken into account when determining the extent of the additional work needed at the final audit?

(1)    The significance of the assessed risks of material misstatement at the assertion level

(2)    The specific controls that were tested during the interim period, and significant changes to them since they were tested, including changes in the information system, processes, and personnel

(3)    The length of the remaining period

O    1 and 2 only

O    2 and 3 only

O    1 and 3 only

O    1, 2 and 3

68    Which of the following considerations is the **MOST** important when deciding whether or not to rely on the work performed by Carlise's internal audit department?

O    Whether any members of Carlise's internal audit department hold a professional qualification

O    Whether the work performed by the internal audit department relates to specific audit assertions over which UYE & Co has concerns

O    Whether a separate audit committee exists

O    Whether Carlise's internal audit department has a work plan which schedules the work they should perform to the end of the year

69  Carlise's internal audit team is likely to be involved in monitoring the internal controls relating to Carlise's online ticket sales system.

UYE & Co may use the internal audit department to provide direct assistance to it in the audit of this system. Indicate which of the following statements are true, if direct assistance is used?

|  | True | False |
|---|---|---|
| Carlise's internal auditors would perform audit procedures under the direction, supervision and review of UYE & Co's audit team | ☐ | ☐ |
| UYE & Co should only use direct assistance if the risk of material misstatement in relation to the online ticket sales system is high | ☐ | ☐ |
| UYE & Co's audit team should document its review of the work performed by Carlise's internal auditors | ☐ | ☐ |
| Carlise's internal auditors will be separately liable for any material misstatements in the work they have performed | ☐ | ☐ |

70  Indicate which of the following are true of UYE & Co's policies regarding the assembly and retention of audit files.

|  | True | False |
|---|---|---|
| UYE & Co's policy of assembling files within 60 days of the auditor's report is stricter than what is required by ISAs | ☐ | ☐ |
| It is incompatible with ISAs for even minor further procedures to be added to the audit files after the 60 day period | ☐ | ☐ |
| It is acceptable to make administrative changes to an audit file after 60 days, so it is not strictly necessary to 'lock' the files to comply with ISAs | ☐ | ☐ |
| It is acceptable for files to be disposed of after 3 years have passed since the date of the auditor's report | ☐ | ☐ |

(Total = 10 marks)

# 71 Sleeptight                                                                   54 mins

It is 1 July 20X5. You are an audit senior for Mills & Co. Mills & Co was recently appointed as external auditors of Sleeptight Co for the year ending 31 August 20X5 and you are in the process of planning the audit. The previous auditors issued an unmodified audit opinion last year and access to prior year working papers has been granted.

Sleeptight's principal activity is the manufacture and sale of expensive high quality beds which are largely sold to luxury hotels and owners of holiday apartments. Each bed is crafted by hand in the company's workshop. Construction of each bed only begins once a customer order is received, as each customer will usually want their bed to have a unique feature or to be in a unique style.

The business is family run and all the shares in Sleeptight are owned by the two joint managing directors. The directors are two sisters, Anna and Sophie Jones, and they both have a number of other business interests. As a result they only spend a few days a week working at the company and rely on the small accounts department to keep the finances in order and to keep them informed. There is no finance director but the financial controller is a qualified accountant.

Sleeptight requires customers who place an order to pay a deposit of 40% of the total order value at the time the order is placed. The beds will take 4 to 8 weeks to build, and the remaining 60% of the order value is due within a week of the final delivery. Risks and rewards of ownership of the beds do not pass to the customer until the beds are delivered and signed for. Beds also come with a two-year guarantee and the financial controller has made a provision in respect of the expected costs to be incurred in relation to beds still under guarantee.

Although the company does have some employees working in the workshop, it often uses external subcontractors to help make the beds in order to fulfil all its orders. These subcontractors should invoice Sleeptight at the end of each month for the work they have carried out, but sometimes do not get round to it until the following month.

The company undertakes a full count of raw materials at the year end. The quantities are recorded on inventory sheets and the financial controller assigns the costs based on the cost assigned in the previous year or, if there was no cost last year, using the latest invoice. Most beds are made of oak or other durable woods and the cost of these raw materials is known to fluctuate considerably.

It is expected that work in progress will be insignificant this year, but there will be a material amount of finished goods awaiting dispatch. Anna Jones will estimate the value of these finished goods and has said she will take into account the order value when doing so.

There has been steady growth in sales in recent years and in June 20X5 Sleeptight purchased a building close to its existing workshop. Anna and Sophie plan to turn this into another workshop which should more than double its existing manufacturing capacity. The new workshop is currently undergoing extensive refurbishment in order to make it suitable for bed manufacturing.

The purchase of the new premises was funded by a bank loan repayable in monthly instalments over 12 years and has covenants attached to it. These covenants are largely profit related measures and if they are breached the bank has the option to make the remaining loan balance repayable immediately.

(a) Auditors are required to plan and perform an audit with professional scepticism, to exercise professional judgement and to comply with ethical standards.

**Required**

(i) Explain what is meant by 'professional scepticism' and why it is so important that the auditor maintains professional scepticism throughout the audit. **(3 marks)**

(ii) Define 'professional judgement' and describe **TWO** areas where professional judgement is applied when planning an audit of financial statements. **(3 marks)**

(b) Using the information provided, describe **EIGHT** audit risks, and explain the auditor's response to each risk, in planning the audit of Sleeptight.

| Audit risk | Auditor's response |
|---|---|
|  |  |

**(16 marks)**

(c) Describe Mills & Co's responsibilities in relation to the physical inventory count that will take place at the year end. **(4 marks)**

(d) The workshop currently in use is owned by the company and will be included in the financial statements at its revalued amount rather than at cost. The company has always adopted this policy for land and buildings and the valuation of the workshop is to be brought up to date at 31 August 20X5 by an external valuer.

**Required**

Describe the procedures the auditor should carry out to gain evidence over the adequacy of the value of the workshop and the related disclosures included in the financial statements. **(4 marks)**

**(Total = 30 marks)**

# 72 Peony (Mar/Jun 19)                                    36 mins

It is 1 July 20X5. You are an audit supervisor of Daffodil & Co and are planning the audit of Peony Co for the year ending 31 May 20X5. The company is a food retailer with a large network of stores across the country and four warehouses. The company has been a client of your firm for several years and the forecast profit before tax is $28·9m. The audit manager has attended a planning meeting with the finance director and has provided you with the following notes of the meeting.

## Planning meeting notes

Peony Co has an internal audit (IA) department which undertakes controls testing across the network of stores. Each store is visited at least once every 18 months. The audit manager has discussed with the finance director that the external audit team may rely on the controls testing which is undertaken by IA.

During the meeting, the finance director provided some forecast financial information. Revenue for the year is expected to increase by 3% as compared to 20X4; the gross margin is expected to increase from 56% to 60%; and the operating margin is predicted to decrease from 21% to 18%.

Peony Co values inventory in line with industry practice, which is to use selling price less average profit margin. The directors consider this to be a close approximation to cost.

The company does not undertake a full year-end inventory count and instead undertakes monthly perpetual inventory counts, each of which covers one-twelfth of all lines in stores and the warehouses. As part of the interim audit which was completed in January, an audit junior attended a perpetual inventory count at one of the warehouses and noted that there were a large number of exceptions where the inventory records showed a higher quantity than the physical inventory which was present in the warehouse. When discussing these exceptions with the financial controller, the audit junior was informed that this had been a recurring issue.

During the year, IA performed a review of the non-current assets physically present in around one-third of the company's stores. A number of assets which had not been fully depreciated were identified as obsolete by this review.

The company launched a significant TV advertising campaign in January 20X5 in order to increase revenue. The directors have indicated that at the year end a current asset of $0·7m will be recognised, as they believe that the advertisements will help to boost future sales in the next 12 months. The last advertisement will be shown on TV in early May 20X5.

Peony Co decided to outsource its payroll function to an external service organisation. This service organisation handles all elements of the payroll cycle and sends monthly reports to Peony Co which detail wages and salaries and statutory obligations. Peony Co maintained its own payroll records until 31 December 20X4, at which point the records were transferred to the service organisation. Peony Co is planning to expand the company by opening three new stores during July 20X5 and in order to finance this, in March 20X5 the company obtained a $3m bank loan. This is repayable in arrears over five years in quarterly instalments. In preparation for the expansion, the company is looking to streamline operations in the warehouses and is planning to make approximately 60 employees redundant after the year end. No decision has been made as to when this will be announced, but it is likely to be in May 20X5.

## Required

(a)  Define and explain materiality and performance materiality.                    **(4 marks)**

(b)  Describe **EIGHT** audit risks and explain the auditor's response to each risk in planning the audit of Peony Co.

| Audit risk | Auditor's response |
| --- | --- |
|  |  |

**(16 marks)**

**(Total = 20 marks)**

# 73 Walters (2014 Specimen Exam)          36 mins

It is 1 July 20X5. You are the audit senior of Holtby & Co and are planning the audit of Walters Co (Walters) for the year ended 30 September 20X5. The company produces printers and has been a client of your firm for two years; your audit manager has already had a planning meeting with the finance director. He has provided you with the following notes of his meeting and financial statement extracts.

Walters's management were disappointed with the 20X4 results and so in 20X5 undertook a number of strategies to improve the trading results. This included the introduction of a generous sales-related bonus scheme for their salespeople and a high profile advertising campaign. In addition, as market conditions are difficult for their customers, they have extended the credit period given to them.

The finance director of Walters has reviewed the inventory valuation policy and has included additional overheads incurred this year as he considers them to be production related.

The finance director has calculated a few key ratios for Walters; the gross profit margin has increased from 44.4% to 52.2% and the receivables collection period has increased from 61 days to 71 days. He is happy with the 20X5 results and feels that they are a good reflection of the improved trading levels.

FINANCIAL STATEMENT EXTRACTS FOR YEAR ENDED 30 SEPTEMBER

|  | Draft 20X5 $m | Actual 20X4 $m |
|---|---|---|
| Revenue | 23.0 | 18.0 |
| Cost of sales | (11.0) | (10.0) |
| Gross profit | 12.0 | 8.0 |
| Operating expenses | (7.5) | (4.0) |
| Profit before interest and taxation | 4.5 | 4.0 |
| Inventory | 2.1 | 1.6 |
| Receivables | 4.5 | 3.0 |
| Cash | – | 2.3 |
| Trade payables | 1.6 | 1.2 |
| Overdraft | 0.9 | – |

**Required**

(a)   Using the information above:

(i)   Calculate an additional **THREE** ratios, for **BOTH** years, which would assist the audit senior in planning the audit.          **(3 marks)**

(ii)   From a review of the above information and the ratios calculated, describe **SIX** audit risks and explain the auditor's response to each risk in planning the audit of Walters Co.          **(12 marks)**

| Audit risk | Auditor's response |
|---|---|
|  |  |

(b)   Describe the procedures that the auditor of Walters Co should perform in assessing whether or not the company is a going concern.          **(5 marks)**

(Total = 20 marks)

# 74 Harlem (Sep/Dec 19)

**54 mins**

This scenario relates to five requirements.

It is 1 July 20X5. You are an audit supervisor of Brooklyn & Co and are planning the audit of Harlem Co for the year ending 30 September 20X5. The company has been a client of your firm for several years and manufactures car tyres, selling its products to wholesalers and retailers. The audit manager attended a planning meeting with the finance director and has provided you with the following notes of the meeting and financial statements extracts:

## Planning meeting notes

Harlem Co sells approximately 40% of its tyres to wholesale customers. These customers purchase goods on a sale or return basis. Under the terms of the agreement, wholesale customers have 60 days during which any returns can be made without penalty. The finance director has historically assumed a return rate of 10%, however, he now feels that this is excessive and intends to change this 5%.

The company purchased patent on 30 September 20X4 for $800,000, which was capitalised in the prior year as an intangible asset. This patent gives Harlem Co the exclusive right to manufacture specialised wet weather tyres for four years. In preparation for the manufacture of the wet weather tyres, this year the company conducted a review of its plant and machinery. As part of this review, surplus items of plant and machinery were sold, resulting in a loss on disposal of $160,000.

In May 20X5, the financial controller of Harlem Co was dismissed after it was alleged that she had carried out a number of fraudulent transactions against the company. She has threatened to sue the company for unfair dismissal as she disputes the allegations. The company has only recently started to investigate the extent of the fraud in order to quantity the required adjustment.

A problem occurred in June 20X5, during production of a significant batch of tyres, which affected their quality. The issue was identified prior to any good being dispatched and management in investigating whether the issues can be rectified and the tyres can subsequently be sold.

Harlem Co's finance director has informed you that in March 20X5 a significant customer was granted a payment break of six months, as it has been experiencing financial difficulties. Harlem Co maintains an allowance for trade receivables and it is anticipated that this will remain at the same level as prior year.

The report to management issued by Brooklyn & Co following last year's audit highlighted significant deficiencies relating to Harlem Co's purchases cycle.

The finance directors has informed you that the company intends to restructure its debt finance after the year end and will be looking to consolidate its loans to reduce the overall cost of borrowing. As a result of the planned restructuring of debt, Harlem Co has not paid its shareholders a dividend this year, choosing instead to undertake a bonus issue of its $0.50 equity shares.

You have been asked by the audit manager to complete the preliminary analytical review and she has provided you with the following information:

## Financial statements extracts for year ending 30 September

|  | Forecast 20X5 $'000 | Actual 20X4 $'000 |
|---|---|---|
| Revenue | 23,200 | 21,900 |
| Cost of sales | (18,700) | (17,300) |
| **Gross profit** | **4,500** | **4,600** |
|  |  |  |
| Finance costs | 290 | 250 |

|  | Forecast 20X5 $'000 | Actual 20X4 $'000 |
|---|---|---|
| Profit before tax | 450 | 850 |
| Intangible asset | 800 | 800 |
| Inventory | 2,100 | 1,600 |
| Long and short-term borrowings | 13,000 | 11,000 |
| Total equity | 10,000 | 9,500 |

The audit assistant has already calculated some key ratios for Harlem Co which you have confirmed as accurate. She has ascertained that the trade receivables collection period has increased from 38 to 51 days.

**Required**

(a) Describe the auditor's responsibilities in relation to the prevention and detection of fraud and error. **(4 marks)**

(b) Calculate the **FOUR** ratios listed in the table below, for **BOTH** years, to assist you in planning the audit of Harlem Co.

| Ratio | 20X5 | 20X4 |
|---|---|---|
| Gross profit margin |  |  |
| Inventory holding period |  |  |
| Gearing |  |  |
| Interest cover |  |  |

Note: formulae are not required to be shown.

**(4 marks)**

(c) Using the information provided and the ratios calculate, describe **EIGHT** audit risks and explain the auditor's response to each risk in planning the audit of Harlem Co. **(16 marks)**

| Audit risk | Auditor's response |
|---|---|
|  |  |

(d) Describe the substantive procedures the auditor should perform to obtain sufficient appropriate audit evidence in relation to the **VALUATION** of trade receivables in the current year. **(3 marks)**

(e) Describe the substantive procedures the auditor should perform to obtain sufficient appropriate audit evidence in relation to the **DISPOSAL** of plant and machinery in the current year. **(3 marks)**

**(Total = 30 marks)**

# 75 Scarlet (Mar/Jul 20)                                54 mins

This scenario relates to four requirements.

It is 1 July 20X5. You are an audit supervisor of Orange & Co planning the audit of a new client, Scarlet Co, for the year ended 31 May 20X5. Scarlet Co manufactures chemicals for use in domestic and commercial cleaning products.

The company's financial accountant was taken ill suddenly in May 20X5 and is unable to undertake the preparation of the year-end draft financial statements. As a result, the company recruited a temporary financial accountant in early June 20X5 who will prepare the draft financial statements. The year-end financial statements need to be finalised quickly as the company is looking to raise finance through a bank loan to replace three machines in the production facility. The bank has asked for a copy of the audited year-end financial statements by the end of September 20X5 before they will agree to the loan and the directors are keen to report strong results in order to obtain this financing.

In the year, the company also purchased a specialised machine to develop a new range of chemicals for a major customer. Only trained staff are allowed to operate this machine and staff members had to undertake two days of training, followed by an assessment at the end of the training period. The training costs of $15,000 have been capitalised as part of the cost of the asset.

The company sources many if its raw materials to be used in the chemical manufacturing process from an international supplier and goods can be in transit for up to three weeks. The agreement with the international supplier contains a clause which states that Scarlet Co is responsible for the goods as soon as they leave the supplier's warehouse.

You have carried out a preliminary analytical review which indicates that the receivables collection period has increased from the 38 days to 52 days. The credit controller has confirmed that some customers are currently taking longer to pay than in previous years as they are awaiting payment from their customers.

On 29 May 20X5, the directors announced that one of its brand was being discontinued due to a fall in demand for the product. This resulted in four staff members being made redundant. The payroll department has calculated the levels of termination costs associated with the redundancy and they will be paid in the July 20X5 payroll run.

The directors each received a significant bonus in the year which has been included in the payroll charge for the year in the statement of profit or loss. Local legislation requires separate disclosure of directors' bonuses in the financial statements.

During the year the company sold a batch of chemicals to s customer for $120,000. At the beginning of May 20X5, the customer returned these chemicals because the chemical mix was not in line with the customer's specifications. A credit note is yet to be issued to the customer and the chemicals have been written down to their scrap value within inventory.

The company usually pays its suppliers by the end of each month. However, due to the financial accountant's illness, the payment run for May 20X5 was not performed until 1 June 20X5. The finance director has informed you that in order to show consistent results with the prior year, this payment run is shown as an unpresented item on the year-end bank reconciliation.

## Required

ISA 210 *Agreeing the terms of audit engagements* requires auditors to issue an engagement letter.

(a)   Explain the PURPOSE of an audit engagement letter and list FOUR items which should be included in an audit engagement letter.                    **(4 marks)**

(b) Explain WHY the following factors should have been considered by Orange & Co prior to accepting Scarlet Co as a new audit client.

| Pre-acceptance factors | Explanation |
|---|---|
| The outgoing auditor's response | |
| Management integrity | |
| Pre-conditions for an audit | |
| Independence and objectivity | |
| Resources available at the time of the audit | |

(5 marks)

(c) Describe EIGHT audit risks, and explain the auditor's response to each risk, in planning the audit of Scarlet Co.

| Audit risk | Auditor's response |
|---|---|
| | |

(16 marks)

(d) Describe substantive procedures the auditor should perform to obtain sufficient and appropriate audit evidence in respect of the redundancy costs.　(5 marks)

(Total = 30 marks)

# 76 Corley Appliances Co (Mar/Jun 21)　36 mins

**This scenario relates to three requirements.**

It is 1 July 20X5. You are an audit supervisor with Woodward & Co and you are in the process of planning the audirt of Corley Appliances Co, a company which sells domestic electrical appliances such as fridge freezers, TVs, and washing machines. The company's ear end is 31 August 20X5 and forecast revenue for the year is $12.2m, total assets are $6.8m and profit before tax is $2.8m. The audit manager held a meeting with the finance director and the notes from that meeting are provided below.

**Notes from meeting with finance director**

The company operates nationwide with 20 branches located across the country and sells goods to memebers of the public and to retailers. The company has returns policy which allows a customer to return goods within 28 days of purchase if they are not satisfied with the product. Historically, 5% of customers returns goods within the return period. The company also provides a six-month warranty on its products which requires Corley Appliances to repair any defects, at its own cost, which arise within the warranty period. It is anticipated that the warranty provision in the draft financial statementswill be lower than the prior year as the directors are confidednt the producst will be sold by the company are built to a very high standard.

The company is based in Europe and its main supplier of appliances is based in Asia. Goods are shipped to the company's central warehouse by sea and are usually in transit for up to one month. Corley Appliances Co has responsibility for goods in transit from the points of dispatch by the supplier.  The cebtral warehouse nand all  20 branches will be carrying out a full year-end inventory count on 31 August 20X5 anf it is expected that the value of inventory in Corley Appliances Co's financial statements wil be $0.95m.

Over the last six months, the finance director has noticed that the company's receivables collection period is now an average of 55 days, whereas the company's target is 42 days. The credit controller has informed the finance director that she is confident that all receivables will eventually pay as increases in receivables collection periods are starting to become common in the industry. The finance director believes it is unlike that any increase in the allowance for receivables will be necessary at the year end as compared to the prior year.

In June 20X5, a fraud was uncovered in the finance department. A payables ledger supervisor had diverted funds from the company's bank account using a fictitious supplier on the payables ledger. The employee was immediately dismissed, and the value of the fraud will be recognised as an expense in the statement of profit or loss. Since the dismissal of the supervisor, purchase invoices have not been recorded in the payables ledger and it is unlikely that this backlog on invoices will be cleared by the year end.

During the year, the company purchased and installed a new automated dispatch system for its central warehouse. The cost of the dispatch system was $0.9m and has been recognised as an addition to property, plantand equipmentr. These capitalised costs include the purchase price of $0.6m, installation costs of 0.2m and staff training costs of $0.1m.

Due to the costs incurred in purchasing the new dispatch system and the increase in the receivables collection period, the company's overdraft facility has increased significalntly and at one point went over the agreed limit of $0.7m in early June 20X5. The bank has expressed concern about the way that the company is operating its bank overdraft facility, which the company is dependent on. The auditor's report is due to be signed in October 20X5.

ISA 210 Agreeing the Terms of Audit Engagements states that auditors should only accept, or continue an existing audit engagement, oif the preconditions for an audit are present.

(a)  Describe the PRECONDITIONS required for an audit.                        **(3 marks)**

(b)  Describe SEVEN audit risks and explain the auditor's response to each risk in planning the audit of Corley Appliances Co.

| Audit risk | Auditor's response |
|---|---|
|  |  |

**(14 marks)**

(c)  Define the term 'professional scepticism' and explain TWO examples from the audit of Corley Appliances Co where the auditor should apply professional scepticism.    **(3 marks)**

**(Total = 20 marks)**

# 77 Kangaroo Construction Co (Jun 13) (amended) 36 mins

It is 1 July 20X5. You are the audit senior of Rhino & Co and you are planning the audit of Kangaroo Construction Co (Kangaroo) for the year ended 31 August 20X5. Kangaroo specialises in building houses and provides a five-year building warranty to its customers. Your audit manager has held a planning meeting with the finance director. He has provided you with the following notes of his meeting and financial statement extracts.

Kangaroo has had a difficult year; house prices have fallen and, as a result, revenue has dropped. In order to address this, management has offered significantly extended credit terms to their customers. However, demand has fallen such that there are still some completed houses in inventory where the selling price may be below cost. During the year, whilst calculating depreciation, the directors extended the useful lives of plant and machinery from three years to five years. This reduced the annual depreciation charge.

The directors need to meet a target profit before interest and taxation of $0.5 million in order to be paid their annual bonus. In addition, to try to improve profits, Kangaroo changed its main material supplier to a cheaper alternative. This has resulted in some customers claiming on their building warranties for extensive repairs. To help with operating cash flow, the directors borrowed $1 million from the bank during the year. This is due for repayment at the end of 20X5.

FINANCIAL STATEMENT EXTRACTS FOR YEAR ENDED 31 AUGUST

|  | Draft 20X5 $m | Actual 20X4 $m |
|---|---|---|
| Revenue | 12.5 | 15.0 |
| Cost of sales | (7.0) | (8.0) |
| Gross profit | 5.5 | 7.0 |
| Operating expenses | (5.0) | (5.1) |
| Profit before interest and taxation | 0.5 | 1.9 |
| Inventory | 1.9 | 1.4 |
| Receivables | 3.1 | 2.0 |
| Cash | 0.8 | 1.9 |
| Trade payables | 1.6 | 1.2 |
| Loan | 1.0 | – |

## Required

(a) Explain the concepts of materiality and performance materiality in accordance with ISA 320 *Materiality in Planning and Performing an Audit*. **(4 marks)**

(b) Using the information above:

   (i) Calculate the following ratios, for BOTH years, which would assist the audit senior in planning the audit.

| Ratio | 20X5 | 20X4 |
|---|---|---|
| Inventory holding period |  |  |
| Inventory turnover |  |  |
| Receivables collection period |  |  |
| Payables payment period |  |  |

**(4 marks)**

(ii)   Using the information provided and the ratios calculated, describe **SIX** audit risks, and explain the auditor's response to each risk in planning the audit of Kangaroo Construction Co.

| Audit risk | Auditor's response |
|---|---|
|  |  |

(12 marks)

(Total = 20 marks)

# 78 Hart Co (Sep/Dec 20)                          54 mins

**This scenario relates to four requirements.**

It is 1 July 20X5. You are an audit supervisor with Morph & Co responsible for planning the final audit of a new client, Hart Co, for the year ending 30 September 20X5. Hart Co specialises in the design and construction of customised playgrounds. The Audit manager recently met with Hart Co's finance director and has provided you with the following notes:

## Planning meeting notes

Hart Co has a forecast profit before tax of $12.2m (20X4:$9.8m) and total assets are expected to be $28.5m (20X4: $24.3m). The finance director has indicated that the directors are very pleased with the forecast performance for the year as the directors are paid a bonus based on a percentage of profit before tax.

Hart Co is undertaking the construction of playgrounds at 16 sites in various locations across the country. All playgrounds are constructed to specific customer specifications. Customers pay a 25% deposit on signing the contract, with the balance payable when control of the playground is transferred to the customer.

The balance of work in progress (WIP) at 30 June 20X5 is $7.6m in respect of the playgrounds under construction. A WIP count and valuation will be carried out at all sites on 30 September 20X5. Arrangements have been made for the audit team to attend only five of the WIP counts. Hart Co offers its customers a warranty at no extra cost, which guarantees that the playgrounds will function as expected for a period of three years. The warranty provision for the current year has been calculated as 2% of revenue. In the previous year the warranty was based on 6% of revenue. The finance director has made this change despite no significant difference in construction techniques or the level of claims in the year.

Hart Co has incurred expenditure of $1.8m relating to the research and development of a new type of environmentally-friendly building material. $0.6m of the expenditure to date has been written off to the statement of profit or loss. The remaining $1.2m has been capitalised as an intangible asset. No amortisation has been recognised to date as the material has not yet been brought into use.

In June 20X5, the company contracted to purchase new machinery costing $2.4m. It paid $1m on signing the contract to secure the machinery, which was due to be delivered in July 20X5. Due to a supplier problem, the delivery is delayed and is now scheduled to be delivered in October 20X5. In order to finance the research and development costs and the machinery purchase, Hart Co made a rights issue to existing shareholders at a price of $0.75 for each $0.50 share.

Hart Co's payroll function is outsourced to an external service organisation, Chaz Co, which is responsible for all elements of payroll processing and maintenance of payroll records.

Hart Co's directors correctly disclosed their remuneration details in the forecast financial statements in line with IFRS Standards, however, local legislation in the country in which Hart Co is based, requires more extensive disclosure. The directors have stated that they consider this onerous and so do not intend to provide the additional information.

ISA 300 *Planning an audit of financial statements* provides guidance to assist in planning an audit.

**BPP** LEARNING MEDIA

## Required

(a)  Explain the benefits of audit planning. **(4 marks)**

(b)  Describe **EIGHT** audit risks and explain the auditor's response to each risk in planning the audit of Hart Co.

| Audit risk | Auditor's response |
|------------|--------------------|
|            |                    |

**(16 marks)**

(c)  Describe substantive procedures the auditor should perform to obtain sufficient and appropriate audit evidence in relation to Hart Co's directors' bonuses. **(5 marks)**

At the end of the planning meeting, the finance director of Hart Co mentioned to the audit manager that one of the key reasons Morph & Co was appointed as auditor was because of its knowledge of the industry. There were some concerns however, as to how Morph & Co would keep information obtained during the audit confidential as it audits three other construction companies specialising in environmentally-friendly building materials, including Hart Co's main competitor.

(d)  Explain the safeguards which Morph & Co should implement to ensure that this conflict of interest is properly managed. **(5 marks)**

**(Total = 30 marks)**

# 79 Prancer Construction Co (Sep/Dec 17)     36 mins

It is 1 July 20X5. You are an audit supervisor of Cupid & Co, planning the final audit of a new client, Prancer Construction Co, for the year ending 30 September 20X5. The company specialises in property construction and providing ongoing annual maintenance services for properties previously constructed. Forecast profit before tax is $13.8m and total assets are expected to be $22.3m, both of which are higher than for the year ended 30 September 20X4.

You are required to produce the audit strategy document. The audit manager has met with Prancer Construction Co's finance director and has provided you with the following notes, a copy of the August management accounts and the prior year financial statements.

## Meeting notes

The prior year financial statements recognise work in progress of $1.8m, which was comprised of property construction in progress as well as ongoing maintenance services for finished properties. The August 20X5 management accounts recognise $2.1m inventory of completed properties compared to a balance of $1.4m in September 20X4. A full year-end inventory count will be undertaken on 30 September at all of the eleven building sites where construction is in progress. There is not sufficient audit team resource to attend all inventory counts.

In line with industry practice, Prancer Construction Co offers its customers a five-year building warranty, which covers any construction defects. Customers are not required to pay any additional fees to obtain the warranty. The finance director anticipates this provision will be lower than last year as the company has improved its building practices and therefore the quality of the finished properties.

Customers who wish to purchase a property are required to place an order and pay a 5% non-refundable deposit prior to the completion of the building. When the building is complete, customers pay a further 92.5%, with the final 2.5% due to be paid six months later. The finance director has informed you that although an allowance for receivables has historically been maintained, it is anticipated that this can be significantly reduced.

## Information from management accounts

Prancer Construction Co's prior year financial statements and August 20X5 management accounts contain a material overdraft balance. The finance director has confirmed that there are minimum profit and net assets covenants attached to the overdraft.

A review of the management accounts shows the payables payment period was 56 days for August 20X5, compared to 87 days for September 20X4. The finance director anticipates that the September 20X5 payables payment period will be even lower than those in August 20X5.

**Required**

(a) Describe the process Cupid & Co should have undertaken to assess whether the **PRECONDITIONS** for an audit were present when accepting the audit of Prancer Construction Co. **(3 marks)**

(b) Identify **THREE** main areas, other than audit risks, which should be included within the audit strategy document for Prancer Construction Co, and for each area provide an example relevant to the audit. **(3 marks)**

(c) Using all the information provided, describe **SEVEN** audit risks, and explain the auditor's response to each risk, in planning the audit of Prancer Construction Co.

| Audit risk | Auditor's response |
|---|---|
|  |  |

**(14 marks)**

**(Total = 20 marks)**

# 80 Blackberry Co (Mar/Jun 18)        36 mins

You are an audit senior of Loganberry & Co and are planning the audit of Blackberry Co for the year ending 31 March 20X8. The company is a manufacturer of portable music players and your audit manager has already had a planning meeting with the finance director. Forecast revenue is $68.6m and profit before tax is $4.2m.

She has provided you with the following notes of the meeting:

**Planning meeting notes**

Inventory is valued at the lower of cost and net realisable value. Cost is made up of the purchase price of raw materials and costs of conversion, including labour, production and general overheads. Inventory is held in three warehouses across the country. The company plans to conduct full inventory counts at the warehouses on 2, 3 and 4 April, and any necessary adjustments will be made to reflect post year-end movements of inventory. The internal audit team will attend the counts.

During the year Blackberry Co paid $1.1m to purchase a patent which allows the company the exclusive right for three years to customise their portable music players to gain a competitive edge in their industry. The $1.1m has been expensed in the current year statement of profit or loss. In order to finance this purchase, Blackberry Co raised $1.2m through issuing shares at a premium.

In November 20X7 it was discovered that a significant teeming and lading fraud had been carried out by four members of the sales ledger department who had colluded. They had stolen funds from wholesale customer receipts and then to cover this they allocated later customer receipts against the older receivables. These employees were all reported to the police and subsequently dismissed. As a result of the vacancies in the sales ledger department, Blackberry Co decided to outsource its sales ledger processing to an external service organisation. This service provider handles all elements of the sales ledger cycle, including sales invoicing and chasing of receivables balances and sends monthly reports to Blackberry Co detailing the sales and receivable amounts. Blackberry Co ran its own sales ledger until 31 January 20X8, at which point the records were transferred to the service organisation.

In December 20X7 the financial accountant of Blackberry Co was dismissed. He had been employed by the company for nine years, and he has threatened to sue the company for unfair dismissal. As a result of this dismissal, and until his replacement commences work in April, the financial accountant's responsibilities have been adequately allocated to other members of the finance department. However, for this period no supplier statement reconciliations or purchase ledger control account reconciliations have been performed.

BPP
LEARNING
MEDIA

In January 20X7 a receivable balance of $0.9m was written off by Blackberry Co as it was deemed irrecoverable as the customer had declared itself bankrupt. In February 20X8, the liquidators handling the bankruptcy of the company publicly announced that it was likely that most of its creditors would receive a pay-out of 40% of the balance owed. As a result, Blackberry Co has included a current asset of $360,000 within the statement of financial position and other income in the statement of profit or loss.

**Required**

(a) Describe Loganberry & Co's responsibilities in relation to the prevention and detection of fraud and error. **(4 marks)**

(b) Describe **EIGHT** audit risks and explain the auditor's response to each risk in planning the audit of Blackberry Co.

| Audit risk | Auditor's response |
|---|---|
|  |  |

**(16 marks)**

**(Total = 20 marks)**

# 81 Darjeeling Co (Sep/Dec 18) 54 mins

It is 1 July 20X5. You are an audit supervisor of Earl & Co and are planning the audit of Darjeeling Co for the year ending 30 September 20X5. The company develops and manufactures specialist paint products and has been a client of your firm for several years. The audit manager has attended a planning meeting with the finance director and has provided you with the following notes of the meeting and financial statement extracts. You have been asked by the audit manager to undertake preliminary analytical procedures using the financial statement extracts.

**Planning meeting notes**

During the year Darjeeling Co has spent $0.9m, which is included within intangible assets, on the development of new product lines, some of which are in the early stages of their development cycle. Additionally, as the company is looking to expand production, during the year it purchased and installed a new manufacturing line. All costs incurred in the purchase and installation of that asset have been included within property, plant and equipment. These capitalised costs include the purchase price of $2.2m, installation costs of $0.4m and a five-year servicing and maintenance plan costing $0.5m. In order to finance the development projects and the new manufacturing line, the company borrowed $4m from the bank which is to be repaid in instalments over eight years and has an interest rate of 5%. Developing new products and expanding production is important as the company intends to undertake a stock exchange listing in the next 12 months.

The company started a number of initiatives during the year in order to boost revenue. It offered extended credit terms to its customers on the condition that their sales order quantities were increased. In addition, Darjeeling Co made an announcement in October 20X4 of its 'price promise': that it would match the prices of any competitor for similar products purchased. Customers who are able to prove that they could purchase the products cheaper elsewhere are asked to claim the difference from Darjeeling Co, within one month of the date of purchase of goods, via its website. The company intends to include a refund liability of $0.25m, which is based on the monthly level of claims to date, in the draft financial statements.

The finance director informed the audit manager that a problem arose in June 20X5 in relation to the mixing of materials within the production process for one particular product line. A number of these faulty paint products had already been sold and the issue was identified following a number of complaints from customers about the paint consistency being incorrect. As a precaution, further sales have been stopped and a product recall has been initiated for any of these specific paint products sold since June. Management is investigating whether the paint consistency of the faulty products can be rectified and subsequently sold.

Financial statement extracts for year ending 30 September

|  | Forecast 20X5 $'000 | Actual 20X4 $'000 |
|---|---|---|
| Revenue | 19,850 | 16,990 |
| Cost of sales | (12,440) | (10,800) |
| Gross profit | 7,410 | 6,190 |
| Inventory | 1,850 | 1,330 |
| Trade receivables | 2,750 | 1,780 |
| Bank | (810) | 560 |
| Trade payables | 1,970 | 1,190 |

**Required**

(a)   Explain why analytical procedures are used during THREE stages of an audit.   **(3 marks)**

(b)   Calculate THREE ratios, for BOTH years, which would assist you in planning the audit of Darjeeling Co.   **(3 marks)**

(c)   Using the information provided and the ratios calculated, describe EIGHT audit risks and explain the auditor's response to each risk in planning the audit of Darjeeling Co.

| Audit risk | Auditor's response |
|---|---|
|  |  |

**(16 marks)**

(d)   Describe substantive procedures the auditor should perform in relation to the faulty paint products held in inventory at the year end.   **(3 marks)**

(e)   Describe substantive procedures the auditor should perform to obtain sufficient and appropriate evidence in relation to Darjeeling Co's revenue.   **(5 marks)**

**(Total = 30 marks)**

INTERNAL CONTROL

Questions 82–118 cover Internal controls, the subject of Part C of the BPP Workbook for Audit and Assurance.

## Flowers Anytime (AIR Dec 02) (amended)　　　18 mins

The following scenario relates to questions 82–86.

You are an audit manager in a medium-sized audit firm. You are currently planning the audit of Flowers Anytime (Flowers) for the year ended 31 March 20X7. Flowers, a traditional flower wholesaler, is a new audit client for your firm.

As this is the first year you are auditing Flowers, it is necessary to understand and evaluate the company's system of internal control. The audit firm's policy requires the following steps to be taken when performing first year audits:

(1)　Perform walkthrough tests
(2)　Complete flowcharts and internal control evaluation questionnaires
(3)　Revise the audit strategy and audit plan
(4)　Perform tests of control

You have obtained the following background information about your new client. When customers call the company, their orders are taken by clerks who take details of the flowers to be delivered, the address to which they are to be delivered, and the account details of the customer. The clerks input these details into the company's computer system (whilst the order is being taken) which is integrated with the company's inventory control system.

The audit junior has made the following notes on the system for the receipt, processing and recording of the orders:

• All orders are recorded on pre-printed, three-part sequentially numbered order forms. One copy is kept by the sales clerk, one copy is forwarded to the warehouse for the dispatch of inventory, and one copy is sent to the customer as evidence of the order.

• The sales clerk regularly performs reviews of the standing data on the system, matching the price of flowers against an up to date price list.

• To ensure completeness of orders, a sequence check is performed on the sales invoices manually by the sales clerk and any missing documents are investigated.

• Sales invoices are posted on a weekly basis to the sales day book and accounts receivable ledger.

82　Drag each of the four options below to the right hand side to show the correct order in which the steps required by the firm's policy for first year audits would take place.

| Steps | | Order |
|---|---|---|
| (1) | Perform walkthrough tests | (1) |
| (2) | Complete flowcharts and internal control evaluation questionnaires | (2) |
| (3) | Revise the audit strategy and audit plan | (3) |
| (4) | Perform tests of control | (4) |

83 The audit junior has asked you whether internal control questionnaires (ICQs) should be completed as well as internal control evaluation questionnaires (ICEQs).

Which of the following statements is correct in relation to ICQs and ICEQs?

○ ICEQs determine whether controls exist which meet specific control objectives; ICQs determine whether there are controls which prevent or detect specified errors or omissions.

○ ICEQs are generally easier to apply to a variety of different systems than ICQs.

○ ICQs are likely to overlook how internal controls deal with unusual transactions; this will normally have to be recorded using ICEQs.

○ ICQs can give the impression that all controls are of equal weight; this issue is resolved by using ICEQs.

84 Tick the appropriate box to show whether the internal control activities identified in the audit junior's notes would satisfy the objective of preventing/detecting a material misstatement if it is operating effectively.

| Audit junior's notes | Yes | No |
|---|---|---|
| All orders are recorded on pre-printed, three-part sequentially numbered order forms. One copy is kept by the sales clerk, one copy is forwarded to the warehouse for the dispatch of inventory, and one copy is sent to the customer as evidence of the order. | ☐ | ☐ |
| The sales clerk regularly performs reviews of the standing data on the system, matching the price of flowers against an up to date price list. | ☐ | ☐ |
| To ensure completeness of orders, a sequence check is performed on the sales invoices manually by the sales clerk and any missing documents are investigated. | ☐ | ☐ |
| Sales invoices are posted on a weekly basis to the sales day book and accounts receivable ledger. | ☐ | ☐ |

85 You instruct the audit junior to confirm whether the post is opened by more than one individual.

Over which of the following internal control objectives would this provide assurance?

(1) Cash receipts are not misappropriated

(2) All cash receipts that occurred are recorded

(3) Cash receipts are recorded at the correct amounts in the ledger

(4) Cash receipts are posted to the correct receivables accounts and to the general ledger

○ 1 only

○ 2 only

○ 3 and 4

○ 1 and 4

86 During the course of the audit, the audit team identified numerous deficiencies in internal control relating to the sales system. The amounts exposed to the deficiencies were high and you have concluded that it is likely that the deficiencies would result in material misstatements in the financial statements. A deficiency was also identified in the purchases system but further investigation showed this to be a minor, isolated issue.

Which of the following statements is correct regarding the deficiencies which must be included in the report to management?

O The deficiencies identified in the sales system only

O The deficiencies identified in the purchases system only

O The deficiencies identified in the sales and purchases system

O Neither the deficiencies identified in the sales system nor the purchases system

(Total = 10 marks)

# KLE Co                                                                                18 mins

The following scenario relates to questions 87–91.

You are an audit manager in the internal audit department of KLE Co, a listed retail company. The internal audit department is auditing the company's procurement system. The system operates as follows:

## Ordering

KLE's ordering department consists of six members of staff: one chief buyer and five purchasing clerks.

All orders are raised on pre-numbered purchase requisition forms, and are sent to the ordering department.

In the ordering department, each requisition form is approved and signed by the chief buyer. A purchasing clerk transfers the order information onto an order form and identifies the appropriate supplier for the goods.

Part one of the two-part order form is sent to the supplier and part two to the accounts department. The requisition is thrown away.

## Goods received

When goods are received, the goods inwards department immediately raises a two-part pre-numbered goods received note (GRN).

- Part one is sent to the ordering department, which then forwards the GRN to the accounts department.

- Part two is filed in order of the reference number for the goods being ordered (obtained from the supplier's goods dispatched documentation), in the goods inwards department.

KLE Co's management is concerned that a number of inefficiencies in the procurement system may be having a negative financial impact on the company. As a result, they have requested the internal audit department to carry out a value for money audit focused on the company's procurement practices.

87 Which of the following is **NOT** a likely effect of the deficiencies in the internal control system for ordering described above?

O Purchases may be made unnecessarily at unauthorised prices.

O Subsequent queries on orders cannot be traced back to the original requisition.

O The order forms may contain errors that are not identified.

O Goods could be ordered twice in error or deliberately.

88 Which of the following statements are valid recommendations with regards to improving the internal controls for goods received described above?

(1) The ordering department should match orders to GRNs and mark orders as closed once all goods have been received, to enable any outstanding orders to be chased up.

(2) The first copy of the GRN should be sent directly to the accounts department, without first going through the ordering department, to prevent delays in recording the purchase.

(3) The goods inwards department should review the goods for their condition, in order to identify and return any damaged goods.

(4) GRNs should be filed in date order or by purchase order number, instead of by the supplier's reference number, to ensure that they can be matched easily to orders.

○ 1 and 3

○ 1, 2 and 3

○ 1, 2 and 4

○ 1, 3 and 4

89 As part of your audit of the procurement system, you have recommended that the goods inwards department should ensure that the goods received are valid business purchases, by matching all deliveries to an authorised order form before issuing a GRN.

Which of the following would be an appropriate test of control to confirm that the control is operating effectively?

○ For a sample of orders, check that there is a matching GRN

○ Check that the numerical sequence of purchase orders is complete

○ For a sample of GRNs check that there is an authorised purchase order

○ Check that the numerical sequence of GRNs is complete

90 KLE Co's management is keen to increase the range of assignments that the company's internal audit undertake.

Which of the following assignments could the internal audit department be asked to perform by management?

○ Undertake 'mystery shopper' reviews, where they enter the store as a customer, purchase goods and rate the overall shopping experience

○ Assist the external auditors by requesting bank confirmation letters

○ Provide advice on the implementation of a new payroll package for the payroll department

○ Review the company's financial statements on behalf of the board

91    Which of the following best summarises the meaning of 'efficiency' in the context of a Value for Money audit as requested by KLE Co's management?

○    The lowest cost at which the appropriate quantity and quality of physical, human and financial resources can be achieved

○    Producing the required goods and services in the shortest time possible

○    The extent to which an activity is achieving its policy objectives

○    The relationship between goods and services produced and the resources used to produce them

(Total = 10 marks)

# SouthLea (2007 Pilot Paper) (amended)          18 mins

The following scenario relates to questions 92–96.

SouthLea Co, your audit client, is a large unlisted construction company (building houses, offices and hotels) employing a large number of workers on various construction sites.

As part of planning for the audit of the financial statements for the year ended 31 December 20X6, you are reviewing the cash wages systems within the company.

The following information is available concerning the wages systems:

(i)    Hours worked are recorded using a clocking in/out system. On arriving for work and at the end of each day's work, each worker enters their unique employee number on a keypad.

(ii)    Workers on each site are controlled by a foreman. The foreman has a record of all employee numbers and can issue temporary numbers for new employees.

(iii)    Any overtime is calculated by the computerised wages system and added to the standard pay.

(iv)    The two staff in the wages department make amendments to the computerised wages system in respect of employee holidays and illness, as well as setting up and maintaining all employee records.

(v)    The computerised wages system calculates deductions from gross pay, such as employee taxes, and net pay. Every month a wages clerk checks the gross pay and deductions for a sample of employees. Finally a list of net cash payments for each employee is produced.

(vi)    Cash is delivered to the wages office by secure courier.

(vii)    The two staff place cash into wages packets for each employee along with a handwritten note of gross pay, deductions and net pay. The packets are given to the foreman for distribution to the individual employees.

SouthLea's finance director has mentioned to you that an allegation of suspected fraud had been made against a member of the senior management team during the year. This is currently being investigated by the internal audit team and the finance director hopes that the audit may shed further light on the matter.

SouthLea has an internal audit department of six staff. The chief internal auditor appoints staff within the internal audit department, although the chief executive officer is responsible for appointing the chief internal auditor. The chief internal auditor reports directly to the finance director. The chief internal auditor decides on the scope of work of the internal audit department. SouthLea does not currently have an audit committee.

92  In preparation for the audit planning meeting, the audit junior has identified a number of areas requiring audit focus.

Based on the information regarding the wages system, which **TWO** of the following are likely to introduce the highest risk of material misstatement?

☐   Completeness of wages

☐   Accuracy of deductions from gross pay

☐   Cut-off of starters' and leavers' wages

☐   Potential fraud risk factors

---

93  During the previous audit, the audit team had recommended SouthLea's management to ensure that any amendments to standing data on the wages system are reviewed by an authorised manager.

Which of the following is a test of control designed to provide evidence that the recommended internal control is operating effectively?

○   Review overtime lists for evidence of authorisation

○   Review the log of amendments to standing data for evidence of review

○   Perform a proof in total using the number of employees and average wage

○   Obtain printouts of employee wage rates and compare these to HR records

---

94  Which of the following statements about the responsibilities of external and internal auditors with regards to fraud is **NOT** correct?

○   The external auditor must maintain an attitude of professional scepticism throughout the audit, recognising the possibility that a material misstatement due to fraud could exist.

○   The internal auditor must always consider the potential of management overriding controls and modify their audit procedures accordingly when performing internal audit engagements.

○   It is not the responsibility of the external auditors to detect fraud within a client.

○   The work of internal auditors in reviewing the company's system of internal control helps management to fulfil its responsibility for preventing and detecting fraud.

---

95  Which of the following recommendations are appropriate in increasing the independence of SouthLea's internal audit department?

(1)   The chief internal auditor should be appointed by the board of directors.

(2)   The chief internal auditor should report to the board of directors.

(3)   The finance director should decide on the scope of the internal audit work.

○   (1) and (2) only

○   (1) and (3) only

○   (2) and (3) only

○   (1), (2) and (3)

96    You have been told by the finance director that the senior management team is looking to upgrade the company's computerised accounting system in a year's time. This is partly because the senior management team believes that due to the increasing size and complexity of the business, the company will need more robust general IT controls in the future.

Which **TWO** of the following are general IT controls?

☐    Full testing procedures using test data when developing computer applications

☐    One for one checking

☐    Disaster recovery procedures

☐    Hash totals

(Total = 10 marks)

# Cherry (Jun 15) (amended)                                    18 mins

The following scenario relates to questions 97–101.

Cherry Blossom Co (Cherry) manufactures custom made furniture and its year end is 30 April.

You are the audit supervisor of Poplar & Co and are developing the audit programmes for Cherry's forthcoming interim audit.

You have ascertained that Cherry purchases its raw materials from a wide range of approved suppliers. When production supervisors require raw materials, they complete a requisition form and this is submitted to the purchase ordering department. Requisition forms do not require authorisation and no reference is made to the current inventory levels of the materials being requested.

Cherry has an internal audit department which has provided you with details of the internal controls around the non-current assets cycle. One such control is that upon receipt of a new asset, each asset is assigned a unique serial number and this is recorded on the asset and in the non-current assets register.

97    As part of audit planning, the audit team needs to obtain an understanding of the company's system of internal control. Peter, the audit junior, is unsure what a company's internal control comprises.

Which of the following is **NOT** a component of an entity's internal control?

O    The control environment

O    Control activities relevant to the audit

O    The selection and application of accounting policies

O    The information system and communication

98    Which of the following are the most likely consequences of the internal control deficiency described in the requisition system for raw materials?

(1)    Fraudulent purchases may be made, leading to funds being diverted to third parties for illegal purposes.

(2)    Stock-outs may occur, resulting in the company being unable to meet orders and lost revenue.

(3)    Unnecessary purchases may be made, resulting in excess obsolescent raw materials accumulating in inventory requiring to be written down.

(4)    Raw materials of poor quality may be purchased, resulting in low quality products being produced, customer goodwill being lost and going concern risks.

○    1 and 3

○    2 and 3

○    1 and 4

○    2 and 4

99    While reviewing Cherry's purchases cycle, you identified that goods received notes for raw material purchases are not sequentially numbered.

Which of the following areas would you consider to be most at risk of material misstatement, as a result of this internal control deficiency?

○    Rights and obligations of inventory

○    Valuation of payables

○    Existence of inventory

○    Completeness of payables

100    You now turn your attention to Cherry's non-current assets cycle.

Which of the following statements is correct regarding audit procedures concerning the non-current assets cycle?

○    If the same ordering documentation is used in the non-current assets cycle as in the purchases cycle, it will not be necessary to produce additional systems documentation.

○    Because there are likely to be fewer capital purchases than standard purchases in the year, it may not be cost efficient to undertake tests of controls.

○    Because the control risk around the non-current assets cycle is likely to be high, it is important to perform tests of controls.

○    The non-current assets cycle is likely to have a lower risk of material misstatement than the purchases cycle.

101 In relation to the control relating to the receipt of a new asset, which of the following describe the **MOST RELIABLE** audit procedures which enable the auditor to assess whether this control is operating effectively?

    (1) Select a sample of capital additions on site, agree that a serial number is recorded on the asset and confirm it is included in the non-current assets register

    (2) Select a sample of assets recorded on the non-current assets register, confirm that it includes a serial number for each asset and agree the number to the physical asset

    (3) Inspect the non-current asset register and verify that there are no duplicated serial numbers

    (4) Observe the receipt of assets to confirm that serial numbers are assigned and recorded

    ○ 1 and 3

    ○ 2 and 3

    ○ 1 and 4

    ○ 2 and 4

(Total = 10 marks)

# Swan

**18 mins**

The following scenario relates to questions 102–106.

You are the audit senior on the interim audit of Swan Co. The company introduced a new system at the beginning of this financial year. You have discussed the new system with the sales director, and have noted the following two points in particular:

(1) Existing and new customers input their orders into computerised order forms on Swan Co's website. The order notes the items requested, the billing and sales addresses, and the customer number (if any). The system checks whether goods are in stock and approves the order instantly if so. The order is forwarded automatically to the sales department to be prepared.

(2) When an order is ready to send out, the sales department inputs the details into their system, and if it matches the order, a goods outward note is produced and the invoicing department is notified automatically. Staff have experienced multiple issues of goods outward notes not matching on the system, and have often resorted to simply printing the order and using it as a goods outward note. The printed order is then taken to the invoicing department for invoicing.

The partner has requested that you document the new system fully during the interim audit. She wants the system notes to be easy to update, and to contain an element of evaluation of the system.

102 In relation to orders received through the website which of the following control objectives is met?

    ○ Goods are sold to customers with good credit ratings.

    ○ The company is able to fulfil the orders.

    ○ Customers do not exceed credit limits.

    ○ Changes in customer data are authorised.

103 Your audit junior has identified four possible risks arising from the use of the printed order as a goods outward note and subsequent hand delivery to the invoicing department.

Which **TWO** of the below risks arise from the identified system deficiency?

☐ Orders are not fulfilled.

☐ Goods are sent out but not invoiced.

☐ Goods are invoiced but not sent out.

☐ Wrong goods are sent to customers.

104 You are reviewing the audit plan for tests of controls over invoicing, which reads:

(1) Observe the invoicing clerk to ensure that prices are checked to the official price list.

(2) Review a sample of invoices to ensure their numerical sequence.

(3) Review a sample of goods out notes to ensure they have been matched to sales invoices.

(4) Review a sample of sales invoices to verify evidence that the calculations were checked before they were sent to customers.

Which **TWO** of the procedures relate to the completeness assertion?

☐ Observe the invoicing clerk to ensure that prices are checked to the official price list.

☐ Review a sample of invoices to ensure their numerical sequence.

☐ Review a sample of goods out notes to ensure they have been matched to sales invoices.

☐ Review a sample of sales invoices to verify evidence that the calculations were checked before they were sent to customers.

105 Your audit junior is seeking to understand when deficiencies in internal control would be judged to be significant and therefore should be reported to those charged with governance.

Which **TWO** of the following factors would influence your judgement of whether the control deficiencies identified at Swan are significant?

☐ The likelihood of material misstatement resulting

☐ The fact that the system is new

☐ The number of deficiencies identified

☐ The fact that the deficiencies are associated with the sales system

106 In the light of the partner's request concerning documentation, you are considering different options for recording the system.

Which of the following recording methods most suits her requirements?

○ A computerised ICEQ

○ Computerised narrative notes

○ A flowchart

○ Copying the company's control manual

(Total = 10 marks)

# 107 Chuck (Dec 11) (amended)                                    54 mins

## Introduction and client background

You are the audit senior of Blair & Co and your team has just completed the interim audit of Chuck Industries Co, whose year-end is 31 January 20X2. You are in the process of reviewing the systems testing completed on the payroll cycle, as well as preparing the audit programmes for the final audit.

Chuck Industries Co manufactures lights and the manufacturing process is predominantly automated; however, there is a workforce of 85 employees who monitor the machines, as well as approximately 50 employees who work in sales and administration. The company manufactures 24 hours a day, 7 days a week. The payroll system operates as follows.

## Factory workforce

The company operates three shifts every day with employees working eight hours each. They are required to clock in and out using an employee swipe card, which identifies the employee number and links into the hours worked report produced by the computerised payroll system. Employees are paid on an hourly basis for each hour worked. There is no monitoring/supervision of the clocking in/out process.

On a weekly basis, the payroll department calculates the cash wages to be paid to the workforce. This is calculated based on the hours worked report multiplied by the hourly wage rate, with appropriate tax deductions. These calculations are not checked by anyone as they are generated by the payroll system. During the year the hourly wage was increased by the human resources (HR) department and this was notified to the payroll department verbally.

Each Friday, the payroll department prepares the pay packets and physically hands these out to the workforce, who operate the morning and late afternoon shifts, upon production of identification. The pay packets for night shift workers are given to the factory supervisor to distribute. If any night shift employees are absent on pay day then the factory supervisor keeps these wages and returns them to the payroll department on Monday.

## Sales and administration staff

The sales and administration staff are paid monthly by bank transfer. Employee numbers do fluctuate and during July two administration staff joined; however, due to staff holidays in the HR department, they delayed informing the payroll department, resulting in incorrect salaries being paid out.

## Required

(a)     Identify and explain **SIX DEFICIENCIES** of Chuck Industries Co's payroll system and provide a recommendation to address each of these deficiencies.

| Control deficiency | Control recommendation |
| --- | --- |
|  |  |

(12 marks)

(b)     Describe substantive procedures the auditor should perform to obtain sufficient appropriate audit evidence relating to the accuracy and completeness of Chuck Industries Co's payroll charge.                                                                (6 marks)

(c)     Last week the company had a visit from the tax authorities who reviewed the wages calculations and discovered that incorrect levels of tax had been deducted by the payroll system, as the tax rates from the previous year had not been updated. The finance director has queried with the audit team why they did not identify this non-compliance with tax legislation during last year's audit.

### Required

Explain the responsibilities of management and auditors of Chuck Industries Co in relation to compliance with law and regulations under ISA 250 (Revised) Consideration of Laws and Regulations in an Audit of Financial Statements.                                (4 marks)

(d) Chuck Industries Co has decided to outsource its sales ledger department and as a result it is making 14 employees redundant. A redundancy provision, which is material, will be included in the draft accounts.

**Required**

Describe substantive procedures you should perform to confirm the redundancy provision at the year end. **(5 marks)**

(e) Chuck Industries Co is considering establishing an internal audit (IA) department next year. The finance director has asked whether the work performed by the IA department can be relied upon by Blair & Co.

**Required**

Explain the factors that should be considered by an external auditor before reliance can be placed on the work performed by a company's internal audit department. **(3 marks)**

**(Total = 30 marks)**

# 108 Freesia (Mar/Jun 19) 54 mins

Freesia Co is a company listed on a stock exchange. It manufactures furniture which it supplies to a wide range of retailers across the region. The company has an internal audit (IA) department and the company's year end is 31 January 20X5. It is 1 July 20X5. You are an audit supervisor with Zinnia & Co, preparing the draft audit programmes and reviewing extracts from the internal controls documentation in preparation for the interim audit.

## Sales

Freesia Co generates revenue through visits by its sales staff to customers' premises. Sales ledger clerks, who work at head office, carry out credit checks on new customers prior to being accepted and then set their credit limits. Sales staff visit retail customers' sites personally and orders are completed using a four-part pre-printed order form. One copy is left with the customer, a second copy is returned to the sales ordering department, the third is sent to the warehouse and the fourth to the finance department at head office. Each sales order number is based on the sales person's own identification number in order to facilitate monitoring of sales staff performance.

Retail customers are given payment terms of 30 days and most customers choose to pay their invoices by bank transfer. Each day Lily Shah, a finance clerk, posts the bank transfer receipts from the bank statements to the cash book and updates the sales ledger. On a monthly basis, she performs the bank reconciliation.

## Purchases and inventory

Receipts of raw materials and goods from suppliers are processed by the warehouse team at head office, who agree the delivery to the purchase order, check the quantity and quality of goods and complete a sequentially numbered goods received note (GRN). The GRNs are sent to the finance department daily. On receipt of the purchase invoice from the supplier, Camilla Brown, the purchase ledger clerk, matches it to the GRN and order and the three documents are sent for authorisation by the appropriate individual. Once authorised, the purchase invoices are logged into the purchase ledger by Camilla, who utilises document count controls to ensure the correct number of invoices has been input.

The company values its inventory using standard costs, both for internal management reporting and for inclusion in the year-end financial statements. The basis of the standard costs was reviewed approximately 18 months ago.

## Payroll

Freesia Co employs a mixture of factory staff, who work a standard shift of eight hours a day, and administration and sales staff who are salaried. All staff are paid monthly by bank transfer. Occasionally, overtime is required of factory staff. Where this occurs, details of overtime worked per employee is collated and submitted to the payroll department by a production clerk. The payroll department pays this overtime in the month it occurs. At the end of each quarter, the company's payroll department sends overtime reports which detail the amount of overtime worked to the production director for their review.

Freesia Co's payroll package produces a list of payments per employee which links into the bank system to produce a list of automatic bank transfer payments. The finance director reviews the total to be paid on the list of automatic payments and compares this to the total payroll amount to be paid for the month per the payroll records. If any issues arise, then the automatic bank transfer can be manually changed by the finance director.

**Required**

(a)     Auditors are required to document a company's accounting and internal control systems as part of their audit process. Two methods available for documenting systems of internal control are narrative notes and questionnaires.

For each of the two methods, NARRATIVE NOTES and QUESTIONNAIRES:

(i)     Describe the method for documenting systems of internal control; and

(ii)    Explain an ADVANTAGE of using this method.

Note. The total marks will be split equally between each part.          **(4 marks)**

(b)     In respect of the internal controls of Freesia Co:

(i)     Identify and explain SIX deficiencies;

(ii)    Recommend a control to address each of these deficiencies; and

(iii)   Describe a TEST OF CONTROL the external auditors should perform to assess if each of these controls, if implemented, is operating effectively to reduce the identified deficiency.

| Control deficiency | Control recommendation | Test of control |
|---|---|---|
|  |  |  |

**(18 marks)**

Freesia Co deducts employment taxes from its employees' wages and salaries on a monthly basis and pays these to the local taxation authorities in the following month. At the year end, the financial statements will contain an accrual for employment tax payable.

**Required**

(c)     Describe the substantive procedures the auditor should perform to obtain sufficient and appropriate audit evidence in respect of Freesia Co's year-end accrual for employment tax payable.          **(4 marks)**

The listing rules of the stock exchange require compliance with corporate governance principles and the directors of Freesia Co are confident that they are following best practice in relation to this. However, the chairman recently received correspondence from a shareholder, who is concerned that the company is not fully compliant. The company's finance director has therefore requested a review of the company's compliance with corporate governance principles.

Freesia Co has been listed for over eight years and its board comprises four executive and four independent non-executive directors (NEDs), excluding the chairman. An audit committee comprised of the NEDs and the finance director meets each quarter to review the company's internal controls.

The directors' remuneration is set by the finance director. NEDs are paid a fixed fee for their services and executive directors are paid an annual salary as well as a significant annual bonus based on Freesia Co's profits. The company's chairman does not have an executive role and so she has sole responsibility for liaising with the shareholders and answering any of their questions.

**Required**

(d) Describe TWO corporate governance deficiencies faced by Freesia Co and provide a recommendation to address each deficiency to ensure compliance with corporate governance principles.

| Deficiency | Recommendation |
|---|---|
|  |  |

(4 marks)

(Total = 30 marks)

# 109 Tinkerbell (Jun 11)                                    54 mins

### Introduction

Tinkerbell Toys Co (Tinkerbell) is a manufacturer of children's building block toys; they have been trading for over 35 years and they sell to a wide variety of customers including large and small toy retailers across the country. The company's year-end is 31 May 20X1.

The company has a large manufacturing plant, four large warehouses and a head office. Upon manufacture, the toys are stored in one of the warehouses until they are dispatched to customers. The company does not have an internal audit department.

Sales ordering, goods dispatched and invoicing

Each customer has a unique customer account number and this is used to enter sales orders when they are received in writing from customers. The orders are entered by an order clerk and the system automatically checks that the goods are available and that the order will not take the customer over their credit limit. For new customers, a sales manager completes a credit application; this is checked through a credit agency and a credit limit entered into the system by the credit controller. The company has a price list, which is updated twice a year. Larger customers are entitled to a discount; this is agreed by the sales director and set up within the customer master file.

Once the order is entered an acceptance is automatically sent to the customer by mail/email confirming the goods ordered and a likely dispatch date. The order is then sorted by address of customer. The warehouse closest to the customer receives the order electronically and a dispatch list and sequentially numbered goods dispatch notes (GDNs) are automatically generated. The warehouse team packs the goods from the dispatch list and, before they are sent out, a second member of the team double checks the dispatch list to the GDN, which accompanies the goods.

Once dispatched, a copy of the GDN is sent to the accounts team at head office and a sequentially numbered sales invoice is raised and checked to the GDN. Periodically a computer sequence check is performed for any missing sales invoice numbers.

### Fraud

During the year a material fraud was uncovered. It involved cash/cheque receipts from customers being diverted into employees' personal accounts. In order to cover up the fraud, receipts from subsequent unrelated customers would then be recorded against the earlier outstanding receivable balances and this cycle of fraud would continue.

The fraud occurred because two members of staff 'who were related' colluded. One processed cash receipts and prepared the weekly bank reconciliation; the other employee recorded customer receipts in the sales ledger. An unrelated sales ledger clerk was supposed to send out monthly customer statements but this was not performed. The bank reconciliations each had a small unreconciled amount but no one reviewed the reconciliations after they were prepared. The fraud was only uncovered when the two employees went on holiday at the same time and it was discovered that cash receipts from different customers were being applied to older receivable balances to hide the earlier sums stolen.

**Required**

(a) Recommend **SIX** tests of controls the auditor would normally carry out on the sales system of Tinkerbell, and explain the objective for each test. **(12 marks)**

(b) Describe substantive procedures the auditor should perform to confirm Tinkerbell's year-end receivables balance. **(8 marks)**

(c) Identify and explain controls Tinkerbell should implement to reduce the risk of fraud occurring again and, for each control, describe how it would mitigate the risk. **(6 marks)**

(d) Describe substantive procedures the auditor should perform to confirm Tinkerbell's revenue. **(4 marks)**

**(Total = 30 marks)**

# 110 Trombone (Jun 14) 54 mins

Trombone Co (Trombone) operates a chain of hotels across the country. Trombone employs in excess of 250 permanent employees and its year end is 31 August 20X4. You are the audit supervisor of Viola & Co and are currently reviewing the documentation of Trombone's payroll system, detailed below, in preparation for the interim audit.

**Trombone's payroll system**

Permanent employees work a standard number of hours per week as specified in their employment contract. However, when the hotels are busy, staff can be requested by management to work additional shifts as overtime. This can either be paid on a monthly basis or taken as days off.

Employees record any overtime worked and days taken off on weekly overtime sheets which are sent to the payroll department. The standard hours per employee are automatically set up in the system and the overtime sheets are entered by clerks into the payroll package, which automatically calculates the gross and net pay along with relevant deductions. These calculations are not checked at all. Wages are increased by the rate of inflation each year and the clerks are responsible for updating the standing data in the payroll system.

Employees are paid on a monthly basis by bank transfer for their contracted weekly hours and for any overtime worked in the previous month. If employees choose to be paid for overtime, authorisation is required by department heads of any overtime in excess of 30% of standard hours. If employees choose instead to take days off, the payroll clerks should check back to the 'overtime worked' report; however this report is not always checked.

The 'overtime worked' report, which details any overtime recorded by employees, is run by the payroll department weekly and emailed to department heads for authorisation. The payroll department asks department heads to only report if there are any errors recorded. Department heads are required to arrange for overtime sheets to be authorised by an alternative responsible official if they are away on annual leave; however there are instances where this arrangement has not occurred.

The payroll package produces a list of payments per employee; this links into the bank system to produce a list of automatic payments. The finance director reviews the total list of bank transfers and compares this to the total amount to be paid per the payroll records; if any issues arise then the automatic bank transfer can be manually changed by the finance director.

**Required**

(a) In respect of the payroll system of Trombone Co:

(i) Identify and explain **FIVE** deficiencies;

(ii) Recommend a control to address each of these deficiencies; and

(iii) Describe a test of control Viola & Co should perform to assess if each of these controls is operating effectively.

| Control deficiency | Control recommendation | Test of control |
|---|---|---|
|  |  |  |

(15 marks)

(b) Explain the difference between an interim and a final audit. (5 marks)

(c) Describe substantive procedures you should perform at the final audit to confirm the completeness and accuracy of Trombone Co's payroll expense. (6 marks)

Trombone deducts employment taxes from its employees' wages on a monthly basis and pays these to the local taxation authorities in the following month. At the year end the financial statements will contain an accrual for income tax payable on employment income. You will be in charge of auditing this accrual.

### Required

(d) Describe the audit procedures required in respect of the year-end accrual for tax payable on employment income. (4 marks)

(Total = 30 marks)

# 111 Castle Courier Co (Mar/Jun 21)                    54 mins

**This scenario relates to five requirements.**

It is 1 July 20X5. You are an audit supervisor of Apple & Co and are in the process of reviewing extracts of the systems documentation which has been completed on the payroll cycle of the Castle Courier Co, as well as preparing the audit programmes for the forthcoming final audit for the year ending 30 September 20X5. Castle Courier Co is a package delivery company which operates from a large distribution centre.

### Payroll

The company employs 200 staff whom 120 of these staff are delivery drivers. All staff work a standard eight-hour shift each day and are paid monthly. All sraff members are required to clockin and out using a sequentially numbered key card which contains their unique employee number and name. Sequence checks on the key cards and the data recorded in the clocking-in system are carried out by the human resources (HR) supervisor on a regular basis. The clocking-in process is monitored by a camera on entry to the distribution centre and weekly checks are carried out by HR department who review the video footage to ensure that no staff member clocks-in for someone else. Recordings are kept in date order in the HR department and logged on a spredsheet together with the name of the person who has reviewed the footage.

The clocking-in system is directly linked to the payroll system and information regarding the hours worked by the staff is automatically transferred into the payroll system. The payroll system then automatically calculates gross pay, deductions and net pay. The payroll clerk confirms that the transfer or hours and calculations has been done correctly by recalculating a sample of employees' gross to net pay. A payroll supervisor then reviews this check whick is evidenced by the supervisor's signature.

All staff are entitled to 22 days holiday a year. Employees are paid for any holiday which has not been taken at the end of the year. Department managers are required to approve all holiday requests bu authorising employees' holiday forms, however thias does not always occur.

The payroll system is password-protected, and the password is changed on a monthly basis by the payroll manager using a rasndom password generator.

Once the payroll has been agreed by the payroll supervisor, the payroll clerk provides details of the net pay due to each employee to the financial controller who then prepares and authorises the bank transfer to be paid to the employees' bank accounts.

Each month, as part of the month-end procedures, the finance director undertakes a payroll control account reconciliation and investigates any differences to ensure that the payroll figures have been posted into the accounting records correctly.

The company's HR department is responsible for processing starters and leaves using a joiner/leaver form to notify the payroll department of the change. On receipt of the joiner/leaver form a payroll clerk updates the payroll system. An edit report is generated which records the changes made but this report is not reviewed. Two staff members from the HR department have been absent for some time due to illness. As a result, the operations manager has processed six newly recruited temporary delivery drivers and instructed the payroll department to set up the new employees.

Delivery drivers are sometimes required to wqork overtime, particul;arly in busy periods. Where overtimesd is necessary, the operations manager has to authorise overtime in excess of five hours per week.

Some temporary delivery drivers receive their wages in cash. The delivery driver collects their pay packet from the fionance department when it is ready. The member of staff in the finance department will ask for the delivery driver's name to check that there is a pay packet prepared and, if there is, they provide the delivery driver with they pay packet.

The company has to pay employment taxes to the tax authority by the end of each month. Each month the payroll supervisor calculates the total liability due to the tax authority and this is then passed to the financial controller who checks the calculations prior to the payment being made.

To encourage delivery drivers to make deliveries on time, the company pays a discretionary bonus to delivery drivers on a quarterly basis. The operations manager decides on the bonus to be paid and notifies the payroll clerk in writing every quarter as to who will receive a bonus and how much it will be.

As delivery drivers spend the majority of their day driving the company vehicles, they are required by law to take a 15-minute paid break in the morning and afternoon, as well as a one-hour lunch break. The company has no way of monitoring the length of these breaks as the delivery drivers are out on deliveries.

(a)     Describe the following methods for documenting internal control systems and for each explain a **DISADVANTAGE** of using this method.

| Method | Explanation | Disadvantages |
|---|---|---|
| Narrative Notes | | |
| Internal control questionnaires | | |

(4 marks)

(b)     (i)     Identify and explain **FOUR DIRECT CONTROLS** in Castle Courier Co's payroll system which the auditor may seek to place reliance on; and

        (ii)    Describe a **TEST OF CONTROL** the auditor should perform to assess if each of these direct controls is operating effectively.

*Note: The marks will be split equally between each part.*

| Direct control | Test of control |
|---|---|
| | |
| | |
| | |
| | |

(8 marks)

(b)    Identify and explain **SIX DEFICIENCIES** in Castle Courier Co's payroll system and provide a control recommendation to address each of these deficiencies.

| Control deficiency | Control recommendation |
|---|---|
|  |  |
|  |  |
|  |  |
|  |  |
|  |  |
|  |  |

(12 marks)

(c)    Describe substantive procedures the auditor should perform to obtain sufficient and appropriate audit evidence in relation to Castle Courier Co's payroll expense.    **(6 marks)**

(Total = 30 marks)

# 112 Bluesberry (Dec 10)                                          36 mins

Bluesberry Hospital is located in a country where healthcare is free, as the taxpayers fund the hospitals which are owned by the Government. Two years ago management reviewed all aspects of hospital operations and instigated a number of measures aimed at improving overall 'value for money' for the local community. Management have asked that you, an audit manager in the hospital's internal audit department, perform a review over the measures which have been implemented.

Bluesberry has one centralised buying department and all purchase requisition forms for medical supplies must be forwarded here. Upon receipt the buying team will research the lowest price from suppliers and a purchase order is raised. This is then passed to the purchasing director, who authorises all orders. The small buying team receives in excess of 200 forms a day.

The human resources department has had difficulties with recruiting suitably trained staff. Overtime rates have been increased to incentivise permanent staff to fill staffing gaps; this has been popular, and reliance on expensive temporary staff has been reduced. Monitoring of staff hours had been difficult but the hospital has implemented time card clocking in and out procedures and these hours are used for overtime payments as well.

The hospital has invested heavily in new surgical equipment which, although very expensive, has meant that more operations could be performed and patient recovery rates are faster. However, currently there is a shortage of appropriately trained medical staff. A capital expenditure committee has been established, made up of senior managers, and they plan and authorise any significant capital expenditure items.

**Required**

(a)    Explain the purpose of a value for money audit.                                          **(4 marks)**

(b)    (i)    Identify and explain **FOUR STRENGTHS** within Bluesberry's operating environment.
                                                                                              **(6 marks)**

        (ii)    For each strength identified, describe how Bluesberry might make further improvements to provide best value for money.                                          **(4 marks)**

(c)    Describe **TWO** substantive procedures the external auditor of Bluesberry should adopt to verify **EACH** of the following assertions in relation to an entity's property, plant and equipment:

        (i)    Valuation;
        (ii)    Completeness; and
        (iii)    Rights and obligations.

        *Note.* Assume that the hospital adopts IFRS.                                          **(6 marks)**

(Total = 20 marks)

# 113 Snowdon (Mar/Jul 20)

**36 mins**

This scenario relates to four requirements.

It is 1 July 20X5. You are an audit supervisor with Rocky & Co, reviewing extracts from the internal controls documentation in preparation for the interim audit of Snowdon Co. The company's year end is 30 September 20X5. The company provides training services for individuals looking to become qualified engineers. Snowdon Co's customers are the employers that send their employees for training on a weekly basis. Snowdon Co runs classes in its 45 training centres across the country.

The company has a small internal audit (IA) department, which has experienced significant staff shortages and is currently under-resourced. This has resulted in a reduction in their programme of work for the year in many areas.

## Non-current assets

Snowdon Co's training centres are either owned by the company or are held under a long-term lease. The company also has a head office and central warehouse for storage of training materials. Each training centre is set up as a separate department and is given an annual capital expenditure budget but some departments have already significantly exceeded their annual budgets.

When new equipment is acquired the finance department classifies the expenditure between capital and revenue, noting the classification on the purchase order. The classification is made with reference to guidelines established by the finance director, who sample checks that the capital or revenue expenditure allocation has been correctly applied.

Part of the work which Snowdon Co's IA department is required to carry out is a comparison of the assets per the non-current assets register and those physically present in each of the centres. This year's programme of visits, which has been planned and carried out on the same basis as previous years, means that by the year end IA will only have visited the four largest centres and five of the other centres randomly selected.

## Payroll

Snowdon Co has a human resources (HR) department, responsible for setting up all new joiners. Pre-printed joiners' forms, which require all necessary data, are completed by HR for new employees and once verified, a copy is sent to the payroll department so that the employee can be set up for payment. The joiner's form includes the staff member's assigned employee number and the system requires the new joiner's employee number to be entered before they can be added to payroll. All members of the payroll department can amend employees' standing data in the payroll system as they have access to the password, which is changed by the payroll director on a quarterly basis.

On a monthly basis the employees are paid by bank transfer. The senior payroll manager reviews the list of bank payments and agrees this to the payroll records. If any discrepancies are noted, the senior payroll manager always makes the adjustment in the payroll records.

## Sales and bank

After passing a credit check, new customers are set up in the receivables ledger master file and a credit limit is set by the sales director. The credit limits then remain unchanged in the system unless a review is requested by the customer.

Each new customer is allocated a client services manager from Snowdon Co, who is responsible for managing the customer relationship and maximising sales. Standard credit terms for customers are 30 days and on a monthly basis sales invoices which are over 90 days outstanding are notified to the relevant client services manager to chase payment directly with the customer.

Every month, the cashier reconciles the bank statements to the cash book. The reconciliations are reviewed by the financial controller, who also investigates all reconciling items and evidences his review by way of a signature.

## Required

Auditors are required, under ISA 265 *Communicating deficiencies in internal control with those charged with governance and management*, to communicate in writing to those charged with governance any significant deficiencies in internal control.

(a)  Describe **FOUR** matters the auditor may consider in determining whether a deficiency in internal control is significant. **(4 marks)**

(b)  In respect of the internal control system of Snowdon Co:

(i)  Identify and explain **THREE DIRECT CONTROLS** on which the auditor may place reliance; and

(ii)  Describe a **TEST OF CONTROL** the auditor should perform to assess if each of these direct controls is operating effectively.

| Direct control | Test of control |
|----------------|-----------------|
|                |                 |

**(6 marks)**

(c)  Identify **FIVE DEFICIENCIES** in Snowdon Co's internal control system and provide a recommendation to address each of these deficiencies.

| Control deficiency | Control recommendation |
|--------------------|------------------------|
|                    |                        |

**(10 marks)**

**(Total = 20 marks)**

# 114 Swift Co (Sep/Dec 20) 36 mins

This scenario relates to four requirements.

It is 1 July 20X5. Swift Co prints books which it sells online and supplies to retailers across the country. The company's year end is 30 September 20X5. You are an audit supervisor with Toucan & Co, preparing the draft audit programmes and reviewing the internal controls documentation in preparation for the interim audit.

## Payroll

Swift Co employs factory staff who are required to work a standard shift of eight hours per day. No staff members are required to work overtime. All staff members are paid monthly by bank transfer. The company has a resources (HR) department which is responsible for setting up all new joiners and a payroll department which processes wages and salaries.

When a new employee joins the company, HR completes a joiners' form which includes a unique employee number for each new employee. The joiners' form is then sent to the payroll department so that the new employee can be set up for payment. The unique employee number must be entered into the payroll system before the employee can be added to payroll. On a monthly basis, an exception report relating to changes to the payroll standing data is produced and reviewed by the payroll manager who evidences this review.

Employee hours worked and their hourly wage rates are present into the system, which automatically calculates the gross and net pay along with relevant deductions and generates employee payslips. The payroll supervisor selects a sample of the payslips, re-performs the gross to net pay calculations and investigates any discrepancies. The sampled payslips are then signed as evidence of this review.

## Purchases

The company has a purchasing department based at its head office. When raw materials are required, the production supervisors submit a requisition form to the purchasing department. A multi-part purchase order is generated and the purchasing manager authorizes all orders up to $5,000. Orders over $5,000 are authorized by the purchasing director.

The warehouse team processes goods received from suppliers. They agree the goods received to the purchase order and check the quantity and the quality of the goods. On completion of those checks a goods received note (GRN) is produced. One copy of the GRN is then signed and filed in the warehouse. Another copy of the GRN is sent to the finance department.

A payable ledger clerk logs the purchase invoices in batches of 20 into the purchase day book utilizing control totals. A batch control sheet is completed for each set of 20 invoices and the clerk signs to evidence the checks undertaken.

Supplier statement reconciliations are performed on a monthly basis. All differences are fully investigated, and the financial controller reviews these reconciliations. Invoices are paid in accordance with the supplier's credit terms. The finance director authorizes the bank transfer payment list for suppliers having first agreed the amounts to be paid to supporting documentation and having reviewed the list for duplicate payments.

Auditors are required to document a company's accounting and internal control systems as part of their audit process. Three methods available for documenting internal controls are narrative notes, flowcharts and questionnaires.

### Required

(a) For each of the **THREE** methods identified in the table:

   (i) Describe the method for documenting systems of internal control; and

   (ii) Explain an ADVANTAGE of using this method. **(6 marks)**

|  | Description | Advantage |
|---|---|---|
| Narrative notes |  |  |
| Flowcharts |  |  |
| Questionnairs |  |  |

(b) In respect of the internal control system of Swift Co:

   (i) Identify and explain SEVEN DIRECT CONTROLS which the auditor may seek to place reliance on; and

   (ii) Describe a TEST OF CONTROL the auditor should perform to assess if each of these direct controls is operating effectively.

| Direct control | Test of control |
|---|---|
|  |  |

**(14 marks)**

**(Total = 20 marks)**

# 115 Amberjack (Sep/Dec 19)                    36 mins

This scenario relates to two requirements.

Amberjack Co manufactures and distributes car tyres to a wide customer base both in its country and across the rest of the continent. Its year end was 30 April 20X5. It is 1 July 20X5. You are an audit manager of Pinfish & Co and you are reviewing extracts of the documentation describing Amberjack Co's sales and dispatch system following completion of the interim audit.

Amberjack Co has grown in size over the previous 18 months. All new customers undergo credit checks prior to being accepted and credit limits are subsequently set by the receivables ledger clerks who record the new customer details, assign a unique customer number and set credit limits in the master data file. The company's credit controller is currently on secondment to the internal audit department for six months and no replacement has been appointed.

Customers wishing to order goods, telephone the company's sales order department and provide their unique account details. Sequentially numbered four-part sales orders are generated for all orders, after checking available inventory levels. One copy is retained by the sales ordering team to enable them monitor progress of the sales orders, one copy is sent to customer, one copy is sent to one of the company's warehouses for dispatch and the final copy is sent to the finance department. Upon dispatch, a three-part goods dispatch note (GDN) is completed which is assigned the same sequential number as the order number; one copy is sent with the goods, one remains with the warehouse and one is sent to the finance department.

Due to the recent growth of the company, and as there are a large number of sales invoices, additional temporary staff members have been appointed to help the sales clerks to produce the sales invoices. The sales invoices are prepared using quantities from the GDNs and prices from the authorised sales prices list, which is updated every six months. This year, in line with its main competitors, the company offered a 10% discount on all orders placed during one weekend in late November. Where a discount has been given, this has to be manually entered by the sales clerks onto the sequentially numbered invoice.

Customer statements are no longer being generated and sent out. The company only reconciles the receivables ledger control account at the end of April in order to verify the year-end balance.

**Required**

(a)    List FOUR control objectives of Amberjack Co's sales and despatch system.    **(4 marks)**

(b)    As the external auditor of Amberjack Co, write a report to management in respect of the sales and despatch system described which:

(i)    Identifies and explains SEVEN deficiencies in the sales and despatch system and recommends a control to address each of these deficiencies.

(ii)    Includes a covering letter.

Note. Two marks will be awarded within this requirement for the covering letter.

(16 marks)

(Total = 20 marks)

# 116 Comet Publishing Co (Sep/Dec 17)            54 mins

You are an audit supervisor of Halley & Co and you are reviewing the documentation describing Comet Publishing Co's purchases and payables system in preparation for the interim and final audit for the year ending 30 September 20X7. The company is a retailer of books and has ten stores and a central warehouse, which holds the majority of the company's inventory.

Your firm has audited Comet Publishing Co for a number of years and as such, audit documentation is available from the previous year's file, including internal control flowcharts and detailed purchases and payables system notes. As far as you are aware, Comet Publishing Co's system of internal control has not changed in the last year. The audit manager is keen for the team to utilise existing systems documentation in order to ensure audit efficiency. An extract from the existing systems notes is provided below.

### Extract of purchases and payables system

Store managers are responsible for ordering books for their shop. It is not currently possible for store managers to request books from any of the other nine stores. Customers who wish to order books, which are not in stock at the branch visited, are told to contact the other stores directly or visit the company website. As the inventory levels fall in a store, the store manager raises a purchase requisition form, which is sent to the central warehouse. If there is insufficient inventory held, a supplier requisition form is completed and sent to the purchase order clerk, Oliver Dancer, for processing. He sends any orders above $1,000 for authorisation from the purchasing director.

Receipts of goods from suppliers are processed by the warehouse team, who agree the delivery to the purchase order, checking quantity and quality of goods and complete a sequentially numbered goods received note (GRN). The GRNs are sent to the accounts department every two weeks for processing.

On receipt of the purchase invoice from the supplier, an accounts clerk matches it to the GRN. The invoice is then sent to the purchase ordering clerk, Oliver, who processes it for payment. The finance director is given the total amount of the payments list, which she authorises and then processes the bank payments. Due to staff shortages in the accounts department, supplier statement reconciliations are no longer performed.

### Required

(a)     Explain the steps the auditor should take to confirm the accuracy of the purchases and payables flowcharts and systems notes currently held on file.     **(5 marks)**

(b)     In respect of the purchases and payables system for Comet Publishing Co:

    (i)      Identify and explain **FIVE** deficiencies;

    (ii)     Recommend a control to address each of these deficiencies; and

    (iii)    Describe a **TEST OF CONTROL** the auditor should perform to assess if each of these controls, if implemented, is operating effectively to reduce the identified deficiency.

| Control deficiency | Control recommendation | Test of control |
|---|---|---|
|  |  |  |

**(15 marks)**

(c)     Describe substantive procedures the auditor should perform to obtain sufficient and appropriate evidence in relation to Comet Publishing Co's purchases and other expenses.     **(5 marks)**

### Other information – conflict of interest

Halley & Co has recently accepted the audit engagement of a new client, Edmond Co, who is the main competitor of Comet Publishing Co. The finance director of Comet Publishing Co has enquired how Halley & Co will keep information obtained during the audit confidential.

(d)     Explain the safeguards which Halley & Co should implement to ensure that the identified conflict of interest is properly managed.     **(5 marks)**

**(Total = 30 marks)**

# 117 Raspberry Co (Mar/Jun 18)

**54 mins**

Raspberry Co operates an electric power station, which produces electricity 24 hours a day, seven days a week. The company's year-end is 30 June 20X8. You are an audit manager of Grapefruit & Co, the auditor of Raspberry Co. The interim audit has been completed and you are reviewing the documentation describing Raspberry Co's payroll system.

## Systems notes – payroll

Raspberry Co employs over 250 people and approximately 70% of the employees work in production at the power station. There are three shifts every day with employees working eight hours each. The production employees are paid weekly in cash. The remaining 30% of employees work at the head office in non-production roles and are paid monthly by bank transfer.

The company has a human resources (HR) department, responsible for setting up all new joiners. Pre-printed forms are completed by HR for all new employees and, once verified, a copy is sent to the payroll department for the employee to be set up for payment. This form includes the staff member's employee number and payroll cannot set up new joiners without this information. To encourage staff to attend work on time for all shifts, Raspberry Co introduced a discretionary bonus, paid every three months for production staff. The production supervisors determine the amounts to be paid and notify the payroll department. This quarterly bonus is entered into the system by a clerk and each entry is checked by a senior clerk for input errors prior to processing. The senior clerk signs the bonus listing as evidence of undertaking this review.

Production employees are issued with clock cards and are required to swipe their cards at the beginning and end of their shift. This process is supervised by security staff 24 hours a day. Each card identifies the employee number and links into the hours worked report produced by the payroll system, which automatically calculates the gross and net pay along with relevant deductions. These calculations are not checked.

In addition to tax deductions from pay, some employees' wages are reduced for such items as repayments of student loans owed to the central government. All employers have a statutory obligation to remit funds on a timely basis and to maintain accounting records which reconcile with annual loan statements sent by the government to employers. At Raspberry Co student loan deduction forms are completed by the relevant employee and payments are made directly to the government until the employee notifies HR that the loan has been repaid in full.

On a quarterly basis exception reports relating to changes to the payroll standing data are produced and reviewed by the payroll director. No overtime is worked by employees. Employees are entitled to take 28 holiday days annually. Holiday request forms are required to be completed and authorised by relevant line managers, however this does not always occur.

On a monthly basis, for employees paid by bank transfer, the senior payroll manager reviews the list of bank payments and agrees this to the payroll records prior to authorising the payment. If any errors are noted, the payroll senior manager amends the records.

For production employees paid in cash, the necessary amount of cash is delivered weekly from the bank by a security company. Two members of the payroll department produce the pay packets, one is responsible for preparing them and the other checks the finished pay packets. Both members of staff are required to sign the weekly payroll listing on completion of this task. The pay packets are then delivered to the production supervisors, who distribute them to employees at the end of the employees' shift, as they know each member of their production team.

Monthly management accounts are produced which detail variances between budgeted amounts and actual. Revenue and key production costs are detailed however, as there are no overtime costs, wages and salaries are not analysed.

**Required**

(a)     In respect of the payroll system for Raspberry Co:

     (i)     Identify and explain **FIVE DIRECT CONTROLS** which the auditor may seek to place reliance on; and

     (ii)    Describe a **TEST OF CONTROL** the auditor should perform to assess if each of these direct controls is operating effectively.

| Direct control | Test of control |
|---|---|
|  |  |

**(10 marks)**

(b)     Identify and explain **FIVE DEFICIENCIES** in Raspberry Co's payroll system and provide a recommendation to address each of these deficiencies.

| Control deficiency | Control recommendation |
|---|---|
|  |  |

**(10 marks)**

The finance director is interested in establishing an internal audit department (IAD). In the company she previously worked for the IAD carried out inventory counts, however as this is not relevant for Raspberry Co, she has asked for guidance on what other assignments an IAD could be asked to perform.

**Required**

(c)     Describe assignments the internal audit department of Raspberry Co could carry out.

**(5 marks)**

Raspberry Co deducts employment taxes from its employees' wages on a weekly/monthly basis and pays these to the local taxation authorities in the following month. At the year end the financial statements will contain an accrual for income tax payable on employment income.

**Required**

(d)     Describe the substantive procedures the auditor should perform to confirm the year-end accrual for tax payable on employment income.     **(5 marks)**

**(Total = 30 marks)**

# 118 Camomile Co (Sep/Dec 18)                                        36 mins

(a)     ISA 260 *Communication with Those Charged with Governance* provides guidance to auditors in relation to communicating with those charged with governance on matters arising from the audit of an entity's financial statements.

     **Required**

     (i)     Explain why it is important for auditors to communicate throughout the audit with those charged with governance; and

     (ii)    Identify TWO examples of matters which the auditor may communicate to those charged with governance.

          *Note:* The total marks will be split equally between each part.     **(4 marks)**

(b)     Camomile Co operates six restaurant and bar venues which are open seven days a week. The company's year-end is 31 December 20X8. You are the audit supervisor reviewing the internal controls documentation in relation to the cash receipts and payments system in preparation for the interim audit, which will involve visiting a number of the venues as well as the head office. The company has a small internal audit (IA) department based at head office.

The purchasing department based at the company's head office is responsible for ordering food and beverages for all six venues. In addition, each venue has a petty cash float of $400, held in the safe, which is used for the purchase of sundry items. When making purchases of sundries, employees are required to obtain the funds from the restaurant manager, purchase the sundries and return any excess money and the receipt to the manager. At any time, the petty cash sum held and receipts should equal the float of $400 but it has been noted by the company's IA department that on some occasions this has not been the case.

Each venue has five cash tills (cash registers) to take payments from customers. Three are located in the bar area and two in the restaurant area. Customers can pay using either cash or a credit card and for any transaction either the credit card vouchers or cash are placed in the till by the employee operating the till. To speed up the payment process, each venue has a specific log on code which can be used to access all five tills and is changed every two weeks.

At each venue at the end of the day, the tills are closed down by the restaurant manager who counts the total cash in all five tills and the sum of the credit card vouchers and these totals are reconciled with the aggregated daily readings of sales taken from each till. Any discrepancies are noted on the daily sales sheet. The daily sales sheet records the sales per the tills, the cash counted and the total credit card vouchers as well as any discrepancies. These sheets are scanned and emailed to the cashier at head office at the end of each week.

Approximately 30% of Camomile Co's customers pay in cash for their restaurant or bar bills. Cash is stored in the safe at each venue on a daily basis after the sales reconciliation has been undertaken. Each safe is accessed via a key which the restaurant manager has responsibility for. Each key is stored in a drawer of the manager's desk when not being used. Cash is transferred to the bank via daily collection by a security company. The security company provides a receipt for the sums collected, and these receipts are immediately forwarded to head office. The credit card company remits the amounts due directly into Camomile Co's bank account within two days of the transaction.

At head office, on receipt of the daily sales sheets and security company receipts, the cashier agrees the cash transferred by the security company has been banked for all venues. She agrees the cash per the daily sales sheets to bank deposit slips and to the bank statements. The cashier updates the cash book with the cash banked and details of the credit card vouchers from the daily sales sheets. On a monthly basis, the credit card company sends a statement of all credit card receipts from the six venues which is filed by the cashier.

Every two months, the cashier reconciles the bank statements to the cash book. The reconciliations are reviewed by the financial controller who evidences her review by signature and these are filed in the accounts department. All purchases of food and beverages for the venues are paid by bank transfer. At the relevant payment dates, the finance director is given the total amount of the payments list which he authorises.

### Required

Identify and explain **EIGHT DEFICIENCIES** in Camomile Co's cash receipts and payments system and provide a recommendation to address each of these deficiencies.

| Control deficiency | Control recommendation |
|---|---|
|  |  |

(16 marks)

(Total = 20 marks)

AUDIT EVIDENCE

Questions 119–163 cover Audit evidence, the subject of Part D of the BPP Workbook for Audit and Assurance.

## Expert (Dec 08) (amended)                                    18 mins

The following scenario relates to questions 119–123.

You are the audit manager in the firm of WSD & Co, an audit firm. You are planning the audit of Truse Co, which operates as a high street retailer and has 15 shops.

All of the shops are owned by Truse Co and have always been included in the financial statements at cost less depreciation. The shops are depreciated over 50 years. However, you know from discussions with management that the company intends to include one of the shops, the flagship store, at a revalued amount rather than cost in the current accounting period. The revalued amount is expected to be materially above the carrying value of the shop. The valuation will be based on a management estimate.

Management has explained that the reason for the revaluation is because the flagship store is located in an area where property prices have risen much more quickly compared to other shop locations. They consider the flagship store to be significantly undervalued on the statement of financial position.

Management will not depreciate the revalued amount allocated to the flagship store's building because they maintain the building to a high standard.

119    In his notes for the audit planning meeting, the audit junior made several statements in relation to the valuation of the shops.

Which **TWO** of the below statements are correct?

☐    Truse Co is allowed under IAS 16 Property, Plant and Equipment to revalue the flagship shop while continuing to measure its three other shops at cost less depreciation.

☐    The revaluation constitutes a change in accounting policy, so we will need to consider the adequacy of the disclosures made in respect of this.

☐    The flagship store should be depreciated on its revalued amount.

☐    We must confirm that all repairs and maintenance costs have been capitalised.

120    Indicate whether the following assertions are relevant to the audit of tangible non-current assets.

| Assertion | Yes | No |
|---|---|---|
| Existence | ☐ | ☐ |
| Occurrence | ☐ | ☐ |
| Classification | ☐ | ☐ |
| Presentation | ☐ | ☐ |

121 Which of the following procedures will provide appropriate audit evidence in respect of the completeness of non-current assets?

- ○ For a sample of assets selected by physical inspection, agree that they are listed on the non-current assets register
- ○ For a sample of non-current assets listed on the non-current assets register, physically inspect the asset
- ○ For a sample of assets on the assets register, recalculate the carrying amount in accordance with the entity's accounting policies
- ○ For a sample of assets on the assets register, inspect relevant purchase invoices or deeds

122 At the planning meeting, it was decided that an auditor's expert should be sought in relation to the valuation of Truse Co's properties as the company has not used an independent valuer.

ISA 620 *Using the Work of an Auditor's Expert* states that the nature, timing and extent of audit procedures to evaluate the work of the auditor's expert depend on the circumstances of the engagement.

Which of the following matters should the audit team **NOT** consider in determining the nature, timing and extent of these audit procedures?

- ○ The risk of material misstatement associated with Truse Co's properties
- ○ WSD & Co's experience with previous work performed by the expert
- ○ Whether the expert is subject to WSD & Co's quality management policies and procedures
- ○ The existence of any interests in or relationships with Truse Co that might pose a threat to the expert's objectivity

123 The audit junior has been assigned to the audit of the bank and cash balances of Truse Co. He has noted down the audit evidence he plans to obtain in respect of the bank and cash balances:

(1) Bank reconciliation carried out by the cashier
(2) Bank confirmation report from Truse Co's bank
(3) Verbal confirmation from the directors that the overdraft limit is to be increased
(4) Cash count carried out by the audit junior himself

Indicate, by using the table below, the order of reliability of the audit evidence, starting with the most reliable first.

| Audit evidence | Order |
|---|---|
| (1) Bank reconciliation carried out by the cashier | (1) |
| (2) Bank confirmation report from Truse Co's bank | (2) |
| (3) Verbal confirmation from the directors that the overdraft limit is to be increased | (3) |
| (4) Cash count carried out by the audit junior himself | (4) |

(Total = 10 marks)

# Newthorpe

**18 mins**

The following scenario relates to questions 124–128.

You are an audit manager, auditing the financial statements of Newthorpe Engineering Co, a listed company, for the year ended 30 April 20X7.

Newthorpe's management has provided you with a schedule of the realisable values of the inventories. A full inventory count was carried out at 30 April 20X7.

Audit tests have confirmed that the inventory counts are accurate and there are no purchases or sales cut-off errors.

One of the company's factories was closed on 30 April 20X7. The plant and equipment and inventories were to be sold. By the time the audit work commenced in June 20X7, most of the inventory had been sold.

You have instructed the audit junior to evaluate the valuation of the inventory related to the closing factory at the year end. The audit junior has sent you a list of planned audit procedures.

On 17 March 20X7, Newthorpe's managing director was dismissed for gross misconduct. It was decided that the managing director's salary should stop from that date, and that no redundancy or compensation payments should be made.

The managing director has claimed unfair dismissal and is taking legal action against the company to obtain compensation for loss of his employment. The managing director says he has a service contract with the company which would entitle him to two years' salary at the date of dismissal. The directors believe that there is a 35% chance of the managing director succeeding in his claim.

The financial statements for the year ended 30 April 20X7 record the resignation of the director. However, they do not mention his dismissal and no provision for any damages has been included in the financial statements.

124 Which **TWO** of the following statements are true regarding the auditor's attendance at the inventory count?

☐    It is the auditor's responsibility to organise the inventory count.

☐    The auditor observes client staff to determine whether inventory count procedures are being followed.

☐    The auditor reviews procedures for identifying damaged, obsolete and slow-moving inventory.

☐    If the results of the auditors' test counts are not satisfactory, the auditor should insist that the inventory is recounted.

125 Which of the audit procedures below is **NOT** appropriate in auditing the valuation assertion for Newthorpe's inventory?

○    Agree the selling prices of inventory sold since the year end to sales invoices and the cash book.

○    Assess the reasonableness of management's point estimates of realisable value of inventory that has not yet been sold by reviewing sales before the year end, comparing the values with inventory that has been sold since the year end and considering offers made which have not yet been finalised.

○    For a sample of inventory sold just before and just after the year end, match dates of sales invoices/date posted to ledgers with date on related goods dispatched notes.

○    For unsold inventory, assess reasonableness of provisions for selling expenses by comparison of selling expenses with inventory sold.

126 Using the drop down lists, complete the sentence below to show the correct accounting treatment for the legal claim made by the managing director for unfair dismissal and the reason for this treatment.

The legal claim should [                                ] because

[                          ].

Options for drop down list:

First list:

be recorded as a provision

not be recorded as a provision but disclosed as a contingent liability

Second list:

a present obligation exists, but the outflow of economic resources is not probable

a possible obligation exists, depending on whether or not some uncertain future event occurs

---

127 Which of the following audit procedures is likely to provide the auditor with the **MOST** reliable audit evidence regarding the legal claim?

○ Review the minutes of the disciplinary hearing to understand whether the company has acted in accordance with employment legislation and its internal rules

○ Review correspondence between the company and its lawyers regarding the likely outcome of the case

○ Request a written representation from management supporting their assertion that the claim will not be successful

○ Send an enquiry letter to Newthorpe's lawyers to obtain their view as to the probability of the claim being successful

---

128 The dismissal of Newthorpe's managing director has alerted you to the possibility that the company may not have complied with employment regulations. You therefore need to determine the impact that such non-compliance may have on the audit.

ISA 250 (Revised) *Consideration of Laws and Regulations in an Audit of Financial Statements* sets out the responsibilities of the auditor in relation to the entity's compliance with laws and regulations.

Which of the following responsibilities is **CORRECT** regarding the responsibilities of Newthorpe's auditors in relation to compliance with employment regulations?

○ To obtain sufficient appropriate evidence regarding compliance, as they have a direct effect on the financial statements

○ To perform specific audit procedures to identify possible non-compliance

○ The auditors do not have any responsibility, as the employment regulations do not have a direct effect on the financial statements

○ To prevent and detect all non-compliance with the regulations

---

(Total = 10 marks)

# Tirrol (Jun 09) (amended)                                      18 mins

The following scenario relates to questions 129–133.

Your audit firm Cal & Co has just gained a new audit client, Tirrol Co, in a tender in which Cal & Co offered competitively low audit fees. You are the manager in charge of planning the audit work. Tirrol Co's year end is 30 June 20X9 with a scheduled date to complete the audit of 15 August 20X9. The date now is 3 June 20X9.

Tirrol Co provides repair services to motor vehicles from 25 different locations. All inventory, sales and purchasing systems are computerised, with each location maintaining its own computer system. The software in each location is the same because the programs were written specifically for Tirrol Co by a reputable software house. Data from each location is amalgamated on a monthly basis at Tirrol Co's head office to produce management and financial statements.

You are currently planning your audit approach for Tirrol Co. One option being considered is to rewrite Cal & Co's audit software to interrogate the computerised inventory systems in each location of Tirrol Co (except for head office) as part of inventory valuation testing. The testing will need to take place while the system is live. You are aware that July is a major holiday period for Tirrol Co.

129    The audit junior is concerned about various circumstances of the audit, which are likely to increase audit risk. He has written to you with some suggestions.

Which **TWO** of the following suggestions are valid?

☐  We should budget for the extra time required to document an understanding of the entity, its environment and its systems, and to verify material opening balances.

☐  Given the tight reporting deadline, a combined approach should be adopted on the audit, relying on tests of controls wherever possible.

☐  We must agree a clear timetable with the client for the testing of the computerised inventory systems, setting out availability of access to the system, files and personnel required to complete testing.

☐  As this is our first year of audit, we should agree separate fees with the client for any additional audit procedures required. If the client refuses, we should consider withdrawing from the audit as Cal & Co would be deemed to be lowballing.

---

130    Which **TWO** of the following are benefits of using audit software in auditing the inventory of Tirrol Co?

☐  The ability to test all 25 of Tirrol Co's locations using the same audit software, resulting in time and cost savings

☐  The ability to test internal controls relating to the input of data, thus giving greater assurance over the existence of inventory

☐  The ability to select and extract a sample of inventory data for testing, thus reducing sampling risk

☐  The ability to calculate the error rate in sample and thus determine whether further audit procedures are required

---

131  It has been decided that systematic sampling would be applied to the audit of Tirrol Co's inventory.

Which of the following sampling methods correctly describes systematic sampling?

○　A sampling method which is a type of value-weighted selection in which sample size, selection and evaluation results in a conclusion in monetary amounts

○　A sampling method which involves having a constant sampling interval; the starting point for testing is determined randomly

○　A sampling method in which the auditor selects a block(s) of contiguous items from within the population

○　A sampling method in which the auditor selects a sample without following any particular structured technique

---

132  Tirrol Co's internal audit department is going to assist with the statutory audit. The chief internal auditor will provide you with documentation on the computerised inventory systems at Tirrol Co. The documentation provides details of the software and shows diagrammatically how transactions are processed through the inventory system. This documentation can be used to significantly decrease the time needed to understand the computer systems and enable audit software to be written for this year's audit.

Which of the following is **NOT** a matter the audit team should consider in determining whether or not the internal auditor's work is adequate for the purposes of the audit?

○　Whether the work was properly planned, performed, supervised, reviewed and documented

○　Whether there are any significant threats to the objectivity of the internal auditor

○　Whether sufficient appropriate evidence was obtained to allow the internal auditors to draw reasonable conclusions

○　Whether the conclusions reached are appropriate in the circumstances and the reports prepared are consistent with the results of the work done

---

133  The audit junior has obtained the following extract of the aged inventory report:

| Inventory code | Days in inventory | Original cost $ | Selling price $ | Costs to sell $ | Carrying amount $ |
|---|---|---|---|---|---|
| X070003 | 98 | 12,000 | 20,200 | 2,000 | 12,000 |
| X079001 | 127 | 14,500 | 16,000 | 2,500 | 14,500 |
| X084000 | 109 | 18,000 | 26,000 | 3,000 | 23,000 |

What is the impact on the value of inventory if no adjustments are made to the carrying amounts above?

○　Inventory should be $44,500, inventory is overstated.

○　Inventory should be $43,500, inventory is overstated.

○　Inventory should be $54,700, inventory is understated.

○　Inventory should be $62,200, inventory is understated.

---

(Total = 10 marks)

# Wright

**18 mins**

The following scenario relates to questions 134–138.

You are the audit manager in the firm of Wright & Co, a large accountancy firm with 30 offices.

It is January 20X6, and a new intake of graduates and apprentices has recently started work at the audit department after completing their first ACCA exams. Julie, one of the new recruits, has been allocated to the audit of Wilbur Co, your audit client, for the year ended 31 December 20X5. You are responsible for providing guidance to her and have asked her to assist in the audit of trade payables and cash at bank.

## Trade payables

Julie has performed a reconciliation of key trade payables balances as follows and has concluded that no further work is required:

| | Balance per purchase ledger $'000 | Cash in transit $'000 | Goods in transit $'000 | Balance per supplier statement $'000 |
|---|---|---|---|---|
| Supplier XX1 | 400 | – | 100 (1) | 500 |
| Supplier XX2 | 650 | 50 (2) | – | 700 |
| Supplier XX3 | 100 | – | – | 100 |
| | 1,150 | | | 1,300 |

*Notes*

1 Agreed to GRN dated 31 December 20X5

2 Agreed to cheque posted in the cash book 30 December 20X5

Your follow-up work on this identifies that:

- The goods in transit received from supplier XX1 were recognised in inventory at 31 December 20X5

- The cheque payment to supplier XX2 appeared on the bank statement on 2 January 20X6

- There is a nil balance on the purchase accruals account

## Cash at bank

In order to gain assurance over the company's bank balance, you asked Julie to arrange for a bank confirmation letter to be sent to Wilbur Co's bank.

Julie has also prepared a bank reconciliation. This shows a significant number of lodgements which were recorded in the cash book on 31 December 20X5. You are concerned that the cash book may have been kept open to include remittances actually received after the year end.

134 Julie has approached you with the following query:

'I know that as auditors, we have to collect audit evidence in order to support our audit opinion. But how can we tell how much audit evidence we need to get?'

Which of the below factors influence the auditor's judgement regarding the sufficiency of the evidence obtained?

(1) The materiality of the account

(2) The size of the account

(3) The source and quality of the evidence available

(4) The amount of time allocated to the audit

- ○ 1 and 3
- ○ 2 and 4
- ○ 2 and 3
- ○ 1 and 4

---

135 Which of the in-transit items included in the supplier statement reconciliations indicate that there is a cut-off problem?

(1) Cash in transit

(2) Goods in transit

○ 1 only

○ 2 only

○ 1 and 2

○ Neither 1 nor 2

---

136 What further evidence, if any, is required in relation to the balance due to XX3 to determine if trade payables is understated?

○ A review of post year end purchase orders from supplier XX3

○ A confirmation request must be sent to supplier XX3

○ No further evidence is required

○ A review of credit notes issued by Wilbur Co should be performed

---

137 Which of the following summarises the steps Julie should take in preparing the bank confirmation letter you have requested?

○ Written on the audit firm's headed paper; information requested to be sent directly to the auditor

○ Written on the client's headed paper; information requested to be sent directly to the auditor

○ Written on the audit firm's headed paper; information requested to be sent directly to the client

○ Written on the client's headed paper; information requested to be sent directly to the client

---

138 Which of the following pieces of audit evidence would provide the most reliable audit evidence that the lodgements recorded on 31 December 20X5 do not relate to amounts received after the period end?

○ Bank statement showing the lodgements cleared by the bank

○ The date on the cheque paid by the supplier

○ The date on the remittance advice

○ The bank's date stamp on the paying-in slip

---

(Total = 10 marks)

# Lodestar

**18 mins**

The following scenario relates to questions 139–143.

You are an audit senior of Beacon & Co and are currently conducting the audit of Lodestar Co (Lodestar) for the year ended 30 September 20X1. You are reviewing the work of your audit assistant.

## Trade receivables

Your audit assistant has carried out a direct confirmation (a receivables circularisation) on trade receivables at Lodestar. She selected the 10 largest balances, representing 85% of the sales ledger at year end, including 2 items that were individually material. Seven customers agreed the sales ledger balance, two replied noting discrepancies which she has followed up and one has not replied.

The audit working papers contain the following work in respect of the two balances with discrepancies.

| Customer | Balance per sales ledger $ | Balance per customer confirmation $ | Comments |
|---|---|---|---|
| Polaris Co | 23,400 | 19,250 | Balance is payment sent out on 30 September, agreed to cash book 2 October. |
| Sirius Co | 45,000 | 39,000 | Balancing item is credit requested for goods customer claims were defective in February. Production manager confirms no credit will be issued. |

## Allowance for doubtful accounts

The company has an accounting policy of creating an allowance for doubtful accounts at 2% of year-end sales ledger balance.

139 You are analysing the sample selection with regard to the direct confirmation.

Which of the following statements in relation to the sample selection is **TRUE**?

- ○ The sample is appropriate and, at 85% of the balance, gives good assurance about the overall balance.

- ○ As 15% of the ledger balance has not been sampled, the sample is inappropriate.

- ○ The sample selection does not address the risk of understatement as it has focused on the ten largest balances.

- ○ The sample should have been stratified to provide a representative sample.

140 The audit assistant has identified further procedures to be carried out in respect of the customer who has not responded to the circularisation request as follows.

(1) Send out a follow-up request.

(2) Inspect the sales invoices in the customer account at year end.

(3) Ask the credit controller whether the customer exists.

(4) Reconcile cash receipts after date with pre year end invoices in the customer account.

Which of these procedures would provide audit evidence of the **EXISTENCE** of this receivable?

○ 1, 2 and 3

○ 1, 2 and 4

○ 3 and 4

○ 1 and 2

---

141 You are reviewing the work carried out on the disputed balances.

What is the misstatement arising from the above issues and the resultant impact on current assets?

○ Trade receivables should be $10,150 lower, current assets are overstated.

○ Trade receivables should be $6,000 lower, current assets are overstated.

○ Trade receivables should be $4,150 lower, no net effect on current assets as balance is in cash.

○ Trade receivables should be $10,150 higher, current assets are understated.

---

142 Your audit assistant has heard that auditing accounting estimates can be problematic and has asked you to explain why this is the case.

Which of the following statements concerning auditing accounting estimates is **INCORRECT**?

○ It can be difficult to obtain evidence concerning accounting estimates as management use judgement in their estimation.

○ Accounting estimates are high risk as they can be subject to management bias.

○ Auditors can formulate a point estimate to compare to management's estimate.

○ Auditors should use their own estimate in the financial statements, as auditor-generated evidence is more conclusive than management-generated evidence.

---

143 The audit junior has suggested the following tests could be carried out to test the allowance for doubtful accounts:

(1) Review cash receipts after year end
(2) Review an aged debt analysis of the sales ledger
(3) Ask the credit controller what debts are considered to be doubtful
(4) Review sales invoices relating to overdue accounts

Which of the following correctly ranks these tests in terms of their appropriateness to the **VALUATION** assertion (most appropriate being listed first)?

○ 1, 2, 3, 4

○ 2, 4, 3, 1

○ 1, 2, 4, 3

○ 3, 2, 1, 4

---

**(Total = 10 marks)**

# Porthos

The following scenario relates to questions 144–148.

Porthos, a limited liability company, is a retailer of sports equipment, specialising in racquet sports such as tennis, squash and badminton. The company purchases equipment from a variety of different suppliers and then resells this online. Customers place their orders directly on the company website. The ordering/sales software automatically verifies the order details, customer address and credit card information prior to orders being verified and goods dispatched.

Once the order has been verified the system produces a pre-numbered picking note. The order is then picked in the warehouse and a goods dispatched note (GDN) is produced. A copy of this is scanned in to the system and a sequentially numbered invoice is automatically produced and sent to the customer.

You are the audit senior working on the audit of Porthos for the year ended 31 December 20X7.

As the sales system is highly automated the audit manager has decided that computer-assisted audit techniques (CAATs) should be used where possible in the audit of the sales account. You identified the key steps to be taken in planning the application of CAATs, as follows:

(1)     Define the types of transactions to be tested

(2)     Set the objective of the CAAT application

(3)     Define the procedures to be performed on the data

(4)     Determine the content and accessibility of the entity's files

The manager has also decided that test data would be used to test the input of details into the ordering system. You identified the following test data which could be used:

(i)     Orders for unusually large quantities
(ii)    Orders with fields left blank
(iii)   Orders with invalid inventory codes
(iv)    Orders with complete and valid details

In addition to the sales income generated from the sale of sports equipment Porthos earns a small amount of rental income by renting out surplus warehouse space to a local company. The rental agreement shows that the annual rent from 1 March 20X7 was $24,000, increased from $21,600 per annum.

144    Which of the following identifies the correct order in which the steps to be taken in planning the application of CAATs should be performed?

    O     2, 4, 1, 3

    O     1, 4, 2, 3

    O     2, 1, 3, 4

    O     4, 2, 3, 1

145    Which of the test data identified by the audit junior should be used to confirm the completeness and accuracy of input into the sales system?

    O     (ii) only

    O     (ii) and (iii) only

    O     (i), (ii) and (iii) only

    O     (i), (ii), (iii) and (iv)

146  Which of the following procedures would provide evidence that sales cut-off for Porthos has been applied correctly?

- O    For sales invoices issued before 31 December 20X7 use audit software to determine whether there is a matching GDN dated before 31 December 20X7

- O    For sales invoices issued before 31 December 20X7 use audit software to determine whether there is a matching GDN dated after 31 December 20X7

- O    For picking notes issued before 31 December 20X7 use audit software to determine whether there is a matching GDN dated before 31 December 20X7

- O    For picking notes issued before 31 December 20X7 use audit software to determine whether there is a matching GDN dated after 31 December 20X7

147  As part of substantive audit procedures, you perform a sequence check on the sales invoice numbers issued by Porthos over the year.

What is the purpose of the sequence check you have performed on the sales invoice numbers?

- O    To give assurance that cut-off has been applied accurately

- O    To give assurance over the occurrence of the sales transactions recorded

- O    To provide audit evidence over the completeness of the recording of sales

- O    To provide audit evidence that the sales figure has been calculated accurately

148  You are using a proof in total calculation to assess the accuracy of the rental income.

Which of the following correctly shows the calculation which would be used?

- O    $24,000 × 12/12

- O    $21,600 × 12/12

- O    (21,600 × 2/12) + (24,000 × 10/12)

- O    (21,600 × 10/12) + (24,000 × 2/12)

(Total = 10 marks)

# Lancaster Co (Mar/Jun 21)                     18 mins

The following scenario relates to questions 149–153.

It is 1 July 20X5. You are an audit supervisor at York & Co and you are involved in the audit of Lancaster Co for the year ended 31 May 20X5. The company owns a significant amount of non-current assets including a number of properties.

### Additions, disposal and depreciation

Lancaster Co depreciates its properties, on the straight-line basis, at a rate of 5% per annum. The draft depreciation charge on buildings for 20X5 is $2m compared with $1.7m in 20X4.

On 31 May 20X5, Property A was sold for sales proceeds equal to 40% of its original cost. The property initially cost $6m and had been owned and depreciated for seven years.

The audit programme includes the following tests to be carried out in relation to additions made during the year:

1    Agree a sample of additions recorded in the non-current asset register to the cash book and purchase invoice ensuring that the purchase date is accurate and it is recorded at the correct amount

2    Compare total budgeted additions to actual additions in the year and investigate and corroborate any significant differences

BPP
LEARNING
MEDIA

**Revaluation**

On 31 May 20X5, the directors had all of the company's remaining buildings revalued by an external expert. In the detailed audit approach it states that York & Co will rely on this valuation as part of the current year audit procedures.

149 Which **TWO** of the following audit procedures would test for **OVERSTATEMENT** of Lancaster Co's non-current assets?

☐ Agree disposals recorded in the non-current asset register to cash book and sales invoice

☐ Physically inspect a sample of assets selected from the non-current asset register

☐ Inspect a sample of assets found at a location and agree to the non-current asset register

☐ Inspect the condition of assets held to determine the need for any impairment

150 Which of the following assertions are tested by the procedures included in the audit programme for additions?

(1) Completeness

(2) Classification

(3) Existence

(4) Accuracy, valuation and allocation

O 1 and 3 only

O 2 and 4 only

O 1, 3 and 4 only

O 1, 2, 3 and 4

151 You are now considering substantive audit procedures for depreciation across all categories of non-current assets held by Lancaster Co.

Which **TWO** of the following are substantive audit procedures for testing depreciation?

☐ Review the non-current asset register to ensure that all assets are assigned a useful life

☐ Perform a proof in total for the depreciation charge of $2m included in the financial statements and investigate any significant differences

☐ Review the board minutes for evidence of approval of useful lives

☐ Discuss with management the reasons for the $300,000 difference in the current year depreciation compared to the prior year

152 Recalculate the expected loss on disposal of Property A, giving your answer to ONE decimal place.

$ [        ] m

153 In respect of the revaluation, which **TWO** of the following statements regarding reliance on the external expert are **TRUE**?

☐ In line with ISA 620 *Using the Work of an Auditor's Expert*, reliance can only be placed on an expert appointed by York & Co

☐ Obtaining the valuation report would constitute sufficient and appropriate evidence over the carrying amount of the buildings

☐ Reference to the work of the external expert should not be included in the auditor's report

☐ The objectivity of the valuer must be assessed before placing reliance on the valuation report

# 154 Lily (Dec 12)                                      54 mins

It is 1 July 20X5. Lily Window Glass Co (Lily) is a glass manufacturer, which operates from a large production facility, where it undertakes continuous production 24 hours a day, 7 days a week. Also on this site are two warehouses, where the company's raw materials and finished goods are stored. Lily's year end is 31 July.

Lily is finalising the arrangements for the year-end inventory count, which is to be undertaken on 31 July 20X5. The finished windows are stored within 20 aisles of the first warehouse. The second warehouse is for large piles of raw materials, such as sand, used in the manufacture of glass. The following arrangements have been made for the inventory count.

The warehouse manager will supervise the count as he is most familiar with the inventory. There will be ten teams of counters and each team will contain two members of staff, one from the finance and one from the manufacturing department. None of the warehouse staff, other than the manager, will be involved in the count.

Each team will count an aisle of finished goods by counting up and then down each aisle. As this process is systematic, it is not felt that the team will need to flag areas once counted. Once the team has finished counting an aisle, they will hand in their sheets and be given a set for another aisle of the warehouse. In addition to the above, to assist with the inventory counting, there will be two teams of counters from the internal audit department and they will perform inventory counts.

The count sheets are sequentially numbered, and the product codes and descriptions are printed on them but no quantities. If the counters identify any inventory which is not on their sheets, then they are to enter the item on a separate sheet, which is not numbered. Once all counting is complete, the sequence of the sheets is checked and any additional sheets are also handed in at this stage. All sheets are completed in ink.

Any damaged goods identified by the counters will be too heavy to move to a central location, hence they are to be left where they are but the counter is to make a note on the inventory sheets detailing the level of damage.

As Lily undertakes continuous production, there will continue to be movements of raw materials and finished goods in and out of the warehouse during the count. These will be kept to a minimum where possible.

The level of work in progress in the manufacturing plant is to be assessed by the warehouse manager. It is likely that this will be an immaterial balance. In addition, the raw materials quantities are to be approximated by measuring the height and width of the raw material piles. In the past this task has been undertaken by a specialist; however, the warehouse manager feels confident that he can perform this task.

**Required**

(a) For the inventory count arrangements of Lily Window Glass Co:

(i) Identify and explain **SIX** deficiencies; and

(ii) Provide a recommendation to address each deficiency.

The total marks will be split equally between each part.                    **(12 marks)**

You are the audit senior of Daffodil & Co and are responsible for the audit of inventory for Lily. You will be attending the year-end inventory count on 31 July 20X5.

In addition, your manager wishes to utilise computer-assisted audit techniques for the first time for controls and substantive testing in auditing Lily Window Glass Co's inventory.

**Required**

(b)     Describe the procedures to be undertaken by the auditor **DURING** the inventory count of Lily Window Glass Co in order to gain sufficient appropriate audit evidence.     **(6 marks)**

(c)     For the audit of the inventory cycle and year-end inventory balance of Lily Window Glass Co:

(i)     Describe **FOUR** audit procedures that could be carried out using automated tools and techniques

(ii)     Explain the potential advantages of using automated tools and techniques; and

(iii)     Explain the potential disadvantages of using automated tools and techniques.

The total marks will be split equally between each part.     **(12 marks)**

**(Total = 30 marks)**

# 155 Westra Co                                                        54 mins

Westra Co assembles mobile telephones in a large factory. Each telephone contains up to 100 different parts, with each part being obtained from 1 of 50 authorised suppliers.

Like many companies, Westra Co's accounting systems are partly manual and partly computerised. In overview, the systems include:

(i)     Design software

(ii)     A computerised database of suppliers (bespoke system written in-house at Westra Co)

(iii)     A manual system for recording goods inwards and transferring information to the accounts department

(iv)     A computerised payables ledger maintained in the accounts department (purchased off-the-shelf and used with no program amendments)

(v)     Online payment to suppliers, also in the accounts department

(vi)     A computerised nominal ledger which is updated by the payables ledger

Mobile telephones are assembled in batches of 10,000 to 50,000 telephones. When a batch is scheduled for production, a list of parts is produced by the design software and sent, electronically, to the ordering department. Staff in the ordering department use this list to place orders with authorised suppliers. Orders can only be sent to suppliers on the suppliers' database. Orders are sent using electronic data interchange and confirmed by each supplier using the same system. The list of parts and orders is retained on the computer in an 'orders placed' file, which is kept in date sequence.

Parts are delivered to the goods inwards department at Westra Co. All deliveries are checked against the orders placed file before being accepted. A handwritten pre-numbered goods received note (GRN) is raised in the goods inwards department showing details of the goods received with a cross-reference to the date of the order. The top copy of the GRN is sent to the accounts department and the second copy retained in the goods inwards department. The orders placed file is updated with the GRN number to show that the parts have been received.

Paper invoices are sent by all suppliers following dispatch of goods. Invoices are sent to the accounts department, where they are stamped with a unique ascending number. Invoice details are matched to the GRN, which is then attached to the invoice. Invoice details are then entered into the computerised payables ledger. The invoice is signed by the accounts clerk to confirm entry into the payables ledger. Invoices are then retained in a temporary file in number order while awaiting payment.

After 30 days, the payables ledger automatically generates a computerised list of payments to be made, which is sent electronically to the chief accountant. The chief accountant compares this list to the invoices, signs each invoice to indicate approval for payment, and then forwards the electronic payments list to the accounts assistant. The assistant uses online banking to pay the suppliers. The electronic payments list is filed in month order on the computer.

### Required

(a) Describe the substantive audit procedures you should perform to confirm the assertions of completeness, occurrence and cut-off for purchases in the financial statements of Westra Co. For each procedure, explain the purpose of that procedure. **(12 marks)**

(b) Describe the audit procedures you should perform on the trade payables balance in Westra Co's financial statements. For each procedure, explain the purpose of that procedure. **(8 marks)**

(c) Describe the internal controls that should be in place over the standing data on the trade payables master file in Westra Co's computer system. **(5 marks)**

(d) Discuss the extent to which audit data analytics techniques might be used in your audit of purchases and payables at Westra Co. **(5 marks)**

**(Total = 30 marks)**

## 156 Purrfect Co (Mar/Jun 21)                    36 mins

**This scenario relates to four requirements.**

It is 1 July 20X5. Purrfect co manufactures and sells a variety of food for dogs and cats. Your firm, Kirano & Co, has audited the company for a number of years. You are about to commence the final audit for the year ended 31March 20X5 and the draft financial statements show profit before tax of $23.1 m and total assets of $99.2m.

### Vego Dog – inventory valuation

Purrfect Co launched a new brand of vegan dog food, Vego Dog, in December 20X4 but sales have been lower than expected and the doirectors are considering a discounted sales price. Vego Dog products are valued using a standard costing method and the standard costing comprises raw materials, labour costs and production overheads. As at 31March 20X5, Vego Dog products with a standard cost of $2.4m were included as finished goods in inventory.

### Receivable – Ellah Co

One of the Purrfect Co's major customers, Ellah Co, operates a chain of pet stores with 23 stores across the country. There have been reports in the press for several months that Ellah Co's sales and profits have been falling and, in March 20X5, Ellah Co announced that 11 of its stores were to close in May 20X5. As at 31 March 20X5, Purrfect Co's trade receivables include $2.6m outstanding from Ellah Co and no allowance has been included for this balance at the year end.

### Contamination – legal claims

On 25 February 20X5, it was discovered that a batch of canned cat food had been contaminated with insecticide, which could be harmful to cats. This batch had been dispatched in November 20X4 to 247 retail stores. By 31 March 20X5, Purrfect Co had received legal claims totalling $1.9m from consumers whose cats had eaten the contaminated food.

(a) Describe substantive procedures the auditor should perform to obtain sufficient and appropriate audit evidence in relation to the matters identified regarding the inventory valuation of Vego Dog products. **(6 marks)**

(b) Describe substantive procedures the auditor should perform to obtain sufficient and appropriate audit evidence in relation to the receivable balance due from Ellah Co. **(4 marks)**

(c) Describe substantive procedures the auditor should perform to obtain sufficient and appropriate audit evidence in relation to the legal claims following the contamination. **(5 marks)**

The final audit is now nearing completion. The audit team is satisfied that legal claims received to date have been appropriately reflected in the financial statements.

However, Purrfect Co's lawyer has advised you that it is possible that significant additional legal claims may be made by customers in future in respect of the contamination. The audit engagement partner has confirmed that this is a contingent liability that requires disclosure. The finance director has agreed to disclose some detail of the potential claims in the financial statements but the audit team is yet to confirm the adequacy of these disclosures.

(d)    Discuss the issues and describe the impact on the auditor's report of Purrfect Co of both adequate AND inadequate disclosure of the contingent liability.    **(5 marks)**

**(Total = 20 marks)**

## 157 Rose (Dec 12) (amended)                    36 mins

Rose Co operates a chain of health and fitness clubs. Its year end was 31 March 20X6. You are the audit manager and the year-end audit is due to commence shortly. The following three matters have been brought to your attention.

### Trade payables and accruals

Rose Co's finance director has notified you that an error occurred in the closing of the purchase ledger at the year end. Rather than it closing on 1 April, it accidentally closed one week earlier on 25 March. All purchase invoices received between 25 March and the year-end have been posted to the 20X7 year-end purchase ledger.

### Receivables

Rose Co's trade receivables have historically been low as most members pay monthly in advance. However, during the year a number of companies have taken up group memberships at Rose and hence the receivables balance is now material. The audit senior has undertaken a receivables circularisation for the balances at the year-end; however, there are a number who have not responded and a number of responses with differences.

### Reorganisation

The company recently announced its plans to reorganise its health and fitness clubs. This will involve closing some clubs for refurbishment, retraining some existing staff and disposing of some surplus assets. These plans were agreed at a board meeting in March and announced to their shareholders on 29 March. Rose is proposing to make a reorganisation provision in the financial statements.

### Required

(a)    Describe substantive procedures the auditor should perform to obtain sufficient and appropriate audit evidence in relation to the issues identified with the trade payables and accruals balance.    **(6 marks)**

(b)    Describe substantive procedures the auditor should perform to obtain sufficient appropriate evidence in relation to the year-end receivables balance.    **(5 marks)**

(c)    Describe substantive procedures the auditor should perform to obtain sufficient appropriate evidence in relation to the proposed reorganisation.    **(4 marks)**

(d)    Explain the purpose of, and procedures for, obtaining written representations.    **(5 marks)**

**(Total = 20 marks)**

# 158 Hyacinth (Mar/Jun 19)

Hyacinth Co develops and manufactures computer components and its year end was 31 March 20X5. It is 1 July 20X5. The company has a large factory, and two warehouses, one of which is off-site. You are an audit supervisor of Tulip & Co and the final audit is due to commence shortly. Draft financial statements show total assets of $23·2m and profit before tax of $6·4m. The following three matters have been brought to your attention:

## Inventory valuation

Your firm attended the year-end inventory count for Hyacinth Co and confirmed that the controls and processes for recording work in progress (WIP) and finished goods were acceptable. WIP and finished goods are both material to the financial statements and the audit team was able to confirm both the quantity and stage of completion of WIP.

Before goods are dispatched, they are inspected by the company's quality control department. Just prior to the inventory count, it was noted that a batch of product line 'Crocus', which had been produced to meet a customer's specific technical requirements, did not meet that customer's quality and technical standards. This inventory had a production cost of $450,000. Upon discussions with the production supervisor, the finance director believes that the inventory can still be sold to alternative customers at a discounted price of $90,000.

## Research and development

Hyacinth Co includes expenditure incurred in developing new products within intangible assets once the recognition criteria under IAS 38 *Intangible Assets* have been met. Intangible assets are amortised on a straight line basis over four years once production commences. The amortisation policy is based on past experience of the likely useful lives of the products. The opening balance of intangible assets is $1·9m.

In the current year, Hyacinth Co spent $0·8m developing three new products which are all at different stages of development.

## Sales tax liability

Hyacinth Co is required by the relevant tax authority in the country in which it operates to charge sales tax at 15% on all products which it sells. This sales tax is payable to the tax authority. When purchasing raw materials and incurring expenses in the manufacturing process, the company pays 15% sales tax on any items purchased and this can be reclaimed from the tax authority. The company is required to report the taxes charged and incurred by completing a tax return on a quarterly basis, and the net amount owing to the tax authority must be remitted within four weeks of the quarter end. The draft financial statements contain a $1·1m liability for sales tax for the quarter ended 31 March 20X5.

## Required

(a)   Describe substantive procedures the auditor should perform to obtain sufficient and appropriate audit evidence in relation to the VALUATION of Hyacinth Co's inventory.

**(6 marks)**

(b)   Describe substantive procedures the auditor should perform to obtain sufficient and appropriate audit evidence in relation to Hyacinth Co's research and development expenditure. **(4 marks)**

(c)   Describe substantive procedures the auditor should perform to obtain sufficient and appropriate audit evidence in relation to Hyacinth Co's year-end sales tax liability.

**(4 marks)**

The audit is now almost complete and the auditor's report is due to be signed shortly. The following matter has been brought to your attention:

On 3 May 20X5, a flood occurred at the off-site warehouse. This resulted in some damage to inventory and property, plant and equipment. However, there have been no significant delays to customer deliveries or complaints from customers. Hyacinth Co's management has investigated the cause of the flooding and believes that the company is unlikely to be able to claim on its insurance. The finance director of Hyacinth Co has estimated that the value of damaged inventory and property, plant and equipment was $0·7m and that it now has no scrap value.

**Required**

(d) (i) Explain whether the 20X5 financial statements of Hyacinth Co require amendment in relation to the flood; and

   (ii) Describe audit procedures which should be performed in order to form a conclusion on any required amendment.

   Note. The total marks will be split equally between each part. **(6 marks)**

   **(Total = 20 marks)**

# 159 Sagittarii & Co (Sep/Dec 20)     36 mins

**This scenario relates to four requirements.**

It is 1 July 20X5. You are an audit manager of Sagittarii & Co and you are in charge of two final audits which are due to commence shortly. Vega Vista Co and Canopus Co are both existing clients with a financial year ended 30 March 20X5. Vega Vista Co is a not-for-profit charitable organisation which raises funds for disadvantaged families and the draft financial statements shoe revenue of $0.8m. Canopus Co manufactures paint products in seven factories across the country and the draft financial statements show total equity and liabilities of $11.6m.

The following matters have been brought to your attention for each company:

## Vega Vista Co

### Income

Vega Vista Co generates income in a number of ways. The main source of income is via an annual food and music festival held in September every year. Tickets, which cost $35, are sold in the nine-month period prior to the event and can be purchased in advance online or on the day of the event for cash. Approximately 15,000 people attended the September 20X4 event and more are anticipated for 20X5. At the event there are a number of stalls selling food and the charity receives a fixed percentage of these sundry sales. Also, during the festival, volunteers of the charity sign up individuals to make monthly donations, and these are paid by bank transfer to the charity. During the audit planning, the completeness and cut-off of income was flagged as a key audit risk.

## Canopus Co

### Restructuring provision

Canopus Co recently announced plans to fundamentally restructure its production processes due to a change in the focus of the company's operations. It has included a £2.1m restructuring provision in the draft financial statements. The restructure involves a refurbishment of the factories, the purchase of new plant and equipment and retraining of existing staff. These plans were finally agreed at a board meeting in March 20X5 and announced to shareholders and employees just before the year end.

### Bank loans

In readiness for the operational changes, the directors of Canopus Co decided to restructure the company's bank loans. As a result, several long-term loans were repaid early and a new ten-year bank loan of $4.8m was taken out of 1 January 20X5. Repayments of $150,000 are due quarterly in arrears which includes interest.

**Required**

(a) Describe substantive procedures the auditor should perform to obtain sufficient and appropriate audit evidence in relation to Vega Vista Co's income.

   Note. You should assume that the charity adopts International Financial Reporting Standards.

   **(5 marks)**

(b) Describe substantive procedures the auditor should perform to obtain sufficient and appropriate audit evidence in relation to Canopus Co's restructuring provision. **(5 marks)**

(c) Describe substantive procedures the auditor should perform to obtain sufficient and appropriate audit evidence in relation to Canopus Co's bank loans. **(5 marks)**

During the audit of Canopus Co's restructuring provision, the audit team discovered that $270,000 of costs included did not meet the criteria for inclusion as per IAS 37 *Provisions, Contingent Liabilities and Contingent Assets*. The finance director has suggested that no adjustment is made in the 20X5 financial statements as the provision is a matter of judgment and the provision has been deemed reasonable by the board.

(d) Discuss the issue and describe the impact on the auditor's report, if any, should the issue remain unresolved. **(5 marks)**

**(Total = 20 marks)**

# 160 Encore (Mar/Jul 20)          36 mins

This scenario relates to four requirements.

It is 1 July 20X5. You are an audit supervisor with Velo & Co and you are working on the final audit of Encore Co for the year ended 30 April 20X5. Encore Co is a waste management company, supplying its services to a variety of governmental and business organisations. Encore Co's draft profit before tax is $5.3m (20X4: $4.6m) and total assets are $40.1m (20X4: $33.9m). You have been provided with the following information regarding the draft financial statements.

### Vehicle additions and disposals

On 1 February 20X5, Encore Co replaced 20 of its recycling vehicles. The old vehicles had a carrying amount of $1.8m, as recorded in the non-current assets register and were given in part-exchange against new vehicles costing $4.6m. Cash consideration of $3.9m was also paid.

### Trade receivables

Encore Co's credit controller left the company in January 20X5 and has only recently been replaced. The trade receivables collection period increased from 49 days as at 31 December 20X4 to 66 days as at 30 April 20X5. Year-end trade receivables amounted to $9.1m (20X4: $7.1m) and an allowance for irrecoverable receivables of $182,000 (20X4: $142,000) has been made.

### Potential breach of transport regulations

In March 20X5, a former employee of Encore Co made a complaint to the transport authority, alleging that Encore Co has breached the regulations concerning maximum driving hours and compulsory rest breaks for drivers on a number of occasions. The transport authority has launched an investigation but the directors of Encore Co are not intending to disclose this issue or make any provision as they do not believe that the potential fine, which is $50,000 per breach, is material.

### Required

(a) Describe substantive procedures the auditor should perform to obtain sufficient and appropriate audit evidence in relation to Encore Co's vehicle additions and disposals.

**(6 marks)**

(b) Describe substantive procedures the auditor should perform to obtain sufficient and appropriate audit evidence in relation to the VALUATION of Encore Co's trade receivables.

**(5 marks)**

(c) Describe substantive procedures the auditor should perform to obtain sufficient and appropriate audit evidence in relation to the potential breach of transport regulations by Encore Co. **(4 marks)**

It is now 26 August 20X5 and the auditor's report for Encore Co is being finalised. On 12 August 20X5, the transport authority announced that it was taking legal action against Encore Co in respect of 17 breaches of the regulations. Encore Co's lawyers have advised that it is probable that Encore Co will be found guilty of all the breaches. Encore Co's directors have informed you that no provision will be made in respect of this matter, as the decision by the authority to take legal action was made after the year end, but they have agreed to disclose the issue in the notes to the financial statement.

(d)     Discuss the issue and describe the impact on the auditor's report, if any, should this issue remain unresolved. **(5 marks)**

**(Total = 20 marks)**

# 161 Airsoft Co (Mar/Jun 17) 36 mins

It is 1 July 20X5. Airsoft Co is a listed company which manufactures stationery products. The company's profit before tax for the year ended 31 May 20X5 is $16.3m and total assets as at that date are $66.8m. You are an audit supervisor of Biathlon & Co and you are currently finalising the audit programmes for the year-end audit of your existing client Airsoft Co. You attended a meeting with your audit manager where the following matters were discussed:

## Trade payables and accruals

Airsoft Co purchases its raw materials from a large number of suppliers. The company's policy is to close the purchase ledger just after the year end and the financial controller is responsible for identifying goods which were received pre year-end but for which no invoice has yet been received. An accrual is calculated for goods received but not yet invoiced (GRNI) and is included within trade payables and accruals.

The audit strategy has identified a risk over the completeness of trade payables and accruals. The audit team will utilise computer assisted audit techniques (CAATs), in the form of audit software while auditing trade payables and accruals.

## Bank overdraft and savings accounts

Airsoft Co's draft financial statements include a bank overdraft of $2.6m, which relates to the company's main current account. In addition Airsoft Co maintains a number of savings accounts. The savings account balances are classified as cash and cash equivalents and are included in current assets. All accounts have been reconciled at the year end.

## Directors' remuneration

Airsoft Co's board is comprised of eight directors. Their overall remuneration consists of two elements: an annual salary, paid monthly; and a significant annual discretionary bonus, which is paid in a separate payment run on 20 May. All remuneration paid to directors is included within wages and salaries. Local legislation requires disclosure of the overall total of directors' remuneration broken down by element and by director.

## Required

(a)     Describe substantive procedures the auditor should perform to obtain sufficient and appropriate audit evidence in relation to the **COMPLETENESS** of Airsoft Co's trade payables and accruals. **(4 marks)**

Excluding procedures included in part (a):

(b)     Describe audit software procedures which could be carried out during the audit of Airsoft Co's trade payables and accruals. **(3 marks)**

(c)     Describe substantive procedures the auditor should perform to obtain sufficient and appropriate audit evidence in relation to Airsoft Co's year-end bank balances. **(5 marks)**

(d)     Describe substantive procedures the auditor should perform to confirm the directors' remuneration included in the financial statements at the year end. **(3 marks)**

A member of your audit team has asked for information on ISA 701 *Communicating Key Audit Matters in the Independent Auditor's Report* as she has heard this standard is applicable to listed clients such as Airsoft Co.

**Required**

(e) Identify what a key audit matter (KAM) is and explain how the auditor determines and communicates KAM. **(5 marks)**

**(Total = 20 marks)**

# 162 Gooseberry Co (Mar/Jun 18)      36 mins

You are an audit manager of Cranberry & Co and you are currently responsible for the audit of Gooseberry Co, a company which develops and manufactures health and beauty products and distributes these to wholesale customers. Its draft profit before tax is $6.4m and total assets are $37.2m for the financial year ended 31 January 20X8. The final audit is due to commence shortly and the following matters have been brought to your attention:

### Research and development

Gooseberry Co spent $1.9m in the current year developing nine new health and beauty products, all of which are at different stages of development. Once they meet the recognition criteria under IAS 38 *Intangible Assets* for development expenditure, Gooseberry Co includes the costs incurred within intangible assets. Once production commences, the intangible assets are amortised on a straight line basis over three years. Management believe that this amortisation policy is a reasonable approximation of the assets' useful lives, as in this industry there is constant demand for innovative new products.

### Depreciation

Gooseberry Co has a large portfolio of property plant and equipment (PPE). In March 20X7, the company carried out a full review of all its PPE and updated the useful lives, residual values, depreciation rates and methods for many categories of asset. The finance director felt the changes were necessary to better reflect the use of the assets. This resulted in the depreciation charge of some assets changing significantly for this year.

### Bonus

The company's board is comprised of seven directors. They are each entitled to a bonus based on the draft year-end net assets, excluding intangible assets. Details of the bonus entitlement are included in the directors' service contracts. The bonus, which related to the 20X8 year end, was paid to each director in February 20X8 and the costs were accrued and recognised within wages and salaries for the year ended 31 January 20X8. Separate disclosure of the bonus, by director, is required by local legislation.

**Required**

(a) Describe substantive procedures the auditor should perform to obtain sufficient and appropriate audit evidence in relation to Gooseberry Co's research and development expenditure. **(5 marks)**

(b) Describe substantive procedures the auditor should perform to obtain sufficient and appropriate audit evidence in relation to the matters identified regarding depreciation of property, plant and equipment. **(5 marks)**

(c) Describe substantive procedures the auditor should perform to obtain sufficient and appropriate audit evidence in relation to the directors' bonuses. **(5 marks)**

During the audit, the team discovers that the intangible assets balance includes $440,000 related to one of the nine new health and beauty products development projects, which does not meet the criteria for capitalisation. As this project is ongoing, the finance director has suggested that no adjustment is made in the 20X8 financial statements. She is confident that the project will meet the criteria for capitalisation in 20X9.

**BPP** LEARNING MEDIA

**Required**

(d)   Discuss the issue and describe the impact on the auditor's report, if any, should this issue remain unresolved.

(5 marks)

(Total = 20 marks)

# 163 Spadefish (Sep/Dec 19)                                   36 mins

This scenario relates to four requirements.

It is 1 July 20X5 and you are an audit manager of Spadefish & Co and you are currently responsible for the audits of two existing clients:

Triggerfish Co manufactures hair products and its year ended on 31 May 20X5. You are finalising the audit programmes for the forthcoming year-end audit.

Marlin Co is a distributor of electronic goods and its year ended on 30 April 20X5. The audit is almost complete and the auditor's report is due to be signed shortly.

The following matters have been brought to your attention for each company.

## Triggerfish Co – Receivables

Triggerfish Co's draft year-end trade receivables are $3.85m ($20X4: $2.45m) and revenue for the year is slightly increased on 20X4. Triggerfish Co has a large number of customers with balances ranging from $5,000 to $45,000. A positive receivables circularisation has been undertaken based on the year-end balances. The majority of responses from customers agreed to the balances as per Triggerfish Co's receivables ledger, however, the following exceptions were noted:

|  | Balance per Triggerfish | Response from customer |
|---|---|---|
| Albacore Co | $36,558 | Nil response |
| Floundrer Co | $24,115 | $18,265 |
| Menhaden Co | -$5,360 (Credit) | $3,450 |

Due to the increase in receivables, Triggerfish Co has recently recruited an additional credit controller to chase outstanding receivables. As a result of the additional focus on chasing outstanding receivables the finance director thinks it is not necessary to continue to maintain a significant allowance for receivables and has reduced the closing allowance from $125,000 to $5,000.

**Required**

(a)   Describe procedures the auditor should perform to resolve the exceptions noted for each customer during the positive receivables circularisation for Triggerfish Co.

| Customer name | Procedures |
|---|---|
| Albacore Co |  |
| Flounder Co |  |
| Menhaden Co |  |

(8 marks)

(b)   Describe substantive procedures the auditor should perform to obtain sufficient and appropriate audit evidence in relation to the allowance for receivables in the current year.

(4 marks)

(c)   Identify and explain THREE potential indicators that Marlin Co is NOT a going concern.

(3 marks)

(d)   Describe the audit procedures the auditor should perform in assessing whether or not Marlin Co is a going concern.

(5 marks)

(Total = 20 marks)

REVIEW AND REPORTING

Questions 164–203 cover Review and reporting, the subject of Part E of the BPP Workbook for Audit and Assurance.

# Chestnut (Jun 15) (amended)                    18 mins

The following scenario relates to questions 164–168.

It is 1 July 20X5. You are the audit manager of Chestnut & Co and are reviewing the key issues identified in the files of two audit clients.

The first audit client is Palm Industries Co (Palm), a listed company. Palm's year end was 31 March 20X5 and the draft financial statements show revenue of $28.2m, receivables of $5.6m and profit before tax of $4.8m. The fieldwork stage for this audit has been completed.

A customer of Palm owed an amount of $350,000 at the year end. Testing of receivables in April highlighted that no amounts had been paid to Palm from this customer as they were disputing the quality of certain goods received from Palm. The finance director is confident the issue will be resolved and no allowance for receivables was made with regards to this balance.

The second audit client is Ash Trading Co (Ash). Ash is a new client of Chestnut & Co, its year end was 31 January 20X5 and the firm was only appointed as auditor in February 20X5, as the previous auditor was suddenly unable to undertake the audit. The fieldwork stage for this audit is currently ongoing.

The inventory count at Ash's warehouse was undertaken on 31 January 20X5 and was overseen by the company's internal audit department. Neither Chestnut & Co nor the previous auditors attended the count. Detailed inventory records were maintained but it was not possible to undertake another full inventory count subsequent to the year end.

The draft financial statements show a profit before tax of $2.4 million, revenue of $10.1 million and inventory of $510,000.

164  Which of the following audit procedures should be performed in order to form a conclusion on whether an amendment is required in Palm's 20X5 financial statements in respect of the disputed balance?

| | | |
|---|---|---|
| Review whether any payments have subsequently been made by this customer since the audit fieldwork was completed | PERFORM | DO NOT PERFORM |
| Match the total of the aged receivables listing to the sales ledger control account | PERFORM | DO NOT PERFORM |
| Vouch the balance owed by the customer at the year end to sales invoices | PERFORM | DO NOT PERFORM |
| Review the latest customer correspondence with regards to an assessment of the likelihood of the customer making payment | PERFORM | DO NOT PERFORM |

BPP
LEARNING
MEDIA

165 Which of the following correctly summarises the effect of the issue relating to the inventory count of Ash at the year end?

| | Material | Financial statement impact |
|---|---|---|
| ○ | No | Current assets are understated |
| ○ | No | Gross profit may be understated |
| ○ | Yes | Opening inventory may be materially misstated |
| ○ | Yes | Gross profit may be overstated |

166 The audit engagement partner for Ash has requested that additional audit procedures be performed in order to conclude on the level of adjustment needed in relation to the above inventory issue.

Which **TWO** of the following audit procedures should be performed in order to form a conclusion as to whether Ash's 20X5 financial statements require amendment?

☐ Obtain a copy of the aged inventory report and use computer-assisted audit techniques to verify the accuracy of the report. Discuss the valuation of slow-moving inventory with the production director.

☐ Review the internal auditors' reports of the inventory count to identify the level of adjustments made to the records, in order to assess the reasonableness of relying on the inventory records for the purpose of the year-end audit.

☐ Perform test counts of inventory in the warehouse and compare these first to the inventory records, and then from inventory records to the warehouse, in order to assess the reasonableness of the inventory records maintained by Ash.

☐ Review Ash's sales order book for February, March and April 20X5 to estimate the level of inventory that will need to be produced in the new accounting period to fulfil customer demand.

167 Following the inability to attend the inventory count of Ash, an engagement quality reviewer has been appointed to the audit.

Indicate which of the following should be included within the engagement quality review?

| | | |
|---|---|---|
| Evaluation of all significant audit judgments | INCLUDE | EXCLUDE |
| Evaluation of the performance of specific audit procedures performed | INCLUDE | EXCLUDE |
| Evaluation of the cost-effectiveness of the audit process | INCLUDE | EXCLUDE |
| Evaluation of conclusions reached in formulating auditor's report | INCLUDE | EXCLUDE |

168 Alternative procedures, performed as a result of Chestnut & Co being unable to attend the inventory count of Ash, did not provide sufficient appropriate audit evidence regarding the inventory balance in the statement of financial position.

From the options below indicate the audit opinion which would be given in these circumstances and the appropriate disclosure in the auditor's report.

| | Audit opinion | Disclosure in the auditor's report |
|---|---|---|
| O | Qualified | Basis for qualified opinion |
| O | Disclaimer | Basis for disclaimer of opinion |
| O | Qualified | Key audit matters section |
| O | Disclaimer | Emphasis of matter |

(Total = 10 marks)

# Humphries (Dec 11) (amended)                     18 mins

The following scenario relates to questions 169–173.

It is 1 July 20X5. Humphries Co, your audit client, operates a chain of food wholesalers across the country and its year end was 30 April 20X5. The final audit is nearly complete and it is proposed that the financial statements and auditor's report will be signed on 13 July. Revenue for the year is $78 million and profit before taxation is $7.5 million.

The following information comes to light:

Humphries Co has three warehouses; following extensive rain on 20 June, rain and river water flooded the warehouse located in Bass. All of the inventory in the warehouse was damaged and has been disposed of. The insurance company has been contacted. No amendments or disclosures have been made in the financial statements.

A customer of Humphries Co has been experiencing cash flow problems and its year-end balance is $0.3 million. The company has just become aware that its customer is experiencing significant going concern difficulties. The management of Humphries Co believes that as the company has been trading for many years, they will receive some, if not full, payment from the customer; hence they have not adjusted the receivable balance.

A key supplier of Humphries Co is suing them for breach of contract. The lawsuit was filed prior to the year end, and the sum claimed by them is $1 million. This has been disclosed as a contingent liability in the notes to the financial statements.

Correspondence has just arrived from the supplier indicating that they are willing to settle the case for a payment by Humphries Co of $0.6 million. It is likely that the company will agree to this.

169 Which of the following audit procedures would identify subsequent events occurring up to the date of the auditor's report?

(1) Enquire of management whether there have been any unusual accounting adjustments

(2) Enquire of management whether there have been any issues of shares/debentures, or changes in business structure

(3) Review management procedures for identifying subsequent events to ensure that such events are identified

(4) Obtain written representation that all subsequent events requiring adjustment or disclosure have been adjusted or disclosed

○    1 and 2

○    1 and 3

○    1, 3 and 4

○    1, 2, 3 and 4

---

170    Which **TWO** of the following statements correctly describe the likely impact that the flooding of the warehouse will have on Humphries Co's financial statements for the year ended 30 April 20X5?

☐    Inventory should be written down, because the flood damage is an adjusting event.

☐    Inventory should not be written down, because the damage is not an adjusting event.

☐    If a material amount of inventory is uninsured, it may be necessary to disclose the event and an estimate of the financial losses.

☐    If insurance proceeds are more likely than not to be received, a contingent asset should be recognised.

---

171    Which **TWO** of the following audit procedures should be performed in order to form a conclusion on the amendment required to Humphries Co's 20X5 financial statements in respect of the $0.3 million owed by the customer experiencing financial difficulties?

☐    Reviewing the post year end period for payments received from the customer in respect of the year-end debt

☐    Reviewing correspondence with the customer to assess the likelihood of Humphries Co recovering the $0.3 million

☐    Writing to the customer to request confirmation of the amount owed to Humphries Co at the year end

☐    Ask management to produce a revised cash flow forecast covering at least 12 months after the year end

---

172    Complete the following sentence regarding the auditor's report by selecting from the options provided.

The lawsuit relating to the breach of contract is considered to be [            ] and therefore if the financial statements are not revised in the light of the new information then the auditor's opinion will be [            ].

| Impact of breach of contract | Auditor's opinion |
|---|---|
| material | adverse |
| material and pervasive | disclaimer |
| not material | qualified 'except for' – due to insufficient appropriate evidence |
| | qualified 'except for' – due to material misstatement |
| | unmodified |
| | unmodified with emphasis of matter |

173 It is now 13 July 20X5. The auditor's report has been signed. The financial statements are due to be issued on 25 July 20X5.

Which of the following statements correctly describes the auditor's responsibility in relation to subsequent events occurring between now and 25 July?

○ The auditor must design procedures to obtain sufficient appropriate audit evidence that all events up to that date that may require adjustment or disclosure have been identified.

○ The auditor must perform procedures on matters examined during the audit, which may be susceptible to change after the year end.

○ The auditor has no obligation to perform procedures, or make enquiries regarding the financial statements. Any subsequent events should be noted and considered in the next period's audit.

○ If the auditor becomes aware of a fact that, had it been known to the auditor at the date of the auditor's report, may have caused the auditor to amend the auditor's report, the auditor shall discuss the need for any adjustments with management.

(Total = 10 marks)

# Greenfields (Dec 10) (amended)                     18 mins

The following scenario relates to questions 174–178.

It is 1 July 20X5. Greenfields Co specialises in manufacturing equipment which can help to reduce toxic emissions in the production of chemicals. The company has grown rapidly over the past eight years and this is due partly to the warranties that the company gives to its customers. It guarantees its products for five years and if problems arise in this period it undertakes to fix them, or to provide a replacement product.

You are the manager responsible for the audit of Greenfields Co. You are performing the final review stage of the audit and have come across the following issues.

### Receivable balance owing from Yellowmix Co

Greenfields Co has a material receivable balance owing from its customer, Yellowmix Co. During the year-end audit, your team reviewed the ageing of this balance and found that no payments had been received from Yellowmix Co for over six months, and Greenfields Co would not allow this balance to be circularised. Instead management has assured your team that they will provide a written representation confirming that the balance is recoverable.

## Warranty provision

The warranty provision included within the statement of financial position is material. The audit team has performed testing over the calculations and assumptions which are consistent with prior years. The team has requested a written representation from management confirming that the basis and amount of the provision are reasonable. Management has yet to confirm acceptance of this representation.

## Other information

You have reviewed a financial summary which is to be included in the annual report and have found that the details are inconsistent with the financial statements. Your investigations have shown that the error is in the summary and not the financial statements.

174    Assuming you received the written representations as described above for both the receivables balance and the warranty provision, in respect of which balances is the auditor most likely to conclude that sufficient appropriate evidence has been obtained?

    O      Receivables balance only

    O      Warranty provision only

    O      Receivables balance and warranty provision

    O      Neither the receivables balance nor the warranty provision

175    Which **TWO** of the following audit procedures could the audit team carry out to obtain independent evidence relating to the recoverability of the debt from Yellowmix Co?

    ☐      Review correspondence with Yellowmix Co regarding the late payment

    ☐      Trace a sample of goods dispatched notes for Yellowmix Co to sales invoices

    ☐      Trace the entries in Yellowmix Co's account in the receivables ledger to invoices and remittances

    ☐      Perform a review of post year-end cash receipts

176    Management has now stated that it is not prepared to confirm that the basis and amount of the warranty provision are reasonable.

Indicate which of the following actions you must perform in accordance with ISA 580 *Written Representations?*

| | | |
|---|---|---|
| Discuss with management why they have refused to provide the representations requested | PERFORM | DO NOT PERFORM |
| Reassess the integrity of management and consider the implications for any other representations | PERFORM | DO NOT PERFORM |
| Seek legal advice | PERFORM | DO NOT PERFORM |
| Resign as auditor | PERFORM | DO NOT PERFORM |

177 You have discussed the matter with management but they are still not prepared to provide the representations you have requested.

What type of modified opinion would be issued and what would be the basis for this modification?

| | Audit opinion | Reason |
|---|---|---|
| O | Qualified | Material misstatement |
| O | Disclaimer | Inability to obtain sufficient appropriate evidence |
| O | Adverse | Material misstatement |
| O | Qualified | Inability to obtain sufficient appropriate evidence |

178 You have notified the directors of the error in the summary financial statements.

Which of the following correctly summarises the impact on the auditor's report if the directors do not correct this error?

| | Audit opinion | Disclosure |
|---|---|---|
| O | Modified | Other Information section stating that there is nothing to report |
| O | Modified | Other Information section would not be required as there is nothing to report |
| O | Unmodified | Other Information section including a description of the uncorrected misstatement |
| O | Unmodified | Other Matter paragraph including a description of the uncorrected misstatement |

(Total = 10 marks)

# Strawberry (Jun 12) (amended)                    18 mins

The following scenario relates to questions 179–183.

You are the audit manager of Kiwi & Co. Your client is Strawberry Kitchen Designs Co (Strawberry), which is a kitchen manufacturer. The company's year-end is 30 April 20X2.

Strawberry has had a challenging year. Grape Co, a major customer of Strawberry which owes $0.6m, is experiencing financial difficulties. However, the balance is included within the financial statements. The sales director has recently left Strawberry and has yet to be replaced. As a result Strawberry has struggled to win any new business in the last six months.

The monthly cash flow has shown a net cash outflow for the last two months of the financial year and is forecast as negative for the forthcoming financial year.

You have performed some analytical procedures on the draft financial statements and have calculated the following ratios:

| | 20X2 Draft | 20X1 Actual |
|---|---|---|
| Inventory holding period (days) | 95 | 97 |
| Receivables collection period (days) | 65 | 49 |
| Payables payment period (days) | 120 | 86 |

Due to its poor cash flow, Strawberry missed a loan repayment and, as a result of this breach in the loan covenants, the bank has asked that the loan of $4.8m be repaid in full within 6 months.

BPP
LEARNING
MEDIA

179 Which of the following are potential indicators that Strawberry is not a going concern?

(1) The breach of the loan covenants

(2) The departure of the sales director

(3) The fall in the inventory holding period

(4) The negative cash flow figures

O 1, 2 and 3

O 2, 3 and 4

O 1, 3 and 4

O 1, 2 and 4

180 You are reviewing the management's assessment of Strawberry's ability to continue as a going concern.

What period must management's assessment cover?

O At least 12 months from the date of the auditor's report

O At least 12 months from the date of the financial statements

O A maximum of 12 months from the date of the auditor's report

O A maximum of 12 months from the date of the financial statements

181 You are concerned that the debt due from Grape Co may not be recoverable and believe that this would have a significant effect on the viability of Strawberry.

Which of the following would provide you with the most reliable evidence regarding the recoverability of this debt?

O A management representation confirming its recoverability

O The response from the customer to your circularisation performed earlier in the audit confirming the amount owed

O Identification during your subsequent events review of a cash receipt for the full amount

O Correspondence between Strawberry's lawyer and Grape Co's lawyers confirming that the amount will be paid

182 You have raised your concerns with management regarding the ability of Strawberry to repay the $0.6m loan in 6 months. The directors have assured you that this will be possible as they have a contingency plan.

Which of the following courses of action by the directors would provide you with the most assurance that Strawberry will be able to meet this commitment?

O Plans to dispose of a property valued at $5.2m in August 20X2

O The reopening of negotiations regarding the terms of the loan with the current provider

O Plans to substantially cut production costs by moving production to Asia

O Agreement by an alternative financial institution to lend Strawberry $4.8m in September 20X2

183    You have concluded that Strawberry is not a going concern.

If the directors refuse to amend the financial statements which of the following correctly describes the impact on the auditor's report?

| | Auditor's opinion | Explanation of circumstances |
|---|---|---|
| O | Adverse opinion | Basis for adverse opinion |
| O | Qualified opinion | Basis for qualified opinion |
| O | Adverse opinion | Material uncertainty related to going concern |
| O | Qualified opinion | Material uncertainty related to going concern |

(Total = 10 marks)

# Clarinet (Jun 14) (amended)                                          18 mins

The following scenario relates to questions 184–188.

It is 1 July 20X5. Clarinet Co (Clarinet) is a computer hardware specialist and has been trading for over five years. The company is funded partly through overdrafts and loans and also by several large shareholders; the year end is 30 April 20X5.

Clarinet has experienced significant growth in previous years; however, in the current year a new competitor, Drums Design Co (Drums), has entered the market and through competitive pricing has gained considerable market share from Clarinet including one of its largest customers. Clarinet is looking to develop new products to differentiate itself from the rest of its competitors. It has approached its shareholders to finance this development; however, they declined to invest further in Clarinet. Clarinet's loan is long term and it has met all repayments on time. The overdraft has increased significantly over the year and the directors have informed you that the overdraft facility is due for renewal next month and they believe it will be renewed.

The directors have produced a cash flow forecast which shows a significantly strengthening position over the coming 12 months. They are confident with the new products being developed and, in light of their trading history of significant growth, believe it is unnecessary to make any disclosures in the financial statements regarding going concern.

At the year end, Clarinet received notification from one of its customers that the hardware installed by Clarinet for the customers' online ordering system has not been operating correctly. As a result, the customer has lost significant revenue and has informed Clarinet that they intend to take legal action against them for loss of earnings. Clarinet has investigated the problem post year end and discovered that other work in progress is similarly affected and inventory should be written down by $375,000. The finance director believes that as this misstatement was identified after the year end, it can be amended in the 20X6 financial statements. Draft financial statements for the year ended 30 April 20X5 showed profit after tax of $2.5m.

184    Which of the following correctly summarises whether the uncorrected misstatement of inventory is material and its impact on the 20X5 financial statements?

| | Material | Adjust in 20X5 financial statements |
|---|---|---|
| O | No | No |
| O | No | Yes |
| O | Yes | Yes |
| O | Yes | No |

185 Which of the following factors are indicators that may cast doubt on Clarinet's ability to continue as a going concern?

(1) The entry of the new competitor reducing Clarinet's market share

(2) The significant increase in the overdraft

(3) The company has a long-term loan

(4) The reluctance of the shareholders to provide further investment in Clarinet

O 1, 2 and 3

O 1, 2 and 4

O 1, 3 and 4

O 2, 3 and 4

186 As part of your assessment of going concern you have reviewed the cash flow forecast. This is based on the assumption of significant increases in revenue.

Which of the following procedures would provide the most reliable evidence regarding the validity of this assumption?

O Email correspondence between the sales director and potential new customers

O A review of board minutes showing details of new customers won

O A review of post year-end sales and the order book

O Discussions with management regarding their plans for obtaining new business

187 You have concluded that circumstances exist which cast significant doubt on Clarinet's ability to continue as a going concern.

Which of the following must you include in your communication with those charged with governance in accordance with ISA 570 *Going Concern*?

(1) Whether the circumstances you have identified constitute a material uncertainty

(2) Whether the use of the going concern basis of accounting is appropriate in the preparation and presentation of the financial statements

(3) The adequacy of the related disclosures

(4) The period of time your assessment has covered if less than 12 months from the date of the financial statements

O 1, 2 and 3

O 1, 2 and 4

O 1, 3 and 4

O 2, 3 and 4

188 The auditors have been informed that Clarinet's bankers will not make a decision on the overdraft facility until after the auditor's report is completed. The directors have now agreed to include some going concern disclosures and you believe these disclosures are adequate.

Which of the following correctly summarises the impact on the auditor's report of Clarinet if the auditor believes the company is a going concern but that this is subject to a material uncertainty?

| | Opinion | Disclosure |
|---|---|---|
| O | Modified | Key audit matters |
| O | Unmodified | Material uncertainty related to going concern |
| O | Unmodified | Key audit matters |
| O | Modified | Material uncertainty related to going concern |

(Total = 10 marks)

# Czech & Dawson                                              18 mins

The following scenario relates to questions 189–193.

It is 1 July 20X5. You are the audit manager of Savage & Co. It is a busy time of year for you as you have several ongoing audit clients at the moment and you are in the process of dealing with a number of outstanding issues and queries from members of your audit teams.

### Czech Co (Czech)

Czech is a pharmaceutical company. The fieldwork has been completed and you are currently reviewing the audit file. The audit senior is not sure how to deal with the following issue.

Czech has incurred $2.1m and development expenditure of $3.2m during the year, all of which has been capitalised as an intangible asset. Profit before tax is $26.3m.

### Dawson Co (Dawson)

The fieldwork on this audit is also complete with the exception of the following issue which the audit senior has been unable to deal with.

Dawson's computerised wages program is backed up daily; however, for a period of two months the wages records and back-ups have been corrupted, and therefore cannot be accessed. Wages and salaries for these 2 months are $1.1m. Profit before tax is $10m.

189 You have just received a phone call from one particular audit senior who is unsure about the steps to take in relation to uncorrected misstatements.

Which of the following statements correctly describe the auditor's responsibility in respect of misstatements?

O   ISA 450 *Evaluation of Misstatements Identified During the Audit* states that the auditor only has a responsibility to accumulate material misstatements identified during the audit.

O   Where misstatements are not material the auditor should request that management correct the misstatements in the following accounting period.

O   If management refuses to correct some or all of the misstatements, the auditor should consider the implications of this for their audit opinion.

O   A written representation should be requested from management to confirm whether they believe that the effects of the unadjusted misstatements are immaterial, both individually and in aggregate, to the financial statements as a whole.

190 Which **TWO** of the following audit procedures should be performed in order to form a conclusion on whether an amendment is required to Czech's financial statements in respect of the research and development expenditure?

- [ ] Discuss the requirements of IAS 38 *Intangible Assets* with the directors in order to determine whether they understand the required accounting treatment of research and development expenditure

- [ ] Obtain a breakdown of the $5.3m capitalised as an intangible asset and agree to supporting documentation to determine the nature of the projects to which the expenditure relates

- [ ] Review minutes of board meetings to determine whether the expenditure was authorised

- [ ] Visit the laboratory where the current research is being undertaken and to confirm occurrence of the research expenditure

191 Which of the following options correctly summarises the impact on the auditor's report for Czech if the issue remains unresolved?

- ○ Unmodified opinion with key audit matters paragraph
- ○ Qualified opinion with key audit matters paragraph explaining the issue
- ○ Qualified opinion
- ○ Adverse opinion

192 Which of the following correctly summarises the effect of the issue relating to the wages balance in the financial statements of Dawson?

| | Material | Financial statement impact |
|---|---|---|
| ○ | No | Liabilities to tax authorities may be understated |
| ○ | No | Profit may be overstated |
| ○ | Yes | Wages may be materially misstated |
| ○ | Yes | Proper accounting records have not been kept |

193 Based on the above information, which of the following options correctly summarises the impact of the wages and salaries issue on the auditor's report for Dawson?

| | Audit opinion | Disclosure in the auditor's report |
|---|---|---|
| ○ | Qualified | Basis for qualified opinion |
| ○ | Disclaimer | Basis for disclaimer of opinion |
| ○ | Qualified | Key audit matters section |
| ○ | Qualified | Emphasis of matter |

(Total = 10 marks)

# Medimade (Jun 10) (amended)

**18 mins**

The following scenario relates to questions 194–198.

It is 1 July 20X5. Medimade Co is an established pharmaceutical company that has for many years generated 90% of its revenue through the sale of two specific cold and flu remedies. Medimade Co has lately seen a real growth in the level of competition that it faces in its market and demand for its products has significantly declined.

You are the audit manager responsible for the audit of Medimade Co's financial statements for the year ended 31 March 20X5.

In addition to recruiting staff, Medimade Co needed to invest $2m in plant and machinery. The company wanted to borrow this sum but was unable to agree suitable terms with the bank; therefore it used its overdraft facility, which carried a higher interest rate. Consequently, some of Medimade Co's suppliers have been paid much later than usual and hence some of them have withdrawn credit terms meaning the company must pay cash on delivery.

194    Which **TWO** of the following statements are correct with regard to the going concern basis of accounting?

- ☐  The going concern basis of accounting is used when the entity will be able to continue in business for the foreseeable future.

- ☐  The foreseeable future is defined for accounting purposes as 6 months from the company's reporting date.

- ☐  The going concern basis of accounting assumes that the entity will be able to realise its assets and discharge its liabilities in the normal course of business.

- ☐  Financial statements that are prepared on a going concern basis assert that the company will be in the position of having net current assets for the next 12 months.

195    Which **TWO** of the following statements describe the most direct impact the withdrawal of supplier credit has on Medimade Co's use of the going concern basis of accounting?

- ☐  Medimade Co now has to pay cash on delivery and this adds further cash flow strain imposed by the overdraft.

- ☐  Some suppliers may end their relationship with Medimade Co, preventing the company from producing its products, thus further reducing sales.

- ☐  Medimade Co will have to seek alternative suppliers, who may not meet Medimade Co's quality control standards.

- ☐  The bank may impose strict covenants on the overdraft, restricting the way Medimade Co can conduct its future operations.

196    The directors have informed you that the bank overdraft facility is due for renewal next month, after the auditor's report is signed. They are confident that it will be renewed.

Which of the following audit procedures would be most effective in assessing whether or not Medimade is a going concern?

- ○  Agree current overdraft level to bank letter

- ○  Obtain confirmation from the bank that the overdraft facility will be renewed

- ○  Obtain written representation from management that they consider the going concern assumption to be appropriate

- ○  Review board minutes for meetings held after the year end for evidence which indicates further financial difficulties or evidence of alternative sources of finance

197 The directors have now agreed to include going concern disclosures, while continuing to use the going concern basis of accounting.

You agree with Medimade Co's management that the going concern basis of accounting is appropriate under the circumstances. You have reviewed the draft disclosures and believe they are correct and adequate.

Indicate which form of audit opinion would be appropriate and how the going concern issue would be disclosed in the auditor's report.

| Audit opinion | Disclosure in the auditor's report |
|---|---|
| ○ Disclaimer | ○ Describe the nature of the going concern uncertainty in the Material uncertainty related to going concern section |
| ○ Unmodified opinion | ○ Describe the nature of the going concern uncertainty in the Key audit matters section |
| ○ Qualified opinion | ○ Describe the nature of the going concern uncertainty in the Basis for adverse opinion section |
| ○ Adverse opinion | ○ Describe the nature of the going concern uncertainty in the Basis for qualified opinion section |

---

198 The audit is completed. The auditor's report and the financial statements have been signed but not yet issued.

The finance director of Medimade Co has just informed the audit team that he has been informed by the bank that the overdraft facility will not be renewed. Medimade Co currently does not have any other source of finance.

What actions, if any, should you now take in order to meet the auditor's responsibilities under ISA 560 *Subsequent Events*?

○ No actions required as the auditor's report and financial statements have already been signed.

○ Discuss with management about their plans for the company and determine whether the 20X5 financial statements should now be prepared on a break-up basis. If yes, request management to adjust the financial statements, audit the adjustments and provide a new auditor's report.

○ Discuss with management about their plans for the company and determine whether disclosures should be revised in the 20X5 financial statements. If yes, request management to revise the disclosures and redraft the auditor's report to refer to the revised disclosures.

○ Request that management adjust for this event in the 20X8 financial statements, as it occurred in the year ending 31 March 20X6.

(Total = 10 marks)

# Brown & Green Co (Sep/Dec 20)    18 mins

The following scenario relates to questions 199–203.

It is 1 July 20X5. You are an audit manager of Brown & Green Co and you are currently working on the completion stage of the audit of Strawberry Co, a listed company specialising in the manufacture of smart phone accessories, for the year ended 31 March 20X5. The draft financial statements of Strawberry Co show revenue for the year of $500m and total assets of $210m.

You are reviewing the outcome of the audit work documented by your team. You have become aware of the following two issues:

## Issue 1 – Reduction in sales

On 18 March 20X5, the board of directors approved a strategic plan which will help it increase the sales of smart phone chargers in the future. The strategic plan is to upgrade Strawberry Co's manufacturing facilities, which will allow it to manufacture higher quality and technologically advanced products. To fund the planned upgrade, the company issued equity share capital to the general public in May 20X5, which generated cash of $4m.

## Issue 2 – Letter from the government environmental agency

Strawberry Co received a letter dated 15 May 20X5, from the government environmental agency advising that water samples taken from a public lake close to Strawberry Co's manufacturing site have shown traces of a harmful substance which is produced during its manufacturing process. The agency has concluded that Strawberry Co is the source of the contamination and is liable for a fine. The board of directors has denied any responsibility and have forwarded the case to the company's legal advisers.

199    Which of the following statements correctly describes Brown & Green Co's responsibility in relation to subsequent events occurring between the date on which the auditor's report is signed and the date on which the financial statements are issued?

- ○    Brown & Green Co should obtain sufficient and appropriate audit evidence and design audit procedures to ensure that all subsequent events are identified.

- ○    Brown & Green Co should obtain a list of subsequent events from the directors of Strawberry Co and include these in the written representation letter.

- ○    Brown & Green Co has no duty to perform any procedures after the date on which the auditor's report is signed and therefore any subsequent events in this period will be dealt with in next year's audit.

- ○    Brown & Green Co should discuss any subsequent events they become aware of with the directors of Strawberry Co to determine whether the financial statements need amending.

200 Explain, by choosing the relevant boxes in the statements below, how the issue of share capital should be treated in the financial statements of Strawberry Co.

The issue of share capital is [ **an adjusting** ] [ **a non-adjusting** ] event

because it

| **was approved prior to year end and so gives information about events existing at year-end date** | **gives new information about an event that did not exist at year-end date** |
|---|---|

and it is material

therefore it requires

| **to be accounted for in the current year financial statements** | **to be disclosed in the current year financial statements** | **no treatment in the current year financial statements** |
|---|---|---|

---

201 The audit team has performed various substantive procedures in order to obtain sufficient and appropriate audit evidence relating to the potential fine for environmental damage.

Which **TWO** of the following are appropriate audit procedures to perform in respect of the letter from the government environmental agency?

☐ Send a letter addressed to the government environmental agency to confirm the matter

☐ Examine post year-end board meeting minutes to identify any reference to further developments of the case

☐ Review the correspondence with the company's legal advisers to assess the probable outcome of the case

☐ Test the effectiveness of the client's system of internal control in relation to the prevention of environmental damage

---

202 Assuming 'Issue 2' is a material subsequent event, match the relevant audit opinion to the following two outcomes.

| Audit opinion |
|---|
| Unmodified with emphasis of matter |
| Qualified |
| Adverse |
| Disclaimer |
| Modified with emphasis of matter |

| Outcome 1 |
|---|
| It is probable that the government agency will win the case, but as the letter was received after the year end, the directors did not plan to account for or disclose it in the financial statements. |

| Outcome 2 |
|---|
| It is possible but not probable that the government agency will win the case and therefore the directors have disclosed the matter in the financial statements. |

---

BPP LEARNING MEDIA

203 The two issues will be included in a written representation from management. All audit work will be finished by 31 July 20X5. The auditor's report is due to be signed by Brown & Green Co on 28 September 20X5. Strawberry Co's board plans to issue the financial statements on 21 October 20X5 which will be followed by an annual general meeting on 30 October 20X5.

Which of the following would be the most appropriate date for the directors of Strawberry Co to sign the written representation?

O    31 July 20X5

O    28 September 20X5

O    21 October 20X5

O    30 October 20X5

# 204 Panda (6/13)                                                        36 mins

Panda Co manufactures chemicals and has a factory and four offsite storage locations for finished goods. Panda Co's year end was 30 April 20X3. The final audit is almost complete and the financial statements and auditor's report are due to be signed next week. Revenue for the year is $55 million and profit before taxation is $5.6 million.

The following two events have occurred subsequent to the year end. No amendments or disclosures have been made in the financial statements.

### Event 1 – Defective chemicals

Panda Co undertakes extensive quality control checks prior to the dispatch of any chemicals. Testing on 3 May 20X3 found that a batch of chemicals produced in April was defective. The cost of this batch was $0.85 million. In its current condition it can be sold at a scrap value of $0.1 million. The costs of correcting the defect are too significant for Panda Co's management to consider this an alternative option.

### Event 2 – Explosion

An explosion occurred at the smallest of the four offsite storage locations on 20 May 20X3. This resulted in some damage to inventory and property, plant and equipment. Panda Co's management have investigated the cause of the explosion and believe that they are unlikely to be able to claim on their insurance. Management of Panda Co has estimated that the value of damaged inventory and property, plant and equipment was $0.9 million and it now has no scrap value.

### Required

(a)    Explain the five elements of an assurance engagement.                    **(5 marks)**

(b)    For each of the two events above:

   (i)    Explain whether the financial statements require amendment; and

   (ii)   Describe audit procedures that should be performed in order to form a conclusion on any required amendment.

   *Note.* The total marks will be split equally between each event.            **(10 marks)**

(c)    The directors do not wish to make any amendments or disclosures to the financial statements for the explosion (Event 2).

   *Required*

   Discuss the issue and explain the impact on the auditor's report, if any, should this issue remain unresolved.                                                          **(5 marks)**

   **(Total = 20 marks)**

# Q205–206 March 2017

**7 mins**

## Comments from the examining team (March 2017)

Section A

The following two questions are reviewed with the aim of giving future candidates an indication of the types of questions asked, guidance on dealing with exam questions and to provide a technical debrief on the topics covered by the specific questions selected.

205   Following discussions with one of your firm's clients, the audit engagement partner has advised that detailed testing will need to be performed on the valuation of inventory due to some concerns over the net realisable value of certain products.

Which of the following matters disclosed by the client is an indicator that net realisable value could be lower than cost?

○   General market prices for individual gemstones have remained static for the last three years.

○   Demand for certain items of jewellery has increased marginally over the past year.

○   Trade discounts given by suppliers have increased in the past year.

○   There has been an increase in the average time taken to manufacture each individual jewellery piece.

206   You are an audit senior and have been asked to draft the auditor's report.

Which of the following are elements which should be included in an unmodified auditor's report for a listed company as per ISA 700 (Revised) *Forming an Opinion and Reporting on Financial Statements*?

(1)   Basis for opinion paragraph

(2)   Other reporting responsibilities

(3)   Key audit matters

(4)   Other matters paragraph

○   (1), (3) and (4)

○   (1), (2) and 4)

○   (1), (2) and (3)

○   (2), (3) and (4)

# Q207–208 June 2017

**7 mins**

## Comments from the examining team (June 2017)

Section A in the June 2017 examination included questions on the following areas:

- Professional ethics and application of ACCA's *Code of Ethics and Conduct*
- Internal audit
- Corporate Governance
- Substantive testing including testing on tangible assets, receivables, bank and cash and using the work of others
- Subsequent events; and
- Auditor's reports

The following two questions are reviewed with the aim of giving future candidates an indication of the types of questions asked, guidance on dealing with exam questions and to provide a technical debrief on the topics covered by the specific questions selected. Candidates are reminded that there will be a mix of application and knowledge questions in section A and it is imperative that they ensure their knowledge of the International

Standards on Auditing (ISAs) and financial reporting is adequate. The following questions have been selected to demonstrate the importance of these key areas.

207 Which **TWO** of the following matters should the auditor consider prior to placing reliance on the work of the expert?

☐ The availability of alternative sources of audit evidence

☐ The technical expertise required to perform the valuation

☐ The availability of audit staff to complete the evaluation of the expert on a timely basis

☐ The extent to which the use of the expert can be referred to in the auditor's report

---

208 Which of the following procedures should be performed in relation to the revaluation recorded in the year?

(1) Recalculate the depreciation charge for the year using the updated valuation.

(2) Verify that all the assets in the same class have been revalued in line with IAS 16 *Property, Plant and Equipment.*

(3) Agree the value to the expert's report and recalculate the revaluation adjustment recorded by Gates Co.

(4) Agree that the revaluation surplus has been recorded in the statement of profit or loss.

○ (1), (2) and (3) only

○ (1), (2) and (4) only

○ (3) and (4) only

○ (1), (2), (3) and (4)

---

# Q209–210 September 2017

**7 mins**

## Comments from the examining team (September 2017)

Section A

Section A in the September 2017 examination included, but was not limited to, questions on the following areas:

- The concept of assurance and other assurance engagements

- Substantive testing including testing on trade payables, bank and cash and share capital

- Going concern

- Audit finalisation and the final review; and

- Auditor's reports

The following two questions are reviewed with the aim of giving future candidates an indication of the types of questions asked, guidance on dealing with exam questions and to provide a technical debrief on the topics covered by the specific questions selected. Candidates are reminded that there will be a mix of application and knowledge questions.

209   Which of the following audit procedures will test for the **EXISTENCE** of bank and cash?

○   Review all relevant bank statements to verify that the accounts are held under the company name

○   Attend the cash count at the year end and re-perform the count

○   Agree a sample of accounts detailed in the bank confirmation letter to the trial balance

○   Review the disclosure included in the financial statements to verify only bank accounts as per the bank letter are disclosed

---

210   The company issued 100,000 $1 ordinary shares in August 20X7. This is currently not reflected in the financial statements for the year ended 31 July 20X7.

If no changes are made to the financial statements which of the following audit opinions will be issued?

○   Unmodified opinion as the share issue occurred after the year end

○   Qualified opinion as the financial statements are materially misstated

○   Qualified opinion as the auditor has not gathered sufficient, appropriate evidence in respect of the share issue

○   Unmodified opinion with an Emphasis of Matter paragraph drawing shareholders' attention to the share issue

---

# Q211–212 December 2017

## Comments from the examining team (December 2017)

Section A in the December 2017 examination included, but was not limited to, questions on the following areas:

- Professional ethics and application of ACCA's *Code of Ethics and Conduct*
- Substantive testing including testing on wages and salaries, revenue and tangible assets.
- Subsequent events
- Audit finalisation and the final review; and
- Auditor's reports

The following two questions are reviewed with the aim of giving future candidates an indication of the types of questions asked, guidance on dealing with exam questions and to provide a technical debrief on the topics covered by the specific questions selected. Candidates are reminded that there will be a mix of application and knowledge questions in Section A and it is imperative that they ensure their knowledge of the International Standards on Auditing (ISAs), and important areas of the syllabus such as audit procedures is at an appropriate level. The following questions have been selected to demonstrate the importance of these key areas.

211 Which of the following procedures would **NOT** test for **UNDERSTATEMENT** of the wages accrual in Scarborough Co's statement of financial position?

- ○ Agree the payment of the final week's wages from post year-end bank statements to the accrual listing
- ○ Agree the final week's wage cost from the payroll listing to the accrual listing
- ○ Compare the accrual in the financial statements to the prior year and investigate any significant differences
- ○ Select a sample of employees from the final week's payroll listing and recalculate deductions

---

212 One objective of the final overall review is to ensure that the evidence gathered in the course of the audit supports the audit opinion.

Which **TWO** of the following questions, which are answered as part of the final review, support this objective?

- ☐ Was the audit plan suitably modified to allow for changing circumstances?
- ☐ Has the audit firm's continued independence been considered?
- ☐ Is other information published within the annual report consistent with the financial statements?
- ☐ Has work been performed in accordance with relevant auditing, legal and professional standards?

---

# Q213–214 March 2018

## Comments from the examining team (March 2018)

Section A in the March 2018 examination included but was not limited to, questions on the following areas:

- Professional ethics and application of ACCA's *Code of Ethics and Conduct*
- Substantive testing including testing on non-current assets and inventory
- Written representations
- Audit finalisation and review
- Auditor's reports

The following questions are reviewed with the aim of giving future candidates an indication of the types of questions asked, guidance on dealing with exam questions and to provide a technical debrief on the topics covered by the specific questions selected. Candidates are reminded that there will be a mix of application and knowledge questions in Section A and it is imperative that they ensure their knowledge of the International Standards on Auditing (ISAs), and important areas of the syllabus such as audit procedures is at an appropriate level.

213   Which TWO of the following statements relating to codes of professional ethics are correct?

☐   Codes of professional ethics are prescriptive ethical rules which professional accountants should consider in every situation

☐   A code of professional ethics allows a professional accountant to apply fundamental ethical principles to a given situation

☐   A code of professional ethics encourages professional accountants to think about more than just legal compliance

☐   Compliance with codes of professional ethics is a legal requirement for professional accountants

214   As a starting point for the audit testing of inventory the audit assistant has carried out ratio analysis on the draft financial statements of Well Heeled Co.

Which of the following ratios would be useful in relation to testing inventory?

○   Gross profit margin

○   Quick ratio

○   Current ratio

○   Return on assets

# Q215–216 June 2018

## Comments from the examining team (June 2018)

Section A in the June 2018 examination included, but was not limited to, questions on the following areas:

- Professional ethics and application of ACCA's *Code of Ethics and Conduct*
- The level of assurance provided by review engagements
- Substantive testing including testing on revenue, trade receivables and tangible assets
- Going concern
- Audit finalisation and the final review; and
- Auditor's reports

The following questions are reviewed with the aim of giving future candidates an indication of the types of questions asked, guidance on dealing with exam questions and to provide a technical debrief on the topics covered by the specific questions selected. Candidates are reminded that there will be a mix of application and knowledge questions in Section A and it is imperative that they ensure their knowledge of the International Standards on Auditing (ISAs), and important areas of the syllabus such as audit procedures and going concern is at an appropriate level.

215 Which of the following statements summarise the auditor's responsibilities in relation to going concern?

    (1) Evaluate management's assessment of the entity's ability to continue as a going concern

    (2) Determine whether or not an entity can prepare its financial statements using the going concern basis of accounting

    (3) Remain alert throughout the audit for events or conditions which may cast significant doubt on the entity's ability to continue as a going concern

    (4) Obtain evidence to determine whether a material uncertainty exists if events are identified which may cast doubt on the entity's ability to continue as a going concern

    ○ (1), (3) and (4) only

    ○ (1), (2) and (4) only

    ○ (2) and (3) only

    ○ (1), (2), (3) and (4)

216 Which of the following describes the level of assurance, which will be provided by Red & Co following the review of the five-year profit forecast?

    ○ Limited assurance, positive conclusion

    ○ Reasonable assurance, negative conclusion

    ○ Limited assurance, negative conclusion

    ○ No assurance

# Q217–218 September 2018

## Comments from the examining team (September 2018)

Section A in the September 2018 examinations included, but was not limited to, questions on the following areas:

- Professional ethics and application of ACCA's *Code of Ethics and Conduct*

- Corporate Governance

- Substantive testing including testing on tangible and intangible non-current assets and investments

- Subsequent events

- Audit finalisation and review

- Auditor's reports

The following questions are reviewed with the aim of giving future candidates an indication of the types of questions asked, guidance on dealing with exam questions and to provide a technical debrief on the topics covered by the specific questions selected. Candidates are reminded that there will be a mix of application and knowledge questions in Section A and it is imperative that they ensure their knowledge of the International Standards on Auditing (ISAs), and important areas of the syllabus such as audit procedures is at an appropriate level.

217  Which **TWO** of the following are objectives of the external auditor?

☐ To consider the adequacy of the accounting records which have been maintained

☐ To confirm the company will continue trading for the foreseeable future

☐ To obtain an understanding of the internal control system in place

☐ To access the books and records of the company

---

218  X Co has a year ended 30 June 20X8. At the end of June 20X8 the company's corporate headquarters building was revalued by a reputable firm of surveyors.

Assuming a reliable valuation is obtained, which of the following procedures should be performed to obtain sufficient appropriate substantive evidence about the carrying amount of X Co's corporate headquarters?

(1) Review the board minutes to ensure that the decision to revalue the headquarters was approved by the board.

(2) Agree the revalued amount in the valuation statement to the amount recorded in the non-current asset register.

(3) Recalculate the revaluation adjustment and agree that it is correctly recorded in the revaluation surplus.

(4) Confirm with the directors that all other assets in the same class as the headquarters have been revalued and agree this to the accounting policy disclosure.

○ 2 and 3 only

○ 1, 2 and 3

○ 2, 3 and 4

○ 1 and 4 only

---

# Q219–220 December 2018

## Comments from the examining team (December 2018)

Section A in the December 2018 examination included, but was not limited to, questions on the following areas:

- Professional ethics and application of ACCA's *Code of Ethics and Conduct*

- Corporate governance

- Substantive testing including analytical procedures, revenue, bank and cash and trade payables

- Subsequent events

- Audit finalisation and review

- Auditor's reports

The following questions are reviewed with the aim of giving future candidates an indication of the types of questions asked, guidance on dealing with exam questions and to provide a technical debrief on the topics covered by the specific questions selected. Candidates are reminded that there will be a mix of application and knowledge questions in Section A and it is imperative that they ensure their knowledge of the International Standards on Auditing (ISAs), relevant financial accounting and important areas of the syllabus such as audit procedures is at an appropriate level.

219     Which of the following details should be disclosed in respect of the revaluation of the head office if the auditor is to conclude that the disclosures are adequate?

      (1)     Effective date of the revaluation

      (2)     Name of the valuer

      (3)     The amount of the revaluation increase

      (4)     Carrying amount of the head office under the cost model

      O     1, 2 and 3 only

      O     1, 3 and 4 only

      O     2, 3 and 4 only

      O     1, 2, 3 and 4

220     All adjustments required by the auditors of X Co have been made to the financial statements with the exception of an adjustment relating to faulty goods held in inventory at the year end. The audit work concluded that the cost of this inventory exceeded its net realisable value by $2.9m. The directors dispute the audit team's figures and believe that the realisable value of the inventory still exceeds its cost. Profit before tax for the year was $131.4m.

      Which of the following correctly describes the effect of this matter on the auditor's report?

      O     Unmodified opinion with no further disclosure

      O     Unmodified opinion with disclosure in an emphasis of matter paragraph

      O     Qualified opinion due to material misstatement

      O     Qualified opinion due to inability to obtain sufficient appropriate audit evidence

### Comments from the examining team (March 2019)

Section A in the March 2019 examination included, but was not limited to, questions on the following areas:

- Concepts of assurance
- Professional ethics and application of ACCA's *Code of Ethics and Conduct*
- Substantive testing including analytical procedures, revenue, expenses, PPE and estimates
- Written representations
- Auditor's reports

The following questions are reviewed with the aim of giving future candidates an indication of the types of questions asked, guidance on dealing with exam questions and to provide a technical debrief on the topics covered by the specific questions selected. Candidates are reminded that there will be a mix of application and knowledge questions in Section A and it is imperative that they ensure their knowledge of the International Standards on Auditing (ISAs), relevant financial accounting and important areas of the syllabus such as auditor's reports is at an appropriate level. Recent Examiner's reports have noted that performance on knowledge questions was poor and this continued to be the case in March 2019. Questions may test specific details of an ISA, therefore candidates must ensure that they have studied the ISAs in sufficient depth.

221 Which of the following must be included in an unmodified auditor's report?

(1) A statement that the auditor believes the audit evidence obtained is sufficient and appropriate

(2) Title indicating the report is that of the independent auditor

(3) Description of the meaning of materiality

(4) A statement that the auditor is independent of the entity and has fulfilled their ethical responsibilities

○ 1, 2 and 3 only

○ 1 and 3 only

○ 2 and 4 only

○ 1, 2, 3 and 4

---

222 The auditors have discovered that the chairman's report of XYZ Co, a listed company, is inconsistent with the financial statements and it has been determined that the material inconsistency is in the chairman's report.

Complete the following sentence by dragging and dropping the appropriate audit opinion and type of communication in the auditor's report.

If the directors refuse to amend the inconsistency, then the auditor's opinion will be [          ] and the inconsistency will be explained in a [          ]

| Auditor's opinion | Inconsistency explained in |
|---|---|
| Unmodified | Other matters paragraph |
| Qualified on the grounds of a material misstatement | Other information section |
| Qualified on the grounds of an inability to obtain sufficient appropriate audit evidence | Emphasis of matter paragraph |
| Adverse | Key audit matters section |
| Disclaimer of opinion | |

# Q223–224 June 2019

**7 mins**

### Comments from the examining team (June 2019)

Section A in the June 2019 examination included, but was not limited to, questions on the following areas:

- Corporate governance

- Substantive procedures including analytical procedures, revenue, expenses, bank and cash and share capital

- Written representations

- Going concern

- Subsequent events

- Auditor's reports

The following questions are reviewed with the aim of giving future candidates an indication of the types of questions asked, guidance on dealing with exam questions and to provide a technical debrief on the topics covered by the specific questions selected. Candidates are reminded that there will be a mix of application and knowledge questions in Section A and it is imperative that they ensure their knowledge of the International Standards on Auditing (ISAs), relevant financial accounting and important areas of the syllabus such as auditor's reports is at an appropriate level. Recent Examiner's reports have noted that performance on knowledge questions was poor and this continued to be the case in June 2019. Questions may test specific details of examinable documents including ISAs, ACCA's *Code of Ethics and Conduct* and the Corporate Governance Code, therefore candidates must ensure that they have studied these in sufficient depth.

223 X Co is a listed company and has an audit committee.

Identify, by clicking on the relevant box in the table below, whether each of the following statements is true or false.

| | | |
|---|---|---|
| The audit committee's terms of reference should include reviewing and monitoring the external auditor's independence and objectivity | TRUE | FALSE |
| The audit committee's terms of reference should include appointing and removing the external auditors | TRUE | FALSE |
| The audit committee's terms of reference should include evaluating and monitoring the effectiveness of the internal audit function | TRUE | FALSE |

224 A & Co is the auditor of Z Co for the year ended 31 December 20X8. The detailed audit work is due to be completed by 30 June 20X9. The directors are planning to approve the financial statements on 31 July 20X9 and then issue them to the shareholders on 15 August 20X9. The management of Z Co has performed an assessment of the company's ability to continue as a going concern based on a cash flow forecast prepared to 31 December 20X9.

Complete the following sentence by dragging and dropping the appropriate date.

A & Co's evaluation of management's assessment of Z Co's ability to continue as a going concern must cover the period up to [          ] .

| Dates |
|---|
| 30 June 20X9 |
| 31 July 20X9 |
| 15 August 20X9 |
| 31 December 20X9 |

# Q225–226 September 2019

## Comments from the examining team (September 2019)

It was very pleasing to see that once again almost all candidates attempted all 15 questions, across the three OT cases. Candidates preparing for future sessions are advised to work through the past exams which are available and to carefully review how each of the correct answers were derived. Section A questions aim to provide a broad coverage of the syllabus, and future candidates should aim to revise all areas of the Audit and Assurance syllabus, rather than attempting to question spot.

Section A in the September 2019 examination included, but was not limited to, questions on the following areas:

- Professional ethics and application of ACCA's Code of Ethics and Conduct
- Substantive procedures including bank and cash, share capital and inventory
- Audit finalisation and review
- Auditor's reports

The following questions are reviewed with the aim of giving future candidates an indication of the types of questions asked, guidance on dealing with exam questions and to provide a technical debrief on the topics covered by the specific questions selected. Candidates are reminded that there will be a mix of application and knowledge questions in Section A and it is imperative that they ensure their knowledge of the International Standards on Auditing (ISAs), relevant financial accounting and important areas of the syllabus such as auditors' reports is at an appropriate level. Questions may test specific details of examinable documents including ISAs, ACCA's *Code of Ethics and Conduct* and the Corporate Governance Code, therefore candidates must ensure that they have studied these in sufficient depth. Candidates must also ensure that they have studied all areas of the syllabus. The syllabus includes audit evidence learning outcomes relating to a wide range of specific items, any of which may be examined.

225 You have been assigned to the audit of bank and cash for X Co. X Co has a number of bank accounts and due to the nature of its business will hold a significant amount of cash at head office at the year end.

Which of the following audit procedures included in the audit programme will test for EXISTENCE of bank and cash?

○ Agree a sample of accounts detailed on the bank confirmation letters to the trial balance

○ Review all relevant bank statements to verify that the accounts are held under X Co

○ Attend the cash count at the year end and reperform the count

○ Review the disclosure included in the financial statements to verify only bank accounts per the bank letters are disclosed

226 One objective of the final overall review stage of the audit is to ensure that the evidence gathered in the course of the audit supports the audit opinion.

Which of the following questions, which are answered as part of the final review, support this objective?

(1) Was the audit plan suitably modified to allow for changing circumstances?

(2) Has the audit firm's continued independence been considered?

(3) Have all deficiencies in internal control been communicated to management?

(4) Has work been performed in accordance with relevant auditing, legal and professional standards?

○ 1 and 4

○ 1 and 2

○ 2 and 3

○ 3 and 4

# Q227–228 December 2019

## Comments from the examining team (December 2019)

Section A It was very pleasing to see that once again almost all candidates attempted all 15 questions, across the three OT cases. Candidates preparing for future sessions are advised to work through the past exams which are available and to carefully review how each of the correct answers were derived. Section A questions aim to provide a broad coverage of the syllabus, and future candidates should aim to revise all areas of the Audit and Assurance syllabus, rather than attempting to question spot. Section A in the December 2019 examination included, but was not limited to, questions on the following areas:

- Principles of assurance
- Corporate Governance
- Substantive procedures including non-current assets
- Audit finalisation and review

227 You are an audit manager working for W & Co which has audited X Co for the last seven years. The board has decided that X Co should be listed on a stock exchange and the board has asked W & Co to advise the company on how to become compliant with corporate governance guidelines.

Which of the following are typical requirements contained within best practice corporate governance guidelines?

(1) The remuneration committee should only consist of independent non-executive directors

(2) The chief executive officer should be responsible for leadership of the board and ensuring its effectiveness

(3) The non-executive directors should provide constructive challenge and strategic guidance

(4) The audit committee's key role is appointing and liaising with the external auditor

- O   1 and 3 only
- O   2 and 4 only
- O   1, 3 and 4
- O   2, 3 and 4

228 It is 1 July 20X5. You are an audit supervisor of Y & Co and have been assigned responsibility for completing the detailed going concern testing for Z Co for the year ended 30 April 20X5. Z Co's audit should be finalised and the financial statements signed by 30 September 20X5. Management's assessment of Z Co's ability to continue as a going concern covers the period to 30 November 20X5.

Which of the following actions should Y & Co take in relation to Z Co's going concern assessment?

- O   Request that management extends the assessment period to 30 September 20X6
- O   Request that management extends the assessment period to 30 April 20X6
- O   Perform additional audit procedures to confirm Z Co's going concern status
- O   Review management's assessment to 30 November 20X5 and only request that it is extended if it raises doubt that Z Co is a going concern

# Q229–230 March 2020

**Comments from the examining team (March 2020)**

It was very pleasing to see that once again almost all candidates attempted all 15 questions, across the three OT cases. Candidates preparing for future sessions are advised to work through the past exams which are available and to carefully review how each of the correct answers were derived. Section A questions aim to provide a broad coverage of the syllabus, and future candidates should aim to revise all areas of the AA syllabus, rather than attempting to question spot.

Section A in the March 2020 examination included, but was not limited to, questions on the following areas:

- Professional ethics and application of ACCA's Code of Ethics and Conduct
- Substantive procedures including payables and inventory
- Audit finalisation and review
- Auditor's reports

229  Which **TWO** of the following statements should be included in a written representation letter?

☐  All transactions have been recorded in the accounting records and are reflected in the financial statements

☐  Due to inherent limitations of the audit, there is a risk that some material misstatements will not be detected

☐  Professional judgement and scepticism have been exercised throughout the course of the audit

☐  Significant assumptions used in making accounting estimates are reasonable

230  It is 1 July 20X5. You are an audit manager at X & Co, currently finalising the audit of Y Co for the year ended 31 March 20X5. You are performing the final review in preparation for signing the auditor's report. During the year one of the company's properties was revalued by an independent expert valuer.

Which **TWO** of the following are audit procedures X & Co should perform in conducting its overall review of the financial statements of Y Co?

☐  Make an assessment of Y Co's ability to continue as a going concern

☐  Design and perform analytical procedures to confirm the financial statements are consistent with the auditor's understanding of the entity

☐  Undertake money laundering identification procedures to reconfirm the identity of the directors of Y Co

☐  Assess the information obtained from the external expert in respect of the property revaluation

☐  Obtain and retain documentation to confirm the legal title of all non-current assets

☐  Reassess materiality to confirm whether it remains appropriate in the context of Y Co's final financial statements

## Comments from the examining team (July 2020)

It was very pleasing to see that once again almost all candidates attempted all 15 questions, across the three OT cases. Candidates preparing for future sessions are advised to work through the past exams which are available and to carefully review how each of the correct answers were derived. Section A questions aim to provide a broad coverage of the syllabus, and future candidates should aim to revise all areas of the AA syllabus, rather than attempting to question spot.

Section A in the July 2020 examination included, but was not limited to, questions on the following areas:

- Principles of assurance
- Substantive procedures including non-current assets, provisions and contingencies
- Going concern
- Auditors' reports

231 It is 1 July 20X5. You are an audit supervisor and are conducting the year-end audit of X Co. You are currently undertaking the audit testing in relation to non-current assets.

Which **TWO** of the following procedures would provide substantive audit evidence in respect of the **COMPLETENESS** assertion for plant and machinery?

☐ For a sample of assets held in the factory and warehouse record the asset identity number as marked on the asset and trace back to the relevant entry in the non-current asset register

☐ Review board minutes to confirm that all major items of capital expenditure are noted and have been authorised

☐ Trace a sample of costs recognised in the repairs and maintenance account to invoices and determine the nature of the expenditure and assess whether any capital items have been expensed

☐ For a sample of fully depreciated assets, enquire with management to confirm whether the assets are still being used in the operations of X Co

232 It is 1 July 20X5. A & Co are the external auditors of B Co for the year ended 31 March 20X5. B Co has sourced external finance for the first time during the year. The draft financial statements show non-current liabilities in relation to loan finance of $1.2m.

Which of the following procedures should be performed to confirm the loan liability balance at the year end?

(1) Review directors' board minutes for evidence of approval of the external finance

(2) Agree the loan payments recorded in the general ledger to the bank statement to confirm capital has been repaid

(3) Agree the year-end loan liability balance to the bank confirmation letter

(4) Compare loan liabilities at the end of the year to balances in the previous year

O 1 and 2

O 3 and 4 only

O 1, 3 and 4

O 2 and 3

# Answers

# BJM Co

1   The correct answer is: The external audit is an exercise carried out by auditors in order to give an opinion on whether the financial statements of a company are fairly presented.

The external audit is carried out by external auditors, who are independent of the company so that they can provide an independent opinion on whether the company's financial statements are prepared, in all material respects, in accordance with an applicable financial reporting framework. The principal aim of the audit is not in relation to the control system in place or to identify other areas of deficiency, although deficiencies and recommendations may be suggested by the external auditors as a by-product of the external audit in a report to management at the conclusion of the audit.

2   The correct answer is: YHT & Co should perform specific audit procedures to identify possible non-compliance.

ISA 250 (Revised) distinguishes between regulations which have a direct effect on the financial statements (in the sense of directly affecting the determination of balances) and those which do not have a direct effect but can still have a material effect (such as an operating licence).

The hygiene regulations do not have a direct effect but they may have a material effect. The external auditor must therefore perform audit procedures to help identify any non-compliance which might have a material effect on the financial statements, ie any breaches of the hygiene regulations that could result in material fines or restaurant closures.

3   The correct answer is: The determination of materiality

This review engagement is an example of an assurance engagement. There are five elements to an assurance engagement: criteria, report, evidence, subject matter and three-party relationship (CREST) (IFAC, 2016).

4   The correct answer is: Limited; Negative.

A review engagement, such as a review of compliance with hygiene regulations, is an assurance engagement where the practitioner carries out limited procedures on BJM's internal controls relating to hygiene compliance.

As the procedures are limited, the practitioner will gain only enough evidence to provide a negative expression of opinion. This means the practitioner gives assurance that nothing has come to their attention which indicates that BJM's internal controls relating to hygiene compliance are not, in all material respects, compliant with national regulation.

5   The correct answer is: The lucrative nature of the review engagement may make the external audit team less inclined to require management to make adjustments or to issue a modified audit opinion, for fear of losing the review engagement.

The fees from the review engagement are likely to be very lucrative, so there is a risk that YHT & Co will not seek adjustments during the external audit process for fear of upsetting the board of BJM and losing the review engagement work.

The provision of non-audit services to unlisted audit clients is not specifically prohibited. While YHT & Co should be alert to self-review threats, in this case it seems unlikely: the scenario states that the review engagement does not include the provision of accounting advice or the preparation of figures in the financial statements. A firm is not required to turn down work when a 15% limit is exceeded. Where fee income from a listed audit client is expected to exceed 15% of the audit firm's total fee revenue, this fact should be disclosed to those charged with governance and a separate review may be required (ACCA *Code of Ethics and Conduct*: para. R410.4-6). However, the 15% fee cap is not a major concern to YHT & Co in this instance because BJM is unlisted.

# Conoy

6    The correct answers are:

direction, supervision, performance and review; may be performed, but is not mandatory.

The engagement partner is responsible for the direction, supervision, performance and review of the audit, but this does not mean that they are the only individual involved in discharging their responsibilities. The partner directs the audit. The partner will supervise and review some of the audit directly, but some of this role is likely to be delegated to senior members of the audit team. The partner is likely to delegate all or almost all of the performance of the audit to the audit team.

Regarding the question of a quality review of the Conoy audit, since Conoy is not listed such a review is not required as such. Instead, it would only be a requirement where the auditor determines that it is necessary. In relation to the final option, the audit should not be accepted if ethical requirements are not complied with, although it is the case that detecting ethical breaches may form part of a quality review (in order to ensure that the audit complies with professional and regulatory standards).

7    The correct answer is:

|  | Strength | Deficiency |
|---|---|---|
| The audit team as a whole takes collective responsibility for the audit. | ☐ | ☑ |
| At the audit planning meeting, Karolina Hernandez emphasised that each member of the audit team is required exercise professional scepticism through the Conoy audit. | ☑ | ☐ |
| Karolina Hernandez is scheduled to review the formal written communications to be sent to Conoy's management after the date of the auditor's report. | ☑ | ☐ |

The audit team does not bear collective responsibility for the audit. Rather, ultimate responsibility rests with the audit engagement partner, Karolina Hernandez, who must then ensure that the audit team conducts the engagement in accordance with ISAs.

It is a strength of the quality management of the Conoy audit that Karolina Hernandez emphasised the need for the team to exercise professional scepticism. As the engagement partner, she is ultimately responsible for the audit, and by directing the team in this way she is helping to discharge this responsibility appropriately.

Finally, it is also a strength that the engagement partner is scheduled to review the communications with management after the date of the auditor's report. This is the normal time for such communications to be made, and it is encouraging that there is a schedule for making them.

8    The correct answer is:

| Proposed member | Include in audit committee | Do not include in audit committee |
|---|---|---|
| Adrian Muse | | X |
| Penny Dinty | | X |
| Sharon Header | X | |
| Fredrick Rowe | X | |

The audit committee has a monitoring role and should therefore comprise at least three independent non-executive directors, one of whom should have relevant financial expertise.

Adrian Muse is the chief internal auditor and so should not be part of the audit committee because he manages the team that will report to the audit committee.

Whilst Penny Dinty has some financial experience, she is already an executive director and so should not be a member of the audit committee as well.

The two new non-executive directors should be appointed to the audit committee provided that they are sufficiently independent and have the relevant skills.

9    The correct answer is: The audit committee will have at least one member who has relevant financial experience, so that they can monitor the integrity of the financial statements.

Conoy's finance director has left and had not yet been replaced. It appears that no one else has appropriate financial reporting knowledge required by Conoy. The audit committee should contain at least one member who has financial experience so that they can monitor the integrity of the financial statements. This may give the bank the confidence it needs before it lends Conoy the money.

Guaranteeing the loan or standing in as interim finance director are not acceptable options, as that will impair the independence of the audit committee.

Substantiating evidence for information used in financial reporting is a function of internal audit, not the audit committee.

10   The correct answer is:

| | True | False |
|---|---|---|
| A key drawback of data analytics software is that it is difficult to tailor to each particular audit client | ☐ | ☑ |
| Data analytics routines enable auditors to examine complex data using simple visualisation techniques | ☑ | ☐ |
| Although powerful, data analytics routines must be applied to strictly limited quantities of data so as to extrapolate correctly from a sample | ☐ | ☑ |

A key advantage of data analytics routines over the older CAATs is precisely that they do not require significant tailoring time – they are standardised and may be applied quickly.

Another advantage of data analytics is that they can be applied to large quantities of data – there is no need to restrict the amount of data they are applied to.

# Stark

11   The correct answer is:

| Advocacy | Intimidation | Self-interest |
|---|---|---|
| (4) only | (3) only | (2) and (3) |

Including Mr Day's daughter, Zoe, is unusual but should not raise any significant risks to the audit.

The gift of the balloon flight represents a self-interest threat.

The tax fee represents a self-interest threat as Ali & Co will want to save as much tax as possible in order to charge as high a tax fee as possible. There is also an intimidation threat created by the request as the finance director may make Ali & Co feel that it has to accept the method of calculating tax fees in order to keep Stark as a tax client.

The fact that Stark expects Ali & Co to represent it in a dispute with the tax authorities creates an advocacy threat to audit independence.

12   The correct answer is: The gift should only be accepted if its value is trivial and inconsequential to the recipients

Gifts and hospitality should only be accepted where the value is trivial and inconsequential. In this case it is likely that the value of the gift is too high, so the balloon flight should be declined.

13  The correct answer is: The audit engagement partner should be removed from the audit team.

Stark is a public interest entity, so the audit engagement partner should only remain on the audit team for a maximum of seven years before being rotated. It would also be beneficial for an independent engagement review partner to be appointed but Mr Day should not take on this role as, following rotation, he should have no involvement with the audit client for a 'cooling off' period of five years (ACCA *Code of Ethics and Conduct*: para. R540.11).

14  The correct answer is: 4, 5, 1, 2, 3

This is the process by which the IAASB develops new standards.

15  The correct answer is: Auditors may disclose matters to third parties without their client's consent if it is in the public interest, and they must do so if there is a statutory duty to do so.

There is no blanket prohibition on disclosure, nor is there any general right of the police or taxation authorities to demand information. Auditors have an implied contractual duty of confidentiality. There is no statutory duty of confidentiality.

# Tangerine Tech Co

16  The correct answer is: 1 and 3 only

The board as a whole should take on the responsibility for liaising with shareholders, not just the chairman. (The board should state in the annual report the steps it has taken to ensure that the members of the board, and in particular the non-executive directors, develop an understanding of the views of the major shareholders about the company) (FRC *UK Corporate Governance Code*: Introduction).

As the chairman and one of the NEDs are former executive directors they were previously employed by the company and as a result this raises questions about their independence. Independent non-executive directors should be appointed to the board of Tangerine.

Tangerine is not required to have an internal audit function (however, where there is no internal audit function, the audit committee is required annually to consider the need for one).

17  The correct answer is:

| Deficiency 1 | Deficiency 2 |
|---|---|
| The directors should be subject to annual re-election | At least 50% of the board, excluding the Chair, must be comprised of non-executive directors whom the board considers to be independent |

The directors should be subject to annual re-election by the shareholders (FRC *UK Corporate Governance Code*: para. 18). They are re-elected by the shareholders, not the chairman.

There should be an appropriate balance of executives and NEDs to ensure that the board makes the correct objective decisions. At least half of the board, excluding the Chair, should be comprised of NEDs whom the board considers to be independent (FRC *UK Corporate Governance Code*: para. 11).

18  The correct answer is: 2 only

The audit committee is supposed to be made up of independent NEDs. The chairman should not be a member of the audit committee (FRC *UK Corporate Governance Code*: para. 24).

All four members of the audit committee were previously involved in sales and production related roles. At least one member of the audit committee should have recent and relevant financial experience. (FRC *UK Corporate Governance Code*: para. 24)

19     The correct answer is:

| To review internal controls annually | To report on internal controls to shareholders |
| --- | --- |
| Yes | Yes |

The directors are responsible for implementing and monitoring the company's system of internal control. An annual assessment of internal control should be conducted to confirm that the board has considered all significant aspects of internal control. The directors should report on its review as part of the annual report. (FRC *UK Corporate Governance Code*: para. 29)

20     The correct answer is: 1 and 3 only

The board is responsible for a company's internal control. The establishment of an internal audit function is one of the practical ways in which the board can meet its responsibility to monitor and review internal controls. However, as with all key decisions, costs versus benefits will be assessed too.

The directors are responsible for the prevention and detection of fraud. Whilst the internal audit function may assist the directors in this, the directors retain the ultimate responsibility.

# LV Fones

21     The correct answer is:

Self-interest: 1, 3 and 4

Self-review: 2 only

The audit team have previously been offered a 10% discount on luxury phones from LV Fones (LV) which will potentially have a high value. As only goods with a trivial and inconsequential value can be received, if the same discount is again offered, it will constitute a self-interest threat.

The fee income from LV is 16% of Jones & Co's total fees. If, after accounting for non-recurring fees such as the secondment, it remains at this percentage of total fees on a recurring basis there is likely to be a self-interest threat because of undue dependence on this client.

The overdue fees (60% of the total fee) may be perceived as a loan which is prohibited, but may also create a self-interest threat. This is because Jones & Co may be less robust than it should be when it disagrees with management out of fear it may not recover the fees.

The audit senior probably prepared a significant proportion of the records to be audited; this creates a self-review threat as he will review his own work during the audit.

22     The correct answer is:

Threats: Familiarity and self-interest

Safeguards: Rotation of audit partner

The partner and finance director of LV have been on holiday together and appear to have a longstanding close relationship. This results in a familiarity and self-interest threat. Both are senior in their respective organisation and any onlooker would perceive independence to be threatened. The audit firm does not need to resign but the partner should no longer be involved in the audit.

23    The correct answer is: Unless the value of the discount is trivial and inconsequential to the
      audit team members, the offer should be declined.

|  | True | False |
|---|---|---|
| The audit team can accept the discount as it is on the same terms as that offered to staff | ☐ | ☑ |
| Junior members of the audit team are allowed to accept the discount, but the audit manager and audit partner should not | ☐ | ☑ |
| Unless the value of the discount is trivial and inconsequential to the audit team members, the offer should be declined | ☑ | ☐ |
| The audit team is only allowed to accept a discount of up to 5% | ☐ | ☑ |

The ACCA *Code of Ethics and Conduct* states that unless the value of a gift is trivial and
inconsequential it should be declined. 10% of the value of a smartphone is unlikely to be
trivial and inconsequential. (ACCA *Code of Ethics and Conduct*: para. R420.3)

24    The correct answer is: 2 and 3

For the audit of a public interest entity (which includes listed companies), where total fees
from the client exceed more than 15% of the firm's total fees for 2 consecutive years, the
auditor must disclose this to those charged with governance and arrange for a review to be
conducted (either pre-issuance or post-issuance). Provided these mandatory safeguards are
applied the firm is not required to resign from the audit (ACCA *Code of Ethics and Conduct*:
para. R410.4-6).

25    The correct answer is:

|  | Service can be provided | Service cannot be provided |
|---|---|---|
| Design and implementation of IT systems over financial reporting | | X |
| Assistance with preparation of tax return | X | |
| Accounting services | | X |
| Recruiting service for the position of credit controller | X | |

In general terms audit firms can provide other services provided that the firm does not
assume a management responsibility. The provision of certain services is deemed to create
such a threat to independence that safeguards will not be adequate to reduce this to an
acceptable level. Additional restrictions will apply to LV as it is a public interest entity. The
provision of IT services re accounting systems and accounting services cannot be made to
LV, as these services have a direct impact on the financial statements that would be audited.
Assistance with preparation of a tax return would be allowed as it is generally based on
historical information. Provision of the recruitment service would be possible in this instance
as the role is for a credit controller. The recruitment of senior management would be
prohibited.

# Orange

26    The correct answer is:

|     |                                                                                                      | Yes | No |
|-----|------------------------------------------------------------------------------------------------------|-----|-----|
| (1) | The engagement partner has been asked to attend meetings with potential investors.                   | X   |     |
| (2) | Currant & Co has been offered the opportunity to provide other services to Orange Financials.        |     | X   |
| (3) | Currant & Co has been asked to produce the financial statements of Orange Financials.                |     | X   |
| (4) | There is a suggestion that a partner who previously worked for Orange Financials should be the review partner. |     | X   |

Risk (1) represents an advocacy threat as this may be interpreted as the audit firm promoting investment in Orange Financials Co.

Risk (2) Currant & Co would like to conduct other assignments for Orange Financials Co.

This gives rise to a potential self-interest threat as the total fees generated from this client may form a substantial proportion of the fees of the firm which may have an impact on the firm's objectivity.

Risk (3) Currant & Co have been asked to produce the financial statements of Orange Financials Co.

This represents a possible self-review threat as Currant & Co would be both preparing and auditing the same information.

Risk (4) The assistant finance director of Orange Financials Co has joined Currant & Co as a partner and it has been suggested that he should be the independent review partner.

This represents a self-review threat as the same individual would be responsible for reviewing the audit of financial statements which he has been involved in preparing.

27    The correct answers are: Intimidation and self-interest

This gives rise to an intimidation threat as the audit team may feel under pressure not to perform a thorough audit in order to comply with this request. There is also a self-interest threat as Currant & Co will be keen to win the additional work.

28    The correct answers are: (1) Not accepted (2) Not accepted

As the value of the hospitality is unlikely to be inconsequential no safeguards would be adequate to reduce the threat to an acceptable level. The offer of the weekend away should be declined politely.

If the loan had been made at normal commercial rates then the senior would be able to accept without any consequences for independence.

In this case as the terms are preferential the loan must be declined.

29    The correct answer is: Total fees from Orange Financials Co makes up more than 15% of Currant & Co's total fees for the second consecutive year.

The mandatory safeguards apply to public interest entity audits therefore would be applied to the audit of Orange Financials Co when it is listed.

30    The correct answer is:

| | True | False |
|---|---|---|
| The audit committee should be made up of independent non-executive directors | X | |
| The audit committee normally appoints the external auditors at the AGM | | X |
| The audit committee monitors and reviews the internal audit function | X | |
| The audit committee sets out the scope of the external auditor's work | | X |

The audit committee makes recommendations about the appointment of external auditors but the shareholders are responsible for appointing them at the AGM.

The scope of the external auditor's work is determined by the audit engagement partner on the basis of the requirements of auditing standards. The scope of the audit may be discussed with the audit committee but the audit committee does not set out the scope of the work as the audit must be an independent exercise.

# SGCC

31    The correct answer is:

SGCC should appoint a new chief executive officer or board chairman.

Corporate governance codes indicate that there should be a clear division of responsibilities between running the board of directors and running the company's business so that no individual has unfettered powers of decision (FRC *UK Corporate Governance Code:* Principle G).

32    The correct answer is:

SGCC should appoint three new non-executive directors to the board.

Corporate governance codes indicate that the board should have a balance of executive and non-executive directors. SGCC currently has five executive and two non-executive directors and should therefore appoint a further three non-executive directors in order to balance the board. This is so that at least half the board, excluding the Chair, will be non-executive directors whom the board considers to be independent (FRC *UK Corporate Governance Code:* para. 11).

33    The correct answers are:

Once SGCC has an audit committee and an internal audit department, the head of the internal audit department should report to the audit committee.

SGCC should not rely on the external audit to inform them of deficiencies in internal controls.

SGCC should establish an audit committee with at least three independent non-executive directors (FRC *UK Corporate Governance Code:* para. 24).

Listed companies should review the need for an internal audit department at least annually. They are not automatically required to have an internal audit department (FRC *UK Corporate Governance Code:* para. 25).

34    The correct answer is:

Taking responsibility for the implementation of a new sales ledger system

The internal audit function is a review and monitoring function. It should not take operational responsibility for any part of the accounting or information systems.

35    The correct answer is:

| Consideration | | Employed | Outsourced |
|---|---|---|---|
| (1) | Greater availability of specialist industry skills as required | | X |
| (2) | Flexibility regarding staff numbers in response to changing circumstances | | X |
| (3) | Elimination of direct training costs | | X |
| (4) | Development of skills increasing the human resource strength of the entity | X | |

Where the internal audit department is outsourced to an external firm, SGCC is likely to benefit from specialist industry skills and will benefit from the greater flexibility in staffing numbers as the team can be modified depending on the workload at a particular point in time. SGCC will also be shielded from the direct costs of training staff. However, if the staff are employed by SGCC, this increases the skills held within the business and therefore increases the value of the workforce which is a strength of the company.

# Bridgford

36    The correct answer is:

| Area | | Audit strategy document | Detailed audit plan |
|---|---|---|---|
| (1) | The availability of the client's data and staff (including internal audit) | X | |
| (2) | The allocation of responsibility for specific audit procedures to audit team members | | X |
| (3) | The audit procedures to be undertaken for each area of the financial statements | | X |
| (4) | The potential for using automated tools and techniques to gather evidence | X | |

The audit strategy includes areas such as identifying the characteristics of the engagement, the reporting objectives, timing and nature of communications, knowledge gained from previous audits and during the preliminary risk assessments and the nature, timing and extent of resources in terms of using appropriate personnel.

The availability of the client's data and staff (including internal audit) and the potential for using CAATs are included in the characteristics of the engagement.

The auditor will take the overall audit strategy and convert it into a more detailed audit plan. This will include the allocation of work to audit team members and the audit procedures to be undertaken for each area of the financial statements.

37    The correct answer is:

Performance materiality refers to the amounts set by the auditor at higher than the materiality level for particular classes of transactions, account balances or disclosures where the materiality level might otherwise mean that such items are not tested.

The auditor sets performance materiality at an amount which is lower than the materiality level for the financial statements as a whole. This is so that the impact of misstatements for particular classes of transactions, account balances or disclosures will be considered even if they are not material to the financial statements as a whole (ISA 320).

38 The correct answer is:

Perform a trend analysis on current year and prior year monthly revenue, to identify whether revenue is overstated as a result of fraud or error

An overstatement of revenue would result in a reduction, not an increase in the receivables collection period.

39 The correct answer is:

That the financial statements include balances due from credit customers which are not recoverable

The audit risk relates to the concern about receivables taking 127 days to settle their invoices rather than the permitted 90 days (3-month credit terms), and that some customers are refusing to pay for products due to the reliability issues encountered. This means that the financial statements may include balances from receivables that are not recoverable. This would result in an overstatement of assets, and gives rise to concerns about the valuation of receivables.

Despite the worsening working capital position indicated by the increase in the receivables collection period, on its own it is unlikely to give rise to doubts over Bridgford's going concern status.

40 The correct answers are:

Determine how often inventory counts are performed and the level of corrections required to the inventory system

Test the operation of the inventory system using CAATs

The risk which has been identified relates to inventory quantities. Testing the operation of the inventory system using CAATs and reviewing the level of corrections required to the system would provide evidence regarding the operation of the system used to record the number of units of inventory held.

Reviewing purchase requisitions is a test to determine whether authorisation controls are in place to prevent orders of unnecessary items. The comparison of cost and net realisable value is a valid audit procedure; however it provides evidence regarding the valuation of inventory rather than quantity.

# EuKaRe

41 The correct answer is:

| | | |
|---|---|---|
| Detection risk will increase due to the increased risk of cash donations being misappropriated and revenue being overstated | | X |
| Inherent risk will increase as the nature of EuKaRe's transactions means that income may be misstated either in error or deliberately. | X | |
| Control risk will increase as internal controls may be weak due to the large number of volunteers used by EuKaRe | | X |
| Business risk will increase due to the level of volunteers used by EuKaRe | | X |

Inherent risk is the risk that an item will be misstated due to the characteristics of that item. High levels of income in the form of cash increase the risk that income may be misstated either in error or deliberately. In addition, there may be no other independent source to show what the income should be. For example in this instance there would not be any formal record to support the majority of the takings (eg invoice or receipt) collected in the buckets.

Detection risk is the risk that the auditor's substantive procedures will not detect material misstatements. This is likely to increase but the principal risk is of revenue being understated (since some of it may be stolen / misappropriated).

Control risk is the risk that EuKaRe's internal controls will not prevent or detect misstatements. However the explanation states that this will be high due to the reliance on volunteers rather than due to transactions being in the form of cash.

Business risk is the risk that the business will not achieve its objectives and is not an element of audit risk.

42 The correct answer is:

|  | True | False |
| --- | --- | --- |
| The risk assessment will help the audit team gain an understanding of the entity for audit purposes | ☑ | ☐ |
| The risk assessment will enable the audit senior to produce an accurate budget for the audit assignment | ☐ | ☑ |
| The risk assessment will form the basis of the audit strategy and the detailed audit plan | ☑ | ☐ |
| Once the risks have been assessed, TEY & Co can select audit team members with sufficient skill and experience to maximise the chance of those risks being addressed | ☑ | ☐ |

Whilst an audit firm is a commercial and profit-making organisation, ISA 315 is not concerned with the auditor's budget but rather with ensuring that the auditor has a sufficient understanding of the business. This is so that they can select appropriate audit procedures in order to minimise the risk of undetected material misstatements.

43 The correct answer is:

Obtain a breakdown of the income recorded from the cash that was collected in buckets, and vouch a sample of entries back to the volunteer in order to determine which volunteer collected the relevant donations

This will provide evidence of the occurrence of income, but the key risk here is completeness of income.

44 The correct answer is:

The auditor is not responsible for the **prevention** of fraud or error. However, they are responsible for obtaining **reasonable assurance** that the financial statements are free from material misstatement whether caused by fraud or error. (ISA 240).

The directors, or rather here the trustees, are ultimately responsible for the prevention and detection of fraud and error within EuKaRe. The auditor needs to obtain reasonable assurance that the financial statements are not materially misstated due to fraud or error.

45 The correct answers are:

EuKaRe's finance department relies on volunteers who may not have accounts experience.

Understaffing in the finance department at certain times is due to the ad hoc nature of volunteer working hours.

The fact that EuKaRe has a detailed constitution which explains how the charity's income can be spent is a positive influence on the control environment, as it indicates that there is a benchmark in place against which the suitability of EuKaRe's expenditure can be measured.

The fact that the income of EuKaRe is primarily cash increases inherent risk but does not automatically mean that the control environment is weak.

# South

46 The correct answers are: To ensure appropriate attention is devoted to important areas of the audit; To assist in the co-ordination of work done by any auditor's experts.

The main aim of planning is not to ensure the audit is completed within budget restraints, but to ensure that it is carried out in an effective manner as described by the other statements (ISA 300).

The determination of whether the audit engagement is ethically acceptable should have been done before the planning stage, and is not therefore an objective of planning.

47 The correct answer is:

| Procedure | Assertion |
|---|---|
| Review financial statement notes | Presentation |
| Read minutes of board meetings for evidence of share issues | Completeness |
| Recalculate the closing balance on the share capital account | Accuracy, valuation and allocation |
| Review Memorandum and Articles of Association and compare their requirements with issued share capital | Existence |

Comparing issued share capital with the Memorandum and Articles of Association relates to existence because 'equity' that is not issued pursuant to those documents does not legally exist.

48 The correct answer is: Inspect invoices capitalised within the cost of the new till system to determine whether they are directly attributable to the cost of the new till system

The audit risk relates to the concern that South may have capitalised costs which are revenue in nature. As such the appropriate response is to review the invoices which have been capitalised not just for their amount but also to determine the nature of the expense to which the invoice relates.

49 The correct answers are: Perform analytical procedures by comparing daily/weekly sales by store with both the prior year and with expectations, in order to determine whether any unusual patterns have occurred following the installation of the new system; Obtain a copy of the training manual relating to the new till system and discuss with directors the extent of training staff have received on the new system.

The audit risk relates to the concern that the system may not be reliable, that not all invoices have been recorded and that staff may not be familiar with the system.

Vouching the revenue per the system back to till receipts is not a valid response to the audit risk. Given that one concern is that revenue is understated, testing should be from the till receipts to the system to ensure that all sales have been recorded. Similarly, agreeing revenue from till receipts to the cashbook is also the wrong way around – this test should begin with the cashbook in order to test for completeness.

50 The correct answers are: To assess whether a provision for customer compensation is required in South's financial statements; To determine whether disclosure of the nature and financial effect of the legal claim is required in South's financial statements.

The concern over deficiencies in South's internal controls is a valid concern, but the review of legal correspondence is unlikely to be an appropriate response to this as the auditor would need to review internal controls. The impact on the reputation of South is also a valid concern as it could have implications for the viability of the company but again it is unlikely that information specifically relating to this would be available in the legal correspondence reviewed.

# Mason

51 The correct answer is: Revenue may be overstated if it is recognised according to the contract date rather than over the relevant accounting period.

There is a risk that the revenue for the annual fees is not properly recognised in the period to which it relates, leading to revenue (and deferred income) being materially misstated in the financial statements. Revenue should be recognised according to the accounting period in which the related performance obligations of the contract are met.

52 The correct answers are: Obtain a breakdown of the capitalised costs and agree a sample of items to invoices to determine the nature of the expenditure; Inspect management's review of whether the value of the aircraft has been impaired.

The auditor should obtain a breakdown of the capitalised costs and vouch them back to invoices to determine whether they relate to a capital or revenue expense. They can then determine whether they have been recognised appropriately in accordance with IAS 16 *Property, Plant and Equipment*.

The large amount of refitting work could also indicate that something is wrong with the aircraft and that their value has become impaired.

53 The correct answer is: Mason's going concern status may be at risk if the contract is not renewed.

The key risk here is going concern. It is possible that the company will lose one of only four customers. In addition, a bank loan is being renegotiated and it is expected that costs will increase. This may threaten Mason's ability to continue as a going concern.

54 The correct answers are: Review Mason's contracts with its other three customers to determine whether they contain a break clause, in order to determine the likelihood of losing any further contracts to other aircraft providers; Review the short-term and long-term funding facilities which are available to Mason.

The main risk here is to the going concern assumption, if Mason loses other key sources of revenue. The auditor would therefore want to consider whether this is likely, by reviewing the other contracts. If, as appears likely, they do, then Mason would need a source of funding to survive.

It would not be appropriate to contact an audit client's customer directly in relation to a matter such as this.

The issue of disclosure would only need to be considered once the going concern status of Mason had been determined.

55    The correct answer is:

| | Audit concern | Not audit concern |
|---|---|---|
| Non-current assets | ☐ | ☑ |
| Inventory | ☑ | ☐ |
| Completeness | ☐ | ☑ |
| Accuracy, valuation and allocation | ☑ | ☐ |

Specialist equipment has been removed from the aircraft and is now included in inventory. Inventory should be valued at the lower of cost and net realisable value, not at amortised cost. The fact that the equipment has been replaced suggests that its net realisable value is lower than its cost. This may mean that inventory is overstated in the financial statements.

# Severn

56    The correct answer is:

| | | |
|---|---|---|
| The proposed fee for the initial audit of Severn Co | INCLUDE | |
| A description of Rivers & Co, including the curriculum vitae of key staff likely to be assigned to the client | INCLUDE | |
| Overall level of materiality to be used in the audit | | EXCLUDE |
| A summary of potential other services Rivers & Co could provide to Severn Co | INCLUDE | |

The materiality level used is included in the audit plan, not the audit tender document. The proposed fee is a critical part of the tender, as is a description of the firm and the key personnel to be associated with Severn.

While there will be limits associated with what other services can be offered to Severn (as it is a listed entity), it would still be appropriate for the firm to list the services it offers, tailored to areas where it might be possible to offer services, as this might be a critical factor for Severn.

57    The firm is independent of the potential client; The firm has the appropriate resources to conduct the audit of the potential client.

These two issues are important when tendering for any audit, but particularly in this case, where Severn Co would represent a major client, and therefore self-interest issues might apply (for instance, the firm might consider it would become over reliant on the fee).

In addition, given the significance of Severn Co to Rivers & Co, it is particularly important to consider whether the firm has the resources (eg number of audit staff available at the appropriate time of year) to provide this audit service.

While the existence of preconditions of audit is an essential part of accepting an audit, in this instance, the firm has already identified that the company applies an applicable financial reporting framework, acknowledges its responsibilities and is prepared to confirm this in writing, so this is of less significance to consider prior to tendering in this circumstance.

While the issue of access to working papers might influence the audit approach in the first year and hence impact on budgeting and fee setting, it is not a reason not to tender, so again, less important to consider than items 1 and 2.

58    The correct answer is: A reply from the outgoing auditors stating that they declined to seek reappointment to the audit of Severn Co due to a disagreement over accounting policies.

A reply from the outgoing auditors stating that they declined to seek reappointment to the audit of Severn Co due to a disagreement over accounting policies

This would imply a lack of integrity on the part of the director who asserted the firm had not been re-elected due to familiarity issues. Disagreement over accounting policies suggests the opposite of familiarity risk, which was the reason the company gave the firm for the change in auditors. It also raises the threat of possible future intimidation, if there may be disagreements concerning accounting policy. It is even possible that the company has deliberately asked a relatively small firm to tender in order to have more sway over them.

It is not necessary to have an engagement letter set up prior to acceptance, although this should be dealt with soon after acceptance.

Although the ACCA *Code of Ethics and Conduct* contains a 15% benchmark in relation to fees from one audit client, it recommends safeguards which could be implemented to mitigate the threat, and the firm could actively seek other clients to replace the lost client and hence lower the proportion represented by Severn Co (ACCA *Code of Ethics and Conduct*: para. 410.A3).

Similarly, although the apparent lack of resources in March is an issue, it is an issue that the firm may be able to work around, by negotiating different audit timetables with other clients, or by coming to a different arrangement with Severn Co. It is not a reason to automatically decline.

59    The correct answer is:

|  | Include in engagement letter | Do not include in engagement letter |
|---|---|---|
| Scope of the audit | ✓ | ☐ |
| Responsibilities of management of Severn Co | ✓ | ☐ |
| Timetable for the provision of accounting information by Severn Co | ☐ | ✓ |
| Fees and billing arrangements | ☐ | ✓ |

The scope of the audit and the responsibilities of Severn Co's management must be included in the engagement letter. The remaining options may be included, but they are not mandatory elements according to ISA 210 (ISA 210).

60    The correct answers are: Before accepting the audit of Severn Co, Rivers & Co should **obtain references concerning the directors**. Once the audit has been accepted, then Rivers & Co should begin to **submit the letter of engagement**.

References concerning the directors should be obtained before the engagement is accepted. The letter of engagement is then submitted after acceptance but before beginning to perform procedures.

# Goofy Co

61 The correct answers are:

Inform the audit committees of both Goofy and Mickey of the potential conflict of interest and obtain their consent to act for both parties

Prevent unauthorised physical access to the information relating to both company audits

The management of both Goofy and Mickey should be informed and their consent obtained.

Separate audit teams should be used including audit partners and independent review partners.

Confidentiality agreements should be signed by NAB & Co's staff, not by the client.

62 The correct answer is:

| Threat to independence | | Familiarity | Self-interest |
|---|---|---|---|
| (1) | Audit engagement partner has been in the position for six years | X | |
| (2) | Audit engagement partner's daughter works for Goofy | X | |
| (3) | Audit engagement partner's daughter's bonus would be in the form of shares | | X |
| (4) | 5% bonus offered if audit is completed three weeks earlier than last year | | X |

The long association of the audit engagement partner with Goofy represents a familiarity threat as she may not maintain professional scepticism and objectivity. Similarly the audit engagement partner's daughter being employed by Goofy is also a familiarity threat, although there would not be a need for additional safeguards as a warehouse manager is unlikely to influence the financial statements.

A self-interest threat arises from the financial interest in Goofy which the audit engagement partner's daughter will receive if she is awarded a bonus. As an immediate family member of the partner this creates an indirect interest in a client which is not permitted by the ACCA (ACCA *Code of Ethics and Conduct*: para. R510.4).

A bonus relating to the audit being completed three weeks earlier than last year creates a self-interest threat, as there is a danger NAB & Co will be less thorough in order to achieve the deadline and not risk losing the client as a result of not meeting it.

63 The correct answer is:

(1) Communicate with Mickey's existing auditors
(2) Perform client screening procedures, including an assessment of Mickey's risk profile
(3) Ensure that the existing auditor's resignation has been properly conducted
(4) Submit an engagement letter to Mickey's management

NAB & Co should contact the existing auditor before accepting nomination, in order to find out whether there are any reasons behind Mickey's decision to change its auditors about which NAB & Co should be aware. Once this is done, client screening must be performed.

Ensuring that the existing auditor's resignation has been properly conducted and issuing an engagement letter are procedures which should be taken after accepting nomination.

64 The correct answer is:

Management's responsibility to prevent and detect fraud

Although management is responsible for the prevention and detection of fraud, this is not one of the matters included in the agreement obtained by the auditors to establish that the preconditions of an audit exist.

65 The correct answer is:

| | | |
|---|---|---|
| The auditor has the right of access to the books, records and vouchers of the company | TRUE | |
| The auditor has the right to be heard at general meetings on matters relating to the audit | TRUE | |
| The auditor is appointed by, and answerable to, those charged with governance of the company | | FALSE |
| An auditor can be removed by a simple oral resolution in line with the common law | | FALSE |

# Carlise

66 The correct answer is:

| Audit procedures | | Interim audit | Final audit |
|---|---|---|---|
| (1) | Update documentation relating to Carlise's accounting systems which has been prepared in prior year audits. | X | |
| (2) | Obtain third-party confirmations relating to receivables, payables and cash at bank. | | X |
| (3) | Review the directors' assessment of whether Carlise is a going concern. Consider whether the assumptions made by the directors are reasonable and whether it is appropriate to prepare the accounts on the going concern basis. | | X |
| (4) | Perform preliminary analytical procedures in order to identify any major changes in the business or unexpected trends. | X | |

Audit procedures performed during an interim audit are likely to include analytical procedures, tests of controls, updating risk assessments and substantive testing of transactions which have occurred during the first part of the year.

When it comes to the final audit a trial balance or draft set of financial statements will be available, so detailed substantive testing of year-end balances will be conducted. This is in addition to completing the tests of controls and substantive procedures started during the interim audit.

67 The correct answer is:

1, 2 and 3

All of the factors should be taken into account.

68 The correct answer is:

Whether the work performed by the internal audit department relates to specific audit assertions over which UYE & Co have concerns

Where the external auditor plans to rely on the work of the internal audit department, they must ensure that the internal auditors' work has been performed to a good standard. However, most important is the requirement that the work performed by the internal audit department must be relevant to the evidence the external auditor is trying to gather.

69    The correct answers are:

|  | True | False |
|---|:---:|:---:|
| Carlise's internal auditors would perform audit procedures under the direction, supervision and review of UYE & Co's audit team | ✓ | |
| UYE & Co should only use direct assistance if the risk of material misstatement in relation to the online ticket sales system is high | | ✓ |
| UYE & Co's audit team should document its review of the work performed by Carlise's internal auditors | ✓ | |
| Carlise's internal auditors will be separately liable for any material misstatements in the work they have performed | | ✓ |

Direct assistance describes the use of internal auditors to perform audit procedures under the direction, supervision and review of the external auditor (ISA 620).

The external auditor should document their review of the work performed by the internal auditors.

The external auditor is likely to be less inclined to use direct assistance where the assessed risk of material misstatement is high, as this increases audit risk. The auditor must take full responsibility for their audit opinion regardless of whether they rely on the work of others.

70    The correct answers are:

|  | True | False |
|---|:---:|:---:|
| UYE & Co's policy of assembling files within 60 days of the auditor's report is stricter than what is required by ISAs | | ✓ |
| It is incompatible with ISAs for even minor further procedures to be added to the audit files after the 60 day period | ✓ | |
| It is acceptable to make administrative changes to an audit file after 60 days, so it is not strictly necessary to 'lock' the files to comply with ISAs | ✓ | |
| It is acceptable for files to be disposed of after 3 years have passed since the date of the auditor's report | | ✓ |

ISA 230 *Audit documentation* requires the assembly of the final audit file within 60 days of the auditor's report, so UYE & Co's policy is in line with this (and is not therefore stricter than required).

Once this time has passed, it is acceptable for changes can be made where they are administrative in nature – but further procedures would not be administrative and would thus not be acceptable. The files do not necessarily have to be 'locked'.

It is not acceptable to dispose of audit files after just 3 years – ISA 230 requires audit files to be kept for 5 years from the date of the auditor's report.

# 71 Sleeptight

**Workbook references. Chapters 6 and 13.**

**Top tips.** This 30-mark case study style question contains a mixture of knowledge-based questions and questions requiring application to a long scenario.

Part (a) requires you to recall your knowledge of professional scepticism and judgement. In part (ii), notice that your examples of areas to apply professional judgement should be limited to the planning stage.

Part (b) worth 16 marks contains a common requirement where you are asked to explain audit risks and then suggest appropriate responses. Audit risks will be related to potential material misstatements of the financial statements and this should be in the forefront of your mind throughout when you are answering this part of the question. When you are explaining your risk you should therefore state how the financial statements are affected.

Responses are the auditor's responses, not management responses. These will therefore be procedures or actions the auditor will carry out to mitigate the risks.

In part (c) you should have realised that the auditor must attend the inventory count and is required to perform certain procedures specified by ISA 501.

In part (d), although you would assess the reliability of the expert, don't forget there are also other important procedures such as reviewing the disclosures and the revaluation adjustments.

**Easy marks.** In part (a), easy marks are available for explaining professional scepticism and defining professional judgement.

## Marking scheme

| | | | Marks |
|---|---|---|---|
| (a) | (i) | Professional scepticism<br>1 mark per valid point up to a maximum of | 3 |
| | (ii) | Professional judgement<br>1 mark per valid point up to a maximum of | 3 |
| (b) | | Risks and responses<br>1 mark per well-explained risk (maximum of 8) and<br>1 mark for each valid response (maximum of 8) up to a total<br>maximum of | 16 |
| (c) | | Inventory count attendance<br>1 mark per valid point up to a maximum of | 4 |
| (d) | | Audit procedures for value of property and disclosure<br>Up to 1 mark per procedure to a maximum of | 4 |
| | | **Maximum marks** | **30** |

(a)    (i)    **Professional scepticism**

Professional scepticism is an attitude that includes having a questioning mind, being alert to conditions which may indicate possible misstatement due to error or fraud, and subjecting audit evidence to a critical assessment rather than just taking it at face value (ISA 200).

It is important that professional scepticism is maintained throughout the audit to reduce the risks of overlooking unusual transactions, of overgeneralising when drawing conclusions, and of using inappropriate assumptions in determining the nature, timing and extent of audit procedures and evaluating the results of them.

Professional scepticism is necessary to the critical assessment of audit evidence. This includes questioning contradictory audit evidence and the reliability of documents and responses from management and those charged with governance.

(ii)    **Professional judgement**

Professional judgement is the application of relevant training, knowledge and experience in making informed decisions about the appropriate courses of action in

BPP
LEARNING
MEDIA

the circumstances of the audit engagement. The auditor must exercise professional judgement when planning an audit of financial statements (ISA 200).

Professional judgement will be required in many areas when planning. For example, the determination of materiality for the financial statements as a whole and performance materiality levels will require professional judgement.

Professional judgement will also be required when deciding on the nature, timing and extent of audit procedures.

(b)

| Audit risk | Auditor's response |
| --- | --- |
| The firm has recently been appointed as auditor. There is a lack of cumulative knowledge and understanding of the business, which may result in a failure to identify events and transactions which impact on the financial statements. Furthermore, opening balances may be misstated. | Adopt procedures to ensure opening balances are properly brought forward and corresponding amounts are correctly classified and disclosed.<br><br>Review previous auditor's working papers and consider performing additional substantive procedures on opening balances. |
| The directors only work part time at Sleeptight and there is no finance director. This may promote a weak control environment, resulting in undetected errors or frauds. There is also a control risk if the directors fail to implement an appropriate system of internal control. | The controls will need to be documented and evaluated. If these are deficient then the level of substantive testing will need to be increased accordingly. |
| The requirement for customers to pay 40% on ordering and the remainder following delivery could result in revenue recorded before it should be, if the deposit is recorded as a sale and not deferred until delivery. This would result in revenue being overstated.<br><br>Alternatively, revenue could be understated if the final payment were only recognised when it is received, rather than on delivery of the bed. | Enquire of management the point at which revenue is actually recognised, and review the system of accounting for deposits to ensure they are not included in revenue until goods are delivered and signed for.<br><br>For a sample of transactions within eight weeks of the year end, ensure the revenue recorded is only in respect of beds delivered to customers in the same period and ensure they have been signed for. |
| The two-year guarantee on the beds gives rise to a provision, the measurement of which involves a high degree of judgement, and therefore carries a risk of misstatement. This risk is increased by the fact the loan covenants are profit related and there is an incentive to manipulate areas of the financial statements based on judgements. | Establish the basis of the amount provided for and assumptions made by the financial controller.<br><br>Reperform any calculations and establish the level of warranty costs in the year, and compare with the previous provision.<br><br>Review the level of repair costs incurred post year end and use these to assess the reasonableness of the provision. |
| Contractors are required to invoice at the end of each month but often there is a delay in receiving these. There is therefore a risk the company will not accrue for costs, resulting in incomplete liabilities and understatement of expenses. | Review invoices and payments to contractors after the year end and, if they relate to work undertaken before the year end, ensure they are included as accruals. |

| Audit risk | Auditor's response |
|---|---|
| The current year raw materials costs for materials also in inventory last year are based on prices at least a year old. They should be based on the actual cost or reasonable average cost. Given that prices fluctuate the value of year-end raw materials may be over- or undervalued due to price rises/decreases occurring during the year. | For a sample of materials to include the cost of wood, compare material costs to actual prices on invoices. Investigate and resolve any significant differences and evaluate the potential impact on the inventory value in the financial statements. |
| The finished goods value is to be estimated by Anna Jones, who appears to be basing her estimate on order value rather than applying the IAS 2 rule that goods should be valued at the lower of cost and net realisable value (NRV) (IAS 2). This could result in inventory being overstated in the financial statements. | For beds awaiting dispatch, establish the lower of cost and NRV and compare with the figures provided by Anna Jones. Investigate any differences and evaluate the potential impact on the inventory value in the financial statements. |
| The new workshop is undergoing refurbishment that could result in inappropriate treatment of capital or non-capital items, potentially misstating non-current assets, or repair costs in the statement of profit or loss. Again, this risk is increased by the fact the loan covenants are profit related and there is an incentive to manipulate areas of the financial statements based on judgements. | Obtain a breakdown of the related costs and establish which are included as non-current assets and which are treated as repair costs. Review the nature of items included in non-current assets to ensure only capital items are included and review repairs to ensure no capital items are included. |
| The new premises purchase was funded by a bank loan which may not be classified correctly between current and non-current liabilities, or may not be properly presented or disclosed as required by IFRSs. | Reperform the calculation of the split between current and non-current liabilities and ensure the loan is properly presented and terms are disclosed as required by IFRSs. |
| There is a risk the company may fail to comply with the loan covenants, resulting in the loan being recalled. This could then possibly lead to going concern issues.<br><br>There is also a risk of manipulation, resulting in overstated profits, in order to meet the covenant conditions in relation to profit. | Obtain and review (or reperform) covenant calculations to identify any breaches. If there are any, the likelihood of the bank demanding repayment will need to be assessed, along with the potential impact on the company. The need to avoid breaching the covenants reinforces the audit team's need to maintain professional scepticism in areas that could be manipulated. |

*Note.* Only 8 risks and 8 related responses were needed to gain 16 marks.

(c)  ISA 501 *Audit Evidence – Specific Considerations for Selected Items* sets out the responsibilities of auditors in relation to the physical inventory count. It states that where inventory is material, auditors shall obtain sufficient appropriate audit evidence regarding its existence and condition by attending the physical inventory count (ISA 501).

At the count attendance, Mills & Co will need to evaluate management's instructions and procedures for recording and controlling the result of the physical inventory count.

It must also observe the performance of the count procedures to assess whether they are properly carried out.

In addition, Mills & Co should inspect the inventory to verify that it exists and look for evidence of damaged or obsolete inventory. It will also perform test counts to assess the accuracy of the counts carried out by the company.

Mills & Co is also required by ISA 501 to perform audit procedures over the entity's final inventory records to determine whether they accurately reflect the count results (ISA 501).

**BPP**
LEARNING
MEDIA

(d)     **Procedures in relation to property valuation and related disclosures**

Obtain a copy of the valuer's report and consider the reliability of the valuation after taking account of:

- The basis of valuation
- Independence/objectivity
- Qualifications
- Experience
- Reputation of the valuer

Compare the valuation with the value of other similar properties in the locality and investigate any significant difference.

Reperform the calculation of the revaluation adjustments and ensure the correct accounting treatment has been applied.

Inspect notes to the financial statements to ensure appropriate disclosures have been made in accordance with IFRSs.

# 72 Peony

**Workbook references.** Chapter 6.

**Top tips.** Part (a), on materiality and performance materiality, involved an element of recall. The more difficult marks were for the explanation, particularly of performance materiality, but you should be aiming to score at least three marks on a requirement like this.

Part (b) was an application-based requirement. It is essential that you only include eight audit risks in your solution; the 16 marks available divide themselves into one each for describing the audit risk and then for the auditor's response to it. Your description of the audit risk should say what is happening and then, crucially, why this poses an audit risk. This statement of why could address a problem that could be encountered during the audit (eg due to lack of available information), or simply which balances could be over or understated. The auditor's response is then focused on reducing the audit risks.

**Easy marks.** There are marks in (b) for giving a simple description of each audit risk from the scenario (the marks for identification), and these are easy to get.

**Examining team's comments.** As noted in previous Examining team's Reports a fundamental factor in planning and assessing the risks of an audit of an entity is an assessment of audit risk, and this remains a highly examinable area. Audit risk questions typically require a number of audit risks to be identified (½ marks each), explained (½ marks each) and an auditor's response to each risk (1 mark each). Typically candidates can be required to identify and explain in the region of six to eight risks and responses.

A significant minority of candidates stated the risk was 'under/over stated' when it was clearly one or the other. They were not awarded credit and this scattergun approach is not recommended. Additionally, candidates must state the specific area of the financial statements impacted, as opposed to a general statement. As an example, a significant loss on disposal is indicative of an inappropriate depreciation policy resulting in 'property, plant and equipment being overstated or depreciation being understated'. No credit would be awarded just for stating 'assets are overstated' or 'profit is overstated'.

An auditor's response does not have to be a detailed audit procedure, rather an approach the audit team will take to address the identified risk. In common with previous sessions, auditor responses were sometimes too weak e.g. 'discuss with management' or 'obtain a breakdown and confirm it is reasonable'. In addition, it was noted that some candidates focussed on what management should do rather than the auditor, and/or, gave responses that were inappropriate to the scenario. For example, in this session a company had encountered significant fraud in its warehouse, some candidates recommended that 'the company install CCTV cameras'. This is an inappropriate auditor response and so would have gained no marks as it addresses the issue from the perspective of the company and not the audit. 'Peony Co' from the 'Sample March/June 2019 Questions' is a good scenario based question on audit risks and responses to practise.

Marks

(a) Materiality and performance materiality
   Materiality definition                                                    1
   Material due to size or nature                                            1
   Materiality benchmarks                                                    1
   Depends on judgement and risk                                            1
   Performance materiality definition                                       1
   Used for testing individual balances                                     1
   Set at lower level than materiality                                      1
   Restricted to                                                            4
(b) Audit risks and responses (only 8 required)
   Reliance on internal audit – increased detection risk                    2
   Unusual movement in margins                                              2
   Inventory valuation policy                                               2
   Perpetual inventory system                                               2
   Obsolete PPE                                                             2
   Advertising expenditure                                                  2
   Use of payroll service organisation                                      2
   Transfer of data to service organisation                                 2
   Bank loan                                                                2
   Redundancy plan                                                          2
   Max 8 issues, 2 marks each                                              16

**Total marks**                                                           20

(a) **Materiality and performance materiality**

Materiality and performance materiality are dealt with under ISA 320 *Materiality in Planning and Performing an Audit*. Auditors need to establish the materiality level for the financial statements as a whole, as well as assess performance materiality levels, which are lower than the overall materiality for the financial statements as a whole.

**Materiality**

Materiality is defined in ISA 320 as follows: 'Misstatements, including omissions, are considered to be material if they, individually or in the aggregate, could reasonably be expected to influence the economic decisions of users taken on the basis of the financial statements.'

If the financial statements include a material misstatement, then they will not present fairly (give a true and fair view) the position, performance and cash flows of the entity.

A misstatement may be considered material due to its size (quantitative) and/or due to its nature (qualitative) or a combination of both. The quantitative nature of a misstatement refers to its relative size. A misstatement which is material due to its nature refers to an amount which might be low in value but due to its prominence and relevance could influence the user's decision, for example, directors' transactions.

As per ISA 320, materiality is often calculated using benchmarks such as 5% of profit before tax or 1% of total revenue or total assets. These values are useful as a starting point for assessing materiality, however, the assessment of what is material is ultimately a matter of the auditor's professional judgement. It is affected by the auditor's perception of the financial information, the needs of the users of the financial statements and the perceived level of risk; the higher the risk, the lower the level of overall materiality.

In assessing materiality, the auditor must consider that a number of errors each with a low value may, when aggregated, amount to a material misstatement.

 **BPP** LEARNING MEDIA

ANSWERS

### Performance materiality

Performance materiality is defined in ISA 320 as follows: 'The amount set by the auditor at less than materiality for the financial statements as a whole to reduce to an appropriately low level the probability that the aggregate of uncorrected and undetected misstatements exceeds materiality for the financial statements as a whole.'

Hence performance materiality is set at a level lower than overall materiality for the financial statements as a whole. It is used for testing individual transactions, account balances and disclosures. The aim of performance materiality is to reduce the risk that the total of all of the errors in balances, transactions and disclosures exceeds overall materiality.

(b) **Audit risks and auditor's response**

| Audit risk | Auditor's response |
|---|---|
| The external audit team may place reliance on the controls testing work undertaken by the IA department.<br><br>If reliance is placed on irrelevant or poorly performed testing, then the external audit team may form an incorrect conclusion on the strength of the internal controls at Peony Co. This could result in them performing insufficient levels of substantive testing, thereby increasing detection risk. | The external audit team should meet with IA staff, read their reports and review their files relating to store visits to ascertain the nature of the work undertaken.<br><br>Before using the work of IA, the audit team will need to evaluate and perform audit procedures on the entirety of the work which they plan to use, in order to determine its adequacy for the purposes of the audit. In addition, the team will need to re-perform some of the testing carried out by IA to assess its adequacy. |
| Forecast ratios from the finance director show that the gross margin is expected to increase from 56% to 60% and the operating margin is expected to decrease from 21% to 18%.<br><br>This movement in gross margin is significant and inconsistent with the fall in operating margin. There is a risk that costs may have been omitted or included in operating expenses rather than cost of sales. Misclassification of expenses would result in understatement of cost of sales and overstatement of operating expenses. | The classification of costs between cost of sales and operating expenses should be reviewed in comparison to the prior year and any inconsistencies investigated. |
| Peony Co's inventory valuation policy is selling price less average profit margin, as this is industry practice. Inventory should be valued at the lower of cost and net realisable value (NRV).<br><br>IAS 2 *Inventories* allows this as a cost calculation method as long as it is a close approximation to cost. If this is not the case, then inventory could be under or overvalued. | Testing should be undertaken to confirm cost and NRV of inventory and that on a line-by-line basis the goods are valued correctly.<br><br>In addition, valuation testing should focus on comparing the cost of inventory to the selling price less margin for a sample of items to confirm whether this method is actually a close approximation to cost. |

| Audit risk | Auditor's response |
|---|---|
| The company utilises a perpetual inventory system at its warehouse rather than a full year-end count. Under such a system, all inventory must be counted at least once a year with adjustments made to the inventory records on a timely basis. Inventory could be under or overstated if the perpetual inventory counts are not all completed, such that some inventory lines are not counted in the year.<br><br>During the interim audit, it was noted that there were significant exceptions with the inventory records being higher than the inventory in the warehouse. As the year-end quantities will be based on the records, this is likely to result in overstated inventory. | The timetable of the perpetual inventory counts should be reviewed and the controls over the counts and adjustments to records should be tested.<br><br>In addition, the level of adjustments made to inventory should be considered to assess their significance. This should be discussed with management as soon as possible as it may not be possible to place reliance on the inventory records at the year end, which could result in the requirement for a full year-end inventory count. |
| A number of assets which had not been fully depreciated were identified as being obsolete.<br><br>This is an indication that the company's depreciation<br><br>policy of non-current assets may not be appropriate, as depreciation in the past appears to have been understated.<br><br>If an asset is obsolete, it should be written off to the statement of profit or loss. Therefore depreciation may be understated and profit and assets overstated. | Discuss the depreciation policy for non-current assets with the finance director and assess its reasonableness.<br><br>Enquire of the finance director if the obsolete assets have been written off. If so, review the adjustment for completeness. |
| Peony Co is planning to include a current asset of $0·7m, which relates to advertising costs incurred and adverts shown on TV before the year end.<br><br>The costs were incurred and adverts shown in the year ending 20X5 and there is no basis for including them as a current asset at the year end. The costs should be recognised in operating expenses in the current year financial statements. If these costs are not expensed, current assets and profits will be overstated. | Discuss with management the rationale for including the advertising as a current asset. Request evidence to support the assessment of probable future cash flows, and review for reasonableness.<br><br>Review supporting documentation for the advertisements to confirm that all were shown before the 20X5 year end. Request that management remove the current asset and record the amount as an expense in the statement of profit or loss. |
| During the year, Peony Co outsourced its payroll function to an external service organisation. A detection risk arises as to whether sufficient and appropriate evidence is available at Peony Co to confirm the completeness and accuracy of controls over the payroll cycle and liabilities at the year end. | Discuss with management the extent of records maintained at Peony Co for the period since January 20X5 and any monitoring of controls which has been undertaken by management over payroll.<br><br>Consideration should be given to contacting the service organisation's auditor to confirm the level of controls in place, a type 1 or type 2 report could be requested. |

ANSWERS

| Audit risk | Auditor's response |
|---|---|
| The payroll function was transferred to the service organisation from 1 January 20X5, which is five months prior to the year end. If any errors occurred during the transfer process, these could result in wages and salaries being under/overstated. | Discuss with management the transfer process undertaken and any controls which were put in place to ensure the completeness and accuracy of the data.<br><br>Where possible, undertake tests of controls to confirm the effectiveness of the transfer controls. In addition, perform substantive testing on the transfer of information from the old to the new system. |
| A $3m loan was obtained in March 20X5. This finance needs to be accounted for correctly, with adequate disclosure made. The loan needs to be allocated between non-current and current liabilities. Failure to classify the loan correctly could result in misclassified liabilities. | Re-perform the company's calculations to confirm that the split of the loan note is correct between non-current and current liabilities and that total financing proceeds of $3m were received.<br><br>In addition, the disclosures for this loan note should be reviewed in detail to ensure compliance with relevant accounting standards. |
| Peony Co is planning to make approximately 60 employees redundant after the year end.<br><br>The timing of this announcement has not been confirmed; if it is announced to the staff before the year end, then under IAS 37 *Provisions, Contingent Liabilities and Contingent Assets*, a redundancy provision will be required at the year end as a constructive obligation will have been created.<br><br>Failure to provide or to provide an appropriate amount will result in an understatement of provisions and expenses. | Discuss with management the status of the redundancy announcement; if before the year end, review supporting documentation to confirm the timing. In addition, review the basis of and recalculate the redundancy provision. |

# 73 Walters

**Workbook references.** Chapters 7 and 19.

**Top tips.** In part (a), make sure you read the requirement carefully and calculate the required number of ratios. The risks and the auditor's response to each risk need to be clearly explained: the ratios must be linked to the audit risks, and specific audit procedures should be stated. Again, you will not be awarded marks for vague responses such as 'check cut-off is appropriate'.

**Easy marks.** Part (a)(i) should not pose a problem, and part (b) also contains easy marks

Marks

(a)  (i)  ½ mark per ratio calculation per year.
Operating margin
Inventory holding period
Payables payment period
Current ratio
Quick ratio

3

(ii)  Up to 1 mark per well-explained audit risk, maximum of 6 marks for risks and up to 1 mark per audit response, maximum of 6 marks for responses.
Management manipulation of results
Sales cut-off
Revenue growth
Misclassification of costs between cost of sales and operating
Inventory valuation
Receivables valuation
Going concern risk

12

(b)  1 mark per well-explained point – if the procedure does not clearly explain how this will help the auditor to consider going concern then a ½ mark only should be awarded.
Review cash flow forecasts
Review bank agreements, breach of key ratios
Review post year end sales and order book
Review supplier's correspondence
Inquire of lawyers for any litigation
Subsequent events
Board minutes
Management accounts
Consider additional disclosures under IAS 1
Written representation

$$\frac{5}{20}$$

(a)  (i)  **Additional ratios**

|  |  | 20X5 | 20X4 |
|---|---|---|---|
| Operating margin | PBT/Revenue | 4.5/23 = 19.6% | 4/18 = 22.2% |
| Inventory holding period | Inventories/COS × 365 days | 2.1/11 × 365 = 70 days | 1.6/10 × 365 = 58 days |
| Payables payment period | Payables/COS × 365 days | 1.6/11 × 365 = 53 days | 1.2/10 × 365 = 44 days |
| Current ratio | Current assets/Current liabilities | 6.6/2.5 = 2.6 | 6.9/1.2 = 5.8 |
| Quick ratio | (Current assets – inventories)/Current liabilities | (6.6 – 2.1)/2.5 = 1.8 | (6.9 – 1.6)/1.2 = 4.4 |

*(Note.* Only three ratios were required. Also note that the formulae are provided here to help with your revision, and would not be required in the actual exam.)

(ii) **Audit risks and responses**

| Audit risk | Auditor's response |
|---|---|
| Management were disappointed with the 20X4 results and are under pressure to improve the trading results in 20X5. There is a risk that management have a greater incentive to manipulate the results by adopting a more aggressive approach in relation to accounting estimates (ie provisions), resulting in an overstatement of provisions and an understatement of expenses. | The audit team will need to remain alert to the risk of creative accounting throughout the audit. It is important that they exercise professional scepticism and evaluate any assumptions made by management in auditing accounting estimates. Current year balances should be compared to the prior year to highlight any unusual trends. |
| A generous sales-related bonus scheme has been introduced for the company's salespeople. This increases the risk of misstatements arising from sales cut-off (most likely overstatement of sales) as the sales staff seek to maximise their bonus. | Increased sales cut-off testing will be required. Post year end sales returns should be reviewed, as they may provide evidence of incorrect cut-off. |
| Revenue has grown by 28%, while cost of sales has only increased by 10%. The gross profit margin has increased significantly. Although the bonus scheme and the advertising campaign may explain the growth in revenue, the fact that the cost of sales has seen a corresponding increase needs to be investigated. The principal risks are of overstatement of revenue and understatement of cost of sales. | Inquiries should be made of management regarding the reason why cost of sales has not increased in line with sales. Substantive procedures should be performed on an increased sample of costs, with an aim to identify any costs omitted or misclassified. |
| Although the gross margin has increased from 44.4% to 52.2%, the operating margin has decreased from 22.2% to 19.6%. This trend is unusual. While the bonus scheme and advertising campaign could account for some of the increase in operating expenses, there is a possibility that costs may have been misclassified from cost of sales to operating expenses. This would understate cost of sales and operating profit, and overstate gross profit and operating expenses. | The classification of costs between cost of sales and operating expenses will be compared with the prior year to ensure consistency. A detailed breakdown of operating expenses and cost of sales should be reviewed for evidence of misclassification. The main components of costs of sales and operating expenses should be identified and compared to the prior year. Any unusual trends (for example, significant costs in the prior year not present in the current year, and vice versa) should be discussed with management. |
| The inventory valuation policy has been changed, with additional overheads to be included within inventory. This would mean that more costs were included within the valuation of inventory than would otherwise be the case. This could therefore mean that costs that would have been expensed against profit or loss would now be held as current assets. | The change in the inventory valuation policy should be discussed with management. The additional overheads included should be reviewed, to confirm that they are related to production. Detailed cost and net realisable value testing should be performed and the aged inventory report should be reviewed to assess whether a write down is required. |

| Audit risk | Auditor's response |
|---|---|
| The inventory holding period has increased from 58 to 70 days.<br>There is a risk that inventory is overvalued and thus overstated. | |
| The receivables collection period has increased from 61 to 71 days and management have extended the credit period given to customers.<br>This leads to an increased risk of unrecoverable receivables and a concomitant overstatement of the receivables balance in the financial statements | Extended post year end cash receipts testing and a review of the aged receivables ledger should be performed to assess the need for any write-offs or provision. |
| The current ratio and quick ratio have both decreased significantly. In addition, the company's positive cash balance of $2.3m in 20X4 has become an overdraft of $0.9m.<br>Taken together with the growth in revenue and the increase in operating expenses, this may indicate overtrading. A going concern risk should be considered. | Detailed going concern testing to be performed during the audit. Cash flow forecasts covering at least 12 months from the year end should be reviewed, and the assumptions discussed with management. |

(b) **Going concern procedures**

(i) Obtain Walters' cash flow forecast and review the cash payments and receipts. Assess the assumptions for reasonableness and discuss the findings with management to understand if the company will have sufficient cash flows.

(ii) Review any current agreements with the bank to determine whether any covenants in relation to the overdraft have been breached.

(iii) Read minutes of the meetings of shareholders, the board of directors and important committees for reference to financing difficulties and for evidence of any future financing plans.

(iv) Review the company's post year end sales and order book to assess the levels of trade. Evaluate whether the revenue figures in the cash flow forecast are reasonable.

(v) Review post year end correspondence with suppliers to identify any restriction in credit that may not be reflected in the cash flow forecasts.

(vi) Inquire of the lawyers of Walters as to the existence of litigation and claims.

(vii) Perform audit tests in relation to subsequent events to identify any items that might indicate or mitigate the risk of going concern not being appropriate.

(viii) Review post year end management accounts to assess if it is in line with cash flow forecast.

(ix) Consider whether any additional disclosures as required by IAS 1 *Presentation of Financial Statements* in relation to material uncertainties over going concern should be made in the financial statements.

(x) Confirm the existence, legality and enforceability of arrangements to provide or maintain financial support with related and third parties and assess the financial ability of such parties to provide additional funds.

(xi) Consider Walters' position concerning any unfulfilled customer orders.

(xii) Obtain a written representation confirming the director's view that Walters is a going concern.

*Note.* Only five procedures were required.

# 74 Harlem

## Marking scheme

| | | Marks |
|---|---|---|
| (a) | **Auditor's responsibility for fraud** | |
| | Obtain reasonable assurance that financial statements are free from material misstatement | 1 |
| | Identify and assess risk of misstatement due to fraud | 1 |
| | Obtain sufficient and appropriate evidence | 1 |
| | Respond appropriately to fraud or suspected fraud | 1 |
| | Maintain professional scepticism | 1 |
| | Discuss risk of fraud with engagement team | 1 |
| | **Restricted to** | **4** |
| | | |
| (b) | **Ratios** | |
| | Gross profit margin | 1 |
| | Inventory holding period | 1 |
| | Gearing | 1 |
| | Interest cover | 1 |
| | | **4** |
| (c) | **Audit risks and responses** (only 8 required) | |
| | Sale or return assumption | 2 |
| | Intangible asset amortisation | 2 |
| | Significant losses on disposal | 2 |
| | Financial controller dismissal | 2 |
| | Unfair dismissal claim | 2 |
| | Inventory valuation | 2 |
| | Recoverability of receivables | 2 |
| | Purchases cycle control deficiencies | 2 |
| | Intention to restructure finance | 2 |
| | Bonus issue of shares | 2 |
| | **Max 8 issues, 2 marks each** | **16** |

(d) **Substantive procedures – Valuation of trade receivables**

| | |
|---|---|
| Discuss with management adequacy of allowance for trade receivables | 1 |
| Outcome of prior year allowance | 1 |
| Review aged trade receivables listing to identify old balances | 1 |
| Cash after-date testing | 1 |
| Review customer correspondence for evidence of disputes | 1 |
| Recalculate potential irrecoverable balances and assess adequacy of provision | 1 |
| **Restricted to** | **3** |

(e) **Substantive procedures – Disposal of plant and machinery**

| | |
|---|---|
| Obtain breakdown of disposals, cast and agree removal to non-current asset register | 1 |
| Select sample of disposals and agree sales proceeds to invoice | 1 |
| Recalculate the profit/loss on disposal and agree to trial balance | 1 |
| Recalculate depreciation to confirm applied on a pro rata basis | 1 |
| Review disclosures and confirm in line with accounting standards | 1 |
| **Restricted to** | **3** |
| **Total marks** | **30** |

---

(a) **Fraud responsibility**

Auditors conduct an audit in accordance with ISA *240 The Auditor's Responsibilities Relating to Fraud in an Audit of Financial Statements* and are responsible for obtaining reasonable assurance that the financial statements taken as a whole are free from material misstatement, whether caused by fraud or error.

In order to fulfil this responsibility, the auditor is required to identify and assess the risks of material misstatement of the financial statements due to fraud.

The auditor needs to obtain sufficient appropriate audit evidence regarding the assessed risks of material misstatement due to fraud through designing and implementing appropriate responses. In addition, the auditor must respond appropriately to fraud or suspected fraud identifies during the audit.

When obtaining reasonable assurance, the auditor is responsible for maintaining professional scepticism throughout the audit, considering the potential for management override of controls and recognising the fact that audit procedures which are effective in detecting error may not be effective in detecting fraud.

To ensure that the whole engagement team is aware of the risks and responsibilities for fraud and error, ISA 240 requires that a discussion is held within the team. For members not present at the meeting, the audit engagement partner should determine which matters should be communicated to them.

(b) **Ratios**

| | 20X5 | 20X4 |
|---|---|---|
| Gross profit margin | 4,500/23,200 = 19.4% | 4,600/21,900 = 21% |
| Inventory holding period | 2,100/18,700 × 365 = 41 days | 1,600/17,300 × 365 = 34 days |
| Gearing ration | 13,000/(10,000 + 13,000) = 56.5% | 11,000/9,500 + 11,000 = 53.7% |
| **OR** | 13,000/10,000 = 130% | 11,000/9,500 = 116% |
| Interest cover | (450 + 290)/290 = 2.6 | (850 + 250)/250 = 4.4 |

(c) **Audit risks and auditor's response**

| Audit risk | Auditor's response |
|---|---|
| The finance director is planning on reducing the estimated return rate for goods sold on a sale or return basis to wholesale customers from 10% to 5%. | Discuss the basis of the revised assumption of a 5% return rate with the finance director. Review a period of 60 days to quantify the levels of return in the specified period and compare this to the assumed rate of 5%. Discuss any significant variations with the finance directors. |
| IFRS® 15 *Revenue from Contracts with Customers* provides that revenue and cost of sales should only be accounted for to the extent that the company foresees that the goods will not be returned. For the goods which may be returned, the company should recognise a refund liability. If, after 60 days, the goods are not returned, then this liability is reversed and revenue is recognised. | |
| By reducing the return rate, there is a risk that revenue and cost of sales may be overstated and liabilities understated. | |
| The company purchased a patent for $800,000 at the end of the prior year which has a useful life of four years. The carrying amount in the forecast financial statements is $800,000 which is the sane as prior year. | Agree the useful life of the patent is four years to supporting documentation. The amortisation charge should be calculated and the appropriate journal adjustment discussed with management, in order to ensure the accuracy of the charge and that the intangible is correctly valued at the year end. |
| In accordance with IAS® 38 *Intangible Assets*, this intangible asset should be amortised over its four-year life. It does not appear that management has correctly accounted for the amortisation and as a result, intangible assets and profits are overstated. | |
| Surplus plant and machinery was sold during the year, resulting in a loss on disposal of $160,000. | Recalculate the loss on disposal calculations and agree all items to supporting documentation. |

| Audit risk | Auditor's response |
|---|---|
| Significant profits or losses on disposal are an indication that the depreciation policy of plant and machinery may not be appropriate. Therefore depreciation may be understated and profit and assets overstated. | Discuss the depreciation policy for plant and machinery with the finance director to assess its reasonableness<br><br>Review for other significant gains or losses on disposal of property, plant and equipment to assess the reasonableness of the company's depreciation policies. |
| Harlem Co's financial controller has allegedly carried out a number of fraudulent transactions at the company. The investigation into the extent of the fraud has only recently commenced. | Discuss with the finance director the details of the fraud perpetrated by the financial controller and what procedures have been adopted to date to identify any adjustments which are needed in the financial statements |
| There is a risk that she may have under level of fraudulent transactions leading to an increased control risk which has not yet been identified. These would need to be written off to the statement of profit or loss. If these have not been uncovered by the year end, the financial statements could include errors resulting in the misstatement of profits. | Additional substantive testing should be conducted over the affected areas of the accounting records.<br><br>In addition, the team should maintain their professional scepticism and be alert to the risk of further fraud and errors. |
| In May 20X5, the financial controller was dismissed and is threatening to sue the company foe unfair dismissal. | The audit team should discuss with management and request confirmation from the company's lawyers of the existence and likelihood of success of any claim from the former financial controller. |
| If it is probable that Harlem Co will make payment to the financial controller, a provision for unfair dismissal is required to comply with IAS 37 *Provisions, Contingent Liabilities and Contingent Assets*. If the payment is possible rather than probable, a contingent liability disclosure would be necessary. If Harlem Co has not done this, there is a risk over the completeness of any provisions or contingent liabilities disclosures. | |
| Harlem Co has had production problems which have affected the quality of a significant batch of tyres. In addition, the inventory holding period has increased from 34 to 41 days. | Discuss with the finance director whether any write downs will be made to the affected tyres, and what, if any, modifications may be required with regards to the quality. |
| Inventory may be overvalued as its net realisable value (NRV) may be below its cost. If the tyres can be rectified, the rectification costs may mean that cost exceeds net realisable value. If the tyres cannot be rectified, the inventory may need to be written off completely | Testing should be undertaken to confirm cost and NRV of the affected products in inventory and that all inventory on a line-by-line basis is valued correctly |

| Audit risk | Auditor's response |
|---|---|
| A significant customer has been granted a six-month payment break and the receivables collection period has increased from 38 to 51 days. An allowance for receivables has historically been maintained, and it is anticipated that it will remain at the prior year level.<br><br>There is a risk that receivables will be overvalued; some balances may not be recoverable and so will be overstated if not adequately provided for. | Review and test the controls surrounding how the finance director identifies old or potentially irrecoverable receivables balances and credit control to ensure that they are operating effectively.<br><br>Discuss with the director the rationale for maintaining the allowance for receivables at the same level as the prior year, despite the increase in receivables collection period and the payment break granted to a large customer.<br><br>Extended post year-end cash receipts testing and a review of the aged receivables ledger to be performed to assess valuation and the need for an increased level of allowance for receivables. |
| The report to management issued after the prior year audit highlighted significant deficiencies relating to the purchases cycle. | Discuss with management whether the purchases cycle recommendations suggested by Brooklyn & Co were implemented successfully this year. If so, undertake tests of these controls to assess of they are operating efficiently.<br><br>If the controls are not in a place or operating efficiently, adopt a fully substantive approach for confirming the completeness and accuracy of cost of sales and other expenses and trade payables. |
| If these deficiencies have not been rectified, the controls over purchases and payables may continue to be weak leading to increased control risk and risk misstatements arising. Cost of sales, expenses and trade payables may not be complete or accurate. | |
| Harlem Co intends to restructure its debt finance after the year end. However, the interest cover has declined from 4.4 to 2.6 and the level of gearing has increased from 53.7% to 56.5%<br><br>In order to maximise the chances of securing the debt finance restructure, Harlem Co will need to present financial statements which show the best possible position and performance. The worsening interest cover and gearing ratio increases the risk that the directors may manipulate the financial statements, by overstating profits and assets and understanding debt liabilities. | Brooklyn & Co should ensure that there is a suitably experienced audit team. Also, adequate time should be allocated for team members to obtain an understanding of the company and the significant risks of overstatement of profits and assets and understatement of debt, including attendance at an audit team briefing.<br><br>The team needs to maintain professional scepticism and be alert to the increased risk of manipulation.<br><br>Significant estimates and judgements should be carefully reviewed in light of the misstatement risk. |
| Harlem Co has issued shares during the year via a bonus issue. Share capital within equity should increase by the value of the shares and a reserve should decrease accordingly. | Review the treatment of the bonus issue and agree the increase in shares to the share register and share certificates, and agree that the corresponding reduction in reserves is correct. |

| Audit risk | Auditor's response |
|---|---|
| If the company has not accounted for a bonus issue before, there is a risk that it could have been incorrectly treated with equity being under or overstated. In addition, legal issues may arise if the shares have not been issued in accordance with the company's statutory constitution. | Review board minutes for authorisation and terms of the bonus issue and review if the transaction has been conducted in line with this approval. Review the statutory constitution documents to confirm the legality of the share issue. |
| Additionally, bonus issues require disclosure in the financial statements and there is a risk that these may be incomplete or inaccurate. | Review the adequacy of the bonus issue disclosures in the financial statements. |

(d) **Substantive procedures for valuation of trade receivables**

- Discuss with the finance director the rationale for not increasing the allowance for trade receivables and review its overall adequacy.

- Obtain a breakdown of the opening allowance and consider if the receivables provided for in the prior year have been recovered to assess the reasonableness of the prior levels of allowances.

- Review the aged trade receivables ledger to identify any slow moving or old receivable balances and discuss the status of these balances with the credit controllers to assess whether they are likely to be received.

- Review whether there are any after-date cash receipts for slow moving/old receivable balances.

- Review customer correspondence with the significant customer and others to identify any balances which are in dispute or are unlikely to be paid.

- Review board minutes to identify whether there are any significant concerns in relation to payments by customers.

- Calculate the potential level of trade receivables which are not recoverable and assess whether this is material or not and discuss with management.

(e) **Substantive procedures for disposals of plant and machinery**

- Obtain a breakdown of disposals, cast the list and review the non-current assets register to confirm that all assets have been removed.

- Select a sample of disposals and agree sale proceeds to supporting documentation such as sundry sales invoices.

- Recalculate the depreciation charge for a sample of disposals to confirm the calculations are correctly applied as per the company policy of a pro rata basis or a full year in the year of acquisition and none in the year of disposal.

- Review the disposal of the disposals in the draft financial statements and ensure it is in line with IAS 16 *Property, Plant and Equipment*

# 75 Scarlet

**Workbook references.** Chapters 5, 6 and 7.

**Top tips.** Maintaining focus is essential on a long 30-mark question such as this one. A common theme throughout this question is the risk of answering the question you hoped would come up, rather than the question actually being asked.

In part (a) you were given a straight knowledge question about the engagement letter, which was not difficult and should have helped you to get off to a good start on the question.

Part (b) continued the theme, although the question was slightly deceptive in that you needed to make sure that your explanations really warranted a full mark each. It may be helpful here to think about trying to get two half marks here in order to extend your answer enough to get the full mark.

BPP
LEARNING
MEDIA

Part (c) was the standard risk and response requirement, for which you need to work through the scenario carefully, drawing out the consequences of the hints contained therein.

Part (d) rounded off the question by asking for substantive procedures. It is crucial here that you do not, for example, stray into writing down tests of controls or audit evidence points. Each procedure should be something that the audit team can do.

**Easy marks.** Part (a) was a relatively painless start to the question (and to the exam, if this had been your real exam).

## Marking scheme

|  |  |  | Marks |
|---|---|---|---|
| (a) | **Purpose and contents of engagement letter** | | |
| | Purpose | 2 | |
| | Four examples of items to be included (1/2 mark each) | 2 | |
| | | | 4 |
| (b) | **Factors to consider prior to acceptance** | | |
| | Outgoing auditor's response | 1 | |
| | Management integrity | 1 | |
| | Pre-conditions | 1 | |
| | Independence and objectivity | 1 | |
| | Resources | 1 | |
| | | | 5 |
| (c) | **Audit risk and response (only 8 risks required)** | | |
| | New client | 2 | |
| | Temporary accountant | 2 | |
| | FS preparation deadline for bank loan application | 2 | |
| | Training costs capitalised | 2 | |
| | Goods in transit | 2 | |
| | Increase in receivables days | 2 | |
| | Redundancy provision | 2 | |
| | Directors' bonus disclosure | 2 | |
| | Credit note for faulty goods | 2 | |
| | Late supplier payment run | 2 | |
| | Max 8 issues, 2 marks each | | 16 |
| (d) | **Substantive procedures for redundancy costs** | | |
| | 1 mark per well-described procedure | | |
| | Restricted to | | 5 |
| | Total marks | | 30 |

### (a) Engagement letters

**Purpose of an engagement letter**

The letter of engagement outlines the responsibilities of both the audit firm and the audit client. Its purpose is to:

- minimise the risk of any misunderstanding between the auditor and the client;

- confirm acceptance of the engagement; and

- forms the basis of the contract by outlining the terms and conditions of the engagement

**Items to be included in an engagement letter**

- the objective and scope of the audit;

- the responsibilities of the auditor;

- responsibilities of management;

- identification of the financial reporting framework used in the preparation of the financial statements;

- expected form and content of any reports to be issued;

- elaboration of the scope of the audit with reference to legislation;

- the form of any other communication of the results of the audit;

- the fact that some material misstatements may not be discovered;

- arrangements concerning the planning and performance of the audit, including the composition of the audit team;

- the expectation that management will provide written representations;

- the basis on which the audit firm will calculate its fees;

- a request for management to agree to the terms of the audit engagement and acknowledge receipt of the letter of engagement;

- arrangements concerning the involvement of internal audit and other staff employed at the company;

- any obligations to provide audit working papers to third parties;

- any restrictions on the auditor's liability; and

- arrangements to make available draft financial statements and any other information.

(b) **Factors to consider prior to accepting Scarlet Co as a new audit client**

| Pre-acceptance factors | Explanation |
|---|---|
| The outgoing auditor's response | Prior to accepting an audit engagement, the auditor is required to contact the previous auditors, after obtaining permission from Scarlet Co, to ask for all information relevant to the decision as to whether or not the firm should accept appointment. The auditor should consider the outgoing auditor's response to assess whether there are any ethical or professional reasons why the firm should not accept appointment. |
| Management integrity | If Orange & Co's audit engagement partner has reason to believe that Scarlet Co's management lack integrity, there is a greater risk of fraud and intimidation. Orange & Co need to consider management integrity because if there are serious concerns regarding this, Orange & Co must not accept the audit engagement. |

| Pre-acceptance factors | Explanation |
|---|---|
| Pre-conditions for an audit | Orange & Co can only accept an audit engagement if the preconditions are present. The preconditions confirm that management will use an acceptable financial reporting framework under which they will prepare the financial statements and confirms that management acknowledges and understands its responsibilities for:<br><br>• Preparing the financial statements in accordance with the applicable financial reporting framework;<br><br>• Internal control necessary for the preparation of the financial statements to be free from material misstatement; and<br><br>• Providing the auditor with access to information relevant for the audit and access to staff within the entity to obtain audit evidence.<br><br>If the preconditions are not present, Orange & Co cannot accept the audit engagement. |
| Independence and objectivity | The auditor must consider whether there are any threats to independence and objectivity which cannot be reduced to an acceptably low level by the use of appropriate safeguards, such as if any of Orange & Co's staff have shares in Scarlet Co or are related to staff employed at Scarlet Co. If such threats are present and cannot be sufficiently mitigated, Orange & Co must not accept the audit engagement. |
| Resources available at the time of the audit | Orange & Co must have adequate resources with the relevant experience available at the time the audit of Scarlet Co is likely to be carried out. All audit staff deployed to the audit of Scarlet Co must be capable of carrying out the audit in accordance with International Standards on Auditing (ISAs). If adequate resources will not be available, Orange & Co must not accept the audit engagement. |

(c)     **Audit risks and auditor's responses**

| Audit risk | Auditor's response |
|---|---|
| Scarlet Co is a new audit client of the firm. The audit engagement team will be unfamiliar with the accounting policies, transactions and balances of the client, hence there will be increased detection risk on the audit.<br><br>In addition, there is less assurance over opening balances as Orange & Co did not perform last year's audit. | Orange & Co should ensure that it has a suitably experienced team deployed on the audit. In addition, sufficient time must be set aside so that the team members can familiarise themselves with the new client document its systems and controls and understand the risks of material misstatement.<br><br>Increased audit procedures should be performed on the opening balances to confirm their reasonableness. |
| The company's financial accountant was taken ill suddenly in May 20X5 and a temporary accountant has been drafted in to help prepare the financial statements.<br><br>There is an increased risk of errors in the financial statements as the temporary financial accountant may not be familiar with the company's activities and so errors/omissions may go unnoticed. | Discuss with management the technical competency and experience of the temporary financial accountant. In addition, the audit engagement team should ensure that increased substantive procedures are undertaken on the material areas of the financial statements to reduce audit risk, particularly those requiring judgement. |
| The year-end financial statements have to be prepared by the end of September 20X5 in order to secure bank finance and management wish to report strong results.<br><br>This increases the risk that the directors may manipulate the financial statements, by overstating profits and assets and understating liabilities. | The audit engagement team should maintain professional scepticism throughout the course of the audit. Detailed cut-off testing on areas such as revenue, inventory and payables should be performed to ensure that cut-off has been correctly applied and substantive procedures performed on estimates and judgements to ensure accuracy. |
| A specialised machine was acquired and staff members had to be trained in the machine's use at a cost of $15,000 which has been capitalised as part of the cost of the machine.<br><br>IAS® 16 Property, Plant and Equipment prohibits training costs from being capitalised and therefore profits and property, plant and equipment will be overstated, and expenses understated if the training costs are not written off to the statement of profit or loss. | Discuss the accounting treatment with the directors and request that an adjustment is made to ensure appropriate treatment of the training costs. Obtain a breakdown of the remaining capitalised costs and agree to supporting documentation to ensure that they meet the recognition criteria in IAS 16. |
| The delivery time of three weeks from the company's international supplier is likely to result in goods in transit at the year end. The company has advised that the contract with the supplier means that Scarlet Co will be responsible for goods from dispatch and therefore inventory should be recorded when the products are sent by the supplier.<br><br>There is a risk that inventory is not recorded on dispatch and therefore inventory and liabilities are understated at the year end. | Discuss with management the point at which inventory is recorded and review the contract with the supplier to verify the requirements in place.<br><br>Review the controls the company has in place to ensure that inventory is recorded from the point of dispatch.<br><br>Extend cut-off testing by reviewing pre and post year-end GRNs and supplier dispatch notes to verify that inventory is recorded at the correct point. |

ANSWERS

| Audit risk | Auditor's response |
|---|---|
| Preliminary analytical procedures indicate that the receivables collection period has increased from 38 days to 52 days due to customers taking longer to pay.<br><br>There is a risk that some receivables may not be recoverable and an allowance for receivables is required, hence receivables may be overstated and the allowance for receivables understated. | Extend post year-end cash receipts testing and perform a review of the aged receivables listing to assess the valuation of receivables. Discuss with management the adequacy of any allowance for receivables. |
| On 29 May 20X5, the directors announced that a brand was being discontinued resulting in four members of staff being made redundant. The costs of redundancy are being included in the July 20X5 payroll run.<br><br>As there is a present obligation for which the costs can be reliably measured, and which will result in an outflow of funds, IAS 37 Provisions, Contingent Assets and Contingent Liabilities would require this provision to be recognised in the financial statements. If a provision is not recognised profit would be overstated and liabilities and payables would be understated. | Obtain the calculation of the redundancy payments and agree that a provision has been included as a liability in the year-end financial statements.<br><br>Agree the redundancy payments have been paid post year end. |
| The directors have each been paid a significant bonus at the year end and separate disclosure of this is required in the financial statements by local legislation.<br><br>The directors' remuneration disclosure will be incomplete and inaccurate if the bonus paid is included in the payroll charge for the year and not separately disclosed in accordance with the local legislation. | Discuss this matter with management and review the disclosure in the financial statements to ensure it complies with local legislation. |
| A customer has returned $120,000 of faulty goods to the company prior to the year-end but a credit note is yet to be issued.<br><br>As this sale occurred pre year end there is a risk that revenue and receivables are overstated if the credit note is not correctly recorded prior to the year end. | Inspect a copy of the credit note and confirm an adjustment to revenue and receivables has been recorded pre-year end. |
| The company's suppliers have been paid on 1 June 20X5 and the payment has been included as an unpresented item in the year-end bank reconciliation.<br><br>This is possible evidence of window dressing which results in understated payables and bank balances. | Request that the bank reconciliation is amended to remove the supplier payments at the year-end as these should be accounted for in the 31 May 20X6 financial statements.<br><br>Review the journal entry correcting the payables and bank balances at the year end. |

(d)    Substantive procedures for the redundancy costs

- Review the board minutes for evidence of the decision to discontinue the brand of chemicals prior to the year-end.

- Review supporting documentation to confirm that the decision to discontinue the brand was notified to the four members of staff prior to the year end.

- Obtain details of the redundancy calculated by employee, cast the schedule and agree to the trial balance/financial statements.

- Recalculate the redundancy provision to confirm completeness and agree components of the cost to supporting documentation such as employee contracts.

- Agree the redundancy payments made in July 20X5 to the cash book/payroll records and compare these to the provision in the financial statements.

- Obtain a written representation from management confirming the completeness of the costs.

- Review the disclosures included in the financial statements to verify they are in compliance with requirements of IAS 37 Provisions, Contingent Assets and Contingent Liabilities.

# 76 Corley Appliances Co

**Workbook references.** Chapters 5 and 6.

**Top tips.** Part (a) of this question is largely knowledge, which could mean either that you have a nice easy start to the question (if you know it) or that you struggled. The key here is whether you have done enough preparation for your exam.

For part (b) of the question it is important that you describe the audit risks clearly. A common mistake in this type of question is to simply identify a risk factor from the question eg the company has reduced the amount of its warranty provision. This is a risk factor, ie something about the way in which the business operates that increases audit risk. The risk itself is the potential issue that this causes. For example in this case the risk would be that the reduction is not reasonable leading to an understatement of provisions in the statement of financial position and an overstatement of profit for the period. Notice that to score well you must both identify the risk factor and then explain the associated risk.

Part (c) then asks you about professional scepticism. This has been a topical area in the profession for some time and continues to be so. The three marks that are available for this part divide themselves neatly into one for your definition (knowledge), and then two for your examples (application). If you read through the model answer, you will find that you do not need to say anything intimidatingly profound to get the marks. You do, however, need to select some appropriate areas where the auditor could be sceptical, and try to use the right audit terminology when describing the potential problems. For example, terms such as 'management bias' and 'manipulation'. Finally, it is instructive that the model answer is specific about the risk that professional scepticism would want to address, stating where possible what the effect might be on the financial statements were a problem to go unaddressed.

Take care with timing. Part (c) is for only three marks but it is important that you attempt all parts of the question.

**Easy marks.** Part (a) should represent easy marks as you should be familiar with the concept of the preconditions for an audit.

Marks

(a)     **Preconditions for the audit**

1 mark per well-explained point

**Restricted to**                                                                         3

(b)     **Audit risks and auditor's responses** (only 7 required)

Refund liability                                                                          2

Reduced warranty provision                                                                2

Goods in transit                                                                          2

Inventory count attendance                                                                2

Allowance for receivables                                                                 2

Fraud                                                                                     2

Payables ledger backlog                                                                   2

Training costs capitalised                                                                2

Renewal of overdraft facility                                                            _2_

**Max 7 issues, 2 marks each**                                                          _14_

(c)     **Professional scepticism and examples where professional scepticism should be applied**

Professional scepticism definition                                                        1

Examples                                                                                   2

                                                                                         _3_

**Total marks**                                                                         _20_

---

(a)     **Preconditions required for an audit**

Auditors should only accept a new audit engagement or continue an existing audit engagement if the preconditions for an audit are present.

ISA 210 *Agreeing the Terms of Audit Engagements* requires the auditor to:

- Determine whether the financial reporting framework to be applied in the preparation of the financial statements is acceptable (for example IFRS® Standards). In considering this, the auditor should have assessed the nature of the entity, the nature and purpose of the financial statements and whether law or regulation prescribes the applicable reporting framework.

- Obtain the agreement of management that it acknowledges and understands its responsibilities for the following:

    - preparing the financial statements in accordance with the applicable financial reporting framework;

    - internal control necessary for the preparation of the financial statements to be free from material misstatement whether due to fraud or error; and

    - providing the auditor with access to information relevant for the audit and access to staff within the entity to obtain audit evidence.

(b) **Audit risks and auditor's responses**

| Audit risk | Auditor's response |
|---|---|
| The company has a returns policy allowing a customer to return goods within 28 days of purchase if they are dissatisfied with the product.<br><br>IFRS® 15 *Revenue from Contracts with Customers* requires that revenue should only be recognised to the extent that goods will not be returned. The company should recognise a refund liability for goods which are expected to be returned.<br><br>If the company has not correctly accounted for the refund liability, revenue will be overstated and the refund liability understated. | Enquire with the finance director how the returns policy has been applied at the year end and whether the provisions in IFRS 15 have been reflected.<br><br>Review the assumptions underpinning the refund liability for reasonableness and whether they meet the historic 5% value of returns.<br><br>Compare the level of post year-end returns to the refund liability and discuss any significant differences with management. |
| The company provides a six-month warranty on its products which require defects to be repaired at Corley Appliances Co's own cost. The directors have reduced this provision during the year on the grounds they feel the products they sell are built to a high standard.<br><br>The company does not manufacture the goods (they only sell them) and therefore this is not a reasonable reason for reduction, hence if the company has reduced the warranty provision excessively at the year end, liabilities and expenses may be understated. | Review the calculation of the warranty provision and assess its reasonableness in light of the value of claims received in the period.<br><br>Review the assumptions underpinning the warranty provision for reasonableness.<br><br>Review the level of claims made under warranty post year end to assess the reasonableness of the reduced provision. |
| The company purchases their goods from its main supplier in Asia and has responsibility for goods at the point of dispatch, the goods are in transit for up to one month.<br><br>At the year end, there is a risk that the cut-off of purchases may not be accurate as they may not correctly recognise the goods from the point of dispatch. There is also a risk that inventory and trade payables are understated at the year end. | Discuss with management the point at which inventory is recorded and review the contract with the supplier to verify the requirements in place.<br><br>Review the controls the company has in place to ensure that inventory is recorded from the point of dispatch.<br><br>The audit team should undertake detailed cut-off testing of purchases of goods at the year end and the sample of shipping documentation immediately before and after the year end relating to goods from its main supplier in Asia should be increased to ensure that cut-off is complete and accurate. |
| The company's central warehouse and all 20 branches will be carrying out an inventory count at the year-end date of 31 August.<br><br>It is unlikely that the auditor will be able to attend all sites which increases detection risk. It may not be possible to gain sufficient appropriate audit evidence over the inventory counting controls and completeness and existence of inventory for those sites which are not visited. | The audit team should assess which of the inventory counts they will attend. This should include the count for the central warehouse and a sample of branches which contain the most material balances of inventory and those which have historically had exceptions reported during the inventory count.<br><br>For those not visited, the auditor will need to review the level of exceptions noted during the count and discuss any issues which arose during the count with management. |

| Audit risk | Auditor's response |
|---|---|
| Over the last six months, the receivables collection period has increased from 42 days to 55 days and the allowance for receivables will be at the same level as the prior year. | Review and test the controls surrounding the way in which the finance director assesses the recoverability of receivables balances and other credit control processes to ensure that they are operating effectively. |
| Some receivables may not be recoverable and if an additional allowance for receivables is not included in the financial statements, receivables will be overstated and the allowance for receivables understated. | Perform extended post year-end cash receipts testing and a review of the aged receivables ledger in order to assess valuation and the need for an increased allowance for irrecoverable receivables. |
| | Discuss with the finance director whether an additional allowance for receivables will be required against balances older than the company's credit terms. |
| The payables ledger supervisor was dismissed in June 20X5 due to a fraud. The value of this fraud has been recognised as an expense in the draft statement of profit or loss. | Discuss with the finance director the details of the fraud perpetrated by the payables ledger supervisor and what procedures have been adopted to date to identify any further adjustments which are needed in the financial statements. In addition, discuss with the finance director what additional controls have been put in place to prevent any similar frauds. |
| If additional frauds committed by the payables ledger supervisor are not discovered, this could result in expenses being understated and payables being overstated. Control risk is also increased if the fraud has gone undetected for a period of time. | The audit team should undertake additional substantive procedures over the payables balance, particularly the fictitious supplier set up on the payables ledger to ensure this has been removed. |
| | In addition, the team should maintain professional scepticism and be alert to the risk of further fraud. |
| Since the dismissal of the payables ledger supervisor, purchase invoices have yet to be logged onto the payables ledger. | Review the unprocessed invoices file at the year end to identify any invoices which relate to the supply of pre year‐end goods and ensure they have been properly accrued for in the year-end financial statements and recognised as a liability. |
| There is a risk that the purchases and trade payables balance at the year end will be understated if these invoices are not logged onto the payables ledger before it is closed down for the year or accrued for. | Discuss with the finance director the approach to be adopted to resolve the issue of unprocessed purchase invoices. |
| The company purchased and installed a new dispatch system. The costs which have been capitalised include staff training costs ($0.1m). | Discuss the accounting treatment with the finance director and request that the training costs are written off to profit or loss to ensure treatment is in accordance with IAS 16. If adjusted, review the journal entry for accuracy. |
| As per IAS® 16 Property, Plant and Equipment, the cost of an asset includes its purchase price and directly attributable costs only. IAS 16 does not allow staff training costs to be capitalised as part of the cost of a non-current asset, as these costs are not directly related to the cost of bringing the asset to its working condition. | |
| The training costs should be charged to profit or loss. Therefore property, plant and equipment (PPE) and profits are overstated. | |

| Audit risk | Auditor's response |
|---|---|
| The company breached the terms of its overdraft facility in June 20X5 and the bank will only confirm the decision whether, or not, to continue to support the business in November 20X5, which is after the auditor's report will be signed. The company is dependent on the overdraft facility.<br><br>If the bank refuses to continue to support the company, there may be doubts as to the company's ability to continue as a going concern. The uncertainties may not be adequately disclosed in the financial statements. | Discuss with the finance director the availability of alternative financing if the bank is unwilling to continue to support the company and review the adequacy of any going concern disclosures in the financial statements.<br><br>The audit team should undertake detailed going concern testing, in particular, reviewing the impact of a non-renewal of the overdraft facility. |

(c) **Professional scepticism and examples where professional scepticism should be applied**

Professional scepticism is defined in ISA 200 *Overall Objectives of the Independent Auditor and the Conduct of an Audit in Accordance with International Standards on Auditing* as an attitude which includes a questioning mind, being alert to conditions which may indicate possible misstatement due to fraud or error, and a critical assessment of audit evidence.

Examples where the auditor should apply professional scepticism for Corley Appliances Co are as follows:

### Revenue recognition

ISA 240 *The Auditor's Responsibilities Relating to Fraud in an Audit of Financial Statements* contains a rebuttable presumption that fraud in relation to revenue is high risk and hence the auditor must apply professional scepticism to Corley Appliances Co's revenue recognition policies, especially in relation to the company's returns policy which due to the judgement involved may be used as a way to manipulate revenue.

### Warranty provision

Accounting for warranty provisions will include an element of estimation based on previous experiences of the costs incurred by the company to repair defective goods. The auditor should maintain professional scepticism keeping in mind that warranty provisions may include management bias to either deliberately over or understate the provision. Management has reduced the warranty provision in the year on the grounds they feel the goods they sell are built to a high standard. As the company is not involved in the manufacturing of the goods they sell, it may be unreasonable to reduce the warranty provision on this basis.

### Fraud

As a fraud has been committed during the year, the auditor must maintain professional scepticism recognising the fact that internal controls may be weak, hence allowing for employee manipulation of such internal control deficiencies. The auditor must also consider the possibility that other frauds may have taken place during the year through management override of the entity's internal controls.

### Bank overdraft

The company is reliant on its bank overdraft due to the significant levels of expenditure which it has incurred during the year on the new dispatch system. Management may want to deliberately overstate profit and understate liabilities so that the bank renews the overdraft facility.

### Receivables valuation

The receivables collection period has been increasing over the past six months, but the finance director does not envisage that an increase in the allowance for receivables is required. The auditor must apply professional scepticism in considering whether management's assessment of recoverability is reasonable, as any increase in the allowance will reduce profits.

# 77 Kangaroo Construction Co

## Marking scheme

| | | | Marks |
|---|---|---|---|

(a)   Up to 1 mark per well-explained point.

- Materiality for financial statements as a whole and also performance materiality levels
- Definition of materiality
- Amount or nature of misstatements, or both
- 5% profit before tax or 1% revenue or total expenses
- Judgement, needs of users and level of risk
- Small errors aggregated
- Performance materiality                                                              4

(b)   (i)   ½ mark per ratio calculation per year.

- Gross margin
- Operating margin
- Inventory holding period
- Inventory turnover
- Receivables collection period
- Payables payment period                                                             4

(ii)   Up to 1 mark per well-described audit risk and up to 1 mark per well-explained audit response.

- Receivables valuation
- Inventory valuation
- Depreciation of plant and machinery
- Management manipulation of profit to reach bonus targets
- Completeness of warranty provision
- Disclosure of bank loan of £1 million
- Going concern risk                                                                   12
                                                                                       ___
                                                                                       20
                                                                                       ═══

## (a) Materiality and performance materiality

Materiality is not specifically defined in ISA 320 *Materiality in Planning and Performing an Audit* but it does state that misstatements are material if they could reasonably be expected to influence the economic decisions of users (either individually or in aggregate) (ISA 320). ISA 320 also states that judgements about materiality are affected by the size and/or nature of a misstatement (ISA 320). Auditors set their own materiality levels, based on their judgement of risk. During audit planning, the auditor will set materiality for the financial statements as a whole and this involves the exercise of professional judgement. Benchmarks and percentages are often used to calculate a materiality level for the financial statements as a whole, eg 5% of profit before tax or 1–2% of total assets, but ultimately, the level of materiality set is down to the auditor's professional judgement, and may be revised during the course of the audit.

The auditor also has to set performance materiality, which is lower than materiality for the financial statements as a whole. Performance materiality is defined in ISA 320 as the amount or amounts set by the auditor at less than materiality for the financial statements as a whole to reduce to an appropriately low level the probability that the aggregate of uncorrected and undetected misstatements exceeds materiality for the financial statements as a whole (ISA 320).

## (b) (i) Ratios

| Ratio | 20X5 | 20X4 |
|---|---|---|
| Inventory turnover (cost of sales/inventory) | 7/1.9 = 3.7 | 8/1.4 = 5.7 |
| Inventory holding period (inventory/cost of sales × 365) | 1.9/7 × 365 = 99 days | 1.4/8 × 365 = 64 days |
| Receivables collection period (receivables/sales × 365) | 3.1/12.5 × 365 = 91 days | 2/15 × 365 = 49 days |
| Payables payment period (payables/cost of sales × 365) | 1.6/7 × 365 = 83 days | 1.2/8 × 365 = 55 days |

| Audit risk | Auditor's response |
|---|---|
| The company offers a five-year building warranty on its houses. During the year, as a result of switching to a cheaper supplier, some customers have claimed on their guarantees. There is a risk that the warranty provision is understated in the financial statements. | As this is a judgemental area, the auditors need to discuss the basis of calculating the provision with the directors and assess the reasonableness of any assumptions made. They should also review a sample of guarantees claimed during the year and vouch amounts to repairs invoices. They should review the level of claims made in the year and assess whether the provision needs revising in light of this. |
| The company has had a difficult year due to a fall in house prices. In addition, the company has had to take out a loan of $1m during the year to help with operating cash flow. The payables collection period has also increased from 55 days to 83 days, indicating that the company is having problems paying suppliers. The current and quick ratios have also fallen significantly from the prior year. There is therefore a risk that the company may not be a going concern. | The auditors must discuss with directors whether they believe that the company is still a going concern in light of the results of the ratio analysis, and review cash flow forecasts and budgets for the forthcoming year. |

| Audit risk | Auditor's response |
|---|---|
| The receivables collection period has increased from 49 days to 91 days as a result of the directors increasing the credit terms offered to customers. There is a risk that the receivables balance at year end is materially overstated as customers may not be able to pay. | The auditors should carry out post year end testing and cut-off testing on receivables balances to verify the accuracy of the year-end balance. The auditors should also review the aged receivables listing to identify any balances that need writing off. |
| There is a risk that inventory is overstated in the financial statements as there may be some houses whose selling price is less than cost. The inventory holding period has also increased from 64 days to 99 days, and inventory turnover has fallen from 5.7 to 3.7. Inventory should be valued at the lower of cost and net realisable value. | Detailed audit work on inventory should be carried out as this is likely to be a material balance. An auditor's expert may need to be used to independently verify the value of inventory at the year end. |
| There is a risk that revenue has been deliberately overstated and that costs have been deliberately understated in the financial statements, in order for the directors to meet the target profit before interest and taxation figure of $0.5m so as to get their bonuses (window dressing). This is also indicated by the fact that the directors have changed the useful economic life of plant and machinery from three to five years to reduce the depreciation charge for the year and hence inflate the profit figure to attain the minimum target figure. | The auditors need to maintain professional scepticism throughout the audit and carry out detailed cut-off testing on revenue and expenses to confirm that the figures are correctly stated. |
| There is a risk that the depreciation charge for the year is understated and non-current assets on the statement of financial position are overstated as the directors have amended the useful economic life of plant and machinery from three to five years. | The auditors should discuss the change and the reasons for it with the directors and assess whether it is reasonable or not. They should also examine a sample of plant and machinery assets to assess whether the change is appropriate. |
| The company has taken out a loan of $1m from the bank which is repayable within a year. There is a risk that this loan has been incorrectly disclosed in the financial statements. It should be disclosed as a current liability as it is repayable within a year. | The auditors should review the terms of the loan agreement to verify the repayment date and the amount borrowed. They should review the draft financial statements to confirm the correct disclosure of the loan. |

*Note.* Only **six** audit risks were required.

# 78 Hart Co

## Marking scheme

| | | Marks |
|---|---|---|
| (a) | **Benefits of audit planning** | |
| | Appropriate attention to important areas | 1 |
| | Identify/resolve potential problems/risks | 1 |
| | Effective/efficient performance | 1 |
| | Assists in selection of audit team/assignment of work | 1 |
| | Facilitates direction/supervision/review | 1 |
| | Assists in coordination of work performed by experts | 1 |
| | **Restricted to** | **4** |
| (b) | **Audit risk and response** (only 8 risks required) | |
| | New client | 2 |
| | Directors' bonus | 2 |
| | Payment of deposit | 2 |
| | Audit team not attending all WIP counts | 2 |
| | Warranty provision decrease | 2 |
| | Treatment of R&D costs | 2 |
| | Payment for PPE in advance | 2 |
| | Rights issue | 2 |
| | Outsourced payroll function | 2 |
| | Directors' remuneration disclosure | 2 |
| | **Max 8 issues, 2 marks each** | **16** |
| (c) | **Substantive procedures for directors' bonuses** | |
| | 1 mark per well-described procedure | |
| | **Restricted to** | **5** |
| (d) | **Safeguards** | |
| | 1 mark per well-explained point | |
| | Restricted to | **5** |
| **Total marks** | | **30** |

(a)    Audit planning is addressed by ISA 300 *Planning an Audit of Financial Statements*.

It states that adequate planning benefits the audit of financial statements in several ways:

- Helping the auditor to devote appropriate attention to important areas of the audit.

- Helping the auditor to identify and resolve potential problems on a timely basis.

- Helping the auditor to properly organise and manage the audit engagement so that it is performed in an effective and efficient manner.

- Assisting in the selection of engagement team members with appropriate levels of capabilities and competence to respond to anticipated risks and the proper assignment of work to them.

- Facilitating the direction and supervision of engagement team members and the review of their work.

- Assisting, where applicable, in coordination of work done by experts.

(b)    **Risks and responses**

| Audit risk | Auditor's response |
|---|---|
| Hart Co is a new client for Morph & Co. As the audit team is not familiar with the accounting policies, transactions and balances of Hart Co, there will be an increased detection risk on the audit. There is also less assurance over opening balances as Morph & Co did not perform the audit last year. | Morph & Co should ensure it has a suitably experienced team assigned to the audit and that adequate time is allowed for team members to obtain an understanding of the company and the risks of material misstatement, including a detailed team briefing to cover the key areas of risk. Increased audit procedures should be performed over opening balances. |
| The directors are paid a bonus based on a percentage of profit before tax for the year. There is a risk that the directors will try to overstate the profit, and therefore their bonuses by increasing the revenue and income recorded and decreasing expenses. This is a particular risk relating to judgemental areas such as provisions and estimates. | The audit team should be aware of the increased risks of manipulation and should assign more experienced audit members to significant estimates and judgemental areas. Also, adequate time should be allocated for team members to obtain an understanding of the company and the significant risks of overstatement of profit, including attendance at an audit team briefing. The team needs to maintain professional scepticism and be alert to the increased risk of manipulation. Increased testing should be performed relating to adjusting journal entries. |
| Customers pay a 25% deposit on signing the contract to purchase the playgrounds. The deposits should not be recognised as revenue immediately and instead should be recognised as deferred income (contract liabilities) within current liabilities until the performance obligations, as per the contracts, have been satisfied. This is likely to be at a point in time, when control of the playground is passed to the customer. There is a risk that revenue is overstated and current liabilities understated if the deposits have been recorded within revenue. | The audit team should obtain a copy of the contracts with customers and review them to understand the performance obligations. They should discuss with management the criteria for determining whether performance obligations have been satisfied and the treatment of deposits received to ensure it is appropriate and consistent with relevant standards. During the final audit, the audit team should undertake increased testing over the cut-off of revenue and the completeness of deferred income (contract liabilities). |

| Audit risk | Auditor's response |
|---|---|
| The audit team will only attend the WIP counts at five of the 16 sites.<br><br>WIP is a material balance and the valuation of WIP is a judgemental area. As the audit team is not attending all sites, detection risk is increased as the team will be unable to directly obtain evidence relating to WIP. | The auditor should assess which inventory counts the team will attend, most likely to be those with the most material WIP balances or which are assessed as having the greatest risk of misstatement.<br><br>For those inventory counts not attended, the audit team will need to obtain and review documentation relating to the controls surrounding the counts and will need to review reports from any experts used to value the WIP, and any exceptions noted during the count and discuss with management any issues which arise during the count. |
| Hart Co offers its customers a warranty at no extra cost, which guarantees the playgrounds will function as expected for three years. The provision is calculated as 2% of revenue in the current year against 6% in the prior year, despite there being no changes in the construction techniques or the level of claims.<br><br>Under IAS 37 *Provisions, Contingent Liabilities and Contingent Assets* this should be recognised as a warranty provision. Calculating warranty provisions requires judgement as it is an uncertain amount.<br><br>There is a risk that the warranty provision could be understated, leading to understated expenses and liabilities. | The audit team should discuss with management the basis of the provision calculation and compare this to industry averages and the level of post year-end claims, if any, made by customers. In particular, they should discuss the rationale behind reducing the level of provision this year.<br><br>The audit team should also compare the prior year provision with the actual level of claims in the year, to assess the reasonableness of the judgements made by management. |
| Hart Co has recognised $0.6m of research expenditure in profit or loss with the remaining $1.2m having been capitalised as development expenditure.<br><br>IAS 38 *Intangible Assets* has strict criteria as to which costs can be capitalised as development expenditure. There is a risk that the requirements of the standard have not been applied correctly.<br><br>If research costs have been incorrectly classified as development expenditure, there is a risk that intangible assets could be overstated and research expenses understated. | The audit team should obtain a breakdown of the research expenditure recognised in profit or loss and of the development costs capitalised and review supporting documentation to determine whether they have been correctly classified. Any development expenditure should then be agreed as meeting the relevant criteria for capitalisation as set out in IAS 38.<br><br>The team should also discuss the accounting treatment with the finance director and ensure it is in accordance with IAS 38. |

| Audit risk | Auditor's response |
|---|---|
| Hart Co placed an order for $2.4m of machinery, paying $1m in advance. The machinery was due to be received in July 20X5 but will now be delivered post year end. | Review the non-current asset register to determine if the $1m paid in advance has been capitalised. Discuss the correct accounting treatment with management to confirm that the amount paid in advance is recognised as a prepayment and if incorrectly recognised review the correcting journal entry. |
| Only assets which physically exist at the year end should be capitalised as property, plant and equipment (PPE). The $1m deposit paid in advance should be recognised as a prepayment. If the deposit of $1m paid in advance has been capitalised within PPE then prepayments are understated and PPE will be overstated. | |
| Hart Co made a rights issue in the year. This is a non-standard transaction and there is increased risk that the issue has not been recorded correctly. | The audit team should obtain legal documentation in support of the rights issue to agree the number of shares issued and the rights price. They should recalculate the split of share capital and share premium and agree this to the journal entry to record the rights issue. |
| The rights issue has been made at a premium and therefore requires to be split into its share capital and share premium elements. | |
| There is a risk that the split between share capital and share premium has not been accounted for correctly and that these balances are misstated. There is also a risk that the rights issue has not been disclosed in accordance with accounting standards and local company legislation. | The audit team should also agree that disclosures are adequate and consistent with standards and legislation. |
| Hart Co's payroll function is outsourced to an external service organisation. | Discuss with management any changes to the extent of records maintained at Hart Co since the prior year audit and any monitoring of controls which has been undertaken by management over payroll. |
| A detection risk arises as to whether sufficient and appropriate evidence is available at Hart Co to confirm the completeness and accuracy of controls over the payroll cycle and liabilities at the year end. | Consideration should be given to contacting the auditor of the service organisation, Chaz Co, to confirm the level of controls in place. A type 1 or type 2 report could be requested. Consider the extent to which sufficient appropriate audit evidence can be obtained from records held at Hart Co in respect of the wages and salaries expense and liabilities. |
| Consideration should be given to the level of controls in place at the service organisation and whether the data is reliable. If any errors occurred these could result in the wages and salaries expense and any accruals being misstated. | |
| Directors' remuneration disclosures have been made in line with IFRS® Standards but not local legislation. | Discuss this matter with management and review the requirements of local legislation to determine if the disclosure in the financial statements is included appropriately. |
| Where the local legislation is more comprehensive than IFRS Standards it is likely that the company must comply with local legislation. | |
| The directors' remuneration disclosure will not be complete if the additional information is not disclosed. | |

(c) **Substantive procedures for directors' bonuses**

- Obtain a schedule of the directors' bonus and cast the schedule to ensure its accuracy. Agree the amount to that disclosed in the financial statements.

- Review the schedule of current liabilities and confirm the bonus accrual is included as a year-end liability.

- Agree the individual bonus payments to the post year-end payroll records.

- Recalculate the bonus payments and agree the criteria to supporting documentation and the percentage rates to be paid to the directors' service contracts.

- Confirm the amount of each bonus paid by agreeing to the post year-end cash book and bank statements.

- Compare the profit before tax used in the bonus calculation to the final profit before tax figure to confirm whether any adjustment is required to the bonus paid and discuss any differences with management.

- Agree the amounts paid to each director to board minutes and contracts to ensure the amounts included in the current year financial statements are fully accrued and disclosed.

- Review the board minutes to identify whether any additional payments relating to this year have been agreed for any directors.

- Obtain a written representation from management confirming the completeness of directors' remuneration including the bonus.

- Review the disclosures made regarding the bonus paid to directors and assess whether these are in compliance with local legislation.

(d) **Safeguards**

- Both Hart Co and its competitor should be notified that Morph & Co would be acting as auditors for each company and consent should be obtained from management of each company.

- Morph & Co should consider advising one or both clients to seek additional independent advice.

- Morph & Co must ensure it appoints separate engagement teams, with different engagement partners and team members to each client; once an employee has worked on one audit, such as Hart Co, then they should be prevented from being on the audit of the competitor for a period of time.

- Adequate procedures should be in place within the firm to prevent access to information, for example, strict physical separation of both teams, confidential and secure data filing.

- Morph & Co must set out clear guidelines for members of each engagement team on issues of security and confidentiality. These guidelines could be included within the audit engagement letters sent to each client.

- Morph & Co should consider the use of confidentiality agreements signed by all members of the engagement teams of Hart Co and the competitor.

- Work performed should be reviewed by an appropriate reviewer who is not involved in the audit to assess whether key judgements and conclusions are appropriate.

- Regular monitoring of the application of the above safeguards should be undertaken by a senior individual in Morph & Co not involved in either audit.

# 79 Prancer Construction Co

**Workbook references.** Chapters 4 and 6.

**Top tips.** This question is a typical scenario based question testing the area of audit risk. Part (a), on the preconditions of an audit, is an area that can easily be tested for a few marks and so you need to be familiar with them.

Both parts (a) and (b) were for 3 marks each, so you need to be looking for at least 2 marks on each question part to pass this part of the question.

Part (c) accounted for the majority of marks in this question, and required you to read the scenario closely in order to identify audit risks. The requirement asks you to 'describe' the audit risks, so it is important that you do not just state what the risk is, but also say why it is a risk, thinking in particular about how it might affect the financial statements and specifically which balances might be over or understated.

**Easy marks.** You should have found parts (a) and (b) reasonably straightforward.

**Examining team's comments.** This area of the syllabus requires an understanding of how the auditor obtains and accepts audit engagements, obtains an understanding of the entity and its environment, assesses the risk of material misstatement and plans an audit of the financial statements.

Questions on assessing audit risks tend to be scenario based with candidates having to identify and explain the risks from a scenario and give an auditor's response to address the risks. Other questions in this area of the syllabus tend to be more factual knowledge based questions and hence depend on the ability of students to recall their knowledge in the exam.

In this session it was disappointing to see a significant number of candidates were unable to answer the knowledge marks in this syllabus area. Some answers scored zero marks as points made were completely unrelated to the question asked. It is important in factual questions that candidates answer the question set rather than the one they would like to see. This unsatisfactory performance also indicates a lack of preparation and awareness of the knowledge areas relating to planning and risk.

As noted in previous Examining team's Reports a fundamental factor in planning and assessing the risks of an audit of an entity is an assessment of audit risk, and this remains a highly examinable area. Audit risk questions require a number of audit risks to be identified (½ marks each), explained (½ marks each) and an auditor's response to each risk (1 mark each). Typically candidates can be required to identify and explain in the region of six to eight risks and responses.

The scenarios usually contain more issues than are required to be discussed. It is pleasing that candidates planned their time carefully and generally only attempted to list the required number of issues. However, in common with other sessions, a significant number of candidates often did not explain how each issue could impact on the audit risk and therefore were not awarded the second ½ mark. To explain audit risk candidates need to state the area of the accounts impacted with an assertion (eg cut off, valuation, etc), or, a reference to under/over/misstated, or, a reference to inherent, control or detection risk. Misstated was only awarded if it was clear that the balance could be either over or understated.

Auditor's responses still continue to be weak and while an auditor's response does not have to be a detailed audit procedure, rather an approach the audit team will take to address the identified risk. The responses given were sometimes too vague, eg "discuss with the finance director" or they were impractical such as "recruit more audit staff" for the risk of the auditor not attending all the company's inventory counts. Additionally, candidates continue to concentrate their responses on what management should do rather than the auditor.

Marks

(a) **Preconditions for the audit**

| | Marks |
|---|---|
| Determination of acceptable framework | 1 |
| Agreement of management responsibilities | 1 |
| Preparation of financial statements | 1 |
| Internal control | 1 |
| Access to information | 1 |
| **Restricted to** | 3 |

(b) **Audit strategy document**

| | Marks |
|---|---|
| Main characteristics of the audit | 1 |
| Reporting objectives | 1 |
| Significant factors affecting the audit | 1 |
| Preliminary engagement activities | 1 |
| Nature, timing and extent of resources | 1 |
| **Restricted to** | 3 |

(c) **Audit risks and responses** (only 7 risks required)

| | Marks |
|---|---|
| New client | 2 |
| Work in progress | 2 |
| Increased inventory | 2 |
| Warranty provision | 2 |
| Attendance at inventory counts | 2 |
| Deferred income not correctly recognised | 2 |
| Receivables allowance and valuation | 2 |
| Overdraft covenants | 2 |
| Trade payables | 2 |
| | |
| Max 7 issues, 2 marks each | 14 |
| **Total marks** | 20 |

(a) **Preconditions for the audit**

ISA 210 *Agreeing the Terms of Audit Engagements* states that auditors should only accept a new audit engagement when it has been confirmed that the preconditions for an audit are present.

To assess whether the preconditions for an audit are present, Cupid & Co should have determined whether the financial reporting framework to be applied in the preparation of Prancer Construction Co's financial statements is acceptable. In considering this, the auditor should have assessed the nature of the entity, the nature and purpose of the financial statements and whether law or regulation prescribes the applicable reporting framework

In addition, the firm should have obtained the agreement of Prancer Construction Co's management that it acknowledges and understands its responsibility for the following:

- Preparation of the financial statements in accordance with the applicable financial reporting framework, including where relevant their fair presentation;

- For such internal control as management determines is necessary to enable the preparation of financial statements which are free from material misstatement, whether due to fraud or error; and

- To provide Cupid & Co with access to all relevant information for the preparation of the financial statements, any additional information which the auditor may request from management and unrestricted access to personnel within Prancer Construction Co from whom the auditor determines it necessary to obtain audit evidence.

(b)   **Areas to be included in the audit strategy document**

The audit strategy sets out the scope, timing and direction of the audit and helps the development of the audit plan. The revised ISA 220 *Quality Management for an Audit of Financial Statements* understands proper planning to be a key part of providing a high quality audit. ISA 300 *Planning an Audit of Financial Statements* sets out areas which should be considered and documented as part of the audit strategy document and are as follows:

### Main characteristics of the engagement

The audit strategy should consider the main characteristics of the engagement, which define its scope. For Prancer Construction Co, the following are examples of things which should be included:

- Whether the financial information to be audited has been prepared in accordance with the relevant financial reporting framework.

- Whether computer-assisted audit techniques will be used and the effect of IT on audit procedures.

- The availability of key personnel at Prancer Construction Co.

### Reporting objectives, timing and nature of communication

It should ascertain the reporting objectives of the engagement to plan the timing of the audit and the nature of the communications required, such as:

- The audit timetable for reporting including the timing of interim and final stages.

- Organisation of meetings with Prancer Construction Co's management to discuss any audit issues arising.

- Any discussions with management regarding the reports to be issued.

- The timings of the audit team meetings and review of work performed.

### Significant factors affecting the audit

The strategy should consider the factors which, in the auditor's professional judgement, are significant in directing Prancer Construction Co's audit team's efforts, such as:

- The determination of materiality for the audit.

- The need to maintain a questioning mind and to exercise professional scepticism in gathering and evaluating audit evidence.

### Preliminary engagement activities and knowledge from previous engagements

It should consider the results of preliminary audit planning activities and, where applicable, whether knowledge gained on other engagements for Prancer Construction Co is relevant, such as:

- Results of any tests over the effectiveness of internal controls.

- Evidence of management's commitment to the design, implementation and maintenance of sound internal controls.

- Volume of transactions, which may determine whether it is more efficient for the audit team to rely on internal controls.

- Significant business developments affecting Prancer Construction Co, such as the improvement in building practices and construction quality.

### Nature, timing and extent of resources

The audit strategy should ascertain the nature, timing and extent of resources necessary to perform the audit, such as:

- The selection of the audit team with experience of this type of industry.

- Assignment of audit work to the team members.

- Setting the audit budget.

(c) **Audit risks and auditor's responses**

| Audit risk | Auditor's response |
|---|---|
| Prancer Construction Co is a new client for Cupid & Co. As the team is not familiar with the accounting policies, transactions and balances of the company, there will be an increased detection risk on the audit. | Cupid & Co should ensure they have a suitably experienced team. In addition, adequate time should be allocated for team members to obtain an understanding of the company and the risks of material misstatement including a detailed team briefing to cover the key areas of risk. |
| Prancer Construction Co is likely to have a material level of work in progress at the year end, being construction work in progress as well as ongoing maintenance services, as Prancer Construction Co has annual contracts for many of the buildings constructed. The level of work in progress will need to be assessed at the year end. Assessing the percentage completion for partially constructed buildings is likely to be quite subjective, and the team should consider if they have the required expertise to undertake this. If the percentage completion is not correctly calculated, the inventory valuation may be under or overstated. | The auditor should discuss with management the process they will undertake to assess the percentage completion for work in progress at the year end. This process should be reviewed by the auditor while attending the year-end inventory counts. In addition, consideration should be given as to whether an independent expert is required to value the work in progress or if a management expert has been used. If the work of an expert is to be used, then the audit team will need to assess the competence, capabilities and objectivity of the expert. |
| The August 20X5 management accounts contain $2.1 million of completed properties; this balance was $1.4 million in September 20X6. The increase in inventory may be due to an increased level of pre year-end orders. Alternatively, it may be that Prancer Construction Co is struggling to sell completed properties, which may indicate that they are overvalued. IAS 2 *Inventories* requires that inventory should be stated at the lower of cost and NRV. | Detailed cost and net realisable value (NRV) testing to be performed at the year end and the aged inventory report to be reviewed to assess whether inventory requires to be written down. |

| Audit risk | Auditor's response |
|---|---|
| At the year end there will be inventory counts undertaken at all 11 of the building sites in progress.<br><br>It is unlikely that the auditor will be able to attend all of these inventory counts, increasing detection risk, and therefore they need to ensure that they obtain sufficient evidence over the inventory counting controls, and completeness and existence of inventory for any sites not visited. | The auditor should assess for which of the building sites they will attend the counts. This will be those with the most material inventory or which according to management have the most significant risk of misstatement.<br><br>For those not visited, the auditor will need to review the level of exceptions noted during the count and discuss with management any issues, which arose during the count. |
| Prancer Construction Co offers its customers a building warranty of five years, which covers any construction defects. A warranty provision will be required under IAS 37 *Provisions, Contingent Liabilities and Contingent Assets*. Calculating warranty provisions requires judgement as it is an uncertain amount.<br><br>The finance director anticipates this provision will be lower than last year as the company has improved its building practices and the quality of its finished properties. However, there is a risk that this provision could be understated, especially in light of the overdraft covenant relating to a minimum level of net assets and is being used as a mechanism to manipulate profit and asset levels. | Discuss with management the basis of the provision calculation, and compare this to the level of post year-end claims, if any, made by customers. In particular, discuss the rationale behind reducing the level of provision this year.<br><br>Compare the prior year provision with the actual level of claims in the year, to assess the reasonableness of the judgements made by management. |
| Customers who wish to purchase a property are required to place an order and a 5% non-refundable deposit prior to the completion of the building.<br><br>These deposits should not be recognised as revenue in the statement of profit or loss until the performance obligations as per the contracts have been satisfied, which is likely to be when the building is finished and the sale process is complete. Instead, they should be recognised as deferred income within current liabilities.<br><br>Management may have incorrectly treated the deferred income as revenue, resulting in overstated revenue and understated liabilities. | Discuss with management the treatment of deposits received in advance, to ensure it is appropriate.<br><br>During the final audit, undertake increased testing over the cut-off of revenue and completeness of deferred income. |

| Audit risk | Auditor's response |
|---|---|
| An allowance for receivables has historically been maintained, but it is anticipated that this will be reduced.<br><br>There is a risk that receivables will be overvalued; some balances may not be recoverable and so will be overstated if not provided for.<br><br>In addition, reducing the allowance for receivables will increase asset values and would improve the covenant compliance, which increases the manipulation risk further.<br><br>Prancer Construction Co has a material overdraft which has minimum profit and net assets covenants attached to it. If these covenants were to be breached, the overdraft balance would become instantly repayable.<br><br>If the company does not have sufficient cash to meet this repayment, then there could be going concern implications.<br><br>In addition, there is a risk of manipulation of profit and net assets to ensure that covenants are met. | Review and test the controls surrounding how the finance director identifies old or potentially irrecoverable receivables balances and credit control to ensure that they are operating effectively.<br><br>Discuss with the director the rationale for reducing the allowance for receivables.<br><br>Extended post year-end cash receipts testing and a review of the aged receivables ledger to be performed to assess valuation and the need for an allowance for receivables.<br><br>Review the covenant calculations prepared by the company at the year end and identify whether any defaults have occurred; if so, determine the effect on the company.<br><br>The team should maintain their professional scepticism and be alert to the risk that profit and/or net assets have been overstated to ensure compliance with the covenants. |
| Preliminary analytical review of the August management accounts shows a payables payment period of 56 days for August 20X5, compared to 87 days for September 20X4. It is anticipated that the year-end payables payment period will be even lower.<br><br>The forecast profit is higher than last year, indicating an increase in trade, also the company's cash position has continued to deteriorate and therefore, it is unusual for the payables payment period to have decreased.<br><br>There is an increased risk of errors within trade payables and the year-end payables may be understated. | The audit team should increase their testing on trade payables at the year end, with a particular focus on completeness of payables. A payables circularisation or review of supplier statement reconciliations should be undertaken. |

# 80 Blackberry Co

**Workbook references.** Chapter 6.

**Top tips.** Part (a) dealt with responsibilities for fraud. This is a simple area that you should be familiar with.

Part (b) was an application-based requirement. It is essential that you only include eight audit risks in your solution, the 16 marks available divide themselves into one each for describing the audit risk and then for the auditor's response to it. Your description of the audit risk should say what is happening and then, crucially, why this poses an audit risk in terms of problems that could be encountered during the audit (perhaps due to lack of available information) or which balances could be over or understated. The auditor's response is then focused on reducing the audit risks.

BPP
LEARNING
MEDIA

**Easy marks.** You should have found part (a) reasonably straightforward. There are marks in (b) for giving a simple description of each audit risk from the scenario (the marks for identification), and these are easy to get.

**Examining team's comments.** This area of the syllabus requires an understanding of how the auditor obtains and accepts audit engagements, obtains an understanding of the entity and its environment, assesses the risk of material misstatement and plans an audit of the financial statements.

As noted in previous Examining team's Reports a fundamental factor in planning and assessing the risks of an audit of an entity is an assessment of audit risk, and this remains a highly examinable area. Audit risk questions typically require a number of audit risks to be identified (½ marks each), explained (½ marks each) and an auditor's response to each risk (1 mark each). Typically candidates can be required to identify and explain in the region of six to eight risks and responses.

The scenarios usually contain more issues than are required to be discussed. It is pleasing that candidates planned their time carefully and generally only attempted to list the required number of issues. However, in common with other sessions, a significant number of candidates often did not explain how each issue could impact on the audit risk and therefore were not awarded the second ½ mark. To explain audit risk candidates need to state the area of the financial statements impacted with an assertion (e.g. cut off, valuation etc.), a reference to under/over/misstated, or, a reference to inherent, control or detection risk. Misstated was only awarded if it was clear that the balance could be either over or understated.

Candidates should note that an auditor's response does not have to be a detailed audit procedure, rather an approach the audit team will take to address the identified risk. However, the responses given were sometimes too weak e.g. "discuss with management". Responses also sometimes focussed on what management should do rather than the auditor, and/or, were inappropriate to the scenario.

## Marking scheme

|  |  | Marks |
|---|---|---:|
| (a) | **Fraud and error** | |
|  | ISA 240 responsibilities | 2 |
|  | Respond appropriately | 2 |
|  |  | **4** |
| (b) | **Audit risks and responses (only 8 risks required)** | |
|  | Inventory valuation | **2** |
|  | Inventory count after year-end date | **2** |
|  | Accounting treatment of patent | 2 |
|  | Share issue | 2 |
|  | Sales ledger fraud | 2 |
|  | Use of service organisation | 2 |
|  | Transfer of data to service organisation | 2 |
|  | Claim for unfair dismissal | 2 |
|  | Direct controls not performed | **2** |
|  | Contingent asset | **2** |
|  | **Max 8 issues, 2 marks each** | **16** |
|  | **Total marks** | **20** |

(a)    **Fraud responsibility**

Loganberry & Co must conduct an audit in accordance with ISA 240 *The Auditor's Responsibilities Relating to Fraud in an Audit of Financial Statements* and is responsible for obtaining reasonable assurance that the financial statements taken as a whole are free from material misstatement, whether caused by fraud or error.

In order to fulfil this responsibility, Loganberry & Co is required to identify and assess the risks of material misstatement of the financial statements due to fraud.

They need to obtain sufficient appropriate audit evidence regarding the assessed risks of material misstatement due to fraud through designing and implementing appropriate responses. In addition, Loganberry & Co must respond appropriately to fraud or suspected fraud identified during the audit.

When obtaining reasonable assurance, Loganberry & Co is responsible for maintaining professional scepticism throughout the audit, considering the potential for management override of controls and recognising the fact that audit procedures which are effective in detecting error may not be effective in detecting fraud.

To ensure that the whole engagement team is aware of the risks and responsibilities for fraud and error, ISA 240 requires that a discussion is held within the team. For members not present at the meeting, Blackberry Co's audit engagement partner should determine which matters should be communicated to them.

(b)    **Audit risks and auditor's response**

| Audit risk | Auditor's response |
|---|---|
| Blackberry Co values its inventory at the lower of cost and net realisable value. Cost includes both production and general overheads. | Discuss with management the nature of the overheads included in inventory valuation. If general overheads are included, request management remove them from the valuation to be included in the draft financial statements. |
| IAS 2 *Inventories* requires that costs included in valuing goods and services should only be those incurred in bringing inventory to its present location and condition. Although production overheads meet these criteria, general overheads do not. If these are included in inventory cost, then this will result in over-valued inventory. | Review supporting documentation to verify those overheads deemed to be of a production nature are valid. |
| The company is planning to undertake the full year-end inventory counts after the year end and then adjust for movements from the year end. | The auditor should attend the inventory count held after the year end and note details of goods received and despatched post year end, in order to agree to the reconciliation. |
| If the adjustments are not completed accurately, then the year-end inventory could be under or overstated. | During the final audit, the year-end inventory adjustments schedule should be reviewed in detail and agreed to supporting documentation obtained during the inventory count for all adjusting items. |
| | The audit team should increase the extent of inventory cut-off testing at the year end and at the date of the count. |

BPP
LEARNING
MEDIA

| Audit risk | Auditor's response |
|---|---|
| A patent has been purchased for $1.1m and this grants Blackberry Co the exclusive right for three years to customise their portable music players to gain a competitive advantage in their industry. Management has expensed the full amount paid to the current year statement of profit or loss.

In accordance with IAS 38 *Intangible Assets*, this should have been included as an intangible asset and amortised over its three-year life. As the sum has been fully expensed and not treated in accordance with IAS 38, intangible assets and profits are understated. | The audit team will need to agree the purchase price to supporting documentation and confirm the useful life is three years as per the contract.

Discuss with management the reason for fully expensing the $1.1m paid, and request they correct the treatment.

The correcting journal should be reviewed and the amortisation charge should be recalculated in order to ensure the accuracy of the charge and that the intangible is correctly valued at the year end. |
| During the year Blackberry Co has raised new finance through issuing $1.2m of shares at a premium. This needs to be accounted for correctly, with adequate disclosure made and the equity finance needs to be allocated correctly between share capital and share premium.

If this is not done, then the accounts may be misstated due to a lack of disclosure or share capital and share premium may be misstated. | The audit team should confirm that proceeds of $1.2m were received and that the split of share capital and share premium is correct and appropriately recorded.

In addition, the disclosures for this finance should be reviewed in detail to ensure compliance with relevant accounting standards and local legislation. |
| In November 20X7, it was discovered that a significant teeming and lading fraud had been carried out by four members of the sales ledger department.

There is a risk that the full impact of the fraud has not been quantified and any additional fraudulent transactions would need to be written off in the statement of profit or loss. If these have not been uncovered, the financial statements could be misstated.

In addition, individual receivable balances may be under/overstated as customer receipts have been misallocated to other receivable balances. | Discuss with the finance director what procedures they have adopted to fully identify and quantify the impact of the teeming and lading fraud. In addition, discuss with the finance director, what controls have been put in place to identify any similar frauds.

Review the receivables listing to identify any unusual postings to individual receivable balances as this could be further evidence of fraudulent transactions.

In addition, the team should maintain their professional scepticism and be alert to the risk of further fraud and errors. |
| During the year Blackberry Co outsourced its sales ledger processing to an external service organisation. A detection risk arises as to whether sufficient and appropriate evidence is available at Blackberry Co to confirm the completeness and accuracy of controls over the sales and receivables cycle and balances at the year end. | Discuss with management the extent of records maintained at Blackberry Co for the period since February 20X8 and any monitoring of controls undertaken by management over sales and receivables.

Consideration should be given to contacting the service organisation's auditor to confirm the level of controls in place. |

| Audit risk | Auditor's response |
|---|---|
| The sales ledger processing transferred to the service organisation from 1 February 20X8. If any errors occurred during the transfer process, these could result in sales and receivables being under/overstated. | Discuss with management the transfer process undertaken and any controls put in place to ensure the completeness and accuracy of the data.<br><br>Where possible, undertake tests of controls to confirm the effectiveness of the transfer controls. In addition, perform substantive testing on the transfer of information from the old to the new system. |
| In December 20X7, the financial accountant of Blackberry Co was dismissed and is threatening to sue the company for unfair dismissal.<br><br>If it is probable that Blackberry Co will make a payment to the financial accountant, a provision for unfair dismissal is required. If the payment is possible rather than probable, a contingent liability disclosure would be necessary. If Blackberry Co has not done this, there is a risk over the completeness of any provisions or contingent liabilities. | The audit team should request confirmation from the company's lawyers of the existence and likelihood of success of any claim from the former financial accountant. |
| No supplier statement or purchase ledger control account reconciliations have been performed in the period from December 20X7 to the year end.<br><br>This a direct control which is being overridden and as such there is an increased risk of errors within trade payables and the year-end payables balance may be under or overstated. | The audit team should increase their testing on trade payables at the year end, including performing supplier statement reconciliations, with a particular focus on completeness of trade payables.<br><br>Request management prepare a year-end purchase ledger control account reconciliation. The audit team should undertake a detailed review of this reconciliation with a focus on any unusual reconciling items. |
| A current asset of $360,000 has been included within the statement of profit or loss and assets. It represents an anticipated pay out from liquidators handling the bankruptcy of a customer who owed Blackberry Co $0.9m. The sum of $0.9m was written off in the prior year accounts.<br><br>However, the company has not received a formal notification from the liquidators confirming the payment and this would therefore represent a possible contingent asset. To comply with IAS 37 *Provisions, Contingent Liabilities and Contingent Assets*, this should not be recognised until the receipt is virtually certain. With no firm response to date, the inclusion of this sum overstates profit and current assets. | Discuss with management whether any notification of payment has been received from the liquidators and review the related correspondence. If virtually certain, the treatment adopted is correct. If payment has been received, agree to post-year end cash book.<br><br>If receipt is not virtually certain, management should be requested to remove it from profit and receivables. If the receipt is probable, the auditor should request management include a contingent asset disclosure note. |

ANSWERS

# 81 Darjeeling Co

**Workbook references.** Chapter 6, 13 and 14.

**Top tips.** Part (a) was a simple knowledge requirement on which you should have a chance of scoring at least two marks. If you were not sure of your knowledge here, then you could think about what the stages of an audit would be, and then consider why analytical procedures might be used at each stage.

Part (b) simply asked for three ratios for both years – so six calculations in total. These did not need to be complex, but it is important that you worked carefully and picked up the right figures from the question. Be careful not to waste time by calculating more ratios than are needed, or writing out the formula for each ratio.

Part (c) was an application-based requirement. It is essential that you only include eight audit risks in your solution; the 16 marks available divide themselves into one each for describing the audit risk and then for the auditor's response to it. Your description of the audit risk should say what is happening and then, crucially, why this poses an audit risk. This statement of why could address a problem that could be encountered during the audit (eg due to lack of available information), or simply which balances could be over or understated. The auditor's response is then focused on reducing the audit risks.

Part (d) asked for substantive procedures on the faulty paint inventory. When writing your procedures you need to be as specific as possible, and should say **why** the procedure should be performed. Do not overlook procedures that begin with 'Discuss with management' – you could have scored two out of three marks here merely for 'discuss' procedures.

Part (e) was similar to (d) but focused on revenue. Many of these are generic points that would apply to many different situations, but there are easy marks available for thinking of procedures that are specific to Darjeeling Co and its sales price promise.

**Easy marks.** There are marks in (c) for giving a simple description of each audit risk from the scenario (the marks for identification), and these are easy to get.

**Examining team's comments.** As noted in previous examiner's reports a fundamental factor in planning and assessing the risks of an audit of an entity is an assessment of audit risk, and this remains a highly examinable area. Audit risk questions typically require a number of audit risks to be identified (½ marks each), explained (½ marks each) and an auditor's response to each risk (1 mark each). Typically candidates can be required to identify and explain in the region of six to eight risks and responses.

The scenarios usually contain more issues than are required to be discussed. It is pleasing that candidates planned their time carefully and generally only attempted to list the required number of issues. However, in common with other sessions, a significant number of candidates often did not explain how each issue could impact on the audit risk and therefore were not awarded the second ½ mark. To explain audit risk candidates need to state the area of the financial statements impacted with an assertion (eg cut off, valuation etc), a reference to under/over/misstated or, a reference to inherent, control or detection risk. Misstated was only awarded if it was clear that the balance could be either over or understated.

Candidates should note that an auditor's response does not have to be a detailed audit procedure, rather an approach the audit team will take to address the identified risk. However, the responses given were sometimes too weak eg 'discuss with management'. Responses also sometimes focussed on what management should do rather than the auditor, and/or, were inappropriate to the scenario.

As in previous sessions, in this session a number of audit risk questions were combined with a requirement to calculate ratios, these ratios then link into the risk and responses requirement. 'Darjeeling Co' from the 'Sample September/December 2018 Questions' is a good question to practice the skill of calculating ratios and applying these to a risk and response question. Candidates tend to score well in calculating ratios, however a few points to note are as follows:

- Do not calculate more than the required number of ratios as this wastes time
- Do not provide the formula for ratios, as no credit is available

|  |  | Marks |
|---|---|---|
| (a) | Analytical procedures | |
|  | Must be used at planning as risk assessment tool | 1 |
|  | Can be used to gather evidence during fieldwork | 1 |
|  | Must be used at completion to confirm overall conclusion | 1 |
|  |  | 3 |
| (b) | Ratios | |
|  | Gross profit margin | 1 |
|  | Inventory holding period | 1 |
|  | Receivables collection period | 1 |
|  | Payables payment period | 1 |
|  | Current ratio | 1 |
|  | Quick ratio | 1 |
|  | Max 3 ratios, ½ for each calc | 3 |
| (c) | Audit risks and responses (only 8 risks required) | 2 |
|  | Treatment of research and development costs | 2 |
|  | Incorrect capitalisation of PPE costs | 2 |
|  | New significant loan finance | 2 |
|  | Finance costs | 2 |
|  | Risk of manipulation due to potential listing | 2 |
|  | Recoverability of receivables | 2 |
|  | Accounting for 'price promise' | 2 |
|  | Product recall | 2 |
|  | Inventory valuation | 2 |
|  | Significant increase in revenue and gross margin | 2 |
|  | Cash flow difficulties | 2 |
|  | Max 8 issues, 2 marks each | 16 |

(d)  Substantive procedures – faulty inventory

| | |
|---|---|
| Obtain schedule of faulty inventory, cast and agree to inventory listing | 1 |
| Agree quantities affected to manufacturing and sales records | 1 |
| Agree a sample of returns to relevant documentation | 1 |
| Discuss issue with management and likelihood of subsequent sale | 1 |
| Agree any post year-end sales to invoice and assess NRV | 1 |
| Agree costs of faulty goods to supporting documentation | 1 |
| Discuss any write down with management | 1 |
| Inspect board minutes for evidence of resale or additional costs | 1 |
| Restricted to | 3 |
| **Total marks** | **30** |

(a)  **Analytical procedures**

Analytical procedures can be used at all stages of an audit, however, ISA 315 *Identifying and Assessing the Risks of Material Misstatement* and ISA 520 *Analytical Procedures* identify three particular stages.

During the planning stage, analytical procedures must be used as risk assessment procedures in order to help the auditor to obtain an understanding of the entity and assess the risk of material misstatement.

During the final audit, analytical procedures can be used to obtain sufficient appropriate evidence. Substantive procedures can either be tests of detail or substantive analytical procedures.

At the final review stage, the auditor must design and perform analytical procedures which assist them when forming an overall conclusion as to whether the financial statements are consistent with the auditor's understanding of the entity.

(b)  **Ratios**

Ratios to assist the audit supervisor in planning the audit:

| | 20X5 | 20X4 |
|---|---|---|
| Gross margin | (7,410/19,850) * 100 = 37.3% | (6,190/16,990) * 100 = 36.4% |
| Inventory holding period | (1,850/12,440) * 365 = 54 days | (1,330/10,800) * 365 = 45 days |
| OR | | |
| Inventory turnover | 12,440/1,850 = 6.7 times | 10,800/1,330 = 8.1 times |
| Receivables collection period | (2,750/19,850) * 365 = 51 days | 1,780/16,990 * 365 = 38 days |
| Payables payment period | (1,970/12,440) * 365 = 58 days | 1,190/10,800 * 365 = 40 days |
| Current ratio | (4,600/[1,970 + 810]) = 1.65 | 3,670/1,190 = 3.08 |
| Quick ratio | (2,750/[1,970 + 810]) = 0.99 | (3,670 – 1,330)/1,190 = 1.97 |

(c)

| Audit risk | Auditor's response |
|---|---|
| During the year, Darjeeling Co has spent $0.9m on developing new product lines, some of which are in the early stages of their development cycle. This expenditure is classed as research and development under IAS 38 *Intangible Assets*. The standard requires research costs to be expensed to profit or loss and only development costs to be capitalised as an intangible asset.<br><br>The company has included all of this expenditure as an intangible asset. If research costs have been incorrectly classified as development expenditure, there is a risk that intangible assets could be overstated and expenses understated. | Obtain a breakdown of the expenditure and verify that it relates to the development of the new products. Review expenditure documentation to determine whether the costs relate to the research or development stage. Discuss the accounting treatment with the finance director and ensure it is in accordance with IAS 38. |
| Darjeeling Co purchased and installed a new manufacturing line. The costs include purchase price ($2.2m), installation costs ($0.4m) and a five-year servicing and maintenance plan ($0.5m).<br><br>As per IAS 16 *Property, Plant and Equipment*, the cost of an asset includes its purchase price and directly attributable costs only. IAS 16 does not allow servicing and maintenance costs to be capitalised as part of the cost of a non-current asset, as they are not directly related to the cost of bringing the asset to its working condition.<br><br>The servicing costs relate to a five-year period and so should be charged to profit or loss over this time. The upfront payment represents a prepayment for five years; as the services are received, the relevant proportion of the cost should be charged to profit or loss. If the service for 20X5 has been carried out, then $0.1m ($0.5m/5) should be charged to profit or loss. Therefore property, plant and equipment (PPE) and profits are overstated and prepayments are understated. | Review the purchase documentation for the new manufacturing line to confirm the exact cost of the servicing and that it does relate to a five-year period.<br><br>Discuss the accounting treatment with the finance director and the level of any necessary adjustment to ensure treatment is in accordance with IAS 16. |
| The company has borrowed $4m from the bank via an eight-year loan. This loan needs to be correctly split between current and non-current liabilities in order to ensure correct disclosure. | During the audit, the team would need to confirm that the $4 million loan finance was received. In addition, the split between current and non-current liabilities and the disclosures for this loan should be reviewed in detail to ensure compliance with relevant accounting standards and local legislation.<br><br>Details of security should be agreed to the bank confirmation letter. |

| Audit risk | Auditor's response |
|---|---|
| As the level of debt has increased, there should be additional finance costs as the loan has an interest rate of 5%. There is a risk that this has been omitted from the statement of profit or loss leading to understated finance costs and overstated profit. | The finance costs should be recalculated and any increase agreed to the loan documentation for confirmation of the 5% interest rate. Interest payments should be agreed to the cash book and bank statements to confirm the amount was paid and is not therefore a year-end payable. |
| Darjeeling Co intends to undertake a stock exchange listing in the next 12 months.<br><br>In order to maximise the success of the potential listing, Darjeeling Co will need to present financial statements which show the best possible position and performance. The directors therefore have an incentive to manipulate the financial statements, by overstating revenue, profits and assets. | Earl & Co should ensure that there is a suitably experienced audit team. Also, adequate time should be allocated for team members to obtain an understanding of the company and the significant risks of overstatement of revenue, profits and assets, including attendance at an audit team briefing. The team needs to maintain professional scepticism and be alert to the increased risk of manipulation.<br><br>Significant estimates and judgements should be carefully reviewed in light of the misstatement risk. |
| The receivables collection period has increased from 38 to 51 days and management has extended the credit terms given to customers on the condition that sales order quantities were increased. The increase in receivable days could be solely due to these increased credit terms. However, it could also be due to an increased risk over recoverability of receivables as they may be overvalued and expenses understated. | Review and test the controls surrounding how Darjeeling Co identifies receivables balances which may not be recoverable and procedures around credit control to ensure that they are operating effectively.<br><br>Extended post year-end cash receipts testing and a review of the aged receivables ledger to be performed to assess valuation. Also consider the adequacy of any allowance for receivables |
| This year the company made a 'price promise' to match the price of its competitors for similar products. Customers are able to claim the difference from the company for one month after the date of purchase of goods.<br><br>The company should account for the price promise in accordance with IFRS 15 *Revenue from Contracts with Customers*. As the company may be required to provide a refund, the anticipated refund amount should not be initially recognised as revenue but instead as a refund liability until the one-month price promise period has ended.<br><br>This is a highly subjective area, with many judgements required with regards to the level of likely refund due. As this is a new liability, the directors may not have correctly accounted for this sum resulting in overstated revenue, under/overstated profits and liabilities. | Discuss with management the basis of the refund liability of $0.25m and obtain supporting documentation to confirm the reasonableness of the assumptions and calculations. |

| Audit risk | Auditor's response |
|---|---|
| Darjeeling Co has stopped further sales of one of its paint products and a product recall has been initiated for any goods sold since June.<br><br>This product recall will result in Darjeeling Co paying refunds to customers. The sales will need to be removed from the 20X5 financial statements and a refund liability recognised. Also inventory will need to be reinstated, albeit at a possibly written down value. Failing to account for this correctly could result in overstated revenue, understated liabilities and misstated inventory. | Review the list of sales of the paint product made between June and the date of the recall, agree that the sales have been removed from revenue and the inventory included. If the refunds have not been paid before the year end, review the draft financial statements to confirm that it is included within current liabilities. |
| The company is holding a number of damaged paint products in inventory and overall the inventory holding period has increased from 45 days to 54 days.<br><br>Due to the issue with the paint consistency, the quality of these products is questionable and management is investigating whether these products can be rectified. There is a risk that this inventory may be overvalued as its net realisable value may be below cost. | Discuss with the finance director whether any write downs will be made to this product, and what, if any, modifications will be required to rectify the quality of the product.<br><br>Testing should be undertaken to confirm cost and NRV of the affected paint products held in inventory and that on a line by line basis the goods are valued correctly. |
| Revenue has increased by 16.8% in the year; and the gross margin has increased slightly from 36.4% to 37.3%. This is a significant increase in revenue and, along with the increase in gross margin, may be related to the increased credit period and price promise promotion or could be due to an overstatement of revenue. | During the audit a detailed breakdown of sales will be obtained, discussed with management and tested in order to understand the sales increase. Also increased cut-off testing should be undertaken to verify that revenue is recorded in the right period and is not overstated. |
| The payables payment period has increased from 40 to 58 days. The current ratio has decreased from 3.08 to 1.65. The quick ratio has also decreased from 1.97 to 0.99.<br><br>In addition, the bank balance has moved from $0.56m to an overdraft of $0.81m.<br><br>These are all indicators that the company could be experiencing a reduction in its cash flow which could result in going concern difficulties or uncertainties. These uncertainties may not be adequately disclosed in the financial statements. | Detailed going concern testing to be performed during the audit, including the review of cash flow forecasts and the underlying assumptions. These should be discussed with management to ensure that the going concern basis is reasonable. |

(d) **Faulty inventory**

- Obtain a breakdown of the damaged goods held in inventory and returned from customers and cast to confirm its accuracy.

- From the breakdown, agree the damaged goods quantities manufactured since June to production records; and agree to sales records the quantities sold.

- Agree on a sample basis the returns from customers as per the breakdown back to sales returns documentation to confirm the existence of the returns quantities.

- Discuss with management the current status of their plans for this product line and whether they are able to rectify the damage and then sell the goods on. If so, agree the costs of rectification to supporting documentation.

- If the damaged inventory has been rectified and sold post year end, agree to the sales invoice to assess NRV in line with the new cost of the product.

- Agree the cost of damaged goods to supporting documentation to confirm the raw material cost, labour cost and any overheads attributed to the cost.

- Discuss with management if the goods have been written down; if so, follow through the write down to the inventory valuation to confirm.

- Inspect monthly board meeting minutes from June 20X5 onwards to obtain further information regarding the faulty paint and its possible resale value.

(e) **Revenue**

- Compare the overall level of revenue against prior years and budget for the year and investigate any significant fluctuations.

- Perform a proof in total calculation for revenue, creating an expectation of the average price for the main paint products multiplied by the increased sales volumes for this year. This expectation should be compared to actual revenue and any significant fluctuations should be investigated.

- Obtain a schedule of sales for the year broken down into the main product categories and compare this to the prior year breakdown and for any unusual movements, discuss with management.

- Calculate the final gross profit margin for Darjeeling Co and compare this to the prior year and investigate any significant fluctuations.

- Select a sample of sales invoices for customers and agree the sales prices back to the price list or customer master data information to ensure the accuracy of invoices.

- For a sample of invoices, recalculate invoice totals including discounts and sales tax.

- Select a sample of credit notes raised, trace through to the original invoice and ensure the invoice has been correctly removed from sales.

- Select a sample of customer orders and agree these to the despatch notes and sales invoices through to inclusion in the sales ledger and revenue general ledger accounts to ensure completeness of revenue.

- Select a sample of despatch notes both pre and post year end and follow these through to sales invoices in the correct accounting period to ensure that cut-off has been correctly applied.

- For sales made under the price promise, compare the level of claims made to date with the refund liability recognised and assess whether it is reasonable.

- For a sample of sales invoices issued between June and the product recall, trace to subsequent credit notes to confirm that the sale has been removed from revenue.

# Flowers Anytime

82    The correct answer is:

(1)    Complete flowcharts and internal control evaluation questionnaires
(2)    Perform walkthrough tests
(3)    Perform tests of control
(4)    Revise the audit strategy and audit plan

The first step should be to document the system of internal control – this is done using the flowchart and internal control evaluation questionnaire. The second step should be to confirm the auditor's understanding of the system – this is done with a walkthrough test. Tests of control are then performed to obtain audit evidence about the effectiveness of the design and operation of internal controls. Finally, if controls testing reveals any deficiencies in internal controls that have not been previously identified, the audit strategy and the audit plan should be revised as required.

83    The correct answer is:

ICEQs are generally easier to apply to a variety of different systems than ICQs.

In the first option, the descriptions of ICQs and ICEQs are reversed. Neither ICQs nor ICEQs are likely to capture how internal controls deal with unusual transactions: narrative notes are needed to do this. Both ICQs and ICEQs give the impression that all controls are of equal importance. The significance of each control would only be highlighted in narrative notes.

84    The correct answer is:

| Audit junior's notes | Yes | No |
|---|---|---|
| All orders are recorded on pre-printed, three-part sequentially numbered order forms. One copy is kept by the sales clerk, one copy is forwarded to the warehouse for the dispatch of inventory, and one copy is sent to the customer as evidence of the order. | | X |
| The sales clerk regularly performs reviews of the standing data on the system, matching the price of flowers against an up to date price list. | | X |
| To ensure completeness of orders, a sequence check is performed on the sales invoices manually by the sales clerk and any missing documents are investigated. | X | |
| Sales invoices are posted on a weekly basis to the sales day book and accounts receivable ledger. | | X |

A sequence check of the invoices is an effective control, be it carried out manually or electronically. Order forms should have four, not three, parts. No copy of the order is sent to the accounts receivables clerk – as a result, the recording of receivables may be incomplete or delayed, and outstanding balances may remain uncollected. The sales clerk should not be reviewing the standing data themselves – this review should be performed by an independent, senior member of staff. Sales invoices should be posted automatically to the sales day book and the accounts receivables ledger immediately after the order is taken.

85    The correct answer is:

1 only

This simply reduces the risk that cash will be misappropriated. It does not provide any assurance that subsequent recording will be complete or accurate.

86    The correct answer is:

The deficiencies identified in the sales system only

ISA 265 *Communicating Deficiencies in Internal Control to those Charged with Governance and Management* requires the auditor to communicate significant deficiencies in internal control (ISA 265). The fact that the amounts exposed to the deficiencies in the sales system were high and that it is likely that the deficiencies would result in material misstatements in the financial statements are indicators that the deficiencies are significant (ISA 265).

# KLE Co

87    The correct answer is: Purchases may be made unnecessarily at unauthorised prices.

The fact that the ordering clerk transfers information from the order requisition to the order form without any subsequent approval increases the risk that errors on the order form go unnoticed. The fact that the order requisition is thrown away means that any subsequent queries cannot be traced back to the original order. The facts that the ordering department does not retain copies of the order forms means that orders may be duplicated, either in error or deliberately. The chief buyer authorises the order requisitions and determines the appropriate supplier, so the risk of purchases being made at unauthorised prices is reduced.

88 The correct answer is: 1, 3 and 4

It is important that the ordering department receives a copy of the GRN, so that they can monitor which orders are closed and which remain outstanding. To ensure efficiency and to avoid delays, a three-part GRN could be used – one for the ordering department, one for the goods inwards department and one for the accounts department.

89 The correct answer is: For a sample of GRNs check that there is an authorised purchase order

The direction of the test is important here. The sample is taken from goods received notes as these represent deliveries. The auditor can then check that each delivery is supported by a valid order. If the sample is chosen from purchase orders (as in the first option) the test would confirm whether orders have been fulfilled. The remaining options are tests of controls regarding completeness of accounting information.

90 The correct answer is: Undertake 'mystery shopper' reviews, where they enter the store as a customer, purchase goods and rate the overall shopping experience

Bank confirmations should always be carried out by the auditor. Providing advice on the implementation of a new payroll system would impair the internal auditors' independence. Reviewing the financial statements on behalf of the board is the responsibility of the audit committee, not internal audit.

91 The correct answer is: The relationship between goods and services produced and the resources used to produce them

A value for money audit focuses on three Es: Economy, Efficiency and Effectiveness. The first option describes economy. The third option describes effectiveness. The second option only describes one aspect of efficiency.

## SouthLea

92 The correct answers are:

Cut-off of starters' and leavers' wages

Potential fraud risk factors

The facts that the foreman is authorised to issue new employee numbers, and that the two wages clerks are responsible for setting up employee records, make it more likely for bogus employees to be set up on the system than for bona fide employees to be omitted. This is likely to give rise to questions around the occurrence of wages, not their completeness. The fact that a wages clerk reviews the calculations for the deductions from gross pay should reduce the risk of computerised errors.

93 The correct answer is:

Review the log of amendments to standing data for evidence of review

Reviewing overtime lists for evidence of authorisation is a test of control over the authorisation of wages. The other two procedures can identify unauthorised amendments to standing data, but they are substantive procedures.

94 The correct answer is:

The internal auditor must always consider the potential of management overriding controls and modify their audit procedures accordingly when performing internal audit engagements.

The need to consider the potential of management override applies mainly to the external auditors. The external auditor's objective is to conclude whether the financial statements are free from material misstatement, whether from error or fraud. Audit procedures that are effective in detecting error may not be appropriate in detecting fraud due to the nature of fraud.

95  The correct answer is:

(1) and (2) only

In the absence of the audit committee the work of the internal audit department should be directed by the board. The scope being set by the finance director reduces independence.

96  The correct answers are:

Full testing procedures using test data when developing computer applications

Disaster recovery procedures

One for one checking and hash totals are application controls.

# Cherry

97  The correct answer is: The selection and application of accounting policies

The selection and application of accounting policies is one of the areas in which the auditor is required to gain an understanding, as part of the auditor's risk assessment procedures. It is not a component of internal control. The other components of internal control are the entity's risk assessment process and the entity's process to monitor the system of internal control.

98  The correct answer is: 2 and 3

The fact that raw materials are being ordered without reviewing inventory levels means that both stock-outs and excess obsolescent inventory are likely. The lack of authorisation means that fraudulent purchases could be made, but there is an approved supplier list and money-laundering risks seem far-fetched. Likewise, poorer quality goods may be ordered but the approved supplier list does act as a control here – and going concern risks are irrelevant.

99  The correct answer is: Completeness of payables

The fact that goods received notes (GRNs) are not sequentially numbered means that GRNs may be omitted from accounting records and it would be difficult to trace the unrecorded GRNs. As a result, the risk is that payables (and inventory) is understated.

100  The correct answer is: Because there are likely to be fewer capital purchases than standard purchases in the year, it may not be cost efficient to undertake tests of controls.

It is likely that the number of capital purchases in the year will be less than the number of standard purchases in the year. If the invoices are not segregated, it may not be cost efficient to test the controls over this area, in which case substantive testing would have to be undertaken. Although controls around the non-current assets cycle will probably resemble those around the purchases cycle, the auditor should still understand how the company's system records capital invoices. The risk of material misstatement in relation to the non-current assets cycle is high, because orders are likely to be of a less routine nature, larger amounts may be involved, and there may be an incentive to account creatively for tax or other purposes.

101  The correct answer is: 1 and 3

The direction of the test is important here. If the sample of serial numbers were taken from the non-current assets register, the physical assets which were not assigned serial numbers and/or were not recorded would not be identified. Reviewing the non-current register to identify duplicate serial numbers will identify instances when the serial numbers assigned were not unique, making it difficult to trace the related assets. Observation is a valid audit procedure, but it provides a weak form of audit evidence, since it does not assure the auditor that the control would be operated when the auditor is not there to observe it.

# Swan

102    The correct answer is:

The company is able to fulfil the orders.

It is a deficiency in the system that the other three objectives do not appear to be met.

103    The correct answers are:

Goods are sent out but not invoiced.

Wrong goods are sent to customers.

This is because there is a risk that the printed orders will not be invoiced properly as they may be lost or overlooked (being outside the electronic system), hence the second risk. In addition, if the reason the GRN details do not match is that they have been fulfilled incorrectly (rather than due to simple typographical errors), the staff member may assume it is a typing issue and simply print the order, but not double check the goods properly against it, hence the fourth risk. In this situation, a customer might be sent 50 goods rather than the ordered 5, but only be invoiced for 5, as the invoice is generated from the order.

This issue should not cause goods to be invoiced without being sent out, as invoices are generated from goods out notes or orders being used as goods out notes.

It should also not cause orders not to be fulfilled, as the issue arises when the order has been processed, so the order has not been overlooked.

104    The correct answers are:

Review a sample of invoices to ensure their numerical sequence.

Review a sample of goods out notes to ensure they have been matched to sales invoices.

The other two procedures relate to accuracy.

105    The correct answers are:

The likelihood of material misstatement resulting

The number of deficiencies identified

The likelihood of material misstatement occurring is a key factor in determining whether the deficiency is significant. The number of deficiencies is a factor, as deficiencies may become significant if there is a significant combination of deficiencies.

A control deficiency does not increase in significance simply due to the area of business it relates to, but may become significant if there is a risk of fraud. There is no more significant risk of fraud in the sales system than in other systems, for example, the purchases system or payroll system, so the business area is not a critical factor.

Similarly, a deficiency is a deficiency regardless of whether the related control is new or not. In fact, an old deficiency might be more significant than a new one if, say, it had been previously reported and not acted on.

106    The correct answer is:

A computerised ICEQ

This is the only option that has the element of evaluation that the partner requires. The fact that it is computerised should also influence how easy it is to update, therefore addressing her second issue.

# 107 Chuck

**Workbook references.** Chapters 6, 10, 11, 17 and 20.

**Top tips.** As always in the long 30-mark questions you should make sure you keep to time for each individual part and the question as a whole.

In part (a) you should identify and explain the deficiencies of the payroll system from the scenario and recommend a control to address each one.

In (b) keep your answers focused on substantive procedures, not tests of control. Also your procedures should remain relevant to the assertions stated in the question – completeness and accuracy of the payroll charge. Don't forget simple procedures such as casting the payroll records since this will also help to confirm accuracy and completeness.

Part (c) was on the auditor's responsibility in relation to laws and regulations. Remember the auditor's opinion will be on the financial statements, so the auditor's responsibility will be focused on those laws and regulations that could have a material effect on the financial statements, whether direct or indirect. There are a number of substantive procedures you could have suggested in (d) in respect of the redundancy provision, but the most you could gain is four marks so it is important you did not carry on stating more than four procedures and risk exceeding your time allocation of eight minutes. Part (e) was relatively straightforward in relation to reliance on internal audit as long as you knew the four key factors of objectivity, technical competence, due professional care and communication.

**Easy marks.** These were available in parts (d) and (e), but all in all it was possible to score well in every part of this question.

**Examining team's comments.** In part (a) the scenario contained an abundance of deficiencies and so on the whole candidates were able to easily identify enough points. A small minority of candidates provided implications and recommendations for general deficiencies which were not specified within the scenario; these points would not have gained credit as the question requirement clearly stated that points needed to be raised for the deficiencies identified in the scenario. A significant proportion of candidates wasted time by writing out the deficiencies from the scenario; there were no marks available for deficiencies, only for the implications and recommendations.

Performance was mixed in part (b). As noted in previous examining team's reports, candidates are often confused with the differences between tests of controls and substantive tests. The requirement verb was to 'describe' therefore sufficient detail was required to score the one mark available per test.

Part (c) was answered unsatisfactorily by most candidates. Most candidates focused on management's responsibility for preparing financial statements and implementing controls and auditors' responsibility to provide a true and fair opinion. These points are not related to laws and regulations. Part (d) was answered unsatisfactorily by many candidates. Candidates must tailor their knowledge to the scenario in order to pick up application marks and those candidates who performed well were able to produce detailed procedures which related to the scenario. In relation to the popular answer of obtaining written representations this procedure needs to be phrased with sufficient detail to obtain credit. 'Obtain a written representation from management' would not have scored any marks as it does not specify what the representation is for. Candidates performed well on part (e), with many attaining full marks.

(a)    Up to 1 mark per well-explained control deficiency and up to 1 mark for each well-explained recommendation.

    No monitoring/supervision of clocking in and out

    Payroll calculations not checked

    Verbal notification of payroll changes by HR

    Night shift wages susceptible to risk of theft

    Absent night shift employees' pay not secure over weekend

    Joiners not notified on timely basis    12

(b)    Up to 1 mark per substantive procedure.

    Agree wages and salaries per payroll to trial balance

    Cast payroll records

    Recalculate gross and net pay

    Recalculate statutory deductions, agree relevant to current year rates

    Compare total payroll to prior year

    Review monthly payroll to prior year and budget

    Proof in total of payroll

    Verify joiners/leavers and recalculate first/last pay

    Agree salaries paid per payroll to bank transfer list and cash book

    Agree total cash withdrawn from bank equates to wages paid and surplus cash banked

    Agree tax liabilities to payroll and post year end cash book

    Agree the individual wages and salaries as per the payroll to the personnel records and records of hours worked per clocking in cards    6

(c)    Up to 1 mark per valid point.

    Management responsibility to comply with law and regulations

    Auditors not responsible for preventing non-compliance

    Auditors – reasonable assurance financial statements free from material error

    Law and regulations – direct effect responsibility

    Law and regulations – indirect effect responsibility

    Remain alert/Professional scepticism    4

(d) Up to 1 mark per substantive procedure.

Discuss with directors whether formal announcement made of redundancies

Review supporting documentation to confirm present obligation

Review board minutes to confirm payment probable

Cast breakdown of redundancy provision

Recalculate provision and agree components of calculation to supporting documentation

Review post year end period to compare actual payments to amounts provided

Written representations to confirm completeness

Review disclosures for compliance with IAS 37 *Provisions, Contingent Liabilities and Contingent Assets*                 5

(e) Up to 1 mark per well-explained point.

Objectivity – independence, status and to whom report

Technical competence – qualifications and experience

Due professional care – properly planned and performed

Communication – between internal and external auditors                 $\underline{3}$

$\underline{\underline{30}}$

(a) **Chuck Industries – payroll system**

| Control deficiency | Control recommendation |
|---|---|
| There are no monitoring/supervision procedures relating to the clocking in and clocking out of employees. This means that staff may ask colleagues to clock them in when they are not actually present resulting in a payroll cost in excess of that expected for the actual hours worked. | Clocking in and out should be monitored by a supervisor of an appropriate level, or by CCTV cameras installed to deter employees from clocking in for one another. Furthermore, employees should be automatically clocked out at the end of their shift, and should be required to clock back in if they are completing pre-agreed overtime. |
| Payroll calculations are not reviewed and 100% reliance is placed on the accuracy of the payroll system. This means that any errors made, for example as a result of standing or underlying data being incorrect or errors occurring during payroll processing, then they would not be discovered. This may lead to overpayments or underpayments (and incorrect payroll costs) and may result and lead to losses or disgruntled employees. | A payroll supervisor should periodically recalculate the net pay based on the gross pay and expected deductions, then compare the result with the computer generated figures for a sample of employees. The review should be evidenced by a signature and wages should not be paid until this signed review is completed. |
| The HR department has used verbal authorisation to inform the payroll department of pay increases. This indicates a lack of authorisation at board level and could lead to invalid increases in employee wages (eg for HR personnel's friends or relatives). | HR should be required to gain written board authorisation for any proposed wage increase before passing this to payroll. Similarly, payroll should be informed only to action a wage increase or other change on receipt of written authorisation approved by the board. |

| Control deficiency | Control recommendation |
| --- | --- |
| The factory supervisor is trusted with substantial cash sums in advance of the distribution of wages to the night shift. This cash is susceptible to theft and loss while not with employees or securely stored. | Payroll officials should be available for certain hours during the night shift to distribute wages. The night shift workers should also be required to produce identification before they are given their pay packets. Alternatively Chuck may decide to pay the night shift via bank transfer. |
| The factory supervisor keeps absent employees' wages over the weekend before handing back to payroll and this further increases the risk of loss or theft of cash wages. | Any amounts not paid out on Fridays should be kept by payroll in a safe or other secure means until Monday when the employee can collect from payroll. |
| Staff holidays in the HR department have meant that payroll information relating to new joiners was not communicated on a timely basis, which in turn meant that joiners were not paid on time leading to disgruntled employees and inaccurate payroll records. | HR staff duties and responsibilities should be reallocated when staff are ill or on holiday, including the responsibility of immediate communication of new joiners (and leavers) to payroll. In addition, new joiner forms showing start date should be completed and authorised, and then passed to payroll so that they are aware of the need to update the payroll records. |

(b)     **Substantive procedures – Payroll cost**

(i)     Compare the total payroll expense to the previous year and investigate any significant variances.

(ii)    Review monthly payroll charges and compare this to the prior year monthly charges and to budgets. Discuss significant variances with management.

(iii)   Reconcile the total wages and salaries expense per the payroll records to the cost in the financial statements and investigate any differences.

(iv)    Agree amounts owed to the tax authorities to the payroll records and with the amount subsequently paid and clearing the bank statement post year end to ensure completeness.

(v)     Cast a sample of payroll records to confirm completeness and accuracy of the payroll expense.

(vi)    Recalculate the gross and net pay for a sample of employees and agree to the payroll to confirm accuracy.

(vii)   Recalculate statutory deductions to confirm whether the correct deductions are included within the payroll expense.

(viii)  Perform a proof in total of total factory workforce wages by taking last year's expense, dividing by last year's average employee numbers to arrive at an average wage and multiplying by current year average employee numbers (the calculation should also incorporate the pay increase). Compare this estimate of the current year charge with the actual wages cost in the financial statements and investigate significant differences.

(ix)    Agree the start or leaving date to supporting documentation for a sample of joiners and leavers, and recalculate their first or last pay packet to ensure it was accurately calculated and properly recorded.

(x)     Agree the total net salaries paid on the payroll records to the bank transfer listing of payments for sales and administrative staff, and to the cash book for weekly paid employees.

(xi)  Agree the total cash withdrawn for wage payments equates to the weekly wages paid plus any leftover cash subsequently banked to confirm completeness and accuracy.

(xii)  Agree individual wages and salaries per the payroll to the personnel records and records of hours worked per the swipe card system.

*Note.* Only six procedures were needed to gain full marks.

(c)  **Responsibilities – Laws and regulations**

It is Chuck Industries Co's management that have a responsibility to ensure that the entity complies with the relevant laws and regulations (ISA 250). It is not the auditor's responsibility to prevent or detect non-compliance with laws and regulations.

The auditor's responsibility is to obtain reasonable assurance that the financial statements are free from material misstatement and, in this respect, the auditor must take into account the legal and regulatory framework within which the entity operates (ISA 250).

ISA 250 (Revised) *Consideration of Laws and Regulations in an Audit of Financial Statements* distinguishes the auditor's responsibilities in relation to compliance with two different categories of laws and regulations:

- Those that have a direct effect on the determination of material amounts and disclosures in the financial statements

- Those that do not have a direct effect on the determination of material amounts and disclosures in the financial statements but where compliance may be fundamental to the operating aspects, ability to continue in business, or to avoid material penalties (ISA 250).

For the first category, the auditor's responsibility is to obtain sufficient appropriate audit evidence about compliance with those laws and regulations (ISA 250). For the second category, the auditor's responsibility is to undertake specified audit procedures to help identify non-compliance with laws and regulations that may have a material effect on the financial statements (ISA 250).

Blair & Co must also maintain professional scepticism and be alert to the possibility that other audit procedures may bring instances of identified or suspected non-compliance with laws and regulations. (ISA 250)

(d)  **Substantive procedures – Redundancy provision**

- Obtain an analysis of the redundancy calculations (cost by employee) and cast it to ensure completeness.

- Obtain written representation from management confirming the completeness of the provision.

- In order to establish that a present obligation exists at the year end, ask the directors whether they formally announced their intention to make the sales ledger department redundant during the year.

- If the redundancies have been announced pre year end, review any documentation corroborating that the decision has in fact been formally announced.

- Review the board minutes to assess the probability the redundancy payments will be paid.

- Recalculate the redundancy provision to confirm completeness and agree components of the calculation to supporting documents.

- Confirm whether any redundancy payments have been made post year end and compare any amounts paid to amounts provided to assess the adequacy of the provision.

- Review the disclosure of the redundancy provision to ensure it complies with IAS 37 *Provisions, Contingent Liabilities and Contingent Assets*.

*Note.* Only five procedures were needed to gain full marks.

(e)    **Factors to consider – Reliance on work performed by internal audit**

The following important criteria will be considered by the external auditors when determining if the work of internal auditors is likely to be adequate.

*Extent to which its objectivity is supported*

The auditor must consider the extent to which the internal audit function's objectivity is supported by its organisational status, relevant policies and procedures. Considerations include to whom the internal auditors report, any conflicting responsibilities, any constraints or restrictions, whether those charged with governance oversee employment decisions regarding internal auditors and whether management acts on recommendations made.

*Level of technical competence*

The auditor must consider whether internal auditors are members of relevant professional bodies, whether they have adequate technical training and proficiency and whether there are established policies for hiring and training.

*Whether a systematic and disciplined approach is taken*

The auditor must also consider whether internal audit activities are systematically and properly planned, supervised, reviewed and documented; and whether suitable audit manuals, work programmes and internal audit documentation exist. The auditor must also consider whether the function has appropriate quality management procedures in place.

# 108 Freesia

---

**Workbook references.** Chapters 3, 10 and 16.

**Top tips.** Part (a) was the knowledge-based part, and as such you should be aiming for full marks here. It is important that you stick to the requirement precisely, eg you should only give an advantage of each method – one advantage, with no marks available for disadvantages. The marks for describing each method were among the easiest in the exam.

Part (b) was the core of this question, and asked for six deficiencies for which you needed to develop controls and then tests of control. Your response should therefore be connected across all three columns. As ever, the requirement is to 'identify and explain' each deficiency, which suggests that your answer could be structured as two sentences / paragraphs within the left column, the first of which says what is happening (identifying the problem), and the second of which says why this is a problem (or why it is wrong). Your control and test of control must then be explained in enough detail to get a full mark each. It is a good idea to think of these two columns together – try to suggest a control for which you can easily suggest a test.

Part (c) asked for substantive procedures in relation to the employment tax accrual; quite a lot of the points here should not be difficult to think of, so this requirement is a good opportunity to score marks.

Part (d) covered corporate governance. This requirement is not actually asking a great deal here, particularly given the length of the related scenario, so again this should not have been overly taxing.

**Easy marks.** Part (a) was knowledge-based and should have been within your reach.

**Examination team comments.** Internal control questions remain a highly examinable area and performance in June 2019 was mixed. The scenarios included in exam questions contain more issues than are required to be discussed. It was pleasing in this session that candidates were generally able to identify (for ½ mark each) the required number of issues from the scenarios. However some candidates were unable to correctly identify the deficiency from the scenario. They were able to pick the relevant fact from the scenario but failed to spot what the actual deficiency was. For example, from the scenario candidates identified 'invoices have a unique number' but the actual issue was that the unique numbers were not sequential. Additionally, this session there was an increase in the number of answers with irrelevant deficiencies being given. This seems to stem from a lack of understanding of the scenario and possibly due to a lack of question practice.

---

In common with previous sittings many candidates did not clearly explain the implication of the deficiencies. It is important that the explanation fully details the impact to the company. As an example, for a deficiency of 'purchase invoices are not sequentially numbered' a suitable, well-explained implication would be 'this could result in the recording of purchases and payables being incomplete and suppliers being paid late'. Many candidates did not go on to explain the impact on the company in sufficient detail, for example just stating, 'this could result in invoices being missed'.

Most candidates were able to provide good recommendations to address the deficiencies they identified. However, some of the recommendations were either poorly described, did not clearly address the specific control deficiency identified or were impractical suggestions. Many candidates just repeated the converse of the deficiency and to obtain the one mark for the recommendation more detail is needed. For example, for the deficiency 'a lack of segregation of duties around inventory management' some candidates stated a recommendation of 'segregation should be introduced'. However, to obtain the full mark this recommendation needed to cover what elements of the role should be separated. Additionally, as with ethics and corporate governance questions, recommendations must be actions rather than just objectives.

## Marking scheme

|  |  | Marks |
|---|---|---|
| (a) | Methods of documenting systems of internal control | |
| | Narrative notes | 2 |
| | Questionnaires | 2 |
| | | 4 |
| (b) | Control deficiencies, recommendations and tests of control (only 6 required) | |
| | Credit limits | 3 |
| | No sequential numbering of orders | 3 |
| | Segregation of duties – cash receipts | 3 |
| | Insufficient copies of GRN | 3 |
| | Controls over inputting of invoices | 3 |
| | Out-of-date standard costs | 3 |
| | Overtime not authorised | 3 |
| | Authorisation of bank transfer | 3 |
| | Max 6 issues, 3 marks each | 18 |
| (c) | Substantive procedures – accrual for employment tax | |
| | Compare to prior year and investigate differences | 1 |
| | Agree accrual to year-end payroll records | 1 |
| | Recalculate accrual and consider reasonableness | 1 |
| | Perform proof in total and investigate variances | 1 |
| | Confirm post year-end payment | 1 |
| | Review correspondence with tax authorities for any additional liabilities | 1 |
| | Review disclosure and confirm in line with accounting standards | 1 |
| | Restricted to | 4 |

(d)    Corporate governance weakness and recommendations (2 issues required)

Composition of audit committee                                                   2

Finance director sets remuneration                                               2

Executive directors' remuneration                                                2

Only chairman liaises with shareholders                                          2

Max 2 issues, 2 marks each                                                       4

**Total marks**                                                                  **30**

(a)    **Documenting systems**

|  | Description | Advantage |
|---|---|---|
| Narrative notes | Narrative notes consist of a written description of the system. They detail what occurs in the system at each stage and include any controls which operate at each stage. | They are simple to record; after discussion with staff members, these discussions are easily written up as notes.<br><br>They can facilitate understanding by all members of the audit team, especially more junior members who might find alternative methods too complex. |
| Questionnaires | Internal control questionnaires (ICQs) or internal control evaluation questionnaires (ICEQs) contain a list of questions for each major transaction cycle; ICQs are used to assess whether controls exist whereas ICEQs assess the effectiveness of the controls in place. | Questionnaires are quick to prepare, which means they are a timely method for recording the system.<br><br>They ensure that all controls present within the system are considered and recorded, hence missing controls or deficiencies are clearly highlighted to the audit team. |

(b)    **Deficiencies, controls and test of controls**

| Control deficiency | Control recommendation | Test of control |
|---|---|---|
| Customer credit limits are set by sales ledger clerks. Sales ledger clerks are not sufficiently senior and so may set limits too high, leading to irrecoverable debts, or too low, leading to a loss of sales. | Credit limits should be set by a senior member of the sales department and not by sales ledger clerks. These limits should be regularly reviewed by a responsible official. | For a sample of new customers accepted in the year, review the authorisation of the credit limit, and ensure that this was performed by a responsible official.<br><br>Enquire of sales ledger clerks as to who can set credit limits. |

| Control deficiency | Control recommendation | Test of control |
|---|---|---|
| Customer orders are given a number based on the sales person's own identification number. These numbers are not sequential. Without sequential numbers, it is difficult for Freesia Co to identify missing orders and to monitor if all orders are being dispatched in a timely manner. If they are not, this could lead to a loss of customer goodwill. | Sales orders should be sequentially numbered. On a regular basis, a sequence check of orders should be undertaken to identify any missing orders. | Re-perform the control by undertaking a sequence check of sales orders.<br><br>Discuss any gaps in the sequence with sales ordering staff. |
| Lily Shah, a finance clerk, is responsible for several elements of the cash receipts system as she posts the bank transfer receipts from the bank statements to the cash book, updates the sales ledger and performs the bank reconciliations.<br><br>There is a lack of segregation of duties and errors will not be identified on a timely basis. There is also an increased risk of fraud. | The key roles of posting bank receipts, updating the sales ledger and performing bank reconciliations should be split between different individuals.<br><br>If this is not practical, then as a minimum, the bank reconciliations should be undertaken by another member of the finance team. | Review the file of completed bank reconciliations to identify who prepared them.<br><br>Review the log of IDs of individuals who have posted bank receipts and updated the sales ledger to assess whether these are different individuals.<br><br>Discuss with the financial controller which members of staff undertake the roles of processing of bank receipts and updating of the cash book and sales ledger. |
| GRNs are only sent to the finance department. Failing to send a copy to the purchase ordering department means that it is not possible to monitor the level of unfulfilled orders. This could result in a significant level of unfulfilled orders leading to stock-outs and a consequent loss of sales.<br><br>In addition, if the GRN is lost, then it will not be possible for the finance department to match the invoice to proof of goods being received. This could result in a delay to the invoice being paid and a loss of supplier goodwill. | The GRN should be created in three parts with one copy of the GRN being sent to the ordering department. The second copy should be held at the warehouse and the third sent to the finance department.<br><br>A purchase ordering clerk should agree their copy of the GRN to the purchase order and change the order status to complete. On a regular basis, a review should be undertaken for all unfulfilled orders and these should be followed up with the relevant supplier. | Review the file of copy GRNs held by the purchase ordering department and review for evidence that these are matched to orders and flagged as complete.<br><br>Review the file of unfulfilled purchase orders for any overdue items and discuss their status with an ordering clerk. |

ANSWERS

| Control deficiency | Control recommendation | Test of control |
|---|---|---|
| Camilla Brown, the purchase ledger clerk, only utilises document count controls when inputting invoices into the purchase ledger. <br><br> Document count controls can confirm the completeness of input. However, they do not verify the accuracy or validity of input. <br><br> If the invoices are not input correctly, suppliers may not be paid on time, or paid incorrect amounts leading to an overpayment or loss of supplier goodwill who may withdraw credit facilities. | The purchase ledger clerk should instead input the invoices in batches and apply application controls, such as control totals, rather than just completeness checks to ensure both completeness and accuracy over the input of purchase invoices. In addition, sequence checks should be built into the system to ensure completeness of input. | The audit team should utilise test data procedures to assess whether data can be entered without the use of batch control totals and also whether sequence checks are built into the system. <br><br> Observe the inputting of purchase invoices and identify what application controls are utilised by the clerk. |
| The company values its inventory using standard costs, which are not being kept up-to-date. <br><br> If the standard costs were reviewed 18 months ago, there is the risk that the costs are misstated as changes in raw materials and wages inflation may not have been adjusted for. This could result in inventory being under or overvalued and profits being misstated. <br><br> In addition for year-end reporting, IAS 2 *Inventories* only allows standard costs to be used for valuation purposes if they are a close approximation to actual costs, which is unlikely if the standard costs remain unchanged for a long period of time. Therefore the valuation may not be in line with IAS 2. | A review of all standard costs currently in use should be undertaken by a senior manager in the production department. Actual costs for materials, labour and overheads should be ascertained and compared to the proposed standard costs to ensure they are a close approximation. <br><br> The revised standard costs should be reviewed by the production director who should evidence this review. At least annually, a review of the standard costs should be undertaken to ensure they are up-to-date. | Obtain a copy of the standard costs used for inventory valuation, assess when the review was last undertaken and inspect for evidence of review by the production director. |

| Control deficiency | Control recommendation | Test of control |
|---|---|---|
| Overtime worked is not authorised prior to being paid. The information per employee is collated and submitted to payroll by a production clerk, but not authorised. The production director is only informed about overtime levels via quarterly reports.<br><br>These reports are reviewed sometime after the payments have been made which could result in unauthorised overtime or amounts being paid incorrectly and Freesia Co's payroll cost increasing. | All overtime should be authorised by a responsible official prior to the payment being processed by the payroll department. This authorisation should be evidenced in writing. | Review the overtime report for evidence of authorisation and note the date this occurred to ensure that this was undertaken prior to the payment of the overtime. |
| The finance director compares the total of the list of bank transfers with the total to be paid per the payroll records.<br><br>There could be employees omitted or fictitious employees added to the payment listing so that, although the total payments list agrees to payroll totals, there could be fraudulent or erroneous payments being made. | The finance director, when authorising the payments, should on a sample basis perform checks from the human resource department's staff records to payment list and vice versa to confirm that payments are complete and only made to *bona fide* employees.<br><br>The finance director should sign the payments list as evidence that these checks have been undertaken. | Obtain a sample of payments lists and review for signature by the finance director as evidence that the control is operating correctly. |

(c)  **Accrual for employment tax payable**

Substantive procedures the auditor should adopt in respect of auditing this accrual include:

- Compare the accrual for employment tax payable to the prior year, investigate any significant differences.

- Agree the year-end employment tax payable accrual to the payroll records to confirm accuracy.

- Re-perform the calculation of the accrual for a sample of employees to confirm the accuracy.

- Undertake a proof in total test for the employment tax accrual by multiplying the payroll cost for January 20X5 with the appropriate tax rate. Compare this expectation to the actual accrual and investigate any significant differences.

- Agree the subsequent payment to the post year-end cash book and bank statements to confirm completeness.

- Review any correspondence with tax authorities to assess whether there are any additional outstanding payments due. If so, confirm they are included in the year-end accrual.

- Review any disclosures made of the employment tax accrual and assess whether these are in compliance with accounting standards and legislation.

(d) **Corporate governance deficiencies and recommendations**

| Weakness | Recommendation |
|---|---|
| The finance director is a member of the audit committee.<br><br>The audit committee should be made up entirely of independent NEDs. The role of the committee is to maintain objectivity with regards to financial reporting; this is difficult if the finance director is a member of the committee as the finance director will be responsible for the preparation of the financial statements. | The audit committee must be comprised of independent NEDs only; therefore the finance director should resign from the committee. |
| The remuneration for directors is set by the finance director.<br><br>However, no director should be involved in setting their own remuneration as this may result in excessive levels of pay being set. | There should be a fair and transparent policy in place<br><br>for setting remuneration levels. The NEDs should form a remuneration committee to decide on the remuneration of the executives. The board as a whole should decide on the pay of the NEDs. |
| Executive remuneration includes a significant annual profit related bonus. Remuneration should motivate the directors to focus on the long-term growth of the business, however, annual targets can encourage short-term strategies rather than maximising shareholder wealth. | The remuneration of executives should be restructured to include a significant proportion based on long-term company performance. For example, executives could be granted share options, as this would encourage focus on the longer term position. |
| The chairman has sole responsibility for liaising with the shareholders and answering any of their questions.<br><br>However, this is a role which the board as a whole should undertake. | All members of the board should be involved in ensuring that satisfactory dialogue takes place with shareholders, for example, all should attend meetings with shareholders such as the annual general meeting.<br><br>The board should state in the annual report the steps they have taken to ensure that the members of the board, and in particular the non-executive directors, develop an understanding of the views of major shareholders about the company. |

# 109 Tinkerbell

**Workbook reference.** Chapters 9, 10 and 14.

**Top tips.** Read the examining team's comments below carefully in relation to part (a). You must be able to differentiate between a test of control and a substantive procedure or you risk losing a high proportion of marks on some questions. A test of control must provide evidence that a control is operating effectively (or otherwise).

Parts (b) and (d) were relatively straightforward and you should have been able to come up with enough procedures to gain the majority of marks. You should use the scenario to help you to generate tests, for example identifying procedures in relation to the discounts offered to large customers.

Part (c) could be answered in a tabular format to help address both mini-requirements – (1) identify and explain controls and (2) describe how the risk of fraud is mitigated. The description of the 'teeming and lading' fraud uncovered in the year pointed out the current lack of controls, so this could form the basis of your controls which should fill the gap. For example, customer statements were not sent out and this is one of the reasons the fraud was not uncovered before, so making sure that they are sent out in the future is a valid control.

**Easy marks.** These are available in parts (b) and (d) where you are asked for substantive procedures in relation to receivables and revenue.

**Examining team's comments.** In part (a) most candidates performed inadequately. The main problems encountered were that candidates struggled to differentiate between tests of control and substantive tests and hence often provided long lists of substantive procedures, which scored no marks. In addition, a significant minority of candidates did not read the question carefully and, instead of providing tests of controls, gave control procedures management should adopt. The approach candidates should have taken was to firstly identify from the scenario the controls present for Tinkerbell; they then should have considered how these controls could be confirmed by the auditor. In addition, candidates' explanations of tests were vague, such as 'check that credit limits are set for all new customers'. This procedure does not explain how the auditor would actually confirm that the control for new customer credit limits operates effectively. Tests that start with 'check' are unlikely to score many marks as they do not explain how the auditor would actually check the control. Future candidates should practise generating tests, both substantive and tests of controls, which do not start with the word 'check'.

The second part of this requirement was to explain the objective of the test of control provided. Again, this was not answered well. A common answer was to state that the objective was 'to ensure that the control is operating effectively'. This was far too vague. Instead, candidates should have considered the aim of the specific control being tested. Therefore the objective of a test over credit limits is 'to ensure that orders are not accepted for poor credit risks'.

As noted in previous examining team's reports candidates are often confused with the differences between tests of controls and substantive tests. Candidates must ensure that they understand when tests of controls are required and when substantive procedures are needed. They need to learn the difference between them and should practice questions requiring the generation of both types of procedures.

Part (b) for eight marks required substantive procedures the auditor should perform on year-end receivables. This was answered well by many candidates. Candidates were able to provide variety in their procedures including both tests of detail and analytical review tests.

The most common mistakes made by some candidates were providing tests of control rather than substantive procedures, providing substantive procedures for revenue rather than receivables, not generating enough tests for eight marks and describing the process for a receivables circularisation at length (this was not part of the question requirement).

Part (c) for six marks required identification and explanation of controls that Tinkerbell should adopt to reduce the risk of fraud occurring again, as well as an explanation of how this control would mitigate the fraud risk. This question was answered well by most candidates, with some scoring full marks.

The scenario provided details of a 'teeming and lading fraud' which had occurred during the year and candidates needed to think practically about how Tinkerbell could reduce the risk of this occurring again. However, candidates' performance on the second requirement to describe how the control would mitigate the risk of fraud occurring again was mixed.

The main problem was that answers were not specific enough; frequently vague answers such as 'this will reduce the risk of fraud and error occurring' were given.

Part (d) for four marks required substantive procedures the auditor should perform on Tinkerbell's revenue. This requirement was not answered well. Some candidates confused this requirement with that of 1b, which required receivables tests, and so provided the same tests from 1b again. In addition, a significant number of candidates provided procedures to confirm bank and cash rather than revenue.

Those candidates who performed well were able to provide a good mixture of analytical procedures such as 'compare revenue to prior year or to budget' and 'review monthly sales against prior year' and also detailed tests such as confirming cut-off of sales.

Marks

(a) Up to 1 mark per well-explained point and up to 1 mark for each objective.

Process order for fictitious order

Sales order over credit limit

Inspect credit applications

Agree prices used to relevant price list

Confirm discounts used on invoices agree to customer master file

Attempt to process a discount for a small customer

Inspect orders to confirm order acceptance generated

Observe sales order clerk processing orders to see if acceptance generated

Observe goods dispatch process

Agree goods dispatch notes (GDN) to invoices

Sequence checks over invoices                                                12

(b) Up to 1 mark per well-explained procedure.

Trade receivables circularisation, follow up any non-replies

Review the after-date cash receipts

Calculate average receivables collection period

Reconciliation of sales ledger control account

Cut-off testing of GDN

Aged receivables report to identify any slow-moving balances

Review customer correspondence to assess whether there are any invoices in dispute

Review board minutes

Review post year end credit notes

Review for any credit balances

Agree to GDN and sales order to ensure existence                              8

(c) Up to 1 mark per well-explained control and up to 1 mark for how it mitigates risk.

Relatives not permitted to work in the same department

Cash receipts processed by two members of staff

Monthly customer statements sent

Bank reconciliations reviewed by responsible official

Rotation of duties within finance department

Sales ledger control account reconciliation regularly performed

Consider establishing an internal audit department                           6

(d)   Up to 1 mark per well-explained procedure.

Analytical review over revenue compared to budget and prior year

Analytical review of major categories of toy sales compared to prior year

Gross margin review

Recalculate discounts allowed for larger customers

Recalculate sales tax

Follow order to goods dispatched note to sales invoice to sales ledger

Sales cut-off

Review post year end credit notes

4<br>――<br>30

(a)   **Tinkerbell – Tests of control and test objectives for the sales cycle**

| Test of control | Test objective |
|---|---|
| Enter an order for a fictitious customer account number and ensure the system does not accept it. | To ensure that orders are only accepted and processed for valid customers. |
| Inspect a sample of processed credit applications from the credit agency and ensure the same credit limit appears in the sales system. | To ensure that goods are only supplied to customers with acceptable credit ratings. |
| For a sample of invoices, agree that current prices have been used by comparing them with prices shown on the current price list. | To ensure that goods are only sold at authorised prices. |
| For a sample of invoices showing discounts, agree the discount terms back to the customer master file information. | To ensure that sales discounts are only provided to those customers the sales director has authorised. |
| For a sample of orders ensure that an order acceptance email or letter was generated. | To ensure that all orders are recorded completely and accurately. |
| Visit a warehouse and observe whether all goods are double checked against the GDN and dispatch list before sending out. | To ensure that goods are dispatched correctly to customers and are of an adequate quality. |

> **Top tips.** Six tests of controls and six objectives such as those shown above were enough to gain the 12 marks available. However, other valid tests and objectives you may have come up with are shown below.

| Test of control | Test objective |
|---|---|
| With the client's permission, attempt to enter a sales order which will take a customer over the agreed credit limit and ensure the order is rejected as expected. | To ensure that goods are not supplied to poor credit risks. |
| Attempt to process an order with a sales discount for a customer not normally entitled to discounts to assess the application controls. | To ensure that sales discounts are only provided to valid customers. |

BPP
LEARNING
MEDIA

| Test of control | Test objective |
|---|---|
| Observe the sales order clerk processing orders and look for proof that the order acceptance is automatically generated (eg email in sent folder). | To ensure that all orders are recorded completely and accurately. |
| Inspect a sample of GDNs and agree that a valid sales invoice has been correctly raised. | To ensure that all goods dispatched are correctly invoiced. |
| Review the latest report from the computer sequence check of sales invoices for omissions and establish the action taken in respect of any omissions found. | To ensure completeness of income for goods dispatched. |

(b) **Substantive procedures to confirm Tinkerbell's year-end receivables balance**

(i) Circularise trade receivables for a representative sample of the year-end balances. If authorised by Tinkerbell's management, send an email or reminder letter to follow up non-responses.

(ii) Review cash receipts after the year end in respect of pre year end receivable balances to establish if anything is still outstanding. Where amounts are unpaid investigate whether an allowance is needed.

(iii) Review the reconciliation of the receivables ledger control account (sales ledger control account) to the list of receivables (sales ledger) balances and investigate unusual reconciling items.

(iv) Review the aged receivables report to identify any old balances and discuss the probability of recovery with the credit controller to assess the need for an allowance.

(v) Calculate average receivables collection period and compare this to prior year and expectations, investigating any significant differences.

(vi) Select a sample of goods dispatched notes just before and just after the year end to ensure the related invoices are recorded in the correct accounting period.

(vii) Review a sample of credit notes raised after the year end to identify any that relate to pre year end transactions and confirm that they have not been included in receivables.

(viii) Review the aged receivables ledger for any credit balances and inquire of management whether these should be reclassified as payables.

> **Top tips.** Eight substantive procedures like the ones shown above were enough to gain the eight marks available. However, other valid procedures you may have come up with are shown below.

(ix) For slow-moving/aged balances, review customer correspondence files to assess whether there are any invoices in dispute which require an allowance.

(x) Review board minutes to assess whether there are any material disputed receivables.

(xi) Select a sample of year-end receivable balances and agree back to a valid GDN and sales order to ensure existence.

(c) Controls to reduce the risk of fraud reoccurring and explanation of how the risk is mitigated

| Control | Explanation of how risk is mitigated by control |
|---|---|
| Related members of staff should not be allowed to work in the same department where they can seek to override segregation of duty controls. | The risk of related staff colluding and being able to commit a fraud without easily being discovered will be reduced. |
| Customer statements should be sent out each month to all customers. The receivables ledger supervisor should check that all customers have been sent statements. | Customers receiving statements may notice anomalies in the allocation of payments (either timing or amount) and may alert the company of these anomalies. This may draw attention to the sort of fraud that occurred at Tinkerbell (known as 'teeming and lading'). |
| Bank reconciliations should be reviewed regularly by someone of an appropriate level of management who is not involved in its preparation. Unreconciled amounts should be investigated and resolved at the time of review. | Any compensating material balances netted off to a small difference on the bank reconciliation will be discovered quickly, increasing the probability of uncovering fraud on a timely basis. |

**Top tips.** Three controls such as those shown above along with three explanations were enough to gain the six marks available. However, other valid controls and explanations are given below.

| Control | Explanation of how risk is mitigated by control |
|---|---|
| Two members of staff should process cash receipts. | This would mean another collusion would be necessary (on top of the one that has already occurred) to steal cash receipts. This therefore reduces the risk of reoccurrence. |
| Staff within the finance department should rotate duties on a regular basis. | Rotation will act as a deterrent to fraud. This is because staff will be less likely to commit fraudulent activities due to an increased risk of the next person to be rotated to their position uncovering any wrongdoing. |

| Control Study | Explanation of how risk is mitigated by control |
|---|---|
| The receivables ledger should be reconciled to the receivables ledger control account on at least a monthly basis. The reconciliation should be reviewed by a responsible official and anomalies investigated. | This will increase the chance of discovering errors in the receivable balances and help to create a strong control environment likely to deter fraud. |
| Management should consider establishing an internal audit department to assess and monitor the effectiveness of controls, identify any deficiencies, and carry out specific fraud investigations. | The presence of an internal audit department would help to deter employees committing fraud and identification of fraud would be more likely due to ongoing monitoring of internal controls. |

(d) **Substantive procedures to confirm Tinkerbell's revenue**

(i) Compare the total revenue with that reported in previous years and the revenue budgeted, and investigate any significant fluctuations.

(ii) For a sample of customer orders, trace the details to the related dispatch notes and sales invoices and ensure there is a sale recorded in respect of each (to test the completeness of revenue).

(iii) For a sample of sales invoices for larger customers, recalculate the discounts allowed to ensure that these are accurate.

(iv) Select a sample of dispatch notes in the month immediately before and month immediately after the year end. Trace these through to the related sales invoices and resultant accounting entries to ensure each sale was recorded in the appropriate period.

> **Top tips.** Four procedures such as those shown above would have been sufficient to gain full marks on this part of the question. However, other procedures are given below.

(v) Obtain an analysis of sales by major categories of toys manufactured and compare this to the prior year breakdown and discuss any unusual movements with management.

(vi) Calculate the gross profit margin for Tinkerbell for the year and compare this to the previous year and expectations. Investigate any significant fluctuations.

(vii) Recalculate the sales tax for a sample of invoices and ensure that the sales tax has been correctly applied to the sales invoice.

(viii) Select a sample of credit notes issued after the year end and trace these through to the related sales invoices to ensure sales returns were recorded in the proper period.

# 110 Trombone

> **Workbook references.** Chapters 7, 9 and 10.
>
> **Top tips.** Part (a) asks you to identify deficiencies in the control system for payroll, to recommend improvements and to describe a relevant test of control. Make sure that your answer addresses all three requirements. A tabular format is a particularly useful way of presenting your answer.
>
> Part (c) tests your knowledge of the difference between an interim audit and a final audit. You should find this relatively straightforward.
>
> **Easy marks.** Easy marks can be found in part (b).
>
> **Examining team's comments.** The first two parts of part (a) were answered satisfactorily by candidates; however, the tests of controls proved challenging for many.
>
> The requirement for tests of controls was answered unsatisfactorily. Many candidates are still confusing substantive procedures and test of controls. A significant number of candidates suggested substantive procedures such as 'recalculating gross and net pay calculations', rather than a test of control which might be to 'review evidence of the recalculation of payroll'. Candidates need to review their understanding of these different types of audit procedures and ensure that they appreciate that substantive tests focus on the number within the financial statements whereas tests of controls are verifying if client procedures are operating.
>
> In many instances candidates focused on reperforming the control rather than testing that it had operated. Observation of a control was commonly suggested by candidates; however, in many cases this is not an effective way of testing that a control has operated throughout the year. Part (c) was answered very poorly by a significant number of candidates, demonstrating a worrying lack of knowledge about substantive procedures and tests of controls. This is an important area which needs to be addressed.

Part (b) was generally answered well by candidates. A minority of candidates incorrectly suggested that planning procedures would be undertaken at the interim audit and that they were undertaken by internal auditors. Also a significant minority confused this requirement with a comparison of internal and external audit roles. Candidates must remember to read the question carefully and think and plan before writing to ensure that they answer the question asked.

## Marking scheme

| | | Marks |
|---|---|---|
| (a) | **Internal control deficiencies, recommendations and tests of control** Up to 1 mark per well-explained deficiency, up to 1 mark for each well-explained recommendation and up to 1 mark for each well-described test of control. Overall maximum of 5 marks each for deficiencies, controls and tests of control. Payroll calculations not checked Payroll clerks update standing data for wages increases Authorisation of overtime sheets only undertaken if overtime exceeds 30% of standard hours Time off as payment for overtime not checked to overtime worked report Review of overtime worked reports by department heads Authorisation of overtime sheets when department heads on annual leave Finance director only reviews totals of payroll records and payments list **Maximum marks** | 15 |
| (b) | **Final audit and interim audit** Up to 1 mark per well-explained point, maximum of 3 marks each for interim and final audit, overall maximum of 5 marks. Interim audit Final audit | 5 |
| (c) | Up to 1 mark per well-described substantive procedure. Agree wages and salaries per payroll to trial balance Cast payroll records Recalculate gross and net pay Recalculate statutory deductions Compare total payroll to prior year Review monthly payroll to prior year and budget Proof in total of payroll and agree to the financial statements Verify joiners/leavers and recalculate first/last pay Agree wages and salaries paid per payroll to bank transfer list and cash book Agree the individual wages and salaries as per the payroll to the personnel records Agree sample of weekly overtime sheets to overtime payment in payroll records | 6 |
| (d) | Up to 1 mark per well-described procedure. Agree to the payroll records to confirm the accuracy of the accrual Reperform the calculation of the accrual Agree the subsequent payment to the post year end cash book and bank statements Review any correspondence with tax authorities to assess whether there are any additional outstanding payments due, if so, agree they are included in the year-end accrual Review disclosures and assess whether these are adequate and in compliance **Maximum marks** | 4 / 30 |

(a)

| Deficiencies | Recommended controls | Test of control |
|---|---|---|
| The gross and net pay automatically calculated by the payroll package are not checked at all.<br><br>The lack of checking increases the risk that errors are being accumulated without being detected. This could lead to wages being over- or understated.<br><br>Additional wages may be paid as a result. Statutory deductions may be over- or underpaid, giving rise to compliance issues. There is also likely to be a loss of employee goodwill. | A senior member of the payroll department should reperform a sample of the gross and net pay calculations. Any discrepancies should be investigated. The automatic gross and net pay calculations must be reviewed and approved before payments are made. | Obtain the recalculations performed by the senior payroll reviewer for evidence that the automatic calculations have been reviewed.<br><br>Review a sample of the gross and net pay calculations generated by the payroll system for evidence that they have been approved and signed off. |
| The clerks update the standing data to reflect the increase of wages each year.<br><br>The apparent lack of authorisation to changes in standing data increases the risk of errors, leading to the over- or understatement of wages, and the incorrect payment of wages.<br><br>This also increases the risk of fraud, as the clerks have the ability to make unauthorised changes to standing data. | Payroll clerks should not be allowed to make standing data changes.<br><br>Changes to the standing data to reflect the annual wage increase should be made by a senior member of the payroll department. These changes should be checked by another responsible official to identify any errors or inconsistencies. | Observe a payroll clerk attempting to make changes to payroll standing data, to determine whether the system rejects the changes.<br><br>Review the log of changes made to the standing data for evidence that they were made by a senior member of the payroll department.<br><br>Review the log of changes made to the standing data for evidence that they have been reviewed by another responsible official. |
| Only payment for overtime in excess of 30% of the standard hours are authorised by department heads.<br><br>This increases the risk of employees claiming for overtime not worked, leading to additional payroll costs. | All overtime hours worked, whether in lieu of pay or holidays, must be authorised by the relevant department head. The authorisation should be evidenced by signatures. | Review a sample of the weekly overtime sheets for evidence of signature by the head of the department concerned. |
| The payroll clerks do not always check the overtime worked report before employees take time off in lieu of overtime worked.<br><br>This increases the risk of employees taking unauthorised leave, leading, again, to wages being paid for days which have not been worked. | Payroll clerks must agree holidays taken in lieu to the overtime report, and record that this has been done. Where inconsistencies are identified, the payroll clerks should notify the relevant department head. | Review a sample of holidays taken in lieu of overtime to verify whether the payroll clerk has agreed the time taken in lieu to the overtime report. |

| Deficiencies | Recommended controls | Test of control |
|---|---|---|
| The overtime worked report is emailed by the payroll department to department heads, who report only by exception if errors are identified.<br><br>The authorisation of overtime sheets by an alternative responsible official while the department heads are on leave does not always occur.<br><br>The fact that the department heads only report by exception can cause the payroll department to mistakenly assume that the overtime report is correct when it is not – leading to the payment of incorrect overtime.<br><br>The lack of holiday cover for the authorisation of overtime can lead to overtime pay being delayed, resulting in the loss of employee goodwill. | Departments should be required to respond to the payroll department regarding each overtime worked report, regardless of whether it is correct.<br><br>The department heads should be reminded of the procedures with regards to holiday cover.<br><br>No payment should be made until the report has been authorised by the relevant official.<br><br>The payroll department should monitor the authorisation of the overtime worked report and follow up with each relevant head where no response has been received. | For a sample of overtime worked reports, inspect the responses received from each department head.<br><br>For a sample of overtime payments, compare the dates on which authorisation has been received with the dates on which overtime payment is made, to confirm that payment is only made after authorisation has been obtained.<br><br>Make enquiries of payroll clerks regarding the process of obtaining authorisation for overtime sheets while the department heads are on leave. |
| The finance director reviews the total list of bank transfers and compares this to the total payable per the payroll records.<br><br>This process does not prevent employees to be omitted from the payroll. There is equally a risk of fictitious employees, or employees who have left the company, appearing on payroll. As a result, fraudulent payments could be made. | The finance director should agree a sample of the employees on the payroll records to the payment list, and vice versa, to ensure that payments are complete, and made only to bona fide employees.<br><br>These checks should be evidenced by the finance director's signature. | Inspect payment lists for evidence that the finance director has agreed a sample of payees to the payroll records, and vice versa. |

(b) The differences between an interim and a final audit can be summarised as follows:

| Type of audit | When it occurs | Purpose | Procedures performed |
|---|---|---|---|
| Interim audit | During the period of review | To carry out procedures that would be difficult to perform at the year end because of time constraints.<br><br>No statutory requirement to perform interim audit. | • Inherent risk assessment and gaining an understanding of the entity<br><br>• Documenting and evaluating the entity's system of internal control<br><br>• Carrying out tests of control on the company's internal controls to ensure they are operating as expected<br><br>• Performing substantive testing of profit or loss transactions/balances to gain evidence that the books and records are a reliable basis for the preparation of financial statements<br><br>• Identification of issues that may have an impact on work to take place at the final audit |

| Type of audit | When it occurs | Purpose | Procedures performed |
|---|---|---|---|
| Final audit | After the year end | To express an audit opinion on the financial statements covering the entire period being audited.<br><br>The performance of the final audit is a statutory requirement. | Substantive procedures involving verification of statement of financial position balances and amounts in the statement of profit or loss<br><br>• Obtaining third-party confirmations<br>• Analytical procedures relating to figures in the financial statements<br>• Subsequent events review<br>• Agreeing the financial statements to the accounting records<br>• Examining adjustments made during the process of preparing the financial statements<br>• Consideration of the going concern status of the entity<br>• Performing tests to ensure that the conclusions formed at the interim audit are still valid<br>• Obtaining written representations |

(c) **Payroll substantive procedures**

(i) Agree the total wages and salaries expense per the payroll system to the trial balance, investigate any differences.

(ii) Cast a sample of payroll records to confirm completeness and accuracy of the payroll expense.

(iii) For a sample of employees, recalculate the gross and net pay and agree to the payroll records to confirm accuracy.

(iv) Reperform the calculation of statutory deductions to confirm whether correct deductions for this year have been made in the payroll.

(v) Compare the total payroll expense to the prior year and investigate any significant differences.

(vi) Review monthly payroll charges, compare this to the prior year and budgets and discuss with management for any significant variances.

(vii) Perform a proof in total of total wages and salaries, incorporating joiners and leavers and the annual pay increase. Compare this to the actual wages and salaries in the financial statements and investigate any significant differences.

(viii) Select a sample of joiners and leavers, agree their start/leaving date to supporting documentation, recalculate that their first/last pay packet was accurately calculated and recorded.

(ix) Agree the total net pay per the payroll records to the bank transfer listing of payments and to the cash book.

(x) Agree the individual wages and salaries per the payroll to the personnel records for a sample.

(xi) Select a sample of weekly overtime sheets and trace to overtime payment in payroll records to confirm completeness of overtime paid.

(d)    **Accrual for income tax payable on employment income**

Procedures the auditor should adopt in respect of auditing this accrual include:

(i)    Agree the year-end income tax payable accrual to the payroll records to confirm accuracy.

(ii)    Reperform the calculation of the accrual to confirm accuracy.

(iii)    Agree the subsequent payment to the post year end cash book and bank statements to confirm completeness.

(iv)    Review any correspondence with tax authorities to assess whether there are any additional outstanding payments due; if so, agree they are included in the year-end accrual.

(v)    Review any disclosures made of the income tax accrual and assess whether these are in compliance with accounting standards and legislation.

# 111 Castle Courier

**Workbook references.** Chapters 9, 10 and 16.

**Top tips.** The requirements for this question are typical of the Audit and Assurance exam, with the scenario being about controls and tests of control within a particular system. There is a lot to do in this question, so there is a risk of overrunning on the time. Make sure you stick to time for each part of the question and move on to the next requirement once the time is up.

Part (a) is a knowledge-based requirement. The CBE would have given you a table in which to complete your answer, which would help you to get one mark for each method / explanation / advantage.

Part (b) requires you to make good use of the tabular format for the controls and tests of control. – go through the scenario line by line and make notes on the controls that appear to be particularly important in the system, and then consider how you might go about testing whether the control works as it should do. Your tests of control need to be sufficiently detailed to gain the marks. Note that you should not be mentioning financial statement assertions here because we are dealing with test of control rather than substantive procedures.

Part (c) is on controls deficiencies and recommendations. This is the biggest part of the question so it is important that you stick to your time here. Your recommendations should be as specific as possible, including details of the actions that will need to be taken and why they should be taken.

Part (d) asks for substantive procedures on the payroll expense. This is a standard area for AA, and should be within your reach; if you struggled here then it is important that you prepare yourself for questions of this type in your exam.

**Easy marks.** Part (a) on methods of documenting internal controls is knowledge based for four marks and relatively straightforward. Part (d) asks for substantive procedures for payroll. This is worth six marks and, provided your procedures are adequately detailed, you should be able to score well here.

Marking scheme

|  | | Marks |
|---|---|---|
| (a) | **Methods for documenting internal control systems** | |
| | Narrative notes | 2 |
| | Internal control questionnaires | 2 |
| | | 4 |

**BPP**
LEARNING
MEDIA

Answers    **225**

| | | Marks |
|---|---|---|

**(b)**     **Direct controls and tests of control** (only 4 required)

| | |
|---|---|
| Sequence checks on key cards/data | 2 |
| HR review of clocking in process | 2 |
| Payroll calculations reperformed | 2 |
| Password updated monthly | 2 |
| Control account reconciliations performed | 2 |
| Tax liability calculation reviewed | 2 |
| **Max 4 issues, 2 marks each** | **8** |

**(c)**     **Control deficiencies and recommendations** (only 6 required)

| | |
|---|---|
| Holiday requests not authorised | 2 |
| FC prepares and authorises bank transfer | 2 |
| Edit report not checked | 2 |
| Temporary staff not processed by HR | 2 |
| Only overtime above five hours authorised | 2 |
| Cash wages collected without identification | 2 |
| No approved bonus parameters | 2 |
| Drivers breaks not monitored | 2 |
| **Max 6 issues, 2 marks each** | **12** |

**(d)**     **Substantive procedures for payroll expense**

| | |
|---|---|
| 1 mark per well-described procedure | |
| **Restricted to** | **6** |
| **Total marks** | **20** |

**(a)**     **Methods for documenting internal control systems**

| Method | Explanation | Disadvantage |
|---|---|---|
| Narrative notes | Narrative notes consist of a written description of the internal control system. They detail what occurs in the system at each stage including related controls which operate at each stage. | They may prove to be time-consuming and cumbersome if the internal control system is complex.<br><br>It may make it more difficult to identify if any internal controls are missing in narrative notes. |
| Internal control questionnaires | Internal control questionnaires contain a list of questions for each major transaction cycle. They use questions designed to assess whether internal controls exist. | Internal controls may be overstated if the client is aware that the auditor is looking for a particular answer.<br><br>Unusual controls may not be included on a standard questionnaire and hence may not be identified. |

(b) Direct controls and tests of control

| Direct control | Test of control |
| --- | --- |
| All staff members are issued with a sequentially numbered key card. Sequence checks and checks on the data recorded are carried out by the human resources (HR) supervisor.<br><br>This ensures that payroll records are complete, that employees are paid for hours worked and that all hours are recorded. | For a sample of key cards and data recorded in the clocking-in system, carry out a sequence check to identify if there are any gaps in the sequence.<br><br>Review details of checks carried out by the HR supervisor to identify any gaps in the sequence and check they have evidenced their review by way of signature. |
| The clocking-in process is monitored by a camera on entry to the distribution centre and video footage is reviewed by HR every week.<br><br>This will prevent staff members fraudulently clocking-in for other employees and hence employees will only be paid for actual hours worked. | For a sample of weeks, review the log of the recordings to identify who reviewed that week's footage to ensure it has been reviewed by a member of the HR department.<br><br>Review the log for any gaps in the review process and discuss these findings with HR. |
| The payroll clerk confirms the transfer of hours and calculations has been done accurately by recalculating, for a sample of employees, their gross to net pay. This check is also reviewed by the payroll supervisor who evidences their review.<br><br>This reduces the risk that errors occur in the automated transfer and calculations during the payroll processing. Any errors would be identified on a timely basis to prevent salaries being over or under paid. | For a sample of months, review the calculations of gross to net pay for evidence that the calculations have been performed. Confirm the signature of the payroll supervisor as evidence that they have reviewed the report. For any anomalies, enquire of the reasons and what action was taken to resolve the issue.<br><br>For a sample of months, reperform the gross to net pay calculations and compare to the payroll system and the calculations prepared by the payroll clerk. Discuss any discrepancies with the payroll supervisor. |
| The payroll system is password-protected and the payroll manager changes the password on a monthly basis using a random password generator.<br><br>This reduces the risk of fraud by preventing unauthorised changes being made to the standing data and unauthorised access to sensitive payroll information. | Attempt to login to the payroll system using a password which should be out of date. Confirm that the system has rejected access. |
| Each month, the finance director carries out a payroll control account reconciliation and investigates any differences.<br><br>This will ensure the payroll expense and employment tax liability is accurate and is not misstated in the year-end financial statements. | For a sample of months, review the control account reconciliations and make enquiries of the finance director of any errors on the control account, how they arose and what action was taken to ensure they do not arise in the future.<br><br>Reperform a sample of control account reconciliations and compare results with those prepared by the finance director. Discuss any discrepancies with the finance director. |

| Direct control | Test of control |
|---|---|
| The amount due to the tax authority is calculated by the payroll supervisor who then passes it to the financial controller for review. | Review a sample of calculations of the monthly employment tax liability for evidence of review by the financial controller confirming the calculation is correct and that payment can be made. |
| This ensures that the amount paid to the tax authority is correct. It also creates segregation of duties between the payroll supervisor calculating the liability and the financial controller reviewing the calculation which reduces the risk of error. | |

(c) **Deficiencies and recommendations**

| Control deficiency | Control recommendation |
|---|---|
| Department managers are required to approve all employees' holiday forms, however, this does not always occur. | Employees should receive written confirmation when their holiday has been approved and should be informed that they will not be able to take holiday without this notification. |
| This could result in employees taking unauthorised leave which could lead to operational difficulties if there are shortages of staff at critical periods. In addition, payments for untaken holiday may be made in error as holiday records may be incorrect. | Any payments for unused holiday should be authorised by department managers prior to payment. |
| The financial controller prepares the bank transfers for the payroll and also authorises these to be paid. | Once the bank transfer has been prepared by the financial controller, it should be passed to the finance director to be reviewed and authorised for payment. The review and authorisation should be evidenced by the finance director. |
| This lack of segregation of duties increases the risk of fraud/error as the financial controller could pay themselves or certain employees more than they are due without this being detected. | |
| The payroll clerk amends the payroll and an edit report of changes is produced but this report is not reviewed. | The payroll supervisor or a member of the finance team should review all edit reports and agree changes made to the details on the joiner/leavers forms. Any discrepancies should be investigated promptly and the payroll system updated for any errors or omissions. |
| As the edit report is not checked, errors made by the payroll clerk when updating the system will not be identified promptly. This may result in new employees not being paid at all, errors being made in payments to new employees or leavers being paid after they have left the company. This would lead to loss of employee goodwill and errors in accounting records for wages and salaries. | The payroll supervisor should evidence their review on the edit report with their signature. |
| It could also result in an increased risk of fraud as fictitious employees could be added by the payroll clerk. | |

| Control deficiency | Control recommendation |
|---|---|
| The HR department is responsible for processing joiners and leavers, but due to staff illness, the operations manager has processed temporary new drivers and notified payroll.<br><br>The operations manager may not carry out all the required procedures for processing temporary new drivers as the manager may not be using appropriate documentation.<br><br>This could result in temporary employees not being set up in the payroll records correctly, resulting in the late payment of wages, incorrect statutory deductions being calculated and incomplete payroll records. | All staff appointments, including temporary staff, should only be processed by the HR department to ensure that correct procedures are followed.<br><br>If it is not possible for the HR department to carry out all of the detailed processing due to staff shortages, a member of the HR team should review the leaver/joiner form and authorise it before it is sent to the payroll department.<br><br>The payroll department should be notified not to accept any new joiner information unless approved by a member of HR. |
| Only overtime in excess of five hours per week needs authorisation by the operations manager.<br><br>This means that employees could claim to have worked up to five hours overtime without authorisation resulting in payments being made to employees for hours not worked and additional payroll costs. | All overtime, including that below five hours, should be authorised by a responsible official before being processed in the payroll. This authorisation should be evidenced by way of signature. |
| Where cash wages are paid, the driver is only required to provide their name to collect their pay packet.<br><br>Payment of wages without proof of identity or signature increases the risk that wages could be paid to incorrect employees either in error or due to fraud resulting in a loss of cash. | All drivers collecting cash pay packets should provide a form of identification to the finance staff member before the pay packet is handed to them. The driver should also be required to sign for their pay packet. |
| The operations manager decides on the bonus to be paid to delivery drivers each quarter and there are no approved parameters for the bonus levels.<br><br>Without approved parameters, the operations manager may award excessive bonuses or pay additional sums to friends and family members resulting in additional payroll costs. | Approved bonus parameters should be established by the board. All bonuses should be determined by a senior official, such as the sales director, in line with these parameters, who should communicate the bonus in writing to the payroll department. |
| Delivery drivers must take breaks throughout the day which are not monitored.<br><br>Drivers could take longer breaks than those authorised resulting in payments being made to employees for time not worked. Conversely, if drivers do not take the required breaks, they may be in breach of law and regulations which require drivers to take regular breaks, hence the company is at risk of fines. | The company should monitor the activity of the delivery drivers through electronic means, for example, by using tracking devices attached to their vehicles to ensure that the prescribed breaks are taken by the employees.<br><br>Data should be downloaded and reviewed by a responsible official on a regular basis. |

(d)    **Substantive procedures on payroll expense**

- Cast a sample of payroll records to confirm completeness and accuracy and agree the total wages and salaries expense per the payroll system to the trial balance.

- Recalculate the gross and net pay figures for a sample of employees and agree to the payroll records.

- For a sample of wage payments, agree the total net pay per the payroll records to the bank transfer listing and to the cash book.

- Perform a proof in total of wages and salaries, incorporating joiners and leavers and the pay increase/bonuses. Compare this to the actual wages and salaries expense in the financial statements and investigate any significant differences.

- Compare the total payroll figure this year to the prior year, identify any significant differences and discuss with management.

- Review monthly payroll charges, compare this to the prior year and budgets and discuss any significant differences with management.

- Calculate overtime costs as a percentage of total wages. Compare this to the prior year and discuss any significant differences with management.

- Agree a sample of individual wages and salaries per the payroll to personnel records and records of hours worked per the clocking-in system.

- Reperform the calculation of statutory deductions and agree to supporting documentation to confirm whether correct deductions for this year have been made in the payroll.

- Select a sample of joiners and leavers, agree their start/leaving date to supporting documentation, recalculate their first/last salary to ensure it is accurate.

- Recalculate holiday pay for a sample of employees and agree to holiday records and daily rate applied.

- Select a sample of employees from HR records and agree salaries per HR records to the payroll records to confirm the accuracy of the payroll expense.

- Agree the payroll control account reconciliation to accounting records and investigate any differences.

# 112 Bluesberry

**Workbook references.** Chapters 5 and 12.

**Top tips.** You should have been familiar with the purpose of a value for money audit in part (a) – just remember to focus on the **purpose** and not just provide a definition of a value for money audit.

The most important thing for (b)(i) is to understand the requirement. Don't be fazed by the fact you are asked for strengths instead of weaknesses or deficiencies. The scenario actually gives examples of problems that have been solved by certain procedures, so you should have recognised that these were strengths (for example the overtime scheme has seen reliance on expensive temporary staff reduced). As you were pulling out the strengths in the operating environment you could also have been considering the areas for improvement to help in answering part (b)(ii). In fact a good approach would have been to lay out your answer so that you could answer (b)(i) and (b)(ii) together.

Part (c) depends on you knowing your assertions so you can stay focused on the relevant substantive procedures. For each assertion ask yourself, what am I trying to prove with this procedure? For example, with completeness you are trying to prove no material items are missing from non-current assets. You therefore need to suggest procedures that might highlight missing assets.

**Easy marks.** Parts (a) and (c) were more straightforward than (b).

## Marking scheme

Marks

(a)  Up to 1 mark per valid point.

Explanation of value for money audit

Economy – description

Efficiency – description

Effectiveness – description                                                                 4

(b)  0.5 marks for identification and up to 1 mark for explanation of each well-explained strength and up to 1 mark per improvement. If not well explained 0.5 marks for each, but overall maximum of 4 points.

Internal audit department

Centralised buying department buys from lowest cost supplier

Authorisation of all purchase orders by purchasing director

Reduction in use of temporary staff

Employee clocking in cards to monitor hours worked

New surgical equipment leading to better recovery rates

Capital expenditure committee                                                             10

(c)  Up to 1 mark per substantive procedure.

Valuation (i)

Review depreciation policies for reasonableness

Recalculate the depreciation charge

Proof in total calculation of depreciation

For revalued assets, consider reasonableness of valuer

For revalued assets, agree the revalued amounts to valuation report

Surgical equipment additions – vouch the cost to invoice                        2

Completeness (ii)

Reconcile PPE schedule to general ledger

Physical inspection of assets

Reconciliation of non-current asset register to the general ledger

Review the repairs and maintenance expense account                    2

Rights and obligations (iii)

Verify ownership of property via inspection of title deeds

Additions agree to purchase invoices to verify invoice relates to entity

Review any new lease agreements

Inspect vehicle registration documents                                              2

Total for (c)                                                                                          6
                                                                                                          20

---

(a)    **Purpose of a value for money (VFM) audit**

VFM focuses on the best combination of services for the lowest level of resources. The purpose of a VFM audit is to examine the **economy**, **efficiency** and **effectiveness** of the activity or process in question.

- **Economy**: attaining the appropriate quantity and quality of physical, human and financial resources (inputs) at lowest cost

- **Efficiency**: the relationship between goods or services produced (outputs) and the resources used to produce them

- **Effectiveness**: concerned with how well an activity is achieving its policy objectives or other intended effects

(b)

| Strength (i) | Improvement (ii) |
|---|---|
| The buying department researches the lowest price from suppliers before raising a purchase order. This helps with economy of the process, attaining resources at the lowest cost. | In order to also ensure the goods are of the required quality, an approved list of suppliers could be built up, with purchases only being permitted from those suppliers on the list. |
| Overtime rates have been increased and this has incentivised staff to fill staffing gaps. As a result the hospital has saved money by decreasing the level of expensive temporary staff. Additionally, the permanent staff may be more effective as they are familiar with the hospital's systems and the level of patient care expected at Bluesberry. | The increased hours will affect overall efficiency given that the same staff are now carrying out extended shifts, as overtime rates are higher than basic rates, even though overtime cost appears to be lower than temporary staff.<br><br>There is also an increased risk of mistakes due to tiredness which could have adverse effects on the reputation of the hospital. Ideally the hospital should recruit enough permanent staff of the required level to fill shifts without then working overtime. |

| Strength (i) | Improvement (ii) |
|---|---|
| The hospital has implemented time card clocking in to ensure employees are only paid for those hours worked. It also provides a means for recording hours worked which is valuable management information. Before this there would have been no definitive record of actual hours worked. | The system appears to allow payable overtime to accumulate simply because an employee clocks out late, even if there is no staff gap to fill. The system should be set to automatically clock out after the normal number of shift hours. Staff will then need to clock back in for their overtime if they have an authorised shift. Overtime hours each month should be reviewed by the department head for consistency with agreed extra shifts. |
| A capital expenditure committee of senior managers has been set up to authorise significant capital expenditure items. This will help prevent cash outflows for unnecessary assets, or assets not budgeted for. | In a hospital there will be very expensive equipment purchases, such as the recently acquired new surgical equipment. It is better that these are authorised at board level rather than by senior managers. An authorisation policy should be drawn up setting out the different levels of authorisation needed (the highest being at board level) depending on the amount of expenditure for capital items. |

> **Top tips.** You were only asked for four strengths and related improvements. Others you may have come up with in place of those given in the answer above are as follows.

| Strength (i) | Improvement (ii) |
|---|---|
| The hospital has an internal audit department monitoring the internal control environment and advising on value for money. | The remit of internal audit could be extended to advising on implementation. |
| Orders are authorised by a purchasing director to help ensure expenditure incurred is necessary expenditure. | The volume of forms (200 per day) will no doubt take valuable time away from the director which could be used on more pressing matters. Orders below a certain monetary level should be authorised by the next level (down) of management. Orders over the specified monetary value should still be reserved for purchase director authorisation. |
| New surgical equipment purchased has improved the rate of operations and patient recovery rates. This is an improvement in the effectiveness of the hospital. | The equipment is not used as efficiently as it could be due to lack of trained medical staff. The hospital should look at providing targeted training for existing medical staff and look to recruit staff that have the appropriate skills. |

(c) **Substantive procedures – property, plant and equipment (non-current assets)**

(i) *Valuation*

- Review depreciation rates applied in relation to asset lives, past experience of profits and losses on disposals, and consistency with prior years and disclosed accounting policies.

BPP
LEARNING
MEDIA

- If assets have been revalued, consider:

  - Experience and independence of valuer
  - Scope of the valuer's work
  - Methods and assumptions used
  - Whether valuation bases are in line with IFRSs

(ii) *Completeness*

- Compare non-current assets in the general ledger with the non-current assets register and obtain explanations for differences.

- For a sample of assets which physically exist agree that they are recorded in the non-current asset register.

(iii) *Rights and obligations*

- Verify title to land and buildings by inspection of:

  - Title deeds
  - Land registry certificates
  - Leases

- Examine documents of title for other assets (including purchase invoices, contracts, hire purchase or lease agreements).

> **Top tips.** Only two substantive procedures were needed for each assertion. You may have come up with alternative procedures including:
>
> *Valuation*
>
> - Recalculate the depreciation charge for a sample of assets and agree the charges to the asset register
> - Perform a depreciation proof in total taking into account timing of additions/disposals and investigate any differences
> - Agree the cost of a sample of additions of surgical equipment to purchase invoices
>
> *Completeness*
>
> - Reconcile the schedule of non-current assets with the general ledger
> - Review the repairs and maintenance expense account in the SOCI for capital items
>
> *Rights and obligations*
>
> - Review new lease agreements to ensure properly classified as a finance lease or an operating lease in accordance with IFRSs
> - Inspect vehicle registration documents (eg ambulances) to confirm ownership of motor vehicles

# 113 Snowdon

> **Workbook reference.** Chapters 9, 10, 12 and 15.
>
> **Top tips.** This was a reasonable question on internal controls and began, in part (a), with a theoretical requirement on significant deficiencies. This part of the question was not entirely straightforward and many of the points listed in the answer may seem strange, particularly if you were not familiar with the requirements of ISAs in this area. If you struggled then you will need to ensure that you are able to cope with this kind of requirement in your exam.
>
> Part (b), on direct controls and tests of controls, was scenario-focused and to score well here you needed to make sure that you developed your points sufficiently to get the marks on offer.
>
> Part (c) was again based on the scenario and is typical of the way this area is likely to be examined.
>
> **Easy marks.** Part (a) was considered by the examining team to be easy but may not have been - so you would have to have scored well in parts (b) and (c) to make up for this.

Marks

(a) **Significant deficiencies**

| | | |
|---|---|---|
| Likelihood of leading to material misstatement | 1 | |
| Susceptibility to loss or fraud | 1 | |
| Subjectivity and complexity of amounts | 1 | |
| Amount exposed to deficiency | 1 | |
| Volume of activity | 1 | |
| Importance to financial reporting process | 1 | |
| Cause and frequency of exceptions | 1 | |
| Interaction with other deficiencies | 1 | 4 |

**Restricted to**

(b) **Direct controls and tests of control** (only 3 required)

| | | |
|---|---|---|
| Capital expenditure classification | 2 | |
| HR department/payroll department | 2 | |
| Processing new joiners | 2 | |
| Bank reconciliations | 2 | |
| **Max 3 issues, 2 marks each** | | 6 |

(c) **Control deficiencies and recommendations** (only 5 required)

| | | |
|---|---|---|
| IA staff shortages | 2 | |
| Capital expenditure over budget | 2 | |
| Physical verification of assets | 2 | |
| Amendment of standing data | 2 | |
| Changes made in payroll records | 2 | |
| Credit limits not reviewed | 2 | |
| Invoices only chased after 90 days | 2 | |
| **Max 5 issues, 2 marks each** | | 10 |

| | | |
|---|---|---|
| **Total marks** | | **20** |

(a) **Significant deficiencies**

Examples of matters the external auditor may consider in determining whether a deficiency in internal controls is significant include:

- The likelihood of the deficiencies leading to material misstatements in the financial statements in the future.

- The susceptibility to loss or fraud of the related asset or liability.

**BPP** LEARNING MEDIA

- The subjectivity and complexity of determining estimated amounts.
- The financial statement amounts exposed to the deficiencies.
- The volume of activity that has occurred or could occur in the account balance or class of transactions exposed to the deficiency or deficiencies.
- The importance of the controls to the financial reporting process.
- The cause and frequency of the exceptions detected as a result of the deficiencies in the controls.
- The interaction of the deficiency with other deficiencies in internal control.

(b)    **Direct controls and tests of control**

| Direct control | Test of control |
|---|---|
| Capital expenditure purchase orders are classified by the finance department between capital and revenue using guidelines established by the finance director, this is noted on the purchase order. The finance director also sample checks the classification is correctly applied.<br><br>The use of finance department guidelines and sample checks by the finance director should reduce the risk of an incorrect assessment and of understated/overstated profits, assets and incorrect depreciation charges. | Select a sample of capital expenditure purchase orders and review evidence of the classification being noted.<br><br>For a sample of orders compare the classification noted with the finance director's guidelines to assess whether the classification was correctly undertaken.<br><br>Review purchase orders for evidence of the finance director's sample checks for example, by signature. |
| Snowdon Co has a separate human resources (HR) department, which is responsible for setting up all new employees.<br><br>Having a segregation of roles between HR and payroll departments reduces the risk of fictitious employees being set up and also being paid. | Review the job descriptions of payroll and HR to confirm the split of responsibilities with regards to setting up new joiners.<br><br>Discuss with members of the payroll department the process for setting up new joiners and agree new joiners to documentation initiated by HR. |
| Pre-printed forms are completed by HR for new employees, and includes assignment of a unique employee number, and once verified a copy is sent to the payroll department. The payroll system is unable to process new joiners without the inclusion of the employee's unique number.<br><br>As payroll is unable to set up new joiners without the forms and employee number it reduces the risk of fictitious employees being set up by payroll. | Select a sample of new employees added to the payroll during the year, review the joiner forms for evidence of completion and the allocation of a unique employee number which was received by payroll prior to being added to the system.<br><br>Select a sample of edit reports for changes to payroll during the year; agree a sample of new employees added to payroll to the joiner's forms.<br><br>Attempt to add a new joiner to the payroll system without a unique employee number, the system should reject this addition. |

| Direct control | Test of control |
|---|---|
| The cashier reconciles the bank statements to the cash book monthly and this reconciliation is reviewed and investigated by the financial controller, who evidences his review by way of signature on the bank reconciliation.<br><br>The bank reconciliation is a direct control which reduces the risk of fraud. Monthly review and investigation ensure that fraud and errors are identified on a timely basis. | Review the file of bank reconciliations to confirm that there is one for each month. Inspect a sample of monthly bank reconciliations for evidence of investigation and review by the financial controller.<br><br>For a sample of months reperform the bank reconciliation and where differences have occurred discuss and investigate these with the financial controller. |

(c) Control deficiencies and recommendations

| Control deficiency | Control recommendation |
|---|---|
| Snowdon Co has experienced significant staff shortages within its internal audit (IA) department, and the department is currently under-resourced. This has resulted in a reduction in their programme of work for the year.<br><br>Maintaining an IA department is an important control as it enables senior management to test whether controls are operating effectively within the company. If the team has staff shortages, this reduces the effectiveness of this monitoring control. | Senior management should consider recruiting additional employees to join the IA department or outsourcing the IA function.<br><br>In the interim, employees from other departments, such as finance, could be seconded to IA to assist them with audits. It must be ensured that these reviews do not cover controls operating in the department in which the employees normally work. |
| Some departments have already significantly exceeded their annual capital expenditure budgets.<br><br>It appears that purchase orders for capital expenditure are being placed without being agreed back to annual capital budgets, resulting in overspends.<br><br>The increased expenditure may be due to increased levels of services being provided, or it could be due to a lack of control over the capital expenditure process, resulting in increased costs and reduced profits. | The company's monthly management accounts should include an analysis of capital expenditure against budget and prior year per department. Each department head should include narrative which explains the significant variances to date.<br><br>Capital purchase orders should be compared to the annual department budgets as part of the authorisation process. Any spend in excess of the budget should be referred for authorisation to the finance director. |
| The IA department undertakes physical verification of assets each year for the four largest centres as well as five of the other centres, randomly selected. The company has 45 centres as well as a head office and warehouse, hence if each year the four largest sites are visited this can result in the other sites only being visited every eight years.<br><br>If the non-current assets register is not physically verified on a regular basis, there is an increased risk of assets being misappropriated as there is no check that the assets still exist in their correct location. In addition, obsolete assets will not be identified on a timely basis. | IA should review its programme of visits to assess if additional resources could be devoted to ensuring that all sites are visited over a shorter period, for example, five years. This would ensure that physical verification of all assets could be completed more regularly. For sites visited any assets which cannot be located should be investigated fully. If it cannot be located, then it should be written off.<br><br>Each centre should submit a list of assets with serial numbers to IA, who should compare these to the PPE register. Those sites with significant variations should be prioritised for a site visit by IA. |

| Control deficiency | Control recommendation |
|---|---|
| All members of the payroll department can amend employees' standing data in the payroll system as they have access to the password.<br><br>As all members of payroll can amend standing data this may result in errors or unauthorised changes being made, leading to incorrect payment of wages and increased risk of fraud. | The password to amend standing data should be changed and only communicated to senior members of the payroll department.<br><br>If all members of payroll need the ability to amend standing data, the system should be changed to require authorisation of all changes by a senior member of payroll.<br><br>Edit reports should be generated for all standing data changes with clear reference to who made the change and who authorised it. These edit reports should be regularly reviewed by a responsible official and they should evidence this review with a signature. |
| The senior payroll manager reviews the bank transfer listing prior to authorising the payments and if any discrepancies are noted, always makes the adjustment in the payroll records for any changes required.<br><br>Discrepancies may arise due to the payroll records or the bank transfer listing being incorrect. Assuming the discrepancies are always in the payroll records may result in incorrect records may result in incorrect amendments being made to payroll or incorrect amounts paid to employees.<br><br>In addition, there is a lack of segregation of duties as it is the payroll team which processes the amounts and the senior payroll manager who authorises payments. The senior manager could fraudulently increase or incorrectly amend the amounts to be paid to certain employees, process this payment as well as amend the records. | The senior payroll manager should not be able to process changes to the payroll system as well as authorise payments. Discrepancies should be thoroughly investigated, and adjustments made in the relevant record as required.<br><br>The authorisation of the bank transfer listing should be undertaken by an individual outside the payroll department, such as the finance director. |
| After passing a credit check a credit limit is set for all new customers by the sales director, but these credit limits are not reviewed after this unless a review is requested by the customer.<br><br>If credit limits are not reviewed regularly, they could be out of date, resulting in limits being too high and sales being made to poor credit risks or too low and Snowdon Co losing potential revenue. | Credit limits should continue to be set by the sales director; however, these limits should be reviewed and amended as appropriate on a regular basis by a responsible official. |
| Client services managers are given responsibility to chase customers directly for payment once an invoice is outstanding for 90 days. This is considerably in excess of the company's credit terms of 30 days which will lead to poor cash flow.<br><br>Further, client services managers are more likely to focus on customer relationships and generating further revenues rather than chasing payments. This could result in an increase in irrecoverable balances and reduced profit and cash flows. | A credit controller should be appointed, and it should be their role, rather than the client services managers, to chase any outstanding sales invoices which are more than 30 days old. |

# 114 Swift Co

## Marking scheme

| | | Marks |
|---|---|---|
| (a) | **Methods of documenting internal controls** | |
| | Narrative notes | 2 |
| | Flowcharts | 2 |
| | Questionnaires | 2 |
| | | 6 |
| | | |
| (b) | **Direct controls and test of controls** (only 7 required) | |
| | Segregation of duties – HR and payroll | 2 |
| | Unique employee number to process joiners | 2 |
| | Review of exception report | 2 |
| | Recalculation of gross to net pay | 2 |
| | Authorisation of purchase orders | 2 |
| | Goods agreed to purchase order/quality/quantity | 2 |
| | Control totals used for invoice input | 2 |
| | Supplier statement reconciliations | 2 |
| | Authorisation of bank transfer list | 2 |
| | **Max 7 issues, 2 marks each** | 14 |
| **Total marks** | | 20 |

(a) **Documenting systems**

| | Description | Advantage |
|---|---|---|
| **Narrative notes** | Narrative notes Narrative notes consist of a written description of the system. They detail what occurs in the system at each stage and include details of any controls which operate at each stage. | They are simple to record; after discussion with staff members, these discussions are easily written up as notes.<br><br>They can facilitate understanding by all members of the audit team, especially more junior members who might find alternative methods too complex. |

|  | Description | Advantage |
|---|---|---|
| Flowcharts | Flowcharts are a diagrammatic illustration of the internal control system. Lines usually demonstrate the sequence of events and standard symbols are used to signify controls or documents | With flowcharts it is easy to view the system in its entirety as it is all presented together in one diagram.<br><br>Due to the use of standard symbols for controls, it can be effective in identifying missing controls. |
| Questionnaires | Questionnaires Internal control questionnaires (ICQs) or internal control evaluation questionnaires (ICEQs) contain a list of questions for each major transaction cycle; ICQs are used to assess whether controls exist whereas ICEQs assess the effectiveness of the controls in place. | Questionnaires are quick to prepare, which means they are a timely method for recording the system.<br><br>If drafted thoroughly they ensure that all controls present within the system are considered and recorded, hence missing controls or deficiencies are clearly highlighted by the audit team. |

(b)  **Direct controls and tests of control**

| Direct control | Test control |
|---|---|
| Swift Co has a separate human resources (HR) department, which is responsible for setting up all new employees.<br><br>Having a segregation of roles between HR and payroll departments reduces the risk of fictitious employees being set up and also being paid. | Review the job descriptions of payroll and HR to confirm the split of responsibilities with regards to setting up new joiners.<br><br>Discuss with members of the payroll department the process for setting up new joiners and agree new joiners to documentation initiated by HR. |
| All new employees are assigned a unique employee number by HR. The payroll system is unable to process new joiners without the inclusion of the unique employee number.<br><br>As payroll staff are unable to set up new joiners without the employee number from the joiner form it reduces the risk of fictitious employees being set up by payroll. | Attempt to add a new joiner to the payroll system without a unique employee number, the system should reject this addition. |
| On a monthly basis an exception report of changes to payroll standing data is produced and reviewed by the payroll manager.<br><br>This ensures that any unauthorised amendments to standing data are identified and investigated on a timely basis so that the data used when the payroll is run is valid and accurate | Select a sample of monthly exception reports and review for evidence of review and follow up of any unexpected changes by the payroll manager. |

| Direct control | Test control |
|---|---|
| The payroll supervisor selects a sample of payslips and recalculates the gross to net pay calculations, compares the results to the output from the payroll system and investigates any discrepancies.<br><br>This reduces the risk that the automated system generates errors during the payroll processing. Any errors would be identified on a timely basis to prevent wages being over or under paid. | Review the monthly payslips sampled by the payroll supervisor for their signature for evidence the review of calculations has been undertaken.<br><br>For a sample of monthly payrolls reperform the gross to net pay calculation and compare to the payroll system, discuss any discrepancies with the payroll supervisor. |
| Purchase orders up to $5,000 are authorised by the purchasing manager and above $5,000 by the purchasing director.<br><br>This ensures that goods are only purchased which are required by Swift Co and relate to genuine business expenses. | Select a sample of purchase orders and review for evidence of authorisation in accordance with authorisation limits. Agree this to the appropriate signature on the approved signatories list. |
| The warehouse department agrees the receipt of goods from suppliers to a copy of the purchase order and confirms the quantity and quality of the goods received and signs the goods received notes (GRNs) to evidence the checks.<br><br>This ensures that Swift Co is not recording liabilities and subsequently paying for the receipt of inferior quality goods or for goods it did not order. | During the interim audit observe the warehouse department when receiving goods to understand the level of checks being undertaken.<br><br>Review a sample of GRNs held in the warehouse department for signature, as evidence of checks being undertaken on receipt of goods. |
| Purchase invoices are logged into the purchase day book in batches, utilising control totals.<br><br>Utilising control totals ensures both completeness and accuracy over the input of purchase invoices. If the invoices are not all input completely and accurately payables may be misstated. | Select a sample of control total sheets and review for evidence of control totals being utilised and the clerk's signature. |
| Supplier statement reconciliations are undertaken on a monthly basis and these are reviewed by the financial controller.<br><br>This ensures that any errors in the recording of purchases and payables are identified and corrected in a timely manner and therefore that payables are complete and accurate. | Review the file of reconciliations to ensure that they are being performed on a regular basis and that they have been reviewed by a responsible official.<br><br>Re-perform a sample of the reconciliations to ensure that they have been carried out appropriately and discrepancies investigated. |
| The finance director authorises the bank transfer payment list for suppliers after agreeing the amounts to be paid to supporting documentation and reviewing for any duplicate payments.<br><br>This reduces the risk that suppliers could be being paid an incorrect amount, or that sums are being paid to fictitious suppliers. | Review the payments list for evidence of review by the finance director.<br><br>Enquire of accounts staff what supporting documentation the finance director requests when undertaking this review. |

ANSWERS

# 115 Amberjack Co

## Marking scheme

|  |  | Marks |
|---|---|---|
| (a) | **Control objectives for sales and dispatch system** | |
| | Orders only accepted if goods are available | 1 |
| | All orders are recorded completely and accurately | 1 |
| | Goods are not supplied to poor credit risks | 1 |
| | Goods are dispatched for all orders | 1 |
| | Quantity and quality of goods dispatched appropriate | 1 |
| | All goods dispatched are invoiced for correctly | 1 |
| | Completeness of income for goods dispatched | 1 |
| | Sales discounts are only given during valid period | 1 |
| | **Restricted to** | 4 |
| (b) | **Control deficiencies and recommendations** (only 7 required) | |
| | Customer credit limits | 2 |
| | Customer master data not reviewed | 2 |
| | Credit controller not replaced | 2 |
| | Goods dispatch notes (GDNs) not sequentially numbered | 2 |
| | Insufficient copies of GDN | 2 |
| | Sales invoice processing | 2 |
| | Manual recording of discounts | 2 |
| | Customer statements no longer raised | 2 |
| | Receivables ledger control account only reconciled annually | 2 |
| | **Max 7 issues, 2 marks each and 2 marks available for covering letter** | 16 |
| **Total marks** | | 20 |

(a) Control objectives for sales and dispatch system

- To ensure that orders are only accepted if goods are available to be processed for customers.
- To ensure that all orders are recorded completely and accurately.
- To ensure that goods are not supplied to poor credit risks.
- To ensure that goods are dispatched for all orders on a timely basis.
- To ensure that the correct quantity of goods are dispatched and they are of an adequate quality.
- To ensure that all goods dispatched are correctly invoiced at authorised prices.
- To ensure completeness of income for goods dispatched.
- To ensure that sales discounts are only provided during the valid period.

(b) Report to management

Board of directors
Amberjack Co
21 Under the Sea
Shorelife City
Shark Country

1 July 20X5

Dear Sirs,

Audit of Amberjack Co for the year ended 30 April 20X5

Please find enclosed the report to management on deficiencies in internal controls identified during the audit for the year ended 30 April 20X5. The appendix to this report considers deficiencies in the sales and dispatch system and recommendations to address those deficiencies.

Please note that this report only addresses the deficiencies identified during the audit and if further testing had been performed, then more deficiencies may have been reported.

This report is solely for the use of management and if you have any further questions, then please do not hesitate to contact us.

Yours faithfully

An audit firm

Appendix

| Control deficiency | Control recommendation |
|---|---|
| Customer credit limits are set by receivables ledger clerks. Receivables ledger clerks are not sufficiently senior and so may set limits too high, leading to irrecoverable debts, or too low, leading to a loss of sales. | Credit limits should be set by a senior member of the receivables ledger department and not by receivables ledger clerks. These limits should be regularly reviewed by a responsible official. |
| Receivables ledger clerks record new customer details and credit limits in the customer master data file and these changes are not reviewed. There is a risk that customers could be set up incorrectly resulting in a loss of customer goodwill and sales revenue. In addition, the receivables ledger clerks are not senior enough to be given access to making changes to master file data as this could increase the risk of fraud. | Receivables ledger clerks should not be able to access the master data file to add new customer or make amendments. Any such additions/amendments to master file data should be restricted so that only supervisors and above can make changes. An exception report of changes made should be generated and reviewed by a responsible official |

| Control deficiency | Control recommendation |
|---|---|
| Amberjack Co's credit controller is currently on secondment for six months to the internal audit department and has not been replaced. During this period, it does not appear that anyone else has been responsible for monitoring ageing receivables.<br><br>This could result in an increased risk of irrecoverable debts and lead to customers not paying their outstanding balances on time, or at all, leading to reduced cash flows. | During the period of the secondment, an alternative member of the finance department should be trained in the credit control role and assigned responsibility for reviewing the aged receivables listing and following up on any overdue customers. |
| Goods dispatch notes (GDN) are given the same number as the order number to which they relate. The sales invoices are only raised on receipt of a GDN, and without separate sequential numbers, it is difficult for Amberjack Co to identify if any GDNs are missing as they are not likely to be raised in the same sequence as the sales orders.<br><br>If GDNs are missing and the company fails to raise invoices in a timely manner, this could lead to a loss of revenue. | GDNs should all be sequentially numbered using a sequence which is different to the order number. On a regular basis, a sequence check of GDNs should be undertaken to identify any missing dispatch notes. |
| Once orders are processed, copies of GDNs are sent to the finance department, customer and remain in the warehouse. However, the sales order department of Amberjack Co does not receive a copy of the GDN.<br><br>If the sales order department does not receive a copy of the completed GDNs, they are not able to monitor if orders are being fulfilled on a timely basis. This could result in a loss of revenue and customer goodwill. | The GDN should be amended to be at least four-part. One copy should be sent to the sales order department.<br><br>Once the copy of the GDN has been received by the order department, it should be matched to the order. A regular review of unmatched orders should be undertaken by the sales order department to identify any unfulfilled orders. |
| Additional staff has been drafted in to help the sales clerks produce the sales invoices. As the extra staff will not be as experienced as the sales clerks, there is an increased risk of mistakes being made in the sales invoices. This could result in customers being under or overcharged leading to misstated revenue or dissatisfied customers. | Only the sales clerks should be able to raise sales invoices. As Amberjack Co is expanding, consideration should be given to recruiting and training more permanent sales clerks who can produce sales invoices.<br><br>If this is not currently possible, temporary staff should be adequately trained and additional input checks on invoices should be introduced. |
| Discounts given to customers who purchased goods during the 10% off weekend are manually entered onto the sales invoices by sales clerks.<br><br>This could result in unauthorised sales discounts being given as there does not seem to be any authorisation required. In addition, a clerk could forget to manually enter the discount or enter an incorrect level of discount for a customer, leading to the sales invoice being overstated and a loss of | During the period of any special offers, such as the 10% off weekend, the authorised sales prices file should be updated by a responsible official. These changes should be reviewed for any input errors, this review should be evidenced. The invoicing system should confirm that orders were placed during the discount weekend. Hence the sales invoices for these periods should automatically contain the reduced prices.<br><br>The invoicing system should be amended to |

| Control deficiency | Control recommendation |
|---|---|
| customer goodwill. Unauthorised discounts in excess of 10% would result in a loss of revenue, either due to error or fraud. | prevent sales clerks from being able to manually enter sales discounts onto invoices. |
| Customer statements are no longer being generated and sent to customers. If statements are not sent regularly, this increases the likelihood of errors and any disputed invoices not being quickly identified and resolved by Amberjack Co. This could lead to cash flow issues. | Amberjack Co should produce monthly customer statements for all customers and send them out promptly. |
| The receivables ledger control account is only reconciled at the end of April in order to verify the year-end balance. If the receivables ledger is only reconciled annually, there is a risk that errors will not be spotted promptly and receivables may be misstated. | The receivables ledger control account should be reconciled on a monthly basis to identify any errors which should be investigated and corrected. The reconciliations should be reviewed by a responsible official and they should evidence their review by way of signature. |

# 116 Comet Publishing Co

**Workbook references.** Chapters 4, 9, 10 and 16.

**Top tips.** Part (a) was a straightforward and should have been within your reach. Part (b) was the core of the question. It was important that you attempted five deficiencies as required, and that you filled in each column (for parts (i), (ii) and (iii)) for each of them.

Part (c), on substantive procedures in relation to purchases and other expenses, was not difficult. When answering requirements like this one it is important that you are as specific as possible, stating what the procedure would be, the documents it might involve, and most importantly why you would be performing it (verb-document-reason). You could try to get into the habit of writing your answer as a sentence with two parts – the first part says what the procedure is, and the second part says 'in order to' and then explains the purpose of the procedure.

The key to a good answer to part (d) is to think about safeguards that are practical and specific to this scenario.

**Easy marks.** Part (b)(ii) should have represented easy marks provided that you were able to think of different examples of internal controls, make sure you use your everyday experience of life to generate ideas.

**Examining team's comments.** This area of the syllabus requires both an ability to describe and evaluate internal controls techniques and audit tests, and, also an ability to make appropriate recommendations.

BPP LEARNING MEDIA

Internal controls questions remain a highly examinable area and performance in this sitting was mixed. Most candidates were able to provide good recommendations to address the deficiencies they identified. However some of the recommendations were either poorly described, did not clearly address the specific control weakness identified or were impractical suggestions.

Additionally, this session a significant minority of candidates identified issues from the scenario which were not actually deficiencies. For example some stated that 'the warehouse team process receipt of goods from suppliers' and that this was a deficiency as it resulted in a lack of segregation of duties. This is not a deficiency.

Disappointingly, the requirements for tests of controls that the auditor should perform were often not well explained by candidates (e.g. repeated use of the word "check"), did not address the controls identified, were vague in the repeated use of 'observe' or quite commonly were substantive audit procedures rather than tests of control.

Tests of controls are a key requirement in internal control questions and future candidates must ensure they practice these types of questions in advance of their exam.

## Marking scheme

| | | Marks |
|---|---|---|
| (a) | **Steps to confirm prior year flowcharts and system notes** | |
| | Review PY notes and confirm all stages covered | 1 |
| | Review PY file for weaknesses not actioned | 1 |
| | Review PY report to management | 1 |
| | Review client system documentation for changes | 1 |
| | Interview client staff to confirm client processes | 1 |
| | Walk-through tests to confirm notes | 1 |
| | Walk-through tests to confirm procedures | 1 |
| | Restricted to | 5 |
| (b) | **Control deficiencies, recommendations and tests of control (only 5 issues required)** | |
| | No inter-branch transfers | 3 |
| | Not all purchase orders are authorised | 3 |
| | GRNs not processed regularly | 3 |
| | GRNs not sent to purchasing department | 3 |
| | Segregation of duties in relation to purchases | 3 |
| | Authorisation of bank payments | 3 |
| | Supplier statement reconciliations not performed | 3 |
| | Max 5 issues, 3 marks each | 15 |
| (c) | **Substantive tests for purchases and other expenses** | |
| | Calculate operating and gross margin and compare to PY | 1 |
| | Review monthly purchases and investigate unexpected difference | 1 |
| | Discuss changes in key suppliers and compare to PL | 1 |
| | Recalculate a sample of invoices | 1 |
| | Recalculate prepayments and accruals | |

|  | Marks |
|---|---|
| Review post year-end invoices for pre year-end liabilities | 1 |
| Sample of cash book payments to appropriate expense account | 1 |
| GRNs to purchase invoice to purchase day book | 1 |
| Cut-off testing using GRNs | 1 |
| Restricted to | 5 |

(d) Safeguards to deal with conflict of interest

|  | Marks |
|---|---|
| Notify both parties and obtain consent | 1 |
| Advise clients to seek independent advice | 1 |
| Separate engagement teams | 1 |
| Prevent access to information | 1 |
| Clear guidelines on security and confidentiality provided to client | 1 |
| Confidentiality agreements | 1 |
| Monitor safeguards | 1 |
| Restricted to | 5 |
| Total marks | 30 |

(a) **Steps to confirm prior year flowcharts and system notes**

- Obtain the system notes from last year's audit and ensure that the documentation on the purchases and payables system covers all expected stages and is complete.

- Review the audit file for indications of weaknesses in the system and note these for investigation this year.

- Review the prior year report to management to identify any recommendations which were made over controls in this area as this may highlight potential changes which have been made in the current year.

- Obtain system documentation from the client, potentially in the form of a procedure manual. Review this to identify any changes made in the last 12 months.

- Interview client staff to ascertain whether systems and controls have changed including the stores and warehouse to ensure that the flowcharts and notes produced last year is correct.

- Perform walk-through tests by tracing a sample of transactions through the purchases and payables system to ensure that the flowcharts and systems notes contained on the audit file are accurate.

- During the walk-through tests, confirm the systems notes and flowcharts accurately reflect the control procedures which are in place and can be used to identify controls for testing.

(b)    Control deficiencies, control recommendations and tests of control

| Control deficiency | Control recommendation | Test of control |
|---|---|---|
| It is not possible for a store to order goods from other local stores for customers who request them. Instead, customers are told to contact the other stores or use the company website. Customers are less likely to contact individual stores themselves and this could result in the company losing valuable sales.<br><br>In addition, some goods which are slow moving in one store may be out of stock at another; if goods could be transferred between stores, then overall sales may be maximised. | An inter-branch transfer system should be established between stores, with inter-branch inventory forms being completed for store transfers.<br><br>This should help stores whose inventory levels are low but are awaiting their deliveries from the suppliers. | During the interim audit, arrange to visit a number of the stores, discuss with the store manager the process for ordering of inventory items, in particular whether it is possible to order from other branches.<br><br>At each store, inspect a sample of completed inter-branch inventory forms for confirmation the control is operating. |
| Purchase orders below $1,000 are not authorised and are processed solely by the purchase order clerk who is also responsible for processing invoices.<br><br>This could result in non-business related purchases and there is an increased fraud risk as the clerk could place orders for personal goods up to the value of $1,000, which is significant. | All purchase orders should be authorised by a responsible official.<br><br>Authorised signatories should be established with varying levels of purchase order authorisation. | Select a sample of purchase orders and review for evidence of authorisation, agree this to the appropriate signature on the approved signatories list. |
| Goods received notes (GRNs) are sent to the accounts department every two weeks.<br><br>This could result in delays in suppliers being paid as the purchase invoices could not be agreed to a GRN and also recorded liabilities being understated. Additionally, any prompt payment discounts offered by suppliers may be missed due to delayed payments. | A copy of the GRNs should be sent to the accounts department on a more regular basis, such as daily.<br><br>The accounts department should undertake a sequence check of the GRNs to ensure none are missing for processing. | Enquire of the accounts clerk as to the frequency of when GRNs are received to assess if they are being sent promptly.<br><br>Undertake a sequence check of GRNs held by the accounts department, discuss any missing items with the accounts clerk. |

| Control deficiency | Control recommendation | Test of control |
|---|---|---|
| GRNs are only sent to the accounts department. Failing to send a copy to the ordering department could result in a significant level of unfulfilled orders leading to a loss of sales and stock-outs. | The GRN should be created in three parts and a copy of the GRN should be sent to the purchase order clerk, Oliver Dancer, who should agree this to the order and change the order status to complete. On a regular basis he should then review for all unfulfilled orders and chase these with the relevant supplier | Review the file of copy GRNs held by the purchase ordering clerk, Oliver Dancer, and review for evidence that these are matched to orders and flagged as complete. Review the file of unfulfilled purchase orders for any overdue items and discuss their status with Oliver Dancer. |
| The purchase ordering clerk, Oliver Dancer, has responsibility for ordering goods below $1,000 and for processing all purchase invoices for payment. There is a lack of segregation of duties and this increases the risk of fraud and non-business related purchases being made. | The roles of purchase ordering and processing of the related supplier invoices should be allocated to separate members of staff. | Observe which member of staff undertakes the processing of purchase invoices and confirm this is not the purchase ordering clerk, Oliver Dancer. Inspect a copy of the company's organisation chart to identify if these tasks have now been allocated to different roles. |
| The finance director authorises the bank transfer payment list for suppliers; however, she only views the total amount of payments to be made. Without looking at the detail of the payments list, as well as supporting documentation, there is a risk that suppliers could be being paid an incorrect amount, or that sums are being paid to fictitious suppliers. | The finance director should review the whole payments list prior to authorising. As part of this, she should agree the amounts to be paid to supporting documentation, as well as reviewing the supplier names to identify any duplicates or any unfamiliar names. She should evidence her review by signing the bank transfer list. | Review the payments list for evidence of review by the finance director. Enquire of accounts staff what supporting documentation the finance director requests when undertaking this review. |
| Supplier statement reconciliations are no longer performed. This may result in errors in the recording of purchases and payables not being identified in a timely manner. | Supplier statement reconciliations should be performed on a monthly basis for all suppliers and these should be reviewed by a responsible official. | Review the file of reconciliations to ensure that they are being performed on a regular basis and that they have been reviewed by a responsible official. Re-perform a sample of the reconciliations to ensure that they have been carried out appropriately. |

(c) **Substantive procedures for purchases and other expenses**

- Calculate the operating profit and gross profit margins and compare them to last year and budget and investigate any significant differences.

- Review monthly purchases and other expenses to identify any significant fluctuations and discuss with management.

- Discuss with management whether there have been any changes in the key suppliers used and compare this to the purchase ledger to assess completeness and accuracy of purchases.

- Recalculate the accuracy of a sample of purchase invoice totals and related taxes and ensure expense has been included in the correct nominal code.

- Recalculate the prepayments and accruals charged at the year end to ensure the accuracy of the expense charge included in the statement of profit or loss.

- Select a sample of post year-end expense invoices and ensure that any expenses relating to the current year have been included.

- Select a sample of payments from the cash book and trace to expense account to ensure the expense has been included and classified correctly.

- Select a sample of goods received notes (GRNs) from throughout the year; agree them to purchase invoices and the purchase day book to ensure the completeness of purchases.

- Select a sample of GRNs just before and after the year end; agree to the purchase day book to ensure the expense is recorded in the correct accounting period.

(d) **Safeguards to deal with conflict of interest**

- Both Comet Publishing Co and its rival competitor, Edmond Co, should be notified that Halley & Co would be acting as auditors for each company and, if necessary, consent should be obtained from each.

- Advising one or both clients to seek additional independent advice.

- The use of separate engagement teams, with different engagement partners and team members; once an employee has worked on one audit, such as Comet Publishing Co, then they would be prevented from being on the audit of the competitor for a period of time.

- Procedures to prevent access to information, for example, strict physical separation of both teams, confidential and secure data filing.

- Clear guidelines for members of each engagement team on issues of security and confidentiality. These guidelines could be included within the audit engagement letters.

- Potentially the use of confidentiality agreements signed by employees and partners of the firm.

- Regular monitoring of the application of the above safeguards by a senior individual in Halley & Co not involved in either audit.

# 117 Raspberry Co

**Workbook references.** Chapters 5, 10 and 16.

**Top tips.** In part (a), it was important that you stuck to the number of controls required (five). The ten available marks divide themselves into five for part (i) and five for part (ii). Notice that (a)(i) asks you to identify and explain the controls – there is half a mark available for each of these things (ie half for identifying and half for explaining). Your answer must therefore contain the right level of detail to get both of them and so you should extract the information from the scenario to identify the control and then explain the benefit of the control to Raspberry Co.

As with (a), so with (b) – the requirement is to 'identify and explain' each deficiency, which suggests that your answer could be structured as two sentences / paragraphs within the left column, the first of which says what is happening (identifying the problem), and the second of which says why this is a problem (or why it is wrong). You must also make a practical recommendation to address the deficiency, this should be clearly explained with sufficient detail to know what specific action to take to solve the problem.

Part (c) was fairly knowledge-based, and was a matter of recalling the possible assignments for internal audit, and then thinking about how they might apply to Raspberry Co.

Part (d) required you to suggest substantive procedures. It was therefore critical that you did not suggest tests of control here, which would not garner any marks.

**Easy marks.** Part (c) was knowledge-based and should have been within your reach.

**Examination team comments.** This 30-mark question was based on Raspberry Co, a company which operates an electric power station. This question tested candidates' knowledge of direct controls and control deficiencies, recommendations and tests of control, internal audit departments, and, substantive procedures for accruals.

**Part (a)** for 10 marks required candidates to identify and explain from the scenario five direct controls in respect of the payroll system described which the auditor may seek to place reliance on, and, describe a test of control the auditor should perform to assess if each of the direct controls is operating effectively. Candidates' performance on this requirement was disappointing.

In common with previous exams, candidates continue to find tests of control challenging. Many candidates confused substantive procedures for tests of control and tests were often vague or incomplete.

**Part (b)** for 10 marks, required candidates to identify and explain from the scenario five deficiencies in respect of the payroll system and provide a recommendation to address each of these deficiencies. Many candidates performed well in this requirement.
The scenario in the exam contained more issues than were required to be discussed and it was pleasing that many candidates identified the required number of issues noted in the question.

Many candidates were able to provide good recommendations to address the deficiencies identified. However, some of the recommendations were not described in enough detail.

Internal controls questions remain a highly examinable area and future candidates need to ensure that they have undertaken adequate question practice.

**Part (c)** for five marks required candidates to describe assignments the internal audit department of Raspberry Co would carry out. Up to 1 mark was awarded for each well described point. Performance was mixed.

Common misunderstandings by a number of candidates were 'the internal auditor prepares the financial statements' and 'internal auditors implement the controls'.

Some candidates described the differences between internal and external audit, which was not the purpose of the requirement.

In addition some candidates described assignments, which would not be relevant to an electric power station client, for example 'internal auditors undertaking mystery shopping'. This is principally a knowledge area, which has been tested in previous exams.

**Part (d)** for five marks required candidates to describe substantive procedures the auditor should perform to confirm the year-end accrual for tax payable on employment income.

The substantive procedures were often vague, for example 'agree payment' rather than 'agree to the post year-end cashbook'. Candidates are once again reminded that a well described substantive procedure will clearly detail the source of the evidence.

In addition, many candidates did not focus on the year-end accrual and noted general substantive procedures for tax, which did not gain credit.

Candidates are reminded to read the question requirement carefully and to ensure that they are not only answering the question set but also fully describing each substantive procedure.

## Marking scheme

| | | Marks |
|---|---|---|
| **(a)** | **Direct controls and tests of control (only 5 controls required)** | |
| | Separate HR department set up employees | 2 |
| | Pre-printed joiners forms | 2 |
| | Data processing checks on bonus information | 2 |
| | Use of clock cards and process supervised | 2 |
| | Direct transfer between clock card and payroll systems | 2 |
| | Exception reports for changes to payroll data | 2 |
| | Security process over cash | 2 |
| | SOD over pay packets | 2 |
| | **Restricted to** | **10** |
| **(b)** | **Control deficiencies, and control recommendations (only 5 issues required)** | |
| | Production bonus set by supervisor | 2 |
| | No independent checks on wage calculations | 2 |
| | No monitoring of student loan payments | 2 |
| | Holiday requests not always authorised | 2 |
| | Lack of SOD in payroll department | 2 |
| | Pay packets not delivered by independent staff/no evidence of distribution | 2 |
| | Monthly management accounts not analysed | 2 |
| | **Max 5 issues, 2 marks each** | **10** |
| **(c)** | **Internal audit assignments** | |
| | Value for money | 1 |
| | Financial/operational review | 1 |
| | Monitoring assets | 1 |
| | Regulatory compliance | 1 |
| | IT systems | 1 |
| | Cash controls | 1 |
| | Fraud investigation | 1 |
| | **Restricted to** | **5** |

(d) **Substantive procedures – tax payable accrual**

| | |
|---|---|
| Compare to prior year and investigate differences | |
| Agree to TB and payroll records | 1 |
| Reperform accrual calculation and discuss with management | 1 |
| Agree subsequent payment to cash book and bank statement | 1 |
| Review correspondence with tax authorities | 1 |
| Review disclosures | 1 |
| **Restricted to** | 5 |
| **Total marks** | 30 |

(a) **Direct controls and tests of control**

| Direct control | Test of control |
|---|---|
| Raspberry Co has a separate human resources (HR) department which is responsible for setting up all new employees. | Review the job descriptions of payroll and HR to confirm the split of responsibilities with regards to setting up new joiners. |
| Having a segregation of roles between human resources and payroll departments reduces the risk of fictitious employees being set up and also being paid. | Discuss with members of the payroll department the process for setting up new joiners and for confirmation that the process is initiated by HR. |
| Pre-printed forms are completed by HR for all new employees, and includes assignment of a unique employee number, and once verified, a copy is sent to the payroll department. Payroll is unable to set up new joiners without information from these forms. | Select a sample of new employees added to the payroll during the year, review the joiner forms for evidence of completion of all parts and that the information was verified as accurate and was received by payroll prior to being added to the system. |
| The use of pre-printed forms ensures that all relevant information, such as tax IDs, is obtained about employees prior to set up. This minimises the risk of incorrect wage and tax payments. In addition, as payroll is unable to set up new joiners without the forms and employee number, it reduces the risk of fictitious employees being set up by payroll. | Select a sample of edit reports for changes to payroll during the year; agree a sample of new employees added to payroll to the joiners forms. |
| The quarterly production bonus is input by a clerk into the payroll system, each entry is checked by a senior clerk for input errors prior to processing, and they evidence their review via signature. | If attending Raspberry Co at the time of bonus processing, observe the clerk inputting and senior clerk checking the bonus payments into the payroll system. |
| This reduces the risk of input errors resulting in over/underpayment of the bonus to employees. | In addition, obtain listings of quarterly bonus payments and review for evidence of signature by the senior clerk who checks for input errors. |
| Production employees are issued with clock cards and are required to swipe their cards at the beginning and end of their shift, this process is supervised by security staff 24 hours a day. | Observe the use of clock cards by employees when entering the power station. |
| This ensures that genuine employees are only paid for the work actually done, | Confirm the security team is supervising the process and following up on discrepancies through discussions with the security staff. |

| Direct control | Test of control |
|---|---|
| and reduces the risk of employees being paid but not completing their eight-hour shift. In addition, due to the supervision it is unlikely that one employee could swipe in others. | |
| The clock card information identifies the employee number and links into the hours worked report produced by the payroll system.<br><br>As the hours worked are automatically transferred into the payroll system, this reduces the risk of input errors in entering hours to be paid in calculating payroll, ensuring that employees are paid the correct amount.<br><br>On a quarterly basis, exception reports of changes to payroll standing data are produced and reviewed by the payroll director.<br><br>This ensures that any unauthorised amendments to standing data are identified and resolved on a timely basis.<br><br>For production employees paid in cash, cash is received weekly from the bank by a security company.<br><br>It is likely the sum of money required to pay over 175 employees would be considerable. It is important that cash is adequately safeguarded to reduce the risk of misappropriation. | Utilise test data procedures to input dummy clock card information, verify this has been updated into the payroll system.<br><br>Select a sample of quarterly exception reports and review for evidence of review and follow up of any unexpected changes by the payroll director.<br><br>Enquire of payroll clerks how cash is delivered to Raspberry Co for weekly pay packets.<br><br>Review a sample of invoices from the security company to Raspberry Co for delivery of cash. |
| The pay packets are prepared by two members of staff with one preparing and one checking the pay packets and this is evidenced by each staff member signing the weekly listing.<br><br>This ensures there is segregation of duties which prevents fraud and errors not being identified. | Observe the preparation of the pay packets ensuring that two members of staff are involved and that pay packets are checked for accuracy.<br><br>For a sample of weeks throughout the year, inspect the weekly payroll listing for evidence of signature by the two members of staff involved in the preparation of the pay packets. |

(b) Deficiencies and recommendations

| Control deficiency | Control recommendation |
|---|---|
| Production supervisors determine the amount of the discretionary bonus to be paid to employees.<br><br>Production supervisors should not determine this as they could pay extra bonuses to friends or family members, resulting in additional payroll costs. | The bonus should be determined by a responsible official, such as the production director and should be formulated based on a written policy. If significant in value, the bonus should be formally agreed by the board of directors. |
| The wages calculations are generated by the payroll system and there are no checks performed.<br><br>Therefore, if system errors occur during the payroll processing, this would not be identified. This could result in wages being over or under calculated, leading to an additional payroll cost or loss of employee goodwill. | The bonus should be communicated in writing to the payroll department.<br><br>A senior member of the payroll team should recalculate the gross to net pay workings for a sample of employees and compare their results to the output from the payroll system. These calculations should be signed as approved before payments are made. |
| Student loan deduction forms are completed by relevant employees and payments are made directly to the third party until the employee notifies HR that the loan has been repaid in full.<br><br>As the payments continue until the employee notifies HR, and employees are unlikely to be closely monitoring payments, there is the risk that overpayments may be made, which then need to be reclaimed, leading to employee dissatisfaction.<br><br>In the case of underpayments, Raspberry Co has an obligation to remit funds on time and to reconcile to annual loan statements. If the company does not make payments in full and on time, this could result in non-compliance by both the company and employee, which could result in fines or penalties. | The payroll department should maintain a schedule, by employee, of payments made to third parties, such as the central government as well as the cumulative balance owing. On a regular basis, at least annually, this statement should be reconciled to the loan statement received from the government and sent to the employee for agreement.<br><br>In accordance with the schedule, payments which are due to cease shortly should be confirmed in writing with the third party, prior to stopping. |
| Holiday request forms are required to be completed and authorised by relevant line managers, however, this does not always occur.<br><br>This could result in employees taking unauthorised leave, resulting in production difficulties if an insufficient number of employees are present to operate the power plant. In addition, employees taking unauthorised leave could result in an overpayment of wages. | Employees should be informed that they will not be able to take holiday without completion of a holiday request form, with authorisation from the line manager.<br><br>Payroll clerks should not process holiday payments without agreement to the authorised holiday form. |
| The senior payroll manager reviews the bank transfer listing prior to authorising the payments and also amends the payroll records for any changes required. | The senior payroll manager should not be able to process changes to the payroll system as well as authorise payments. |

| Control deficiency | Control recommendation |
|---|---|
| There is a lack of segregation of duties as it is the payroll team which processes the amounts and the senior payroll manager who authorises payments. The senior manager could fraudulently increase the amounts to be paid to certain employees, process this payment as well as amend the records. | The authorisation of the bank transfer listing should be undertaken by an individual outside the payroll department, such as the finance director. |
| The pay packets are delivered to the production supervisors, who distribute them to employees at the end of their shift.<br><br>The supervisor is not sufficiently independent to pay wages out. They could adjust pay packets to increase those of close friends whilst reducing others.<br><br>In addition, although the production supervisors know their team members, payment of wages without proof of identity increases the risk that wages could be paid to incorrect employees.<br><br>Monthly management accounts do not analyse the variances between actual and budgeted wages and salaries; this is because there are no overtime costs.<br><br>However, wages and salaries are a significant expense and management needs to understand why variances may have arisen. These could occur due to extra employees being recruited which were not budgeted for, or an increase in wage pay out rates. The board would need to monitor the wages and salaries costs as if they are too high, then this would impact the profitability of the company. | All pay packets should be distributed by the payroll department, directly to employees, upon sight of the employee's clock card and photographic identification as this confirms proof of identity.<br><br>Payroll should undertake a reconciliation of pay packets issued to production supervisors, wages distributed with employee signatures to confirm receipt and pay packets returned to payroll due to staff absences. Any differences should be investigated immediately.<br><br>As employees work eight-hour shifts over 24 hours,<br><br>consideration should be given to operating a shift system for the payroll department on wages pay out day. This will ensure that there are sufficient payroll employees to perform the wages pay out for each shift of employees, with the same level of controls in place.<br><br>The monthly management accounts should be amended to include an analysis of wages and salaries compared to the budgeted costs. These should be broken down to each relevant department and could also include an analysis of headcount numbers compared to budget. |

(c) **Assignments for internal audit department (IAD)**

Value for money review – The IAD could be asked to assess whether Raspberry Co is obtaining value for money in areas such as capital expenditure.

Review of financial/operational controls – The IAD could undertake reviews of controls at head office and the power station and make recommendations to management over such areas as the purchasing process as well as the payroll cycle.

Monitoring asset levels – The IAD could undertake physical verification of property, plant and equipment (PPE) at the production site and head office and compare the assets seen to the PPE register. There is likely to be a significant level of PPE and the asset register must be kept up to date to ensure continuous production. If significant negative differences occur, this may be due to theft or fraud.

Regulatory compliance – Raspberry Co produces electricity and operates a power station, hence it will be subject to a large number of laws and regulations such as health and safety and environmental legislation. The IAD could help to monitor compliance with these regulations.

IT system reviews – Raspberry Co is likely to have a relatively complex computer system linking production data to head office. The IAD could be asked to perform a review over the computer environment and controls.

Cash controls – Raspberry Co's internal auditors could undertake controls testing over cash payments. 70% of employees are paid in cash rather than bank transfer, therefore on a weekly basis cash held is likely to be significant, therefore the cash controls in payroll should be tested to reduce the level of errors.

Fraud investigations – The IAD can be asked to investigate any specific cases of suspected fraud as well as review the controls in place to prevent/detect fraud.

(d)  **Accrual for income tax payable on employment income**

Procedures the auditor should adopt in respect of auditing this accrual include:

- Compare the accrual for income tax payable to the prior year, investigate any significant differences.

- Agree the year-end income tax payable accrual to the general ledger and payroll records to confirm accuracy.

- Re-perform the calculation of the accrual to confirm accuracy and discuss any unexpected variances with management.

- Agree the subsequent payment to the post year-end cash book and bank statements to confirm completeness.

- Review any correspondence with tax authorities to assess whether there are any additional outstanding payments due; if so, agree they are included in the year-end accrual.

- Review any disclosures made of the income tax accrual and assess whether these are in compliance with accounting standards and legislation.

# 118 Camomile Co

**Workbook references.** Chapters 9 and 10.

**Top tips.** Part (a) here was knowledge-based. This is an area that candidates sometimes find difficult, but it need not be. The model answer refers to the relevant ISA but this is not strictly necessary for your answer. It is best to have knowledge of the standard, but you can go quite a long way here by using your common sense – just think about the relationship between the auditor and management, and why it would be necessary to communicate. This then feeds into part (ii), where you need to give two examples. There is a full mark for each example, provided it makes sense and is described in enough detail.

In part (b), it was important that you stuck to the number of deficiencies required (eight). The sixteen available marks divide themselves into eight for the deficiencies and eight for the recommendations. Note that you are asked to identify and explain the deficiencies, so there is effectively half a mark available for each of these things (ie half for identifying and half for explaining).

You must also then make a practical recommendation to address the deficiency (in the right hand column). This should be clearly explained with enough detail to know what specific action to take to solve the problem.

**Easy marks.** Part (a) was knowledge-based and should have been within your reach.

**Examination team comments.** This area of the syllabus requires both an ability to describe and evaluate internal controls techniques and audit tests, and, also an ability to make appropriate recommendations.

Internal controls questions remain a highly examinable area and performance in December 2018 was mixed. The scenarios included in exam questions contain more issues than are required to be discussed. It was pleasing in this session that candidates were generally able to identify (for ½ mark each) the required number of issues from the scenarios. It was however disappointing that some candidates were not able to identify direct controls, often identifying the existence of a control where in fact there was a deficiency. As an example, if the scenario states, 'supplier statement reconciliations are carried out however reconciling items are not investigated' the fact that the company is reconciling supplier statements is not an effective control and would not be awarded a ½ mark for identification. In this instance the correct conclusion to draw would be that the lack of investigation of reconciling items resulted in a control deficiency.

In common with previous sittings many candidates did not clearly explain the implication of deficiencies identified. It is important that the explanation fully details the impact to the company. As an example, for a deficiency of 'purchase orders are not sequentially numbered' a suitable, well explained implication would be 'unfulfilled orders cannot be effectively monitored which could result in stock-outs leading to a loss of customer goodwill'. Many candidates did not go on to explain the impact on the company.

Most candidates were able to provide good recommendations to address the deficiencies they identified. However some of the recommendations were either poorly described, did not clearly address the specific control deficiencies identified or were impractical suggestions. For example, recommending 'production stops during an inventory count' to address the control of movements during a count is inappropriate if the scenario clearly states the company operates 24-hour production. Additionally as with ethics and corporate governance questions, recommendations must be actions rather than just objectives.

Disappointingly, the requirements for tests of controls that the auditor should perform were often not well explained by candidates (eg repeated use of the word 'check'), did not address the controls identified, were vague in the repeated use of 'observe' or quite commonly were substantive audit procedures rather than tests of control.

Tests of controls are a key requirement in internal control questions and future candidates must ensure they practice these types of questions in advance of their exam.

## Marking scheme

| | | | Marks |
|---|---|---|---|
| (a) | (i) | **Importance of communicating with TCWG** | |
| | | Assists understanding of matters related to the audit | 1 |
| | | Obtains information relevant to the audit | 1 |
| | | Assists TCWG discharge their responsibilities | 1 |
| | | Promotes effective two-way communication | 1 |
| | | **Restricted to** | 2 |
| | (ii) | Matters to communicate to TCWG | |
| | | 1 mark for any relevant and well described example | 2 |
| (b) | | **Control deficiencies and recommendations (only 8 issues required)** | |
| | | Petty cash differences | 2 |
| | | Access to tills | 2 |
| | | Tills reconciled in total | 2 |
| | | Lack of SOD – reconciling cash | 2 |
| | | Risk of incomplete daily sales sheets | 2 |

| | Marks |
|---|---|
| Security of cash – access to safes | 2 |
| Lack of SOD – cashier | 2 |
| Credit card statements are not reconciled | 2 |
| Frequency of bank reconciliations | 2 |
| Payment list not adequately reviewed | 2 |
| Max 8 issues, 2 marks each | 16 |
| **Total marks** | **20** |

(a)    (i)    Importance of communicating with those charged with governance

In accordance with ISA 260 *Communication with Those Charged with Governance*, it is important for the auditors to report to those charged with governance as it helps in the following ways:

- It assists the auditor and those charged with governance in understanding matters related to the audit, and in developing a constructive working relationship. This relationship is developed while maintaining the auditor's independence and objectivity.

- It helps the auditor in obtaining, from those charged with governance, information relevant to the audit. For example, those charged with governance may assist the auditor in understanding the entity and its environment, in identifying appropriate sources of audit evidence and in providing information about specific transactions or events.

- It helps those charged with governance in fulfilling their responsibility to oversee the financial reporting process, thereby reducing the risks of material misstatement of the financial statements.

- It promotes effective two-way communication between the auditor and those charged with governance.

(ii)    Matters to be communicated to those charged with governance

- The auditor's responsibilities with regards to providing an opinion on the financial statements and that they have carried out their work in accordance with International Standards on Auditing.

- The auditor should explain the planned approach to the audit as well as the audit timetable.

- Any key audit risks identified during the planning stage should be communicated.

- In addition, any significant difficulties encountered during the audit should be communicated.

- Also significant matters arising during the audit, as well as significant accounting adjustments.

- During the audit, any significant deficiencies in the internal control system identified should be communicated in writing or verbally.

- How the external auditor and internal auditor may work together and any planned use of the work of the internal audit function.

- Those charged with governance should be notified of any written representations required by the auditor.

- Other matters arising from the audit which are significant to the oversight of the financial reporting process.

- If any suspected frauds are identified during the audit, these must be communicated.

- If the auditors are intending to make any modifications to the audit opinion, these should be communicated to those charged with governance.

- For listed entities, a confirmation that the auditors have complied with ethical standards and appropriate safeguards   have been put in place for any ethical threats identified.

(b) **Control deficiencies and recommendations**

| Control deficiency | Control recommendation |
|---|---|
| Each restaurant maintains a petty cash float of $400, and at any point in time the receipts and funds present should equal the float. It has been noted by the internal audit (IA) department that on occasions there are differences due to the fact that no log is maintained of petty cash requests. <br><br> This could be as a result of sundry items being purchased without the relevant receipt or voucher being returned. There is also a possibility that the cash is being misappropriated by staff members, or being spent on non-business related items. | A petty cash log should be maintained so the purchase of sundry items is recorded in the log along with the sum borrowed, date and employee. <br><br> On purchase of the items, the relevant employee should return the relevant receipt or voucher and any funds not spent. The log should be updated to confirm return of funds and receipts. <br><br> On a weekly basis, the restaurant manager should reconcile the petty cash and if any receipts are missing, these should be followed up with the relevant employee. If it is cash which is missing, then this should be investigated further with the employees who made petty cash purchases during that period. |
| To speed up the cash payment by customers, for each venue the tills have the same log on code and these codes are changed fortnightly. <br><br> In the event of cash discrepancies arising in the tills, it would be difficult to ascertain which employees may be responsible as there is no way of tracking who used which till. This could lead to cash being easily misappropriated. | Each employee should be provided with a unique log on code and this is required to be entered when using the tills. <br><br> In order to facilitate the investigation of till differences, employees should be allocated to a specific till point for their shift. <br><br> Any discrepancies which arise should initially be double checked to ensure they are not arithmetical errors. If still present, the relevant employees who had access to the till can be identified and further investigations can be undertaken. |
| The reconciliations of the tills to the daily sales readings are performed in total for all five tills at each venue rather than for each till. This means that when exceptions arise, it will be difficult to identify which till caused the difference and therefore which employees may require further till training or may have undertaken fraudulent transactions. | The reconciliations should be undertaken on an individual till by till basis rather than in aggregate and any discrepancies noted should be investigated immediately. |

| Control deficiency | Control recommendation |
|---|---|
| The cashing up of tills along with the recording of any cash discrepancies is undertaken by just one individual, the restaurant manager. There is a fraud risk as the manager could remove some of the cash and then simply record that there was an exception on the daily sales list.<br><br>In addition, as there is no segregation of duties, the restaurant manager could, fraudulently or by error, record the total sales as per each till incorrectly leading to incorrect identification of discrepancies. | The cashing up process should be undertaken by two individuals together, ideally an assistant manager and the restaurant manager. One should count the cash and the other record it.<br><br>Any exceptions to the till reading should be double checked to confirm that they are not simply arithmetical errors. If still present, the relevant employees who had access to the till can be identified and further investigations can be undertaken. |
| Daily sales sheets are scanned and emailed to head office on a weekly basis.<br><br>There is a possibility that some sales sheets could be misplaced by the restaurant manager resulting in incomplete sales and cash receipts data being recorded into the accounting system | Daily sales sheets for each venue should be sequentially numbered and remitted to head office on a daily basis. At head office, a sequence check should be undertaken on a regular basis to identify any missing sheets and any gaps should be investigated further.<br><br>Once received, the cashier should post the sales and cash data for all six venues on a daily basis. Once processed, they should then be signed as posted by the cashier and filed away securely. |
| Cash is stored in a safe at each venue and the restaurant manager stores the safe key in a drawer of their desk when not in use. Although cash is banked on a daily basis, there could still be a significant sum of cash onsite each day. There is a risk of significant cash losses due to theft if access to the safe key is not carefully controlled. | The current key lock safe should be replaced with a safe with a digital code. Only authorised personnel should have the code which should be updated on a regular basis. |
| The cashier is responsible for several elements of the cash receipts system. She receives the daily sales sheets from restaurants, agrees that cash has cleared into the bank statements, updates the cash book and undertakes the bank reconciliations.<br><br>There is a lack of segregation of duties and errors will not be identified on a timely basis. | These key roles should be split between different members of the finance team, with ideally the bank reconciliations being undertaken by another member of the team. |
| The cashier is not checking that payments made by credit card have resulted in cash being received by Camomile Co. The credit card statements are not reviewed or reconciled, they are just filed away.<br><br>There is a risk that receipts of cash by credit card may have been omitted and this would not be identified on a timely basis as the bank is only reconciled every two months and may result in difficulties in resolving any discrepancies with the credit card company | The cashier should reconcile the credit card vouchers per restaurant to the monthly statement received from the card company. The daily amounts per the statement should be agreed to the bank statement to ensure that all funds have been received.<br><br>This reconciliation should be reviewed by a responsible official, such as the financial controller, who should evidence by signature that the review has been undertaken |

ANSWERS

| Control deficiency | Control recommendation |
|---|---|
| The bank reconciliations are only carried out every two months.<br><br>For a cash-based business, the bank reconciliation is a direct control which reduces the risk of fraud. If it is not reconciled regularly enough, then this reduces its effectiveness as fraud and errors may not be identified on a timely basis. | The bank reconciliations should be performed on a monthly basis rather than every two months. The financial controller should continue to review each reconciliation and evidence her review by way of signature on the bank reconciliation. |
| The finance director only views the total amount of payments to be made rather than the amounts to be paid to each supplier.<br><br>Without looking at the detail of the payments list, as well as supporting documentation, there is a risk that suppliers could be being paid an incorrect amount, or that sums are being paid to fictitious suppliers. | The finance director should review the whole payments list prior to authorising.<br><br>As part of this, he should agree the amounts to be paid to supporting documentation, as well as reviewing the supplier names to identify any duplicates or any unfamiliar names.<br><br>He should evidence his review by signing the bank transfer list. |

## Expert

119    The correct answers are:

The revaluation constitutes a change in accounting policy, so we will need to consider the adequacy of the disclosures made in respect of this.

The flagship store should be depreciated on its revalued amount.

IAS 16 *Property, Plant and Equipment* permits non-current assets to be revalued (16). However, if an item of property, plant and equipment is revalued, the entire class of property, plant and equipment to which that asset belongs must be revalued (IAS 16). Truse Co is therefore entitled to revalue the shop, but it will also need to revalue all of the other shops if it is to comply with IAS 16.

The revaluation does constitute a change of accounting policy, so disclosures do need to be reviewed.

Under IAS 16, all non-current assets used by the entity should be depreciated, even if the fair value is in excess of the carrying amount. Repair and maintenance does not negate the need to depreciate the shop over its useful life (IAS 16).

Repairs and maintenance costs should be expensed as incurred, not capitalised.

120    The correct answer is:

| Assertion | Yes | No |
|---|---|---|
| Existence | X | |
| Occurrence | | X |
| Classification | X | |
| Presentation | X | |

Existence, classification and presentation are all assertions related to tangible non-current assets. Completeness and accuracy, valuation and allocation are also relevant assertions (ISA 315). Occurrence and classification relate to classes of transactions and events recorded in profit or loss (ISA 315).

121 The correct answer is:

For a sample of assets selected by physical inspection, agree that they are listed on the non-current assets register

Physically inspecting assets listed in the non-current assets register tests for existence. Recalculating the carrying amount tests for accuracy, valuation and allocation. Inspecting relevant purchase invoices or deeds tests for rights and obligations.

122 The correct answer is:

The existence of any interests in or relationships with Truse Co that might pose a threat to the expert's objectivity

The existence of threats to the expert's objectivity should be considered as part of determining the competence, capability and objectivity of the auditor's expert (ISA 620). However, it is not a matter to be considered when the auditor determines the overall nature, timing and extent of the audit procedures required to evaluate the auditor's expert and the auditor's expert's work.

Besides the other three matters listed, the auditor should also consider the nature of the matter to which the auditor's expert's work relates (ie the nature of Truse Co's properties) and the significance of the auditor's expert's work in the context of the audit (this depends, in part, on the materiality of the property account).

123 The correct answer is:

(1)     Bank confirmation report from Truse Co's bank

(2)     Cash count carried out by the audit junior himself

(3)     Bank reconciliation carried out by the cashier

(4)     Verbal confirmation from the directors that the overdraft limit is to be increased

Third-party evidence is the most reliable, followed by auditor-generated evidence. Client-generated evidence is deemed to be less reliable – more so when the evidence is verbal.

# Newthorpe

124 The correct answers are:

The auditor observes client staff to determine whether inventory count procedures are being followed.

The auditor reviews procedures for identifying damaged, obsolete and slow-moving inventory.

Management is responsible for organising the inventory count, not the auditor. If the results of the auditor's test counts are not satisfactory, the auditor can request that inventory is recounted, but the auditor cannot insist on a recount. However, if management refuses the auditor's request then the auditor will need to consider the implications of this on the auditor's report.

125 The correct answer is:

For a sample of inventory sold just before and just after the year end, match dates of sales invoices/date posted to ledgers with date on related goods dispatched notes.

All of the suggested audit procedures test the valuation assumption, except for matching the dates of sales invoices with the dates on the related goods dispatched notes, which is an audit procedure around cut-off.

126 The correct answer is:

The legal claim should **not be recorded as a provision but disclosed as a contingent liability** because **a present obligation exists, but the outflow of economic resources is not probable**.

Management believe that there is a 35% chance of the claim succeeding. For an event to be 'probable', it should be more likely than not to occur (ie a 50% probability) (IAS 37). In this case, the outflow of economic resources is therefore not probable, so a provision should not be recognised. A present obligation (not a possible obligation) exists, since the former managing director has sued Newthorpe for unfair dismissal. It is because the likelihood of him succeeding in his claim is not probable that the claim should be treated as a contingent liability instead of a provision.

127 The correct answer is:

Send an enquiry letter to Newthorpe's lawyers to obtain their view as to the probability of the claim being successful

Independent third-party audit evidence is generally considered to be more reliable than client generated or auditor-generated audit evidence. Although all the procedures are valid, only the written confirmation from Newthorpe's lawyers provides an expert, third-party confirmation on the likelihood of the claim being successful. It is also sent directly to the auditor rather than to the client.

128 To perform specific procedures to identify possible non-compliance

ISA 250 (Revised) distinguishes between those laws and regulations which have a direct effect on the financial statements, and those which have an indirect effect (ISA 250). For those which have a direct effect on the financial statements the auditor must undertake specified audit procedures to help identify non-compliance with laws and regulations that may have a material effect on the financial statements (ISA 250).

# Tirrol

129 The correct answers are:

We should budget for the extra time required to document an understanding of the entity, its environment and its systems, and to verify material opening balances.

We must agree a clear timetable with the client for the testing of the computerised inventory systems, setting out availability of access to the system, files and personnel required to complete testing.

As this is Cal & Co's first year of auditing Tirrol Co, additional time should be budgeted for documenting an understanding of the entity and for verifying the opening balances. Because Cal & Co's audit software has to be rewritten and the testing is taking place on a live basis, it is particularly important to plan our CAATs procedures carefully.

The ACCA's *Code of Ethics and Conduct* does not prohibit lowballing as such stating that 'a professional accountant in public practice may quote whatever fee is deemed appropriate' (ACCA *Code of Ethics and Conduct*: para. 330.3 A2), so withdrawing from the audit engagement on this basis is disproportionate. However, the firm should be able to demonstrate that appropriate time and qualified staff are assigned to the audit, and that all applicable standards are being adhered to (ACCA *Code of Ethics and Conduct*: para. 330.3 A3-7). It may not be appropriate to adopt a combined approach if the control risk is deemed to be high. The appropriate audit approach should be determined by the risk assessment, not by time or fee constraints.

130    The correct answers are:

The ability to test all 25 of Tirrol Co's locations using the same audit software, resulting in time and cost savings

The ability to select and extract a sample of inventory data for testing, thus reducing sampling risk

Audit software is used to perform substantive procedures rather than tests of controls and therefore this would not include testing internal controls relating to the input of data. Similarly, the error rate in a sample refers to the number of times a control deficiency is projected to occur in a population and therefore is not relevant to audit software.

131    The correct answer is:

A sampling method which involves having a constant sampling interval, the starting point for testing is determined randomly

The first option describes monetary unit sampling. The third option is an example of block selection. The fourth option describes haphazard sampling.

132    The correct answer is:

Whether there are any significant threats to the objectivity of the internal auditor

The objectivity of the internal auditor should be considered in determining whether or not the work of the internal auditors can be used in the first place. It is not part of evaluating the work itself.

133    The correct answer is:

Inventory should be $43,500, inventory is overstated.

Inventory should be measured at the lower of cost and net realisable value (IAS 2). Net realisable value is defined by IAS 2 as estimated selling price less estimated costs necessary to make the sale (IAS 2). In this case, inventory should be written down by $6,000 and shown at a value of $43,500 in the financial statements.

# Wright

134    The correct answer is: 1 and 3

Material items will require more evidence to support them than immaterial items, which might be tested by comparative analytical review only. If the evidence is of high quality, then less may be required than if it were of poorer quality. Time and budget constraints should never influence the auditor's judgement regarding the sufficiency of audit evidence. The size of the account is considered in determining materiality (ie materiality may be determined as 5% of profit before tax), but the auditor's judgement regarding the sufficiency of audit evidence depends on the level of audit risks associated with each account. The operating effectiveness of the company's internal control systems will also influence this judgement.

135    The correct answer is: 2 only

The goods were received before the year end and have been recognised in inventory. A liability should therefore be recognised in the current accounting period. Although the cheque cleared the bank account after the year end it was issued before the year end and there is nothing to suggest that it has been deliberately held back. The cash in transit is therefore a legitimate reconciling item.

136    The correct answer is: No further evidence is required

As the supplier statement balance agrees with that on the purchase ledger, no further work is required in respect of this account.

Purchase orders made after the year end would not have any effect on current year liabilities.

As a supplier statement is available there would be no need to ask for a direct confirmation of the balance from supplier XX3.

Credit notes issued by Wilbur Co would potentially affect receivables, not payables, balances.

137 The correct answer is: Written on the audit firm's headed paper; information requested to be sent directly to the auditor

The bank confirmation letter must be sent identifiably by the auditor, and responses should be provided directly to the auditor. This is to prevent the information being distorted by any lack of objectivity, or tampering by client management.

138 The correct answer is: The bank's date stamp on the paying-in slip

The bank's stamp on the paying-in slip is the most reliable as it is third-party evidence and shows the date the lodgements were actually paid into the bank.

The bank statement would be a useful source of evidence but there may be a delay between the paying-in date and the date that the balance is cleared by the banking system. Therefore the bank statement date is not necessarily an accurate reflection of when the lodgement was made. There may also be a delay between the date on the cheques/remittance advice and the date it is actually received by Wilbur Co.

# Lodestar

139 The correct answer is: The sample selection does not address the risk of understatement as it has focused on the ten largest balances.

Option A is incorrect as the sample is not appropriate. In order to test **completeness**, the sample selection for a receivables circularisation should consider incorporating nil balances and balances written off in the year to ensure that the balance is not understated. (Hence Option C is correct.)

Option B is incorrect as the nature of sampling means that a percentage of the balance will not be sampled, but conclusions can still be drawn.

Option D is incorrect as stratification is not required (although it may be helpful) and would not necessarily give a 'representative' sample, due to the risks discussed above in relation to Option A.

140 The correct answer is: 1, 2 and 4

Appropriateness refers to relevance and reliability. All the procedures are relevant to the assertion, but only some of them are reliable. Simply asking the credit controller if the client exists is not reliable, as it gives oral evidence generated by management and does not add value to the sales ledger.

Sending out a follow-up request gives the auditor a chance of obtaining evidence direct from a third party, which would be considered very reliable.

Reviewing cash receipts after date gives indirect evidence from a third party as, if someone is paying the debt, it implies it existed in the first place.

Reviewing the sales invoices is auditor-generated evidence that the sale was generated in the first place. It is based on relatively weak internally generated evidence (the invoices) but as it involves auditor analysis (for example, whether the relevant invoices appear in numerical sequence with other genuine invoices and have associated goods outwards notes) it adds a degree of reliability. This evidence would not be sufficient on its own but it might corroborate other evidence.

141 The correct answer is: Trade receivables should be £6,000 lower, current assets are overstated.

The difference caused by the payment by the customer does not require adjustment. The auditor has verified that the payment was received by Lodestar on 2 October, which is consistent with the
third-party evidence that it was sent out on 30 September. As far as Lodestar is concerned, the debt was genuine at 30 September and there is good evidence about its existence and valuation provided by the subsequent payment.

The customer is disputing an invoice and declaring its intention not to accept the debt. Regardless of management's intention to dispute this credit request, that suggests that the **valuation** of the debt is inappropriate (as the customer is only prepared to pay £0 in effect for that invoice), even if the **existence** of the debt can be proved. The invoice should be written off, hence receivables and current assets are overstated by £6,000.

142 The correct answer is: Auditors should use their own estimate in the financial statements, as auditor-generated evidence is more conclusive than management-generated evidence.

Auditors do not prepare the financial statements, management do. It is inappropriate to suggest that the auditors should prepare a figure for the financial statements (and this might cause an ethical threat of self-review). Auditor-generated evidence is considered reliable, so if the auditors did make an estimate which was significantly different from management's, this would be evidence that the allowance was misstated. The auditor will have to bear in mind the risk of management bias in making an estimate, and it is true that it can be difficult to obtain evidence relating to management judgement (particularly in this case if no events occur to 'prove' the debt is doubtful, such as the customer going into liquidation, or management writing the debt off – which they are likely to want to defer in case the debt is eventually paid).

143 The correct answer is: 1, 2, 3, 4

The assertion being tested is **valuation**.

(1) Gives indirect third-party evidence that the valuation of the debt is appropriate (ie in proving that some debts have not been paid)

(2) Gives auditor-generated evidence of the age of some debt and therefore the fact that its valuation is likely to be in doubt (otherwise it would have been paid before)

(3) Gives management evidence relating to the valuation of the debt, which might give the auditor insight into issues they might otherwise be unaware of, such as conversations with customers about when debts are to be paid

(4) Gives very little evidence about current valuation, as it only shows what the value was at the time the invoice was sent, and is of low reliability anyway, as it is internally generated

# Porthos

144 The correct answer is: 2, 4, 1, 3

The steps should be undertaken in this order. The objective of the CAAT procedures should be determined first and foremost. The accessibility of the data files must be considered before the scope and nature of the procedures are determined.

145 The correct answer is: (i), (ii), (iii) and (iv)

Testing orders for unusually large quantities identifies whether any reject controls requiring special authorisation for large orders are effective. Testing orders with fields left blank determines whether controls are in place to prevent orders being placed that can't be fulfilled due to missing information (ie incomplete delivery address). Testing orders with invalid inventory codes identifies whether controls are in place to ensure that the correct goods are dispatched. Finally, orders with correct and complete details should be accepted by the system. This will allow the auditor to inspect the order confirmation to determine whether the order details are transferred accurately into the dispatch system.

146    The correct answer is: For sales invoices issued before 31 December 20X7 use audit software to determine whether there is a matching GDN dated before 31 December 20X7

Sales cut-off will have been correctly applied where goods are dispatched and recognised as sales in the same accounting period. Therefore all GDNs relating to goods dispatched before 31 December 20X7 should be matched by a sales invoice also dated before 31 December 20X7.

The fact that goods are picked and dispatched in the same accounting period does not provide evidence that sales have been recognised in the correct accounting period. Therefore the third and fourth options are not relevant.

147    The correct answer is: To provide audit evidence over the completeness of the recording of sales

Sequence checks on sales invoices provide evidence on the completeness of sales.

148    The correct answer is: (21,600 × 2/12) + (24,000 × 10/12)

The rent recognised in the year should reflect that earned in the period. For January and February this will be based on an annual rental income of $21,600. For the remaining 10 months this would be based on the increased rental. The proof in total should be calculated on the same basis.

# Lancaster

149    The correct answers are: Physically inspect a sample of assets selected from the non-current asset register; Inspect a sample of assets found at a location and agree to the non-current asset register.

This question tests candidates' understanding of the purpose of specific audit procedures relating to non-current assets with the focus being overstatement. When testing for overstatement it is essential to work from the financial statements to source documents or assets. (Working from source documents or assets to the financial statements would test for understatement.) Candidates should also note the number of responses required. In this case two correct answers from four options are required. Selecting assets from the non-current asset register and inspecting them tests the existence assertion which provides evidence regarding potential overstatement – the balance will be overstated if assets included do not exist.

Assessing the need for impairment is a valuation test. If an asset is impaired but the impairment has not been recognised the balance will be overstated. Option 1 provides evidence that disposals which are recorded have actually taken place. This tests for understatement and is therefore not an appropriate response. Option 3 also tests for understatement by confirming that assets physically inspected are recorded in the non-current asset register.

150    The correct answer is: 1, 3 and 4 only.

In respect of test (1), tracing additions per the non-current asset register to the cash book and invoice, checking that the date is correct is an existence check providing evidence that the asset was held by Lancaster Co from that date. Confirming the amount at which the asset is recorded to the cash book and invoice is a valuation test. Test (2) is an analytical procedure. It therefore provides evidence in respect of all the assertions listed with the exception of classification. As the comparison is being performed based on totals, this test would not provide evidence relating to classification.

151    The correct answers are: Perform a proof in total for the depreciation charge of $2m included in the financial statements and investigate any significant differences; Discuss with management the reasons for the $300,000 difference in the current year depreciation compared to the prior year.

Options 2 and 4, a proof in total and a comparison with the prior year are both analytical procedures and are therefore substantive procedures. Reviewing the non-current asset register to ensure that assets have been assigned a useful life and reviewing board minutes for evidence of approval of useful lives are both examples of tests of controls. This question tests candidates' understanding of the different types of procedures which the auditor may perform during the audit, and in particular the distinction between tests of controls and substantive procedures. Substantive procedures are designed to detect material misstatement at the assertion level whereas tests of controls are designed to evaluate the operating effectiveness of controls. It is essential that candidates understand the purpose of these two types of procedure and can distinguish between them, both for Section A and Section B questions. Candidates also need to be aware that substantive procedures include both analytical procedures and tests of detail.

152 The correct answer is: $1.5m.

At the disposal date accumulated depreciation would be: $6m × 0.05 × 7 = $2.1m

The carrying amount of the asset at the date of disposal would be: $6m – $2.1m = $3.9m

Disposal proceeds are: $6m × 40% = $2.4m

The loss on disposal is therefore: $3.9m – $2.4m = $1.5m

This question highlights the importance of candidates having the required Financial Accounting knowledge which underpins the ability to perform an effective audit. The auditor must understand the basis on which the financial statements being audited should have been prepared if misstatements are to be identified. In this instance, if the auditor is to audit the profit or loss on disposal they must be familiar with the components which make up this balance. This particular calculation could be relevant, for example, as part of the analytical procedures performed. The auditor would form their own expectation of the profit or loss on disposal of an asset and then compare this with the profit or loss recognised in the financial statements. Candidates should also take note of the specific instruction provided with this question ie that the answer should be provided to one decimal place. Where specific instructions like this are given in a question it is essential that candidates follow these to avoid losing marks unnecessarily.

153 The correct answers are: Reference to the work of the external expert should not be included in the auditor's report; The objectivity of the valuer must be assessed before placing reliance on the valuation report.

This question tests candidates' understanding of the issues for the auditor when placing reliance on the work of an expert. There are two types of expert which the auditor may rely on during the course of the audit, a management's expert or an auditor's expert. In this instance the expert has been used by Lancaster Co to assist it with the valuation of the buildings which will appear in the financial statements. The expert is therefore a management's expert in accordance with ISA 500 *Audit Evidence*. If information is to be used as audit evidence that has been prepared using the work of a management's expert the auditor must evaluate the objectivity of that expert. The competence and capabilities should also be evaluated. The auditor takes sole responsibility for the audit opinion. If the auditor is to rely on the work of the expert the evidence would have been evaluated with the conclusion that it provides appropriate evidence to support the valuation. No reference therefore to the expert should be made in the auditor's report.

Option 1 is incorrect as in accordance with ISA 500 there may be circumstances where it is appropriate for the auditor to place reliance on a management's expert. Simply obtaining the valuation report would not constitute sufficient and appropriate evidence over the carrying amount of the buildings. In accordance with ISA 500 the auditor would be required to evaluate whether the information is sufficiently reliable for the purposes of the audit. This would include obtaining evidence about the accuracy and completeness of the information and evaluating whether it is sufficiently precise and detailed. Option 2 is therefore incorrect.

# 154 Lily

## Marking scheme

Marks

(a)    Up to 1 mark per well-explained deficiency and up to 1 mark per recommendation. If not well explained then just give ½ mark for each.

Warehouse manager supervising the count

No division of responsibilities within each counting team

Internal audit teams should be checking controls and performing sample counts

No flagging of aisles once counting complete

Additional inventory listed on sheets which are not sequentially numbered

Inventory sheets not signed by counters

Damaged goods not moved to central location

Movements of inventory during the count

Warehouse manager not qualified to assess the level of work in progress

Warehouse manager not experienced enough to assess the quantities of raw materials

12

(b)     Up to 1 mark per well-described procedure.

Observe the counters to confirm if inventory count instructions are being followed

Perform test counts inventory to sheets and sheets to inventory

Confirm procedures for damaged goods are operating correctly

Inspect damaged goods to confirm whether the level of damage is correctly noted

Observe procedures for movements of inventory during the count

Obtain a photocopy of the completed inventory sheets

Identify and make a note of the last goods received notes and goods dispatched notes

Observe the procedures carried out by warehouse manager in assessing the level of work in progress

Discuss with the warehouse manager how he has estimated the raw materials quantities

Identify inventory held for third parties and ensure excluded from count          6

(c)     (i)     Up to 1 mark per well-described procedure, max of 4 procedures.

Calculate inventory holding period

Produce an aged inventory analysis to identify any slow-moving goods

Cast the inventory listing

Select a sample of items for testing to confirm net realisable value (NRV) and/or cost

Recalculate cost and NRV for sample of inventory

Computer-assisted audit techniques (CAATs) can be used to confirm cut-off

CAATs can be used to confirm whether inventory adjustments noted during the count have been updated to inventory records          4

        (ii)    Up to 1 mark per well-explained advantage.

Test a large volume of inventory data accurately and quickly

Cost effective after set-up

Automated tools and techniques can test program controls as well as general IT controls

Test the actual inventory system and records rather than printouts from the system

Automated tools and techniques reduce the level of human error in testing

Automated tools and techniques results can be compared with traditional audit testing

Free up audit team members to focus on judgemental and high risk areas          4

(iii)     Up to 1 mark per well-explained disadvantage.

Costs of using automated tools and techniques in this first year will be high

Team may require training on the specific automated tools and techniques to be utilised

Changes in the inventory system may require costly revisions to the automated tools and techniques

The inventory system may not be compatible with the audit firm's automated tools and techniques

If testing the live system, there is a risk the data could be corrupted or lost

If using copy files rather than live data, there is the risk that these files are not genuine copies

Adequate systems documentation must be available

4
---
30

(a)

| Deficiency (i) | Recommendation (ii) |
|---|---|
| The warehouse manager will supervise the inventory count and is not independent as he has overall responsibility for the inventory. He therefore has an incentive to conceal or fail to report any issues that could reflect badly upon him. | An independent supervisor should be assigned, such as a manager from the internal audit department. |
| Aisles or areas counted will not be flagged. This could result in items being double counted or not counted at all. | Once areas have been counted they should be flagged. At the end of the count the supervisor should check all areas have been flagged and therefore counted. |
| There is no one independent reviewing controls over the count or test counting to assess the accuracy of the counts. | Instead of the internal auditors being involved in the count itself, they should perform secondary test counts and review controls over the count. |
| Damaged goods are being left in their location rather than being stored separately. This makes it more difficult for finance to assess the level of damage to the goods and establish the level of write down needed. Also, if not moved, damaged goods could be sold by mistake. | Damaged goods should be clearly marked as such during the count and at the end of the count they should be moved to a central location. A manager from the finance team should then inspect these damaged goods to assess the level of allowance or write down needed. |

| Deficiency (i) | Recommendation (ii) |
|---|---|
| Due to the continuous production process, there will be movement of goods in and out of the warehouse during the count, increasing the risk of double counting or failing to count inventory. This could mean inventory in the financial statements is under- or overstated. | Although it is not practicable to disrupt the continuous production process, raw materials (RM) required for 31 July should be estimated and separated from the remainder of inventory. These materials should be included as part of work in progress (WIP). Goods manufactured on 31 July should be stored separately, and at the end of the count should be counted once and included as finished goods. Goods received from suppliers should also be stored separately, counted once at the end and included in RM. Goods dispatched to customers should be kept to a minimum during the count. |
| The warehouse manager is going to estimate WIP levels. The warehouse manager is unlikely to have the necessary experience to estimate the WIP levels which is something the factory manager would be more familiar with. Alternatively a specialist may be needed to make the estimate. This could ultimately result in an inaccurate WIP balance in the financial statements. | A specialist should be used to assess the work in progress. |
| The warehouse manager is going to approximate RM quantities. Although he is familiar with the RM, and on the basis that a specialist has been required in the past, the warehouse manager may not have the necessary skill and experience to carry out these measurements. This could result in an inaccurate RM balance in the financial statements. | As in previous years, a specialist should assess the quantities of raw materials, or at least check the warehouse manager's estimate to give comfort that the manager's estimates will be reasonable going forward. |
| There is no indication that inventory sheets are signed or initialled by the counting team, nor a record kept of which team counted which area. This means it will be difficult to follow up on any anomalies noted, as the identity of the counters may not be known. | Inventory sheets should be signed by both team members once an aisle is completed. The supervisor should check the sheets are signed when handed in. |
| Inventory not listed on the sheets is to be entered onto separate sheets. These sheets are not sequentially numbered and the supervisor will be unable to ensure the completeness of all inventory sheets. | Every team should be given a blank sheet on which they can enter any inventory counted which is not on their sheets. The blank sheets should be sequentially numbered, with any unused sheets returned at the end of the count. The supervisor should then check the sequence of all sheets. |
| The responsibilities of each of the two staff members within a counting team is unclear. It does not appear that one has been told to count and the other to check. Therefore errors in counting may not be picked up. | For each area one team member should be asked to count and the second member asked to check that the inventory has been counted correctly. The roles of each can then be reversed for the next area. |

Note. Only six deficiencies and six related recommendations were needed to gain 12 marks.

(b)   **Procedures undertaken during the inventory count**

- For a sample of inventory items, carry out test counts from aisle to inventory sheet to test completeness and from inventory sheets to aisle to test existence.

- Obtain and record details of the last goods received notes (GRNs) and goods dispatched notes (GDNs) for 31 July to form the basis for cut-off procedures at the audit.

- Observe whether teams carrying out the count are adequately following the inventory count instructions.

- For a sample of items marked as damaged on the inventory sheets, inspect the windows to verify that the level of damage has been correctly recorded.

- Observe the procedures for movements of inventory during the count and assess the risk that raw materials or finished goods have been missed or double counted.

- Photocopy the inventory sheets for follow-up and use when performing procedures at the final audit.

- Ascertain how the warehouse manager is assessing the level of work in progress by observing the assessment and by reviewing his assumptions, and consider how consistent his estimate is with observed levels.

- Ask the warehouse manager how he has estimated the raw materials quantities and review his calculations and any assumptions for reasonableness. Reperform a sample of the measurements of height and width forming the basis of any calculation to see if they are accurate.

- Confirm any third-party inventory observed has been excluded from the count.

- Confirm that the procedures for identifying and separately storing damaged goods are operating effectively.

*Note. Only six procedures were needed to gain full marks.*

(c)   **Automated tools and techniques**

(i)   **Audit procedures**

Software can be used to cast the inventory listing to confirm the total is complete and accurate.

Audit software could be used to extract a statistical sample of inventory items in order to verify their cost or net realisable value (NRV).

Calculations of the inventory holding period or inventory turnover could be carried out by audit software, before being used to compare against the same ratios for the prior year or of competitors. This will help to assess the risk of inventory being overstated.

Audit software could be used to help extract an aged inventory analysis. This could in turn be used to identify any obsolete or slow-moving items, which may require a write-down or an allowance.

Audit software can be used to perform calculations during testing of inventory, such as recorded cost (eg weight or quantity multiplied by cost per kg or unit).

Automated tools can be used to confirm whether inventory adjustments recorded during attendance at the count have been correctly recorded in the final inventory records forming the basis of inventory in the financial statements.

Automated tools can be used to verify cut-off by testing whether the dates of the last GRNs and GDNs recorded relate to pre year end, and that any with a date after the year end have been excluded from the inventory records.

*Note. Only four procedures were required.*

(ii) **Automated tools – advantages**

- Automated tools allow the audit team to test a large volume of inventory data more accurately and more quickly than if tested manually.

- Automated tools decrease the scope for human error during testing and can provide evidence of a higher quality.

- By using automated tools, auditors can test actual inventory transactions within the system rather than working on printouts from spool or previewed files which are dependent on other software (and therefore could contain errors or could have been tampered with following export).

- Assuming the inventory system remains unchanged, automated tools used in the audit of Lily year on year should bring time (and therefore cost) savings in the long term, which should more than compensate for any set-up costs.

- Auditors can utilise automated tools to test program controls as well as general internal controls associated with computers.

- Results from automated tools can be compared with results from traditional testing. If the results correlate, overall confidence is increased.

- The use of automated tools allows audit team members more time to focus on risk areas and issues requiring judgement, rather than performing routine calculations that can be carried out by audit software.

Note. Only four advantages were needed to gain full marks.

(iii) **Automated tools – disadvantages**

- Setting up the software needed for automated tools in the first year is likely to be time consuming and expensive.

- Audit staff working on Lily's audit will need to be trained so they have a sufficient level of IT knowledge to apply automated tools when auditing the inventory system.

- If testing is performed on data in the live inventory system, there is a risk that live client data may be corrupted and lost.

- If the inventory system at Lily changed then it may be expensive and time consuming to redesign the automated tools .

- If the inventory system at Lily is not compatible with Daffodil & Co's automated tools software then they will need to be tailored to Lily's system, which may be costly.

- If testing is performed on data from copies of the live files rather than the live data itself, there is the risk that these files have been affected by the copying process or have been tampered with.

- If there is not adequate systems documentation available, it will be difficult to design appropriate techniques due to a lack of understanding of the inventory system at Lily.

Note. Only four advantages were needed to gain full marks.

# 155 Westra Co

## Marking scheme

Marks

(a) **Audit procedures – purchases**, 12 marks. 1 for procedure and 1 for the reason. Limit to 5 marks in each category where stated briefly without full detail.

| Audit procedure | Reason for procedure |
|---|---|
| Parts to GRN | Check completeness |
| Parts no GRN number | System error or cut-off error |
| GRN to computer | Parts received were ordered – occurrence |
| GRN agree to invoice | Completeness of recording |
| Review unmatched GRN file | Completeness of recording of liabilities |
| Paid invoice – GRN attached | Confirms invoice in PDB |
| Invoice details to payables ledger | Completeness and accuracy of recording |
| Review unmatched invoices file | Indicate understatement of liability (lack of completeness) |
| Payables ledger to purchase invoice | Liability belongs to Westra |
| Payables ledger to payments list | Liability properly discharged – payments complete |
| Payment list entries to invoice | Payment made for bona fide liability |
| Payments list to bank statement | Confirms payment to supplier |
| Bank statement entry to payments list | Confirms payment relates to Westra |
| GRN cut-off testing | Accuracy of cut-off |
| **Maximum marks** | |

12

(b) **Audit procedures – payables**, 8 marks. 1 for procedure and 1 for reason. Limit to ½ mark in each category where stated briefly without full detail.

| Audit procedure | Reason for procedure |
|---|---|
| Obtain and cast list of payables | Ensure that the list is accurate |
| Total of payables to the general ledger and financial statements | Confirm that the total has been accurately recorded |
| Analytical procedures | Indicates problems with the accuracy and completeness of payables |
| Agree payables to supplier statements | Confirm balance due from Westra |
| Supplier statement reconciliation | Liabilities exist and belong to Westra |
| Reconcile invoices | Confirms completeness and cut-off assertions |
| Reconcile payments | Payment to correct supplier |
| Review ledger old unpaid invoices | Credits O/S or going concern indicator |
| After-date credit notes | Payables not overstated |
| FS categorisation payables | Classification objective |

| | |
|---|---|
| **Maximum marks** | 8 |

(c) **Controls over standing data**, 5 marks. 1 mark for explaining each control. ½ for poor/limited explanation.

Amendments authorised

How authorised (form or access control)

Reject deletion where outstanding balance

Keep record of amendments

Review list of suppliers – unauthorised amendments

Update supplier list on computer regularly

Review computer control log

Review list of suppliers – unauthorised additions

Other relevant points (each)

| | |
|---|---|
| **Maximum marks** | 5 |

(d) **Use of data analytics**

Link together with other cycles

Analysis of ageing, problem entries

Use of data analytics may be limited by lack of computer system integration

Cost effective – may improve audit effectiveness

Analysis of journal entries

Ratio analysis

Other relevant points (each)

| | |
|---|---|
| **Maximum marks** | 5 |
| | 30 |

(a)   **Substantive procedures**

*Completeness*

| Audit procedure | Purpose |
|---|---|
| Perform analytical procedures on purchases, eg comparison to the prior year on a month by month basis, ratio of purchases to payables, gross profit percentage etc and investigate any significant fluctuations | To provide assurance on the completeness of amounts recorded in the accounts and to highlight any areas of concern for further investigation |
| For a sample of supplier invoices, trace amounts to the GRN, order and payables ledger | To confirm completeness of recording of purchases |
| Inspect the unmatched GRN file and seek explanations for any old unmatched items and trace these to the year-end accruals listing | To provide assurance on completeness as these should be included in the year-end accrual |
| For a sample of amounts on the ledger, agree to the computerised payments list to verify the amount and supplier | To provide assurance that the payment list is complete and accurate |

*Occurrence*

| Audit procedure | Purpose |
|---|---|
| For a sample of amounts in the payables ledger, trace these to the invoice and other supporting documentation such as GRNs | To provide assurance on the occurrence assertion |
| For a sample of GRNs, agree back to the original order details | To provide assurance on occurrence |
| For a sample of payees on the computerised payments list, agree amounts back to the supporting documentation such as invoices and GRNs | To provide assurance that payment has been made for a bona fide liability of the company |
| For a sample of payments made after the year end, trace back to the computerised payments list | To provide assurance that payment relates to the company |
| For a sample of payees on the computerised payments list, trace payment to post year end bank statements | To confirm that payment was made to authorised suppliers of the company |

*Cut-off*

| Audit procedure | Purpose |
|---|---|
| For a sample of GRNs dated shortly before and after the year end, agree that the amounts on invoices are posted to the correct financial year | To ensure that amounts are included in the correct financial period |
| Review the schedule of accruals and agree to GRNs, inspecting the date of receipt of goods to ensure that goods received after the year end are not included | To ensure that amounts are included in the correct financial period |
| Inspect outstanding orders on the 'orders placed' file for any orders completed but not yet invoiced | To ensure that amounts are included in the correct financial period |

(b)    Audit procedures on trade payables

| Audit procedure | Purpose |
|---|---|
| Cast the list of payables balances from the ledger at the year end | To provide assurance that the list is complete and accurate |
| Reconcile the payables list from the payables ledger to the general ledger and accounts | To provide assurance that the figures are complete and accurate and correctly reflected in the financial statements |
| Perform analytical procedures on trade payables, comparing balance to prior year and investigating any significant fluctuations | To provide assurance on completeness and accuracy and to highlight areas of concern |
| For a sample of balances, trace amount to supporting supplier statements | To confirm the existence and accuracy of the amount outstanding at the year end |
| Test cut-off by taking a sample of GRNs either side of the year end and verifying that amounts are included on the payables ledger for goods received before the year end | To ensure that amounts are included in the correct financial period |
| Review disclosure of payables in the draft financial statements | To ensure that payables have been disclosed appropriately in the statement of financial position and notes as either current or long-term liabilities |

(c)    **Control procedures over standing data on trade payables master file**

- Access to the trade payables master file is limited only to authorised staff

- Amendments to standing data can only be made by authorised staff and all amendments must be authorised prior to input

- Access to the file is controlled by logins and passwords and passwords must be prompted to be changed regularly (say, every 90 days)

- Computer log is reviewed regularly by IT department to detect any unauthorised access or attempts to access the trade payables master file

- The list of suppliers should be reviewed regularly by a senior manager and those no longer used should be removed from the system

(d)    **Use of data analytics techniques in audit of Westra**

Data analytics could be used in the audit of purchases and payables at Westra in a number of ways.

Data analytics routines can be used to link together purchase expenses with payables, which could be helpful in testing a variety of areas. This would include the application of the cut-off at the beginning and end of the reporting period, as well as the completeness of payables, all of which should be matched to expenses.

These routines may be able to go further still, and link together several cycles for a sample of transactions, for example; the purchase order could be linked to the expense, which could in turn be linked to the liability (payable). This is then connected to the cash movement for the payment, and to the accounting for the item in inventory (depending on the item being purchased). Finally it may then be possible to trace the inventory item being sold, with entries to revenue, receivables and, ultimately, the cash receipt. In this way, the audit of payables changes from being an isolated area of the financial statements to one that is connected to the wider accounting context.

Within payables, data analytics software could be used to generate detailed payables ageing reports, allowing the auditor to identify potential problem balances. The software can perform a check that all payables calculations are arithmetically accurate, and can highlight gaps in the expected sequence of entries, as well as zero or duplicated entries.

BPP
LEARNING
MEDIA

An analysis of journal entries to payables can be made, helping to identify eg unexpected journals, journals posted to unusual combinations of accounts or by unauthorised users, or to identify trends such as high numbers of postings just below authorisation limits.

Data analytics software could also be used to **reperform** the cost of the total on the file to ensure the file is a complete record of transactions. The software can also be used to perform **ratio calculations** for analytical procedures on the purchases and payables data, and to compare the results of this analysis with expectations.

For this audit, the use of data analytics may be **limited** by the fact that the company uses a mixture of manual and computerised systems. However, it may still be possible for the auditor to improve both audit efficiency and audit quality by making using of data analytics routines where it is appropriate to do so.

# 156 Purrfect Co

> **Workbook reference.** Chapters 13, 14, 16 and 20.
>
> **Top tips.** Parts (a) to (c) ask for substantive procedures in relation to an inventory valuation, a receivables balance, and some legal claims. This is a standard question for AA and you should expect to find something of this nature in your exam.
>
> Part (d), on auditor reporting, was made relatively simple by the requirement to describe the impact of the issue in both possible situations. The important points when considering the effect of a matter on the auditor's report are usually the type of modified opinion that COULD be required, and then the materiality or pervasiveness of the issue. When describing the impact on the auditor's report there are usually easy marks available for describing how the auditor's opinion and basis for opinion paragraphs will change.
>
> **Easy marks.** Part (d) offers easy marks for giving a description of a 'basis for' section in the auditor's report.

## Marking scheme

|  |  | Marks |
|---|---|---|
| (a) | **Substantive procedures for inventory of Vego Dog** | |
| | 1 mark per well-described procedure | |
| | **Restricted to** | 6 |
| (b) | **Substantive procedures for receivable due from Ellah Co** | |
| | 1 mark per well-described procedure | |
| | **Restricted to** | 4 |
| (c) | **Substantive procedures for contamination – legal claims** | |
| | 1 mark per well-described procedure | 1 |
| | **Restricted to** | 5 |
| (d) | **Issue and impact on auditor's report** | |
| | Discussion of issue | 1 |
| | Adequate disclosure | 2 |
| | Inadequate disclosure | 2 |
| | | 5 |
| | **Total marks** | 20 |

(a) **Inventory of Vego Dog**

- Obtain and cast the inventory listing of Vego Dog products and agree the total cost of $2·4m to inventory records.

- Agree the quantity of Vego Dog products shown as held at the year end to the year-end inventory count records.

- Request a breakdown of the cost calculation of each unit of this product and discuss with management how the standard cost was derived.

- Recalculate the cost calculations to confirm that the quantity multiplied by the standard cost is $2·4m.

- For a sample of finished goods items, obtain standard cost cards and agree:

    - raw material costs to recent purchase invoices;

    - labour costs to time sheets or wage records;

    - overheads allocated to invoices and that they are of a production nature.

- Compare sales prices over time to establish if the price has been reduced because of falling demand to determine whether an allowance is required.

- Compare actual sales units per month to budgeted sales per month from before and after the year end to establish how much lower actual sales are than expected and discuss with management.

- Select a sample of items included in inventory of Vego Dog and review post year-end sales invoices to ascertain if net realizable value (NRV) is above cost or if an adjustment is required.

(b) **Receivable due from Ellah Co**

- Review correspondence with Ellah Co to establish if there was a discussion about payment difficulties and whether Ellah Co intends to fully settle the outstanding amount.

- Review the age of the outstanding debt with Ellah Co and discuss the circumstances with the credit controller to establish if it has exceeded the agreed credit terms and consider if an allowance is required.

- Review post year-end receipts from Ellah Co to establish how much of the debt was recovered by the audit completion date and to assess how much of the year-end balance remains outstanding.

- Inspect board minutes to identify whether there are any significant concerns in relation to payments by Ellah Co.

- Discuss with management of Purrfect Co why no allowance has been made in respect of this debt and assess the justification.

(c) **Contamination – legal claims**

- Review customer correspondence to establish the details of the claims and the amounts being claimed.

- Review correspondence with Purrfect Co's lawyers or, with the client's permission, contact the lawyers to establish the likely outcome of the customer claims made to date.

- Discuss with the lawyers the likelihood and amount of potential future claims.

- Inspect board minutes to establish details of the circumstances of the contamination and to ascertain management's view as to the likelihood that the existing claims will be successful and the extent of possible future claims.

- Compare levels of returns and claims to date against sales volumes of the product to assess the potential level of future claims.

- Review post-year end payments for damage settlements and compare with any amounts provided at the year end to assess the reasonableness of the provision.

- Obtain written representations from management that there have been no other contamination incidents and no other product liability claims of which management are aware and for which provision may be required.

- Review the draft financial statements to establish that the legal claims have been appropriately provided for or disclosed in accordance with IAS 37 *Provisions, Contingent Liabilities and Contingent Assets*.

(d)  **Issue and impact on auditor's report**

According to IAS 37, the possibility of additional claims should be disclosed as a contingent liability as it is possible but not probable and quantifiable.

As the claims may be significant, this issue represents a matter which is fundamental to users' understanding of the financial statements. The impact on the auditor's report depends on whether this matter is deemed to be adequately disclosed in the financial statements.

**Adequate disclosure**

If Purrfect Co adequately discloses the issue, then an unmodified audit opinion should be given but the auditor's report should include an emphasis of matter paragraph. This would draw attention to the disclosure in the financial statements by cross-referencing the user to the note in the financial statements which discloses the possible claims, emphasising that the audit opinion is unmodified.

**Inadequate disclosure**

If there is no disclosure in the financial statements or the disclosure is considered to be inadequate, then this indicates that the financial statements are materially misstated. As this lack of adequate disclosure is likely to be material but not pervasive, then a

qualified opinion will be given. A basis for qualified opinion paragraph will be added to the auditor's report discussing the matter and the opinion paragraph will be modified to state that 'except for' the failure to adequately disclose the matter, the financial statements give a true and fair view.

# 157 Rose

---

**Workbook references.** Chapters 14, 16, 17 and 19.

**Top tips.** Parts (a)–(c) required the application of knowledge to three issues.

When you write your answers here, you need to try to be as specific as possible about how the procedures should be performed. You will only get marks if your answer describes the procedures in enough detail. You can also think about saying first *what* the procedure is, and then saying *why* you would be performing it, which will help to demonstrate that you understand the purpose of the procedure.

Part (d) focused on written representations. Although this was a purely knowledge-based requirement, this is an area that you may have found difficult – if this is the case, then you will need to review the solution carefully.

**Easy marks.** These were available in parts (a) and (b), since these parts cover areas that should be very familiar to AA students and which you should be well prepared to answer.

---

Marks

(a) **Trade payables and accruals**

Calculate trade payables payment period

Compare total trade payables and list of accruals against prior year

Discuss with management process to quantify understatement of payables

Discuss with management whether any correcting journal adjustment posted

Sample invoices received between 25 March and year end and follow to inclusion in year-end accruals or trade payables correcting journal

Review after-date payments

Review supplier statements reconciliations

Perform a trade payables circularisation

Cut-off testing pre- and post-year end GRN

**Maximum**  6

(b) **Receivables**

For non-responses arrange to send a follow-up circularisation

With the client's permission, telephone the customer and ask for a response

For remaining non-responses, undertake alternative procedures to confirm receivables

For responses with differences, identify any disputed amounts, identify whether these relate to timing differences or whether there are possible errors in the records

Cash in transit should be vouched to post year end cash receipts in the cashbook

Review receivables ledger to identify any possible mispostings

Disputed balances, discuss with management whether a write down is necessary

**Maximum**  5

(c) **Reorganisation**

Review the board minutes where decision taken

Review the announcement to shareholders in late October

Obtain a breakdown and confirm that only direct expenditure from restructuring is included

Review expenditure to ensure retraining costs excluded

Cast the breakdown of the reorganisation provision

Agree costs included to supporting documentation

Obtain a written representation

Review the adequacy of the disclosures

**Maximum**  4

(d) **Written representations**

Written representations are necessary evidence

Required to confirm directors' responsibilities

Required to support other evidence or required by ISAs

Required to confirm management have communicated all deficiencies in internal controls

Letter addressed to the auditor

Throughout fieldwork identify that require written representations

**Maximum**  5

Total  20

(a) **Trade payables and accruals**

 (1) Ask management about the action they have taken to establish the value of the misstatement of trade payables. If they have ascertained the value of the error assess the materiality of it and the impact of it remaining uncorrected.

 (2) Enquire whether any correcting journal entry has been calculated and whether it has been processed in relation to the misstatement.

 (3) For a sample of purchase invoices received between 25 March and the end of 31 March 20X6, verify that they are included within accruals or as part of trade payables via a journal adjustment.

 (4) Reconcile supplier statements to purchase ledger balances, and investigate any reconciling items.

 (5) Calculate and compare the trade payables payment period with prior years. Significant differences should be investigated.

 (6) Compare trade payables and accruals against the previous year and expectations. Investigate any significant differences and corroborate any explanations for differences to supporting evidence.

 (7) Review the cash book payments and bank statements in the period immediately after the year end for evidence of payments relating to current year liabilities. Ensure any found are included in accruals, trade payables or the trade payables journal.

 (8) For a sample of payable balances, perform a trade payables circularisation. Any non-replies should be followed up and reconciling items between the balance confirmed and the trade payables balance should be investigated.

 (9) For a sample of goods received notes before the year end and after the year end, ensure the related invoices have been recorded in the period to which they relate.

 **Note.** Only six valid procedures were needed.

(b) **Receivables**

 (1) For those receivables who don't respond, the team should arrange to send a follow-up circularisation if agreed by the client.

 (2) For non-responses to the follow-up, and after obtaining client consent, the audit senior should telephone the customer and request the customer responds in writing to the circularisation request.

 (3) Where all follow-ups are unsuccessful, alternative procedures must be carried out to confirm receivables, such as reviewing after-date cash receipts for year-end receivables.

 (4) Where responses highlight differences, these should be investigated to establish if any amounts are disputed or require adjustment.

 (5) Where it is found that differences are in relation to disputed invoices, they should be discussed with management and the need for an allowance or write-off assessed.

 (6) For timing differences identified on responses or otherwise (eg cash in transit), these should be agreed to post year end cash receipts in the cash book and bank statement.

 (7) For those responses highlighting an unresolved difference, the receivables ledger should be reviewed for unusual entries that could suggest errors made when posting transactions.

 **Note.** Only five valid procedures were needed.

(c) **Reorganisation**

(1) Verify the announcement to shareholders was actually made in late March by inspecting documentary evidence of the announcement.

(2) Board minutes should also be reviewed to confirm that the decision to reorganise the business was taken pre year end.

(3) Obtain an analysis of the reorganisation provision and confirm that only expenditure attributable to the restructuring is included.

(4) Cast the breakdown of the reorganisation provision to ensure it has been correctly calculated.

(5) Review the expenditure and confirm retraining costs are not included.

(6) Agree costs included within the provision to supporting documentation to confirm the appropriateness and accuracy of items included.

(7) Review the related disclosures in the financial statements to assess whether they comply with the requirements of IAS 37 Provisions, Contingent Liabilities and Contingent Assets.

(8) Obtain a written representation confirming management discussions in relation to the announcement of the reorganisation.

Note. Only four valid procedures were needed.

(d) **Written representations**

Written representations are necessary information that the auditor requires in connection with the audit of the entity's financial statements. Accordingly, similar to responses to inquiries, written representations are audit evidence.

The auditor needs to obtain written representations from management and, where appropriate, those charged with governance that they believe they have fulfilled their responsibility for the preparation of the financial statements and for the completeness of the information provided to the auditor.

Written representations are needed to support other audit evidence relevant to the financial statements or specific assertions in the financial statements, if determined necessary by the auditor or required by other ISAs. This may be necessary for judgemental areas where the auditor has to rely on management explanations.

Written representations can be used to confirm that management have communicated to the auditor all deficiencies in internal controls of which management are aware.

Written representations are normally in the form of a letter, written by the company's management and addressed to the auditor. The letter is usually requested from management but can also be requested from the chief operating officer or chief financial officer. Throughout the fieldwork, the audit team will note any areas where representations may be required.

During the final review stage, the auditors will produce the written representations which the directors will review and then produce it on their letterhead. It will be signed by the directors and dated as at the date the auditor's report is signed, but not after.

BPP
LEARNING
MEDIA

# 158 Hyacinth

## Marking scheme

|  |  | Marks |
|---|---|---|
| (a) | Substantive procedures – valuation of inventory | |
|  | Agree percentage completion recorded at inventory count to final inventory records | 1 |
|  | Confirm costs to invoice/timesheets | 1 |
|  | Inspect post year-end sales invoices for finished goods to assess NRV | 1 |
|  | Discuss basis of WIP valuation with management | 1 |
|  | Inspect WIP valuation with sales prices less costs to complete | 1 |
|  | Review aged inventory reports and discuss allowance | 1 |
|  | Discuss with management basis of valuation for Crocus products | 1 |
|  | Inspect post year-end sales value of Crocus products | 1 |
|  | Confirm adjustment regarding Crocus products | 1 |
|  | Restricted to | 6 |

(b)    Substantive procedures – R&D expenditure

| | |
|---|---:|
| Obtain schedule, cast and agree to trial balance | 1 |
| Review reasonableness of useful lives | 1 |
| Recalculate amortisation and confirm in line with policy | 1 |
| Discuss with management treatment of costs for new products | 1 |
| Agree research costs expensed | 1 |
| For capitalised costs, confirm IAS 38 criteria met | 1 |
| Inspect budgets to confirm adequate resources to complete | 1 |
| Review disclosure and confirm in line with accounting standards | 1 |
| Restricted to | 4 |

(c)    Substantive procedures – accrual for sales tax liability

| | |
|---|---:|
| Obtain schedule/return, cast and agree to trial balance | 1 |
| Recalculate sales tax in relation to sales and agree to return | 1 |
| Recalculate sales tax in relation to purchases and agree to return | 1 |
| Recalculate overall amount due to tax authority | 1 |
| Compare liability to prior year end, investigate differences | 1 |
| Confirm payment to post year-end cashbook and bank statements | 1 |
| Review correspondence with the tax authority for evidence of additional liability | 1 |
| Review disclosure and confirm in line with IAS 37 | 1 |
| Restricted to | 4 |

(d)    Subsequent event

| | |
|---|---:|
| Discussion of amendment | 3 |
| Audit procedures | 3 |
| **Total marks** | **6** |

(a)    **Inventory valuation**

- Obtain the breakdown of WIP and agree a sample of WIP assessed during the inventory count to the WIP schedule, agreeing the percentage completion to that recorded at the inventory count.

- For a sample of inventory items (finished goods and WIP), obtain the relevant cost sheets and agree raw material costs to recent purchase invoices, labour costs to time sheets or payroll records and confirm overheads allocated are of a production related nature.

- Examine post year-end credit notes to determine whether there have been returns which could signify that a write down is required.

- Select a sample of year-end finished goods and compare cost with post year-end sales invoices to ascertain if net realisable value (NRV) is above cost or if an adjustment is required.

- Discuss the basis of WIP valuation with management and assess its reasonableness.

- Select a sample of items included in WIP at the year end and ascertain the final unit cost price by verifying costs to be incurred to completion to relevant supporting documentation. Compare to the unit sales price included in sales invoices post year-end to assess NRV

- Review aged inventory reports and identify any slow moving goods, discuss with management why these items have not been written down or if an allowance is required.

- For the defective batch of product Crocus, review board minutes and discuss with management their plans for selling these goods, and why they believe these goods have a NRV of $90,000.

- If any Crocus products have been sold post year end, review the sales invoice to assess NRV.

- Agree the cost of $450,000 for product Crocus to supporting documentation to confirm the raw material cost, labour cost and any overheads attributed to the cost.

- Confirm if the final adjustment for the damaged product is $360,000 ($450,000 – $90,000) and discuss with management if this adjustment has been made. If so, follow through the write down to confirm.

(b) **Research and development**

- Obtain and cast a schedule of intangible assets, agree the closing balances to the general ledger, trial balance and draft financial statements.

- Discuss with the finance director the rationale for the four-year useful life and consider its reasonableness.

- Recalculate the amortisation charge for a sample of intangible assets which have commenced production and confirm that it is in line with the amortisation policy of straight line over four years and that amortisation only commenced from the point of production.

- For the three new computing software projects, discuss with management the details of each project along with the stage of development and whether it has been capitalised or expensed.

- For those expensed as research, agree the costs incurred to invoices and supporting documentation and to inclusion in profit or loss.

- For those capitalised as development, agree costs incurred to invoices.

- Confirm technically feasible and intention to complete the project by discussion with development managers or review of feasibility reports.

- Review market research reports to confirm Hyacinth Co has the ability to sell the product once complete and probable future economic benefits will arise.

- Review the costs, projected revenue and cash flow budgets for the each of the three projects to confirm Hyacinth Co has adequate resources to complete the development stage and that probable future economic benefits exist. Agree the budgets to supporting documentation.

- Review the disclosures for intangible assets in the draft financial statements to verify that they are in accordance with IAS 38 *Intangible Assets*.

(c) **Sales tax liability**

- Agree the year-end sales tax liability in the trial balance to the tax return/reconciliation submitted to the tax authority and cast the return/reconciliation.

- Agree the quarterly sales tax charged equates to 15% of the last quarter's sales as per the sales day book.

- Recalculate the sales tax incurred as per the reconciliation is equal to 15% of the final quarter's purchases and expenses as per the purchase day book.

- Recalculate the amount payable to the tax authority as being sales tax charged less sales tax incurred.

- Compare the year-end sales tax liability to the prior year balance or budget and investigate any significant differences.

- Agree the subsequent payment to the post year-end cash book and bank statements to confirm completeness and that it has been paid in line with the terms of the tax authority.

- Review any current and post year-end correspondence with the tax authority to assess whether there are any additional outstanding payments due. If so, confirm they are included in the year-end liability.

- Review any disclosures made of the sales tax liability to ensure that it is shown as a current liability and assess whether disclosures are in compliance with accounting standards and legislation.

(d)  **Subsequent event**

A flood has occurred at the off-site warehouse and property, plant and equipment and inventory valued at $0.7 million have been damaged and now have no scrap value. The directors do not believe they are likely to be able to claim on the company's insurance for the damaged assets. This event occurred after the reporting period and is not an event which provides evidence of a condition at the year end and so this is a non-adjusting event.

The damaged assets of $0.7 million are material as they represent 10.9% ($0.7m/$6.4m) of profit before tax and 3.0% ($0.7m/$23.2m) of total assets. As a material non-adjusting event, the assets do not need to be written down to zero in this financial year. However, the directors should consider including a disclosure note detailing the flood and the value of assets impacted.

The following audit procedures should be applied to form a conclusion on any amendment:

- Obtain a schedule showing the damaged property, plant and equipment and agree the carrying amount to the non-current assets register to confirm the total value of affected assets.

- Obtain a schedule of the water damaged inventory, visit the off-site warehouse and physically inspect the impacted inventory. Confirm the quantity of goods present in the warehouse to the schedule; agree the original cost to pre year-end production costs.

- Review the condition of other PPE and inventory to confirm all damaged assets identified.

- Review the damaged property, plant and equipment and inventory and discuss with management the basis for the zero scrap value assessment.

- Discuss with management why they do not believe that they are able to claim on their insurance; if a claim were to be made, then only uninsured losses would require disclosure, and this may be an immaterial amount.

- Discuss with management whether they will disclose the effect of the flood, as a non-adjusting event, in the year-end financial statements.

# 159 Sagittarii & Co

## Marking scheme

|  |  | Marks |
|---|---|---|
| (a) | **Substantive procedures for income** <br> 1 mark per well-described procedure <br> Restricted to | 5 |
| (b) | **Substantive procedures for restructuring provision** <br> 1 mark per well-described procedure <br> Restricted to | 5 |
| (c) | **Substantive procedures for bank loans** <br> 1 mark per well-described procedure <br> Restricted to | 5 |
| (d) | **Impact on auditor's report** <br> Discussion of issue <br> Materiality calculation and assessment <br> Type of modification required <br> Impact on auditor's report | 1 <br> 1 <br> 2 <br> 1 <br> 5 |
| **Total marks** | | **20** |

### (a) Substantive procedures for Vega Vista Co's income

- Obtain a schedule of all Vega Vista Co's income and cast to confirm completeness and accuracy of the balance and agree to the trial balance.

- Compare the individual categories of income of festival ticket sales, sundry sales and donations against prior years and investigate any significant differences.

- For the annual festival, construct a proof-in-total calculation of the number of tickets sold, approximately 15,000, multiplied by the ticket price of $35. Compare this to the income recorded and discuss any significant differences with management.

- For tickets sold on the day of the festival reconcile from ticket stubs the number of tickets sold multiplied by $35 and agree these sales to cash banked in the bank statement.

- Discuss with management their procedures for ensuring advance ticket sales for the

- September 20X5 festival are excluded from income and instead recognised as deferred income in the statement of financial position.

- Select a sample of advance ticket sales made online, agree that the transaction has been excluded from current year income and follow through to inclusion in deferred income.

- Agree journal entry to transfer prior year deferred income relating to the 20X4 festival to current year income to the ledger and agree figures to prior year financial statements.

- For sundry sales, obtain a breakdown of the income received per stall and agree to supporting documentation provided by each stall holder. Recalculate the fixed percentage received is as per the agreement/contract made with Vega Vista Co.

- Compare sundry sales per stall holder to prior year sales data and investigate any significant differences.

- For monthly donations, trace a sample of donations from sign up documentation to the bank statements, cash book and income listing to ensure that they are recorded completely and accurately.

- For a sample of new donors in the year, agree the monthly sum and start date from their completed forms and trace to the monthly donations received account and agree to the cash book and bank statements.

(b) **Substantive procedures for Canopus Co's restructuring provision**

- Cast the breakdown of the restructuring provision to ensure it is correctly calculated and agree the total to the trial balance.

- Review the board minutes where the decision to restructure the production process was taken and confirm the decision was made in March 20X5.

- Review the announcement to shareholders and employees in late March, to confirm that this was announced before the year end.

- Obtain a breakdown of the restructuring provision and confirm that only direct expenditure relating to the restructuring is included.

- Review the expenditure to confirm that there are no retraining costs of existing staff included.

- For the costs included within the provision, including acquisitions of plant and machinery, agree to supporting documentation, such as purchase invoices, to confirm validity and value of items included.

- Review post year end payments/invoices relating to the expenditure and compare the actual costs incurred to the amounts provided to assess whether the amount of the provision is reasonable.

- Obtain a written representation confirming management discussions in relation to the announcement of the restructuring and to confirm the completeness of the provision.

- Review the adequacy of the disclosures of the restructuring provision in the financial statements and assess whether these are in accordance with IAS® 37 Provisions,

- Contingent Liabilities and Contingent Assets.

(c)    **Substantive procedures for Canopus Co's bank loans**

- Obtain a schedule of opening and closing loans detailing any changes during the year. Cast the schedule to confirm its accuracy and agree the closing balances to the trial balance and draft financial statements.

- For the new loan taken out in the year, review the loan agreement to confirm the amount borrowed, the repayment terms and the interest rate applicable.

- For the new loan taken out in the year, agree the loan proceeds of $4.8 million per the loan agreement to the cash book and bank statements.

- For loans repaid, agree the final settlement amount per bank correspondence to payments out during the year in the cash book and bank statements.

- Agree the quarterly repayment of the new loan of $150,000 paid on 31 March 20X5 to the cash book and bank statement.

- Recalculate the split of the loan repayment made on 31 March 20X5 between interest and principal, recalculate interest and agree to inclusion in statement of profit or loss, and outstanding loan balance reduced by principal amount repaid.

- Review the bank correspondence and loan agreements for confirmation of any early settlement charges incurred on the loans repaid. Agree that these were charged to the statement of profit or loss as a finance charge.

- Obtain direct confirmation at the year-end from the loan provider of the outstanding balances and any security provided. Agree confirmed amounts to the loans schedule.

- Review all loan agreements for details of covenants and recalculate all covenants to identify any potential or actual breaches.

- Review the disclosure of non-current liabilities in the draft financial statements, including any security provided and assess whether these are in accordance with accounting standards and local legislation. Additionally, confirm that the split of current and non-current loans in the financial statements is correct.

(d)    **Impact on Auditor's report**

The restructuring provision of $2.1 million includes $270,000 of costs which do not meet the criteria for inclusion as per IAS 37 *Provisions, Contingent Liabilities and Contingent Assets*. Hence by including this amount the provision and expenses for this year are overstated and profits understated.

The error is material as it represents 2.3% of total equity and liabilities/ total assets (0·27m/11.6m) and hence the finance director should adjust the financial statements by removing this cost from the provision and instead expensing it to profit or loss as it is incurred. The argument that the provision is judgemental and has been deemed reasonable by the board is not valid. IAS 37 has strict criteria for what can and cannot be included within a restructuring provision. For example, training costs for existing staff must be specifically excluded.

If the finance director refuses to amend this error the audit opinion will be modified due to a material misstatement. As management has not complied with IAS 37 and the error is material but not pervasive, a qualified opinion would be appropriate.

A basis for qualified opinion paragraph would be included after the opinion paragraph and would explain the material misstatement in relation to the incorrect treatment of the restructuring provision and the effect on the financial statements. The opinion paragraph would be qualified 'except for'.

# 160 Encore

## Marking scheme

| | | | Marks |
|---|---|---|---|
| (a) | **Substantive procedures for vehicle additions and disposals** | | |
| | 1 mark per well-described procedure | | |
| | Restricted to | | <u>6</u> |
| (b) | **Substantive procedures for valuation of trade receivables** | | |
| | 1 mark per well-described procedure | | |
| | Restricted to | | <u>5</u> |
| (c) | **Substantive procedures for breach of regulations** | | |
| | 1 mark per well-described procedure | | |
| | Restricted to | | <u>4</u> |
| (d) | **Impact on auditor's report** | | |
| | Discussion of issue | 1 | |
| | Materiality calculation and assessment | 1 | |
| | Type of modification required | 2 | |
| | Impact on auditor's report | 1 | |
| | | | <u>5</u> |
| **Total marks** | | | <u><u>20</u></u> |

(a) **Vehicles additions and disposals**

- Cast the schedule of additions to vehicles, cast it and agree the total to the disclosure note for property, plant and equipment. Agree the cost of the vehicles given in part-exchange to the disclosure note to confirm that they have been removed from cost carried forward.

- For a sample of new vehicles on the schedule of additions agree the cost to the purchase invoice, ensuring that the recorded cost includes the cash amount paid plus the trade-in allowance for the old vehicle. Confirm that the invoice is made out to Encore Co.

- Physically inspect a sample of additions, confirming that the registration number of the vehicle agrees to that on the non-current assets register.

- Review the non-current assets register to confirm that the 20 old vehicles were removed and that the 20 new vehicles were included.

- Recalculate the loss on disposal of $1.1m ($1.8 - ($4.6m - $3.9m)) and agree to the trial balance and statement of profit or loss.

- Agree the cash payment of $3.9m to the cash book and bank statement.

- Recalculate the depreciation expense, confirming that the depreciation expense was based on the old vehicles until 1 February and on the cost of the new vehicles after that date.

- Recalculate accumulated depreciation on the vehicles disposed of and confirm that this has been removed from accumulated depreciation carried forward.

- In light of the loss on disposal, review depreciation rates on existing vehicles to establish if the carrying amount of other vehicles may be overstated.

- Discuss with management Encore Co's history of vehicle replacement to establish if vehicles are being used for the entire period of their estimated useful life.

- Discuss with management why trade-in allowances were so much lower than the carrying amounts of the vehicles to provide further evidence as to whether depreciation policies are reasonable.

- Review the notes to the financial statements to ensure that disclosure of the additions and disposals is in accordance with IAS 16 Property, Plant and Equipment.

(b) **Valuation of trade receivables**

- Review the aged receivables listing to identify slow moving or old balances. Discuss the status of these balances with the credit controller to assess whether the customers are likely to pay or if an allowance for receivables is required.

- Review whether there are any after-date cash receipts for slow moving/old receivable balances.

- Review correspondence with customers in order to identify any balances which are in dispute or unlikely to be paid and discuss with management whether any allowance is required.

- Review board minutes to identify whether there are any significant concerns in relation to outstanding receivables balances and assess whether the allowance is reasonable.

- Obtain a breakdown of the allowance for trade receivables. Recalculate it and compare it to any potentially irrecoverable balances to assess if the allowance is adequate.

- Review the payment history for evidence of slow paying by any customers who were granted credit in the period when there was no credit controller and who may not, therefore, have been properly scrutinised.

- Discuss with the finance director the rationale for maintaining the allowance at the same level in light of the increase in the receivables collection period and the absence of a credit controller.

- Inspect post year-end sales returns/credit notes and consider whether an additional allowance against receivables is required.

(c) **Potential breach of regulations**

- Review correspondence with the transport authority to establish details of the complaint and the number of times the breach has allegedly occurred.

- Enquire of the directors why they are unwilling to provide or make disclosure, whether they accept that any breaches took place but believe that the effect is immaterial or whether they dispute their occurrence.

- Review Encore Co's policies and procedures to record driving hours and rest periods and compare to the regulations to determine the likelihood that breaches have occurred and how frequently.

- Review correspondence with the transport authority to establish if there have been discussions about other instances of potential non-compliance.

- Review correspondence with Encore Co's legal advisers or, with the client's permission, contact the lawyers to establish their assessment of the likelihood of the breach being proven and any fines that would be payable.

- Review the board minutes to ascertain management's view as to the likelihood of payment to the transport authority.

- Obtain a written representation to the effect that the directors are not aware of any other breaches of laws or regulations that would require a provision or disclosure in the financial statements.

- Inspect the post year-end cash book and bank statements to identify whether any fines have been paid.

(d) **Auditor's report**

The breaches in regulations and the initial investigation into the breaches occurred before the year end. The announcement by the authorities that they are taking legal action provides further evidence regarding these conditions which existed at the year-end date therefore IAS 10 Events after the Reporting Period would classify this as an adjusting subsequent event. As it seems probable that the fine will be payable, a provision must be included rather than merely the disclosure. Failure to make such a provision will cause profits to be overstated and provisions to be understated.

The potential fine of $850,000 (17 × $50,000) is 16% ($850k/$5.3m) of profit before tax and 2.1% ($850k/$40.1m) of total assets. It is therefore material.

If the directors refuse to make a provision, then Velo & Co should issue a modified opinion on the grounds that there is a material misstatement of profit and liabilities. As this is material but not pervasive a qualified opinion would be appropriate.

A basis for qualified opinion paragraph would be included after the opinion paragraph. This would explain the material misstatement in relation to the non-recognition of the provision and the effect on the financial statements. The opinion paragraph would be qualified 'except for'.

# 161 Airsoft Co

**Workbook references.** Chapters 11, 15, 16, 17 and 20.

**Top tips.** This question tests audit evidence (including audit software) and has several requirements which are presented alongside some scenario information. When generating your audit procedures it is essential that you give audit procedures that address the specific issues relating, for example, to the closing of the purchase ledger, rather than simply preparing generic procedures on payables.

**Easy marks.** The audit of bank balances has been tested reasonably regularly and so you should have found part (c) straightforward.

**Examining team's comments.** This area of the syllabus requires a description of the work and evidence obtained by the auditor required to meet the objectives of audit engagements and the application of International Standards on Auditing.

A key requirement of this part of the syllabus is an ability to describe relevant audit procedures for a particular class of transactions or event. Overall performance in this key syllabus area in this exam session was very disappointing. The March 2017 exam contained a number of questions in this syllabus area covering a variety of areas including trade payables and accruals, bank balances, directors' remuneration, property plant and equipment, inventory and receivables, illustrating that candidates must be prepared to tailor their knowledge of substantive testing to any area of the financial statements. In most cases candidates remain unable to tailor their knowledge of general substantive procedures to the specific issues in the question requirements, with many providing tests of controls rather than substantive procedures, or, provided vague tests. As addressed in previous reports by the examining team candidates must strive to understand substantive procedures. Learning a generic list of tests will not translate to exam success – procedures must be tailored to the specific requirements of the question.

Marks

(a) **Substantive procedures for completeness of Airsoft Co's payables and accruals**

| | |
|---|---|
| – Compare to prior year and investigate differences | 1 |
| – Post y/e cash book payments to ledger | 1 |
| – Supplier statement reconciliations | 1 |
| – Trade payables circularisation | 1 |
| – Review after date invoices and credit notes | 1 |
| – Enquiry of management process for identifying accruals | 1 |
| Maximum | **4** |

(b) **Audit software procedures over trade payables and accruals**

| | |
|---|---|
| – Calculate trade payables payment period | 1 |
| – Cast the payables and accruals schedule | 1 |
| – Select sample for circularisation | 1 |
| – Recalculate accruals | 1 |
| – Cut-off testing on GRNs | 1 |
| Maximum | **3** |

(c) **Substantive procedures in relation to year-end bank balances**

| | |
|---|---|
| – Bank confirmation letter | 1 |
| – Agree to bank reconciliation and TB | 1 |
| – Cast bank reconciliations | 1 |
| – Testing on bank reconciliations (1 mark per relevant procedure) | 4 |
| – Review cash book and bank statements for window dressing | 1 |
| – Examine bank letter for evidence of security granted | 1 |
| – Review financial statement disclosure | 1 |
| Maximum | **5** |

(d) **Substantive procedures in relation to directors' remuneration**

| | |
|---|---|
| – Cast schedule of remuneration | 1 |
| – Agree payments to payroll records | 1 |
| – Confirm bonus payments to cash book | 1 |
| – Review board minutes for additional remuneration | 1 |
| – Review board minutes for approval | 1 |
| – Obtain written representation confirming completeness | 1 |
| – Review financial statement disclosure | 1 |
| Maximum | **3** |

(e) **Key audit matters (KAM)**

| | |
|---|---|
| – Definition of KAM | 1 |
| – Purpose of KAM | 1 |
| – Significant matters and areas of judgement | 1 |
| – Examples of KAM | 2 |
| – KAM disclosure | 1 |
| Maximum | **5** |
| Total | **20** |

(a) Trade payables and accruals

- Compare the total trade payables and list of accruals against prior year and investigate any significant differences.

- Select a sample of post year-end payments from the cash book; if they relate to the current year, follow through to the purchase ledger or accruals listing to ensure they are recorded in the correct period.

- Obtain supplier statements and reconcile these to the purchase ledger balances, and investigate any reconciling items.

- Select a sample of payable balances and perform a trade payables' circularisation, follow up any non-replies and any reconciling items between the balance confirmed and the trade payables' balance.

- Review after date invoices and credit notes to ensure no further items need to be accrued.

- Enquire of management their process for identifying goods received but not invoiced or logged in the purchase ledger and ensure that it is reasonable to ensure completeness of payables.

(b) Audit software procedures using computer assisted audit techniques (CAATs)

- The audit team can use audit software to calculate payables payment period for the year-to-date to compare against the prior year to identify whether the payables payment period has changed in line with trading levels and expectations. If the payables payment period has decreased, this may be an indication that payables are understated.

- Audit software can be used to cast the payables and accruals listings to confirm the completeness and accuracy of trade payables and accruals.

- Audit software can be used to select a representative sample of items for further testing of payables balances.

- Audit software can be utilised to recalculate the accruals for goods received not invoiced at the year end.

- CAATs can be used to undertake cut-off testing by assessing whether the dates of the last GRNs recorded relate to pre year end; and that any with a date of 1 July 20X5 onwards were excluded from trade payables.

(c) Substantive procedures for bank balances

- Obtain a bank confirmation letter from Airsoft Co's bankers for all of its bank accounts.

- Agree all accounts listed on the bank confirmation letter to Airsoft Co's bank reconciliations and the trial balance to ensure completeness of bank balances.

- For all bank accounts, obtain Airsoft Co's bank account reconciliation and cast to ensure arithmetical accuracy.

- Agree the balance per the bank reconciliation to an original year-end bank statement and to the bank confirmation letter.

- Agree the reconciliations balance per the cash book to the year-end cash book.

- Trace all the outstanding lodgements to the pre year-end cash book, post year-end bank statement and also to the paying-in-book pre year end.

- Trace all unpresented cheques through to a pre year-end cash book and post year-end statement. For any unusual amounts or significant delays, obtain explanations from management.

BPP
LEARNING
MEDIA

- Examine any old unpresented cheques to assess if they need to be written back into the purchase ledger as they are no longer valid to be presented.

- Review the cash book and bank statements for any unusual items or large transfers around the year end, as this could be evidence of window dressing.

- Examine the bank confirmation letter for details of any security provided by Airsoft Co or any legal right of set-off as this may require disclosure.

- Review the financial statements to ensure that the disclosure of bank balances is complete and accurate.

(d) Substantive procedures for directors' remuneration

- Obtain a schedule of the directors' remuneration, split by salary and bonus paid in December and cast the schedule to ensure accuracy.

- Agree a sample of the individual monthly salary payments and the bonus payment in December to the payroll records.

- Confirm the amount of each bonus paid by agreeing to the cash book and bank statements.

- Review the board minutes to identify whether any additional payments relating to this year have been agreed for any directors.

- Agree the amounts paid per director to board minutes to ensure the sums included are genuine.

- Obtain a written representation from management confirming the completeness of directors' remuneration including the bonus.

- Review the disclosures made regarding the directors' remuneration and assess whether these are in compliance with local legislation.

(e) Key audit matters

Key audit matters (KAM) are those matters which, in the auditor's professional judgement, were of most significance in the audit of the financial statements of the current period. Key audit matters are selected from matters communicated with those charged with governance.

The purpose of including key audit matters in the auditor's report is to help users in understanding the entity, and to provide a basis for the users to discuss with management and those charged with governance about matters relating to the entity and the financial statements. A key part of the definition is that these are the most significant matters. Identifying the most significant matters involves using the auditor's professional judgement.

ISA 701 *Communicating Key Audit Matters in the Independent Auditor's Report* suggests that in determining key audit matters the auditor should take the following into account:

- Areas of higher assessed risk of material misstatement, or significant risks.

- Significant auditor judgements relating to areas in the financial statements which involved significant management judgement.

- The effect on the audit of significant events or transactions which occurred during the period.

The description of each KAM in the Key Audit Matters section of the auditor's report should include a reference to the related disclosures in the financial statements and covers why the matter was considered to be one of most significance in the audit and therefore determined to be a KAM; and how the matter was addressed in the audit.

# 162 Gooseberry Co

**Workbook references.** Chapters 12, 17 and 20.

**Top tips.** This question tests audit evidence in relation to different types of non-current assets, and then links in with auditor reporting.

Part (a) is on development costs and IAS 38 *Intangible assets*. This is a standard that you will need to be familiar with, but this is a difficult requirement at AA level. Most of the audit procedures come from the financial reporting, so you can use this to help generate your answers.

For part (b), you can use the scenario as a starting point for your description of the procedures to perform to determine whether the depreciation charge is fairly stated.

Part (c) was another detailed requirement on audit evidence, and should be approached by thinking practically about how these bonuses should have been processed, and then considering how you would test them. The bonuses have been awarded to the directors and so these amounts would be material by their nature. Furthermore the scenario tells you that disclosure is required by local legislation and so it is important that your substantive procedures include reviewing whether the required disclosures have been made.

Part (d) probably came as a relief. This is a familiar requirement on the auditor's report and should have been within your reach.

**Easy marks.** Part (d) was likely to have been the easiest part of the question; the marks for materiality were among the simplest to obtain.

**Examining team's comments.** This 20-mark question was based on Gooseberry Co, a company which develops and manufactures health and beauty products and distributes these to wholesale customers. This question tested candidates' knowledge of substantive procedures for research and development, depreciation and directors' bonuses, and, auditor's reports.

Part (a) for five marks required candidates to describe substantive procedures the auditor should perform to obtain sufficient and appropriate audit evidence in relation to Gooseberry's research and development expenditure. Performance on this requirement was mixed.

One mark was awarded for each well described substantive procedure. Hence for a five mark requirement, candidates should have provided at least five substantive procedures. Disappointingly this was not the case, as some answers only contained one or two procedures for each area and these were often not well described, resulting in a maximum of ½ mark each. Candidates are severely limiting the opportunity to score marks and are reminded to ensure that they employ effective exam technique.

Many procedures were vague, often not giving the source for the test, or, stating 'ensure' without explaining how the test would achieve this.

Part (b) for five marks required the candidates to describe substantive procedures the auditor should perform to obtain sufficient and appropriate audit evidence in relation to depreciation. Performance on this requirement was disappointing.

As in part (a), one mark was awarded for each well described substantive procedure. Disappointingly often the substantive procedures were either not well described, or, were not related to depreciation. A significant number of candidates did not clearly answer the specific requirement of the question to describe depreciation substantive procedures.

In general there was clear evidence of a lack of tailoring of knowledge to the specific scenario provided. Candidates have clearly learned that the depreciation charge should be compared to the prior year. However, this substantive procedure is not relevant if there is a change in the useful life of the assets in the year as was detailed in this scenario. As addressed in previous examining team's reports candidates must strive to understand substantive procedures. Learning a generic list of tests will not translate to exam success, as they must be applied to the question requirement.

Part (c) for five marks required the candidates to describe substantive procedures the auditor should perform to obtain sufficient and appropriate audit evidence in relation to the directors' bonuses. Performance on this requirement for many candidates was pleasing.

BPP
LEARNING
MEDIA

Part (d) for five marks required a discussion of an issue and the impact on the auditor's report if the issue remained unresolved. The issue presented related to $440,000 of development costs which had been incorrectly capitalised by the client.

Auditor's report questions have shown a gradual improvement in recent exams so it is disappointing that performance for this question was mixed.

A number of candidates described the impact on the auditor's report if the issue was resolved and also if the issue remained unresolved. The question clearly asked for the impact if the issue remained unresolved. Once again, candidates are advised to read the question requirements carefully.

## Marking scheme

|  |  | Marks |
|---|---|---|
| **(a)** | **Substantive procedures – Research & development** | |
|  | Cast and agree closing balance to TB and draft FS | 1 |
|  | Discuss amortisation policy with management and assess reasonableness | 1 |
|  | Recalculate amortisation charge/commenced in line with production | 1 |
|  | Discuss new projects and stage of development | 1 |
|  | For research costs agree invoices and to profit or loss | 1 |
|  | For development costs agree to invoices and confirm meets criteria | 1 |
|  | Review market research to confirm ability to sell | 1 |
|  | Review disclosures in line with IAS 38 | 1 |
|  | **Restricted to** | **5** |
| **(b)** | **Substantive procedures – depreciation** | |
|  | Discuss reasons for change with management | 1 |
|  | Compare to industry averages and knowledge of business | 1 |
|  | Review capex budgets to assess revised lives appropriate | 1 |
|  | Agree new rates to non-current asset register | 1 |
|  | Recalculate profit/loss on disposal and consider new rates | 1 |
|  | Recalculate depreciation charge for a sample of assets | 1 |
|  | Perform a proof-in-total on depreciation charge | 1 |
|  | Review disclosure is in line with IAS 16 | 1 |
|  | **Restricted to** | **5** |
| **(c)** | **Substantive procedures – directors' bonuses** | |
|  | Cast schedule of bonuses and agree to TB | 1 |
|  | Confirm bonus accrual as current liability | 1 |
|  | Agree bonus payments to payroll records | 1 |
|  | Recalculate bonus payments in line with contracts | 1 |
|  | Confirm post year-end payment to bank statement | 1 |
|  | Review board minutes for additional sums | 1 |
|  | Obtain written representation confirming completeness | 1 |
|  | Review disclosures in line with local legislation | 1 |
|  | **Restricted to** | **5** |
| **(d)** | **Impact on auditor's report** | |
|  | Discussion of issue | 1 |
|  | Materiality calculation and conclusion | 1 |
|  | Type of modification required | 2 |
|  | Impact on auditor's report | 1 |
|  |  | **5** |
| **Total marks** | | **20** |

(a) **Substantive procedures for research and development**

- Obtain and cast a schedule of intangible assets, detailing opening balances, amounts capitalised in the current year, amortisation and closing balances.

- Agree the closing balances to the general ledger, trial balance and draft financial statements.

- Discuss with the finance director the rationale for the three-year useful life and consider its reasonableness.

- Recalculate the amortisation charge for a sample of intangible assets which have commenced production and confirm it is in line with the amortisation policy of straight line over three years and that amortisation only commenced from the point of production.

- For the nine new projects, discuss with management the details of each project along with the stage of development and whether it has been capitalised or expensed.

- For those expensed as research, agree the costs incurred to invoices and supporting documentation and to inclusion in profit or loss.

- For those capitalised as development, agree costs incurred to invoices and confirm technically feasible by discussion with development managers or review of feasibility reports.

- Review market research reports to confirm Gooseberry Co has the ability to sell the product once complete and probable future economic benefits will arise.

- Review the disclosures for intangible assets in the draft financial statements to verify that they are in accordance with IAS 38 *Intangible Assets*.

(b) **Substantive procedures for depreciation**

- Discuss with management the rationale for the changes to property, plant and equipment (PPE) depreciation rates, useful lives, residual values and depreciation methods and ascertain how these changes were arrived at.

- Confirm the reasonableness of these changes, by comparing the revised depreciation rates, useful lives and methods applied to PPE to industry averages and knowledge of the business.

- Review the capital expenditure budgets for the next few years to assess whether the revised asset lives correspond with the planned period until replacement of the relevant asset categories.

- Review the non-current asset register to assess if the revised depreciation rates have been applied.

- Review and recalculate profits and losses on disposal of assets sold/scrapped in the year, to assess the reasonableness of the revised depreciation rates.

- Select a sample of PPE and recalculate the depreciation charge to ensure that the non-current assets register is correct and ensure that new depreciation rates have been appropriately applied.

- Obtain a breakdown of depreciation by asset categories, compare to prior year; where significant changes have occurred, discuss with management and assess whether this change is reasonable.

- For asset categories where there have been a minimal number of additions and disposals, perform a proof in total calculation for the depreciation charged on PPE, discuss with management if significant fluctuations arise.

- Review the disclosure of the depreciation charges and policies in the draft financial statements and ensure it is in line with IAS 16 *Property, Plant and Equipment*.

(c) **Substantive procedures for directors' bonuses**

- Obtain a schedule of the directors' bonus paid in February 20X8 and cast the schedule to ensure accuracy and agree amount disclosed in the financial statements.

- Review the schedule of current liabilities and confirm the bonus accrual is included as a year-end liability.

- Agree the individual bonus payments to the payroll records.

- Recalculate the bonus payments and agree the criteria, including the exclusion of intangible assets, to supporting documentation and the percentage rates to be paid to the directors' service contracts.

- Confirm the amount of each bonus paid post year end by agreeing to the cash book and bank statements.

- Agree the amounts paid per director to board minutes to ensure the sums included in the current year financial statements are fully accrued and disclosed.

- Review the board minutes to identify whether any additional payments relating to this year have been agreed for any directors.

- Obtain a written representation from management confirming the completeness of directors' remuneration including the bonus.

- Review the disclosures made regarding the bonus paid to directors and assess whether these are in compliance with local legislation.

(d) **Impact on auditor's report**

One of the new health and beauty products Gooseberry Co has developed in the year does not meet the recognition criteria under IAS 38 *Intangible Assets* for capitalisation but has been included within intangible assets. This is contrary to IAS 38, as if the criteria are not met, then this project is research expenditure and should be expensed to the statement of profit or loss rather than capitalised.

The error is material as it represents 6.9% of profit before tax (0.44m/6.4m) and 1.2% of net assets (0.44m/37.2m) and hence management should adjust the financial statements by removing this amount from intangible assets and charging it to the statement of profit or loss instead. IAS 38 requires costs to date to be expensed; if the project meets the recognition criteria in 20X9, then only from that point can any new costs incurred be capitalised. Any costs already expensed cannot be written back to assets.

If management refuses to amend this error, then the auditor's opinion will need to be modified. As management has not complied with IAS 38 and the error is material but not pervasive, then a qualified opinion would be necessary.

A basis for qualified opinion paragraph would be needed after the opinion paragraph and would explain the material misstatement in relation to the incorrect treatment of research and development and the effect on the financial statements. The opinion paragraph would be qualified 'except for'.

# 163 Spadefish

## Marking scheme

| | | Marks |
|---|---|---:|
| (a) | **Audit procedures – Trade receivables circularisation** | |
| | Albacore Co | 3 |
| | Flounder Co | 3 |
| | Menhaden Co | 3 |
| | **Restricted to** | **8** |
| | | |
| (b) | **Substantive procedures – Allowance for trade receivables** | |
| | Discuss the rationale and reasonableness with the finance director | 1 |
| | Obtain breakdown of opening allowance and confirm recovered | 1 |
| | Inspect the aged receivables listing and discuss old or slow moving balances | 1 |
| | Perform cash after-date testing on identified slow moving and old balances | 1 |
| | Review customer correspondence for evidence of disputed balances | 1 |
| | Inspect board minutes for balances which may not be recovered | 1 |
| | Recalculate potential level of irrecoverable balance and compare to allowance and discuss differences | 1 |
| | **Restricted to** | **4** |
| (c) | **Going concern indicators** | |
| | Withdrawal of credit – impact explained | 1 |
| | Loss of main supplier – impact explained | 1 |
| | Overdraft facility due for renewal – impact explained | 1 |
| | No final dividend – impact explained | 1 |
| | **Restricted to** | **3** |
| (d) | **Going concern procedures** | |
| | Obtain cash flow forecast and assess assumptions | 1 |
| | Perform sensitivity analysis on cash flow forecast | 1 |
| | Evaluate management's plans for future actions | 1 |
| | Review post year-end order book to assess levels of trade | 1 |
| | Review agreements with the bank to determine whether any covenants breached | 1 |

|                                                                              | Marks |
| ---------------------------------------------------------------------------- | :---: |
| Review bank correspondence for evidence of renewal                           | 1     |
| Review correspondence with suppliers for dispute/legal action                | 1     |
| Inspect contracts with supplier to confirm supply                            | 1     |
| Obtain confirmation from company lawyers about any legal action              | 1     |
| Review post year-end board minutes for any indications of financial difficulties | 1 |
| Review management accounts to assess if in line with cash flow               | 1     |
| Review financial statement disclosure                                        | 1     |
| Consider if going concern basis is appropriate                               | 1     |
| Obtain a written representation                                              | 1     |
| **Restricted to**                                                           | 5     |
| **Total marks**                                                             | **20** |

(a)   **Exceptions in the receivables circularisation**

The following steps should be undertaken in regard to the exceptions arising in the positive receivables circularisation:

**Albacore Co**

- For the non-response from Albacore Co, with the client's permission, the team should arrange to send a follow-up circularisation.

- If Albacore Co does not respond to the follow up, then with the client's permission, the auditor should telephone the customer and ask whether they are able to respond in writing to the circularisation request.

- If there is still no response, then the auditor should undertake alternative procedures to confirm the balance owing from Albacore Co. Such as detailed testing of the balance by agreeing to sales invoices and goods dispatched notes (GDN).

**Flounder Co**

- For the response from Flounder Co, with a difference of $5,850 the auditor should identify any disputed amounts, and identify whether these relate to timing differences or whether there are possible errors in the records of Trigger

- If the difference is due to timing, such as cash in transit, this should be agreed to post year-end cash receipts in the cash book.

- If the difference relates to goods in transit, then this should be agreed to a pre year-end GDN.

**Menhaden Co**

- The reason for the credit balance with Menhaden should be discussed with the credit controller of finance department to understand how a credit balance has arisen.

- Review the payables ledger to identify if Menhaden is a supplier as well as a customer; if so, a purchase invoice may have been posted in error to the receivables rather than payables ledger.

- If the difference is due to credit notes, this should be agreed to pre year-end credit notes dispatched around the year-end date.

- The receivables ledger should be reviewed to identify any possible mis-postings as this could be a reason for the difference with Menhaden Co.

(b) **Substantive procedures for allowance for trade receivables**

- Discuss with the finance director the rationale for not providing against receivables and consider the reasonableness of the allowance.

- Obtain a breakdown of the opening allowance of $125,000 and consider if the receivables provided for in the prior year have been fully recovered as a result of the additional credit control procedures or if they have now been fully written off.

- Inspect the aged trade receivables ledger to identify any slow moving or old receivable balances and discuss the status of these balances with the credit controllers to assess whether they are likely to be received.

- Review whether there are any after any after-date cash receipts for identified slow moving/old receivables balances.

- Review customer correspondence to identify any balances which are in dispute or are unlikely to be paid and confirm if these have been considered when determining the allowance.

- Inspect board minutes to identify whether there are any significant concerns in relation to payments by customers and assess if these have been considered when determining the allowance.

- Recalculate the potential level of trade receivables which are not recoverable and compare to allowance and discuss differences with management.

(c) **Going concern indicators**

Marlin Co has paid some of its suppliers considerably later than usual and only after many reminders; hence some of them have withdrawn credit terms meaning the company must pay cash on delivery. This suggests that the company was struggling to meet their liability as they fell due and will also put significant additional pressure on the company's cash flow, because the company will have to pay for goods on delivery but is likely to have to wait for cash from its receivables due to credit terms.

Marlin Co's main supplier who provides over 60% of the company's specialist equipment has just stopped trading. If the equipment is highly specialised, there is a risk that Marlin Co may not be able to obtain these products from other suppliers which would impact on the company's ability to trade. More likely, there are other suppliers available but they may be more expensive or may not offer favourable credit terms which will increase the outflows of Marlin Co and worsen the cash flow position.

Marlin Co's overdraft has grown significantly during the year and is for renewal within the next month. If the bank does not renew the overdraft and the company is unable to obtain alternative finance, then it may not be able to continue to meet its liabilities as they fall due, especially if suppliers continue to demand cash on delivery, and the company may not be able to continue to trade.

In order to conserve cash, Marlin Co has decided not to pay a final dividend for the year ended 30 April 20X5. This may result in shareholders losing faith in the company and they may attempt to sell their shares; in addition, they are highly unlikely to invest further equity and Marlin Co may need to raise finance to repay their overdraft.

(d) **Going concern procedures**

- Obtain the company's cash flow forecast and review the cash in and outflows. Assess the assumptions for reasonableness and discuss the findings with management to understand if the company will have sufficient cash flows.

- Perform a sensitivity analysis on the cash flows to understand the margin of safety the company has in terms of its net cash in/outflow.

- Evaluate management's plans for future actions, including their contingency plans in relation to ongoing financing and plans for generating revenue, and consider the feasibility of these plans.

- Review the company's post year-end sales and order book to assess if the levels of trade are likely to increase and if the revenue figures in the cash flow forecast are reasonable.

- Review any agreements with the bank to determine whether any covenants have been breached, especially in relation to the overdraft.

- Review any bank correspondence to assess the likelihood of the bank renewing the overdraft facility.

- Review post year-end correspondence with suppliers to identify if any have threatened legal action or any others have refused to supply goods.

- Inspect any contracts or correspondence with suppliers to confirm supply of the company's specialist equipment. If no new supplier has been confirmed, discuss with management their plans to ensure the company can continue to meet customer demand.

- Enquire of the lawyers of Marlin Co as to the existence of any litigation.

- Perform audit tests in relation to subsequent events to identify any items which might indicate or mitigate the risk of going concern not being appropriate.

- Review the post year-end board minutes to identify any other issues which might indicate fur the company.

- Review post year-end management accounts to assess if in line with cash flow forecast.

- Consider whether any additional disclosures as required by IAS 1 *Presentation of Financial Statements* in relation to material uncertainties over going concern should be made in the financial statements.

- Consider whether the going concern basis is appropriate for the preparation of the financial statements.

- Obtain a written representation confirming the directors' view that Marlin Co is a going concern.

## Chestnut

164    The correct answers are:

| | | |
|---|---|---|
| Review whether any payments have subsequently been made by this customer since the audit fieldwork was completed | PERFORM | |
| Match the total of the aged receivables listing to the sales ledger control account | | DO NOT PERFORM |
| Vouch the balance owed by the customer at the year end to sales invoices | | DO NOT PERFORM |
| Review the latest customer correspondence with regards to an assessment of the likelihood of the customer making payment | PERFORM | |

The audit concern here is that receivables are overstated as the balance from this customer does not appear to be recoverable. Audit procedures should therefore focus on the valuation of receivables. Vouching the balance owed by the customer at the year end to sales invoices will provide audit evidence in relation to the existence, rights and obligations of receivables, but not their valuation. Matching the total of the aged receivables listing to the sales ledger control account will provide evidence of completeness.

165 The correct answer is:

| Material | Financial statement impact |
|---|---|
| Yes | Gross profit may be overstated |

Chestnut & Co was only appointed as auditors subsequent to Ash's year end and hence did not attend the year-end inventory count. Therefore, it has not been able to gather sufficient and appropriate audit evidence with regards to the completeness and existence of inventory. This may mean that closing inventory is over- or understated and this will have a resultant impact on gross profit and current assets.

Inventory is a material amount as it represents 21.3% (0.51/2.4m) of profit before tax and 5% (0.51/10.1m) of revenue.

166 The correct answers are:

Review the internal auditor's reports of the inventory count to identify the level of adjustments made to the records, in order to assess the reasonableness of relying on the inventory records for the purpose of the year-end audit.

Perform test counts of inventory in the warehouse and compare these first to the inventory records, and then from inventory records to the warehouse, in order to assess the reasonableness of the inventory records maintained by Ash.

Audit procedures should focus on testing the accuracy of the work performed by the internal audit department at the year end in order to determine whether the year-end inventory quantity exists and is complete.

Testing the accuracy of the aged inventory report will provide evidence over the valuation of inventory.

Reviewing the sales order book for February, March and April 20X5 could provide audit evidence as to the quantity of inventory at the year end but only if it is assessed to determine whether there would have been sufficient inventory at the year end to fulfil customer demand.

167 The correct answer is:

| | | |
|---|---|---|
| Evaluation of all significant audit judgments | INCLUDE | |
| Evaluation of the performance of specific audit procedures performed | | EXCLUDE |
| Evaluation of the cost-effectiveness of the audit process | | EXCLUDE |
| Evaluation of conclusions reached in formulating auditor's report | INCLUDE | |

The evaluation of specific audit procedures would not be part of an engagement quality review – this would be part of the audit team's internal processes of monitoring and review, but is too detailed to be included within this review.

The cost-effectiveness of the audit is not relevant to the engagement quality review, since it does not have a bearing on whether the auditor expresses an appropriate audit opinion.

168 The correct answer is:

**Audit opinion**          **Disclosure in the auditor's report**

Qualified               Basis for qualified opinion

The auditor will need to express a modified opinion as they are unable to obtain sufficient appropriate evidence in relation to inventory. The effect of this is material but not pervasive. Therefore a qualified 'except for' opinion will be required.

The opinion paragraph will explain that the audit opinion is qualified 'except for'. A basis for qualified opinion paragraph will be required to explain the limitation in relation to the lack of evidence over inventory.

# Humphries

169 The correct answer is:

1, 2, 3 and 4

All the procedures are valid in identifying subsequent events occurring up to the date of the auditor's report.

170 The correct answers are:

Inventory should not be written down, because the damage is not an adjusting event.

If a material amount of inventory is uninsured, it may be necessary to disclose the event and an estimate of the financial losses.

The flood damage does not provide evidence of conditions that existed at the year end, and therefore is not an adjusting event as defined by IAS 10 *Events After The Reporting Period*. On this basis, the inventory should not be written down, but the nature and amount of expected uninsured losses may need to be disclosed. It is incorrect to recognise a contingent asset in the 20X5 financial statements: contingent assets should be disclosed, not recognised, and it should only be disclosed when an inflow of economic benefits is probable (IAS 37).

171 The correct answers are:

Reviewing the post year end period for payments received from the customer in respect of the year-end debt

Reviewing correspondence with the customer to assess the likelihood of Humphries Co recovering the $0.3 million

Writing to the customer is likely to be unproductive. In addition, it would only provide persuasive evidence that the receivable existed at the year end, not that it was recoverable. Requesting a cash flow forecast is irrelevant, as it does not give evidence as to the recoverability of the receivable itself and there is no evidence that the going concern assumption needs to be revised.

172 The correct answer is:

The lawsuit relating to the breach of contract is considered to be **material** and therefore if the financial statements are not revised in the light of the new information then the auditor's opinion will be **qualified 'except for' due to material misstatement**.

The probable payment and anticipated adjustment needed is $0.6m representing 8% of profit ($0.6m/$7.5m × 100%). This is material and if management refuse to adjust for the provision, the audit opinion will need to be modified on the basis management has not complied with IAS 37 *Provisions, Contingent Liabilities and Contingent Assets*. The misstatement is material but not pervasive, so a qualified opinion would be expressed. The opinion paragraph would state that 'except for' this issue the financial statements are presented fairly (or show a true and fair view). A 'basis for qualified opinion' section would explain the material misstatement in relation to the $0.6m not provided, and describe the effect on the financial statements.

173    The correct answer is:

If the auditor becomes aware of a fact that, had it been known to the auditor at the date of the auditor's report, may have caused the auditor to amend the auditor's report, the auditor shall discuss the need for any adjustments with management.

The first two options describe the auditor's responsibility with regards to subsequent events occurring before the date of the auditor's report. It is true that the auditor does not have any obligation to perform procedures or make enquiries but, should an adjusting event come to light, adjustments to the financial statements about to be issued must be considered and further audit procedures must be performed as necessary at the time, rather than deferring to next year, hence the third option is incorrect.

# Greenfields

174    The correct answer is: Warranty provision only

The audit team has already carried out some procedures in testing the calculations and assumptions relating to the warranty provision, and has found them to be in line with prior years (and presumably in accordance with expectations). All of the evidence to date is from internal sources, but there is unlikely to be readily available reliable external sources.

It will be difficult for anyone to predict how many warranty claims there will be in the future and the value of any future claims, and written representation on this matter will be one of the few sources of evidence available.

Management have offered a written representation over the recoverability of the receivables balance but have not allowed circularisation of the receivable. The written representation cannot be used as a substitute for evidence which should otherwise be available. The written representation proposed by management is focused on the recoverability and gives only weak evidence over the relevant assertions. Despite being in writing and more reliable than a verbal representation, the internally generated representation is not as good as evidence from an external source (such as any potential response from Yellowmix to the circularisation).

With the other evidence available being limited due to the lack of payment activity over the last six months, without further, more compelling evidence, the representation alone would appear insufficient to conclude that receivables are free from material misstatement.

175    The correct answers are:

Review correspondence with Yellowmix Co regarding the late payment

Perform a review of post year-end cash receipts

Reviewing correspondence with Yellowmix may provide details confirming the likelihood of the debt being repaid. If cash is received in after the period end from Yellowmix this provides evidence that the debt was recoverable at the period end.

Tracing a sample of goods dispatched notes (Option 2) provides evidence of completeness.

Tracing of entries in Yellowmix's account in the receivables ledger provides evidence of existence and accuracy.

176  The correct answers are:

| | | |
|---|---|---|
| Discuss with management why they have refused to provide the representations requested | PERFORM | |
| Reassess the integrity of management and consider the implications for any other representations | PERFORM | |
| Seek legal advice | | DO NOT PERFORM |
| Resign as auditor | | DO NOT PERFORM |

Management has not provided a requested written representation, therefore ISA 580 *Written Representations* requires the auditor to discuss the matter with management and ask why they will not provide the representation relating to the warranty provision.

ISA 580 also requires the auditor to re-evaluate the integrity of management and evaluate the effect this may have on the reliability of any other representations (such as on the Yellowmix balance) and audit evidence in general (ISA 580).

The auditor must then take appropriate actions, including determining the impact on the auditor's opinion in the auditor's report.

177  The correct answer is:

| Audit opinion | Reason |
|---|---|
| Qualified | Inability to obtain sufficient appropriate evidence |

Given the limited evidence available other than the representation, the auditor will be unable to obtain sufficient appropriate evidence over the material warranty provision. Therefore a modification of the auditor's opinion is required. A qualified opinion will be issued because the misstatement, although material, will not be pervasive. A qualified or adverse opinion on the grounds of material misstatement would not be appropriate as the auditor has not been able to obtain sufficient evidence to determine whether a material misstatement has occurred or not.

178  The correct answer is:

| Audit opinion | Disclosure |
|---|---|
| Unmodified | Other Information section including a description of the uncorrected misstatement |

The audit opinion would not be modified as the audit opinion relates to the financial statements and not the 'Other information'. In accordance with ISA 700 *Forming an Opinion and Reporting on Financial Statements* (ISA 700) and ISA 720 *The Auditor's Responsibilities Relating to Other Information* (ISA 720) the auditor's report would be required to include an Other Information section as other information is issued with the financial statements and is available to the auditors. As there is a material misstatement this would be disclosed in the Other Information section. An Other Matter paragraph is not used for these purposes.

## Strawberry

179  The correct answer is: 1, 2 and 4

The fall in inventory holding period means that Strawberry is turning over its inventory more quickly, which if anything would improve its cash cycle and have a positive rather than negative impact on the ability of the company to continue. In this case the change is relatively small so is unlikely to be a significant factor either way.

180 The correct answer is: At least 12 months from the date of the financial statements

In accordance with ISA 570 the assessment must cover a period of at least 12 months from the date of the financial statements. If the period covered is less than this the auditor must request that the assessment period is extended.

181 The correct answer is: Identification during your subsequent events review of a cash receipt for the full amount

The receipt of the balance after the year end confirms that the debt is recoverable at the year end.

The written representation is written evidence but is internally generated.

The response to the circularisation provides evidence of existence but does not provide evidence of recoverability.

The correspondence between the lawyers is externally generated and from trusted parties but is less reliable than the receipt of the payment as it would still be possible for Grape Co to default.

182 The correct answer is: Agreement by an alternative financial institution to lend Strawberry $4.8m in September 20X2

As part of the going concern review the auditor must consider mitigating circumstances. In this case, the agreement with the alternative finance provider gives the most assurance as there is a greater degree of certainty that Strawberry will receive the cash. The first three options may provide the cash required but this cannot be guaranteed. There is also a timing issue as the property may not sell for some time and cost savings will not have an immediate effect.

183 The correct answer is:

| Auditor's opinion | Explanation of circumstances |
| --- | --- |
| Adverse opinion | Basis for adverse opinion |

An adverse opinion would be issued as the matter is material and pervasive ie the auditors disagree with the whole basis on which the financial statements have been prepared. A description of the circumstances would be included in the Basis for adverse opinion paragraph in accordance with ISA 705 (ISA 705).

A qualified opinion would apply if the issue were material, but not pervasive. Disclosure in the Material uncertainty related to going concern section is made when the auditor agrees that the company is a going concern but believes that there is a material uncertainty which needs to be brought to the attention of the shareholders (ISA 570). This does not apply in this case.

# Clarinet

184 The correct answer is:

| Material | Adjust in 20X4 financial statements |
| --- | --- |
| Yes | Yes |

The uncorrected misstatement amounts to 15% of profit after tax (PAT) and on this basis would be material (ie it is over 10% of PAT). It is an adjusting event as the discovery provides evidence as to the value of the inventory at the year end. The 20X5 financial statements should therefore be adjusted.

Adjustment in the 20X5 financial statements would not be required for non-adjusting events ie those which do not provide evidence of conditions which existed at the period end.

185 The correct answer is: 1, 2 and 4

The entry of the competitor has resulted in a loss of market share and the loss of a major customer. There is a risk that this sizeable loss of market share will result in a significant loss of future revenues, as well as reducing future cash flows.

The overdraft has increased significantly and is due for renewal. This suggests liquidity problems. If the bank does not renew the overdraft, and the company fails to obtain alternative finance it may not be able to continue trading.

The failure of Clarinet's shareholders to invest indicate doubts in relation to the company's ability to generate healthy profits in future, or possible liquidity problems. It may also make it less likely for others to invest.

The existence of a bank loan in itself does not give rise to going concern issues. The bank loan is long term so there is no imminent requirement to repay the balance. To date all payments have been made therefore there is no breach of any loan terms which could trigger early repayment.

186 The correct answer is: A review of post year end sales and the order book

All of the procedures provide evidence regarding the assumption used in the cash flow forecast. However, the review of post year end sales and the order book is the most reliable as this shows sales which have actually taken place or sales to which the customer has shown a commitment. Procedures described in the first, second and fourth options are based on possible events.

187 The correct answer is: 1, 2 and 3

The disclosures are set out in ISA 570 paragraph 25.

(4) is incorrect. The management assessment should be at least 12 months from the date of the financial statements. If not the auditors will ask that the assessment period is extended.

188 The correct answer is:

| Opinion | Disclosure |
| --- | --- |
| Unmodified | Material uncertainty related to going concern |

As the auditors agree with the basis of preparation of the financial statements and have concluded that the disclosures are adequate, an unmodified opinion is issued. As a material uncertainty regarding going concern exists, this must be highlighted for the benefit of the shareholders. In accordance with ISA 570 (ISA 570) and ISA 701 (ISA 701) this must be disclosed in a 'Material uncertainty related to going concern' section, and not as a Key audit matter.

# Czech & Dawson

189 The correct answer is: A written representation should be requested from management to confirm whether they believe that the effects of the unadjusted misstatements are immaterial, both individually and in aggregate, to the financial statements as a whole

ISA 450 *Evaluation of Misstatements Identified During the Audit* states that the auditor has a responsibility to accumulate misstatements identified during the audit, other than those that are clearly trivial (ISA 450).

All the accumulated misstatements should be communicated to the appropriate level of management on a timely basis (ISA 450). The auditor must request that management correct the misstatements.

If management refuses to correct some or all of the misstatements, the auditor must obtain an understanding of the reasons for not making the corrections, and take these into account when determining whether the financial statements are free from material misstatement (ISA 450). This may affect the auditor's opinion if this results in the financial statements being materially misstated, but the refusal to correct the misstatements does not affect the opinion.

The auditor should determine whether uncorrected misstatements are material, both individually and in aggregate (ISA 450).

190 The correct answers are:

Discuss the requirements of IAS 38 *Intangible Assets* with the directors in order to determine whether they understand the required accounting treatment of research and development expenditure

Obtain a breakdown of the $5.3m capitalised as an intangible asset and agree to supporting documentation to determine the nature of the projects to which the expenditure relates

Audit procedures should focus on determining the extent of research expenditure which has been incorrectly capitalised.

Whilst it is generally important to authorise expenditure, the issue is not authorisation or occurrence but its classification.

191 The correct answer is: Qualified opinion

Research expenditure of $2.1m has been capitalised within intangible assets. This accounting treatment is incorrect, as IAS 38 *Intangible Assets* requires research expenditure to be expensed to profit or loss (IAS 38).

The error is material as it represents 8% of profit before tax ($2.1m/$26.3m).

Management should adjust the financial statements by removing the $2.1m research expenditure from intangibles and debiting the amount to profit or loss.

If management refuse to make the adjustment, the auditor's opinion will need to be modified. As the error is material but not pervasive, a qualified opinion would seem appropriate.

The basis of opinion section would need to include a paragraph explaining the misstatement and its effect on the financial statements. The opinion paragraph would be qualified 'except for'.

192 The correct answer is:

| Material | Financial statement impact |
| --- | --- |
| Yes | Wages may be materially misstated |

Two months' worth of wages records have been lost and so audit evidence has not been gained in relation to this expense. Wages and salaries for the 2-month period represent 11% of profit before tax ($1.1m/$10m) and so wages and salaries may be materially misstated.

193 The correct answer is:

| Audit opinion | Disclosure in the auditor's report |
| --- | --- |
| Qualified | Basis for qualified opinion |

The auditors should seek alternative audit procedures to audit the wages and salaries account. If no alternative audit procedures are possible, the loss of data would constitute a lack of sufficient appropriate audit evidence.

The auditors will need to modify the auditor's opinion on the basis that they are unable to obtain sufficient appropriate evidence in relation to a material amount in the financial statements. As the two months' salary and wages are not pervasive, a qualified opinion would seem appropriate.

The basis of opinion section would require an explanation of the insufficient audit evidence in relation to wages and salaries. The opinion paragraph would be qualified on the grounds of an inability to obtain sufficient appropriate audit evidence.

BPP
LEARNING
MEDIA

# Medimade

194     The correct answers are:

The going concern basis of accounting is used when the entity will be able to continue in business for the foreseeable future.

The going concern basis of accounting assumes that the entity will be able to realise its assets and discharge its liabilities in the normal course of business.

The term 'foreseeable future' is not defined within ISA 570 *Going Concern*, but IAS 1 *Presentation of Financial Statements* deems the foreseeable future to be a period of 12 months from the end of the entity's reporting period (IAS 1).

The going concern basis of accounting does not require any specific accounting conditions to hold true (such as that the entity will have net current assets for the next 12 months), but rather the more general assumption that the entity will be able to continue in business, ie as a going concern.

195     The correct answers are:

Medimade now has to pay cash on delivery and this adds further cash flow strain imposed by the overdraft

Some suppliers may end their relationship with Medimade, preventing the company from producing its products, thus further reducing sales

Although all of the stated options are possible consequences, only these two options describe the most direct effect on going concern: cash flow difficulties and reducing sales. The main concern with bank covenants (which should already be in place) is that the bank can withdraw finance if and when the covenants are breached – bank covenants do not usually restrict the way in which a company conducts its business.

196     The correct answer is:

Review board minutes for meetings held after the year end for evidence which indicates further financial difficulties or evidence of alternative sources of finance

The bank letter will provide evidence of the current level of overdraft but not about the likelihood of the overdraft being renewed in future.

The scenario clearly states that the bank will not make a decision on the extension of the overdraft facility until after the auditor's report is signed, and banks will not agree to disclose such information to the auditor. While written representations are a valid form of audit evidence, they do not provide sufficient appropriate audit evidence on their own about any of the matters with which they deal.

197     The correct answer is:

| Audit opinion | Disclosure in the auditor's report |
|---|---|
| Unmodified opinion | Describe the nature of the going concern uncertainty in the Material uncertainty related to going concern section |

An unmodified opinion is issued as the auditor agrees with the use of the going concern basis of accounting and the level of disclosure provided. The existence of a material uncertainty in relation to going concern would be disclosed in the 'Material uncertainty related to going concern' section (ISA 570). A qualified opinion would be issued if the going concern basis of accounting is appropriate, but a material uncertainty exists which is not adequately disclosed (ISA 570). An adverse opinion would be issued where the going concern basis of accounting is inappropriate (ISA 570). A disclaimer of opinion would be issued if the auditor is unable to form an opinion.

198 The correct answer is:

Discuss with management about their plans for the company and determine whether the 20X7 financial statements should now be prepared on a break-up basis. If yes, request management to adjust the financial statements, audit the adjustments and provide a new auditor's report.

If Medimade is no longer able to continue its operations, this constitutes an adjusting event and the financial statements must be revised accordingly. IAS 10 *Events After the Reporting Period* states that an entity must not prepare its financial statements on a going concern basis if management determine after the year end that it has no other alternative but to liquidate the company (IAS 10). Now that the bank has withdrawn its overdraft facility, closure has become a very real possibility. In this case, disclosure in the financial statements is no longer appropriate – the financial statements must be prepared on a break-up basis.

Before the financial statements are issued, the auditors have a passive duty to consider the impact of matters which, had they been known at the date of the auditor's report, would have caused the auditor to amend the auditor's report.

# Brown & Green

199 The correct answer is: Brown & Green Co should discuss any subsequent events they become aware of with the directors of Strawberry Co to determine whether the financial statements need amending.

This question tests knowledge of ISA 560 *Subsequent Events* and demonstrates the importance of having a detailed understanding of the ISAs. While the auditor is not required to perform specific procedures after the signing of the auditor's report, if information comes to light between the signing of the auditor's report and the date the financial statements are issued, the auditor is required to discuss the matter with management and determine whether the financial statements should be amended.

The first option sets out the auditor's responsibilities in the period between the year end and the date the auditor's report is signed.

The auditor is required to obtain written representations in respect of subsequent events but this would have been obtained prior to the auditor's report being signed. Therefore, the second option is not a valid response.

While the statement in the third option correctly identifies that the auditor has no duty to perform subsequent events procedures after the auditor's report is signed, it is not always the case that events in this period will be dealt with next year as in certain circumstances the current year financial statements may be amended.

200 The correct answer is: a non-adjusting event, gives new information about an event that did not exist at year-end date, to be disclosed in the current year financial statements.

The issue of share capital is [ **a non-adjusting** ] event

because it [ **gives new information about an event that did not exist at year-end date** ] and it is material

therefore it requires [ **to be disclosed in the current year financial statements** ]

This question requires an understanding of the accounting treatment of events after the reporting period which underpins the auditor's ability to audit subsequent events and highlights the interaction between IAS 10 *Events after the Reporting Period* and ISA 560. Note the importance of looking carefully at any dates given in the question. In this case the shares were issued in May 20X5, which was after the year end. However, the information does not provide evidence of conditions which existed at the year end and therefore the transaction would be a non-adjusting event. As this event is material, however, it would be disclosed in the current year financial statements.

201 The correct answers are: Examine post year-end board meeting minutes to identify any reference to further developments of the case; Review the correspondence with the company's legal advisers to assess the probable outcome of the case.

Reviewing correspondence with the company's legal advisers would provide third party written evidence regarding the probable outcome of the case. Reviewing post year-end board minutes would provide written evidence of discussions by directors regarding any developments which may affect the overall outcome. Both of these procedures should provide the auditor with substantive evidence to enable them to determine whether these events have been appropriately recognised in the financial statements.

The first option would not be appropriate as the auditor does not have the authority to contact the environmental agency directly. The fourth option describes a test of control, not a substantive procedure. The opening statement in the stem of the question indicates that the procedures which have been carried out, and are therefore relevant, are substantive procedures. Mixing up substantive procedures and tests of controls is a common error. Candidates must ensure that they understand the difference and carefully consider the context set within the scenario or the requirement.

202 The correct answer is: Outcome 1: Qualified; Outcome 2: Unmodified with emphasis of matter.

In outcome 1 the directors have failed to comply with IAS 10. It is probable that Strawberry Co will receive a fine but this has not been reflected in the financial statements. On the basis that the financial statements are materially misstated a modified opinion will be issued. As the misstatement is material but not pervasive a qualified opinion would be appropriate.

(An adverse opinion would be issued if the misstatement had been material and pervasive. A disclaimer would be appropriate where the auditor is unable to obtain sufficient, appropriate evidence and the possible effects on the financial statements of any undetected misstatements could be material and pervasive.)

In outcome 2 the correct treatment has been adopted by the directors. As this is the case an unmodified opinion would be appropriate. The emphasis of matter would draw the user's attention to the case disclosed in the notes to the financial statements.

Care should be taken by candidates when considering the use of an emphasis of matter. In accordance with ISA 706 *Emphasis of Matter Paragraphs and Other Matter Paragraphs in the Independent Auditor's Report*, an emphasis of matter paragraph refers to a matter appropriately presented or disclosed (as is the case in outcome 2) that in the auditor's judgement is fundamental to users' understanding of the financial statements. Importantly therefore, it cannot be used as a substitute for a modified opinion. Suggesting that an emphasis of matter should be used where in fact a modified opinion is required is a common mistake.

203 The correct answer is: 28 September 20X5.

In this requirement extra information is provided in addition to the main scenario. Where this type of information is provided candidates must ensure that they read it carefully before attempting the question. This question requires candidates to apply their knowledge of ISA 580 *Written Representations*. The ISA states that the date of written representations must be as near as practicable to, but not after the date of the auditor's report. The auditor's report is due to be signed on 28 September 20X5, therefore this would be the most appropriate date for the directors to sign the written representation.

# 204 Panda

## Marking scheme

|  |  | Marks |
|---|---|---|

(a)  Up to 1 mark per well-explained element.

- Intended user, responsible party, practitioner
- Subject matter
- Suitable criteria
- Appropriate evidence
- Assurance report  5

(b)  Up to 1 mark per valid point, overall maximum of 6 marks per event.
Event 1 – Defective chemicals
- Provides evidence of conditions at the year end
- Inventory to be adjusted to lower of cost and net realisable value
- Calculation of materiality
- Review board minutes/quality control reports
- Discuss with the directors, adequate inventory to continue to trade
- Obtain written representation re going concern
- Obtain schedule of defective inventory, agree to supporting documentation
- Discuss with directors basis of the scrap value  5

Event 2 – Explosion
- Provides evidence of conditions that arose subsequent to the year end
- Non-adjusting event, requires disclosure if material
- Calculation of materiality
- Obtain schedule of damaged property, plant and equipment and agree values to asset register
- Obtain latest inventory records to confirm damaged inventory levels
- Discuss with the directors if they will make disclosures
- Discuss with directors why no insurance claim will be made  5

(c)  Up to 1 mark per well-explained valid point.

- Disclosure required in 20X3 financial statements and adjustment to the assets in 20X4 financial statements
- Material but not pervasive misstatement, modified auditor's report, qualified opinion
- Basis for qualified opinion paragraph required
- Opinion paragraph – except for

5

20

(a)  ### Elements of an assurance engagement

There are five elements of an assurance engagement and these are explained below (IFAC, 2016).

### A three party relationship

The three parties are the intended user, the responsible party and the practitioner. Intended users are the person, persons or class of persons for whom the practitioner prepares the assurance report. The responsible party is the person (or persons) responsible for the subject matter (in a direct engagement) or subject matter information of the assurance engagement.

The practitioner is the individual providing professional services that will review the subject matter and provide the assurance.

### A subject matter

This is the data to be evaluated that has been prepared by the responsible party. It can take many forms, including financial performance (eg historical financial information), non-financial performance (eg key performance indicators), processes (eg internal control) and behaviour (eg compliance with laws and regulations).

### Suitable criteria

The subject matter is evaluated or measured against criteria in order to reach an opinion.

### Evidence

Sufficient appropriate evidence needs to be gathered to support the required level of assurance.

### Assurance report

A report containing the practitioner's opinion is issued to the intended user.

(b)  ### Event 1: Defective chemicals

A batch of chemicals produced before the year end, costing $0.85m to produce, has been found to be defective after the year end. Its scrap value is $0.1m. Inventory should be valued at the lower of cost and net realisable value in accordance with IAS 2 *Inventories* (IAS 2). This is an adjusting event in accordance with IAS 10 *Events after the Reporting Period* (IAS 10). As it stands, the inventory is overstated by $0.75m. This represents 13.4% of profit before tax and 1.4% of revenue and is therefore material to the financial statements.

*Audit procedures to be performed*

- Obtain a schedule to confirm the cost value of the defective batch of $0.85m and documentary proof of the scrap value of $0.1m.

- Discuss with management whether this is the only defective batch or whether there are likely to be other batches affected.

- Review quality control reports to assess the likelihood of other batches being affected and discuss results of testing with technical team members at Panda.

### Event 2: Explosion

An explosion shortly after the year end has resulted in damage to inventory and property, plant and equipment. The amount of inventory and property, plant and equipment damaged is estimated to be $0.9m. It has no scrap value. Inventory and property, plant and equipment are therefore overstated by $0.9m. This represents 16.1% of profit before tax and 1.6% of revenue, and is therefore material. The explosion represents a non-adjusting event in accordance with IAS 10 *Events after the reporting period*. It therefore does not require adjustment in the financial statements but should be disclosed as it is material (IAS 10).

*Audit procedures to be performed*

- Obtain a schedule of the inventory and property, plant and equipment damaged in the explosion to verify the value of $0.9m.

- Visit the site where the explosion took place to assess damage.

- Discuss with directors the need to make disclosure in the financial statements and review any disclosure note drafted.

- Inspect insurance agreement to assess whether any claim can be made on the insurance.

(c) **Effect on auditor's report of the explosion**

The directors should make disclosures in the financial statements about the explosion and the effect on inventory and property, plant and equipment. This is because the amount involved is material and affects the value of opening inventory and property, plant and equipment in the following financial year.

If the directors refuse to make the disclosure, then the auditors would modify the opinion on the financial statements on the basis of a material misstatement. The opinion would be qualified 'except for' as the matter is material but unlikely to be pervasive.

A 'Basis for qualified opinion' paragraph would be included in the auditor's report, describing the auditor's reason for modifying the opinion and the effect of the explosion on the opening balances in the financial statements for the following financial year (ISA 705). The 'basis for qualified opinion' would be placed immediately after the Opinion paragraph.

# Q205–206 March 2017

205   The correct answer is:

There has been an increase in the average time taken to manufacture each individual jewellery piece.

An increase in the average time to manufacture individual items is likely to increase the costs of production (labour and other direct production costs) meaning costs will rise relative to the net realisable value.

The other answers are incorrect for the following reasons:

- The general market price for individual stones remaining static will have no impact on net realisable value or cost.

- An increase in demand for completed items should increase the net realisable value in comparison to cost.

- An increase in trade discounts will reduce the cost of gems being bought for manufacture into jewellery items therefore should increase the difference between net realisable value and cost.

206  The correct answer is:

(1)  Basis for opinion paragraph
(2)  Other reporting responsibilities
(3)  Key audit matters

(1)  A 'basis for opinion' paragraph explains how the audit was conducted

(2)  An 'other reporting responsibilities' paragraph is included if the auditor addresses other reporting responsibilities in the auditor's report on the financial statements that are in addition to the auditor's responsibilities under the ISAs. This paragraph must therefore be included in the auditor's report for a listed company

(3)  Key audit matters are those matters, in the auditor's judgement, which are the most significant from the audit. A 'key audit matters' paragraph is required for all listed companies.

(4)  Is incorrect as an 'other matters paragraph 'draws users' attention to issues outside the scope of the financial statements. This would result in a modified report with an unmodified opinion.

# Q207–208 June 2017

207  The correct answers are:

The availability of alternative sources of audit evidence

The technical expertise required to perform the valuation

Candidates were told in the scenario that management had appointed an expert during the year and therefore the requirements of ISA 500 *Audit Evidence* were applicable in determining whether reliance can be placed on the expert. ISA 500 states that in order to determine reliance, the auditor should consider whether there are other sources of evidence available as if so the level of reliance will be reduced and to consider the technical expertise that the expert should possess in order to carry out the work.

It is not appropriate for the auditor to consider at this stage whether staff can be allocated to perform the work as the availability of staff and the ability to perform the work should have been considered at the acceptance stage.

While the auditor in certain circumstances may need to refer to the fact that an expert has been used the responsibility to gather sufficient and appropriate evidence on which to base the audit opinion remains solely with the auditor. Therefore considering the extent to which reference can be made to the expert is not an appropriate parameter on which to base reliance.

208  The correct answer is:

(1)  Recalculate the depreciation charge for the year using the updated valuation.

(2)  Verify that all the assets in the same class have been revalued in line with IAS 16 *Property, Plant and Equipment*.

(3)  Agree the value to the expert's report and recalculate the revaluation adjustment recorded by Gates Co.

The procedures listed as (1), (2) and (3) would all be reliable and relevant tests for the auditor to perform to verify a revaluation surplus. The test listed at (4) is not valid as the surplus, in the circumstances described, should not be recorded in the statement of profit or loss, but rather should be recorded in other comprehensive income. As such this is not a suitable test to obtain sufficient and appropriate evidence. Many candidates incorrectly selected all four options demonstrating that accounting knowledge in this area was lacking and therefore they were not able to identify procedures to verify appropriate accounting treatment by the client.

# Q209–210 September 2017

209    The correct answer is: Attend the cash count at the year-end and re-perform the count.

Candidates are reminded that tests for existence need to focus on ascertaining whether the balance is genuine at the year end and is not overstated. A good way to approach this style of question is to think about the objective of a test in relation to the identified assertion before assessing each of the procedures in turn to consider whether it would satisfy that objective.

The first test is a test for Rights & Obligations as this test would only confirm that the account was held in the client's name and therefore that the client has the right to the account, but it would not confirm that the balance was not overstated at the year end.

The third test is a Completeness test as starting at the bank confirmation letter and agreeing to the trial balance allows the auditor to confirm that all accounts on the letter are recorded. It would not allow the auditor to confirm that all accounts on the trial balance are genuine.

The fourth test is a Presentation test as it is focused on the disclosure that is included in the financial statements at the year end.

The only test that would confirm that a recorded balance is both genuine and not overstated is to attend the cash count and to re-perform the count.

210    The correct answer is: Qualified opinion as the financial statements are materially misstated

The share issue represents a material non-adjusting subsequent event. So while the transaction will not be recorded until after the year end the event should be disclosed in the financial statements for the year ended 31 July 20X7. This lack of disclosure means that the financial statements are materially misstated and therefore if no changes are made the auditor should issue a qualified opinion.

The majority of candidates selected the fourth answer and candidates are once again reminded that an Emphasis of Matter paragraph can only be used to draw shareholder attention to an issue that is ALREADY disclosed within the financial statements.

# Q211–212 December 2017

211    The correct answer is:

Select a sample of employees from the final week's payroll listing and recalculate deductions.

Candidates are reminded that testing for understatement is about ascertaining whether the balance is COMPLETE at the year end. In this question candidates were asked to identify which of the procedures would NOT cover this objective. Therefore candidates were being asked to identify which of the tests is NOT a test for completeness. A good way to approach this style of question is to think about the objective of a test in relation to the identified assertion before assessing each of the procedures in turn.

The first three tests would all test for understatement of the accrual through agreement to the subsequent payment, year-end client listing or prior year accrual.

The final option, however, would not test for understatement/completeness as the recalculation of deductions is a test for accuracy and will provide the auditor will no assurance that the correct amount has been accrued at the year end.

212    The correct answers are:

Was the audit plan suitably modified to allow for changing circumstances?

Has work been performed in accordance with relevant auditing, legal and professional standards?

While all of these questions will be considered in preparation for finalising the auditor's report only consideration of the suitability of the audit plan and whether the work has been performed in accordance with relevant standards will have an impact on the audit opinion.

BPP
LEARNING
MEDIA

# Q213–214 March 2018

213    The correct answers are:

A code of professional ethics allows a professional accountant to apply fundamental ethical principles to a given situation

A code of professional ethics encourages professional accountants to think about more than just legal compliance

Codes of professional ethics, including ACCA's *Code of Ethics and Conduct* adopt a principles based approach rather than being a prescriptive set of rules. This approach identifies fundamental principles, threats to these principles and safeguards which can be put in place. This approach requires the professional accountant to use professional judgment when applying ethical principles to any given situation. Compliance with codes of professional ethics is a professional requirement.

On this basis, the first and fourth statements are incorrect.

214    The correct answer is:

Gross profit margin.

The key to this question is to consider the assertions which would be relevant to the testing of inventory. In this instance the gross profit margin is relevant to the valuation of inventory. As closing inventory is a component of cost of sales, changes in the gross profit margin could indicate that inventory is misstated.

Candidates should be reminded of the importance of understanding what the results of a ratio show, rather than just having knowledge of the balances which would be included in its calculation. For example, in this instance whilst the inventory balance is included in the current ratio, it is difficult to derive conclusions regarding inventory specifically from its calculation.

# Q215–216 June 2018

215    The correct answer is: (1), (3) and (4) only.

Candidates are reminded to ensure that they understand the different between the auditor's and management responsibilities in relation to going concern and to ensure that they understand the requirements set out in ISA 570 *Going Concern*. Statement (2), which relates to determining the basis on which the financial statements should be prepared, is a management responsibility.

216    The correct answer is:

Limited assurance, negative conclusion.

Candidates should ensure that they understand the difference between reasonable and limited assurance and the circumstances in which each will be offered. Reasonable assurance is a high level of assurance and should only be provided when sufficient and appropriate evidence can be gathered. In the circumstances, which were described, the most appropriate level is assurance was limited assurance provided through a negative conclusion.

# Q217–218 September 2018

217    The correct answers are:

To consider the adequacy of the accounting records which have been maintained

To obtain an understanding of the internal control system in place

The auditor does not guarantee the going concern status of the company. Accessing the books and records of the company represents one of the rights of the auditor which enables them to achieve their objectives.

This question is a straightforward knowledge-based question. Candidates should be reminded of the importance of having a good understanding of the basic principles of the role of the auditor.

This question was not well-answered in the exam, with many candidates misunderstanding the auditor's responsibility regarding going concern and confusing the auditor's rights and responsibilities.

218   The correct answer is: 2 and 3 only.

This question demonstrates two important points. Firstly, candidates should ensure that they understand the difference between a test of control and substantive procedures. The test described in (1) is a test of control (ie it provides evidence as to whether the control of board approval has operated effectively) and therefore does not provide substantive evidence.

The question also highlights the importance of reading all information provided carefully. The test described in (4) is a valid procedure but it provides evidence regarding other assets, not the headquarters as specified in the requirement.

## Q219–220 December 2018

219   The correct answer is: 1, 3 and 4 only.

The effective date of the revaluation, the amount of the revaluation increase and the carrying amount of the head office under the cost model are disclosures required by IAS 16 Property, Plant and Equipment.

This question demonstrates two key points. Firstly it highlights the importance of disclosures to the audit. Obtaining sufficient appropriate evidence during the audit requires an assessment of the adequacy of disclosures included in the financial statements. Secondly candidates should also note the need for accounting knowledge to answer this question. An understanding of key accounting principles is critical to the audit process therefore candidates must ensure that they are familiar with these.

Guidance for candidates regarding the accounting knowledge assumed for this exam is included in the examinable documents list.

220   The correct answer is: Unmodified opinion with no further disclosure.

The amount of the disputed adjustment is not material, being 2.2% of profit before tax, therefore there is no material misstatement. An unmodified opinion would be issued meaning that options three and four are not correct.

The nature of the issue is such that it would not be disclosed in an emphasis of matter paragraph so option two is incorrect. A significant number of candidates chose this option.

Candidates should note the applied nature of this question and the importance of using the information provided in the scenario to come to a conclusion. Candidates must also ensure that they understand that an emphasis of matter paragraph is included in the auditor's report where a matter, appropriately presented or disclosed in the financial statements, is of such importance that it is fundamental to the users' understanding of the financial statements and the auditor wishes to draw attention to that disclosure.

## Q221–222 March 2019

221   The correct answer is: 1, 2, 3 and 4.

Although straightforward many candidates found this question challenging. This question demonstrates the level of detailed knowledge of an ISA which may be tested, in this case ISA 700 Forming an Opinion and Reporting on Financial Statements.

Items described in (1) and (4) would be included in the basis for opinion paragraph.

Item (2) would appear at the start of the auditor's report so that the auditor's report is clearly distinguished from reports issued by others.

The item described in (3) would be included as part of the auditor's responsibilities for the audit of the financial statements section.

222　The correct answer is:

If the directors refuse to amend the inconsistency, then the auditor's opinion will be **unmodified** and the inconsistency will be explained in an **other information section**.

As with the previous question this question requires a detailed knowledge and understanding of an ISA, in this case ISA 720 *The Auditor's Responsibilities Relating to Other Information*.

As the financial statements are not misstated the audit opinion will be unmodified. However, in accordance with ISA 720 as there is an uncorrected material misstatement in the other information, the auditor's report must include a statement describing the issue in the other information section.

# Q223–224 June 2019

223　The correct answer is:

| | | |
|---|---|---|
| The audit committee's terms of reference should include reviewing and monitoring the external auditor's independence and objectivity | TRUE | |
| The audit committee's terms of reference should include appointing and removing the external auditors | | FALSE |
| The audit committee's terms of reference should include evaluating and monitoring the effectiveness of the internal audit function | TRUE | |

This question tests knowledge of corporate governance responsibilities and in particular those of the audit committee and demonstrates the level of detailed knowledge which is required. It also demonstrates the level of care which must be taken when reading the question and thinking through the options.

The audit committee makes recommendations in relation to the appointment and removal of the external auditors but it is the shareholders who are responsible for their appointment and removal. Candidates who rush through this type of question or who word spot without considering the whole of the context of the question are likely to answer incorrectly.

224　The correct answer is:

A & Co's evaluation of management's assessment of Z Co's ability to continue as a going concern must cover the period up to **31 December 20X9**

As with the previous question, this question requires detailed knowledge, in this case of ISA 570 *Going Concern*. However, it also demonstrates the need to be able to apply knowledge to a practical scenario. In accordance with ISA 570, the auditor is required to review the same period as that used by management to determine whether the going concern basis is appropriate. This must be at least 12 months from the end of the reporting period.

The management of Z Co has used a cash flow forecast for 12 months to December 20X9. As this is at least 12 months from the end of the reporting period, this is date to which A & Co's assessment must cover.

# Q225–226 September 2019

225   The correct answer is: Attend the cash count at the year end and reperform the count

This question tests audit procedures relevant to bank and cash but also an ability to relate procedures to a specific assertion. It demonstrates the importance of understanding why a procedure is performed and the specific objective which it achieves.

By attending the cash count and reperforming the count the auditor is able to physically verify the existence of the cash. Agreeing a sample of accounts detailed on the bank confirmation letters to the trial balance provides evidence of completeness of bank and cash balances. Reviewing bank statements to verify that they are in the name of the company provides evidence of rights and obligations and the review of disclosures provides evidence relating to presentation.

226   The correct answer is: 1 and 4

This question demonstrates the need for candidates to have a thorough understanding of all aspects of the syllabus. While the topic of auditors' reports is an important one, candidates are reminded that section E of the syllabus also includes subsequent events, going concern, written representations and audit finalisation and the final review.

Revising the audit plan to allow for changing circumstances helps to ensure that sufficient and appropriate audit evidence is obtained. Performing audit work in accordance with relevant auditing, legal and professional standards enhances the quality of the audit work and therefore the evidence on which the audit opinion is based. The audit firm should ensure that it remains independent throughout the audit and the auditor is required to communicate deficiencies which are of sufficient importance to merit management's attention. However, neither of these issues has a direct effect on the evaluation of audit evidence at the review stage and its suitability for providing the basis for the audit opinion.

# Q227–228 December 2019

227   The correct answer is: 1 and 3 only

This question tests knowledge of corporate governance guidelines. It demonstrates not only the level of detailed knowledge which is required but also the importance of reading the question carefully rather than rushing to a conclusion. It is the chairman, not the chief executive officer who is responsible for the board. The audit committee will liaise with the external auditor, although this is not its key role, but is not responsible for their appointment. The audit committee may make recommendations regarding the appointment of the external auditor but appointment is normally by the shareholders at a general meeting.

228   The correct answer is: Request that management extends the assessment period to 30 April 20X6

This question examines knowledge of ISA 570 *Going Concern*. However it also demonstrates the need to be able to apply the principles to a practical scenario. ISA 570 requires that in evaluating the entity's ability to continue as a going concern the auditor must cover the same period as that used by management to make its assessment. If management's assessment covers a period of less than twelve months from the date of the financial statements the auditor is required to request management to extend its assessment period. In this case the auditor must request that management extend the assessment period to 30 April 20X6. Performing additional audit procedures would not resolve the fact that the assessment period is not as required by ISA 570, therefore the third option is not an appropriate response in this instance.

# Q229–230 March 2020

229 The correct answers are:

- All transactions have been recorded in the accounting records and are reflected in the financial statements

- Significant assumptions used in making accounting estimates are reasonable

This question examines knowledge of ISA 580 *Written Representations*. The ISA requires the auditor to request a number of written representations in relation to management's responsibilities and these include the statement at A above. There are also a number of other ISAs which require subject matter specific written representations. These include a requirement in ISA 540 *Auditing Accounting Estimates, Including Fair Value Accounting Estimates, and Related Disclosures* for a written representation as set out in the fourth option.

This question also demonstrates the need for candidates to think carefully and not to rush to a conclusion to avoid falling for the distracters. The second statement would be included in the letter of engagement and the third in the auditor's report.

230 The correct answers are:

- Design and perform analytical procedures to confirm the financial statements are consistent with the auditor's understanding of the entity

- Reassess materiality to confirm whether it remains appropriate in the context of Y Co's final financial statements

ISA 520 *Analytical Procedures* requires the auditor to perform analytical procedures near the end of the audit to assist the auditor when performing an overall conclusion. ISA 320 *Materiality in Planning and Performing an Audit* states that materiality may need to be revised as the audit progresses. At the review stage of the audit, the auditor considers whether the aggregate of uncorrected misstatements is material. In doing so the auditor must consider whether the materiality level is still appropriate.

This question is a reminder to candidates not to overlook the finalisation and review stage of the audit. It is an essential part of the audit process and candidates must be prepared for questions on this. It also demonstrates the importance of understanding the process of the audit overall and the procedures that are performed at each stage. For example, the third, fourth and fifth procedures are all valid audit procedures but the third procedure is performed as part of the work on acceptance of a client and the fourth and fifth are performed as part of the fieldwork.

The first procedure is not valid as it is management that would make an assessment of the company's ability to continue as a going concern. The auditor is required to gather sufficient and appropriate evidence that management's assessment and use of the going concern basis is appropriate.

# Q231–232 July 2020

231 The correct answers are:

- For a sample of assets held in the factory and warehouse record the asset identity number as marked on the asset and trace back to the relevant entry in the non-current asset register

- Trace a sample of costs recognised in the repairs and maintenance account to invoices and determine the nature of the expenditure and assess whether any capital items have been expensed

Tracing from the asset to the non-current asset register provides evidence of completeness as the total balance for plant and machinery will only be complete if the assets sampled are recorded in the register. (Tracing from the register to the physical asset would provide evidence of existence.) The plant and machinery balance must also include all relevant capital expenditure. If capital expenditure has been expensed in error, then the balance will not be complete.

Reviewing board minutes for evidence of authorisation is a test of controls and therefore does not provide substantive evidence. In addition, the fact that the capital expenditure has been authorised does not mean that the corresponding assets have been included in the accounting records. Enquiry regarding the fully depreciated assets would provide evidence in relation to valuation.

This question demonstrates the need for candidates to be able to apply their knowledge of substantive procedures and the importance of fully understanding the nature of the evidence obtained by performing a specific procedure, in this case to determine whether they are relevant to the completeness assertion. It also highlights the importance of being able to distinguish between a substantive procedure and a test of control. A test of control is an audit procedure designed to evaluate the operating effectiveness of controls, whereas a substantive procedure is designed to detect material misstatement at the assertion level. Confusing tests of controls and substantive procedures is a common error. Candidates must ensure they understand the difference between the two types of test and can provide examples of both as specified in the syllabus.

232 The correct answer is: 2 and 3

Tracing loan payments from the general ledger to the bank statement allows the auditor to confirm how much capital has been repaid and reconcile the closing balance. Confirmation of the balance to the bank letter provides 3rd party evidence of the closing balance.

The procedure described in statement 1 is a test of controls. As such it does not provide evidence of the year-end balance itself. Candidates should be aware that tests of controls may be included as distracters in questions testing substantive procedures and vice versa, therefore it is essential that they understand the difference. Comparing loan liabilities at the end of the current year to the previous year would not be a valid procedure in this instance as the information states that the company has sourced external finance for the first time during the year. As a result, this comparison would be meaningless. Candidates must be able to apply their knowledge of substantive procedures. In this case candidates were required to take in to account the specific circumstances described in the scenario when considering whether a procedure would be appropriate. Candidates must ensure that they answer OT questions within the context set in the scenario rather than responding to them as standalone questions.

# Mock exams

# ACCA

# Applied Skills

# Audit and Assurance

# Mock Examination 1

# September 2016

Time allowed: 3 hours

This mock exam is divided into two sections:

Section A – ALL 15 questions are compulsory and MUST be attempted

Section B – ALL 3 questions are compulsory and MUST be attempted

BPP
LEARNING
MEDIA

# Section A – ALL 15 questions are compulsory and MUST be attempted

Each question is worth 2 marks.

The following scenario relates to questions 1–5.

Note. Assume it is 1 July 20X5

You are an audit senior of Viola & Co and are currently conducting the audit of Poppy Co for the year ended 31 March 20X5.

Materiality has been set at $50,000, and you are carrying out the detailed substantive testing on the year-end payables balance. The audit manager has emphasised that understatement of the trade payables balance is a significant audit risk.

Below is an extract from the list of supplier statements as at 31 March 20X5 held by the company and corresponding payables ledger balances at the same date along with some commentary on the noted differences:

| Supplier | Statement balance $'000 | Payables ledger balance $'000 |
|---|---|---|
| Carnation Co | 70 | 50 |
| Lily Co | 175 | 105 |

### Carnation Co

The difference in the balance is due to an invoice which is under dispute due to faulty goods which were returned on 30 March 20X5.

### Lily Co

The difference in the balance is due to the supplier statement showing an invoice dated 29 March 20X5 for $70,000 which was not recorded in the financial statements until after the year end. The payables clerk has advised the audit team that the invoice was not received until 2 April 20X5.

1   The audit manager has asked you to review the full list of trade payables and select balances on which supplier statement reconciliations will be performed.

   Indicate on the table below if the following items should be included in, or excluded from, your sample.

| | | |
|---|---|---|
| Suppliers with material balances at the year end | Include | Exclude |
| Suppliers which have a high volume of business with Poppy Co | Include | Exclude |
| Major suppliers with nil balances at the year end | Include | Exclude |
| Major suppliers where the statement agrees to the ledger | Include | Exclude |

2   Which of the following audit procedures should be performed in relation to the balance with Lily Co to determine if the payables balance is understated?

   ○   Inspect the goods received note to determine when the goods were received

   ○   Inspect the purchase order to confirm it is dated before the year end

   ○   Review the post year end cash book for evidence of payment of the invoice

   ○   Send a confirmation request to Lily Co to confirm the outstanding balance

3    Which of the following audit procedures should be carried out to confirm the balance owing to Carnation Co?

(1)   Review post year end credit notes for evidence of acceptance of return

(2)   Inspect pre year end goods returned note in respect of the items sent back to the supplier

(3)   Inspect post year end cash book for evidence that the amount has been settled

O    1, 2 and 3

O    1 and 3 only

O    1 and 2 only

O    2 and 3 only

4    The audit manager has asked you to review the results of some statistical sampling testing, which resulted in 20% of the payables balance being tested.

The testing results indicate that there is a $45,000 error in the sample: $20,000 which is due to invoices not being recorded in the correct period as a result of weak controls and additionally there is a one-off error of $25,000 which was made by a temporary clerk.

What would be an appropriate course of action on the basis of these results?

O    The error is immaterial and therefore no further work is required.

O    The effect of the control error should be projected across the whole population.

O    Poppy Co should be asked to adjust the payables figure by $45,000.

O    A different sample should be selected as these results are not reflective of the population.

5    To help improve audit efficiency, Viola & Co is considering introducing the use of computer-assisted audit techniques (CAATs) for some audits. You have been asked to consider how CAATs could be used during the audit of Poppy Co.

Which of the following is an example of using test data for trade payables testing?

O    Selecting a sample of supplier balances for testing using monetary unit sampling

O    Recalculating the ageing of trade payables to identify balances which may be in dispute

O    Calculation of trade payables payment period to use in analytical procedures

O    Inputting dummy purchase invoices into the client system to see if processed correctly

**The following scenario relates to questions 6–10.**

*Note.* Assume it is 1 July 20X5

You are an audit manager at Blenkin & Co and are approaching the end of the audit of Sampson Co, which is a large listed retailer. The draft financial statements currently show a profit before tax of $6.5m and revenue of $66m for the financial year ended 31 March 20X5. You have been informed that the finance director left Sampson Co on 28 February 20X5.

As part of the subsequent events audit procedures, you reviewed post year end board meeting minutes and discovered that a legal case for unfair dismissal has been brought against Sampson Co by the finance director. During a discussion with the human resources (HR) director of

Sampson Co, you established that the company received notice of the proposed legal claim on 10 April 20X5.

The HR director told you that Sampson Co's lawyers believe that the finance director's claim is likely to be successful, but estimate that $150,000 is the maximum amount of compensation which would be paid. However, management does not intend to make any adjustments or disclosures in the financial statements.

6    Blenkin & Co has a responsibility to perform procedures to obtain sufficient, appropriate evidence that subsequent events are appropriately reflected in the financial statements of Sampson Co.

Indicate, by clicking on the timeline, up until which date the auditor should perform subsequent events procedures.

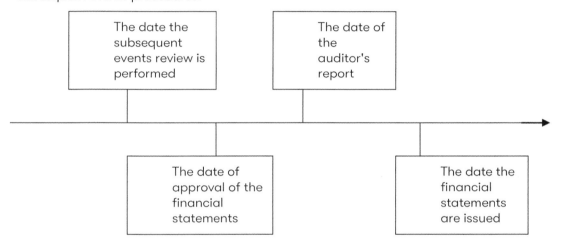

7    If, after the financial statements have been issued, Blenkin & Co becomes aware of a fact which may have caused its report to be amended, the firm should consider several possible actions.

Which **TWO** of the following are appropriate actions for Blenkin & Co to take?

☐    Discuss the matter with management and, where appropriate, those charged with governance

☐    Obtain a written representation from management

☐    Consider whether the firm should resign from the engagement

☐    Enquire how management intends to address the matter in the financial statements where appropriate

8    Which of the following audit procedures should be performed to form a conclusion as to whether the financial statements require amendment in relation to the unfair dismissal claim?

(1)    Inspect relevant correspondence with Sampson Co's lawyers

(2)    Write to the finance director to confirm the claim and level of damages

(3)    Review the post year end cash book for evidence of payments to the finance director

(4)    Request that management confirm their views in a written representation

○     1, 2 and 3

○     1, 2 and 4

○     1, 3 and 4

○     2, 3 and 4

---

9     You are drafting the auditor's report for Sampson Co and the audit engagement partner has reminded you that the report will need to reflect the requirements of ISA 701 *Communicating Key Audit Matters in the Independent Auditor's Report.*

According to ISA 701, which of the following should be included in the 'Key audit matters' paragraph in the auditor's report?

○     Matters which required significant auditor attention

○     Matters which result in a modification to the audit opinion

○     All matters which were communicated to those charged with governance

○     All matters which are considered to be material to the financial statements

---

10    Which of the following audit opinions will be issued if the unfair dismissal case is **NOT** adjusted for or disclosed within the financial statements?

○     A qualified audit opinion as the financial statements are materially misstated

○     A qualified audit opinion as the auditor is unable to obtain sufficient appropriate evidence

○     An unmodified opinion with an emphasis of matter paragraph

○     An unmodified audit opinion

---

**The following scenario relates to questions 11–15.**

Note. Assume it is 1 July 20X5

Sycamore & Co is the auditor of Fir Co, a listed computer software company. The audit team comprises an engagement partner, a recently appointed audit manager, an audit senior and a number of audit assistants. The audit engagement partner has only been appointed this year due to the rotation of the previous partner who had been involved in the audit for seven years. Only the audit senior has experience of auditing a company in this specialised industry. The previous audit manager, who is a close friend of the new audit manager, left the firm before the completion of the prior year audit and is now the finance director of Fir Co.

The board of Fir Co has asked if Sycamore & Co can take on some additional work and have asked if the following additional non-audit services can be provided:

Payroll: Routine maintenance of payroll records

Recruitment:Assistance with the selection of a new financial controller including the checking of references

Tax: Tax services whereby Sycamore & Co would liaise with the tax authority on Fir Co's behalf

Sycamore & Co has identified that the current year fees to be received from Fir Co for audit and other services will represent 16% of the firm's total fee income and totalled 15.5% in the prior year. The audit engagement partner has asked you to consider what can be done in relation to this self-interest threat.

11    Complete the following sentences regarding the audit team by selecting from the options provided.

In relation to the composition of the current audit team, the fundamental principle of

[                    ] is at risk.

An appropriate safeguard to deal with this risk would be to [                    ]

| Fundamental principle |
| --- |
| confidentiality |

| |
| --- |
| professional competence |

| Safeguard |
| --- |
| reinstate the previous partner |

| |
| --- |
| appoint a completely new audit team |

| |
| --- |
| resign from the engagement |

| |
| --- |
| provide industry training for team members |

12    Which of the following identifies the threat which could arise as a result of the finance director's previous employment at Sycamore & Co and recommends an appropriate safeguard?

○      A self-review threat; review the work performed by the previous audit manager

○      A familiarity threat; a different audit manager should be appointed

○      A self-review threat; change the existing audit plan

○      A familiarity threat; the firm should resign from the engagement

13    Ignoring the potential effect on total fee levels, match the non-audit service to the threat to independence which would be created if Sycamore & Co were to provide the proposed services.

| Non-audit service |
| --- |
| Recruitment |

| |
| --- |
| Tax |

| |
| --- |
| Payroll |

| Threat to independence |
| --- |
| Self-review |

| |
| --- |
| Self-interest |

| |
| --- |
| Advocacy |

14    Which of the following safeguards would **NOT** be relevant in mitigating the threat identified in relation to fees?

○    Disclosure to those charged with governance that fees from Fir Co represent more than 15% of Sycamore & Co's total fee income

○    A pre-issuance review to be conducted by an external accountant

○    The use of separate teams to provide the audit and non-audit services

○    A post-issuance review to be conducted by an external accountant or regulatory body

---

15    During the course of the audit of Fir Co, a suspicious cash transfer has been identified. The audit team has reported this to the relevant firm representative as a potential money-laundering transaction.

Which of the following statements is true regarding the confidentiality of this information?

○    Details of the transaction can only be disclosed with the permission of Fir Co.

○    If there is a legal requirement to report money laundering, this overrides the principle of confidentiality.

○    Sycamore & Co is not permitted to disclose details of the suspicious transaction as the information has been obtained during the course of the audit.

○    In order to maintain confidentiality, Sycamore & Co should report its concerns anonymously.

---

**(Total = 30 marks)**

# Section B – ALL THREE questions are compulsory and MUST be attempted

## Question 16

It is 1 July 20X5. Heraklion Co is a manufacturer of footballs and is a new audit client for your firm. You are an audit supervisor of Spinalonga & Co and are currently preparing for the forthcoming interim and final audit for the year ending 30 June 20X5. You are required to document and assess the sales system, recommend control improvements to deal with a specific fraud issue and undertake substantive testing of revenue.

### Sales ordering, goods dispatched and invoicing

Heraklion Co sells footballs to a range of large and small sports equipment retailers in several countries. Sales are made through a network of sales staff employed by Heraklion Co, but new customer leads are generated through a third-party company. Sales staff are responsible for assessing new customers' creditworthiness and proposing a credit limit which is then authorised by the sales director. The sales staff have monthly sales targets and are able to use their discretion in granting sales discounts up to a maximum of 10%. They then record any discount granted in the customer master data file.

The sales staff visit customer sites personally and orders are completed using a two-part pre-printed order form. One copy is left with the customer and the other copy is retained by the salesperson. The sales order number is based on the salesperson's own identification (ID) number.

The company markets itself on being able to dispatch all orders within three working days. Once the order is taken, the salesperson emails the finance department and warehouse dispatch team with the customer ID and the sales order details and from this a pick list is generated. Sequentially numbered goods dispatched notes are completed and filed in the warehouse.

Sequentially numbered invoices are generated using the pick lists for quantities and the customer master data file for prices. Standard credit terms for customers are 30 days and on a monthly basis sales invoices which are over 90 days outstanding are notified to the relevant salesperson to chase payment directly with the customer.

### Payroll fraud

The finance director, Montse Mirabelle, has informed you that a significant fraud took place during the year in the payroll department. A number of fictitious employees were set up on the payroll and wages were paid into one bank account. This bank account belonged to two supervisors, who were married, and were employed by Heraklion Co. One had sole responsibility for setting up new joiners in the payroll system and the other processed and authorised bank transfer requests for wages and supplier payments. These employees no longer work for the company and Montse has asked the audit firm for recommendations on how to improve controls in this area to prevent this type of fraud occurring again. Heraklion Co operates a human resources department.

### Required

(a)     Describe **TWO** methods for documenting the sales system, and for each explain **ONE** advantage and **ONE** disadvantage of using this method.                    **(6 marks)**

(b)     Identify and explain **SEVEN** deficiencies in the sales system of Heraklion Co and provide a recommendation to address each of these deficiencies.

| Control deficiency | Control recommendation |
| --- | --- |
|  |  |

**(14 marks)**

(c)    In relation to the payroll fraud, identify and explain **THREE** controls Heraklion Co should implement to reduce the risk of this type of fraud occurring again and, for each control, describe how it would mitigate the risk. **(6 marks)**

(d)    Describe substantive procedures the auditor should perform to obtain sufficient and appropriate audit evidence in relation to Heraklion Co's revenue. **(4 marks)**

**(Total = 30 marks)**

# Question 17

It is 1 July 20X5. Elounda Co manufactures chemical compounds using a continuous production process. Its year end was 30 April 20X5 and the draft profit before tax is $13.6 million. You are the audit supervisor and the year-end audit is due to commence shortly. The following matters have been brought to your attention:

### Revaluation of property, plant and equipment (PPE)

At the beginning of the year, management undertook an extensive review of Elounda Co's non-current asset valuations and as a result decided to update the carrying value of all PPE. The finance director, Peter Dullman, contacted his brother, Martin, who is a valuer and requested that Martin's firm undertake the valuation, which took place in July 20X4.

### Inventory valuation

Your firm attended the year-end inventory count for Elounda Co and ascertained that the process for recording work in progress (WIP) and finished goods was acceptable. Both WIP and finished goods are material to the financial statements and the quantity and stage of completion of all ongoing production was recorded accurately during the count.

During the inventory count, the count supervisor noted that a consignment of finished goods, compound E243, with a value of $720,000, was defective in that the chemical mix was incorrect. The finance director believes that compound E243 can still be sold at a discounted sum of $400,000.

### Bank loan

Elounda Co secured a bank loan of $2.6 million on 1 July 20X3. Repayments of $200,000 are due quarterly, with a lump sum of $800,000 due for repayment in October 20X5. The company met all loan payments in 20X4 on time, but was late in paying the January and April 20X5 repayments.

### Required

(a)    Describe substantive procedures you should perform to obtain sufficient, appropriate audit evidence in relation to the revaluation of property, plant and equipment (PPE). **(5 marks)**

(b)    Describe substantive procedures you should perform to obtain sufficient, appropriate audit evidence in relation to the inventory valuation. **(6 marks)**

(c)    Describe substantive procedures you should perform to obtain sufficient, appropriate audit evidence in relation to the bank loan. **(4 marks)**

(d)    Describe the procedures which the auditor of Elounda Co should perform in assessing whether or not the company is a going concern. **(5 marks)**

**(Total = 20 marks)**

# Question 18

It is 1 July 20X5. You are an audit supervisor of Chania & Co and are planning the audit of your client, Sitia Sparkle Co, which manufactures cleaning products. Its year end was 30 April 20X5 and the draft profit before tax is $33.6 million. You are supervising a large audit team for the first time and will have specific responsibility for supervising and reviewing the work of the audit assistants in your team.

Sitia Sparkle Co purchases most of its raw materials from suppliers in Africa and these goods are shipped directly to the company's warehouse and the goods are usually in transit for up to three weeks. The company has incurred $1.3 million of expenditure on developing a new range of cleaning products which are due to be launched into the marketplace in August 20X5. In June 20X4, Sitia Sparkle Co also invested $0.9 million in a complex piece of plant and machinery as part of the development process. The full amount has been capitalised and this cost includes the purchase price, installation costs and training costs.

This year, the bonus scheme for senior management and directors has been changed so that, rather than focusing on profits, it is instead based on the value of year-end total assets. In previous years an allowance for receivables, made up of specific balances, which equalled almost 1% of trade receivables, was maintained. However, the finance director feels that this is excessive and unnecessary and has therefore not included it for 20X5 and has credited the opening balance to the profit or loss account.

A new general ledger system was introduced in February 20X5; the finance director has stated that the data was transferred and the old and new systems were run in parallel until the end of May 20X5. As a result of the additional workload on the finance team, a number of control account reconciliations were not completed as at 30 April 20X5, including the bank reconciliation. The finance director is comfortable with this as these reconciliations were completed successfully for both March and May 20X5. In addition, the year-end close down of the purchase ledger was undertaken on 8 May 20X5.

## Required

(a) ISA 300 *Planning an Audit of Financial Statements* provides guidance to assist auditors in planning an audit.

### Required

Explain the benefits of audit planning. **(4 marks)**

(b) Describe **SIX** audit risks, and explain the auditor's response to each risk, in planning the audit of Sitia Sparkle Co.

| Audit risk | Auditor's response |
|---|---|
|  |  |

**(12 marks)**

(c) In line with ISA 220 *Quality Management for an Audit of Financial Statements*, describe the audit supervisor's responsibilities in relation to supervising and reviewing the audit assistants' work during the audit of Sitia Sparkle Co. **(4 marks)**

**(Total = 20 marks)**

# Answers

DO NOT TURN THIS PAGE UNTIL YOU HAVE
COMPLETED THE MOCK EXAM

# Plan of attack

If this were the real Audit and Assurance exam and you had been told to turn over and begin, what would be going through your mind?

An important thing to say (while there is still time) is that it is vital to have a good breadth of knowledge of the syllabus because all the questions are compulsory. However, don't panic. Below we provide guidance on how to approach the exam.

## Looking through the exam

Section A has three objective test cases, each with five questions. This is the section of the exam where the examining team can test knowledge across the breadth of the syllabus. Make sure you read these cases and questions carefully. The distractors are designed to present plausible, but incorrect, answers. Don't let them mislead you. If you really have no idea – guess. You may even be right.

Section B has three longer questions:

- **Question 16** is a 30-mark internal controls question mainly focused on control deficiencies and recommendations in a payroll system. You are also asked to consider controls that would help to prevent fraud. Don't panic – take your time to read the scenario and what you are asked to do. Try to relate your answers to the specific scenario as much as you can.

- **Question 17** is a 20-mark question on audit procedures relating to PPE, inventory, a bank loan and for assessing going concern. You have a number of individual areas to cover here so take care with timing.

- **Question 18** is a 20-mark planning and audit risk question. Make sure you have noticed that part (b) requires you to identify risks **and** explain the auditor's response to these.

## Allocating your time

BPP's advice is to always allocate your time **according to the marks for the question**. However, **use common sense**. If you're doing a question but haven't a clue how to do part (b), you might be better off reallocating your time and getting more marks on another question, where you can add something you didn't have time for earlier on. Make sure you leave time to recheck the OTs and make sure you have answered them all.

## Forget about it!

And don't worry if you found the exam difficult. More than likely other candidates will too. If this were the real thing you would need to forget the exam the minute you left the exam hall and think about the next one. Or, if it is the last one, celebrate!

BPP
LEARNING
MEDIA

# Section A

## ALL 15 questions are compulsory and MUST be attempted

1 The correct answer is:

| Suppliers with material balances at the year end | Include | |
|---|---|---|
| Suppliers which have a high volume of business with Poppy Co | Include | |
| Major suppliers with nil balances at the year end | Include | |
| Major suppliers where the statement agrees to the ledger | | Exclude |

Where completeness is the key assertion, the sample should be selected to verify where the balance may be understated and therefore should include suppliers with material balances, suppliers with a high volume of business with Poppy Co and major suppliers with no outstanding balance at the year end.

2 The correct answer is: Inspect the goods received note to determine when the goods were received.

In order to determine if the balance with Lily Co is understated, the auditor should determine if the goods should be included in payables at the year end by inspecting the goods received note.

3 The correct answer is: 1 and 2 only

To confirm the balance with Carnation Co, the auditor must determine if the liability exists for the disputed items at the year end by reviewing pre year end goods returned notes and post year end credit notes to verify that the goods have been returned and the order cancelled by the supplier.

4 The correct answer is: The effect of the control error should be projected across the whole population.

Although the error is immaterial, the auditor must reach a conclusion on the sample selected and in order to do so the effect of the error must be considered in relation to the whole population.

5 The correct answer is: Inputting dummy purchase invoices into the client system to see if processed correctly

Test data involves inputting fake transactions into the client's system to test how the transactions are processed. The other options are examples of audit software.

6

As per ISA 560 *Subsequent Events*, the auditor has an active responsibility to carry out subsequent events procedures between the date of the financial statements and the date of the auditor's report.

7    The correct answers are:

Discuss the matter with management and, where appropriate, those charged with governance

Enquire how management intends to address the matter in the financial statements where appropriate

As per ISA 560 paragraph 15, in the circumstances described the auditor should initially discuss the matter with management and understand how management intends to address the matter in the financial statements.

8    The correct answer is: 1, 3 and 4

The auditor is unlikely to ask the finance director, who is no longer an officer of the company and the party involved in the claim, to confirm the level of damages payable. All other procedures would be appropriate.

9    The correct answer is: Matters which required significant auditor attention

As per paragraph 9 of ISA 701 *Communicating Key Audit matters in the Independent Auditor's Report*, in determining key audit matters, the auditor shall determine, from the matters communicated to those charged with governance, those which required significant auditor attention.

10    The correct answer is: An unmodified audit opinion

The maximum damages of $150,000 is not material to the financial statements at 2.3% of profit before tax and 0.2% of revenue. Therefore no modification to the audit opinion is required.

11    In relation to the composition of the current audit team, the fundamental principle of **professional competence** is at risk.

An appropriate safeguard to deal with this risk would be to **provide industry training for team members**.

The fundamental principle at risk is professional competence, as many of the audit team are new and do not have relevant experience in relation to the specialised industry in which Fir Co operates. It is not appropriate to reinstate the previous partner as, in line with the ACCA *Code of Ethics and Conduct*, the previous partner has been rotated after seven years to prevent a familiarity threat. The audit firm should offer appropriate training for the audit team to ensure they have the necessary knowledge to carry out the work.

12    The correct answer is: A familiarity threat; a different audit manager should be appointed

As the previous audit manager has taken up employment with the client as the finance director, there is a familiarity threat due to the ongoing relationship between the old and new audit manager. The familiarity threat is not so severe that the firm would need to resign but a new audit manager should be appointed.

13 The correct answer is:

| Non-audit service | Threat to independence |
|---|---|
| | Payroll / Self-review |
| | Recruitment / Self-interest |
| | Tax / Advocacy |

As per the ACCA *Code of Ethics and Conduct*, the following threats would be created from carrying out the non-audit services requested by Fir Co:

Payroll – Self-review as the auditor will also be involved in auditing the figures included in the financial statements in relation to wages and salaries.

Recruitment – Self-interest as the auditor would be involved in selecting an officer of the company who has significant influence over the financial statements.

Tax – Advocacy as the auditor may be perceived to be representing and promoting Fir Co's interest in liaising with the tax authority.

14 The correct answer is: The use of separate teams to provide the audit and non-audit services

Using separate teams will not address the self-interest threat from the fee levels, as separating the teams will not alleviate the firm's potential financial dependence on Fir Co and therefore the risk that work is not carried out independently for fear of losing the client.

15 The correct answer is: If there is a legal requirement to report money laundering, this overrides the principle of confidentiality.

As per the ACCA *Code of Ethics and Conduct* – Confidential information may be disclosed when such disclosure is required by law.

# Section B

# Question 16

## Marking scheme

| | | Marks | |
|---|---|---|---|
| (a) | **Methods for documenting the sales system** | | |
| | • Narrative notes | 3 | |
| | • Questionnaires | 3 | |
| | • Flowcharts | 3 | |
| | Restricted to | | 6 |
| (b) | **Control deficiencies and recommendations** (only 7 issues required) | | |
| | • New customers' creditworthiness assessed by sales staff | 2 | |
| | • Sales staff have discretion to grant discounts up to 10% | 2 | |
| | • Access to master file data | 2 | |
| | • Inventory not checked by salespeople prior to order being placed | 2 | |
| | • No copy of order with the sales ordering department, unable to identify unfulfilled orders | 2 | |
| | • Orders not sequentially numbered | 2 | |
| | • Warehouse dispatch team do not receive a copy of the sales order | 2 | |
| | • Goods dispatch notes filed by warehouse dispatch team | 2 | |
| | • Salesperson responsible for chasing invoices over 90 days old | 2 | |
| | Max 7 issues, 2 marks each | | 14 |
| (c) | **Controls to reduce risk of payroll fraud** | | |
| | • Proof of identity checks undertaken for all new joiners | 2 | |
| | • Review of the number of employees per department to the payroll system | 2 | |
| | • Human resources department initiates request for new joiners | 2 | |
| | • Authorisation of all new joiners by payroll director | 2 | |
| | • Relatives not permitted to undertake interrelated processes | 2 | |
| | • Payroll system reviews same bank account name and number | 2 | |
| | • Bank transfer requests authorised by senior responsible official, independent | 2 | |
| | Restricted to | | 6 |

|  |  |  | Marks |
|---|---|---|---|
| (d) | **Substantive procedures for revenue** | | |
| | • | Analytical review over revenue compared to budget and prior year | 1 |
| | • | Analytical review of main product categories of sales compared to prior year | 1 |
| | • | Gross margin review | 1 |
| | • | Agree sales prices for customers to price list or master file data | 1 |
| | • | Review credit notes | 1 |
| | • | Follow orders to goods dispatched note, to sales invoice and to sales ledger | 1 |
| | • | Sales cut-off | 1 |
| | **Restricted to** | | **4** |
| **Total marks** | | | **30** |

---

## (a)    Documenting the sales system

There are several methods which can be used to document the sales system.

### Narrative notes

Narrative notes consist of a written description of the system; they would detail what occurs in the system at each stage and would include any controls which operate at each stage.

Advantages of this method include:

- They are simple to record; after discussion with staff members, these discussions are easily written up as notes.

- They can facilitate understanding by all members of the audit team, especially more junior members who might find alternative methods too complex.

Disadvantages of this method include:

- Narrative notes may prove to be too cumbersome, especially if the system is complex or heavily automated.

- This method can make it more difficult to identify missing internal controls as the notes record the detail but do not identify control exceptions clearly.

### Questionnaires

Internal control questionnaires (ICQs) or internal control evaluation questionnaires (ICEQs) contain a list of questions; ICQs are used to assess whether controls exist whereas ICEQs assess the effectiveness of the controls in place.

Advantages of this method include:

- Questionnaires are quick to prepare, which means they are a timely method for recording the system.

- They ensure that all controls present within the system are considered and recorded; hence missing controls or deficiencies are clearly highlighted by the audit team.

Disadvantages of this method include:

- It can be easy for the staff members to overstate the level of the controls present as they are asked a series of questions relating to potential controls.

- A standard list of questions may miss out unusual or more bespoke controls used by the company.

### Flowcharts

Flowcharts are a graphic illustration of the internal control system for the sales system. Lines usually demonstrate the sequence of events and standard symbols are used to signify controls or documents.

Advantages of this method include:

- It is easy to view the system in its entirety as it is all presented together in one diagram.

- Due to the use of standard symbols for controls, it can be effective in identifying missing controls.

Disadvantages of this method include:

- They can sometimes be difficult to amend, as any amendments may require the whole flowchart to be redrawn.

- There is still the need for narrative notes to accompany the flowchart and hence it can be a time-consuming method.

Note. Full marks will be awarded for describing **two** methods for documenting the sales system and explaining **one** advantage and **one** disadvantage for each method.

(b) **Deficiencies and controls over the sales system**

| Control deficiency | Control recommendation |
|---|---|
| New customers' creditworthiness is assessed by a salesperson who sets the credit limit, which is authorised by the sales director.<br><br>The sales staff have sales targets, and hence may suggest that new customers are creditworthy simply to meet their targets. This could result in sales being made to poor credit risks. | New customers should complete a credit application which should be checked through a credit agency with a credit limit set. Once authorised by the sales director, the limit should be entered into the system by a credit controller. |
| Sales staff have discretion to grant sales discounts to customers of up to 10%. This could result in a loss of revenue as they may award unrealistic discounts simply to meet sales targets.<br><br>The discounts granted by sales staff are not being reviewed and could result in unauthorised discounts allowed. | All discounts to be granted to customers should be authorised in advance by a responsible official, such as the sales director. If not practical, then the supervisor of the sales staff should undertake this role. |
| Sales staff are able to make changes to the customer master data file, in order to record discounts allowed and these changes are not reviewed.<br><br>There is a risk that these amendments could be made incorrectly resulting in a loss of sales revenue or overcharging of customers. In addition, the sales staff are not senior enough to be given access to changing master file data as this could increase the risk of fraud. | Sales staff should not be able to access the master data file to make amendments. Any such amendments to master file data should be restricted so that only supervisors and above can make changes.<br><br>An exception report of changes made should be generated and reviewed by a responsible official. |

| Control deficiency | Control recommendation |
|---|---|
| Inventory availability does not appear to be checked by the salesperson at the time the order is placed. In addition, Heraklion Co markets itself on being able to dispatch all orders within three working days.<br><br>There is a risk that where goods are not available, the customer would not be made aware of this prior to placing their order, leading to unfulfilled orders and customer dissatisfaction, which would impact the company's reputation. | Prior to the salesperson finalising the order, the inventory system should be checked in order for an accurate assessment of the availability of goods to be notified to customers. |
| Customer orders are recorded on a two-part pre-printed form; one copy is left with the customer and one with the salesperson.<br><br>The sales department of Heraklion Co does not hold these orders centrally and hence would not be able to monitor if orders are being fulfilled on a timely basis. This could result in a loss of revenue and customer goodwill. | The order form should be amended to be at least four-part. The third part of the order should be sent to the warehouse department and the fourth part sent to the finance department.<br><br>The copy the salesperson has should be stored centrally in the sales department. Upon dispatch, the goods dispatch note should be matched to the order; a regular review of unmatched orders should be undertaken by the sales department to identify any unfulfilled orders. |
| Customer orders are given a number based on the salesperson's own identification (ID) number. These numbers are not sequential. Without sequential numbers, it is difficult for Heraklion Co to identify missing orders and to monitor if all orders are being dispatched in a timely manner, leading to a loss of customer goodwill. | Sales orders should be sequentially numbered. On a regular basis, a sequence check of orders should be undertaken to identify any missing orders. |
| The salesperson emails the warehouse dispatch team with the customer ID and the sales order details, rather than a copy of the sales order itself, and a pick list is generated from this.<br><br>There is a risk that incorrect or insufficient details may be recorded by the salesperson and this could result in incorrect orders being dispatched, orders being dispatched late or orders failing to be dispatched at all, resulting in a loss of customer goodwill and revenue. | The third part of the sales order as mentioned previously should be forwarded directly to the warehouse department.<br><br>The pick list should be generated from the original order form and the warehouse team should check correct quantities and product descriptions are being dispatched, as well as checking the quality of goods being dispatched to ensure they are not damaged. |
| Sequentially numbered goods dispatched notes (GDNs) are completed and filed by the warehouse department. If the finance department does not receive a copy of these GDNs, they will not know when to raise the related sales invoices. This could result in goods being dispatched but not being invoiced, leading to a loss of revenue. | Upon dispatch of goods, a four-part GDN should be completed, with copies to the customer, warehouse department, sales department (to confirm dispatch of goods) and finance department. Upon receipt of the GDN, once matched to the fourth part of the sales order form, a clerk should raise the sales invoices in a timely manner, confirming all details to the GDN and order. |

| Control deficiency | Control recommendation |
|---|---|
| The salesperson is given responsibility to chase customers directly for payment once an invoice is outstanding for 90 days. This is considerably in excess of the company's credit terms of 30 days which will lead to poor cash flow.<br><br>Further, as the salespeople have sales targets, they are more likely to focus on generating sales orders rather than chasing payments. This could result in an increase in bad debts and reduced profit and cash flows. | A credit controller should be appointed and it should be their role, rather than that of the salesperson, to chase any outstanding sales invoices which are more than 30 days old. |

(c) Controls to reduce risk of payroll fraud

| Control | Mitigate risk |
|---|---|
| Proof of identity checks should be undertaken by the human resources (HR) department and recorded on individuals' personnel files for all new employees set up on the payroll system. | This should reduce the risk of fictitious employees being set up, as in order to be set up on the system a fictitious set of identification would be required which would be an onerous process. |
| A count should be undertaken of the number of employees in each department of Heraklion Co; this should be reconciled to the number of employees on the payroll system. | This would identify if there are extra employees on the payroll system, which could then be investigated further. |
| The HR department should initiate the process for setting up new joiners by asking new employees to complete a joiner's form which will be approved by the relevant manager and HR. This request should then be forwarded to the payroll department, who should set up the employee. | This control introduces segregation of duties as in order to set up employees both the HR and payroll departments are involved. Without collusion with an HR employee, the payroll supervisor would be unable to set up fictitious employees. |
| All new joiners should only be set up by payroll on receipt of a joiner's form and any additions to the system should be authorised by the payroll director. An edit report should be generated and reviewed by HR. | As all new joiners would be authorised by the payroll director, it is unlikely that payroll employees would risk establishing fictitious joiners. A further review by the HR department would also detect any employees without an authorised joiner form. |
| Where possible, employees who are related should not be allowed to undertake processes which are interrelated whereby they can breach segregation of duty controls for key transaction cycles. A regular review of job descriptions of related employees should be carried out by HR. | This should reduce the risk of related staff colluding and being able to commit a fraud. |
| The payroll system should be amended to run an exception report which identifies any employees with the same bank account name or number and this should be reviewed by HR. | Identifying the same bank account name or number will prevent multiple fraudulent payments being made to the same employee. |

| Control | Mitigate risk |
|---|---|
| All bank transfer requests should be authorised by a senior responsible official, who is independent of the processing of payments; they should undertake spot checks of payments to supporting documentation, including employee identification cards/records. | This would introduce an additional layer of segregation of duties, which would reduce the risk of fraud occurring. In addition, the spot checks to employee identification cards/records would confirm the validity of payments. |

(d) **Revenue substantive procedures**

(i) Compare the overall level of revenue against prior years and budgets and investigate any significant fluctuations.

(ii) Obtain a schedule of sales for the year broken down into the main product categories and compare this to the prior year breakdown and for any unusual movements discuss with management.

(iii) Calculate the gross profit margin for Heraklion Co and compare this to the prior year and investigate any significant fluctuations.

(iv) Select a sample of sales invoices for customers and agree the sales prices back to the price list or customer master data information to ensure the accuracy of invoices.

(v) Select a sample of credit notes raised, trace through to the original invoice and ensure the invoice has been correctly removed from sales.

(vi) Select a sample of customer orders and agree these to the dispatch notes and sales invoices through to inclusion in the sales ledger and revenue general ledger accounts to ensure completeness of revenue.

(vii) Select a sample of dispatch notes both pre and post year end and follow these through to sales invoices in the correct accounting period to ensure that cut-off has been correctly applied.

# Question 17

**Workbook references.** Chapters 12, 13, 17 and 19.

**Top tips.** This is a 20-mark audit evidence and going concern question. In parts (a) to (c), the key is to note that you are being asked for substantive procedures relating to specific aspects eg **revaluation** of PPE, not all aspects of PPE. The examining team's report noted that in relation to inventory a significant proportion of candidates focused on inventory counts rather than **valuation** as required by the question. Make sure you read the information carefully noting important details like these.

You also need to ensure that you tailor your answer to the scenario rather than simply listing out standard audit procedures.

For part (d) make sure you understand the requirement. The question is asking for procedures, not going concern indicators.

**Easy marks.** Overall this is a demanding question due to the care required in reading the information and the need to tailor the answer specifically. However, you should have been able to pick up good marks for substantive procedures relating to the bank loan.

Marks

(a) **Substantive procedures for revaluation of property, plant and equipment (PPE)**
- Cast schedule of PPE revalued this year and agree to TB/FS — 1
- Consider reasonableness of the valuer's qualifications, membership of professional body and experience — 1
- Discuss with management if the valuer has financial interests in the company which along with family relationship may impact his independence — 1
- Agree the revalued amounts to the valuation statement provided by the valuer — 1
- Consider if all items in the same class of assets have been revalued — 1
- Agree the revalued amounts included correctly in the non-current asset register — 1
- Recalculate the total revaluation adjustment and agree recorded in the revaluation surplus — 1
- Recalculate the depreciation charge for the year — 1
- Review the financial statements disclosures for compliance with IAS 16 *Property, Plant and Equipment* — 1

Restricted to — 5

(b) **Substantive procedures for inventory valuation**
- Cast a schedule of all raw materials, finished goods and work in progress (WIP) inventory and agree to TB/FS — 1
- Obtain breakdown and agree sample of WIP from the count to the WIP schedule, agree percentage completion — 1
- For a sample, obtain relevant cost sheets and confirm raw material costs to recent purchase invoices, labour costs to time sheets or wage records and overheads allocated are of a production nature — 1
- For a sample of inventory items, review the calculation for equivalent units and associated equivalent unit cost and recalculate the inventory valuation — 1
- Select a sample of year-end finished goods and review post year end sales invoices to ascertain if net realisable value (NRV) is above cost or if an adjustment is required — 1
- Select a sample of items included in WIP at the year end and ascertain the final unit cost price, verifying to relevant supporting documentation, and compare to the unit sales price included in sales invoices post year end to assess NRV — 1
- Review aged inventory reports, identify slow-moving goods, discuss with management — 1
- Compound E243, discuss with management plans for disposing of goods, why NRV is $400,000 — 1
- If any of defective goods have been sold post year end, agree to the sales invoice to assess NRV — 1
- Agree the cost of $720,000 for compound E243 to supporting documentation — 1

- Confirm the final adjustment for compound E243, discuss with management if adjustment made, if so, follow through the write down to confirm     1
- Review the financial statements disclosures for compliance with IAS 2 *Inventories*     1

  **Restricted to**     6

(c) **Substantive procedures for bank loan**
- Agree the opening balance to the prior year audit file and FS     1
- For loan payments made, agree to cash book and bank statements     1
- Review the bank correspondence for late payment penalties, agree to statement of profit or loss     1
- Obtain direct confirmation of year-end balance from bank, agree to the loan schedule     1
- Review loan agreement for details of covenants and recalculate to identify any breaches     1
- Agree closing balance to the trial balance and draft financial statements and review the disclosure of the current liability bank loan in the draft financial statements     1

  **Restricted to**     4

(d) **Going concern procedures**
- Review cash flow forecasts
- Review bank loan agreements, breach of key ratios or covenants
- Review post year end sales and order book
- Review supplier's correspondence
- Enquire of lawyers for any litigation
- Subsequent events
- Board minutes
- Management accounts
- Consider additional disclosures under IAS 1 *Presentation of Financial Statements*
- Written representation     1

  **Restricted to**     5

**Total marks**     20

---

(a) **Substantive procedures for revaluation of property, plant and equipment (PPE)**

- Obtain a schedule of all PPE revalued during the year and cast to confirm completeness and accuracy of the revaluation adjustment and agree to trial balance and financial statements.

- Consider the competence and capability of the valuer, Martin Dullman, by assessing through enquiry his qualification, membership of a professional body and experience in valuing these types of assets.

- Consider whether the valuation undertaken provides sufficiently objective audit evidence. Discuss with management whether Martin Dullman has any financial interest in Elounda Co which along with the family relationship could have had an impact on his independence.

- Agree the revalued amounts to the valuation statement provided by the valuer.

- Review the valuation report and consider if all assets in the same category have been revalued in line with IAS 16 *Property, Plant and Equipment*.

- Agree the revalued amounts for these assets are included correctly in the non-current assets register.

- Recalculate the total revaluation adjustment and agree correctly recorded in the revaluation surplus.

- Recalculate the depreciation charge for the year to ensure that, for the assets revalued during the year, the depreciation was based on the correct valuation and was for 12 months.

- Review the financial statements disclosures relating to the revaluation to ensure they comply with IAS 16.

(b) **Substantive procedures for inventory valuation**

- Obtain a schedule of all raw materials, finished goods and work in progress (WIP) inventory and cast to confirm completeness and accuracy of the balance and agree to trial balance and financial statements.

- Obtain the breakdown of WIP and agree a sample of WIP assessed during the count to the WIP schedule, agreeing the percentage completion as recorded at the inventory count.

- For a sample of inventory items (finished goods and WIP), obtain the relevant cost sheets and confirm raw material costs to recent purchase invoices, labour costs to time sheets or wage records and overheads allocated are of a production nature.

- For a sample of inventory items, review the calculation for equivalent units and associated equivalent unit cost and recalculate the inventory valuation.

- Select a sample of year-end finished goods and review post year end sales invoices to ascertain if net realisable value (NRV) is above cost or if an adjustment is required.

- Select a sample of items included in WIP at the year end and ascertain the final unit cost price, verifying to relevant supporting documentation, and compare to the unit sales price included in sales invoices post year end to assess NRV.

- Review aged inventory reports and identify any slow-moving goods, discuss with management why these items have not been written down or if an allowance is required.

- For the defective chemical compound E243, discuss with management their plans for disposing of these goods, and why they believe these goods have an NRV of $400,000.

- If any E243 has been sold post year end, agree to the sales invoice to assess NRV.

- Agree the cost of $720,000 for compound E243 to supporting documentation to confirm the raw material cost, labour cost and any overheads attributed to the cost.

- Confirm if the final adjustment for compound E243 is $320,000 (720 – 400) and discuss with management if this adjustment has been made; if so follow through the write down to confirm.

- Review the financial statements disclosures relating to inventory and WIP to ensure they comply with IAS 2 *Inventories*.

(c) **Substantive procedures for bank loan**

- Agree the opening balance of the bank loan to the prior year audit file and financial statements.

- For any loan payments made during the year, agree the cash outflow to the cash book and bank statements.

BPP
LEARNING
MEDIA

- Review bank correspondence to identify whether any late payment penalties have been levied and agree these have been charged to profit or loss account as a finance charge.

- Obtain direct confirmation at the year end from the loan provider of the outstanding balance and any security provided; agree confirmed amounts to the loan schedule and financial statements.

- Review the loan agreement for details of covenants and recalculate to identify any breaches in these.

- Agree closing balance of the loan to the trial balance and draft financial statements and that the disclosure is adequate, including any security provided, that the loan is disclosed as a current liability and that disclosure is in accordance with accounting standards and local legislation.

(d) **Going concern procedures**

- Obtain Elounda's cash flow forecast and review the cash in- and outflows. Assess the assumptions for reasonableness and discuss the findings with management to understand if the company will have sufficient cash flows to meet liabilities as they fall due.

- Discuss with management their ability to settle the next instalment due for repayment to the bank and the lump sum payment of $800k in October 20X5 and ensure these have been included in the cash flow forecast.

- Review current agreements with the bank to determine whether any key ratios or covenants have been breached with regards to the bank loan or any overdraft.

- Review the company's post year end sales and order book to assess the levels of trade and if the revenue figures in the cash flow forecast are reasonable.

- Review post year end correspondence with suppliers to identify whether any restrictions in credit have arisen and, if so, ensure that the cash flow forecast reflects the current credit terms or where necessary an immediate payment for trade payables.

- Enquire of the lawyers of Elounda Co as to the existence of litigation and claims; if any exist, then consider their materiality and impact on the going concern basis.

- Perform audit tests in relation to subsequent events to identify any items which might indicate or mitigate the risk of going concern not being appropriate.

- Review the post year end board minutes to identify any other issues which might indicate financial difficulties for the company.

- Review post year end management accounts to assess if in line with cash flow forecast and to identify any issues which may be relevant to the going concern assessment.

- Consider whether any additional disclosures as required by IAS 1 *Presentation of Financial Statements* in relation to material uncertainties over going concern should be made in the financial statements.

- Obtain a written representation confirming the directors' view that Elounda Co is a going concern.

# Question 18

**Workbook references.** Chapters 4, 6 and 7.

**Top tips.** This is a 20-mark question covering audit planning, audit risk and quality management. As stated below, part (a) and (c) are more straightforward. Part (b) is more demanding as you are required to describe audit risks and provide the auditor's response to address the risk. This is a highly examinable topic and is likely to be examined on a regular basis. One of the key weaknesses in responses to this type of question is a failure to explain the audit risk as well as identifying it. The examining team's report states that to explain audit risk 'candidates need to state the area of the accounts impacted with an assertion, a reference to under/over/misstated, or a reference to inherent, control or detection risk'.

Try to ensure that your answers explain audit risks in this way.

**Easy marks.** Part (a) should represent easy marks as you should be familiar with the benefits of audit planning. You should also be able to score well on part (c) on quality management.

## Marking scheme

Marks

(a) **Benefits of audit planning**
- Important areas of the audit
- Potential problems
- Effective and efficient audit
- Selection of engagement team members and assignment of work
- Direction, supervision and review
- Co-ordination of work

**Restricted to**      4

(b) **Audit risks and responses** (only 6 risks required)

| | Marks |
|---|---|
| • Goods in transit from Africa | 2 |
| • Research and development expenditure | 2 |
| • Capitalisation of costs of plant and machinery | 2 |
| • Senior management bonus scheme | 2 |
| • Allowance for receivables | 2 |
| • Introduction of new general ledger system | 2 |
| • April 20X5 control account reconciliations not undertaken | 2 |
| • Purchase ledger closed down on 8 May | 2 |

**Max 6 issues, 2 marks each**      12

(c) **Supervising and reviewing audit assistants' work**

| | Marks |
|---|---|
| • Monitor the progress of the audit engagement to ensure the audit timetable was met | 1 |
| • Consider the competence and capabilities of team members re sufficient available time, understanding of instructions and if work in accordance with planned approach | 1 |
| • Address any significant matters arising, consider their significance and modifying the approach | 1 |
| • Responsible for identifying matters for consultation/consideration by senior team members | 1 |
| • Work performed in line with professional standards and other requirements | 1 |
| • Work supports conclusions reached and properly documented | 1 |

| | Marks |
|---|---|
| • Significant matters raised for partner attention or further consideration | 1 |
| • Appropriate consultations have taken place with conclusions documented | 1 |
| **Restricted to** | 4 |
| **Total marks** | 20 |

(a) **Benefits of audit planning**

Audit planning is addressed by ISA 300 *Planning an Audit of Financial Statements*. It states that adequate planning benefits the audit of financial statements in several ways:

- Helping the auditor to devote appropriate attention to important areas of the audit

- Helping the auditor to identify and resolve potential problems on a timely basis

- Helping the auditor to properly organise and manage the audit engagement so that it is performed in an effective and efficient manner

- Assisting in the selection of engagement team members with appropriate levels of capabilities and competence to respond to anticipated risks and the proper assignment of work to them

- Facilitating the direction and supervision of engagement team members and the review of their work

- Assisting, where applicable, in co-ordination of work done by experts

(b) **Audit risk and auditor's responses**

| Audit risk | Auditor's response |
|---|---|
| Sitia Sparkle Co purchases its goods from suppliers in Africa and the goods are in transit for up to three weeks. At the year end, there is a risk that the cut-off of inventory, purchases and payables may not be accurate and may be under/overstated. | The audit team should undertake detailed cut-off testing of purchases of goods at the year end and the sample of GRNs from before and after the year end relating to goods from suppliers in Africa should be increased to ensure that cut-off is complete and accurate. |
| Sitia Sparkle Co has incurred expenditure of $1.3 million in developing a new range of cleaning products. This expenditure is classed as research and development under IAS 38 *Intangible Assets*. The standard requires research costs to be expensed to profit or loss and development costs to be capitalised as an intangible asset.<br><br>If the company has incorrectly classified research costs as development expenditure, there is a risk the intangible asset could be overstated and expenses understated.<br><br>In addition, as the senior management bonus is based on year-end asset values, this increases this risk further as management may have a reason to overstate assets at the year end. | Obtain a breakdown of the expenditure and verify that it relates to the development of the new products. Undertake testing to determine whether the costs relate to the research or development stage. Discuss the accounting treatment with the finance director and ensure it is in accordance with IAS 38. |

| Audit risk | Auditor's response |
|---|---|
| In June 20X4, the company invested $0.9 million in a complex piece of plant and machinery. The costs include purchase price, installation and training costs. As per IAS 16 *Property, Plant and Equipment*, the cost of an asset includes its purchase price and directly attributable costs only.<br><br>Training costs are not permitted under IAS 16 to be capitalised as part of the cost and therefore plant and machinery and profits are overstated. | Obtain a breakdown of the $0.9 million expenditure and undertake testing to confirm the level of training costs which have been included within non-current assets. Discuss the accounting treatment with the finance director and the level of any necessary adjustment to ensure treatment is in accordance with IAS 16. |
| The bonus scheme for senior management and directors of Sitia Sparkle Co has been changed; it is now based on the value of year-end total assets. | Throughout the audit, the team will need to be alert to this risk and maintain professional scepticism. |
| There is a risk that management might be motivated to overstate the value of assets through the judgements taken or through the use of releasing provisions or capitalisation policy. | Detailed review and testing on judgemental decisions, including treatment of provisions, and compare treatment against prior years. Any manual journal adjustments affecting assets should be tested in detail.<br><br>In addition, a written representation should be obtained from management confirming the basis of any significant judgements. |
| The finance director of Sitia Sparkle Co believes that an allowance for receivables is excessive and unnecessary and therefore has not provided for it at the year end and has credited the opening balance to profit or loss.<br><br>There is a risk that receivables will be overvalued; some balances may be irrecoverable and so will be overstated if not provided for.<br><br>In addition, releasing the allowance for receivables will increase asset values and hence the senior management bonus which increases the risk further. | Review and test the controls surrounding how Sitia Sparkle Co identifies receivables balances which may require a provision to ensure that they are operating effectively in the current year.<br><br>Discuss with the finance director the rationale for not maintaining an allowance for receivables and releasing the opening provision.<br><br>Extended post year end cash receipts testing and a review of the aged receivables ledger to be performed to assess valuation and the need for an allowance for receivables. |
| A new general ledger system was introduced in February 20X5 and the old and new systems were run in parallel until May 20X5. | The auditor should undertake detailed testing to confirm that all of the balances at the transfer date have been correctly recorded in the new general ledger system. |
| There is a risk of the balances in May being misstated and loss of data if they have not been transferred from the old system completely and accurately. If this is not done, this could result in the auditor not identifying a significant control risk.<br><br>In addition, the new general ledger system will require documenting and the controls over this will need to be tested. | The auditor should document and test the new system. They should review any management reports run comparing the old and new system during the parallel run to identify any issues with the processing of accounting information. |

| Audit risk | Auditor's response |
|---|---|
| A number of reconciliations, including the bank reconciliation, were not performed at the year end; however, they were undertaken in June and August.<br><br>Control account reconciliations provide comfort that accounting records are being maintained completely and accurately. At the year end, it is important to confirm that balances including bank balances are not under- or overstated. This is an example of a control procedure being overridden by management and raises concerns over the overall emphasis placed on internal control. | Discuss this issue with the finance director and request that the July control account reconciliations are undertaken. All reconciling items should be tested in detail and agreed to supporting documentation. |
| The purchase ledger of Sitia Sparkle Co was closed down on 8 May, rather than at the year end of 30 April.<br><br>There is a risk that the cut-off may be incorrect with purchases and payables over- or understated. | The audit team should undertake testing of transactions posted to the purchase ledger between 1 and 8 May to identify whether any transactions relating to the 20X6 year end have been included or any 20X5 balances removed. |

(c)  **Supervision and reviewing of the assistants' work**

**Supervision**

During the audit of Sitia Sparkle Co, the supervisor should keep track of the progress of the audit engagement to ensure that the audit timetable is met and should ensure that the audit manager and engagement partner are kept updated of progress.

The competence and capabilities of individual members of the engagement team should be considered, including whether they have sufficient time to carry out their work, whether they understand their instructions and whether the work is being carried out in accordance with the planned approach to the audit.

In addition, part of the supervision process should involve addressing any significant matters arising during the audit of Sitia Sparkle Co, considering their significance and modifying the planned approach appropriately.

The supervisor would also be responsible for identifying matters for consultation or consideration by the audit manager or engagement partner of Sitia Sparkle Co.

**Review**

The supervisor would be required to review the work completed by the assistants and consider whether this work has been performed in accordance with professional standards and other regulatory requirements and if the work performed supports the conclusions reached and has been properly documented.

The supervisor should also consider whether all significant matters have been raised for partner attention or for further consideration and, where appropriate consultations have taken place, whether appropriate conclusions have been documented.

The overall responsibility for the direction, supervision and review of the audit rests with the audit engagement partner.

# ACCA

# Applied Skills

# Audit and Assurance

# Mock Examination 2

# Specimen exam

Time allowed: 3 hours

This mock exam is divided into two sections:

Section A – ALL 15 questions are compulsory and MUST be attempted

Section B – ALL 3 questions are compulsory and MUST be attempted

# Section A – ALL FIFTEEN questions are compulsory and MUST be attempted

Each question is worth 2 marks.

The following scenario relates to questions 1–5.

You are an audit manager of Buffon & Co, responsible for the audit of Maldini Co, and you have become aware of the following information.

## Audit engagement partner

The audit engagement partner for Maldini Co, a listed company, has been in place for approximately eight years and her son has just been offered a role with Maldini Co as a sales manager. This role would entitle him to shares in Maldini Co as part of his remuneration package.

## Internal audit function

Maldini Co's board of directors are considering establishing an internal audit function, and the finance director has asked the audit firm, Buffon & Co, about the differences in the role of internal audit and external audit. If the internal audit function is established, the directors have suggested that they may wish to outsource this to Buffon & Co.

## Auditor characteristics

Following management's request for information regarding the different roles of internal and external auditors, the audit assistant has collated a list of key characteristics:

(1)    Appointed by audit committee
(2)    Reports are publicly available to shareholders
(3)    Review effectiveness of internal controls to improve operations
(4)    Express an opinion on the truth and fairness of the financial statements

## Fees

The finance director has suggested to the board that if Buffon & Co are appointed as internal as well as external auditors, then fees should be renegotiated with at least 20% of all internal and external audit fees being based on the profit after tax of the company, as this will align the interests of Buffon & Co and Maldini Co. This fee income would be significant to Buffon & Co.

1    Your audit assistant has highlighted a number of potential threats to independence in respect of the audit of Maldini Co.

    Identify which of the following represent valid threats to independence, matching each threat to the appropriate category.

| Facts | Category of threat |
|---|---|
| Length of time the audit engagement partner has been in position | Self-interest |
| Maldini Co's request for advice regarding internal audit | Self-interest |
| Potential holding of shares by audit partner's son | Familiarity |
| Possible provision of internal audit services | Self-review |
| Basis of fee | |

BPP
LEARNING
MEDIA

2    In relation to the audit engagement partner holding the role for eight years, and her son's offer of employment with Maldini Co:

Which of the following safeguards should be implemented in order to comply with ACCA's *Code of Ethics and Conduct*?

○    The audit partner should be removed from the audit team.

○    An independent quality reviewer should be appointed.

○    A third party such as a professional body should be consulted on key audit judgments.

○    Buffon & Co should resign from the audit.

3    In line with ACCA's *Code of Ethics and Conduct*, which **TWO** of the following factors must be considered before the internal audit engagement should be accepted?

☐    Whether the external audit team have the expertise to carry out the internal audit work.

☐    If the assignments will relate to the internal controls over financial reporting.

☐    If management will accept responsibility for implementing appropriate recommendations.

☐    The probable timescale for the outsourcing of the internal audit function.

4    Following management's request for information regarding the different roles of internal and external audit, you have collated a list of key characteristics.

Match the following characteristics to the appropriate auditor.

| Characteristic | Type of auditor |
|---|---|
| 1 | Internal auditor |
| 2 | Internal auditor |
| 3 | External auditor |
| 4 | External auditor |

5    If the internal and external audit assignments are accepted, what safeguards, if any, are needed in relation to the basis for the fee?

○    As long as the total fee received from Maldini Co is less than 15% of the firm's total fee income, no safeguards are needed.

○    The client should be informed that only the internal audit fee can be based on profit after tax.

○    The fees should be based on Maldini Co's profit before tax.

○    No safeguards can be applied and this basis for fee determination should be rejected.

The following scenario relates to Questions 6–10.

It is 1 July 20X5. Balotelli Co operates a number of hotels providing accommodation, leisure facilities and restaurants. You are an audit senior of Mario & Co and are currently conducting the audit of Balotelli Co for the year ended 31 December 20X4. During the course of the audit a number of events and issues have been brought to your attention:

## Non-current assets

Balotelli Co incurred significant capital expenditure during the year updating the leisure facilities at several of the company's hotels. Depreciation is charged monthly on all assets on a straight line (SL) basis and it is company policy to charge a full month's depreciation in the month of acquisition and none in the month of disposal. The audit team has obtained the following extract of the non-current assets register detailing some of the new leisure equipment acquired during the year:

| Date | Description | Original cost | Depreciation policy | Accumulated depreciation | Charge for the year | Carrying value |
|------|-------------|---------------|---------------------|--------------------------|---------------------|----------------|
| | | $ | | $ | $ | $ |
| 01/05/X4 | 15 treadmills | 18,000 | 36 months SL | 0 | 4,000 | 14,000 |
| 15/05/X4 | 20 exercise bikes | 17,000 | 3 years SL | 0 | 5,667 | 11,333 |
| 17/08/X4 | 15 rowing machines | 9,750 | 36 months SL | 0 | 2,167 | 7,583 |
| 19/08/X4 | 10 cross trainers | 11,000 | 36 months SL | 0 | 1,528 | 9,472 |
| | | 55,750 | | 0 | 13,362 | 42,388 |

In order to verify the depreciation charge for the year the audit team has been asked to recalculate a sample of the depreciation charges. The audit team has also been asked to carry out detailed testing on the valuation of non-current assets.

## Food poisoning – litigation

Balotelli Co's directors received correspondence in November 20X4 from a group of customers who attended a wedding at one of the company's hotels. They have alleged that they suffered severe food poisoning from food eaten at the hotel and are claiming substantial damages. Management has stated that, based on discussions with their lawyers, the claim is unlikely to be successful.

## Trade receivables circularisation

The audit team has obtained the following results from the receivables circularisation:

| Customer | Balance per sales ledger | Balance per customer confirmation | Comment |
|----------|--------------------------|-----------------------------------|---------|
| | $ | $ | |
| Willow Co | 42,500 | 42,500 | |
| Cedar Co | 35,000 | 25,000 | Invoice raised 28 December 20X4 |
| Maple Co | 60,000 | 45,000 | Payment made 30 December 20X4 |
| Laurel Co | 55,000 | 55,000 | A balance of $20,000 is currently being disputed by Laurel Co |

## Trade receivables

Balotelli Co's trade receivables have historically been low as most customers are required to pay in advance or at the time of visiting the hotel. However, during the year a number of companies opened corporate accounts which are payable monthly in arrears. As such, the trade receivables balance has risen significantly and is now a material balance.

6   Which of the following correctly calculates the depreciation expense for the new assets for the year ended 31 December 20X4 and explains the resultant impact on non-current assets?

   O   Depreciation should be $10,660, assets are understated

   O   Depreciation should be $18,583, assets are understated

   O   Depreciation should be $9,111, assets are overstated

   O   Depreciation should be $12,549, assets are overstated

7   Which **FOUR** of the following audit procedures are appropriate to test the **VALUATION** assertion for non-current assets?

   ☐   Review board minutes for evidence of disposals during the year and verify that these are appropriately reflected in the non-current assets register

   ☐   Agree a sample of additions included in the non-current asset register to purchase invoice and cash book

   ☐   Review the repairs and maintenance expense account for evidence of items of a capital nature

   ☐   Recalculate the depreciation charge for a sample of assets ensuring that it is being applied consistently and in accordance with IAS 16 *Property, Plant and Equipment*

   ☐   Review physical condition of non-current assets for any signs of damage

   ☐   Ensure disposals are correctly accounted for and recalculate gain/loss on disposal

8   Which of the following audit procedures would provide the auditor with the **MOST** reliable audit evidence regarding the likely outcome of the litigation?

   O   Request a written representation from management supporting their assertion that the claim will not be successful

   O   Send an enquiry letter to the lawyers of Balotelli to obtain their view as to the probability of the claim being successful

   O   Review the correspondence from the customers claiming food poisoning to assess whether Balotelli has a present obligation as a result of a past event

   O   Review board minutes to understand why the directors believe that the claim will not be successful

9   Which **TWO** of the following are benefits of carrying out a trade receivables circularisation?

   ☐   It provides evidence from an independent external source.

   ☐   It provides sufficient appropriate audit evidence over all relevant balance assertions.

   ☐   It improves audit efficiency as all customers are required to respond.

   ☐   It improves the reliability of audit evidence as the process is under the control of the auditor.

10    The audit team has been asked to assess whether any additional audit work is required.

Based on the results of the circularisation, match each customer to the appropriate audit procedure.

| Customer | Audit procedure |
|---|---|
| Willow Co | Agree to post-year end cash book and bank statement |
| Cedar Co | Discuss with management and consider whether amount should be included in allowance for receivables |
| Maple Co | No further audit procedures required |
| Laurel Co | Agree to pre year end invoice |

---

### The following scenario relates to Questions 11–15.

It is 1 July 20X5. Cannavaro.com is a website design company whose year end was 31 December 20X4. The audit is almost complete and the financial statements are due to be signed shortly. Profit before tax for the year is $3.8 million and revenue is $11.2 million.

### Form and content of auditor's report

The company has only required an audit for the last two years and the board of directors has asked your firm to provide more detail in relation to the form and content of the auditor's report. In particular they have queried why the following elements are included:

(1)    Date of report
(2)    Addressee
(3)    Auditor's responsibilities
(4)    Opinion paragraph

### Balance due from Pirlo Co

During the audit it has come to light that a key customer, Pirlo Co, with a receivables balance at the year end of $285,000, has just notified Cannavaro.com that it is experiencing cash flow difficulties and is unable to make any payments for the foreseeable future. The finance director of Cannavaro.com has notified the audit team that he will write this balance off as an irrecoverable debt in the 20X5 financial statements.

### Audit work

The audit partner has asked you to perform the following work in respect of the receivables balance due from Pirlo Co:

(1)    Make an initial assessment of the materiality of the issue and consider the overall impact on the financial statements

(2)    Perform additional procedures in order to conclude on whether the financial statements require adjustment

11  Match the following elements of the unmodified auditor's report, to the correct explanation for its inclusion.

| Element of auditor's report | Reason for inclusion |
|---|---|
| 1 | Explains that the financial statements are presented fairly |
| 2 | Demonstrates the point at which sufficient appropriate evidence has been obtained |
| 3 | Clarifies who may rely on the opinion included in the report |
| 4 | Explains the role and remit of the audit |

12  The audit assistant assigned to the audit of Cannavaro.com wants a better understanding of the effect subsequent events have on the audit and has made the following statements.

Identify, by clicking on the relevant box in the table below, whether each of the following statements is true or false.

| | | |
|---|---|---|
| All material subsequent events require the numbers in the financial statements to be adjusted. | TRUE | FALSE |
| A non-adjusting event is a subsequent event for which **no** amendments to the current year financial statements are required. | TRUE | FALSE |
| The auditor's responsibilities for subsequent events which occur prior to the audit report being signed are different from their responsibilities after the auditor's report has been issued. | TRUE | FALSE |
| The auditor should request a written representation confirming that all relevant subsequent events have been disclosed. | TRUE | FALSE |

13  Which of the following correctly summarises the effect of the outstanding balance with Pirlo Co?

| Option | Material | Impact on accounts |
|---|---|---|
| A | No | Revenue is overstated |
| B | No | Gross profit is understated |
| C | Yes | Profit is overstated |
| D | Yes | The going concern basis is in doubt |

O    Option A

O    Option B

O    Option C

O    Option D

14 Which **TWO** of the following audit procedures should be performed to form a conclusion as to whether the financial statements require amendment?

☐ Discuss with management the reasons for not amending the financial statements

☐ Review the cash book post year end for receipts from Pirlo Co

☐ Send a request to Pirlo Co to confirm the outstanding balance

☐ Agree the outstanding balance to invoices and sales orders

15 The finance director has asked you to outline the appropriate audit opinions which will be provided depending on whether the company decides to amend or not amend the 20X4 financial statements for the issue identified regarding the recoverability of the balance with Pirlo Co.

Complete the following sentences by dragging and dropping the appropriate audit opinions.

If the 20X4 financial statements are not amended, our opinion will be [          ]

If the appropriate adjustment is made to the financial statements, our opinion will be [          ].

| Audit opinion | |
|---|---|
| Adverse | Disclaimer |
| Unmodified with emphasis of matter paragraph | Qualified 'except for' |
| Unmodified | |

(Total = 30 marks)

## Section B – ALL THREE questions are compulsory and MUST be attempted

## Question 16

It is 1 July 20X5. Milla Cola Co (Milla) manufactures fizzy drinks such as cola and lemonade as well as other soft drinks and its year end is 30 September 20X5. You are an audit manager of Totti & Co and are currently planning the audit of Milla. You attended the planning meeting with the audit engagement partner and finance director last week and the minutes from the meeting are shown below. You are reviewing these as part of the process of preparing the audit strategy document.

### Minutes of planning meeting for Milla

Milla's trading results have been strong this year and the company is forecasting revenue of $85 million, which is an increase from the previous year. The company has invested significantly in the cola and fizzy drinks production process at the factory. This resulted in expenditure of $5 million on updating, repairing and replacing a significant amount of the machinery used in the production process.

As the level of production has increased, the company has expanded the number of warehouses it uses to store inventory. It now utilises 15 warehouses; some are owned by Milla and some are rented from third parties. There will be inventory counts taking place at all 15 of these sites at the year end.

A new accounting general ledger has been introduced at the beginning of the year, with the old and new systems being run in parallel for a period of two months. In addition, Milla has incurred expenditure of $4.5 million on developing a new brand of fizzy soft drinks. The company started this process in July 20X4 and is close to launching its new product into the marketplace.

As a result of the increase in revenue, Milla has recently recruited a new credit controller to chase outstanding receivables. The finance director thinks it is not necessary to continue to maintain an allowance for receivables and so has released the opening allowance of $1.5 million.

The finance director stated that there was a problem in April in the mixing of raw materials within the production process which resulted in a large batch of cola products tasting different. A number of these products were sold; however, due to complaints by customers about the flavour, no further sales of these goods have been made. No adjustment has been made to the valuation of the damaged inventory, which will still be held at cost of $1 million at the year end.

As in previous years, the management of Milla is due to be paid a significant annual bonus based on the value of year-end total assets.

### Required

(a)     Explain audit risk and the components of audit risk.                                    **(5 marks)**

(b)     Using the minutes provided, identify and describe **SEVEN** audit risks, and explain the auditor's response to each risk, in planning the audit of Milla.

| Audit risk | Auditor's response |
|---|---|
|  |  |

**(14 marks)**

(c)     Identify the main areas, other than audit risks, which should be included within the audit strategy document for Milla; and for each area provide an example relevant to the audit.
                                                                                                **(4 marks)**

The finance director has requested that the deadline for the 20X6 audit be shortened by a month and has asked the audit engagement partner to consider if this will be possible. The partner has suggested that in order to meet this new tighter deadline the firm may carry out both an interim and a final audit for the audit of Milla to 30 September 20X6.

**Required**

(d)   Explain the difference between an interim and a final audit.   **(3 marks)**

(e)   Explain the procedures which are likely to be performed during an interim audit of Milla and the impact which it would have on the final audit.   **(4 marks)**

**(Total = 30 marks)**

# Question 17

It is 1 July 20X5. Baggio International Co (Baggio) is a manufacturer of electrical equipment. It has factories across the country and its customer base includes retailers as well as individuals, to whom direct sales are made through its website. The company's year-end is 30 September 20X5. You are an audit supervisor of Suarez & Co and are currently reviewing documentation of Baggio's internal control in preparation for the interim audit.

Baggio's website allows individuals to order goods directly, and full payment is taken in advance. Currently the website is not integrated into the inventory system and inventory levels are not checked at the time when orders are placed.

Inventory is valued at the lower of cost and net realisable value.

Goods are dispatched via local couriers; however, they do not always record customer signatures as proof that the customer has received the goods. Over the past 12 months there have been customer complaints about the delay between sales orders and receipt of goods. Baggio has investigated these and found that, in each case, the sales order had been entered into the sales system correctly but was not forwarded to the dispatch department for fulfilling.

Baggio's retail customers undergo credit checks prior to being accepted and credit limits are set accordingly by sales ledger clerks. These customers place their orders through one of the sales team, who decides on sales discount levels.

Raw materials used in the manufacturing process are purchased from a wide range of suppliers. As a result of staff changes in the purchase ledger department, supplier statement reconciliations are no longer performed. Additionally, changes to supplier details in the purchase ledger master file can be undertaken by purchase ledger clerks as well as supervisors.

In the past six months, Baggio has changed part of its manufacturing process and as a result some new equipment has been purchased; however, there are considerable levels of plant and equipment which are now surplus to requirement. Purchase requisitions for all new equipment have been authorised by production supervisors and little has been done to reduce the surplus of old equipment.

**Required**

(a)   In respect of the internal control of Baggio International Co:

  (i)    Identify and explain **SIX** deficiencies;

  (ii)   Recommend a control to address each of these deficiencies; and

  (iii)  Describe a test of control Suarez & Co would perform to assess whether each of these controls, if implemented, is operating effectively.

| Control deficiency | Control recommendation | Test of control |
|---|---|---|
|  |  |  |

**(18 marks)**

(b)   Describe substantive procedures Suarez & Co should perform at the year end to confirm plant and equipment additions.   **(2 marks)**

**(Total = 20 marks)**

# Question 18

It is 1 July 20X5. Vieri Motor Cars Co (Vieri) manufactures a range of motor cars and its year end is 31 March 20X5. You are the audit supervisor of Rossi & Co and are currently preparing the audit programmes for the year-end audit of Vieri. You have had a meeting with your audit manager and he has notified you of the following issues identified during the audit risk assessment process:

## Land and buildings

Vieri has a policy of revaluing land and buildings; this is undertaken on a rolling basis over a five-year period. During the year Vieri requested an external independent valuer to revalue a number of properties, including a warehouse purchased in October 20X4. Depreciation is charged on a pro rata basis.

## Work in progress

Vieri undertakes continuous production of cars, 24 hours a day, 7 days a week. An inventory count is to be undertaken at the year end and Rossi & Co will attend. You are responsible for the audit of work in progress (WIP) and will be part of the team attending the count as well as the final audit. WIP constitutes the partly assembled cars at the year end and this balance is likely to be material. Vieri values WIP according to percentage of completion, and standard costs are then applied to these percentages.

## Required

(a)     Explain the factors Rossi & Co should consider when placing reliance on the work of the independent valuer.                                                                 **(5 marks)**

(b)     Describe the substantive procedures the auditor should perform to obtain sufficient and appropriate audit evidence in relation to the revaluation of land and buildings and the recently purchased warehouse.                                                         **(6 marks)**

(c)     Describe the substantive procedures the auditor should perform to obtain sufficient and appropriate audit evidence in relation to the valuation of work in progress.        **(4 marks)**

During the audit, the team has identified an error in the valuation of work in progress, as a number of the assumptions contain out of date information. The directors of Vieri have indicated that they do not wish to amend the financial statements.

## Required

(d)     Explain the steps Rossi & Co should now take and the impact on the auditor's report in relation to the directors' refusal to amend the financial statements.               **(5 marks)**

(Total = 20 marks)

# Answers

DO NOT TURN THIS PAGE UNTIL YOU HAVE
COMPLETED THE MOCK EXAM

# Plan of attack

If this were the real Audit and Assurance exam and you had been told to turn over and begin, what would be going through your mind?

An important thing to say (while there is still time) is that it is vital to have a good breadth of knowledge of the syllabus because all the questions are compulsory. However, don't panic. Below we provide guidance on how to approach the exam.

## Looking through the exam

Section A has three objective test cases, each with five questions. This is the section of the exam where the examining team can test knowledge across the breadth of the syllabus. Make sure you read these cases and questions carefully. The distractors are designed to present plausible, but incorrect, answers. Don't let them mislead you. If you really have no idea – guess. You may even be right.

Section B has three longer questions:

- **Question 16** is a 30-mark question focused on the planning stage, covering audit risk and the audit strategy document, with an unrelated coda on interim audits. Don't panic – take your time to read the scenario and what you are asked to do.

- **Question 17** is a 20-mark internal controls question. In part (a) it is crucial that you relate your answer to the scenario.

- **Question 18** is a 20-mark question dealing with a number of issues: an independent valuer, revaluations, work in progress, and auditor reporting.

## Allocating your time

BPP's advice is to always allocate your time **according to the marks for the question**. However, **use common sense**. If you're doing a question but haven't a clue how to do part (b), you might be better off reallocating your time and getting more marks on another question, where you can add something you didn't have time for earlier on. Make sure you leave time to recheck the OTs and make sure you have answered them all.

## Forget about it

And don't worry if you found the exam difficult. More than likely other candidates will too. If this were the real thing you would need to forget the exam the minute you left the exam hall and think about the next one. Or, if it is the last one, celebrate!

# Section A

1    The correct answer is:

| Facts | Category of threat |
|---|---|
| Length of time the audit engagement partner has been in position | Familiarity |
| Maldini Co's request for advice regarding internal audit | No threat |
| Potential holding of shares by audit partner's son | Self-interest |
| Possible provision of internal audit services | Self-review |
| Basis of fee | Self-interest |

Fact 1 – Partner has been in role for eight years, this contravenes the Code and represents a familiarity threat.

Fact 2 – Providing information on internal audit is not a threat to independence.

Fact 3 – Partner's son holding shares represents a self-interest threat as a close family member of the partner holds a financial interest.

Fact 4 – Providing internal audit services raises a self-review threat as it is likely that the audit team will be looking to place reliance on the internal control system reviewed by internal audit.

Fact 5 – This represents fees on a contingent basis and raises a self-interest threat as the audit firm's fee will rise if the company's profit after tax increases.

2    The correct answer is: The audit partner should be removed from the audit team.

If the engagement partner's son accepts the role and obtains shares in the company it would constitute a self-interest threat but, as the partner has already exceeded the seven year relationship rule, in line with ACCA's *Code of Ethics and Conduct*, the partner should be rotated off the audit irrespective of the decision made by her son.

As Maldini Co is a listed company an engagement quality reviewer should already be in place in line with ISA 220.

Consulting a third party on key audit judgements would be a potential safeguard in respect of overdependence on fees but would not be adequate in the circumstances described.

It is unlikely that the firm needs to resign from the audit (due to the stated circumstances) as the threat to objectivity can be mitigated.

3    The correct answer is:

If the assignments will relate to the internal controls over financial reporting.

If management will accept responsibility for implementing appropriate recommendations.

Statement 1 is inappropriate as the external and internal audit team should be separate and therefore consideration of the skills of the external audit team is not appropriate in the circumstances.

Statement 4 does not apply because the timescale of the work is not relevant to the consideration of the threats to objectivity.

Statements 2 and 3 are valid considerations – as per ACCA's *Code of Ethics and Conduct*, providing internal audit services can result in the audit firm assuming a management role. To mitigate this, it is appropriate for the firm to assess whether management will take responsibility for implementing recommendations (ACCA *Code of Ethics and Conduct*: para. 605.4). Further, for a listed company the Code prohibits the provision of internal audit services which review a significant proportion of the internal controls over financial reporting as these may be relied upon by the external audit team and the self-review threat is too great (ACCA *Code of Ethics and Conduct*: para. R605.5).

4     The correct answer is:

| Characteristic | | Type of auditor |
|---|---|---|
| (1) | Appointed by audit committee | Internal auditor |
| (2) | Reports are publicly available to shareholders | External auditor |
| (3) | Review effectiveness of internal controls to improve operations | Internal auditor |
| (4) | Express an opinion on the truth and fairness of the financial statements | External auditor |

Internal audit is appointed by the audit committee (external audit usually by the shareholders) and it is the role of internal audit to review the effectiveness and efficiency of internal controls to improve operations. External audit looks at the operating effectiveness of internal controls on which they may rely for audit evidence and a by-product may be to comment on any deficiencies they have found but this is not a key function of the role.

Therefore statements 1 and 3 relate to internal audit.

The external auditor's report is publicly available to the shareholders of the company (internal audit reports are addressed to management/those charged with governance) and the external auditor provides an opinion on the truth and fairness of the financial statements.

Therefore statements 2 and 4 relate to external audit.

5     The correct answer is: No safeguards can be applied and this basis for fee determination should be rejected.

The proposal in relation to the fees is a contingent fee basis which is expressly prohibited by ACCA's *Code of Ethics and Conduct* and therefore the only viable option here is to reject the fee basis (ACCA *Code of Ethics and Conduct*: para. R410.10-11).

6     The correct answer is: Depreciation should be $10,660, assets are understated

Depreciation should be calculated as:

| | |
|---|---|
| Treadmills/exercise bikes = (18,000 + 17,000)/36 × 8 months = | 7,778 |
| Rowing machines/cross trainers = (9,750 + 11,000)/36 × 5 months = | 2,882 |
| Total | 10,660 |

Therefore depreciation should be $10,660 and assets are currently understated as too much depreciation has currently been charged.

The second option is based on depreciation being applied for a full year instead of for the relevant months.

The third option is based on depreciation not being charged in the month of acquisition (ie seven and four months).

The fourth option is based on depreciation for the exercise bikes being divided by the three years instead of allocated on a monthly basis.

7    The correct answer is:

Agree a sample of additions included in the non-current asset register to purchase invoice and cash book

Recalculate the depreciation charge for a sample of assets ensuring that it is being applied consistently and in accordance with IAS 16 *Property, Plant and Equipment*

Review physical condition of non-current assets for any signs of damage

Ensure disposals are correctly accounted for and recalculate gain/loss on disposal

The review of board minutes for evidence of disposals during the year and verify that these are appropriately reflected in the non-current assets register is a test for existence and reviewing the repairs and maintenance expense account for evidence of items of a capital nature is a test for completeness.

All other tests are relevant for valuation.

8    The correct answer is: Send an enquiry letter to the lawyers of Balotelli to obtain their view as to the probability of the claim being successful

While all procedures would be valid in the circumstances, only the written confirmation from the company's lawyers would allow the auditor to obtain an expert, third-party confirmation on the likelihood of the case being successful. This would provide the auditor with the most reliable evidence in the circumstances.

9    The correct answer is:

It provides evidence from an independent external source.

It improves the reliability of audit evidence as the process is under the control of the auditor.

As per ISA 505 *External Confirmations*, the evidence obtained from the trade receivables circularisation should be reliable as it is from an external source and the risk of management bias and influence is restricted due to the process being under the control of the auditor (ISA 505).

Customers are not obliged to answer and often circularisations have a very low response rate. A circularisation will not provide evidence over the valuation assertion for receivables and therefore the second and third statements are drawbacks of a circularisation.

10   The correct answer is:

| Customer | Audit procedure |
|---|---|
| Willow Co | No further audit procedures required |
| Cedar Co | Agree to pre year end invoice |
| Maple Co | Agree to post-year end cash book and bank statement |
| Laurel Co | Discuss with management and consider whether amount should be included in allowance for receivables |

Willow Co – The external confirmation has confirmed the balance and no further work is required.

Cedar Co – The difference represents an invoice in transit and therefore should be confirmed to a pre year end invoice to verify that it is a legitimate timing difference.

Maple Co – The difference represents a payment in transit and should be agreed to post year end payment to confirm that it is a legitimate timing difference.

Laurel Co – The customer is disputing the balance and therefore the need for an allowance against the balance should be assessed.

11    The correct answer is:

| Element of auditor's report | Reason for inclusion |
|---|---|
| Date of report | Demonstrates the point at which sufficient appropriate evidence has been obtained |
| Addressee | Clarifies who may rely on the opinion included in the report |
| Auditor's responsibilities | Explains the role and remit of the audit |
| Opinion paragraph | Explains that the financial statements are presented fairly |

Date of report – The auditor's report shall be dated no earlier than the date on which the auditor has obtained sufficient appropriate audit evidence on which to base the auditor's opinion on the financial statements. The date of the audit report is important in the case of subsequent events which impact the financial statements.

Addressee – Sets out who the report is addressed to (usually the shareholders) and is there to clarify who can place reliance on the audit opinion.

Auditor's responsibilities – This paragraph sets out that the auditor is required to express an opinion on the financial statements and seeks to explain the difference between the role of the auditor and those charged with governance. Thus this paragraph sets out the role and remit of the auditor.

Opinion paragraph – This paragraph sets out the auditor's conclusion on the financial statements. In an unmodified report this takes the form of the auditor confirming that the financial statements present a true and fair view or are presented fairly.

12    The correct answer is:

| | | |
|---|---|---|
| All material subsequent events require the numbers in the financial statements to be adjusted. | | False |
| A non-adjusting event is a subsequent event for which **no** amendments to the current year financial statements are required. | | False |
| The auditor's responsibilities for subsequent events which occur prior to the audit report being signed are different from their responsibilities after the auditor's report has been issued. | True | |
| The auditor should request a written representation confirming that all relevant subsequent events have been disclosed. | True | |

Statement 1 is false as not all subsequent events will require an adjustment to the numbers within the financial statements. IAS 10 *Events After the Reporting Period* makes a distinction between an adjusting and non-adjusting event. Only material adjusting events would require an amendment to the figures within the financial statements (IAS 10).

Statement 2 is false as, while a non-adjusting event would not require a change to the numbers within the financial statements, IAS 10 may require a disclosure to be made. If the non-adjusting event is material, non-disclosure could still result in a modification to the audit report.

Statement 3 is true as the auditor is required to carry out procedures up to the date of the audit report to gain sufficient appropriate audit evidence that all relevant subsequent events have been identified and dealt with appropriately. After the auditor's report is issued, the auditor does not need to actively look for subsequent events but is only required to respond to subsequent events which they become aware of.

Statement 4 is true as ISA 560 *Subsequent Events* requires the auditor to obtain written confirmation from management/those charged with governance that all subsequent events have been identified and dealt with in accordance with the appropriate reporting framework (ISA 560).

13    The correct answer is:

| Option | Material | Impact on accounts |
|--------|----------|--------------------|
| C      | Yes      | Profit is overstated |

The outstanding balance with Pirlo Co is likely to be irrecoverable as the customer is experiencing financial difficulties.

The balance is material at 7.4% of profit before tax and 2.5% of revenue.

Currently profit and assets are overstated by $285,000. Therefore the correct option is C.

14    The correct answer is:

Discuss with management the reasons for not amending the financial statements

Review the cash book post year end for receipts from Pirlo Co

Writing to the customer/agreeing to invoices, while valid procedures during the audit to verify the existence of an outstanding balance, would not allow the auditor to assess the recoverability of the balance which is the key issue in determining whether an adjustment is required.

Post year end cash testing is the best way for the auditor to assess if the balance is recoverable wholly or in part and therefore the cash book should be reviewed for any receipts which will change the assessment of the debt after the year end. The issue should also be discussed with management to understand their reasons for not wanting to amend the financial statements as this may be due to a change in circumstances.

15    The correct answer is: If the 20X4 financial statements are not amended, our opinion will be **qualified on the grounds of material misstatement.**

If the appropriate adjustment is made to the financial statements, our opinion will be **unmodified.**

The debt with Pirlo Co should be provided for and is material to the financial statements at 7.4% of profit before tax and 2.5% of revenue. This represents a material misstatement which is material but not pervasive. As such, if no adjustment is made the auditor will be required to provide a qualified 'except for' opinion. If the required change is made, then no material misstatement exists and therefore the auditor will be able to issue an unmodified opinion.

# Section B

# Question 16

| | | Marks |
|---|---|---|

**(a) Component of audit risk**

| | | |
|---|---|---|
| Explanation of audit risk | 2 | |
| Explanation of components of audit risk: Inherent, control and detection risk | 3 | |
| | | 5 |

**(b) Audit risk and auditor's response** (only 7 risks required)

| | | |
|---|---|---|
| $5 million expenditure on production process | 2 | |
| Inventory counts at 15 warehouses at year end | 2 | |
| Treatment of owned v third-party warehouses | 2 | |
| New general ledger system introduced at the beginning of the year | 2 | |
| Release of opening provision for allowance for receivables | 2 | |
| Research and development expenditure | 2 | |
| Damaged inventory | 2 | |
| Sales returns | 2 | |
| Management bonus based on asset values | 2 | |
| **Max 7 issues, 2 marks each** | | 14 |

**(c) Audit strategy document**

| | | |
|---|---|---|
| Main characteristics of the audit | 1 | |
| Reporting objectives of the audit and nature of communications required | 1 | |
| Factors which are significant in directing the audit team's efforts | 1 | |
| Results of preliminary engagement activities and whether knowledge gained on other engagements is relevant | 1 | |
| Nature, timing and extent of resources necessary to perform the audit | 1 | |
| **Restricted to** | | 4 |

**(d) Difference between interim and final audit**

| | | |
|---|---|---|
| Interim audit | 2 | |
| Final audit | 2 | |
| **Restricted to** | | 3 |

**(e) Procedures/impact of interim audit on final audit**

| | | |
|---|---|---|
| Example procedures | 3 | |
| Impact on final audit | 3 | |
| **Restricted to** | | 4 |

| | | |
|---|---|---|
| **Total marks** | | 30 |

## (a) Audit risk and its components

Audit risk is the risk that the auditor expresses an inappropriate audit opinion when the financial statements are materially misstated. Audit risk is a function of two main components being the risks of material misstatement and detection risk (ISA 200). Risk of material misstatement is made up of two components, inherent risk and control risk.

Inherent risk is the susceptibility of an assertion about a class of transaction, account balance or disclosure to a misstatement which could be material, either individually or when aggregated with other misstatements, before consideration of any related controls (ISA 200).

Control risk is the risk that a misstatement which could occur in an assertion about a class of transaction, account balance or disclosure and which could be material, either individually or when aggregated with other misstatements, will not be prevented, or detected and corrected, on a timely basis by the entity's internal control (ISA 200).

Detection risk is the risk that the procedures performed by the auditor to reduce audit risk to an acceptably low level will not detect a misstatement which exists and which could be material, either individually or when aggregated with other misstatements. Detection risk is affected by sampling and non-sampling risk (ISA 200).

(b)    **Audit risk and auditor's response**

| Audit risk | Auditor's response |
|---|---|
| Milla has incurred $5m on updating, repairing and replacing a significant amount of the production process machinery.<br><br>If this expenditure is of a capital nature, it should be capitalised as part of property, plant and equipment (PPE) in line with IAS 16 *Property, Plant and Equipment*. However, if it relates more to repairs, then it should be expensed to the statement of profit or loss<br><br>If the expenditure is not correctly classified, profit and PPE could be under- or overstated. | The auditor should review a breakdown of these costs to ascertain the split of capital and revenue expenditure, and further testing should be undertaken to ensure that the classification in the financial statements is correct. |
| At the year end there will be inventory counts undertaken in all 15 warehouses.<br><br>It is unlikely that the auditor will be able to attend all 15 inventory counts and therefore they need to ensure that they obtain sufficient appropriate audit evidence over the inventory counting controls, and completeness and existence of inventory for any warehouses not visited. | The auditor should assess which of the inventory sites they will attend the counts for. This will be any with material inventory or which have a history of significant errors.<br><br>For those not visited, the auditor will need to review the level of exceptions noted during the count and discuss with management any issues which arose during the count. |
| Inventory is stored within 15 warehouses; some are owned by Milla and some rented from third parties. Only warehouses owned by Milla should be included within PPE. There is a risk of overstatement of PPE and understatement of rental expenses if Milla has capitalised all 15 warehouses. | The auditor should review supporting documentation for all warehouses included within PPE to confirm ownership by Milla and to ensure non-current assets are not overstated. |
| A new accounting general ledger system has been introduced at the beginning of the year and the old system was run in parallel for two months. There is a risk of opening balances being misstated and loss of data if they have not been transferred from the old system correctly.<br><br>In addition, the new accounting general ledger system will require documenting and the controls over this will need to be tested. | The auditor should undertake detailed testing to confirm that all opening balances have been correctly recorded in the new accounting general ledger system.<br><br>They should document and test the new system. They should review any management reports run comparing the old and new system during the parallel run to identify any issues with the processing of accounting information. |
| Milla has incurred expenditure of $4.5 million on developing a new brand of fizzy drink. This expenditure is research and development under IAS 38 *Intangible Assets*. The standard requires research costs to be expensed and development costs to be capitalised as an intangible asset (IAS 38).<br><br>If Milla has incorrectly classified research costs as development expenditure, there is a risk the intangible asset could be overstated and expenses understated. | Obtain a breakdown of the expenditure and undertake testing to determine whether the costs relate to the research or development stage. Discuss the accounting treatment with the finance director and ensure it is in accordance with IAS 38. |

| Audit risk | Auditor's response |
|---|---|
| The finance director of Milla has decided to release the opening balance of $1.5 million for allowance for receivables as he feels it is unnecessary. There is a risk that receivables will be overvalued, as despite having a credit controller, some balances will be irrecoverable and so will be overstated if not provided against.<br><br>In addition, due to the damaged inventory there is an increased risk of customers refusing to make payments in full. | Extended post year end cash receipts testing and a review of the aged receivables ledger to be performed to assess valuation and the need for an allowance for receivables.<br><br>Discuss with the director the rationale for releasing the $1.5m opening allowance for receivables. |
| A large batch of cola products has been damaged in the production process and will be in inventory at the year end. No adjustment has been made by management.<br><br>The valuation of inventory as per IAS 2 *Inventories* should be at the lower of cost and net realisable value (IAS 2). Hence it is likely that this inventory is overvalued. | Detailed cost and net realisable value testing to be performed to assess how much the inventory requires writing down by. |
| Due to the damaged cola products, a number of customers have complained. It is likely that for any of the damaged goods sold, Milla will need to refund these customers.<br><br>Revenue is possibly overstated if the sales returns are not completely and accurately recorded. | Review the breakdown of sales of damaged goods, and ensure that they have been accurately removed from revenue. |
| The management of Milla receives a significant annual bonus based on the value of year-end total assets. There is a risk that management might feel under pressure to overstate the value of assets through the judgements taken or through the use of releasing provisions. | Throughout the audit, the team will need to be alert to this risk. They will need to maintain professional scepticism and carefully review judgemental decisions and compare treatment against prior years. |

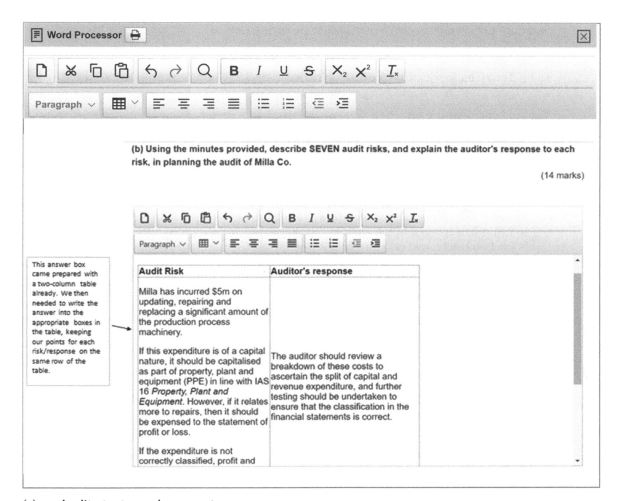

**(b) Using the minutes provided, describe SEVEN audit risks, and explain the auditor's response to each risk, in planning the audit of Milla Co.**

(14 marks)

This answer box came prepared with a two-column table already. We then needed to write the answer into the appropriate boxes in the table, keeping our points for each risk/response on the same row of the table.

| Audit Risk | Auditor's response |
|---|---|
| Milla has incurred $5m on updating, repairing and replacing a significant amount of the production process machinery. | |
| If this expenditure is of a capital nature, it should be capitalised as part of property, plant and equipment (PPE) in line with IAS 16 *Property, Plant and Equipment*. However, if it relates more to repairs, then it should be expensed to the statement of profit or loss. | The auditor should review a breakdown of these costs to ascertain the split of capital and revenue expenditure, and further testing should be undertaken to ensure that the classification in the financial statements is correct. |
| If the expenditure is not correctly classified, profit and | |

(c) **Audit strategy document**

The audit strategy sets out the scope, timing and direction of the audit and helps the development of the audit plan (ISA 300). It should consider the following main areas:

It should identify the main characteristics of the engagement which define its scope. For Milla it should consider the following:

- Whether the financial information to be audited has been prepared in accordance with IFRS

- To what extent audit evidence obtained in previous audits for Milla will be utilised

- Whether computer-assisted audit techniques will be used and the effect of IT on audit procedures

- The availability of key personnel at Milla

It should ascertain the reporting objectives of the engagement to plan the timing of the audit and the nature of the communications required, such as (ISA 300):

- The audit timetable for reporting and whether there will be an interim as well as final audit

- Organisation of meetings with Milla's management to discuss any audit issues arising

- Location of the 15 inventory counts

- Any discussions with management regarding the reports to be issued

- The timings of the audit team meetings and review of work performed

- If there are any expected communications with third parties

The strategy should consider the factors which, in the auditor's professional judgement, are significant in directing Milla's audit team's efforts, such as:

- The determination of materiality for the audit

- The need to maintain a questioning mind and to exercise professional scepticism in gathering and evaluating audit evidence

It should consider the results of preliminary audit planning activities and, where applicable, whether knowledge gained on other engagements for Milla is relevant, such as:

- Results of previous audits and the results of any tests over the effectiveness of internal controls

- Evidence of management's commitment to the design, implementation and maintenance of sound internal control

- Volume of transactions, which may determine whether it is more efficient for the audit team to rely on internal control

- Significant business developments affecting Milla, such as the change in the accounting system and the significant expenditure on an overhaul of the factory

The audit strategy should ascertain the nature, timing and extent of resources necessary to perform the audit, such as:

- The selection of the audit team with experience of this type of industry

- Assignment of audit work to the team members

- Setting the audit budget

Note. The answer is longer than required for four marks but represents a teaching aid.

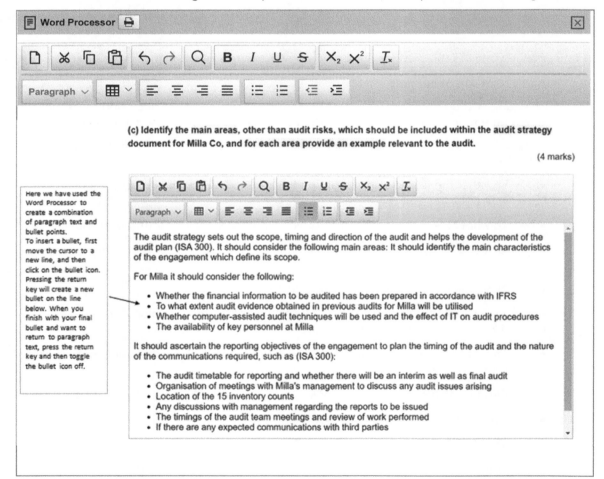

(d) **Differences between an interim and a final audit**

**Interim audit**

The interim audit is that part of the audit which takes place before the year end. The auditor uses the interim audit to carry out procedures which would be difficult to perform at the year end because of time pressure. There is no requirement to undertake an interim audit; factors to consider when deciding upon whether to have one include the size and complexity of the company along with the effectiveness of internal controls.

**Final audit**

The final audit will take place after the year end and concludes with the auditor forming and expressing an opinion on the financial statements for the whole year subject to audit. It is important to note that the final opinion takes account of conclusions formed at both the interim and final audit.

(e) Procedures which could be undertaken during the interim audit include:

- Review and updating of the documentation of accounting systems at Milla

- Discussions with management on the recent growth and any other changes within the business which have occurred during the year to date at Milla to update the auditor's understanding of the company

- Assessment of risks which will impact the final audit of Milla

- Undertake tests of controls on Milla's key transaction cycles of sales, purchases and inventory, and credit control

- Perform substantive procedures on profit and loss transactions for the year to date and any other completed material transactions

**Impact of interim audit on final audit**

If an interim audit is undertaken at Milla, then it will have an impact on the final audit and the extent of work undertaken after the year end. First, as some testing has already been undertaken, there will be less work to be performed at the final audit, which may result in a shorter audit and audited financial statements possibly being available earlier. The outcome of the controls testing undertaken during the interim audit will impact the level of substantive testing to be undertaken. If the controls tested have proven to be operating effectively, then the auditor may be able to reduce the level of detailed substantive testing required as they will be able to place reliance on the controls. In addition, if substantive procedures were undertaken at the interim audit, then only the period from the interim audit to the year end will require testing.

# Question 17

Marking scheme

|  |  | Marks |
|---|---|---|
| (a) | **Control deficiencies, recommendations and tests of controls** | |
| | Website not integrated into inventory system | 3 |
| | Customer signatures | 3 |
| | Unfulfilled sales orders | 3 |
| | Customer credit limits | 3 |
| | Sales discounts | 3 |
| | Supplier statement reconciliations | 3 |
| | Purchase ledger master file | 3 |
| | Surplus plant and equipment | 3 |
| | Authorisation of capital expenditure | 3 |
| | **Max 6 issues, 3 marks each** | 18 |

(b) **Substantive procedures for PPE**

| | Marks |
|---|---|
| Cast list of additions and agree to non-current asset register | 1 |
| Vouch cost to recent supplier invoice | 1 |
| Agree addition to a supplier invoice in the name of Baggio to confirm rights and obligations | 1 |
| Review additions and confirm capital expenditure items rather than repairs and   maintenance | 1 |
| Review board minutes to ensure authorised by the board | 1 |
| Physically verify them on the factory floor to confirm existence | 1 |
| Other | — |
| **Restricted to** | 2 |
| **Total marks** | 20 |

(a) **Baggio International's (Baggio) internal control**

| Deficiency (i) | Control recommendations (ii) | Test of control (iii) |
|---|---|---|
| Currently the website is not integrated into the inventory system. This can result in Baggio accepting customer orders when they do not have the goods in inventory. This can cause them to lose sales and customer goodwill. For goods dispatched by local couriers, customer signatures are not always obtained. This can lead to customers falsely claiming that they have not received their goods. Baggio would not be able to prove that they had in fact dispatched the goods and may result in goods being dispatched twice. | The website should be updated to include an interface into the inventory system; this should check inventory levels and only process orders if adequate inventory is held. If inventory is out of stock, this should appear on the website with an approximate waiting time. Baggio should remind all local couriers that customer signatures must be obtained as proof of delivery and payment will not be made for any dispatches with missing signatures. | Test data could be used to attempt to process orders via the website for items which are not currently held in inventory. The orders should be flagged as being out of stock and indicate an approximate waiting time. Select a sample of dispatches by couriers and ask Baggio for proof of delivery by viewing customer signatures. |
| There have been a number of situations where the sales orders have not been fulfilled in a timely manner. This can lead to a loss of customer goodwill and if it persists will damage the reputation of Baggio as a reliable supplier. | Once goods are dispatched, they should be matched to sales orders and flagged as fulfilled. The system should automatically flag any outstanding sales orders past a predetermined period, such as five days. This report should be reviewed by a responsible official. | Review the report of outstanding sales orders. If significant, discuss with a responsible official to understand why there is still a significant time period between sales order and dispatch date. Select a sample of sales orders and compare the date of order to the goods dispatch date to ascertain whether this is within the acceptable predetermined period. |

| Deficiency (i) | Control recommendations (ii) | Test of control (iii) |
|---|---|---|
| Customer credit limits are set by sales ledger clerks.<br><br>Sales ledger clerks are not sufficiently senior and so may set limits too high, leading to irrecoverable debts, or too low, leading to a loss of revenue. | Credit limits should be set by a senior member of the sales ledger department and not by sales ledger clerks.<br><br>These limits should be regularly reviewed by a responsible official. | For a sample of new customers accepted in the year, review the authorisation of the credit limit, and ensure that this was performed by a responsible official.<br><br>Enquire of sales ledger clerks as to who can set credit limits. |
| Sales discounts are set by Baggio's sales team. In order to boost their sales, members of the sales team may set the discounts too high, leading to a loss of revenue. | All members of the sales team should be given authority to grant sales discounts up to a set limit. Any sales discounts above these limits should be authorised by sales area managers or the sales director.<br><br>Regular review of sales discount levels should be undertaken by the sales director, and this review should be evidenced. | Discuss with members of the sales team the process for setting sales discounts.<br><br>Review the sales discount report for evidence of review by the sales director. |
| Supplier statement reconciliations are no longer performed.<br><br>This may result in errors in the recording of purchases and payables not being identified in a timely manner. | Supplier statement reconciliations should be performed on a monthly basis for all suppliers and these should be reviewed by a responsible official. | Review the file of reconciliations to ensure that they are being performed on a regular basis and that they have been reviewed by a responsible official. |
| Changes to supplier details in the purchase ledger master file can be undertaken by purchase ledger clerks.<br><br>This could lead to key supplier data being accidentally amended or fictitious suppliers being set up, which can increase the risk of fraud. | Only purchase ledger supervisors should have the authority to make changes to master file data. This should be controlled via passwords.<br><br>Regular review of any changes to master file data by a responsible official and this review should be evidenced. | Request a purchase ledger clerk to attempt to access the master file and to make an amendment; the system should not allow this.<br><br>Review a report of master data changes and review the authority of those making amendments. |
| Baggio has considerable levels of surplus plant and equipment. Surplus unused plant is at risk of theft.<br><br>In addition, if the surplus plant is not disposed of, then the company could lose sundry income. | Regular review of the plant and equipment on the factory floor by senior factory personnel to identify any old or surplus equipment.<br><br>As part of the capital expenditure process, there should be a requirement to confirm the treatment of the equipment being replaced. | Observe the review process by senior factory personnel, identifying the treatment of any old equipment.<br><br>Review processed capital expenditure forms to ascertain if the treatment of replaced equipment is as stated. |

**BPP** LEARNING MEDIA

| Deficiency (i) | Control recommendations (ii) | Test of control (iii) |
|---|---|---|
| Purchase requisitions are authorised by production supervisors.<br><br>Production supervisors are not sufficiently independent or senior to authorise capital expenditure. | Capital expenditure authorisation levels to be established. Production supervisors should only be able to authorise low value items; any high value items should be authorised by the board. | Review a sample of authorised capital expenditure forms and identify if the correct signatory has authorised them. |

(b) **Substantive procedures – additions**

- Obtain a breakdown of additions, cast the list and agree to the non-current asset register to confirm completeness of plant and equipment (P&E).

- Select a sample of additions and agree cost to supplier invoice to confirm valuation.

- Verify rights and obligations by agreeing the addition of P&E to a supplier invoice in the name of Baggio.

- Review the list of additions and confirm that they relate to capital expenditure items rather than repairs and maintenance.

- Review board minutes to ensure that significant capital expenditure purchases have been authorised by the board.

- For a sample of additions recorded in P&E, physically verify them on the factory floor to confirm existence.

# Question 18

|  |  | Marks |
|---|---|---|
| (a) | **Reliance on independent valuer** |  |
|  | ISA 500 requires consideration of competence and capabilities of expert | 1 |
|  | Consider if member of professional body or industry association | 1 |
|  | Assess independence | 1 |
|  | Assess whether relevant expertise of type of properties as Vieri Motor Cars | 1 |
|  | Evaluate assumptions | 1 |
|  |  | 5 |
| (b) | **Substantive procedures for revaluation of land and buildings** |  |
|  | Cast schedule of land and buildings revalued this year | 1 |
|  | Agree the revalued amounts to the valuation statement provided by the valuer | 1 |
|  | Agree the revalued amounts included correctly in the non-current assets register | 1 |
|  | Recalculate the total revaluation adjustment and agree recorded in the revaluation surplus | 1 |
|  | Agree the initial cost for the warehouse to invoices to confirm cost | 1 |
|  | Confirm through title deeds that the warehouse is owned by Vieri | 1 |

|  | Marks |  |
|---|---|---|
| Recalculate the depreciation charge for the year | 1 | |
| Review the financial statements disclosures for compliance with IAS 16 *Property, Plant and Equipment* | 1 | |
| Other | — | |
| **Restricted to** | | 6 |

(c) **Substantive procedures for work in progress (WIP)**

| | Marks | |
|---|---|---|
| Discuss with management how the percentage completions are attributed to WIP | 1 | |
| Observe the procedures carried out in the count in assessing the level of WIP; consider reasonableness of the assumptions used | 1 | |
| During the count, agree a sample of percentage completions are in accordance with Vieri's policies | 1 | |
| Discuss with management the basis of the standard costs | 1 | |
| Review the level of variances between standard and actual costs | 1 | |
| Obtain a breakdown of the standard costs and agree a sample of these costs to actual invoices | 1 | |
| Cast the schedule of total WIP and agree to the trial balance and financial statements | 1 | |
| Agree sample of WIP assessed during the count to the WIP schedule, agree percentage completion is correct and recalculate the inventory valuation | 1 | |
| Other | — | |
| **Restricted to** | | 4 |

(d) **Impact on audit report**

| | Marks | |
|---|---|---|
| Discuss with management reasons for non-amendment | 1 | |
| Assess materiality | 1 | |
| Immaterial – schedule of uncorrected adjustments | 1 | |
| Material not pervasive – qualified opinion | 1 | |
| Basis for qualified opinion paragraph | 1 | |
| Opinion paragraph – qualified 'except for' | 1 | |
| **Restricted to** | | 5 |
| **Total marks** | | 20 |

(a) **Reliance on the work of an independent valuer**

ISA 500 *Audit Evidence* requires auditors to evaluate the competence, capabilities including expertise and objectivity of a management expert. This would include consideration of the qualifications of the valuer and assessment of whether they were members of any professional body or industry association (ISA 500).

The expert's independence should be ascertained, with potential threats such as undue reliance on Vieri Motor Cars Co (Vieri) or a self-interest threat such as share ownership considered.

In addition, Rossi & Co should meet with the expert and discuss with them its relevant expertise, in particular whether it has valued similar land and buildings to those of Vieri in the past. Rossi & Co should also consider whether the valuer understands the accounting requirements of IAS 16 *Property, Plant and Equipment* in relation to valuations.

The valuation should then be evaluated. The assumptions used should be carefully reviewed and compared to previous revaluations at Vieri. These assumptions should be discussed with both management and the valuer to understand the basis of any valuations.

BPP
LEARNING
MEDIA

(b) **Substantive procedures for land and buildings**

(1) Obtain a schedule of land and buildings revalued this year and cast to confirm completeness and accuracy of the revaluation adjustment.

(2) On a sample basis, agree the revalued amounts to the valuation statement provided by the valuer.

(3) Agree the revalued amounts for these assets are included correctly in the non-current assets register.

(4) Recalculate the total revaluation adjustment and agree correctly recorded in the revaluation surplus.

(5) Agree the initial cost for the warehouse addition to supporting documentation such as invoices to confirm cost.

(6) Confirm through a review of the title deeds that the warehouse is owned by Vieri.

(7) Recalculate the depreciation charge for the year to ensure that, for assets revalued during the year, the depreciation was based on the correct valuation and for the warehouse addition that the charge was for six months only.

(8) Review the financial statements disclosures of the revaluation to ensure they comply with IAS 16.

(c) **Substantive procedures for work in progress (WIP)**

(1) Prior to attending the inventory count, discuss with management how the percentage completions are attributed to the WIP. For example, is this based on motor cars passing certain points in the production process?

(2) During the count, observe the procedures carried out by Vieri staff in assessing the level of WIP and consider the reasonableness of the assumptions used.

(3) Agree for a sample that the percentage completions assessed during the count are in accordance with Vieri's policies communicated prior to the count.

(4) Discuss with management the basis of the standard costs applied to the percentage completion of WIP, and how often these are reviewed and updated.

(5) Review the level of variances between standard and actual costs and discuss with management how these are treated.

(6) Obtain a breakdown of the standard costs and agree a sample of these costs to actual invoices or payroll records to assess their reasonableness.

(7) Cast the schedule of total WIP and agree to the trial balance and financial statements.

(8) Agree sample of WIP assessed during the count to the WIP schedule, agree percentage completion is correct and recalculate the inventory valuation.

(d) **Auditor's report**

Discuss with the management of Vieri why they are refusing to make the amendment to WIP.

Assess the materiality of the error; if immaterial, it should be added to the schedule of unadjusted differences. The auditor should then assess whether this error results in the total of unadjusted differences becoming material; if so, this should be discussed with management; if not, there would be no impact on the audit report.

If the error is material and management refuses to amend the financial statements, then the auditor's opinion will need to be modified. It is unlikely that any error would be pervasive as, although WIP in total is material, it would not have a pervasive effect on the financial statements as a whole. As management has not complied with IAS 2 *Inventories* and if the error is material but not pervasive, then a qualified opinion would be necessary.

A basis for qualified opinion paragraph would need to be included after the opinion paragraph. This would explain the material misstatement in relation to the valuation of WIP and the effect on the financial statements. The opinion paragraph would be qualified 'except for'.

# ACCA

# Applied Skills

# Audit and Assurance

# Mock Examination 3

# December 2016

Time allowed: 3 hours

This mock exam is divided into two sections:

Section A – ALL 15 questions are compulsory and MUST be attempted

Section B – ALL 3 questions are compulsory and MUST be attempted

BPP
LEARNING
MEDIA

# Section A – ALL 15 questions are compulsory and MUST be attempted

Each question is worth 2 marks.

**The following scenario relates to questions 1–5.**

It is 1 July 20X5. The board of directors of Sistar Co is concerned that they are not currently applying best practice in terms of corporate governance and are seeking to make improvements.

The company currently has three non-executive directors (NEDs) on the board, who are paid a fee which changes annually depending on company performance. The NEDs all sit on the audit, nomination and remuneration committees. There are currently no formal documents setting out the responsibilities of these committees.

At present, Sistar Co does not have an internal audit function but the directors are establishing a team which will be responsible for a range of internal audit assignments.

The following is the current proposed structure for the internal audit (IA) department.

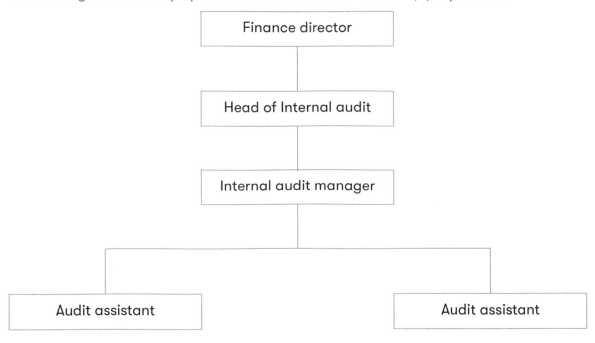

The only role still to be filled is the Head of internal audit. There are two potential candidates: Paul Belling, a consultant who helped design and implement the company's current control system, and Maria Marquez, who is currently an audit manager at Rossi & Bell, an audit firm which has never been used by Sistar Co.

Out of the other three members of the proposed IA department, two of them have moved from other departments in Sistar Co and one of the audit assistants has audit experience.

1   Which of the following should be included in the document setting out the responsibilities of the audit committee?

   (1)    To monitor and review the effectiveness of the newly established internal audit function

   (2)    To evaluate the balance of skills, experience and independence of board members

   (3)    To take responsibility for the appointment and removal of the external auditors

   (4)    To monitor and review the effectiveness of internal financial controls established by the company

○ 1 and 2

○ 1 and 4

○ 2 and 3

○ 3 and 4

2 Indicate which of the following options correctly describes the deficiency relating to NEDs' remuneration and makes a valid recommendation for improvement.

| Option | | Deficiency | Recommendation |
|---|---|---|---|
| ○ | (1) | Compromises NED independence | NEDs should be remunerated on the same basis as the executive team |
| ○ | (2) | Compromises the motivation of NEDs | NEDs' remuneration should be tied to profit targets |
| ○ | (3) | Compromises NED independence | NEDs' remuneration should be a set amount based on time committed |
| ○ | (4) | Compromises the motivation of NEDs | NEDs' remuneration should be linked to individual performance |

3 Complete the sentences below to provide appropriate recommendations to improve the effectiveness and independence of the IA department.

The head of internal audit should report to the [ Report to ]

[ Head of IA ] should be appointed as head of internal audit.

The audit team requires [ Team composition ]

**Picklists for boxes:**

| Reports to | Head of IA | Team composition |
|---|---|---|
| Finance director | Maria Marquez | More senior staff with audit experience |
| Audit committee | Paul Belling | No change to its current composition |
| Chief executive | | More external staff to be appointed |

4 The board has started to compile a list of tasks for the IA department to carry out once it is up and running. It has been agreed that the first assignment to be completed will be for IA to review Sistar Co's processes over capital expenditure to verify if the right items are purchased at an appropriate time and competitive price.

What type of internal audit assignment does this represent?

○ A value for money audit

○ A management audit

○ A financial audit

○ An IT audit

5   When deciding on the role of the IA department in undertaking operational audits, which of the following should the team **NOT** be involved in?

   O    Observing procedures carried out by Sistar Co's staff

   O    Reperforming procedures documented in procedures manuals

   O    Designing and implementing internal control procedures to address deficiencies

   O    Reporting findings directly to the board of directors

---

**The following scenario relates to questions 6–10.**

It is 1 July 20X5. You are an audit manager of Elm & Co and are finalising the audit of the financial statements of Oak Co for the year ended 31 December 20X4. You are reviewing the results of the final analytical procedures and other outstanding points on the audit file, prior to recommending the final audit opinion, which is due to be signed on 12 July 20X5.

The following ratio analysis has been completed as part of the final analytical procedures:

|  | 20X4 final | 20X4 planning | 20X3 final |
| --- | --- | --- | --- |
| Gross profit margin | 9% | 11% | 12% |
| Quick ratio | 0.2 | 0.6 | 0.8 |
| Payables payment period | 45 | 40 | 37 |
| Inventory holding period | 50 | 40 | 42 |

Discussions with the finance director have also revealed the following:

(1)   Oak Co lost a major customer, Beech Co, in December 20X4, but new business has been won post year end which has mitigated the impact of the loss of Beech Co.

(2)   Oak Co is due to repay a substantial loan on 31 August 20X5. Oak Co is currently negotiating revised terms with the bank but it is unlikely that negotiations will be concluded before the auditor's report is signed. This will be disclosed in the financial statements.

The financial statements for the year ended 31 December 20X4 have been prepared on a going concern basis.

6   As part of the going concern assessment, the following additional issues have been noted on the audit file.

   Which **TWO** of the following issues could individually cast doubt over the going concern assumption for Oak Co?

   ☐   A number of personnel in the purchasing department left during the year and have not been replaced.

   ☐   A major supplier to Oak Co has just gone out of business with a number of unfulfilled orders.

   ☐   A new product which was due to account for 30% of revenue has proved to be unsuccessful.

   ☐   A litigation claim has been raised against Oak Co after the year end with potential damages totalling 3% of this year's profit.

7    As part of your review of the final analytical procedures, you compare the results to the following comments on the audit file:

(1)    The company has increased the sales prices charged to customers while maintaining costs at a level comparable to 20X3.

(2)    The company has become more reliant on its overdraft facility during the year.

(3)    Due to cash restrictions, the company has encountered delays in paying suppliers.

(4)    At the year-end inventory count, a lower level of slow-moving inventory was noted compared to the prior year.

Which of the above comments are **INCONSISTENT** with the results of the final analytical procedures?

- O    1 and 2
- O    1 and 4
- O    2 and 3
- O    3 and 4

8    Which of the following procedures would provide the **MOST** reliable evidence in relation to the new business won post year end?

- O    Review of post-year end sales orders from the new customer
- O    Inspect email correspondence between the sales director of Oak Co and the new customer
- O    Obtain a written representation confirming the level of business agreed with the new customer
- O    Review of board minutes discussing the contract with the new customer

9    The initial going concern assessment conducted by the management of Oak Co covers the period to
30 June 20X5.

Which of the following is an appropriate course of action in the circumstances described above?

- O    Request management extend the assessment to the date of the auditor's report
- O    Design and carry out procedures to only assess going concern in the period from 31 December 20X4 to the date of the auditor's report
- O    Request management extend the assessment to cover at least until 31 December 20X5
- O    Accept the time frame used by management as the going concern review is their responsibility

10    The audit engagement partner has concluded that the disclosure included in the financial statements in relation to the loan negotiations is adequate. Additionally, the audit partner has commented that this disclosure is fundamental to the users' understanding of the financial statements.

**Complete the following sentence, identifying what form of auditor's report should be issued.**

The audit engagement partner has concluded that the disclosure included in the financial statements in relation to the loan negotiations is adequate. Additionally, the audit partner has commented that this disclosure is fundamental to the users' understanding of the financial statements.

An auditor's report with | Opinion | Opinion and | Paragraph | paragraph should be issued.

**Picklists for boxes:**

| Opinion | Paragraph |
|---|---|
| a modified | an other matter |
| an unmodified | a material uncertainty relating to going concern |

---

**The following scenario relates to questions 11–15.**

It is 1 July 20X5. You are an audit senior at Jones & Co and are currently performing the final audit of Walker Co for the year ended 30 April 20X5. The company is a manufacturer and retailer of shoes and boots. The current audit senior is ill and you have been asked to complete the audit of payroll in their absence.

On arrival at the head office of Walker Co, you determine the following data from a review of the current year and prior year audit files:

(1)    As at 30 April 20X4, Walker Co had 500 employees.

(2)    On 1 May 20X4, 10% of staff were made redundant, effective immediately, due to discontinuation of a product line.

(3)    On 1 July 20X4, all remaining staff received a 6% pay rise.

(4)    Over the course of the year, sales levels met performance targets which resulted in a fixed bonus of $1,500 being paid to each employee on 30 April 20X5.

11    Which of the following statements explains the **CUT-OFF** assertion for wages and salaries?

    ○    Wages and salaries have been fairly allocated within the statement of profit or loss.

    ○    Wages and salaries have been appropriately calculated taking into account all relevant taxation costs and adjustments.

    ○    Wages and salaries which have been incurred during the period have been accounted for in respect of all personnel employed by Walker Co.

    ○    Wages and salaries accounted for relate to the current year ended 30 April 20X5.

---

12    Order the evidence, in terms of its reliability, starting with the **MOST RELIABLE**.

| Audit evidence | Order of reliability |
|---|---|
| Proof in total calculation performed by an audit team member | 1 – Most |
| Written representation from the directors of Walker Co confirming the accuracy of wages and salaries | 2 |
| Verbal confirmation from the finance director of Walker Co confirming the accuracy of wages and salaries | 3 |
| Recalculation of the gross and net pay for a sample of employees by an internal audit team member of Walker Co | 4 – Least |

13    The prior year financial statements for Walker Co included $17m for wages and salaries in the statement of profit or loss.

What would be the estimated current year wages and salaries expense, ignoring redundancy costs, based upon the data gathered from the review of the audit files?

O      $16,740,000

O      $16,893,000

O      $16,815,000

O      $18,600,000

14    Which **TWO** of the following are substantive **ANALYTICAL PROCEDURES** for wages and salaries?

☐      Trace and agree the total wages and salaries expense per the payroll system to the draft financial statements

☐      Recalculate the gross and net pay for a sample of employees, agree to payroll records and investigate discrepancies

☐      Compare the current year total payroll expense to the prior year and investigate any significant differences

☐      Perform a proof in total calculation and compare expected expense to actual expense within the draft financial statements

15    You have been given a list of procedures to carry out on revenue and you have decided to prioritise those which deal with the key assertion of occurrence.

Which of the following substantive procedures provide evidence over the **OCCURRENCE** assertion for revenue?

(1)    Compare the reported revenue figure to the budget and to the previous year, investigating any significant differences

(2)    Select a sample of goods dispatched notes (GDNs) and agree to invoices in the sales day book

(3)    Select a sample of invoices from the sales day book and agree to GDNs

(4)    Select a sample of invoices and recalculate the invoiced amount agreeing to price list

O    1 and 2

O    1 and 3

O    2 and 4

O    3 and 4

(Total = 30 marks)

## Section B – ALL THREE questions are compulsory and MUST be attempted

## Question 16

It is 1 July 20X5. You are an audit supervisor of Ant & Co and are planning the final audit of Centipede Co, which is a listed company, for the year ended 31 March 20X5. The company purchases consumer packaged goods and sells these through its website and to wholesalers. This is a new client for your firm and your audit manager has already had a planning meeting with the finance director and has provided you with the following notes along with financial statement extracts.

### Client background and notes from planning meeting

Rather than undertaking a full year-end inventory count, the company undertakes monthly perpetual inventory counts, covering one-twelfth of all lines monthly. As part of the interim audit which was completed earlier in the year, an audit assistant attended a perpetual inventory count in September and noted that there were a large number of exceptions where the inventory records were consistently higher than the physical inventory in the warehouse. When discussing these exceptions with the finance director, the assistant was informed that this had been a recurring issue all year. In addition, the audit assistant noted that there were some lines of inventory which, according to the records, were at least 90 days old.

Centipede Co has a head office where the audit team will be based to conduct the final audit fieldwork. However, there are four additional sites where some accounting records are maintained and these sites were not visited during the interim audit. The records for these sites are incorporated monthly through an interface to the general ledger. A fifth site was closed down in the year ending 20X4; however, the building was only sold in 20X5 at a loss of $825,000.

One of Centipede Co's wholesale customers is alleging that the company has consistently failed to deliver goods in a saleable condition and on time, hence it has commenced legal action against Centipede Co for a loss of profits claim.

The directors have disclosed their remuneration details in the financial statements in line with IFRS, which does not require a separate list of directors' names and payments. However, in the country in which Centipede Co is based, local legislation requires disclosure of the names of the directors and the amount of remuneration payable to each director.

FINANCIAL STATEMENT EXTRACTS FOR THE YEAR ENDED 31 MARCH

|  | Draft 20X5 $'000 | Final 20X4 $'000 |
|---|---|---|
| Revenue | 25,230 | 21,180 |
| Cost of sales | (15,840) | (14,015) |
| Gross profit | 9,390 | 7,165 |
| Operating expenses | (4,903) | (3,245) |
|  | 4,487 | 3,920 |
| Inventory | 2,360 | 1,800 |
| Trade receivables | 1,590 | 1,250 |
| Cash | – | 480 |
| Trade payables | 3,500 | 2,800 |
| Overdraft | 580 | – |

**Required**

(a)     Describe the matters which Ant & Co should have considered prior to accepting the audit of Centipede Co.                                                                                                                                                **(5 marks)**

(b)     Calculate **FOUR** ratios, for **BOTH** years, which would assist you in planning the audit of Centipede Co.                                                                                                                                           **(4 marks)**

(c)     From a review of the above information and the ratios calculated, describe **EIGHT** audit risks and explain the auditor's response to each risk in planning the audit of Centipede Co.

| Audit risk | Auditor's response |
|------------|--------------------|
|            |                    |

**(16 marks)**

The finance director of Centipede Co informed Ant & Co that one of the reasons it was appointed as auditors was because of its knowledge of the industry. Ant & Co audits a number of other consumer packaged goods companies, including Centipede Co's main rival. The finance director has enquired into how Ant & Co will keep information obtained during the audit confidential.

**Required**

(d)     Explain the safeguards which Ant & Co should implement to ensure that this conflict of interest is properly managed.                                                                                                                          **(5 marks)**

**(Total = 30 marks)**

# Question 17 (amended)

It is 1 July 20X5. Caterpillar Co is a clothing retailer which operates 45 stores throughout the country. The company's year end is  31 March 20X5. Caterpillar Co has an internal audit department which has undertaken a number of internal control reviews specifically focusing on cash controls at stores during the year. The reviews have taken place in the largest 20 stores as this is where most issues arise. You are an audit supervisor of Woodlouse & Co and are reviewing the internal controls documentation in relation to the cash receipts system in preparation for the interim audit which will involve visiting a number of stores and the head office.

Each of Caterpillar Co's stores has on average three or four cash tills to take customer payments. All employees based at the store are able to use each till and individuals do not have their own log-on codes, although employees tend to use the same till each day. Customers can pay using either cash or a credit card and for any transaction either the credit card payment slips or cash are placed in the till by the cashier. Where employees' friends or family members purchase clothes in store, the employee is able to serve them at the till point.

At the end of each day, the tills are closed down with daily readings of sales taken from each till; these are reconciled to the total of the cash in the tills and the credit card payment slips and any discrepancies are noted. To save time, this reconciliation is done by the store's assistant manager in aggregate for all of the store tills together. Once this reconciliation has taken place, the cash is stored in the shop's small safe overnight and in the morning it is transferred to the bank via collection by a security company. If the store is low on change for cash payments, a junior sales clerk is sent by a till operator to the bank with money from the till and asked to change it into smaller denominations.

The daily sales readings from the tills along with the cash data and credit card payment data are transferred daily to head office through an interface with the sales and cash receipts records. A clerk oversees that this transfer has occurred for all stores. On a daily basis, he also agrees the cash transferred by the security company has been banked in full by agreeing the cash deposit slips to the bank statements, and that the credit card receipts have been received from the credit card company. On a monthly basis, the same clerk reconciles the bank statements to the cash book. The reconciliations are reviewed by the financial controller if there are any unreconciled amounts.

 **BPP** LEARNING MEDIA

### Required

(a) State **TWO** control objectives of Caterpillar Co's cash receipts system. **(2 marks)**

(b) Identify and explain **THREE DIRECT CONTROLS** which the auditor may seek to place reliance on in Caterpillar Co's cash receipts system; and describe a **TEST OF CONTROL** the auditor should perform to assess if each of these direct controls is operating effectively.

| Direct control | Test of control |
| --- | --- |
| | |

**(6 marks)**

(c) Identify and explain **SIX DEFICIENCIES** in Caterpillar Co's cash receipts system and provide a recommendation to address each of these deficiencies.

| Control deficiency | Control recommendation |
| --- | --- |
| | |

**(12 marks)**

**(Total = 20 marks)**

## Question 18

It is 1 July 20X5. You are an audit manager of Snail & Co and you are in charge of two audits which are due to commence shortly. Insects4U Co is a registered charity which promotes insect conservation and has been an audit client for several years. Spider Spirals Co, also an existing audit client, manufactures stationery products and its draft total liabilities are $8.1 million. Both clients' financial years ended on 30 April 20X5. The following matters have been brought to your attention for each company.

### Insects4U Co

(i) **Completeness of income**

Insects4U Co is a not-for-profit organisation which generates income in a number of ways. It receives monthly donations from its many subscribers and these are paid by bank transfer to the charity. In addition, a large number of donations are sent through the post to the charity. Insects4U Co also sells tickets for its three charity events held annually. During the audit planning, completeness of income was flagged as a key risk.

**Note.** Assume that the charity adopts IFRSs. **(4 marks)**

### Spider Spirals Co

(ii) **Trade payables**

The finance director of Spider Spirals Co has informed you that at the year end the purchase ledger was kept open for one week longer than normal as a large bank transfer and cheque payment run was made on 3 May 20X5. Some purchase invoices were received in this week and were recorded in the 20X5 purchase ledger as well as the payment run made on 3 May. **(6 marks)**

(iii) **Trade receivables**

Spider Spirals Co has a large number of small customers; the normal credit terms offered to them is 30 days. However, the finance director has informed you that the average trade receivables collection period has increased quite significantly this year from 34 days to 55 days. This is partly due to difficult trading conditions and also because for six months of the year the role of credit controller was vacant. The company has historically maintained on average an allowance for trade receivables of 1.5% of gross trade receivables. **(5 marks)**

**Required**

(a) Describe substantive procedures the auditor should perform to obtain sufficient and appropriate audit evidence in relation to the above three matters.

*Note.* The mark allocation is shown against each of the three matters above.

(b) The finance director of Spider Spirals Co has informed you that he is not proposing to make an adjustment for the trade payables payment run made on 3 May, as the total payment of $490,000 would only require a change to trade payables and the bank overdraft, both of which are current liabilities.

**Required**

Discuss the issue and describe the impact on the auditor's report, if any, should this issue remain unresolved. **(5 marks)**

**(Total = 20 marks)**

# Answers

DO NOT TURN THIS PAGE UNTIL YOU HAVE
COMPLETED THE MOCK EXAM

# Plan of attack

If this were the real Audit and Assurance exam and you had been told to turn over and begin, what would be going through your mind?

An important thing to say (whilst there is still time) is that it is vital to have a good breadth of knowledge of the syllabus because all the questions are compulsory. However, don't panic. Below we provide guidance on how to approach the exam.

## Looking through the exam

Section A has three objective test cases, each with five questions. This is the section of the exam where the examining team can test knowledge across the breadth of the syllabus. Make sure you read these cases and questions carefully. The distractors are designed to present plausible, but incorrect, answers. Don't let them mislead you. If you really have no idea – guess. You may even be right.

Section B has three longer questions:

- **Question 16** is a 30-mark question focused on the planning stage, covering analytical procedures, audit risk, acceptance procedures and ethics. Read the requirements carefully, taking note in particular of the number of ratios that you have been asked to calculate and that they must be calculated for both years.

- **Question 17** is a 20-mark internal controls question. Here you need to consider strengths in the system as well as identifying weaknesses.

- **Question 18** is a 20-mark question dealing with substantive procedures relating to income, trade payables and trade receivables. You are also asked to consider the impact on the auditor's report of any unresolved issues.

## Allocating your time

BPP's advice is to always allocate your time **according to the marks for the question**. However, **use common sense**. If you're doing a question but haven't a clue how to do part (b), you might be better off reallocating your time and getting more marks on another question, where you can add something you didn't have time for earlier on. Make sure you leave time to recheck the OTs and make sure you have answered them all.

## Forget about it

And don't worry if you found the exam difficult. More than likely other candidates will too. If this were the real thing you would need to forget the exam the minute you left the exam hall and think about the next one. Or, if it is the last one, celebrate!

# Section A

1     The correct answer is: 1 and 4

The audit committee should be responsible for monitoring the effectiveness of the internal audit function and the company's internal control system. Therefore statements 1 and 4 should be included.

2     The correct answer is:

Compromises NED independence, NEDs' remuneration should be a set amount based on time committed

NEDs remuneration should not be tied to the performance of Sistar Co as this can compromise their independence. NEDs remuneration should be based on the time committed to carry out the role.

3     The correct answers are: Audit committee; Maria Marquez; More senior staff with audit experience.

To improve the effectiveness and independence of the internal audit function, the head of internal audit should report to the audit committee. Maria Marquez should be appointed as the head of internal audit as she is completely independent of Sistar Co and the audit team needs more senior staff with relevant experience.

4     The correct answer is: A value for money audit.

The assignment described represents a value for money audit as it is focused on assessing the economy, efficiency and effectiveness of Sistar Co's capital expenditure.

5     The correct answer is: Designing and implementing internal control procedures to address deficiencies

Internal audit should not be involved in designing and then implementing internal control procedures as this would result in a self-review threat to independence.

6     The correct answers are: A major supplier to Oak Co has just gone out of business with a number of unfulfilled orders; A new product which was due to account for 30% of revenue has proved to be unsuccessful.

The loss of a major supplier could have a serious impact on Oak Co if no alternative can be found and poor results in a product line expected to account for 30% of revenue could also have a significant impact on the company going forward

7     The correct answer is: 1 and 4.

Gross margin has dropped which implies that the company is not gaining as good a return as in the prior year - this would most likely be due to an increase in C.O.S or drop in sales price. Therefore the comment regarding increasing sales price contradicts the results of the AR.

The inventory holding period has increased significantly implying that items are taking longer to sell, given the comment regarding the observation made at the inventory count this would warrant further investigation given the increase in the inventory holding period.

Therefore comment 1 and 4 should be investigated and are inconsistent with the final AR.

8     The correct answer is: Review of post-year end sales orders from the new customer

The review of post year-end sales would provide the best evidence that the new customer is genuine and is ordering goods. This to some extent will then allow the auditor to assess the level of sales being made to the new customer and to determine whether this does therefore mitigate for the loss of Beech Co.

9 The correct answer is: Request management extend the assessment to cover at least until 31 December 20X5

As per ISA 570 *Going Concern*, the period of assessment should be at least 12 months from the date of the financial statements.

10 The correct answers are: a modified; a material uncertainty relating to going concern.

As per ISA 570 *Going Concern*, where there is a matter of fundamental importance to the users' understanding regarding an uncertainty over going concern, as long as this is adequately disclosed the auditor should include a material uncertainty paragraph related to going concern. The audit opinion is unmodified in this regard.

11 The correct answer is: Wages and salaries accounted for relate to the current year ended 30 April 20X5.

The cut-off assertion relates to ensuring that transaction are recorded in the correct accounting period, and therefore that wages and salaries accounted for relate to the year ended 30 April 20X5.

12

| Audit evidence | Order of reliability |
|---|---|
| Proof in total calculation performed by an audit team member | 1 – Most |
| Written representation from the directors of Walker Co confirming the accuracy of wages and salaries | 3 |
| Verbal confirmation from the finance director of Walker Co confirming the accuracy of wages and salaries | 4 – Least |
| Recalculation of the gross and net pay for a sample of employees by an internal audit team member of Walker Co | 2 |

13 The correct answer is: $16,740,000

Working:

$17,000,000 \times 90\% \times 2/12 = 2,550,000$

$(17,000,000 \times 106\%) \times 90\% \times 10/12 = 13,515,000$

$450 \times 1,500 = 675,000$

$2,550,000 + 13,515,000 + 675,000 = 16,740,000$

14 The correct answers are:

Compare the current year total payroll expense to the prior year and investigate any significant differences

Perform a proof in total calculation and compare expected expense to actual expense within the draft financial statements.

Comparisons with prior years and proof in total calculations are examples of substantive analytical procedures.

15 The correct answer is: 1 and 3

(2) provides evidence that goods dispatched have been invoiced

(4) provides evidence of accuracy

# Section B

# Question 16

## Marking scheme

|  |  | Marks |
|---|---|---|
| (a) | **Matters to be considered prior to accepting the audit of Centipede Co** | |
| | • Compliance with ACCA's *Code of Ethics and Conduct* | 1 |
| | • Competent | 1 |
| | • Reputation and integrity of directors | 1 |
| | • Level of risk of Centipede Co audit | 1 |
| | • Fee adequate to compensate for risk | 1 |
| | • Write to outgoing auditor after obtaining permission to contact | 1 |
| | • Previous auditor permission to respond | 1 |
| | • Review response for any issues | 1 |
| | **Restricted to** | **5** |
| (b) | **Ratio calculations** (½ mark for each year) | |
| | • Gross margin | 1 |
| | • Operating margin | 1 |
| | • Inventory holding period/Inventory turnover | 1 |
| | • Receivables collection period | 1 |
| | • Payables payment period | 1 |
| | • Current ratio | 1 |
| | • Quick ratio | 1 |
| | **Restricted to** | **4** |
| (c) | **Audit risks and responses** (only 8 risks required) | |
| | • New client, increased detection risk | 2 |
| | • Perpetual inventory count adjustments | 2 |
| | • Valuation of inventory | 2 |
| | • Branch records | 2 |
| | • Disposal of building | 2 |
| | • Legal case | 2 |
| | • Directors' remuneration disclosure | 2 |
| | • Revenue growth | 2 |

|  |  | Marks |
|---|---|---|
| • Misclassification of costs between cost of sales and operating | 2 | |
| • Going concern | 2 | |
| Max 7 issues, 2 marks each | | 16 |

(d) **Safeguards to deal with conflict of interest**

| | Marks |
|---|---|
| • Notify Centipede Co and its competitor | 1 |
| • Advise seek independent advice | 1 |
| • Separate engagement teams | 1 |
| • Procedures prevent access to information | 1 |
| • Clear guidelines on security and confidentiality | 1 |
| • Confidentiality agreements | 1 |
| • Monitoring of safeguards | 1 |
| **Restricted to** | 5 |
| **Total marks** | 30 |

(a) **Matters to be considered prior to accepting the audit of Centipede Co**

ISA 220 *Quality Management for an Audit of Financial Statements* provides guidance to Ant & Co on the steps they should have taken in accepting the new audit client, Centipede Co. It sets out a number of processes which the auditor should perform prior to accepting a new engagement.

Ant & Co should have considered any issues which might arise which could threaten compliance with ACCA's *Code of Ethics and Conduct* or any local legislation, such as the level of fees from Centipede Co, to ensure they are not unduly reliant on these fees, as well as considering whether any conflicts of interest arise with existing clients. If issues arise, then their significance must be considered.

In addition, they should have considered whether they were competent to perform the work and whether they would have appropriate resources available, as well as any specialist skills or knowledge required for the audit of Centipede Co.

Ant & Co should have considered what it already knows about the directors of Centipede Co; it needed to consider the reputation and integrity of the directors. If necessary, the firm may have wanted to obtain references if it does not formally know the directors.

Additionally, Ant & Co should have considered the level of risk attached to the audit of Centipede Co and whether this was acceptable to the firm. As part of this, it should have considered whether the expected audit fee was adequate in relation to the risk of auditing Centipede Co.

Ant & Co should have communicated with the outgoing auditor of Centipede Co to assess if there were any ethical or professional reasons why they should not have accepted appointment. They should have obtained permission from Centipede Co's management to contact the previous auditor; if this was not given, then the engagement should have been refused. Once received, the response from the previous auditor should have been carefully reviewed for any issues which could affect acceptance.

(b) **Ratios**

Ratios to assist the audit supervisor in planning the audit:

|  | 20X5 | 20X4 |
|---|---|---|
| Gross margin | 9,390/25,230 = 37.2% | 7,165/21,180 = 33.8% |
| Operating margin | 4,487/25,230 = 17.8% | 3,920/21,180 = 18.5% |
| Inventory holding period or | 2,360/15,840 × 365 = 54 days | 1,800/14,015 × 365 = 47 days |
| Inventory turnover | 15,840/2,360 = 6.7 | 14,015/1,800 = 7.8 |
| Receivables collection period | 1,590/25,230 × 365 = 23 days | 1,250/21,180 × 365 = 22 days |
| Payables payment period | 3,500/15,840 × 365 = 81 days | 2,800/14,015 × 365 = 73 days |
| Current ratio | 3,950/4,080 = 0.97 | 3,530/2,800 = 1.26 |
| Quick ratio | (3,950 − 2,360)/4,080 = 0.39 | (3,530 − 1,800)/2,800 = 0.62 |

(c) **Audit risks and auditor's responses**

| Audit risk | Auditor's response |
|---|---|
| Centipede Co is a new client for Ant & Co and is a listed company. As the team is not familiar with the accounting policies, transactions and balances of the company, there will be an increased detection risk on the audit. | Ant & Co should ensure it has a suitably experienced team. Also, adequate time should be allocated for team members to obtain an understanding of the company and the risks of material misstatement, including attendance at an audit team briefing. |
| The company utilises a perpetual inventory system at its warehouse rather than a full year-end count. Under such a system, all inventory must be counted at least once a year, with adjustments made to the inventory records on a timely basis. Inventory could be under- or overstated if the perpetual inventory counts are not complete.<br><br>During the interim audit, it was noted that there were significant exceptions with the inventory records being higher than the inventory in the warehouse. As the year-end quantities will be based on the records, this is likely to result in overstated inventory. | The completeness of the perpetual inventory counts should be reviewed and the controls over the counts and adjustments to records should be tested.<br><br>In addition, the level of adjustments made to inventory should be considered to assess their significance. This should be discussed with management as soon as possible as it may not be possible to place reliance on the inventory records at the year end, which could result in the requirement for a full year-end inventory count. |
| During the interim audit, it was noted that there were some lines of inventory which according to the records were at least 90 days old. In addition, the inventory holding period has increased from 47 to 54 days. It would appear that there may be an increase in slow-moving inventory.<br><br>The valuation of inventory as per IAS 2 *Inventories* should be at the lower of cost and net realisable value. Hence there is a risk that obsolete inventory has not been appropriately written down and inventory is overvalued. | The aged inventory report should be reviewed and discussed with management to assess if certain lines of products are slow moving.<br><br>Detailed cost and net realisable value testing to be performed to assess whether an allowance or write down of inventory is required. |

| Audit risk | Auditor's response |
|---|---|
| Centipede Co maintains accounting records at four additional sites which were not visited during the interim audit, and the records from these sites are incorporated monthly into the general ledger.<br><br>Ant & Co needs to ensure that it has obtained sufficient appropriate audit evidence over all the accounting records of the company, not just for those at head office. There is a detection risk if the team does not visit or undertake testing of the records at these sites. Further, if the interface does not occur appropriately, there is a risk that accounting records are incomplete. | Discuss with management the significance and materiality of the records maintained at the four sites. The team may then need to visit some of these sites during the final audit to undertake testing of the records held there.<br><br>In addition, computer-assisted audit techniques could be utilised by the team to sample test the monthly interface of data from each site to head office to identify any errors. |
| During 20X5 a building was disposed of with a loss on disposal of $825,000. There is a risk that the disposal has not been removed appropriately from the accounting records or that the loss on disposal calculation is incorrect.<br><br>In addition, significant profits or losses on disposal are an indication that the depreciation policy for land and buildings may not be appropriate. Therefore depreciation may be understated and consequently assets overstated. | Agree that the asset has been removed from the non-current assets register, recalculate the loss on disposal calculation and agree all items to supporting documentation.<br><br>Discuss the depreciation policy for land and buildings with the finance director to assess its reasonableness. Review the level of losses on disposal generated from other asset sales to ascertain if this is a more widespread issue. |
| A customer of Centipede Co has commenced legal action against Centipede Co for a loss of profits claim.<br><br>If it is probable that the company will make payment to the customer, a legal provision is required. If the payment is possible rather than probable, a contingent liability disclosure would be necessary. If Centipede Co has not done this, there is a risk over the completeness of any provisions and the necessary disclosure of contingent liabilities. | Ant & Co should write to the company's lawyers to enquire of the existence and likelihood of success of any claim from the wholesale customer. The results of this should be used to assess the level of provision or disclosure included in the financial statements. |
| The directors have not disclosed the individual names and payments for each of the directors' remuneration. This is in line with IFRS but disclosure of this is required by local legislation. In cases where the local legislation is more comprehensive than IFRS, it is likely the company must comply with the local legislation.<br><br>The directors' remuneration disclosure will not be complete and accurate if the names and individual payments are not disclosed in accordance with the relevant local legislation and hence the financial statements will be misstated as a result of the non-compliance. | Discuss this matter with management and review the requirements of the local legislation to determine if the disclosure in the financial statements is appropriate. |

| Audit risk | Auditor's response |
| --- | --- |
| Revenue has grown by 19% in the year; however, cost of sales has only increased by 13%. This is a significant increase in revenue and along with the increase in gross margin may be due to an overstatement of revenue. | During the audit a detailed breakdown of sales will be obtained, discussed with management and tested in order to understand the sales increase. Increased cut-off testing should also be undertaken to verify that revenue is recorded in the right period and is not overstated. |
| Gross margin has increased from 33.8% to 37.2%. Operating margin has decreased from 18.5% to 17.8%. This movement in gross margin is significant and there is a risk that costs may have been omitted or included in operating expenses rather than cost of sales. This would risk overstating operating expenses and understating costs of sales, and would in turn overstate the gross margin and understate the operating margin. | The classification of costs between cost of sales and operating expenses will be compared with the prior year to ensure consistency. Also increased cut-off testing should be performed at the year end to ensure that costs are complete. |
| The overall liquidity of the company is in decline, with the current and quick ratios decreasing from 1.26 to 0.97 and 0.62 to 0.39 respectively. In addition, the cash balances have decreased significantly over the year, and the company now has an overdraft of $580,000 at the end of the year. Further, the trade payables payment period has increased from 73 to 81 days, implying the company is struggling to meet its liabilities as they fall due.<br><br>All of these changes in key ratios could signal going concern difficulties. | Detailed going concern testing to be performed during the audit as there may be a doubt over going concern and the basis of accounting should be discussed with management to ensure that the going concern basis is reasonable. |

(d) **Safeguards to deal with conflict of interest**

- Both Centipede Co and its rival competitor should be notified that Ant & Co would be acting as auditors for each company and, if necessary, consent obtained.

- Advising one or both clients to seek additional independent advice.

- The use of separate engagement teams, with different engagement partners and team members; once an employee has worked on one audit, such as Centipede Co, then they should be prevented from being on the audit of the competitor for a period of time.

- Procedures to prevent access to information, for example, strict physical separation of both teams, confidential and secure data filing.

- Clear guidelines for members of each engagement team on issues of security and confidentiality. These guidelines could be included within the audit engagement letters.

- Potentially the use of confidentiality agreements signed by employees and partners of the firm.

- Regular monitoring of the application of the above safeguards by a senior individual in Ant & Co not involved in either audit.

# Question 17

## Marking scheme

|  |  |  | Marks |
|---|---|---|---|
| (a) | **Control objectives – cash receipts system** | | |
| | • To ensure that all valid cash receipts are received and deposited promptly in the bank | 1 | |
| | • To ensure all cash receipts are recorded in the cash book | 1 | |
| | • To ensure that all receipts are recorded at the correct amounts in the cash books | 1 | |
| | • To ensure that cash receipts are correctly posted to the general ledger | 1 | |
| | • To ensure that cash receipts are recorded in the correct accounting period | 1 | |
| | • To ensure that cash is safeguarded to prevent theft | 1 | |
| | • To ensure that management has accurate and timely information regarding the cash position | 1 | |
| | **Restricted to** | | 2 |
| (b) | **Direct controls and tests of control** (3 strengths required) | | |
| | • Internal audit department which undertakes cash control reviews at stores | 2 | |
| | • Daily sales readings taken from tills and reconciled to cash and credit card payment slips, exceptions noted | 2 | |
| | • Cash collected daily and taken to the bank by security company | 2 | |
| | • Daily interface to head office for sales, cash and credit card data into sales and cash receipts books | 2 | |
| | • Daily agreement of cash banked by security company and cash received from credit card company into bank statements | 2 | |
| | • Monthly bank reconciliations undertaken | 2 | |
| | **Max 3 issues, 2 marks each** | | 6 |

(c)     **Control deficiencies and recommendations** (only 6 issues required)

| | Marks |
|---|---|
| • Internal audit only visits 20 largest stores rather than all 45 | 2 |
| • All employees able to use tills and no individual log-on codes | 2 |
| • Employees can serve friends and family members at the till points | 2 |
| • Daily till reading reconciliations performed in aggregate for all tills in store rather than individually | 2 |
| • Cashing up of tills undertaken by just one individual | 2 |
| • Cash stored on site overnight | 2 |
| • Junior sales clerks given cash and sent to the bank to change notes into smaller denominations | 2 |
| • Lack of segregation of duties in head office for recording and reconciling of cash | 2 |
| • Bank reconciliations not always reviewed by the financial controller | 2 |

Max 6 issues, 2 marks each     12

**Total marks**     20

---

(a)     **Control objectives – cash receipts system**

- To ensure that all valid cash receipts are received and deposited promptly in the bank
- To ensure all cash receipts are recorded in the cash book
- To ensure that all receipts are recorded at the correct amounts in the cash book
- To ensure that cash receipts are correctly posted to the general ledger
- To ensure that cash receipts are recorded in the correct accounting period
- To ensure that cash is safeguarded to prevent theft
- To ensure that management has accurate and timely information regarding the cash position

(b)     **Caterpillar Co's cash cycle strengths and tests of control**

| Direct controls | Test of control |
|---|---|
| Caterpillar Co has an internal audit (IA) department which has undertaken a number of internal control reviews, which specifically focused on cash controls at stores during the year.<br><br>This is a strong monitoring control as stores will aim to ensure that company procedures are maintained as they would not wish IA to report any exceptions at their store. As a result of this control risk is reduced for the external audit. | Discuss with IA the programme of their visits to stores and the areas addressed on these visits. This will assess the strength of this monitoring control. In particular, enquire of IA whether over a rolling period all stores will be visited.<br><br>Review the IA department files for the results of the store visits, to confirm that the 20 stores programmed to be visited did all actually take place and for exceptions noted and actions taken. |
| At the end of each day, the tills are closed down with daily readings of sales taken; these are reconciled to the total of the cash in the tills and the credit card payment slips and any discrepancies are noted.<br><br>Daily cashing up procedures should ensure that the cash is controlled and reduces the risk of fraud as employees are aware that the assistant manager will be looking for cash discrepancies. | For a sample of stores visited, the auditor should review the file of daily reconciliations to ascertain if end of day till reconciliations have taken place on a daily basis.<br><br>For reconciliations with discrepancies, discuss with the store manager what actions were taken and how these differences were resolved. |

| Direct controls | Test of control |
|---|---|
| Cash received from customers is taken to the bank daily via collection by a security company.<br><br>This ensures that cash is safeguarded and that the risk of theft when transferring to the bank is minimised. | During the store visits, enquire of staff how the cash is transferred to the bank. A sample of invoices from the collection company should be reviewed and confirmed that they are charging Centipede Co on a daily basis.<br><br>In addition, during these visits observe the cash collection process carried out by the security company. |
| The daily sales readings from the tills along with the cash and credit card data are transferred to head office through a daily interface into the sales and cash receipts records.<br><br>This should ensure that sales and cash records are updated on a prompt basis and are complete and accurate, and that the bank balance is accurate. | During the interim audit at head office, compare the daily sales readings from individual stores, including some visited by the audit team, to the sales and cash receipt records within the general ledger. Review the date on which the sales and cash receipt records were updated to ensure this occurred promptly. Any discrepancies should be discussed with the clerk responsible for overseeing this process. |
| On a daily basis the clerk agrees that the cash banked and the credit card receipts from the credit card company have been credited to the bank statements in full.<br><br>This should ensure the completeness of cash receipts, as they are transferred in from two sources, being the security company and the credit card operator. | Discuss with the clerk responsible for reconciling the cash and credit card receipts the process he undertakes. Review the daily reconciliations he has completed to confirm the process has been undertaken as described. |
| Bank reconciliations are undertaken on a monthly basis.<br><br>This should ensure that any discrepancies between the cash book and the bank statements are identified promptly. | Review the file of bank reconciliations to ascertain if there is one for each month and that they are either fully reconciled, or the financial controller has evidenced their review of any unreconciled amounts. |

(c)  **Caterpillar Co's cash system deficiencies and controls**

| Control deficiency | Control recommendation |
|---|---|
| The IA department only undertakes cash control visits to the 20 largest stores as they feel this is where most issues arise. However, Caterpillar Co has 45 stores in total which means over half of the stores are not being checked. This increases the likelihood of control errors, as these stores may not comply with company procedures and with it being a cash business heightens the chance of frauds occurring. | Caterpillar Co's IA department should have a rolling programme of visits to all 45 stores. This programme can have a bias to large and high risk stores, but it should ensure that all stores are visited on a cyclical basis. |
| All store employees are able to use each till and none have an individual log-on code when using the tills. Allowing all employees access to the till points increases the risk of fraud and error arising. Also in the event of cash discrepancies arising in the tills, it would be difficult to ascertain which employees may be responsible as there is no way of tracking who used which till. | Only employees for whom criminal record/credit checks have been undertaken should be able to use the tills to take customer payments.<br><br>Each employee should have a designated till and a log-on code, which is required for each payment transaction. |

ANSWERS

| Control deficiency | Control recommendation |
|---|---|
| Where employees' friends or family members purchase clothes in store, the employee is able to serve them at the till point.<br><br>There is a significant fraud risk as employees could fail to put the goods through the till, but retain the cash paid by the friend/family members. Additionally, they could give the goods away for free or undercharge for goods sold, thereby granting unauthorised discounts. | Caterpillar Co should instigate a policy whereby employees are unable to serve friends or family members at the till points. They should be required to request that a manager or supervisor put these goods through the till.<br><br>In addition, CCTV cameras could be placed in the shops, near to the till points to record the daily till transactions. This would act as a deterrent to employees as well as provide evidence in the case of fraudulent transactions occurring.<br><br>Caterpillar Co should also carry out regular inventory counts to identify if goods in the stores are below the levels in the inventory records, as this could identify goods being given away for free. |
| The daily reading of sales and reconciliations to the tills is performed in aggregate rather than for each till. This means if exceptions arise, it will be difficult to identify which till caused the difference and therefore which employees may require further till training or have undertaken fraudulent transactions. | The reconciliations should be undertaken on an individual till by till basis rather than in aggregate. |
| The cashing up of tills along with the recording of any cash discrepancies is undertaken by just one individual, the assistant store manager. There is a fraud risk as the store manager could remove some of the cash and then simply record that there was an exception on this till. | The cashing up process should be undertaken by two individuals together, ideally the assistant and the store manager. One should count the cash and the other record it. Any exceptions to the till reading should be double checked to confirm that they are not simply addition errors. |
| The cash is kept at the store overnight in a small safe. Although in a safe, this is not secure as it is likely that the cash sales for one day would be a significant sum. This cash is at risk of being stolen overnight. | The cash should continue to be collected daily by the security company, but rather than in the morning it should be collected as the store closes in the evening so that cash does not have to be stored overnight. |
| If a store needs change, a junior sales clerk is sent to the bank by a till operator to change it into smaller denominations. There is a risk of the cash being misplaced or stolen on the way to the bank or collusion between the junior clerk and till operator as no record appears to be kept of the money removed from the till in these instances and no confirmation of how much cash is returned is carried out. | Caterpillar Co's head office should stipulate a float amount per till and how the note denominations should be comprised. When assigning the cash float in the morning, the store manager should ensure that this policy is adhered to.<br><br>If, during the day, further smaller denomination notes are required, the store manager should authorise a member of staff to obtain cash from the bank and should fully record movements in and out of the till. |

| Control deficiency | Control recommendation |
|---|---|
| One clerk is responsible for several elements of the cash receipts system. He oversees the daily interface from stores, agrees that cash has cleared into the bank statements and undertakes the bank reconciliations.<br><br>There is a lack of segregation of duties and errors will not be identified on a timely basis as well as increasing the risk of fraud. | These key roles should be split between a few individuals, with ideally the bank reconciliations being undertaken by another member of the finance team. |
| The bank reconciliations are only reviewed by the financial controller if there are any unreconciled amounts. The bank reconciliation could reconcile but still contain significant errors as there could be compensating errors which cancel each other out. In addition, for a cash based business, the bank reconciliation is a direct control which reduces the risk of fraud. If it is not reviewed, then this reduces its effectiveness. | The bank reconciliations should be reviewed by the financial controller on a monthly basis, even if there are no exceptions, and he should evidence his review by way of signature on the bank reconciliation. |

# Question 18

**Workbook references.** Chapters 14, 16 and 20.

**Top tips.** This is a 20-mark question which tests substantive procedures relating to income, trade payables and trade receivables, together with auditors' reports. In part (a) you must read the scenario carefully and tailor your substantive procedures. In the past the examining team has commented that candidates often provide lists of standard audit work without consideration of the facts in the question. Also note that in relation to income the question considers the assertion of completeness specifically. Again you must ensure you address this in your answer.

In part (b) the key is to note that you need to discuss the issues as well as commenting on the impact on the auditor's report. Your discussion should support the conclusion you have come to.

**Easy marks.** No specific part of this question is straightforward but there are some easier marks available in part (b).

## Marking scheme

Marks

(a) (i) **Substantive procedures for completeness of Insects4U Co income**
- Cast schedule of all of the company's income    1
- Compare individual categories of income to prior year    1
- Trace monthly donations from bank statements to cash book    1
- New subscribers agree subscription forms to donations received account, cash book and bank statements    1
- For donations, review correspondence from donors, agree to donations account, cash book and bank statements    1
- Perform proof in total of tickets sold multiplied by ticket price, compare to actual and investigate significant difference    <u>1</u>

Restricted to      4

(ii) **Substantive procedures for Spider Spirals Co trade payables**

| | Marks |
|---|---|
| • Calculate trade payables payment period | 1 |
| • Compare total trade payables and list of accruals against prior year | 1 |
| • Discuss with management process to quantify misstatement of payables | 1 |
| • Sample invoices received between 1 and 7 May, if post year end, then agree excluded from ledger | 1 |
| • Review after-date payments | 1 |
| • Review supplier statements reconciliations | 1 |
| • Perform a trade payables circularisation | 1 |
| • Cut-off testing pre and post year end GRN | 1 |
| **Restricted to** | 6 |

(iii) **Substantive procedures for Spider Spirals Co trade receivables**

| | Marks |
|---|---|
| • Aged receivables report to identify any slow-moving balances | 1 |
| • Review customer correspondence to assess whether there are any invoices in dispute | 1 |
| • Review the after-date cash receipts | 1 |
| • Review board minutes | 1 |
| • Calculate level of irrecoverable receivables, assess if material and discuss with management | 1 |
| • Recalculate allowance for receivables | 1 |
| • Post year end sales returns/credit notes | 1 |
| **Restricted to** | 5 |

(b) **Effect of uncorrected misstatement and impact on auditor's report**

| | Marks |
|---|---|
| • Discussion of issue | 1 |
| • Calculation of materiality | 1 |
| • Type of auditor's report modification required | 2 |
| • Impact on auditor's report | 1 |
| **Restricted to** | 5 |
| **Total marks** | 20 |

(a) (i) **Substantive procedures for Insects4U Co income**

- Obtain a schedule of all Insects4U Co's income and cast to confirm completeness and accuracy of the balance.

- Compare the individual categories of income against prior year and investigate any significant differences.

- For monthly donations, trace a sample of donations received in the bank statements to the cash book to ensure that they are recorded completely and accurately.

- For a sample of new subscribers in the year, agree from their completed subscription form the monthly sum and start date, trace to the monthly donations received account and agree to the cash book and bank statements.

- For donations received in the post, review correspondence from donors, agree to the donations account and trace sums received to the cash book and bank statements to ensure all completely recorded.

- For the charity events, undertake a proof in total calculation of the number of tickets sold multiplied by the ticket price, compare this to the income recorded and discuss any significant differences with management.

(ii) **Substantive procedures for Spider Spirals Co trade payables**

- Calculate the trade payables collection period for Spider Spirals Co, compare with prior years and investigate any significant difference, in particular any decrease for this year due to the payment run on 3 May.

- Compare the total trade payables and list of accruals against prior year and investigate any significant differences.

- Discuss with management the process they have undertaken to quantify the misstatement of trade payables due to the late payment run and cut-off error of purchase invoices and consider the materiality of the error in isolation as well as with other misstatements found.

- Select a sample of purchase invoices received between the period of 1 and 7 May, ascertain through reviewing goods received notes (GRNs) if the goods were received pre or post year end; if post year end, then confirm that they have been excluded from the ledger or follow through to the correcting journal entry.

- Review after-date payments; if they relate to the current year, then follow through to the purchase ledger or accrual listing to ensure they are recorded in the correct period.

- Obtain supplier statements and reconcile these to the purchase ledger balances, and investigate any reconciling items.

- Select a sample of payables balances and perform a trade payables circularisation, follow up any non-replies and any reconciling items between the balance confirmed and the trade payables balance.

- Select a sample of GRNs before the year end and after the year end and follow through to inclusion in the correct period's payables balance, to ensure correct cut-off.

(iii) **Substantive procedures for Spider Spirals Co trade receivables**

- Review the aged receivables listing to identify any slow-moving or old receivables balances; discuss the status of these balances with the finance director to assess whether they are likely to pay.

- Review customer correspondence to identify any balances which are in dispute or unlikely to be paid.

- Review whether there are any after-date cash receipts for slow-moving/old receivables balances.

- Review board minutes to identify whether there are any significant concerns in relation to payments by customers.

- Calculate the potential level of receivables which are not recoverable and assess whether this is material or not and discuss with management.

- Recalculate the allowance for receivables and compare to the potentially irrecoverable balances to assess if the allowance is adequate.

- Inspect post year end sales returns/credit notes and consider whether an additional allowance against receivables is required.

(b)     **Impact on auditor's report**

The company made a payment run of $490,000 for payables on 3 May, which is post year end. The trade payables which were outstanding at the year end have been understated as they have been recorded as being paid. In addition, the bank overdraft is overstated as the payments are recorded as coming out of the year-end bank balance. This is evidence of window dressing, as the company has attempted to record a lower level of payable obligations at the year end. The finance director's argument that no adjustment is necessary because the balances affected are both current liabilities is irrelevant as, although both balances are liabilities, they should each still be materially correct.

The amount of the payment run is $490,000 which represents 6.0% of total liabilities (490/8,100) and hence is a material matter.

If management refuses to adjust for the post year end payment run, the auditor's opinion will need to be modified. As trade payables are understated and the bank overdraft is overstated and there is a material misstatement which is not pervasive, a qualified opinion would be necessary. A basis for qualified opinion section would need to be included subsequent to the opinion section. This would explain the material misstatement in relation to the treatment of the trade payables and bank overdraft and the effect on the financial statements. The opinion would be qualified 'except for'.

# ACCA

# Applied Skills

# Audit and Assurance

# Mock Examination 4

# Section B from Sep/Dec 2021 Hybrid Exam

Time allowed: 3 hours

This mock exam is divided into two sections:

Section A – ALL 15 questions are compulsory and MUST be attempted

Section B – ALL 3 questions are compulsory and MUST be attempted

# Section A – ALL 15 questions are compulsory and MUST be attempted

Each question is worth 2 marks.

The following scenario relates to questions 1–5.

You are an audit manager at Horti & Co and you are considering a number of ethical issues which have arisen on some of the firm's long-standing audit clients. It is 1 July 20X5.

## Tree Co

Horti & Co is planning its external audit of Tree Co. Yesterday, the audit engagement partner, Charlie Thrower, discovered that a significant fee for information security services, which were provided to Tree Co by Horti & Co, is overdue. Charlie hopes to be able to resolve the dispute amicably and has confirmed that he will discuss the matter with the finance director, Percy Marsh, at the weekend, as they are both attending a party to celebrate the engagement of Charlie's daughter and Percy's son.

## Bush Co

Horti & Co is the external auditor of Bush Co and also provides other non-audit services to the company. While performing the audit for the year ended 30 November 20X4, the audit engagement partner was taken ill and took an indefinite leave of absence from the firm. The ethics partner has identified the following potential replacements and is keen that independence is maintained to the highest level:

| Brian Smith | who is also the partner in charge of the tax services provided to Bush Co |
| Monty Nod | who was the audit engagement partner for the ten years ended 30 November 20X3 |
| Cassie Dixon | who introduced Bush Co as a client when she joined the firm as an audit partner five years ago |
| Pete Russo | who is also the partner in charge of the payroll services provided to Bush Co |

## Plant Co

Plant Co is a large private company, with a financial year to 31 March, and has been an audit client of Horti & Co for several years. Alan Marshlow, a partner of Horti & Co, has acted as the Engagement Quality Reviewer (EQR) on the last two audits to the year ended 31 March 20X5. At a recent meeting, he advised that he can no longer be EQR on the engagement as he is considering accepting appointment as a non-executive director and will sit on the audit committee of Plant Co.

The board of directors has also asked Horti & Co if they would be able to provide internal audit services to the company.

## Weed Co

Weed Co, a listed company, is one of Horti & Co's largest clients. Last year the fee for audit and other services was $1.2m and this year it is expected to be $1.3m which represents 16.6% and 18.1% of Horti & Co's total income respectively.

1    **Which of the following statements correctly explains the possible threats to Horti & Co's independence and recommends an appropriate safeguard in relation to their audit of Tree Co?**

    (1)        An intimidation threat exists due to the overdue fee and Tree Co should be advised that all fees must be paid prior to the auditor's report being signed

    (2)        A self-review threat exists due to the nature of the non-audit work which has been performed and an engagement quality control review should be carried out

    (3)        A self-interest threat exists due to the relationship between Charlie and Percy and Charlie should be removed as audit partner

    O    1, 2 and 3

    O    1 and 2 only

    O    2 only

    O    3 only

2    **Taking into account the concern of the ethics partner, which of the partners identified as potential replacements should take over the audit of Bush Co for the year ended 30 November 20X4?**

    O    Brian Smith

    O    Monty Nod

    O    Cassie Dixon

    O    Pete Russo

3    **Which of the following options correctly identifies the threats to Horti & Co's independence and proposes an appropriate course of action for the firm if Alan Marshlow accepts appointment as a non-executive director of Plant Co?**

| | Threats | Course of action |
|---|---|---|
| Option 1 | Self-interest and familiarity | Can continue with appropriate safeguards |
| Option 2 | Self-interest and self-review | Must resign as auditor |
| Option 3 | Self-interest and familiarity | Must resign as auditor |
| Option 4 | Familiarity only | Can continue with appropriate safeguards |

    O    Option 1

    O    Option 2

    O    Option 3

    O    Option 4

4    You are separately considering Plant Co's request to provide internal audit services and the remit of these services if they are accepted.

**Which of the following would result in Horti & Co assuming a management responsibility in relation to the internal audit services?**

(1)    Taking responsibility for designing and maintaining internal control systems

(2)    Determining which recommendations should take priority and be implemented

(3)    Determining the reliance which can be placed on the work of internal audit for the external audit

(4)    Setting the scope of the internal audit work to be carried out

○    1 and 3

○    2, 3, and 4

○    1, 2 and 4

○    3 and 4 only

---

5    **Which of the following actions should Horti & Co take to maintain their objectivity in relation to the level of fee income from Weed Co?**

|  | TAKE | DO NOT TAKE |
|---|---|---|
| Communicate level of fee income to those charged with governance | ☐ | ☐ |
| Use separate teams for the audit and non-audit work | ☐ | ☐ |
| Request payment of the current year's audit fee in advance of any work being performed | ☐ | ☐ |
| Request a pre-issuance review be conducted by an external accountant | ☐ | ☐ |

---

**The following scenario relates to questions 6–10.**

Chester Co manufactures and sells pet toys to the wholesale market. It has prepared its financial statements to 28 February 20X5. It is 1 July 20X5. You are an audit assistant with Durham & Co and you have been assigned the current liabilities balances in the audit work plan.

You have calculated the payables payment period to be 66 days in 20X5 (45 days in 20X4) and have asked the directors of Chester Co to provide an explanation as to the increase in days.

Chester Co receives monthly statements from its main suppliers and performs regular supplier statement reconciliations. There were inconsistencies noted in respect of the following at 28 February 20X5:

| Supplier | Balance per purchase ledger ($) | Balance per supplier statement ($) |
|---|---|---|
| Oxford Co | 151,480 | 296,120 |
| Poole Co | (72,168) | 84,235 |
| Bath Co | 82,348 | 92,340 |

## Oxford Co

Chester Co has a credit agreement with Oxford Co under which it receives goods 14 days before the supplier raises the invoice. Chester Co received goods worth $144,640 on 18 February 20X5 for which the invoice was received shortly after the year end in accordance with the agreement. Chester Co entered the transaction into its accounting records at the date of invoice.

## Poole Co

The difference on this balance has still to be investigated.

## Bath Co

Chester Co's finance director has informed you that there was an error in closing the purchase ledger and it was closed three days early. Invoices received 26, 27 and 28 February 20X5 were posted to the 20X6 ledger. The directors of Chester Co have confirmed that following discovery of this error, a manual adjustment was made using the journal book.

6    Which of the following supplier balances would indicate a high risk in relation to the COMPLETENESS of the liability recorded at the year end?

O    A supplier with a high balance at the year end and with a low volume of transactions during the year

O    A supplier with a low balance at the year end and with a high volume of transactions during the year

O    A  supplier with a low balance at the year end and with a low volume of transactions during the year

O    A supplier with a high balance at the year end and with a high volume of transactions during the year

7    Which of the following would correctly explain why the payables payment period has increased from 45 days in 20X4 to 66 days in 20X5?

O    Chester Co received a prompt payment discount from one of its suppliers for the first time in 20X5

O    Chester Co obtained a trade discount from one of its biggest suppliers which has reduced the amount owed to that supplier by 10% in the year

O    Chester Co purchased an unusually high level of goods in February 20X5 to satisfy a large order and had not paid for those goods by the year end

O    Chester Co took advantage of extended credit terms offered by a new supplier in respect of a large order which it had fully settled by the year end

8    Which of the following is an appropriate action in respect of the inconsistency in the balance with Oxford Co?

O    The auditor should take no further action as this is a timing difference which was resolved upon receipt and posting of the invoice

O    The auditor should request that the purchase ledger balance is amended at the reporting date to reflect the recent invoice

O    The auditor should contact the supplier and request a supplier statement as at the current date

O    The auditor should request that an accrual is created in respect of the goods received but not yet invoiced

9    Which of the following would be a valid explanation for the difference in respect of Poole Co?

Complete the following sentences regarding the difference in respect of Poole Co by selecting from the options provided.

An invoice for [＿＿＿＿＿＿＿] has been [＿＿＿＿＿＿＿].

| Invoice amount |
| --- |
| $156,403 |

| |
| --- |
| $84,235 |

| |
| --- |
| $72,168 |

| Explanation |
| --- |
| paid twice |

| |
| --- |
| posted as a debit note |

| |
| --- |
| received and processed prior to receipt of the goods |

10    Which of the following would NOT provide sufficient and appropriate audit evidence over the COMPLETENESS of the purchase ledger balance in respect of Bath Co?

○    Obtain the journal book and confirm that all invoices recorded as received from Bath Co dated 26–28 February have been manually adjusted for

○    Review the accruals listing to ensure goods received from Bath Co post year end for which an invoice has not been received have been recorded in the correct period

○    For post year-end cash book payments to Bath Co, confirm date of matching invoice and if pre year end agree to liability

○    Review a sample of invoices received from Bath Co recorded post year end and match to GRN to determine if they should have been recorded at the year end

## The following scenario relates to questions 11–15.

Viola Co is a manufacturer of shoes. You are an audit manager with Cello & Co and you are performing an overall review of the financial statements for the year ended 31 December 20X4 prior to the issue of the auditor's report. It is 1 July 20X5. Profit before tax for the year was $131.4m (20X3: $120.9m).

### Analytical procedures

As part of your overall review, you have performed analytical procedures over the draft financial statements and have noted that the trade receivables collection period is lower than it was during the interim audit performed in October 20X4. You are aware that the credit controller of Viola Co left the company in November 20X4 and that the directors have said that, as a result, the company is experiencing difficulties in debt collection.

### Disclosures

During the year, Viola Co revalued its head office and as part of your review, you are considering the detail which is disclosed in the property, plant and equipment note in the draft financial statements.

BPP
LEARNING
MEDIA

## Uncorrected misstatements

Your review also includes an assessment of uncorrected misstatements. These have been recorded by the audit team as follows:

|  |  | $000 |
|---|---|---|
| (1) | Interest payable omitted in error | 1,942 |
| (2) | Additional allowance for receivables required | 9,198 |
| (3) | Error in sales invoice processing resulting in understatement of sales | 8,541 |
| (4) | Write off in respect of faulty goods | 2,900 |

## Faulty goods

The adjustment for faulty goods listed as an uncorrected misstatement above, relates to an entire batch of shoes, which was produced on 12 December 20X4. The audit work concluded that the cost of this inventory exceeded its net realisable value by $2.9m. The directors dispute the audit team's figures and believe that the realisable value of the inventory still exceeds its cost.

11  **Which of the following would form part of the auditor's overall review of the financial statements?**

(1) Establishing whether the pre-conditions for an audit are present

(2) Assessing whether the information and explanations obtained during the audit are adequately reflected

(3) Performing a detailed review of the audit working papers to ensure the work has been properly performed

(4) Reviewing the adequacy of the disclosure of accounting policies

○  1 and 2

○  3 and 4

○  1 and 3

○  2 and 4

12  **Which of the following is a valid explanation for the INCONSISTENCY between the results of the analytical procedures on trade receivables and the directors' statement regarding debt collection problems?**

○  A change in sales mix towards high value products

○  An increase in the proportion of cash sales since November 20X4

○  An increase in the rate of sales tax in December 20X4

○  Sales growth of 1% per month over the year

13    Which of the following details should be disclosed in respect of the revaluation of the head office if the auditor is to conclude that the disclosures are adequate?

    (1)    Effective date of the revaluation

    (2)    Name of the valuer

    (3)    The amount of the revaluation increase

    (4)    Carrying amount of the head office under the cost model

    O    1, 2 and 3 only

    O    1, 3 and 4 only

    O    2, 3 and 4 only

    O    1, 2, 3 and 4

14    Which of the uncorrected misstatements numbered (1), (2) and (3) by the audit team MUST be adjusted for if the auditor is to issue an unmodified audit opinion?

    O    Misstatements 2 and 3 only

    O    Misstatements 1 and 3 only

    O    Misstatements 1, 2 and 3

    O    Misstatement 2 only

15    All adjustments required by the auditors have been made to the financial statements with the exception of adjustment (4) relating to the faulty goods.

**Which of the following correctly describes the effect of this matter on the auditor's report?**

    O    Unmodified opinion with no further disclosure

    O    Unmodified opinion with disclosure in an emphasis of matter paragraph

    O    Qualified opinion due to material misstatement

    O    Qualified opinion due to inability to obtain sufficient appropriate audit evidence

(Total = 30 marks)

# Section B – ALL THREE questions are compulsory and MUST be attempted

## Question 16

This scenario relates to five requirements.

It is 1 July 20X5. You are an audit supervisor with Apricot & Co and have been assigned to the audit of Peach Co, a soft drinks manufacturer which sells to wholesale customers. You are currently planning the year-end audit for the year ending 31 August 20X5 and have received the following notes from the audit engagement partner. Materiality for the draft financial statements has been calculated as $153,000, which is 5% of profit before tax.

### Planning meeting notes

A new accounting system was introduced via direct changeover in March 20X5. It had been successfully tested prior to its implementation and management had such confidence in the new system that they did not consider it necessary to undertake further testing after implementation.

Peach Co has been developing a new production process which will help to reduce sugar in its drinks by 50%. Development commenced on 1 November 20X4 and the total amount capitalised was $0.8m. On 1 May 20X5, the food safety authority approved the process and production of the new reduced-sugar soft drinks commenced.

Peach Co has inventories of high-sugar drinks costing $227,000 which it can no longer sell in its home market due to a lack of demand. The directors believe Peach Co can sell the remaining inventories to an international customer at a price that marginally exceeds cost but Peach Co will be responsible for all costs relating to the delivery and shipping of the drinks.

Peach co replaced two items of machinery in its production line to accommodate a change in the type of bottles used. There were significant staff costs involved in preparing the site for the new machinery and in testing that the new machinery was operating correctly. These costs have been included within the wages and salaries expense for the period. Despite the old machinery being sold at a significant loss, during the year the directors of Peach Co decided to extend the useful lives of plant and machinery by an average of five years.

A member of the finance team was dismissed by Peach Co in May 20X5 after it was discovered that they had been fraudulently purchasing non-current assets for personal use. Peach Co started to investigate the fraud at the beginning of June 20X5 by reconciling all physical assets to the non-current asset register but will not have completed the reconciliation by the year-end date.

Peach Co entered into a contract on 1 May 20X5 with a new supplier of bottles. Peach Co has committed to a minimum order quantity of 150,000 bottles per month for a period of 12 months commencing 1 May 20X5. No costs have been accounted for to date as no amounts are payable for the first six months. Three equal instalments are then payable across the remainder of the contract term. Peach Co's previous supplier has launched a legal claim against Peach Co for breach of contract, stating that Peach Co did not have the right to exit the agreement early. Peach Co's lawyers have indicated that it is likely to lose the case and have estimated the amount payable to be in the region of $0.3m.

In order to fund the development of the new production and the purchase of new machinery. Peach Co obtained an interest-bearing bank loan of $1.2m on 1 March 20X5 repayable over the next three years in arrears. In order to secure the bank loan, Peach Co agreed to maintain a minimum net profit margin and meet specific sales targets.

Required

(a) Describe EIGHT audit risks, and explain the auditor's response to each risk, in planning the audit of Peach Co. (16 marks)

| Audit risk | Auditor's response |
|---|---|
| | |
| | |
| | |
| | |
| | |
| | |
| | |
| | |

(b) **Describe Apricot & Co's responsibilities in relation to the prevention and detection of fraud and error.** (4 marks)

Peach co has been an audit client of Apricot & Co for the last 15 years. The audit staff of Apricot & Co and the client staff of Peach Co have always enjoyed a meal together at the start of the final audit. Alan Edward, the managing director of Peach Co has this year suggested that instead of a meal, all the audit staff and client staff go away for the weekend to a luxury hotel at Peach Co's expense.

Alan Edward had also suggested that the current year audit fee is renegotiated to be based on a percentage of Peach Co's net profit for the year.

This year, for the first time, Apricot & Co has been approached by Peach Co to help identify potential targets. Discussions are currently at an early stage and no work has been undertaken at present. The total fees in relation to the audit and other work would fail within acceptable levels in line with ACCA's Code of Ethics and Conduct.

(c) (i) **Identify and explain TWO ethical threats which may affect the independence of Apricot & Co's audit of Peach Co; and**

(ii) **For each threat, recommend an appropriate safeguard to reduce the threat to an acceptable level.** (4 marks)

(d) **Describe substantive procedures the auditor should perform to obtain sufficient and appropriate audit evidence in relation to Peach Co's development expenditure.** (6 marks)

(30 marks)

# Question 17

This scenario relates to two requirements.

It is 1 July 20X5. Pomeranian Co is a manufacturer of fizzy drinks and operates across the country. The company's year end is 30 September 20X5. You are an audit supervisor with Poodle & Co and you are reviewing extracts from the internal controls documentation in preparation for the forthcoming audit.

## Sales

All new customers of Pomeranian Co are required to pass suitable credit checks. Upon passing the credit check customers are set up in the receivables ledger master file and a credit limit is set by the sales director. The credit limits are only then changed when a customer requests an increase.

Customers orders are processed by Pomeranian Co's sales ordering department and goods are dispatched from one of the company's warehouses. Sequentially numbered multi-part goods dispatched notes (GDNs) are completed and a copy is filed in the warehouse when the goods are dispatched. Copies of the GDNs are sent to the sales ordering department and the finance department on a weekly basis.

Pomeranian Co's credit controller is currently on maternity leave for six months and no one has taken over her duties. As part of the month-end procedures, a clerk reconciles the receivables ledger control account to the receivables ledger and the reconciliation are only reviewed by the financial controller if there are any unreconciled differences.

## Non-current assets

An annual capital expenditure budget is set for each department within Pomeranian Co and is referred to as part of the approval process. Board approval is required for any capital items costing more than $0.5m. Capital expenditure below this level can be authorised by the relevant head of department.

Pomeranian Co has a head office and five factories, each of which includes a warehouse. The company has an internal audit (IA) department which is required, over a three-year cycle, to carry out a comparison between all the assets recorded on the non-current assets register to those physically present in each of the company's 11 sites. The programme of visits for the current year means that by the year end, IA will only have completed this comparison at one factory and one warehouse.

## Purchases and inventory

Pomeranian Co maintains a perpetual inventory system in which finished goods and raw materials, stored in the warehouses, are counted monthly throughout the year rather than just being counted at the year end. Each of the five warehouse managers are responsible for supervising the inventory counts at their sites and ensuring that the counting teams are following the issued instructions.

The company calculates the cost of its inventory using standard costs, both for internal management reporting and for inclusion in the year-end financial statements. The basis of the standard costs was reviewed by the production department approximately two years ago.

The company has a central purchasing department which is based at its head office. All members of this department have full access to the supplier master file data and a monthly exception report of any changes to master file date is automatically generated and then filed by a purchasing clerk.

Sequentially numbered goods received notes (GRNs) are produced by the warehouse department when goods are received, a copy of which is promptly sent to the purchases and finance departments. On receipt of the purchase invoices, the finance clerk matches the invoices to the relevant purchase order and then passes the documents to the finance director for authorisation prior to input.

**Required**

In order to obtain sufficient appropriate audit evidence, an auditor cannot place complete reliance on an entity's system of internal control. In addition to performing tests of controls, auditors must always perform some substantive procedures due to the limitations of internal control.

(a)    Described the LIMITATIONS of internal control.

     **Note:** You do not need to refer to the scenario to answer this requirements.    **(4 marks)**

(b)    Identify and explain EIGHT deficiencies in Pomeranian Co's internal control system and provide a control recommendation to address each of these deficiencies.

                                                          **(16 marks)**

                                                          **(20 marks)**

# Question 18

## The scenario relates to five requirements.

It is 1 July 20X5. Danube Co is listed on a stock exchange and sells consumer goods to wholesale customers. The company has a large head office and 18 warehouses. You are an audit supervisor of Mississippi & Co and the final audit for the year ended 31 March 20X5 is due to commence shortly. The draft financial statements show total assets of $198.5m and profit before tax of $56.1m. The following three matters have been brought to your attention.

### Land and buildings

Danube Co historically recorded all property, plant and equipment (PPE) at cost less accumulated depreciation. However during the year, management decided to change the accounting policy for land and buildings from the cost model to the revaluation model. The finance director hired an external independent valuer to undertake the valuation of all land and buildings, and this took place in July 20X4. Depreciation is calculated monthly on a pro rata basis. Danube Co's year-end balance for PPE includes land and buildings of $79.2m (20X4: $64m).

### Trade receivables circularisation

Danube Co's year-end trade receivables balance of $9.3m (20X4: $7.7m) has significantly increased compared to the prior year. Danube Co's receivables ledger is made up of a large number of customers with balances ranging from $15,000 to $150,000. A positive trade receivables circularisation has been undertaken by the audit team based on the year-end balances. The majority of responses from customers agreed to the balances as per Danube Co's receivables ledger at 31 March 20X5, however the following exceptions were noted:

| Customer | Balance per Danube Co | Response from customer |
|----------|----------------------|------------------------|
| Nile Co | $141,102 | No response |
| Congo Co | $136,321 | $122,189 |

### Provision and receivable arising from the sale of defective goods

In December 20X4 Danube Co sold a number of hoverboards to a customer, Kalama Kids Co. It is alleged by Kalama Kids Co that these hoverboards are faulty, as there have been a few instances of the hoverboards overheating and catching fire. As a result, Kalama Kids Co is suing Danube Co for $3.9m. The court case is due to take place in August 20X5 and management believes that Kalama Kids Co's inventory at the year end.

Danube Co purchased the hoverboards from a supplier, Thames Co. In February 20X5 Danube Co contacted Thames Co and requested that they reimburse Danube Co for damages which may become payable as a result of the sale of defective hoverboards. Danube Co is requesting a sum of $3.9m from Thames Co. The draft financial statements contain a provision of $3.9m in respect of the customer's claim and a receivable of $3.9m in respect of Danube Co's counter-claim against its supplier.

### Required

(a) Describe substantive procedures the auditor should perform to obtain sufficient and appropriate audit evidence in relation to Danube Co's land and buildings.    (6 marks)

(b) Describe the procedures the auditor should perform in relation to the exceptions noted during the trade receivables circularisation in respect of Nile Co and Congo Co.

   **Note:** The marks will split equally between each customers.    (4 marks)

| Nile Co - Audit procedures |
| --- |
| |

| Congo Co - Audit procedures |
| --- |
| |

(c) Described substantive procedures the auditor should perform to obtain sufficient and appropriate audit evidence in relation to the PROVISION and the RECEIVABLE arising from the sale of defective goods. (5 marks)

The audit engagement partner has determined that the issue relating to the provision and receivable arising from the sale of defective goods should be communicated as a key audit matter (KAM), in accordance with ISA 701 Communicating Key Audit Matters in the independent Auditor's Report.

(d)   (i)   Describe the factors which the audit engagement partner would have considered in determining that this issue is a KAM; and

   (ii)   Described the content of the KAM section of the auditor's report for Danube Co. (5 marks)

(20 marks)

# Answers

DO NOT TURN THIS PAGE UNTIL YOU HAVE
COMPLETED THE MOCK EXAM

# Plan of attack

If this were the real Audit and Assurance exam and you had been told to turn over and begin, what would be going through your mind?

An important thing to say (whilst there is still time) is that it is vital to have a good breadth of knowledge of the syllabus because all the questions are compulsory. However, don't panic. Below we provide guidance on how to approach the exam.

## Looking through the exam

Section A has three objective test cases, each with five questions. This is the section of the exam where the examining team can test knowledge across the breadth of the syllabus. Make sure you read these cases and questions carefully. The distractors are designed to present plausible, but incorrect, answers. Don't let them mislead you. If you really have no idea – guess. You may even be right.

Section B has three longer questions:

- **Question 16** is a 30-mark question covering audit risks and responses, responsibilities for fraud, ethics and substantive procedures on one area. Read the requirements carefully, and try to relate your answers to the specific scenario as much as you can .

- **Question 17** is a 20-mark question set on the limitations of internal controls, and then control deficiencies and recommendations.

- **Question 18** is a 20-mark question dealing with substantive procedures in relation to land and buildings, procedures for exceptions in receivables circularisations, substantive procedures in relation to an issue, and key audit matters.

## Allocating your time

BPP's advice is to always allocate your time **according to the marks for the question**. However, **use common sense**. If you're doing a question but haven't a clue how to do part (b), you might be better off reallocating your time and getting more marks on another question, where you can add something you didn't have time for earlier on. Make sure you leave time to recheck the OTs and make sure you have answered them all.

## Forget about it

And don't worry if you found the exam difficult. More than likely other candidates will too. If this were the real thing you would need to forget the exam the minute you left the exam hall and think about the next one. Or, if it is the last one, celebrate!

# Section A

1    The correct answer is: 3 only

In line with ACCA's *Code of Ethics and Conduct*, a self-interest threat would arise due to the personal relationship between the audit engagement partner and finance director. A self-interest threat, not intimidation threat, would arise as a result of the overdue fee and due to the nature of the non-audit work, it is unlikely that a self-review threat would arise.

2    The correct answer is: Cassie Dixon

In order to maintain independence, Cassie Dixon would be the most appropriate replacement as audit engagement partner as she has no ongoing relationship with Bush Co. Appointing any of the other potential replacements would give rise to self-review or familiarity threats to independence.

3    The correct answer is: Option 2

If Alan Marshlow accepts the position as a non-executive director for Plant Co, self-interest and self-review threats are created which are so significant that no safeguards can be implemented. Further as per ACCA's *Code of Ethics and Conduct*, no partner of the firm should serve as a director of an audit client and as such, Horti & Co would need to resign as auditor.

4    The correct answer is: 1, 2 and 4

Assuming a management responsibility is when the auditor is involved in leading or directing the company or making decisions which are the remit of management. Designing and maintaining internal controls, determining which recommendations to implement and setting the scope of work are all decisions which should be taken by management.

5    The correct answer is:

|  | TAKE | DO NOT TAKE |
|---|:---:|:---:|
| Communicate level of fee income to those charged with governance | ✓ | ☐ |
| Use separate teams for the audit and non-audit work | ☐ | ✓ |
| Request payment of the current year's audit fee in advance of any work being performed | ☐ | ✓ |
| Request a pre-issuance review be conducted by an external accountant | ✓ | ☐ |

Weed Co is a listed company and the fees received by Horti & Co from the company have exceeded 15% of the firm's total fees for two years. As per ACCA's *Code of Ethics and Conduct*, this should be disclosed to those charged with governance and an appropriate safeguard should be implemented. In this case, it would be appropriate to have a pre-issuance review carried out prior to issuing the audit opinion for the current year.

6    The correct answer is: A supplier with a low balance at the year-end but with a high volume of transactions during the year.

This may indicate that not all liabilities have been recorded at the year-end date.

7    The correct answer is: Chester Co purchased an unusually high level of goods in February 20X5 to satisfy a large order and had not paid for those goods by the year end

A purchase of a large volume of goods close to the year-end would increase the payables payment period. The prompt payment and trade discounts would both decrease the payables payment period, and the extended credit terms in this instance would have no impact as there is no closing balance with the new supplier.

8   The correct answer is: The auditor should request that an accrual is created in respect of the goods received but not yet invoiced

The difference of $144,640 with Oxford Co relates to goods which were received by Chester Co prior to the year-end but were not recorded in the accounting records until after the year-end date. As Chester Co had a liability to pay for the goods at the date of receipt, an accrual should be created for the goods received not yet invoiced.

9   The correct answer is:  An invoice for $156,403 has been paid twice.

The difference in respect of Poole Co may have arisen if the invoice had been paid twice in error as an additional $156,403 will have been debited to the supplier account.

10  The correct answer is: Review the accruals listing to ensure goods received from Bath Co post year end for which an invoice has not been received have been recorded in the correct period

Reviewing the accruals listing would not help the auditor confirm the purchase ledger balance with Bath Co as accruals are recorded separately from the purchase ledger balance.

11  The correct answer is: 2 and 4

As part of the overall review of the financial statements, the auditor should assess whether the information and explanations gathered during the audit and accounting policies are adequately reflected and disclosed. Pre-conditions should be considered as part of the auditor's acceptance procedures and a detailed review of the audit working papers is conducted as part of the firm's quality management procedures.

12  The correct answer is: An increase in the proportion of cash sales since November 20X4

An increase in the proportion of cash sales since the interim audit would increase sales but not trade receivables resulting in a decreased trade receivables collection period.

13  The correct answer is: 1, 3 and 4 only

The effective date of the revaluation, the amount of the revaluation increase and the carrying amount of the head office under the cost model are disclosures required by IAS 16 *Property, Plant and Equipment*.

14  The correct answer is: Misstatements 2 and 3 only

Misstatements (2) and (3) are individually material and would require adjustment for an unmodified opinion to be issued. Misstatement (1) is immaterial and if Viola Co did not make this adjustment, an unmodified opinion could still be issued.

15  The correct answer is: Unmodified opinion with no further disclosure

Misstatement (4) is immaterial at 2.2% of profit before tax ($2.9m/$131.4m) and would not require further disclosure. Therefore as all other adjustments have been made, no material misstatement exists and an unmodified opinion can be issued.

# Section B

# Question 16

## Marking scheme

|  |  |  | Marks |
|---|---|---|---|
| (a) | **Audit risks and auditor's responses (only 8 required)** |  |  |
|  | New accounting system | 1 |  |
|  | Development costs | 1 |  |
|  | Inventory valuation | 1 |  |
|  | Staff costs | 1 |  |
|  | PPE useful lives | 1 |  |
|  | Fraudulent purchases | 1 |  |
|  | New supplier costs | 1 |  |
|  | Legal claim | 1 |  |
|  | New bank loan | 1 |  |
|  | Loan covenants | 1 |  |
|  | Max 8 issues, 2 marks each |  | 16 |
| (b) | **Auditor's responsibilities in relation to the prevention and detection of fraud and error** |  |  |
|  | 1 mark per well-explained point |  |  |
|  | **Restricted to** |  | 4 |
| (c) | **Ethical threats and appropriate safeguards** |  |  |
|  | Luxury weekend provided by client | 2 |  |
|  | Audit fee based on profit | 2 |  |
|  | Corporate finance service | 2 |  |
|  | Max 2 issues, 2 marks each |  | 4 |

(d)   **Substantive procedures for development expenditure**
1 mark per well-described procedure
Restricted to                                                   6

**Total marks**                                               <u>30</u>

---

(a)   **Audit risks and auditor's response**

| Audit risk | Auditor's response |
|---|---|
| A new accounting system was introduced in March 20X5 and post implementation testing has not been conducted.<br><br>There is a risk of opening balances on the new system being misstated and loss of ongoing data if they have not been transferred from the old system correctly. If the new system is not operating effectively there is a risk of misstatement of the accounting records. | The audit team should undertake detailed testing to confirm that all balances have been completely and accurately transferred to the new accounting system.<br><br>They should perform walkthroughs to document the new system and test the controls in place.<br><br>They should discuss with management any issues which have occurred since the new system was implemented. |
| Peach Co has been developing a new production process and $0.8m was capitalised in the year as development expenditure. | The audit team should discuss with management the accounting policy applied, particularly in respect of identifying the research and development stages. |
| IAS® 38 *Intangible Assets* requires research expenditure to be recognised as an expense as incurred and development expenditure capitalised only if strict criteria are satisfied.<br><br>There is a risk that research expenditure has been incorrectly classified as development expenditure resulting in overstated intangible assets and understated research expenses.<br><br>The capitalised expenditure should be amortised over the life of the process, commencing when the new process is first brought into use in May 20X5. There is a risk that amortisation has not been correctly calculated | A detailed review of the costs capitalised and supporting documentation should be carried out to determine the nature of the expenditure. Any development expenditure should then be agreed as meeting the relevant criteria for capitalisation as set out in IAS 38.<br><br>The auditor should discuss the assessment of the useful life of the product with management and assess its reasonableness. They should also reperform amortisation calculations to confirm the amounts are accurate. |
| Peach Co holds inventory of $227,000 that it can no longer sell in its home market. It believes it can be sold to an international customer, but there are significant additional costs that Peach Co will incur.<br><br>There is a risk that the net realisable value (NRV) of the inventory is less than cost and therefore that the inventory is overstated and cost of sales understated. | The audit team should discuss with the directors their belief that the inventory can be sold and should review any agreement with the international customer to determine the likelihood of the sale and the selling price for the inventory. They should also obtain supporting documentation in respect of the delivery and shipping costs in order to establish NRV and discuss with management if a write-down is required. |

| Audit risk | Auditor's response |
|---|---|
| Peach Co has included in wages and salaries, significant staff costs involved in the preparation of the site for the new machinery and in testing the new machinery.<br><br>IAS 16 *Property, Plant and Equipment* states that costs, directly attributable to bringing the asset to the condition necessary for its intended use, are capitalised as part of the cost of the asset. These directly attributable costs include costs of site preparation and costs of testing.<br><br>It appears that an incorrect accounting treatment has been applied in respect of the staff costs resulting in understated property, plant and equipment (PPE) and overstated wages and salaries expense. | The audit team should discuss with management the accounting treatment applied and request that the relevant staff costs are included in the cost of PPE.<br><br>The audit team should undertake a review of the staff costs expensed and the process for allocating staff costs to work undertaken to confirm the amounts that should be capitalised as part of the cost of machinery. If an adjusting journal is made by management this should be reviewed for accuracy. |
| The directors extended the useful lives of plant and machinery by an average of five years despite the fact that machinery had been disposed of at a significant loss.<br><br>Under IAS 16 asset lives should be reviewed annually, and if the asset lives have genuinely increased, then the resulting decrease in depreciation may be reasonable. However, the fact that old items of machinery were sold at a substantial loss in the period does not support the decision to increase useful life.<br><br>As such, it appears that plant and machinery is overstated and depreciation expense understated. | The audit team should discuss with the directors the rationale for any extensions of asset lives and reduction of depreciation rates.<br><br>The revised useful life of a sample of assets should be compared to how often these assets are replaced and any gain or loss on disposal, as this provides evidence of the useful life of assets. |
| A member of Peach Co's finance team fraudulently purchased assets for personal use.<br><br>The reconciliation of physical assets to the non-current assets register will be ongoing at the year end, hence there is a risk that non-current assets are overstated as they may include the personal assets purchased.<br><br>Control risk is also increased if the fraud has gone undetected for a period of time. | The audit team should discuss the fraud with management to understand how the fraud was detected and corrected. They must understand the internal controls in place to prevent other frauds occurring.<br><br>Additional procedures should be performed, particularly in respect of non-current assets additions. When testing non-current assets, they should obtain a list of all non-current assets capitalised in the year and agree the new assets to an authorised purchase order. They should select an increased sample of assets from the non-current assets register to confirm the existence of the assets and that they are used in the business. |

| Audit risk | Auditor's response |
|---|---|
| The directors have not accounted for any costs under the new contract for bottles as no amounts are due to be paid until after the year end.<br><br>There is a risk that the costs incurred to date have not been recognised and therefore costs and liabilities are understated and profit is overstated. | The audit team should review the terms of the contract to understand the amounts payable and terms of payment. They should review the goods received not invoiced accrual listing to ensure that amounts payable to the supplier for bottles received have been accrued despite not being invoiced. |
| A previous supplier has launched a legal claim against Peach Co. The claim has not been settled but Peach Co's lawyers believe that they are likely to have to pay an estimated $0·3m.<br><br>As it appears probable that Peach Co will have to pay the supplier, a provision is required to comply with IAS 37 *Provisions, Contingent Liabilities and Contingent Assets*. There is a risk that provisions and expenses are understated if the company has not recognised a liability in respect of this legal claim. | The audit team should review correspondence with Peach Co's lawyer to understand the likelihood of the supplier winning the case and the amount of the payments to be made to them. |
| Peach Co obtained a new interest-bearing bank loan in the year repayable over three years.<br><br>There is a risk that the loan has not been correctly allocated between current and non-current liabilities which would give rise to a classification error and liabilities being misstated.<br><br>In addition, the finance costs are paid in arrears and may not have been correctly accrued at the year end resulting in understated accruals and finance costs. | The audit team should undertake a review of the loan agreement to confirm the details and reperform the company's calculations to confirm that the loan has been correctly classified between current and non-current liabilities.<br><br>The finance costs should be recalculated and agreed to the accruals schedule. |
| Peach Co has strict covenants in place regarding the loan.<br><br>A breach of covenants could result in fines and penalties or mean the loan would be instantly repayable. There is an increased risk that the existence of covenants gives an incentive to manipulate key balances by overstating revenue and profit to ensure covenants are met. | The audit team should review the loan covenants in detail to understand what Peach Co is required to comply with. They should calculate the covenants to understand whether any breaches have occurred and discuss the impact of any breaches with management.<br><br>The team should maintain their professional scepticism to remain alert to the risk over revenue recognition and judgements which affect profit. |

(b)   **Auditor's responsibilities in relation to the prevention and detection of fraud and error**

- Apricot & Co must conduct an audit in accordance with ISA 240 *The Auditor's Responsibilities Relating to Fraud in an Audit of Financial Statements* and are responsible for obtaining reasonable assurance that the financial statements taken as a whole are free from material misstatement, whether caused by fraud or error.

- Apricot & Co is required to identify and assess the risks of material misstatement of the financial statements due to fraud.

BPP
LEARNING
MEDIA

- The auditor needs to obtain sufficient appropriate audit evidence regarding the assessed risks of material misstatement due to fraud, through designing and implementing appropriate responses.

- Apricot & Co must respond appropriately to fraud or suspected fraud identified during the audit, for example, the fraud regarding the purchase of assets for personal use identified by Peach Co.

- When obtaining reasonable assurance, Apricot & Co is responsible for maintaining professional scepticism throughout the audit, considering the potential for management override of controls and recognising the fact that audit procedures which are effective in detecting error may not be effective in detecting fraud.

- To ensure that the whole engagement team is aware of the risks and responsibilities for fraud and error, ISAs require that a discussion is held within the team.

- Apricot & Co must report any actual or suspected fraud to appropriate parties.

(c) **Ethical threats and appropriate safeguards**

| Ethical threat | Appropriate safeguard |
|---|---|
| The managing director of Peach Co has this year suggested that instead of a meal, all the audit staff and client staff go away for the weekend to a luxury hotel at Peach Co's expense.<br><br>This represents a self-interest and familiarity threat. The acceptance of goods and services, unless trivial and inconsequential in value, is not permitted as it may make the audit staff less likely to challenge Peach Co's assumptions and explanations. | As it is unlikely that the weekend away has an insignificant value, this offer should be politely declined. The normal meal at the start of the audit is likely to be acceptable, particularly if the audit team pay for themselves. |
| Peach Co has suggested that the audit fee is renegotiated to be based on a percentage of Peach Co's net profit. This is a contingent fee and leads to a self-interest threat.<br><br>If the audit fee is based on profit the audit team may feel incentivised to allow incorrect accounting treatments in order to maximise profits. | Apricot & Co should not agree to the proposed basis for the fees and should communicate with those charged with governance to explain that the audit fee needs to reflect the level of work and the experience of the team required to obtain reasonable assurance. |
| Apricot & Co has been approached by Peach Co to assist with the identification of acquisition targets.<br><br>The provision of this type of corporate finance work creates a potential advocacy threat as Apricot & Co may be seen to be promoting Peach Co as an investor. In addition, there may be a self-review threat if the potential acquisition is subsequently reflected in the financial statements and the audit team may be less likely to challenge the figures included. | Apricot & Co may be able to accept this type of work depending on the precise nature and provided that adequate safeguards can be put in place. Care must also be taken not to make management decisions. Safeguards would include using professionals who are not involved in the audit to perform the service (e.g. corporate finance) and having an appropriate reviewer who was not involved in providing the service review the audit work or service performed. |

(d)  **Development expenditure**

–  Obtain a schedule of capitalised costs within intangible assets, cast it and agree the closing balance to the general ledger, trial balance and financial statements.

–  Select a sample of capitalised costs and agree to invoices, payroll records or other source documentation in order to confirm that the amount is correct and that the cost relates to the project.

–  Discuss with the directors the decision to capitalise the costs from 1 November 20X4 onwards and assess whether this is based on the project meeting all of the conditions for capitalisation in IAS 38.

–  Review a breakdown of the nature of the costs capitalised to identify if any research costs have been incorrectly included. If so, request that management remove these and include within profit or loss.

–  Select a sample of costs recorded as research expenses and development costs and agree to supporting documentation confirming the date of the expenditure to ensure that costs were allocated correctly.

–  Review market research reports to confirm that there is a market for the new process and that the selling price is high enough to generate a profit.

–  Review feasibility reports as at 1 November 20X4 and discuss with directors their view that the process was technically feasible at that date.

–  Review the budgets in relation to the development project and the cash flow forecast in order to assess whether Peach Co had access to adequate cash resources to complete the project as at the date of capitalisation. Agree the budgets to supporting documentation.

–  Discuss with the finance director the rationale for the useful life being applied, consider its reasonableness and agree to supporting documentation.

–  Recalculate the amortisation charge and confirm that it covers the period for May to August 20X5.

–  Review the disclosures for intangible assets in the draft financial statements in order to confirm that they are in accordance with IAS 38.

# Question 17

## Marking scheme

| | | | Marks |
|---|---|---|---|
| (a) | **Limitations of internal control**<br>1 mark per well-explained point<br>**Restricted to** | | 4 |
| (b) | **Control deficiencies and recommendations (only 8 required)** | | |
| | Credit limits not reviewed | 2 | |
| | GDNs sent weekly to finance department | 2 | |
| | No credit controller | 2 | |
| | Reconciliations only reviewed if differences | 2 | |
| | Capex authorisation limits too high | 2 | |
| | PPE verification work not as scheduled | 2 | |
| | Warehouse manager supervising inventory counts | 2 | |
| | Standard costs out of date | 2 | |
| | Exception report not checked | 2 | |
| | Purchase invoices not agreed to GRNs | 2 | |
| | **Max 8 issues, 2 marks each** | | 16 |
| **Total marks** | | | **20** |

## (a) Limitations of internal control

There are limitations in any system of internal control which affects the extent to which the auditor can place reliance on it. The limitations are as follows:

### Human error in the design of or application of an internal control

An entity may have an adequate internal control process over a particular area of the financial statements. However, human error in applying that control gives rise to an inherent limitation, for example a staff member may review a bank reconciliation but not identify an error.

There may also be a flaw in the design of internal control whereby there is an error in the design of, or change to, an internal control which means it does not operate as intended.

### Circumvention of internal control

No system of internal control will be completely effective at preventing and detecting fraud and error. Employees may manipulate deficiencies in an entity's internal control for personal gain or to conceal fraudulent activity. This is more likely to be possible where there is collusion between employees.

### Management override of internal control

Management is in a position of power to override an entity's internal control regardless of the strength of the system of internal control. Such management override could be to conceal information or for personal financial gain.

### Use of judgement on the nature and extent of controls

Management is responsible for implementing controls which are designed to prevent, detect and correct material misstatements and safeguard the company's assets. Professional judgement will be needed to determine the type and extent of internal controls needed within the company and certain controls may be absent or ineffective. In particular, systems may be designed to deal with routine transactions and may therefore be inadequate in respect of non-routine transactions.

(b)  **Control deficiencies and recommendations**

| Control deficiency | Control recommendation |
|---|---|
| Credit limits set by the sales director are only changed when a customer requests an increase.<br><br>If credit limits are not reviewed regularly they could be out of date, resulting in limits being too high and therefore sales being made to poor credit risks or, alternatively, too low and therefore Pomeranian Co losing potential revenue. | Credit limits should continue to be set by the sales director, however these limits should be reviewed and amended as appropriate on a regular basis by a responsible official for example the finance director or sales director. |
| Goods dispatched notes (GDNs) are sent to the finance department on a weekly basis.<br><br>If the finance department does not promptly receive GDNs, this could result in goods being dispatched but being invoiced late. This could result in revenue cut-off issues and understated receivables. | The copies of the GDNs should be sent to the finance department on a more frequent basis, such as daily.<br><br>The finance department should undertake a sequence check of the GDNs to ensure none are missing for processing. |
| The company's credit controller is currently on maternity leave for six months and no one has taken over her duties.<br><br>Therefore, during this period no one has been responsible for monitoring and chasing ageing receivables. This could result in an increased risk of irrecoverable receivables and lead to customers not paying their outstanding balances on time, or at all, leading to reduced cash flows. | During the period of the maternity leave an alternative member of the finance department should be trained in the credit control role (or a temporary credit controller recruited) and assigned responsibility for reviewing the aged receivables listing and following up on any overdue customers. |

| Control deficiency | Control recommendation |
|---|---|
| The monthly receivables ledger control account (RLCA) reconciliation is only reviewed by the financial controller if there are any unreconciled differences.<br><br>The RLCA reconciliation could reconcile but still contain significant errors as there could be compensating errors which cancel each other out or it may have been incorrectly prepared or manipulated and this would not be identified. If the reconciliation is not reviewed, then this significantly reduces its effectiveness. | The RLCA reconciliations should be reviewed by the financial controller on a monthly basis, even if there are no exceptions, and the review should be evidenced by way of signature on the reconciliation. |
| Capital expenditure items below $0.5m are authorised by the relevant head of department.<br><br>$0.5m is a significant sum and although department heads undertake the authorisation process, there is still considerable scope for non-business use or surplus assets being purchased leading to reduced profits and cash flow for Pomeranian Co. | The authorisation level for department heads should be significantly reduced to a more appropriate level, such as $25,000. Any sums in excess of this should be approved by the board. If this proves too onerous, a capital expenditure committee of senior employees should be established for authorisation of capital items. This committee should report to the board. |
| The internal audit department (IA) undertakes physical verification of assets each year. It is supposed to verify all assets over a three-year cycle, however in the current year IA will only complete the relevant procedures at one factory and one warehouse.<br><br>The company has five factories and warehouses and a head office. Therefore, on this basis it will take over five years to physically verify all 11 sites. If the non-current assets register is not physically verified on a regular basis, there is an increased risk of assets being misappropriated or obsolete assets still being included in the register, as there is no check that the assets still exist in good working order. | IA should review its programme of visits to assess if additional resources could be devoted to ensure that all 11 sites are visited in line with the policy of three years. This would ensure that physical verification of all assets could be completed more regularly. During visits any assets which cannot be located should be investigated fully to identify where they could be. If they cannot be located then they should be written off. |
| The warehouse manager at each of the company's five sites is responsible for supervising the monthly perpetual inventory counts and ensuring that the counting teams are following their instructions.<br><br>The warehouse managers may wish to hide inefficiencies and inventory discrepancies so that their departments are not criticised. This could result in inventory count records being inaccurate as well as an increase in inventory frauds. | The inventory counts should be supervised by an independent person, such as a member of Pomeranian Co's IA department. |

| Control deficiency | Control recommendation |
|---|---|
| The company costs its inventory using standard costs, which are not being kept up to date.<br><br>If the standard costs were last reviewed two years ago there is the risk that the costs are misstated as changes in raw materials and wages costs may not have been adjusted for. This could result in inventory and profits being misstated.<br><br>In addition, for year-end reporting, IAS 2 *Inventories* only allows standard costs to be used for valuation purposes, if they are a close approximation to actual costs, which is unlikely if the standard costs remain unchanged for a long period of time. Therefore, the inventory cost may not be in line with IAS 2. | A review of all standard costs currently in use should be undertaken by a senior manager in the production department. Actual costs for materials, labour and overheads should be ascertained and compared to the proposed standard costs to ensure they are a close approximation.<br><br>The revised standard costs should be reviewed by the production director who should evidence this review. At least annually, a review of the standard costs should be undertaken by the production director to ensure they are up to date. |
| Access to the master file data for suppliers is available to all those in the purchasing department and the monthly exception report of changes to master file data is not reviewed.<br><br>All members of the purchasing department could amend data and, potentially, add new suppliers to the payables ledger system, and as the exception report is not reviewed it is unlikely that this would be identified. This leads to an increased risk of fraud as clerks could add fictitious suppliers and then place fraudulent orders without detection. | The monthly exception report of changes to master file data should be reviewed by a responsible official, who should evidence this review. Any unauthorised or unexpected changes should be investigated and appropriate action taken.<br><br>The ability to make amendments to master file data should be restricted to those required and authorised to make changes to this data. |
| Purchase invoices are not agreed to the relevant goods received notes (GRNs) prior to authorisation and input.<br><br>This could result in invoices being paid for goods which were not received, resulting in increased costs. | All purchase invoices should be matched to both the purchase order and the related GRN. The details should be agreed prior to the invoice being authorised and logged in the payables ledger. |

# Question 18

## Marking scheme

|  |  |  | Marks |
|---|---|---|---|
| (a) | **Substantive procedures for land and buildings**<br>1 mark per well-described procedure<br>Restricted to |  | 6 |
| (b) | **Procedures for exceptions in the trade receivables circularisation**<br>Nile Co<br>Congo Co | 2<br>2 | 4 |
| (c) | **Substantive procedures for provision and receivable arising from the sale of defective goods**<br>1 mark per well-described procedure<br>Restricted to |  | 5 |
| (d) | **Factors/content for key audit matters**<br>Matter communicated to those charged with governance<br>Assessment of risk<br>Areas of judgement<br>Effect on audit<br>Description of issue<br>Why determined KAM<br>How addressed in audit<br>Restricted to | 1<br>1<br>1<br>1<br>1<br>1<br>1 | 5 |
| **Total marks** |  |  | **20** |

### (a) Land and buildings

- Obtain a schedule of all land and buildings, cast and agree to the trial balance and financial statements.

- Consider the competence and capability of the valuer, by assessing through enquiry their qualification, membership of a professional body and experience in valuing these types of assets.

- Review the assumptions and method adopted by the valuer in undertaking the revaluation to confirm the reasonableness and compliance with principles of IAS 16.

- Agree the schedule of revalued land and buildings to the valuation statement provided by the valuer and to the non-current assets register.

- Agree all land and buildings on the non-current assets register to the valuation report to ensure completeness of the land and buildings valued to ensure all assets in the same category have been revalued in line with IAS 16.

- Recalculate the total revaluation adjustment and agree correctly recorded in the revaluation surplus.

- Recalculate the depreciation charge for the year and confirm that for assets revalued at July 20X4, the depreciation was based on cost before the revaluation and based on the valuation after on a pro rata basis.

- For a sample of land and buildings from the non-current assets register, physically verify to confirm existence.

- For a sample of land and buildings trace back to the non-current assets register and general ledger to confirm completeness.

- Review the financial statements disclosures relating to land and buildings to ensure they comply with IAS 16.

(b) **Exceptions in the trade receivables circularisation**

**Nile Co**

- For the non-response from Nile Co, with the client's permission, the team should arrange to send a follow-up confirmation request.

- If Nile Co does not respond to the follow up, then with the client's permission, the auditor should telephone the customer and ask whether they are able to respond in writing to the confirmation request.

- If there is still no response, then the auditor should undertake alternative procedures to confirm the balance owing from Nile Co. These would include detailed testing of the balance by a review of after date cash receipts and agreeing to sales invoices and goods dispatched notes (GDN).

**Congo Co**

- For the response from Congo Co the auditor should investigate the difference of $14,132, and identify whether this relates to timing differences or whether there are possible errors in the records of Danube Co.

- If the difference is due to timing, such as cash in transit, details of the difference should be agreed to post year-end cash receipts in the cash book.

- If the difference relates to goods in transit, then details should be agreed to a pre year-end GDN.

- The receivables ledger should be reviewed to identify any possible mis-postings as this could be a reason for the difference with Congo Co.

(c) **Provision and receivable arising from the sale of defective goods**

- Review the correspondence with Kalama Kids Co and establish the details of the claim to assess whether a present obligation as a result of a past event has occurred.

- Review correspondence with Thames Co, the supplier of the hoverboards, to assess whether they accept liability for the defect.

- Review correspondence with Danube Co's legal advisers or, with the client's permission, contact the legal advisers to obtain their view as to the probability of either the legal claim from the customer and the request for reimbursement from the supplier being successful as well as any likely amounts to be paid or received.

- Discuss with management/enquire of the legal adviser as to whether any other customers of Danube Co have experienced problems with sales of hoverboards and therefore the likelihood of any potential future claims.

- Review board minutes to establish whether the directors believe that either claim will be successful or not.

- Review the post year-end cash book to assess whether any payments have been made to the customer or cash received from the supplier and compare with the amounts recognised in the financial statements.

- Discuss with management why they have included a receivable for the claim against the supplier as this is possibly a contingent asset and should only be recognised as an asset if the receipt of cash is virtually certain. Consider the reasonableness of the proposed treatment.

- Obtain a written representation confirming management's view that the lawsuit by Kalama Kids Co is likely to be successful and the claim against Thames Co is virtually certain and hence a provision and a receivable are required to be included.

- Review the adequacy of the disclosures of the lawsuit and supplier claim in the draft financial statements to ensure they are in accordance with IAS 37.

(d) **Key audit matters**

(i) **Factors to consider**

As Danube Co is listed, a Key Audit Matters (KAM) section will be required in the auditor's report. The audit partner would have considered whether the matter was communicated to those charged with governance as KAM are selected from matters communicated with those charged with governance. The audit partner would also have considered whether the issue relating to the claims was an area of higher assessed risk of material misstatement or a significant risk and as it is an accounting estimate the level of judgement involved. The audit partner will have also considered whether, in their professional judgement, the matters regarding the claim and counter-claim were of most significance in the audit of Danube Co's financial statements for the year ended 31 March 20X5 therefore requiring significant auditor attention.

(ii) **Contents of KAM section**

The KAM section of the auditor's report should provide a description of the issue. It should detail why this issue was considered to be an area of most significance in the audit and therefore determined to be a KAM. It would include a reference to the audit risk of completeness of the provision and recognition of the receivable and the level of judgement required in making this assessment. It should also explain how the matter was addressed in the audit and the auditor should provide a brief overview of the audit procedures adopted as well as making a reference to any related disclosures.

# Tell us what you think

Got comments or feedback on this book? Let us know.

Use your QR code reader:

Or, visit:

https://bppgroup.fra1.qualtrics.com/jfe/form/SV_cuphESF344D68Mm